INSTRUCTOR'S RESOURCE GUIDE WITH COMPLETE SOLUTIONS

TO ACCOMPANY

UNDERSTANDABLE STATISTICS

SEVENTH EDITION

BRASE/BRASE

Charles Henry Brase
Regis University

Corrinne Pellillo Brase
Arapahoe Community College

Laurel Tech Integrated Publishing Services

HOUGHTON MIFFLIN COMPANY BOSTON NEW YORK

Sponsoring Editor: Lauren Schultz
Assistant Editor: Marika Hoe
Senior Manufacturing Coordinator: Priscilla Bailey
Marketing Manager: Ben Rivera

Printed in the U.S.A.

ISBN: 0-618-20560-8

1 2 3 4 5 6 7 8 9 – CRS – 06 05 04 03 02

Contents

Part I: Teaching Hints

Suggestions for Using the Text 3

Alternate Parts Through the Text 4

Teaching Tips for Each Chapter 5

Hints for Distance Education Courses 17

Suggested References 20

Part II: Hints for Advanced Placement Statistics Courses

AP Features of the Text 23

Information about the AP Statistics Exam 24

Hints for Helping Students Succeed on the AP Statistics Exam 29

Part III: Transparency Masters

Table A Areas of a Standard Normal Distribution 37

Table 1 Random Numbers 38

Table 2 Binomial Coefficients $C_{n,r}$ 40

Table 3 Binomial Probability Distribution $C_{n,r}\,p^r q^{n-r}$ 41

Table 4 Poisson Probability Distribution 45

Table 5 Areas of a Standard Normal Distribution 52

Table 6 Student's t Distribution 55

Table 7 The χ^2 Distribution 56

Table 8 The F Distribution 57

Table 9 Critical Values for Spearman Rank Correlation, r_s 63

Frequently Used Formulas 64

Part IV: Sample Chapter Tests with Answers

Chapter 1 Sample Tests 71
Chapter 2 Sample Tests 77
Chapter 3 Sample Tests 86
Chapter 4 Sample Tests 93
Chapter 5 Sample Tests 100
Chapter 6 Sample Tests 109
Chapter 7 Sample Tests 118
Chapter 8 Sample Tests 125
Chapter 9 Sample Tests 134
Chapter 10 Sample Tests 156
Chapter 11 Sample Tests 163
Chapter 12 Sample Tests 177
Answers to Sample Chapter Tests 186

Part V: Complete Solutions

Chapter 1 Getting Started 213
Chapter 2 Organizing Data 218
Chapter 3 Averages and Variation 259
Chapter 4 Elementary Probability Theory 289
Chapter 5 The Binomial Probability Distribution and Related Topics 318
Chapter 6 Normal Distributions 367
Chapter 7 Introduction to Sampling Distributions 408
Chapter 8 Estimation 434
Chapter 9 Hypothesis Testing 473
Chapter 10 Regression and Correlation 544
Chapter 11 Chi-Square and *F* Distributions 591
Chapter 12 Nonparametric Statistics 628

Part I

Teaching Hints

Suggestions for Using the Text

In writing this text, we have followed the premise that a good textbook must be more than just a repository of knowledge. A good textbook should be an agent interacting with the student to create a working knowledge of the subject. To help achieve this interaction, we have modified the traditional format, to encourage active student participation.

Each chapter begins with Preview Questions, which indicate the topics addressed in each section of the chapter. Next comes a Focus Problem that uses real-world data. The Focus Problems show the students the kinds of questions they can answer when they have mastered the material in the chapter. In fact, students are asked to solve each chapter's Focus Problem as soon as the concepts required for the solution have been introduced.

A special feature of this text are the Guided Exercises built into the reading material. These Guided Exercises, with their completely worked solutions, help the students focus on key concepts in the newly introduced material. The Section Problems reinforce student understanding and sometimes require the student to look at the concepts from a slightly different perspective than that presented in the section. Chapter Review problems are much more comprehensive. They require students to place each problem in the context of all they have learned in the chapter. Data Highlights at the end of each chapter ask students to look at data as presented in newspapers, magazines, and other media and then to apply relevant methods of interpretation. Finally, Linking Concept problems ask students to verbalize their skills and synthesize the material.

We believe that the approach from small-step Guided Exercises to Section Problems, to Chapter Review problems, to Data Highlights, to Linking Concepts will enable the instructor to use his or her class time in a very profitable way, going from specific mastery details to more comprehensive decision-making analysis.

Calculators and statistical computer software take much of the computational burden out of statistics. Many basic scientific calculators provide the mean and standard deviation. Those calculators that support two-variable statistics provide the coefficients of the least-squares line, the value of the correlation coefficient, and the predicted value of y for a given x. Graphing calculators sort the data, and many provide the least-squares line. Statistical software packages give full support for descriptive statistics and inferential statistics. Students benefit from using these technologies. In many examples and exercises in *Understandable Statistics,* we ask students to use calculators to verify answers. Illustrations in the text show TI-83 calculator screens, MINITAB outputs, and ComputerStat outputs, so that students can see the different types of information available to them through the use of technology.

However, it is not enough to enter data and punch a few buttons to get statistical results. The formulas producing the statistics contain a great deal of information about the *meaning* of the statistics. The text breaks down formulas into tabular form so that students can see the information in the formula. We find it useful to take class time to discuss formulas. For instance, an essential part of the standard deviation formula is the comparison of each data value to the mean. When we point this out to students, it gives meaning to the standard deviation. When students understand the content of the formulas, the numbers they get from their calculator or computer begin to make sense.

The seventh edition features Focus Points at the beginning of each section, describing that section's primary learning objectives. Also new to the seventh edition is the change from Calculator Notes to Technology Notes. The Technology Notes briefly describe relevant procedures for using the TI-83 Plus calculator, Microsoft Excel, and MINITAB. In addition, the Using Technology segments have been updated to include Excel material.

For courses in which technologies are strongly incorporated into the curriculum, we provide two separate supplements, the *Technology Guide* (for the TI-83 Plus, MINITAB, and ComputerStat) and the *Excel Guide* (for Microsoft Excel). These guides gives specific hints for using the technologies, and also give Lab Activities to help students explore various statistical concepts.

Alternate Paths Through the Text

Like previous editions, the seventh edition of *Understandable Statistics* is designed to be flexible. In most one-semester courses, it is not possible to cover all the topics. The text provides many topics so you can tailor a course to fit your students' needs. The text also aims to be a *readable reference* for topics not specifically included in your course.

Table of Prerequisite Material

Chapter	Prerequisite Sections
1 Getting Started	**none**
2 Organizing Data	**1.1**
3 Averages and Variation	**1.1, 1.2, 2.2**
4 Elementary Probability Theory	**1.1, 1.2, 2.2, 3.1, 3.2**
5 The Binomial Probability Distribution and Related Topics	**1.1, 1.2, 2.2, 3.1, 3.2, 4.1, 4.2, with 4.3 useful but not essential**
6 Normal Distributions	
with 6.4 omitted	**1.1, 1.2, 2.2, 3.1, 3.2, 4.1, 4.2, 5.1**
with 6.4 included	**add 5.2, 5.3**
7 Introduction to Sampling Distributions	**1.1, 1.2, 2.2, 3.1, 3.2, 4.1, 4.2, 5.1, 6.1, 6.2, 6.3**
8 Estimation	
with 8.3 and parts of 8.4, 8.5 omitted	**1.1, 1.2, 2.2, 3.1, 3.2, 4.1, 4.2, 5.1, 6.1, 6.2, 6.3, 7.1, 7.2**
with 8.3 and all of 8.4, 8.5 included	**add 5.2, 5.3, 6.4**
9 Hypothesis Testing	
with 9.5 and part of 9.7 omitted	**1.1, 1.2, 2.2, 3.1, 3.2, 4.1, 4.2, 5.1, 6.1, 6.2, 6.3, 7.1, 7.2**
with 9.5 and all of 9.7 included	**add 5.2, 5.3, 6.4**
10 Regression and Correlation	
with part of 10.2 and 10.4, 10.5 omitted	**1.1, 1.2, 3.1, 3.2**
with all of 10.2 and 10.4, 10.5 included	**add 4.1, 4.2, 5.1, 6.1, 6.2, 6.3, 7.1, 7.2, 8.1, 9.1, 9.2**
11 Chi-square and *F* Distributions	
with 11.3 omitted	**1.1, 1.2, 2.2, 3.1, 3.2, 4.1, 4.2, 5.1, 6.1, 6.2, 6.3, 7.1, 7.2, 9.1**
with 11.3 included	**add 8.1**
12 Nonparametric Statistics	**1.1, 1.2, 2.2, 3.1, 3.2, 4.1, 4.2, 5.1, 6.1, 6.2, 6.3, 7.1, 7.2, 9.1, 9.5**

Teaching Tips for Each Chapter

CHAPTER 1 GETTING STARTED

Double-Blind Studies (SECTION 1.3)

The double-blind method of data collection, mentioned at the end of Section 1.3, is an important part of standard research practice. A typical use is in testing new medications. Because the researcher does not know which patients are receiving the experimental drug and which are receiving a more familiar drug (or a placebo), the researcher is prevented from subconsciously doing things that might skew the results.

If, for instance, the researcher communicates a more optimistic attitude to patients in the experimental group, this could influence how they respond to diagnostic questions or might actually influence the course of their illness. And if the researcher wants the new drug to prove effective, this could subconsciously influence how he or she handles information related to each patient's case. All such factors are eliminated in double-blind testing.

The following appears in the physician's dosing instructions package insert for the prescription drug QUIXIN™:

> In randomized, double-masked, multicenter controlled clinical trials where patients were dosed for 5 days, QUIXIN™ demonstrated clinical cures in 79% of patients treated for bacterial conjunctivitis on the final study visit day (day 6-10).

Note the phrase "double-masked." This is, apparently, a synonym for "double-blind." Since "double-blind" is widely used in the medical literature and in clinical trials, why do you suppose they chose to use "double-masked" instead?

Perhaps this will provide some insight: QUIXIN™ is a topical antibacterial solution for the treatment of conjunctivitis, i.e., it is an antibacterial eye drop solution used to treat an inflammation of the conjunctiva, the mucous membrane that lines the inner surface of the eyelid and the exposed surface of the eyeball. Perhaps, since QUIXIN™ is a treatment for eye problems, the manufacturer decided the word "blind" shouldn't appear *anywhere* in the discussion.

Source: Package insert. QUIXIN™ is manufactured by Santen Oy, P.O. Box 33, FIN-33721 Tampere, Finland, and marketed by Santen Inc., Napa, CA 94558, under license from Daiichi Pharmaceutical Co., Ltd., Tokyo, Japan.

CHAPTER 2 ORGANIZING DATA

Emphasize when to use the various graphs discussed in this chapter: bar graphs when comparing data sets; circle graphs for displaying how a total is dispersed into several categories; time plots to display how data changes over time; histograms or frequency polygons to display relative frequencies of grouped data; stem-and-leaf displays for displaying grouped data in a way that does not lose the detail of the original raw data.

Drawing and Using Ogives (Section 2.2)

The text describes how an ogive, which is a graph displaying a cumulative frequency distribution, can easily be constructed using a frequency table. However, a graph of the same basic sort can be constructed even more quickly than that. Simply arrange the data values in ascending order and then plot one point for each data value, where the x coordinate is the data value and the y coordinate starts at 1 for the first point and increases by 1 for each successive point. Finally, connect adjacent points with line segments. In the resulting graph, for any x, the corresponding y value will be (roughly) the number of data values less than or equal to x.

Here, for example, is the graph for the data set 64, 65, 68, 73, 74, 76, 81, 84, 85, 88, 92, 95, 95, 99:

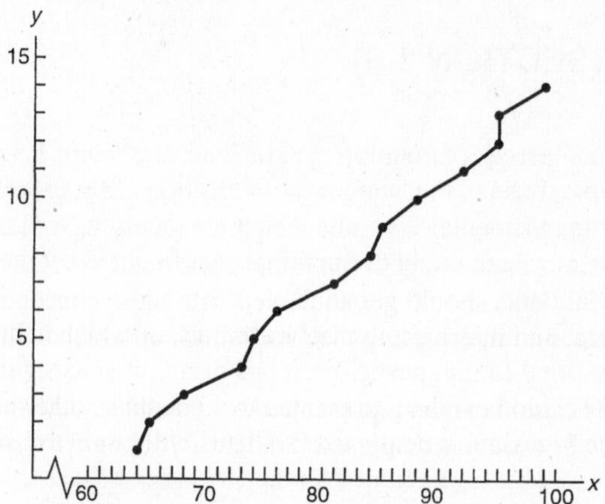

This graph and others like it are not technically ogives, since for one thing, the possibility of duplicate data values (like 95 in this example) means that the graph will not necessarily be a function. But the graph can be used to get a quick fix on the general shape of the cumulative distribution curve. And by implication, the graph can be used to get a quick idea of the shape of the frequency distribution, as illustrated below.

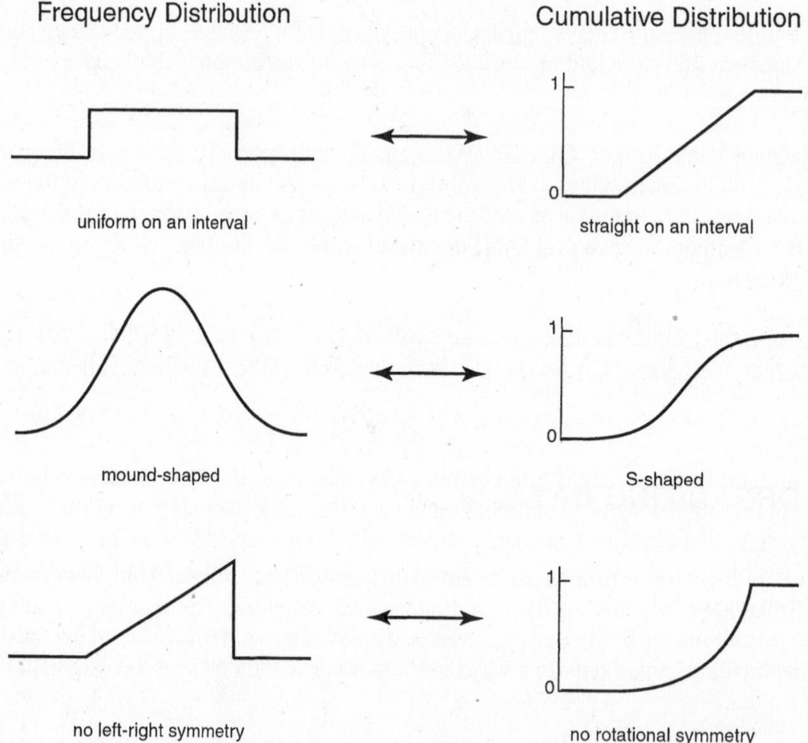

The pseudo-ogive obtained for the example data set suggests a uniform distribution on the interval 63 to 100 or thereabouts.

CHAPTER 3 AVERAGES AND VARIATION

Students should be instructed in the various ways that sets of numeric data can be represented by a single number. The concepts of this section can be motivated to students by emphasizing the need to represent a set of data by a single number.

The different ways this can be done that are discussed in Section 3.1: mean, median, and mode vary in appropriateness according to the situation. In many cases of numeric data, the mean is the most appropriate measure of central tendency. If the mean is larger or smaller than most of the data values, however, then the median may be the number that best represents a set of data. The median is most appropriate usually if the set of data is annual salaries, costs of houses, or any set of data which contains one or a few very large or very small values. The mode would be the most appropriate if the population was the votes in an election or Nielsen television ratings, for example. Students should get aquainted with these concepts by calculating the mean, median, and mode for sets of data, and interpreting their meanings, or which is the most appropriate.

Range, variance, and standard deviation can be represented to students as other numbers that aid in representing a set of data in that they measure how data is dispersed. Students will begin to have a better understanding of these measures of dispersion, like mean, median, and mode, by calculating these numbers for given sets of data, and interpreting their respective meanings. These concepts of central tendency and dispersion of data can also be applied to grouped data, and students should get aquainted with interpreting these measures for given realistic situations in which data have been collected.

Chebyshev's theorem is an important theorem to discuss with students that relates to the mean and standard deviation of *any* data set.

Finally, the mean, median, first and third quartiles, and range of a set of data can be easily viewed in a box-and-whisker plot.

CHAPTER 4 ELEMENTARY PROBABILITY THEORY

Ways To Think About Probability (Section 4.1)

As the text describes, there are several methods for assigning a probability to an event. Probability based on intuition is often called *subjective* probability. Thus understood, probability is a numerical measure of a person's confidence about some event. Subjective probability is assumed to be reflected in a person's decisions: the higher an event's probability, the more the person would be willing to bet on its occurring.

Probability based on relative frequency is often called *experimental* probability, because relative frequency is calculated from an observed history of experiment outcomes. But we are already using the word experiment in a way that is neutral among the different treatments of probability—namely, as the name for the activity that produces various possible outcomes. So when we are talking about probability based on relative frequency, we will call this *observed* probability.

Probability based on equally likely outcomes is often called *theoretical* probability, because it is ultimately derived from a theoretical model of the experiment's structure. The experiment may be conducted only once, or not at all, and need not be repeatable.

These three ways of treating probability are compatible and complementary. For a reasonable, well-informed person, the subjective probability of an event should match the theoretical probability, and the theoretical probability in turn predicts the observed probability as the experiment is repeated many times.

Also, it should be noted that although in statistics, probability is officially a property of *events,* it can be thought of as a property of *statements,* as well. The probability of a statement equals the probability of the event that makes the statement true.

Probability and statistics are overlapping fields of study; if they weren't, there would be no need for a chapter on probability in a book on statistics. So the general statement, in the text, that probability deals with known populations while statistics deals with unknown populations is, necessarily, a simplification. However, the statement does express an important truth: if we confront an experiment we initially know absolutely nothing about, then we can collect data, but we cannot calculate probabilities. In other words, we can only calculate probabilities after we have formed some idea of, or acquaintance with, the experiment. To find the theoretical probability of an event, we have to know how the experiment is set up. To find the observed probability, we have to have a record of previous outcomes. And as reasonable people, we need some combination of those same two kinds of information to set our subjective probability.

This may seem obvious, but it has important implications for how we understand technical concepts encountered later in the course. There will be times when we would like to make a statement, say, about the mean of a population, and then give the probability that this statement is true—that is, the probability that the event described by the statement occurs (or has occurred). What we discover when we look closely, however, is that often this can't be done. Often we have to settle for some other conclusion instead. The Teaching Tips for Sections 8.1 and 9.1 describe two instances of this problem.

CHAPTER 5 THE BINOMIAL PROBABILITY DISTRIBUTION AND RELATED TOPICS

Binomial Probabilities (Section 5.2)

Students should be able to show that $pq = p(1 - p)$ has its maximum value at $p = 0.5$. There are at least three ways to demonstrate this: graphically, algebraically, and using calculus.

Graphical method

Recall that $0 \le p \le 1$. So, for $q = 1 - p$, $0 \le q \le 1$ and $0 \le pq \le 1$. Plot $y = pq = p(1 - p)$ using MINITAB, a graphing calculator, or other technology. The graph is a parabola. Observe which value of p maximizes pq. (Many graphing calculators can find the maximum value and where it occurs.)

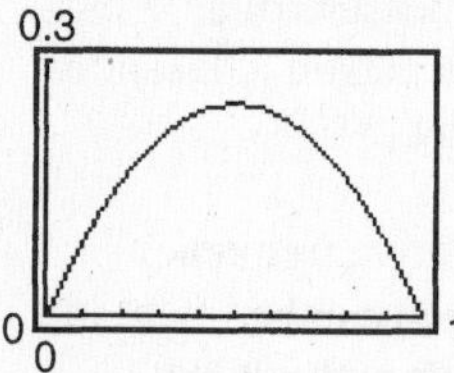

So pq has a maximum value of 0.25, when $p = 0.5$.

Algebraic method

From the definition of q, it follows that $pq = p(1 - p) = p - p^2 = -p^2 + p + 0$. Recognize that this is a quadratic function of the form $ax^2 + bx + c$, where p is used instead of x, and $a = -1$, $b = 1$, and $c = 0$.

The graph of a quadratic function is a parabola, and the general form of a parabola is $y = a(x - h)^2 + k$. The parabola opens up if $a > 0$, opens down if $a < 0$, and has a vertex at (h, k). If the parabola opens up, it has its minimum at $x = h$, and the minimum value of the function is $y = k$. Similarly, if the parabola opens down, it has its maximum value of $y = k$ when $x = h$.

Using the method of completing the square, we can rewrite $y = ax^2 + bx + c$ in the form $y = a(x - h)^2 + k$ to show that $h = -b/2a$ and $k = c - b^2/4a$. When $a = -1$, $b = 1$, and $c = 0$, it follows that $h = 1/2$ and $k = 1/4$. So the value of p that maximizes pq is $p = 1/2$, and then $pq = 1/4$. This confirms the results of the graphical solution.

Calculus-based method
This method is shown on page 31.

This result has implications for confidence intervals for p; see the Teaching Tips for Chapter 8.

CHAPTER 6 NORMAL DISTRIBUTIONS

Emphasize the differences between discrete and continuous random variables with examples of each.

Emphasize how normal curves can be used to approximate the probabilities of both continuous and discrete random variables, and in the cases when the distribution of a set of data can be approximated by a normal curve, such a curve is defined by 2 quantities: the mean and standard deviation of the data. In such a case, the normal curve is defined by the equation $y = \dfrac{e^{-\frac{1}{2}\left(\frac{x-\mu}{\sigma}\right)^2}}{\sigma\sqrt{2\pi}}$.

Review Chebyshev's Theorem from Chapter 3. Emphasize that this theorem implies that for *any* set of data

at *least* 75% of the data lie within 2 standard deviations on each side of the mean; at *least* 88.9% of the data lie within 3 standard deviations on each side of the mean, and at *least* 93.8% of the data lie within 4 standard deviations on each side of the mean.

In comparison, a set of data that has a distribution which is symmetrical and bell-shaped, in particular has a normal distribution, is more restrictive in that

approximately 68% of the data values lie within 1 standard deviation on each side of the mean;
approximately 95% of the data values lie within 2 standard deviations on each side of the mean; and
approximately 99.7% of the data values lie within 3 standard deviations on each side of the mean.

Remind students regularly that a z-value equals the number of standard deviations from the mean for data values of *any* distribution approximated by a normal curve.

Emphasize the connection between the area under a normal curve and probability values of the random variable. That is, emphasize that the area under any normal curve equals 1, and the percentage of area under the curve between given values of the random variable equals the probability that the random variable will be between these values. The values in a z-table are areas *and* probability values.

Emphasize the conditions whereby a binomial probability distribution (discussed in Chapter 5) can be approximated by a normal distribution: $np > 5$ and $n(1-p) > 5$, where n is the number of trials and p is the probability of success in a single trial.

When a normal distribution is used to approximate a discrete random variable (such as the random variable of a binomial probability experiment), the *continuity correction* is an important concept to emphasize to students. A discussion of this important adjustment can be a good opportunity to compare discrete and continuous random variables.

CHAPTER 7 INTRODUCTION TO SAMPLING DISTRIBUTIONS

Emphasize the differences between population parameters and sample statistics. Point out that when knowledge of the population is unavailable, then knowledge of a corresponding sample statistic must be used to make inferences about the population.

Emphasize the main two facts discussed from the Central Limit Theorem:

1) If x is a random variable with a normal distribution whose mean is μ and standard deviation is σ, then the means of random samples for any fixed size n taken from the x distribution is a random variable $\bar{x}$ that has a normal distribution with mean μ and standard deviation $\sigma/\sqrt{n}$.

2) If x is a random variable with *any* distribution whose mean is μ and standard deviation is σ, then the mean of random samples of a fixed size n taken from the x distribution is a random variable $\bar{x}$ that has a distribution that approaches a normal distribution with mean μ and standard deviation $\sigma/\sqrt{n}$ as n increases without limit.

Choosing sample sizes greater than 30 is an important point to emphasize in the situation mentioned in part 2 of the Central Limit Theorem above. This commonly-accepted convention insures that the $\bar{x}$ distribution of Part 2 will have a normal distribution regardless of the distribution of the population from which these samples are drawn.

Emphasize that the Central Limit Theorem allows us to infer facts about populations from sample means having normal distributions.

Emphasize that facts about sampling distributions for proportions relating to binomial experiments can be inferred if the same conditions satisfied by a binomial experiment that can be approximated by a normal distribution are satisfied: that is, $np > 5$ and $n(1-p) > 5$, where n is the number of trials and p is the probability of success in a single trial.

Emphasize the difference in the continuity correction that must be taken into account in a sampling distribution for proportions and the continuity correction for a normal distribution used to approximate the probability distribution of the discrete random variable in a binomial probability experiment. That is, instead of subtracting 0.5 from the left endpoint and adding 0.5 to the right endpoint of an interval involved in a normal distribution approximating a binomial probability distribution, $0.5/n$ must be subtracted from the left endpoint and $0.5/n$ added to the right endpoint of such an interval, where n is the number of trials, when a normal distribution is used to approximate a sampling distribution for proportions.

CHAPTER 8 ESTIMATION

Understanding Confidence Intervals (Section 8.1)

As the text says, nontrivial probability statements involve variables, not constants. And if the mean of a population is considered a constant, then the event that this mean falls in a certain range with known numerical bounds has either probability 1 or probability 0.

However, we might instead think of the population mean as itself a variable, since, after all, the value of the mean is initially unknown. In other words, we may think of the population we are sampling from as one of many populations—a population of populations, if you like. One of these populations has been randomly selected for us to work with, and we are trying to figure out which population it is, or, at least, what its mean is.

If we think of our sampling activity in this way, we can then think of the event "The mean lies between *a* and *b*" as having a non-trivial probability of being true. Can we, now, create a 0.90 confidence interval and then say that the mean has a 90% probability of being in that interval? It might seem so, but in general the answer is no. Even though a procedure might have exactly a 90% success rate at creating confidence intervals that contain the mean, a confidence interval created by such a procedure will not, in general, have exactly a 90% chance of containing the mean.

How is this possible? To understand this paradox, let us turn from mean-finding to a simpler task: guessing the color of a randomly-drawn marble. Suppose a sack contains some red marbles and some blue marbles. And suppose we have a friend who will reach in, draw out a marble, and announce its color while we have our backs turned. The friend can be counted on to announce the correct color *exactly 90% of the time* (that is, with a probability of 90%) and the wrong color the other 10% of the time. So if the marble drawn is blue, the friend will say "blue" 9 times out of 10 and "red" the remaining time. And conversely for a red marble. This is like creating an 0.90 confidence interval.

Now the friend reaches in, pulls out a marble, and announces, "blue." Does this mean that we are 90% sure the friend is holding a blue marble? *It depends on what we think about the mix of marbles in the bag.* Suppose we think that the bag contains three red marbles and two blue ones. Then we expect the friend to draw a red marble 3/5 of the time and announce "blue" 10% of those times, or 3/50 of all draws. And we expect the friend to draw a blue marble 2/5 of the time and announce "blue" 90% of those times, or 18/50 of all draws. This means that the ratio of true "blue" announcements to false ones is 18 to 3, or 6 to 1. And thus we attach a probability of 6/7 = 85.7%, not 90%, to our friend's announcement that the marble drawn is blue, even though we believe our friend to be telling the truth 90% of the time. For similar reasons, if the friend says "red," we will attach a probability of 93.1% to this claim. Simply put, our initial belief that there are more red marbles than blue ones pulls our confidence in a "blue" announcement downward, and our confidence in a "red" announcement upward, from the 90% level.

Now, if we believe that there are an *equal* number of red and blue marbles in the bag, then, as it turns out, we will attach 90% probability to "blue" announcements and to "red" announcements as well. But *this is a special case.* In general, the probabilities we attach to each of our friend's statements will be different from the frequency with which we think he is telling the truth. Furthermore: if we have *no idea* about the mix of marbles in the bag, then we will be *unable* to set probabilities for our friend's statements, because we will be unable to run the calculation for how often his "blue" statements are true and his "red" statements are true. In other words, *we cannot justify simply setting our probability equal, by default, to the test's confidence level.*

This story has two morals. (1) The probability of a statement is one thing, and the success rate of a procedure that tries to come up with true statements is another. (2) Our prior beliefs about the conditions of an experiment are an unavoidable element in our interpretation of any sample data.

Let us apply these lessons to the business of finding confidence intervals for population means. When we create a 0.90 confidence interval, we will in general *not* be 90% sure that the interval contains the mean. It could *happen* to turn out that we were 90% sure, but this will depend on what ideas we had about the population mean going in. Suppose we were fairly sure, to start with, that the population mean lay somewhere between 10 and 20, and suppose we then took a sample that led to the construction of a 0.90 confidence interval which ran from 31 to 46. We would *not* conclude, with 90% certainty, that the mean lay between 31 and 46. Instead, we would have a probability lower than that, because previously we thought the mean was outside that range. At the same time, we would be much more ready to believe that the mean lay between 31 and 46 than we were before, because, after all, a procedure with a 90% success rate produced that prediction. Our exact probability for the "between 31 and 46" statement would depend on our entire initial probability distribution for values of the population mean—something we would have a hard time coming up with, if the question were put to us. Thus, under normal circumstances, our exact level of certainty about the confidence interval could not be calculated.

So the general point made in the text holds, even if we think of a population mean as a variable. The procedure for finding a confidence interval of confidence level *c* does not, in general, produce a statement (about the value of a population mean) that has a probability *c* of being true.

Confidence Intervals for *p* (Section 8.3)

The result obtained in the Teaching Tip for Chapter 5 has implications for the confidence interval for *p*: the most conservative interval estimate of *p*, the widest possible confidence interval in a given situation, is obtained when $E = z_c\sqrt{pq/n}$ is calculated using $p = 1/2$.

CHAPTER 9 HYPOTHESIS TESTING

What a Hypothesis Test Tells Us (Sections 9.1–9.3)

The procedure for hypothesis testing with significance levels may at first confuse some students, especially since the levels are chosen somewhat arbitrarily. Why, the students may wonder, don't we just calculate the likelihood that the null hypothesis is true? Or is that really what we're doing, when we find the *P* value?

Once again we run the risk of confusion over the role of probability in our statistical conclusions. The *P* value is *not* the same thing as the probability, in light of the data, of the null hypothesis. Instead, the *P* value is the probability that the data would turn out the way it did, assuming the null hypothesis to be true. Just as with confidence intervals, here we have to be careful not to think we are finding the probability of a given statement when in fact we are doing something else.

To illustrate: consider two coins in a sack, one fair and one two-headed. One of these coins is pulled out at random and flipped. It comes up heads. Let us take, as our null hypothesis, the statement "The flipped coin was the fair one." The probability of the outcome, given the null hypothesis, is 1/2, because a fair coin will come up heads half the time. This probability is in fact the *P* value of the outcome. On the other hand, the probability that the null hypothesis is true, given the evidence, is 1/3, since out of all the heads outcomes one will see in many such trials, 1/3 are from the fair coin.

Now suppose that instead of containing two coins of known character, the sack contains an unknown mix—some fair coins, some two-headed coins, and possibly some two-tailed coins, as well. Then we can still calculate the *P* value of a heads outcome, because the probability of "heads" with a fair coin is still 1/2. But the probability of the coin's being fair, given that we're seeing heads, *cannot be calculated,* because we know nothing about the mix of coins in the bag. So the *P* value of the outcome is one thing, and the probability of the null hypothesis is another.

The lesson should be now be familiar: without some prior ideas about the character of an experiment, either based on a theoretical model or on previous outcomes, we cannot attach a definite probability to a statement about the experimental setup or its outcome.

This is the usual situation in hypothesis testing. We normally lack the information needed to calculate probabilities for the null hypothesis and its alternative. What we do instead is to take the null hypothesis as defining a well-understood scenario from which we *can* calculate the likelihoods of various outcomes—the probabilities, that is, of various kinds of sample results, given that the null hypothesis is true. By contrast, the alternative hypothesis includes all sorts of scenarios, in some of which (for instance) two population means are only slightly different, in others of which the two means are far apart, and so on. Unless we have identified the likelihoods of all these possibilities, relative to each other and to the null hypothesis, we will not have the background information needed to calculate the probability of the null hypothesis from sample data.

In fact, we will not have the data necessary to calculate what the text calls the power, $1 - \beta$, of a hypothesis test. This is what the text means when it says that finding the power requires knowing the H_1 distribution. Because we cannot specify the H_1 distribution when we are concerned with things like diagnosing disease (instead of drawing coins from a sack and the like), we normally cannot determine the probability of the null hypothesis in light of the evidence. Instead, we have to content ourselves with quantifying the risk, α, of rejecting the hypothesis when it is true.

A Paradox About Hypothesis Tests

The way hypothesis tests work (see the AP Hints for discussion) leads to a result that at first seems surprising. It can sometimes happen that, at a given level of significance, a one-tailed test leads to a rejection of the null hypothesis while a two-tailed test would not. Apparently, one can be justified in concluding that $\mu > k$ (or $\mu < k$ as the case may be) but not justified in concluding that $\mu \neq k$—even though the latter conclusion follows from the former! What is going on here?

This paradox dissolves when one remembers that a one-tailed test is used only when one has appropriate information. With the null hypothesis H_0: $\mu = k$, we choose the alternative hypotheses H_1: $\mu > k$ only if *we are already sure* that μ is not less than H_1: $\mu < k$. This assumption, in effect, boosts the force of any evidence that μ does not equal k—and if it is not less than or equal to k, it must be greater.

In other words, when a right-tailed test is appropriate, rejecting the null hypothesis means concluding *both* that $\mu > k$ and that $\mu \neq k$. But when there is no justification for a one-tailed test, one must use a two-tailed test and needs somewhat stronger evidence before concluding that $\mu \neq k$.

CHAPTER 10 REGRESSION AND CORRELATION

Least-Squares Criteria (Section 10.2)

With some sets of paired data, it will not be obvious which is the explanatory variable and which is the response variable. Here it may be worth mentioning that for linear regression, the choice matters. The results of a linear regression analysis will differ, depending on which variable is chosen as the explanatory variable and which one as the response variable. This is not immediately obvious. We might think that with x as the explanatory variable, we could just solve the regression equation $y = a + bx$ for x in terms of y to obtain the regression equation that we would get if we took y as the explanatory variable instead. But this would be a mistake.

The figure below shows the vertical distances from data points to the line of best fit. The line is defined so as to make the sum of the squares of these vertical distances as small as possible.

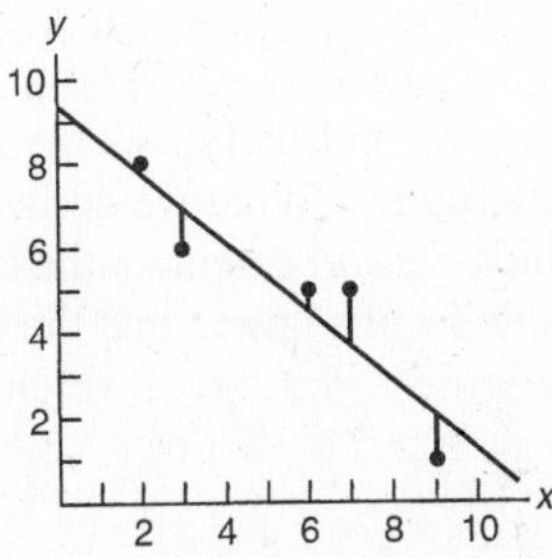

The next figure, now, shows the *horizontal* distances from the data points to the same line. These are the distances whose sum of squares would be minimized if the explanatory and response variables switched roles. With such a switch, the graph would be flipped over, and the horizontal distances would become vertical ones. But the line that minimizes the sum of squares for vertical distances is not, in general, the same line that minimizes the sum of squares for horizontal distances.

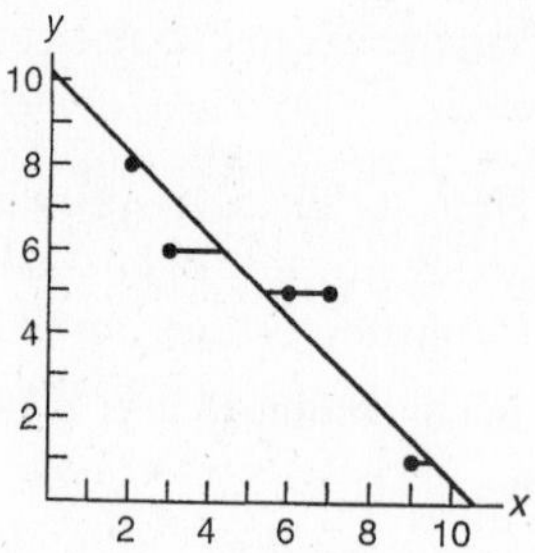

So there is more than one way, mathematically, to definite the line of best fit for a set of paired data. This raises a question: what is the *proper* way to define the line of best fit?

Let us turn this question around: under what circumstances is a best fit based on *vertical* distances the right way to go? Well, intuitively, the distance from a data point to the line of best fit represents some sort of deviation from the ideal value. We can most easily conceptualize this in terms of measurement error. If, now, we treat the error as a strictly vertical distance, then we are saying that in each data pair, the second value is possibly off but the first value is exactly correct. In other words, the least-squares method with vertical distances assumes that the first value in each data pair is measured with essentially perfect accuracy, while the second is measured only imperfectly.

An illustration shows how these assumptions can be realistic. Suppose we are measuring the explosive force generated by the ignition of varying amounts of gunpowder. The weight of the gunpowder is the explanatory variable, and the force of the resulting explosion is the response variable. It could easily happen that we were able to measure the weight of gunpowder with great exactitude—down to the thousandth-ounce—but that our means of measuring explosion force was quite crude, such as the height to which a wooden block was flung into the air by the explosion. We would then have an experiment with a good deal of error in the response variable measurement but for, practical purposes, no error in the explanatory variable measurement. This would all be perfectly in accord with the vertical-distance criterion for finding the line of best fit by the least-squares method.

But now consider a different version of the gunpowder experiment. This time we have a highly refined means of measuring explosive force (some sort of electronic device, let us say) and at the same time we have only a very crude means of measuring gunpowder mass (perhaps a rusty pan balance). In this version of the story, the error would be in the measurement of the response variable, and a horizontal least-squares criterion would be called for.

Now, the most common situation is one in which both the explanatory and the response variables contain some error. The preceding discussion suggests that the most appropriate least-squares criterion for goodness of fit for a line through the cluster of data points would be a criterion in which error was represented as a line lying at some slant, as in the figure.

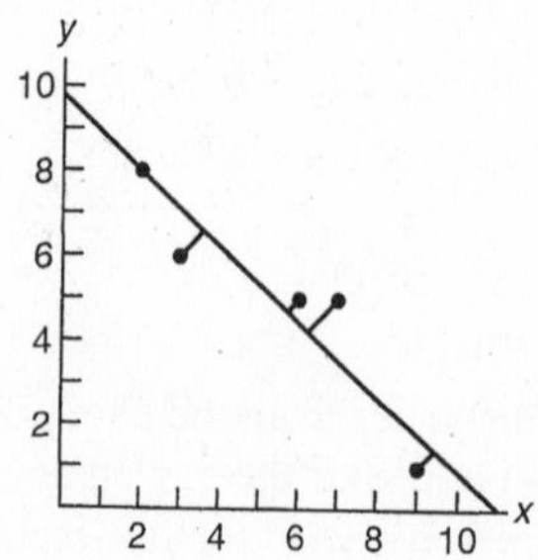

To apply such a criterion, we would have to figure out to define distance in two dimensions when the x and y axis have different units of measure. We will not try to solve that puzzle here. Instead we just summarize what we have learned: there is more than one least-squares criterion for fitting a line to a set of data points, and the choice of which criterion to use implies an assumption about which variable(s) is affected by the error (or other deviation) that moves points off the line representing ideal results.

And, finally, we now see that the standard use of vertical distances in the least-squares method *implies an assumption that the error is predominantly in the response variable.* This is often a reasonable assumption to make, since the explanatory variable is frequently a *control* variable, that is, a variable under the experimenter's control and thus generally capable of being adjusted with a fair amount of precision. The response variable, by contrast, is the one that must simply be measured and cannot be fine-tuned through an experimenter's adjustment. However, it is worth noting that this is only the typical relationship, not a necessary one (as the second gunpowder scenario shows).

Finally, it is also worth nothing that both the vertical and the horizontal least-squares criteria will produce a line that passes through the point $(\overline{x}, \overline{y})$. Thus the vertical- and horizontal-least-squares lines must either coincide (which is atypical but not impossible) or intersect at $(\overline{x}, \overline{y})$. The other thing the two lines have in common is the correlation coefficient, r. It is easy to see, looking at the formula for r, that the value of r does not depend on which variable is chosen as the explanatory one and which as the response one.

Variables and the Issue of Cause and Effect (Sections 10.2 and 10.3)

As remarked at the end of Section 10.3, the relationship between two measured variables x and y may not, in physical terms, be one of cause and effect, respectively. It often is, of course, but it may instead happen that y is the cause and x is the effect. Note that in the example where x = cricket chirps per second and y = air temperature, y is obviously the cause and x the effect. In other situations, x and y will be two effects of a common, possibly unknown, cause. For example, x might be a patient's blood sugar level and y might be the patient's body temperature. Both of these variables could be caused by an illness, which might be quantified in terms of a count of bacterial activity. The point to remember is that although the x-causes-y scenario is typical, strictly speaking the designations "explanatory variable" and "response variable" should be understood not in terms of a causal relationship but in terms of which quantity is initially known and which one is inferred.

CHAPTER 11 CHI-SQUARE AND *F* DISTRIBUTIONS

Emphasize that both the χ^2 distribution and the F distribution are not symmetrical and have only non-negative values.

Emphasize that the applications of the χ^2 distribution include the test for independence of two factors, goodness of fit of a present distribution to a given distribution, and whether a variance (or standard deviation) has changed or varies from a known population variance (or standard deviation). The χ^2 distribution is also used to find a confidence interval for a variance (or standard deviation).

Emphasize that the applications of the F distribution includes the test of whether the variances (or equivalently, standard deviations) of two independent, normal distributions are equal. A second application of the F distribution is the one-way ANOVA test which determines whether a significant difference exists between any of several sample means of groups taken from populations that are each assumed to be normally distributed, independent of one another, and the groups come from distributions with approximately the same standard deviation. A third application of the F distribution is a two-way ANOVA test: a test of whether differences exist in the population means of varying levels of two factors where each level of each factor is assumed to be from a normal distribution and all levels of both factors are assumed to have equal variances.

CHAPTER 12 NONPARAMETRIC STATISTICS

Review the classifications of data discussed in Chapter 1: ratio, interval, ordinal, and nominal.

Emphasize that the methods of nonparametric statistics are quite general and are applied when no assumptions are known about the population distributions from which samples are drawn, such as that the distributions are normal or binomial, for example.

Emphasize that the sign test is used when comparing sample distributions from two populations that are not independent, such as when a sample is measured twice, as in a "before-and-after" study. Emphasize that the sign-test requires that the number of positive and negative signs between the samples number at least 12. Point out that since the proportion of plus signs to total number of plus and minus signs of the sampling distribution for x follows a normal distribution, the critical values for the sign test are based on z values from a normal distribution.

Emphasize that the rank-sum test for testing the difference between sample means can be used when it is not known whether the populations the samples come from are normally distributed or when assumptions about equal population variances are not satisfied. An important point to emphasize is that the rank-sum test requires that the sample size of each sample be at least 8. Emphasize that since the sampling distribution for the sum of ranks R follows a normal distribution, the critical values and sample statistics of the test are z values from a normal distribution.

Emphasize that the Spearman rank correlation is used to compare ranked data from two sources.

Emphasize that for the Spearman rank correlation coefficient r_S, $-1 \le r_S \le 1$, and discuss the meanings of $r_S = 1$, $r_S = -1$, $r_S = 0$, r_S close to 1, and r_s close to -1.

Compare the similarity of r_s to the correlation coefficent r from Chapter 10.

Hints for Distance Education Courses

Distance education uses various media, each of which can be used in one-way or interactive mode. Here is a representative list:

Medium:		One-way	Interactive
	Audio	Cassette tapes	Phone
	Audiovisual	Videotapes, CD-ROMs	Teleconferencing
	Data	Computer-resident tutorials, web tutorials	E-mail, chat rooms, discussion lists
	Print	Texts, workbooks	Mailed-in assignments, mailed-back instructor comments, fax exchanges

Sometimes the modes are given as asynchronous (students working on their schedules) versus synchronous (students and instructors working at the same time), but synchronous scheduling normally makes sense only when this enables some element of interactivity in the instruction.

Naturally the media and modes may be mixed and matched. A course might, for instance, use a one-way video feed with interactive audio, plus discussion lists.

THINGS TO KEEP IN MIND

Even in a very high-tech telecourse, print is a foundational part of the instruction. The textbook is *at least* as important as in a traditional course, since it is the one resource which requires no special equipment to use, and whose use is not made more difficult by the distance separating student and instructor.

Because students generally obtain all course materials at once, before instruction begins, mid-course adjustments of course content are generally not practicable. Plan the course carefully up front, so everything is in place when instruction begins.

In distance courses, students can often be assumed to have ready access to computers while working on their own. This creates the opportunity for technology-based assignments that in a traditional course might be feasible at best as optional work (for example, assignments using ComputerStat, MINITAB, or Microsoft Excel; see the corresponding guides that accompany *Understandable Statistics*). However, any time students have to spend learning how to use unfamiliar software will add to their overall workload and possibly to their frustration level. Remember this when choosing technology-based work to incorporate.

Remember that even (and perhaps especially) in distance education, students take a course because they want to interact with a human being rather than just read a book. The goal of distance instruction is to make that possible for students who cannot enroll in a traditional course. Lectures should not turn into slide shows with voice commentary, even though these may be technologically easier to transmit than, say, real-time video. Keep the human element uppermost.

All students should be self-motivated, but in real life nearly all students benefit from a little friendly supervision and encouragement. This goes double for distance education. Make an extra effort to check in with students one-on-one, ask how things are going, and remind them of things they may be forgetting or neglecting.

CHALLENGES IN DISTANCE EDUCATION

Technology malfunctions often plague distance courses. To prevent this from happening in yours:

- Don't take on too much at once. As the student sites multiply, so do the technical difficulties. Try the methodology with one or two remote sites before expanding.
- Plan all technology use well in advance and thoroughly test all equipment before the course starts.
- Have redundant and backup means for conducting class sessions. If, for instance, a two-way teleconferencing link goes down, plan for continuing the lecture by speakerphone, with students referring to predistributed printed materials as needed.
- Allow enough slack time in lectures for extra logistical tasks and occasional technical difficulties.
- If possible, do a pre-course dry run with at least some of the students, so they can get familiar with the equipment and procedures and alert you to any difficulties they run into.
- When it is feasible, have a facilitator at each student site. This person's main job is to make sure the technology at the students' end works smoothly. If the facilitator can assist with course administration and answer student questions about course material, so much the better.

In a distance course, establishing rapport with students and making them comfortable can be difficult.

- An informal lecture style, often effective in traditional classrooms, can be even more effective in a distance course. Be cheerful and use humor. (But in cross-cultural contexts, remember that what is funny to you may fall flat with your audience.)
- Remember that your voice will not reach the students with the clarity as in a traditional classroom. Speak clearly, not too fast, and avoid over-long sentences. Pause regularly.
- Early in the course, work in some concrete, real-world examples and applications to help the students relax, roll up their sleeves, and forget about the distance-learning aspect of the course.
- If the course is interactive, via teleconferencing or real-time typed communication, get students into "send" mode as soon as possible. Ask them questions. Call on individuals if you judge that this is appropriate.
- A student-site assistant with a friendly manner can also help the students quickly settle into the course.

The distance learning format will make it hard for you to gauge how well students are responding to your instruction. In a traditional course, students' incomprehension or frustration often registers in facial expression, tone of voice, muttered comments—all of which are, depending on the instructional format, either difficult or impossible to pick up on in a distance course. Have some way for students to give feedback on how well the course is going for them. Possibilities:

- Quickly written surveys ("On a scale of 1 to 5, please rate …") every few weeks.
- Periodic "How are things going?" phone calls from you.
- A student-site assistant can act as your "eyes and ears" for this aspect of the instruction, and students may be more comfortable voicing frustrations to him or her than to you.

If students are to mail in finished work, set deadlines with allowance for due to mail delivery times, and with allowance for the possibility of lost mail. This is especially important for the end of the term, when you have a deadline for turning in grades.

Cheating is a problem in any course, but especially so in distance courses. Once again, an on-site facilitator is an asset. Another means of forestalling cheating is to have open-book exams, which takes away the advantage of sneaking a peek at the text.

Good student-instructor interaction takes conscious effort and planning in a distance course. Provide students with a variety of ways to contact you:

- E-mail is the handiest way for most students to stay in touch.
- Phone; a toll-free number is ideal. When students are most likely to be free in the evenings, set the number up for your home address and schedule evening office hours when students can count on reaching you.
- When students can make occasional in-person visits to your office, provide for that as well.

ADVANTAGES IN DISTANCE EDUCATION

Compared to traditional courses, more of the information shared in a distance course is, or can be, preserved for later review. Students can review videotaped lectures, instructor-student exchanges via e-mail can be reread, class discussions are on a reviewable discussion list, and so on.

To the extent that students are on their own, working out of texts or watching prerecorded video, course material can be modularized and customized to suit the needs of individual students: where a traditional course would necessarily be offered as a 4-unit lecture series, the counterpart distance course could be broken into four 1-unit modules, with students free to take only those modules they need. This is especially beneficial when the course is aimed at students who already have some professional experience with statistics and need to fill-in-gaps rather than comprehensive instruction.

STUDENT INTERACTION

Surprisingly, some instructors have found that students interact more with one another in a well-designed distance course than in a traditional course, even when the students are physically separated from one another. Part of the reason may be a higher level of motivation among distance learners. But another reason is the same technologies which facilitate student-instructor communication—things like e-mail and discussion lists—also facilitate student-student communication. In some cases, distance learners have actually done better than traditional learners taking the very same course. Better student interaction was thought to be the main reason.

One implication is that while group projects, involving statistical evaluations of real-world data, might seem more difficult to set up in a distance course, they are actually no harder, and the students learn just as much. The web has many real-world data sources, like the U.S. Department of Commerce (home.doc.gov) which has links to the U.S. Census Bureau (www.census.gov), the Bureau of Economic Analysis (www.bea.gov), and other agencies that compile publicly-available data.

Suggested References

THE AMERICAN STATISTICAL ASSOCIATION

Contact Information

1429 Duke Street
Alexandria, VA 22314-3415
Phone: (703) 684-1221 or toll-free: (888) 231-3473
Fax: (703) 684-2037

ASA Publications

Stats: The Magazine for Students of Statistics
CHANCE magazine
The American Statistician
AmStat News

BOOKS

Huff, Darryll and Geis, Irving (1954). *How to Lie with Statistics.* Classic text on the use and misuse of statistics.

Moore, David S. (2000) *Statistics: Concepts and Controversies,* fifth edition. Does not go deeply in to computational aspects of statistical methods. Good resource for emphasizing concepts and applications.

Tufte, Edward R. (2001). *The Visual Display of Quantitative Information,* second edition. A beautiful book, the first of three by Tufte on the use of graphic images to summarize and interpret numerical data. The books are virtual works of art in their own right.

Tanur, Judith M. (1989) *Statistics: A Guide to the Unknown,* third edition. Another excellent source of illustrations.

REFERENCES FOR DISTANCE LEARNING

Bolland, Thomas W. (1994). "Successful Customers of Statistics at a Distant Learning Site." *Proceedings of the Quality and Productivity Section, American Statistical Association,* pp. 300–304.

Lawrence, Betty and Gaines, Leonard M. (1997). "An Evaluation of the Effectiveness of an Activity-Based Approach to Statistics for Distance Learners." *Proceedings of the Section on Statistical Education, American Statistical Association,* pp. 271–272.

Wegman, Edward J. and Solka, Jeffrey L. (1999). "Implications for Distance Learning: Methodologies for Statistical Education." *Proceedings of the Section on Statistical Education, the Section on Teaching Statistics in the Health Sciences, and the Section on Statistical Consulting, American Statistical Association,* pp. 13–16.

Distance Learning: Principles for Effective Design, Delivery, and Evaluation

University of Idaho website: www.uidaho.edu/evo/distglan.html

Part II

Hints for Advanced Placement Statistics Courses

AP Features of the Text

Understandable Statistics is particularly well-suited for Advanced Placement statistics courses. The standard topics are carefully presented, the Guided Exercises invite students to be active learners, and there is an emphasis on interpreting statistical results in real-world contexts.

Technology support for the TI-83 Plus, MINITAB, and Microsoft Excel are included in the text. Two technology supplements, the *Technology Guide* and the *Excel Guide,* give detailed instructions for the use of various technologies and contain supplemental learning activities to help students use technology to explore statistics.

The seventh edition also incorporates a number of features to make the text even more useful for AP courses:

- The normal distribution table has been changed to the cumulative, left-tailed style provided during the AP exam.
- Section 1.3, Introduction to Experimental Design, is a new section on issues related to the planning of statistical studies.
- Dotplots are discussed in Problems 17, 18, and 19 of Section 2.2.
- Section 5.1, Introduction to Random Variables and Probability Distributions, now includes the mean and standard deviation of a linear transformation of a random variable. The section also includes the mean and standard deviation for linear combinations of independent random variables. (The mean and standard deviation for a linear combination of two random variables are discussed in Problem 16 of Section 10.3.)
- A discussion of normal quantile plots is included in the Using Technology section of Chapter 6.
- Section 7.3, Sampling Distributions for Proportions, is a new section. The topic of this section is also addressed in sections on confidence intervals and the testing of proportions.
- Residual plots for linear regression are discussed in Problems 17 and 18 of Section 10.2.
- Section 10.4, Inferences Concerning Regression Parameters, has been revised. Tests of the correlation coefficient are now done with Student's t distribution rather than a special table for r. Additional topics include testing and confidence intervals for the slope of the least-squares line.
- The Instructor's Annotated Edition now includes margin answers for both odd and even problems. In addition, teaching hints and comments continue to be provided within each section.
- Headers for each example and Guided Exercise in the text quickly identify the statistical analysis being demonstrated. Headers for each of the section and chapter problems identify the field of study from which the application is drawn.

In addition, the Test Item File supplement contains a special section of questions geared to preparing students for the AP Exam. It contains 48 multiple-choice questions and 12 free-response questions. The first 11 free-response questions are similar to the types of questions students will see on the Part A of the free-response section of the AP Exam while the last question is similar to the longer more in-depth free-response question the students will see in Part B.

Information about the AP Statistics Exam

OUTLINE OF MAJOR TOPICS COVERED IN THE AP STATISTICS EXAM

I. Exploring Data: Observing patterns and departures from patterns
Use of graphical and numerical techniques to study patterns and departure from patterns, with an emphasis on interpreting the information from graphical displays and numerical summaries.

A. Single-variable data
Students should be able to construct and interpret graphs such as histograms, stem-and-leaf plots, and box-and-whisker plots. They must also be well-versed in different ways of describing the shape, center, and variability of a distribution of data values and the position of individual values relative to the set.

- A distribution's shape may variously be described as (among other things) either symmetric or asymmetric, approximately normal, or uniform.
- Summary statistics such as the mean, median, and mode give measures of the center.
- Values such as the variance, standard deviation, range, and interquartile range describe the variability.
- Quartiles, percentiles, standardized scores (z-scores) and outlier values give information about the position of an individual data value relative to the overall distribution.

Students should also understand the effect that changing units has on the different summary measures.

B. Data pairs
Students should be able to use scatter diagrams to detect patterns in data pairs and to find the equation of the least-squares regression line. They should know how to use the plot of residuals to judge the appropriateness of a linear model, and how to use the correlation coefficient to judge a linear model's strength. Students should be able to identify outliers and influential points. They should also understand the relation of causation and correlation.

II. Planning a Study: Deciding what and how to measure
In open-ended questions, students need to demonstrate that they understand how to gather data according to a well-developed plan. Methods of data collection such as census, sample survey using simple random samples, experiment, and observational study may be used. Students should demonstrate an awareness of sampling error, sources of bias, and use of stratification to reduce variation. Experimental designs, such as completely randomized design for two treatments and blocking designs, might be required.

III. Anticipating patterns: Producing models using probability and simulation
Under this topic, students use probability as a tool for anticipating what the distribution of data should look like for a given model. Particular topics include

- rules of probability
- law of large numbers
- independence of events
- mean and standard deviation of a random variable
- use of binomial distributions
- normal distributions and sampling distributions of a sample proportion
- sample mean
- difference of two independent sample proportions
- difference between two independent sample means

IV. Statistical inference: Confirming models
Students should know how to select appropriate models for statistical inference.

A. Confidence intervals

- their meaning
- large-sample confidence interval for a proportion
- large-sample confidence interval for a mean
- large-sample confidence interval for a difference between two proportions
- large-sample confidence interval for a difference between two means (unpaired and paired)

B. Tests of significance
   - structure and logic, including null hypothesis, alternate hypothesis, P values, one- and two-tailed tests
   - large-sample tests for a mean and a difference between two means (paired and unpaired)
   - large-sample tests for a proportion and a difference between two proportions
   - chi-square test for goodness of fit, homogeneity of proportions, and independence

C. Special case of normally distributed data
   - Student's t distribution
   - single-sample t procedures
   - two-sample t procedures (independent and matched pairs)
   - inference for slope of least-squares line

TYPES OF QUESTIONS

The AP test has two parts, the first of which is multiple-choice. The second part is a free-response section requiring the student to answer open-ended questions and to complete an investigative task involving more extended reasoning. The two sections are given equal weight in determining the grade for the examination.

DURATION AND GRADING OF THE EXAM

The test is three hours long. The exam consists of two sections, each of which will last 90 minutes and will each account for 50% of the total exam grade: a multiple-choice section that consists of 40 problems, and a second section of six free-response problems. Students will be instructed before the multiple-choice section that they most likely will not have time to answer every multiple-choice problem, and that they do not benefit from guessing because 1/4 of the number of incorrect responses on the multiple-choice section will be deducted from the number of correct responses. The free-response section consists of two parts. Part A will be made up of 5 free-response problems for which they will be allowed 65 minutes. Part A will account for 75% of the free-response section. Part B consists of a longer more in-depth free-response problem. Students will be allowed 25 minutes for this part which will count as 25% of the free-response score.

CALCULATOR

Each student is expected to use a graphing calculator with statistics capabilities during the AP exam. *Understandable Statistics* uses the versatile and widely available TI-83 Plus.

FORMULAS AND TABLES

Formulas and tables are provided for students taking the AP Statistics Examination. The format of the formulas and some of the tables is slightly different from those in the text. Note that the normal distribution table for the AP exam gives areas in the *left tail* of the distribution. (Some references give the area from 0 to z instead; *Understandable Statistics* contains both types of tables.) The table for Student's t distribution provides critical values for areas in the right tail of the distribution, and gives critical values for different confidence levels.

The following formulas are provided during the AP exam.

Descriptive Statistics

$$\overline{x} = \frac{\sum x_i}{n}$$

$$s_x = \sqrt{\frac{1}{n-1}\sum(x_i - \overline{x})^2}$$

$$s_p = \sqrt{\frac{(n_1-1)s_1^2 + (n_2-1)s_2^2}{(n_1-1)+(n_2-1)}}$$

$$\hat{y} = b_0 + b_1 x$$

$$b_1 = \frac{\sum(x_i - \overline{x})(y_i - \overline{y})}{\sum(x_i - \overline{x})^2}$$

$$b_0 = \overline{y} - b_1\overline{x}$$

$$r = \frac{1}{n-1}\sum\left(\frac{x_i - \overline{x}}{s_x}\right)\left(\frac{y_i - \overline{y}}{s_y}\right)$$

$$b_1 = r\frac{s_y}{s_x}$$

$$s_{b_1} = \frac{\sqrt{\frac{\sum(y_i - \hat{y}_i)^2}{n-2}}}{\sqrt{\sum(x_i - \overline{x})^2}}$$

Probability

$$P(A \cup B) = P(A) + P(B) - P(A \cap B)$$

$$P(A|B) = \frac{P(A \cap B)}{P(B)}$$

$$E(X) = \mu_x = \sum x_i p_i$$

$$Var(X) = \sigma_x^2 = \sum(x_i - \mu_x)^2 p_i$$

If X has a binomial distribution with parameters n and p, then:

$$P(X = k) = \binom{n}{k} p^k (1-p)^{n-k}$$

$$\mu_x = np$$

$$\sigma_x = \sqrt{np(1-p)}$$

$$\mu_{\hat{p}} = p$$

$$\sigma_{\hat{p}} = \sqrt{\frac{p(1-p)}{n}}$$

If $\overline{x}$ is the mean of a random sample of size n from an infinite population with mean μ and standard deviation σ, then:

$$\mu_{\overline{x}} = \mu$$

$$\sigma_{\overline{x}} = \frac{\sigma}{\sqrt{n}}$$

Inferential Statistics

Standardized test statistic: $\dfrac{\text{statistic} - \text{parameter}}{\text{standard deviation of statistic}}$

Confidence interval: statistic $\pm$ (critical value) $\cdot$ (standard deviation of statistic)

Single-Sample	
Statistic	Standard Deviation of Statistic
Sample Mean	$\dfrac{\sigma}{\sqrt{n}}$
Sample Proportion	$\sqrt{\dfrac{p(1-p)}{n}}$

Two-Sample	
Statistic	Standard Deviation of Statistic
Difference of sample means	$\sqrt{\dfrac{\sigma_1^2}{n_1}+\dfrac{\sigma_2^2}{n_2}}$ Special case when $\sigma_1 = \sigma_2$ $\sigma\sqrt{\dfrac{1}{n_1}+\dfrac{1}{n_2}}$
Difference of sample proportions	$\sqrt{\dfrac{p_1(1-p_1)}{n_1}+\dfrac{p_2(1-p_2)}{n_2}}$ Special case when $p_1 = p_2$ $\sqrt{p(1-p)}\sqrt{\dfrac{1}{n_1}+\dfrac{1}{n_2}}$

$$\text{Chi-square test statistic} = \sum \frac{(\text{observed} - \text{expected})^2}{\text{expected}}$$

DIFFERENCES IN CONVENTION AND NOTATION BETWEEN *UNDERSTANDABLE STATISTICS* AND THE AP EXAM

Notation and Terminology Correlation Chart	
Understanding Statistics	**AP Statistics Exam**
Box-and-whisker plot	Box Plot
Alternate hypothesis: H_1	Alternate hypothesis: H_a
Smallest level of significance at which to reject the null hypothesis: P-value	Smallest level of significance at which to reject the null hypothesis: p-value
Conditional probability: $P(A \text{ given } B)$	Conditional probability: $P(A \mid B)$
Ogive	Cumulative graph

SOME COMMON STUDENT MISTAKES ON THE AP EXAM

Students taking the AP exam often make the following mistakes:

- Failing to follow through with the answer to a question. For example, students asked to compare two data sets may describe each set but fail to finish with a statement that compares the one to the other.
- Getting mixed up about what the numbers in data sets mean. For example, students will sometimes treat one-variable data in a frequency table as if it were paired data, and construct a scatter diagram when a histogram is called for.
- Misreading the computer printouts that appear as graphics on the test. For example, a student may take a number to represent the slope of the regression line when in fact this number represents the constant term.
- Getting confused by the coding for representing data values of variables. For example, a student may forget that if x represents years after 1900, then the year 1995 is represented by $x = 5$, not $x = 1995$.

MORE INFORMATION AND SAMPLE QUESTIONS

Advanced Placement Program Course Description - Statistics, published by The College Board, contains sample questions, formulas, tables, and a description of the AP Statistics course. This publication is available from the College Board.

The College Board
45 Columbus Avenue
New York, NY 10023-6992
Phone (212) 713-8000

Additionally, old AP Statistics tests are available. The College Board releases the free-response part of the exam every year and the multiple-choice part once every five years. The free-response sections and sample solutions are available for free on the College Board website at www.collegeboard.org/ap/statistics. Copies of the multiple-choice part of the exam can be purchased from the College Board by calling or by visiting the "Shop" section on the College Board website.

Hints for Helping Students Succeed on the AP Statistics Exam

DEVELOP THEIR COMMUNICATION SKILLS

On the free-response portion of the AP Statistics Exam, graders will be looking for students to show that they understand the statistical knowledge and that they are able to communicate that knowledge clearly. Throughout the course, give students lots of opportunities to explain their reasoning. Encourage them to show their thinking in a variety of ways. They should use diagrams where appropriate and words to explain the reasons they choose to use certain techniques. Encourage them to write as if they are explaining their ideas to someone who has not yet mastered statistics.

DEVELOP THEIR GRAPHING CALCULATOR SKILLS

Give students lots of opportunities to develop their skills using a graphing calculator to do statistics. The more familiar they are with the capabilities of their calculator and how to use them, the more time they will have during the AP Statistics Exam to devote to their solution.

DEVELOP THEIR SKILLS USING STATISTICAL TABLES AND FORMULAS

Be sure that students can quickly use the statistical tables and apply the formulas that are provided on the AP Statistics Exam.

EMPHASIZE CONCEPTUAL UNDERSTANDING

Displaying Data

Be sure students know the appropriate uses of the various graphs. They should use

- Bar graphs when comparing data sets;
- Circle graphs for displaying how a total is dispersed into several categories;
- Time plots to display how data change over time;
- Histograms or frequency polygons to display relative frequencies of grouped data;
- Stem-and-leaf displays for displaying grouped data in a way that does not lose the detail of the original raw data.

Drawing and Using Ogives (Section 2.2)

Be sure students understand the relationship between the shapes of the frequency distribution curve and the cumulative distribution curve. The one can be used to infer the other, as illustrated on the next page.

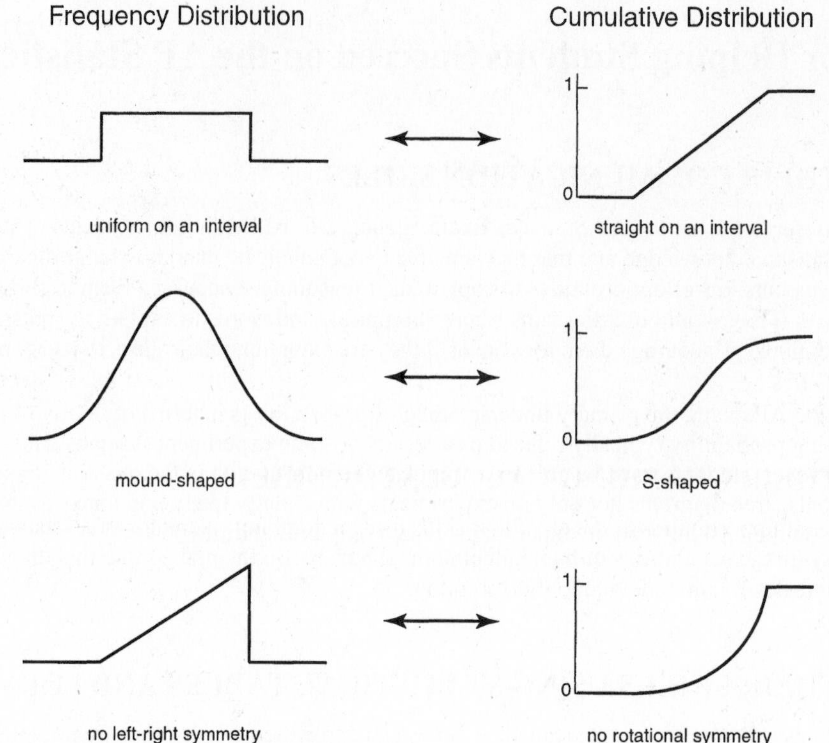

Quartiles

The text mentions, in passing, that there are different conventions for calculating the first and third quartiles of a data set. The convention in the text is that the first quartile is the median of the data set's lower half, *not including* the data set's overall median (the second quartile). Correspondingly, the third quartile is the median of the upper half, not including the overall median. The usual alternate method is to include the overall median in both the upper and the lower half of the data set. Then it plays a role in the calculation of both the first and the third quartile.

To illustrate how it matters which method you choose, use both methods to calculate the first and third quartiles of the data set below, where $N = 15$, an odd number.

Test scores														
59	63	68	73	74	76	81	84 median	85	88	91	95	95	97	98

When the median is left out of the lower and upper halves of the data, the first quartile is the fourth of the first seven values, namely 73, and the third quartile is the fourth of the last seven values, namely 95. When the median is included in the lower and upper halves of the data, the first quartile is halfway between the fourth and fifth of the first eight values, which makes it 73.5. And the third quartile is halfway between the fourth and fifth of the last eight values, which makes it 93.

The two methods always give the same results when N, the size of the data set, is an even number, because then the issue of whether or not to include the median in each half does not arise.

Ways to Think about Probability

As the text describes in Section 4.1, there are several methods for assigning a probability to an event:

- Probability based on intuition is often called *subjective* probability. Thus understood, probability is a numerical measure of a person's confidence about some event. Subjective probability is assumed to be reflected in a person's decisions: the higher an event's probability, the more the person would be willing to bet on its occurring.
- Probability based on relative frequency often called *experimental* probability, because relative frequency is calculated from an observed history of experiment outcomes. It can also be called *observed* probability.
- Probability based on equally likely outcomes is often called *theoretical* probability, because it is ultimately derived from a theoretical model of the experiment's structure. The experiment may be conducted only once, or not at all, and need not be repeatable.

These three ways of treating probability are compatible and complementary. For a reasonable, well-informed person, the subjective probability of an event should match the theoretical probability, and the theoretical probability in turn predicts the observed probability as the experiment is repeated many times.

For purposes of the AP exam, the primary understanding of probability is in terms of relative frequency. Test questions involving probability typically refer to past results of some experiment (such as clinical trials of a medication). However, students must be able to manipulate the information in the question appropriately. They should be able to use tree diagrams not only on experiments with equally likely outcomes, as in Section 4.3 (see the figure below on the left) but also on experiments where only probabilities of various events are given (see the figure on the right).

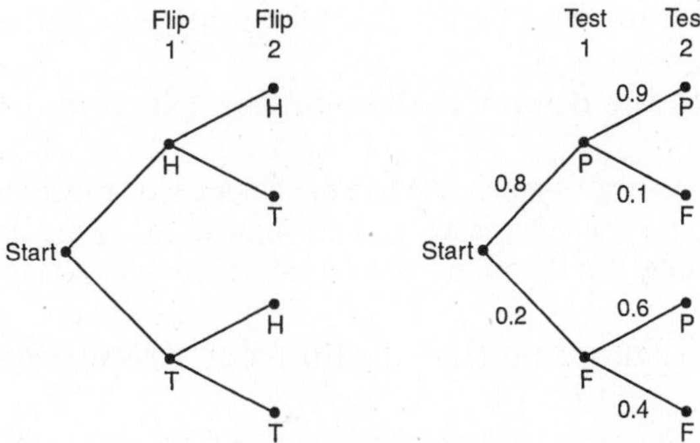

Probability Statements with > and ≥: Discrete versus Continuous Variables

When x is a discrete variable, there is a real difference between, say, $P(x > 5)$, the probability that x is greater than 5, and $P(x \geq 5)$, the probability that x is greater than or equal to 5. The difference comes from the fact that $P(x = 5)$, the probability that x equals 5, is in general greater than zero. By contrast, when x is a continuous variable, $P(x = 5)$ is essentially zero: the probability that the variable takes exactly the value 5 is vanishingly small. This means that there is no important difference between $P(x > 5)$ and $P(x \geq 5)$ when x is a continuous variable.

Binomial Probabilities (Section 5.2)

Students should be able to show that $p(1 - p) = pq$ has its maxim value at $p = 0.5$. There are at least three ways to demonstrate this: graphically, algebraically, and using calculus.

Graphical and algebraic methods

See the Teaching Tips for Chapter 5.

Calculus-based method

Advanced Placement students have probably had (or are taking) calculus, including tests for local extrema. For a function with continuous first and second derivatives, at an extremum the first derivative equals zero and the second derivative is either positive (at a minimum) or negative (at a maximum).

The first derivative of $f(p) = pq = p(1-p)$ is given by

$$\begin{aligned} f'(p) &= \frac{d}{dp}[p(1-p)] \\ &= \frac{d}{dp}[-p^2 + p] \\ &= -2p+1 \end{aligned}$$

Solve $f'(p) = 0: -2p+1=0$

$$p = \frac{1}{2}$$

Now find $f''\left(\frac{1}{2}\right)$: $f''(p) = \frac{d}{dp}[f'(p)]$

$$\begin{aligned} &= \frac{d}{dp}(-2p+1) \\ &= -2 \end{aligned}$$

So $f''\left(\frac{1}{2}\right) = -2.$

Since the second derivative is negative when the first derivative equals zero, $f(p)$ has a maximum at $p = 1/2$.

Normal Approximation to the Binomial Distribution (Section 6.4)

As a test of the suitability of the normal approximation to the binomial distribution, *Understandable Statistics* uses the test $np > 5$, $nq > 5$. The AP exam, however, expects students to use the test $np > 10$, $nq > 10$. This test is based on recent studies indicating that the >5 test is not adequate for very small p or q.

Continuity Correlation in Sampling Distributions for Proportions (Section 7.3)

Emphasize the difference in the continuity correction that must be taken into account in a sampling distribution for proportions and the continuity correction for a normal distribution used to approximate the probability distribution of the discrete random variable in a binomial probability experiment. That is, instead of subtracting 0.5 from the left endpoint and adding 0.5 to the right endpoint of an interval involved in a normal distribution approximating a binomial probability distribution, $0.5/n$ must be subtracted from the left endpoint and $0.5/n$ added to the right endpoint of such an interval, where n is the number of trials, when a normal distribution is used to approximate a sampling distribution for proportions.

Understanding Confidence Intervals (Section 8.1)

Students need to understand that the method for creating confidence intervals is not a procedure that comes up with a statement having a specified probability (like 90%, or 95%) of being true. Instead, it is a procedure that has a specified probability of coming up with a true statement. These are two different things.

To understand the difference, consider a simple task: guessing the color of a randomly-drawn marble. Suppose a sack contains some red marbles and some blue marbles. And suppose we have a friend who will reach in, draw out a marble, and announce its color while we have our backs turned. The friend can be counted on to announce the correct color *exactly 90% of the time* (that is, with a probability of 90%) and the wrong color the other 10% of the time. So if the marble drawn is blue, the friend will say "blue" 9 times out of 10 and "red" the remaining time; and conversely for a red marble. This is like creating an 0.90 confidence interval.

The friend reaches in, pulls out a marble, and announces, "blue." Does this mean that we are 90% sure the friend is holding a blue marble? Not necessarily. Suppose we think that the bag contains three red marbles and two blue ones. Then we expect the friend to draw a red marble 3/5 of the time and announce "blue" 10% of those times, or 3/50 of all draws. And we expect the friend to draw a blue marble 2/5 of the time and announce "blue" 90% of those times, or 18/50 of all draws. This means that the ratio of true "blue" announcements to false ones is 18 to 3, or 6 to 1. And thus we attach a probability of 6/7 = 85.7%, not 90%, to our friend's announcement that the marble drawn is blue, even though we believe our friend to be telling the truth 90% of the time. Simply put, our initial belief that there are more red marbles than blue ones pulls our confidence in a "blue" announcement downward.

Now, if we believe that there are an *equal* number of red and blue marbles in the bag, then, as it turns out, we will attach 90% probability to "blue" announcements and to "red" announcements as well. But *this is a special case.* In general, the probabilities we attach to each of our friend's statements will be different from the frequency with which we think he is telling the truth.

For the same reasons, when we create a 0.90 confidence interval, we will in general not be 90% sure that the interval contains the mean. It could *happen* to turn out that we were 90% sure, but this will depend on what ideas we had about the population mean going in. Suppose we were fairly sure, to start with, that the population mean lay somewhere between 10 and 20, and suppose we then took a sample that led to the construction of a 0.90 confidence interval which ran from 31 to 46. We would *not* conclude, with 90% certainty, that the mean lay between 31 and 46. Instead, we would have a probability lower than that, because previously we thought the mean was outside that range. At the same time, we would be much more ready to believe that the mean lay between 31 and 46 than we were before, because, after all, a procedure with a 90% success rate produced that prediction.

To repeat: the procedure for finding a confidence interval of confidence level c does not, in general, produce a statement (about the value of a population mean) that has a probability c of being true. This issue is discussed somewhat more fully in the Teaching Tips for Chapter 8.

Hypothesis testing and *P* values (Sections 9.1–9.3)

Hypothesis Tests

The hypothesis tests in these sections test the value of a population mean, μ, against some specified value, denoted by k. Be sure students understand when to use each test.

Z-tests are appropriate for testing the null hypothesis $H_0\colon \mu = k$ against one of the three alternative hypotheses: $H_1\colon \mu > k$, $H_1\colon \mu < k$, or $H_1\colon \mu \neq k$ when (1) the data in the sample are known to be from a normal distribution (in which case, the sample may be any size), or when (2) the data distribution is unknown or the data are believed to be from a non-normal distribution, but the sample size is large $(n > 30)$. The z-test requires the population standard deviation σ to be known, but if the sample size n is large, the sample standard deviation, s, is assumed to be close to σ, and can be used instead.

For an upper- or right-tailed test, the alternative hypothesis is $H_1\colon \mu > k$, where k is the hypothesized value of the population mean and the sample mean $\bar{x}$ is greater than k. (If $\bar{x}$ is less than or equal to k, you do not use this test.) This test calculates the sample standard deviation s from the sample data and substitutes s for σ in the formula $z_{calculated} = \frac{\bar{x}-k}{\sigma/\sqrt{n}}$. The P value is then calculated as the probability of getting a z-value as large or larger than the one observed (that is, $z_{calculated}$) if the null hypothesis is true; small P values indicate that the null hypothesis should be rejected.

For a lower- or left-tailed test, the alternative hypothesis is $H_1\colon \mu < k$, where k is the hypothesized value of the population mean and the sample mean $\bar{x}$ is less than k. (If $\bar{x}$ is greater than or equal to k, you do not use this test.) This test calculates the sample standard deviation s from the sample data and substitutes s for σ in the formula $z_{calculated} = \frac{\bar{x}-k}{\sigma/\sqrt{n}}$. The P value is then calculated as the probability of getting a z-value as small or smaller than the one observed (that is, $z_{calculated}$) if the null hypothesis is true; small P values indicate that the null hypothesis should be rejected.

For a two-tailed test, the alternative hypothesis is H_1: $\mu \neq k$, where k is the hypothesized value of the population mean. This test calculates the sample standard deviation s from the sample data and substitutes s for σ in the formula $z_{calculated} = \frac{\bar{x}-k}{\sigma/\sqrt{n}}$. The P value is then calculated as the probability of getting a z-value as far or further away from zero as the one observed (that is, $z_{calculated}$) if the null hypothesis is true. This P value is always double the value found using the appropriate one-tailed test (right-tailed for $\mu > k$, left-tailed for $\mu < k$). Small P values indicate that the null hypothesis should be rejected.

P Values

Suppose you and a friend were tossing a coin 100 times, and if there are more than 50 heads, you buy ice cream for both of you; if there are fewer than 50 heads, your friend buys, and if there are exactly 50 heads, each person buys his or her own ice cream. You and your friend plan to toss the coin and have ice cream every day after school. You reason, correctly, that over the school year, you will buy about half the time, and your friend will buy about half the time IF the coin you are tossing is fair. However, after a week or so, you notice that there seem to be lots of heads and that you seem to be doing most of the buying. You also notice that your friend always seems to have a coin handy, and most of the time you use his coin for the coin toss. Where do you draw the line between "I'm just unlucky" and "That jerk is cheating!"? At 55 heads out of 100 tosses? At 60 heads? At 75 heads? At 90 heads?

The P value is helping to draw the line for you. It tells you how likely you are to see, say, 60 or more heads in 100 tosses of a fair coin. If this probability is, in your opinion, too small, you know whom *not* to call your friend!

Many problems specify testing at level α; in these problems, if the P value is less than α, reject H_0. Frequently-used α are 0.10, 0.05, and 0.01; however, there is nothing sacred or special about these values. If you want to use an alpha of 0.0827 as your cutoff point for "too small," you can. The numbers in the tables for z values and t values were originally obtained by hand, using calculus and old-fashioned mechanical calculators. The amount of work that went into calculating the values cannot be overstated, and when these tables were first printed in the 1920s, 1930s, and 1940s, it made life much easier for practicing statisticians. If you wanted to know which value of Student's t with 14 degrees of freedom cut off an area of 0.04135 (instead of 0.05 or 0.025, say) in the upper tail, you either said that the t-value was between the tabled values 1.761 and 2.145, or you calculated it yourself. Before there were powerful and readily accessible computers, most people said tail areas of 0.05 or 0.025 were good enough for them. And that is why 0.10, 0.05, 0.01, etc., are so common—we have always used these numbers. Even today, at the bottom of z, t, etc., tables in textbooks, you can find statements such as "reprinted with the permission of the *Biometrika* trustees," a reference to the fact that these tables are copies of the tables that originally appeared in the journal *Biometrika* many years ago.

Understanding the Results of a Hypothesis Test

Just as students may get confused about the probability associated with a confidence interval, they may get confused about the probability associated with a hypothesis test. The P value is *not* the probability, in light of the data, of the null hypothesis. Instead, the P value is the probability that the data would turn out the way it did, assuming the null hypothesis to be true.

To illustrate: consider two coins in a sack, one fair and one two-headed. One of these coins is pulled out at random and flipped. It comes up heads. Let us take, as our null hypothesis, the statement "The flipped coin was the fair one." The probability of the outcome, given the null hypothesis, is 1/2, because a fair coin will come up heads half the time. This probability is in fact the P value of the outcome. On the other hand, the probability that the null hypothesis is true, given the evidence, is 1/3, since out of all the heads outcomes one will see in many such trials, 1/3 are from the fair coin.

The meaning of the probability associated with a hypothesis test is more fully discussed in the Teaching Tips for Chapter 9.

Part III

Transparency Masters

TABLE A Areas of a Standard Normal Distribution
(Alternate Version of Appendix II Table 5)

The table entries represent the area under the standard normal curve from 0 to the specified value of z.

z	.00	.01	.02	.03	.04	.05	.06	.07	.08	.09
0.0	.0000	.0040	.0080	.0120	.0160	.0199	.0239	.0279	.0319	.0359
0.1	.0398	.0438	.0478	.0517	.0557	.0596	.0636	.0675	.0714	.0753
0.2	.0793	.0832	.0871	.0910	.0948	.0987	.1026	.1064	.1103	.1141
0.3	.1179	.1217	.1255	.1293	.1331	.1368	.1406	.1443	.1480	.1517
0.4	.1554	.1591	.1628	.1664	.1700	.1736	.1772	.1808	.1844	.1879
0.5	.1915	.1950	.1985	.2019	.2054	.2088	.2123	.2157	.2190	.2224
0.6	.2257	.2291	.2324	.2357	.2389	.2422	.2454	.2486	.2517	.2549
0.7	.2580	.2611	.2642	.2673	.2704	.2734	.2764	.2794	.2823	.2852
0.8	.2881	.2910	.2939	.2967	.2995	.3023	.3051	.3078	.3106	.3133
0.9	.3159	.3186	.3212	.3238	.3264	.3289	.3315	.3340	.3365	.3389
1.0	.3413	.3438	.3461	.3485	.3508	.3531	.3554	.3577	.3599	.3621
1.1	.3643	.3665	.3686	.3708	.3729	.3749	.3770	.3790	.3810	.3830
1.2	.3849	.3869	.3888	.3907	.3925	.3944	.3962	.3980	.3997	.4015
1.3	.4032	.4049	.4066	.4082	.4099	.4115	.4131	.4147	.4162	.4177
1.4	.4192	.4207	.4222	.4236	.4251	.4265	.4279	.4292	.4306	.4319
1.5	.4332	.4345	.4357	.4370	.4382	.4394	.4406	.4418	.4429	.4441
1.6	.4452	.4463	.4474	.4484	.4495	.4505	.4515	.4525	.4535	.4545
1.7	.4554	.4564	.4573	.4582	.4591	.4599	.4608	.4616	.4625	.4633
1.8	.4641	.4649	.4656	.4664	.4671	.4678	.4686	.4693	.4699	.4706
1.9	.4713	.4719	.4726	.4732	.4738	.4744	.4750	.4756	.4761	.4767
2.0	.4772	.4778	.4783	.4788	.4793	.4798	.4803	.4808	.4812	.4817
2.1	.4821	.4826	.4830	.4834	.4838	.4842	.4846	.4850	.4854	.4857
2.2	.4861	.4864	.4868	.4871	.4875	.4878	.4881	.4884	.4887	.4890
2.3	.4893	.4896	.4898	.4901	.4904	.4906	.4909	.4911	.4913	.4916
2.4	.4918	.4920	.4922	.4925	.4927	.4929	.4931	.4932	.4934	.4936
2.5	.4938	.4940	.4941	.4943	.4945	.4946	.4948	.4949	.4951	.4952
2.6	.4953	.4955	.4956	.4957	.4959	.4960	.4961	.4962	.4963	.4964
2.7	.4965	.4966	.4967	.4968	.4969	.4970	.4971	.4972	.4973	.4974
2.8	.4974	.4975	.4976	.4977	.4977	.4978	.4979	.4979	.4980	.4981
2.9	.4981	.4982	.4982	.4983	.4984	.4984	.4985	.4985	.4986	.4986
3.0	.4987	.4987	.4987	.4988	.4988	.4989	.4989	.4989	.4990	.4990
3.1	.4990	.4991	.4991	.4991	.4992	.4992	.4992	.4992	.4993	.4993
3.2	.4993	.4993	.4994	.4994	.4994	.4994	.4994	.4995	.4995	.4995
3.3	.4995	.4995	.4995	.4996	.4996	.4996	.4996	.4996	.4996	.4997
3.4	.4997	.4997	.4997	.4997	.4997	.4997	.4997	.4997	.4997	.4998
3.5	.4998	.4998	.4998	.4998	.4998	.4998	.4998	.4998	.4998	.4998
3.6	.4998	.4998	.4998	.4999	.4999	.4999	.4999	.4999	.4999	.4999

For values of z greater than or equal to 3.70, use 0.4999 to approximate the shaded area under the standard normal curve.

TABLE 1 Random Numbers

92630	78240	19267	95457	53497	23894	37708	79862	76471	66418
79445	78735	71549	44843	26404	67318	00701	34986	66751	99723
59654	71966	27386	50004	05358	94031	29281	18544	52429	06080
31524	49587	76612	39789	13537	48086	59483	60680	84675	53014
06348	76938	90379	51392	55887	71015	09209	79157	24440	30244
28703	51709	94456	48396	73780	06436	86641	69239	57662	80181
68108	89266	94730	95761	75023	48464	65544	96583	18911	16391
99938	90704	93621	66330	33393	95261	95349	51769	91616	33238
91543	73196	34449	63513	83834	99411	58826	40456	69268	48562
42103	02781	73920	56297	72678	12249	25270	36678	21313	75767
17138	27584	25296	28387	51350	61664	37893	05363	44143	42677
28297	14280	54524	21618	95320	38174	60579	08089	94999	78460
09331	56712	51333	06289	75345	08811	82711	57392	25252	30333
31295	04204	93712	51287	05754	79396	87399	51773	33075	97061
36146	15560	27592	42089	99281	59640	15221	96079	09961	05371
29553	18432	13630	05529	02791	81017	49027	79031	50912	09399
23501	22642	63081	08191	89420	67800	55137	54707	32945	64522
57888	85846	67967	07835	11314	01545	48535	17142	08552	67457
55336	71264	88472	04334	63919	36394	11196	92470	70543	29776
10087	10072	55980	64688	68239	20461	89381	93809	00796	95945
34101	81277	66090	88872	37818	72142	67140	50785	21380	16703
53362	44940	60430	22834	14130	96593	23298	56203	92671	15925
82975	66158	84731	19436	55790	69229	28661	13675	99318	76873
54827	84673	22898	08094	14326	87038	42892	21127	30712	48489
25464	59098	27436	89421	80754	89924	19097	67737	80368	08795

TABLE 1 *continued*

67609	60214	41475	84950	40133	02546	09570	45682	50165	15609
44921	70924	61295	51137	47596	86735	35561	76649	18217	63446
33170	30972	98130	95828	49786	13301	36081	80761	33985	68621
84687	85445	06208	17654	51333	02878	35010	67578	61574	20749
71886	56450	36567	09395	96951	35507	17555	35212	69106	01679
00475	02224	74722	14721	40215	21351	08596	45625	83981	63748
25993	38881	68361	59560	41274	69742	40703	37993	03435	18873
92882	53178	99195	93803	56985	53089	15305	50522	55900	43026
25138	26810	07093	15677	60688	04410	24505	37890	67186	62829
84631	71882	12991	83028	82484	90339	91950	74579	03539	90122
34003	92326	12793	61453	48121	74271	28363	66561	75220	35908
53775	45749	05734	86169	42762	70175	97310	73894	88606	19994
59316	97885	72807	54966	60859	11932	35265	71601	55577	67715
20479	66557	50705	26999	09854	52591	14063	30214	19890	19292
86180	84931	25455	26044	02227	52015	21820	50599	51671	65411
21451	68001	72710	40261	61281	13172	63819	48970	51732	54113
98062	68375	80089	24135	72355	95428	11808	29740	81644	86610
01788	64429	14430	94575	75153	94576	61393	96192	03227	32258
62465	04841	43272	68702	01274	05437	22953	18946	99053	41690
94324	31089	84159	92933	99989	89500	91586	02802	69471	68274
05797	43984	21575	09908	70221	19791	51578	36432	33494	79888
10395	14289	52185	09721	25789	38562	54794	04897	59012	89251
35177	56986	25549	59730	64718	52630	31100	62384	49483	11409
25633	89619	75882	98256	02126	72099	57183	55887	09320	72363
16464	48280	94254	45777	45150	68865	11382	11782	22695	41988

Source: Reprinted from *A Million Random Digits with 100,000 Normal Deviates* by the Rand Corporation (New York: The Free Press, 1955). Copyright 1955 by the Rand Corporation. Used by permission.

TABLE 2 Binomial Coefficients $C_{n,r}$

$n \backslash r$	0	1	2	3	4	5	6	7	8	9	10
1	1	1									
2	1	2	1								
3	1	3	3	1							
4	1	4	6	4	1						
5	1	5	10	10	5	1					
6	1	6	15	20	15	6	1				
7	1	7	21	35	35	21	7	1			
8	1	8	28	56	70	56	28	8	1		
9	1	9	36	84	126	126	84	36	9	1	
10	1	10	45	120	210	252	210	120	45	10	1
11	1	11	55	165	330	462	462	330	165	55	11
12	1	12	66	220	495	792	924	792	495	220	66
13	1	13	78	286	715	1,287	1,716	1,716	1,287	715	286
14	1	14	91	364	1,001	2,002	3,003	3,432	3,003	2,002	1,001
15	1	15	105	455	1,365	3,003	5,005	6,435	6,435	5,005	3,003
16	1	16	120	560	1,820	4,368	8,008	11,440	12,870	11,440	8,008
17	1	17	136	680	2,380	6,188	12,376	19,448	24,310	24,310	19,448
18	1	18	153	816	3,060	8,568	18,564	31,824	43,758	48,620	43,758
19	1	19	171	969	3,876	11,628	27,132	50,388	75,582	92,378	92,378
20	1	20	190	1,140	3,845	15,504	38,760	77,520	125,970	167,960	184,756

TABLE 3 Binomial Probability Distribution $C_{n,r}p^rq^{n-r}$

This table shows the probability of *r* successes in *n* independent trials, each with probability of success *p*.

		p																			
n	*r*	.01	.05	.10	.15	.20	.25	.30	.35	.40	.45	.50	.55	.60	.65	.70	.75	.80	.85	.90	.95
2	0	.980	.902	.810	.723	.640	.563	.490	.423	.360	.303	.250	.203	.160	.123	.090	.063	.040	.023	.010	.002
	1	.020	.095	.180	.255	.320	.375	.420	.455	.480	.495	.500	.495	.480	.455	.420	.375	.320	.255	.180	.095
	2	.000	.002	.010	.023	.040	.063	.090	.123	.160	.203	.250	.303	.360	.423	.490	.563	.640	.723	.810	.902
3	0	.970	.857	.729	.614	.512	.422	.343	.275	.216	.166	.125	.091	.064	.043	.027	.016	.008	.003	.001	.000
	1	.029	.135	.243	.325	.384	.422	.441	.444	.432	.408	.375	.334	.288	.239	.189	.141	.096	.057	.027	.007
	2	.000	.007	.028	.057	.096	.141	.189	.239	.288	.334	.375	.408	.432	.444	.441	.422	.384	.325	.243	.135
	3	.000	.000	.001	.003	.008	.016	.027	.043	.064	.091	.125	.166	.216	.275	.343	.422	.512	.614	.729	.857
4	0	.961	.815	.656	.522	.410	.316	.240	.179	.130	.092	.062	.041	.026	.015	.008	.004	.002	.001	.000	.000
	1	.039	.171	.292	.368	.410	.422	.412	.384	.346	.300	.250	.200	.154	.112	.076	.047	.026	.011	.004	.000
	2	.001	.014	.049	.098	.154	.211	.265	.311	.346	.368	.375	.368	.346	.311	.265	.211	.154	.098	.049	.014
	3	.000	.000	.004	.011	.026	.047	.076	.112	.154	.200	.250	.300	.346	.384	.412	.422	.410	.368	.292	.171
	4	.000	.000	.000	.001	.002	.004	.008	.015	.026	.041	.062	.092	.130	.179	.240	.316	.410	.522	.656	.815
5	0	.951	.774	.590	.444	.328	.237	.168	.116	.078	.050	.031	.019	.010	.005	.002	.001	.000	.000	.000	.000
	1	.048	.204	.328	.392	.410	.396	.360	.312	.259	.206	.156	.113	.077	.049	.028	.015	.006	.002	.000	.000
	2	.001	.021	.073	.138	.205	.264	.309	.336	.346	.337	.312	.276	.230	.181	.132	.088	.051	.024	.008	.001
	3	.000	.001	.008	.024	.051	.088	.132	.181	.230	.276	.312	.337	.346	.336	.309	.264	.205	.138	.073	.021
	4	.000	.000	.000	.002	.006	.015	.028	.049	.077	.113	.156	.206	.259	.312	.360	.396	.410	.392	.328	.204
	5	.000	.000	.000	.000	.000	.001	.002	.005	.010	.019	.031	.050	.078	.116	.168	.237	.328	.444	.590	.774
6	0	.941	.735	.531	.377	.262	.178	.118	.075	.047	.028	.016	.008	.004	.002	.001	.000	.000	.000	.000	.000
	1	.057	.232	.354	.399	.393	.356	.303	.244	.187	.136	.094	.061	.037	.020	.010	.004	.002	.000	.000	.000
	2	.001	.031	.098	.176	.246	.297	.324	.328	.311	.278	.234	.186	.138	.095	.060	.033	.015	.006	.001	.000
	3	.000	.002	.015	.042	.082	.132	.185	.236	.276	.303	.312	.303	.276	.236	.185	.132	.082	.042	.015	.002
	4	.000	.000	.001	.006	.015	.033	.060	.095	.138	.186	.234	.278	.311	.328	.324	.297	.246	.176	.098	.031
	5	.000	.000	.000	.000	.002	.004	.010	.020	.037	.061	.094	.136	.187	.244	.303	.356	.393	.399	.354	.232
	6	.000	.000	.000	.000	.000	.000	.001	.002	.004	.008	.016	.028	.047	.075	.118	.178	.262	.377	.531	.735
7	0	.932	.698	.478	.321	.210	.133	.082	.049	.028	.015	.008	.004	.002	.001	.000	.000	.000	.000	.000	.000
	1	.066	.257	.372	.396	.367	.311	.247	.185	.131	.087	.055	.032	.017	.008	.004	.001	.000	.000	.000	.000
	2	.002	.041	.124	.210	.275	.311	.318	.299	.261	.214	.164	.117	.077	.047	.025	.012	.004	.001	.000	.000
	3	.000	.004	.023	.062	.115	.173	.227	.268	.290	.292	.273	.239	.194	.144	.097	.058	.029	.011	.003	.000
	4	.000	.000	.003	.011	.029	.058	.097	.144	.194	.239	.273	.292	.290	.268	.227	.173	.115	.062	.023	.004
	5	.000	.000	.000	.001	.004	.012	.025	.047	.077	.117	.164	.214	.261	.299	.318	.311	.275	.210	.124	.041
	6	.000	.000	.000	.000	.000	.001	.004	.008	.017	.032	.055	.087	.131	.185	.247	.311	.367	.396	.372	.257
	7	.000	.000	.000	.000	.000	.000	.000	.001	.002	.004	.008	.015	.028	.049	.082	.133	.210	.321	.478	.698

TABLE 3 *continued*

		p																			
n	*r*	.01	.05	.10	.15	.20	.25	.30	.35	.40	.45	.50	.55	.60	.65	.70	.75	.80	.85	.90	.95
8	0	.923	.663	.430	.272	.168	.100	.058	.032	.017	.008	.004	.002	.001	.000	.000	.000	.000	.000	.000	.000
	1	.075	.279	.383	.385	.336	.267	.198	.137	.090	.055	.031	.016	.008	.003	.001	.000	.000	.000	.000	.000
	2	.003	.051	.149	.238	.294	.311	.296	.259	.209	.157	.109	.070	.041	.022	.010	.004	.001	.000	.000	.000
	3	.000	.005	.033	.084	.147	.208	.254	.279	.279	.257	.219	.172	.124	.081	.047	.023	.009	.003	.000	.000
	4	.000	.000	.005	.018	.046	.087	.136	.188	.232	.263	.273	.263	.232	.188	.136	.087	.046	.018	.005	.000
	5	.000	.000	.000	.003	.009	.023	.047	.081	.124	.172	.219	.257	.279	.279	.254	.208	.147	.084	.033	.005
	6	.000	.000	.000	.000	.001	.004	.010	.022	.041	.070	.109	.157	.209	.259	.296	.311	.294	.238	.149	.051
	7	.000	.000	.000	.000	.000	.000	.001	.003	.008	.016	.031	.055	.090	.137	.198	.267	.336	.385	.383	.279
	8	.000	.000	.000	.000	.000	.000	.000	.000	.001	.002	.004	.008	.017	.032	.058	.100	.168	.272	.430	.663
9	0	.914	.630	.387	.232	.134	.075	.040	.021	.010	.005	.002	.001	.000	.000	.000	.000	.000	.000	.000	.000
	1	.083	.299	.387	.368	.302	.225	.156	.100	.060	.034	.018	.008	.004	.001	.000	.000	.000	.000	.000	.000
	2	.003	.063	.172	.260	.302	.300	.267	.216	.161	.111	.070	.041	.021	.010	.004	.001	.000	.000	.000	.000
	3	.000	.008	.045	.107	.176	.234	.267	.272	.251	.212	.164	.116	.074	.042	.021	.009	.003	.001	.000	.000
	4	.000	.001	.007	.028	.066	.117	.172	.219	.251	.260	.246	.213	.167	.118	.074	.039	.017	.005	.001	.000
	5	.000	.000	.001	.005	.017	.039	.074	.118	.167	.213	.246	.260	.251	.219	.172	.117	.066	.028	.007	.001
	6	.000	.000	.000	.001	.003	.009	.021	.042	.074	.116	.164	.212	.251	.272	.267	.234	.176	.107	.045	.008
	7	.000	.000	.000	.000	.000	.001	.004	.010	.021	.041	.070	.111	.161	.216	.267	.300	.302	.260	.172	.063
	8	.000	.000	.000	.000	.000	.000	.000	.001	.004	.008	.018	.034	.060	.100	.156	.225	.302	.368	.387	.299
	9	.000	.000	.000	.000	.000	.000	.000	.000	.000	.001	.002	.005	.010	.021	.040	.075	.134	.232	.387	.630
10	0	.904	.599	.349	.197	.107	.056	.028	.014	.006	.003	.001	.000	.000	.000	.000	.000	.000	.000	.000	.000
	1	.091	.315	.387	.347	.268	.188	.121	.072	.040	.021	.010	.004	.002	.000	.000	.000	.000	.000	.000	.000
	2	.004	.075	.194	.276	.302	.282	.233	.176	.121	.076	.044	.023	.011	.004	.001	.000	.000	.000	.000	.000
	3	.000	.010	.057	.130	.201	.250	.267	.252	.215	.166	.117	.075	.042	.021	.009	.003	.001	.000	.000	.000
	4	.000	.001	.011	.040	.088	.146	.200	.238	.251	.238	.205	.160	.111	.069	.037	.016	.006	.001	.000	.000
	5	.000	.000	.001	.008	.026	.058	.103	.154	.201	.234	.246	.234	.201	.154	.103	.058	.026	.008	.001	.000
	6	.000	.000	.000	.001	.006	.016	.037	.069	.111	.160	.205	.238	.251	.238	.200	.146	.088	.040	.011	.001
	7	.000	.000	.000	.000	.001	.003	.009	.021	.042	.075	.117	.166	.215	.252	.267	.250	.201	.130	.057	.010
	8	.000	.000	.000	.000	.000	.000	.001	.004	.011	.023	.044	.076	.121	.176	.233	.282	.302	.276	.194	.075
	9	.000	.000	.000	.000	.000	.000	.000	.000	.002	.004	.010	.021	.040	.072	.121	.188	.268	.347	.387	.315
	10	.000	.000	.000	.000	.000	.000	.000	.000	.000	.000	.001	.003	.006	.014	.028	.056	.107	.197	.349	.599

TABLE 3 *continued*

		p																			
n	*r*	.01	.05	.10	.15	.20	.25	.30	.35	.40	.45	.50	.55	.60	.65	.70	.75	.80	.85	.90	.95
11	0	.895	.569	.314	.167	.086	.042	.020	.009	.004	.001	.000	.000	.000	.000	.000	.000	.000	.000	.000	.000
	1	.099	.329	.384	.325	.236	.155	.093	.052	.027	.013	.005	.002	.001	.000	.000	.000	.000	.000	.000	.000
	2	.005	.087	.213	.287	.295	.258	.200	.140	.089	.051	.027	.013	.005	.002	.001	.000	.000	.000	.000	.000
	3	.000	.014	.071	.152	.221	.258	.257	.225	.177	.126	.081	.046	.023	.010	.004	.001	.000	.000	.000	.000
	4	.000	.001	.016	.054	.111	.172	.220	.243	.236	.206	.161	.113	.070	.038	.017	.006	.002	.000	.000	.000
	5	.000	.000	.002	.013	.039	.080	.132	.183	.221	.236	.226	.193	.147	.099	.057	.027	.010	.002	.000	.000
	6	.000	.000	.000	.002	.010	.027	.057	.099	.147	.193	.226	.236	.221	.183	.132	.080	.039	.013	.002	.000
	7	.000	.000	.000	.000	.002	.006	.017	.038	.070	.113	.161	.206	.236	.243	.220	.172	.111	.054	.016	.001
	8	.000	.000	.000	.000	.000	.001	.004	.010	.023	.046	.081	.126	.177	.225	.257	.258	.221	.152	.071	.014
	9	.000	.000	.000	.000	.000	.000	.001	.002	.005	.013	.027	.051	.089	.140	.200	.258	.295	.287	.213	.087
	10	.000	.000	.000	.000	.000	.000	.000	.000	.001	.002	.005	.013	.027	.052	.093	.155	.236	.325	.684	.329
	11	.000	.000	.000	.000	.000	.000	.000	.000	.000	.000	.000	.001	.004	.009	.020	.042	.086	.167	.314	.569
12	0	.886	.540	.282	.142	.069	.032	.014	.006	.002	.001	.000	.000	.000	.000	.000	.000	.000	.000	.000	.000
	1	.107	.341	.377	.301	.206	.127	.071	.037	.017	.008	.003	.001	.000	.000	.000	.000	.000	.000	.000	.000
	2	.006	.099	.230	.292	.283	.232	.168	.109	.064	.034	.016	.007	.002	.001	.000	.000	.000	.000	.000	.000
	3	.000	.017	.085	.172	.236	.258	.240	.195	.142	.092	.054	.028	.012	.005	.001	.000	.000	.000	.000	.000
	4	.000	.002	.021	.068	.133	.194	.231	.237	.213	.170	.121	.076	.042	.020	.008	.002	.001	.000	.000	.000
	5	.000	.000	.004	.019	.053	.103	.158	.204	.227	.223	.193	.149	.101	.059	.029	.011	.003	.001	.000	.000
	6	.000	.000	.000	.004	.016	.040	.079	.128	.177	.212	.226	.212	.177	.128	.079	.040	.016	.004	.000	.000
	7	.000	.000	.000	.001	.003	.011	.029	.059	.101	.149	.193	.223	.227	.204	.158	.103	.053	.019	.004	.000
	8	.000	.000	.000	.000	.001	.002	.008	.020	.042	.076	.121	.170	.216	.237	.231	.194	.133	.068	.021	.002
	9	.000	.000	.000	.000	.000	.000	.001	.005	.012	.028	.054	.092	.142	.195	.240	.258	.236	.172	.085	.017
	10	.000	.000	.000	.000	.000	.000	.000	.001	.002	.007	.016	.034	.064	.109	.168	.232	.283	.292	.230	.099
	11	.000	.000	.000	.000	.000	.000	.000	.000	.000	.001	.003	.008	.017	.037	.071	.127	.206	.301	.377	.341
	12	.000	.000	.000	.000	.000	.000	.000	.000	.000	.000	.000	.001	.002	.006	.014	.032	.069	.142	.282	.540
15	0	.860	.463	.206	.087	.035	.013	.005	.002	.000	.000	.000	.000	.000	.000	.000	.000	.000	.000	.000	.000
	1	.130	.366	.343	.231	.132	.067	.031	.013	.005	.002	.000	.000	.000	.000	.000	.000	.000	.000	.000	.000
	2	.009	.135	.267	.286	.231	.156	.092	.048	.022	.009	.003	.001	.000	.000	.000	.000	.000	.000	.000	.000
	3	.000	.031	.129	.218	.250	.225	.170	.111	.063	.032	.014	.005	.002	.000	.000	.000	.000	.000	.000	.000
	4	.005	.005	.043	.116	.188	.225	.219	.179	.127	.078	.042	.019	.007	.002	.001	.000	.000	.000	.000	.000
	5	.000	.001	.010	.045	.103	.165	.206	.212	.186	.140	.092	.051	.024	.010	.003	.001	.000	.000	.000	.000
	6	.000	.000	.002	.013	.043	.092	.147	.191	.207	.191	.153	.105	.061	.030	.012	.003	.001	.000	.000	.000
	7	.000	.000	.000	.003	.014	.039	.081	.132	.177	.201	.196	.165	.118	.071	.035	.013	.003	.001	.000	.000
	8	.000	.000	.000	.001	.003	.013	.035	.071	.118	.165	.196	.201	.177	.132	.081	.039	.014	.003	.000	.000
	9	.000	.000	.000	.000	.001	.003	.012	.030	.061	.105	.153	.191	.207	.191	.147	.092	.043	.013	.002	.000
	10	.000	.000	.000	.000	.000	.001	.003	.010	.024	.051	.092	.140	.186	.212	.206	.165	.103	.045	.010	.001
	11	.000	.000	.000	.000	.000	.000	.001	.002	.007	.019	.042	.078	.127	.179	.219	.225	.188	.116	.043	.005
	12	.000	.000	.000	.000	.000	.000	.000	.000	.002	.005	.014	.032	.063	.111	.170	.225	.250	.218	.129	.031
	13	.000	.000	.000	.000	.000	.000	.000	.000	.000	.001	.003	.009	.022	.048	.092	.156	.231	.586	.267	.135
	14	.000	.000	.000	.000	.000	.000	.000	.000	.000	.000	.000	.002	.005	.013	.031	.067	.132	.231	.343	.366
	15	.000	.000	.000	.000	.000	.000	.000	.000	.000	.000	.000	.000	.000	.002	.005	.013	.035	.087	.206	.463

TABLE 3 *continued*

		p																			
n	*r*	.01	.05	.10	.15	.20	.25	.30	.35	.40	.45	.50	.55	.60	.65	.70	.75	.80	.85	.90	.95
16	0	.851	.440	.185	.074	.028	.010	.003	.001	.000	.000	.000	.000	.000	.000	.000	.000	.000	.000	.000	.000
	1	.138	.371	.329	.210	.113	.053	.023	.009	.003	.001	.000	.000	.000	.000	.000	.000	.000	.000	.000	.000
	2	.010	.146	.275	.277	.211	.134	.073	.035	.015	.006	.002	.001	.000	.000	.000	.000	.000	.000	.000	.000
	3	.000	.036	.142	.229	.246	.208	.146	.089	.047	.022	.009	.003	.001	.000	.000	.000	.000	.000	.000	.000
	4	.000	.006	.051	.131	.200	.225	.204	.155	.101	.057	.028	.011	.004	.001	.000	.000	.000	.000	.000	.000
	5	.000	.001	.014	.056	.120	.180	.210	.201	.162	.112	.067	.034	.014	.005	.001	.000	.000	.000	.000	.000
	6	.000	.000	.003	.018	.055	.110	.165	.198	.198	.168	.122	.075	.039	.017	.006	.001	.000	.000	.000	.000
	7	.000	.000	.000	.005	.020	.052	.101	.152	.189	.197	.175	.132	.084	.044	.019	.006	.001	.000	.000	.000
	8	.000	.000	.000	.001	.006	.020	.049	.092	.142	.181	.196	.181	.142	.092	.049	.020	.006	.001	.000	.000
	9	.000	.000	.000	.000	.001	.006	.019	.044	.084	.132	.175	.197	.189	.152	.101	.052	.020	.005	.000	.000
	10	.000	.000	.000	.000	.000	.001	.006	.017	.039	.075	.122	.168	.198	.198	.165	.110	.055	.018	.003	.000
	11	.000	.000	.000	.000	.000	.000	.001	.005	.014	.034	.067	.112	.162	.201	.210	.180	.120	.056	.014	.001
	12	.000	.000	.000	.000	.000	.000	.000	.001	.004	.011	.028	.057	.101	.155	.204	.225	.200	.131	.051	.006
	13	.000	.000	.000	.000	.000	.000	.000	.000	.001	.003	.009	.022	.047	.089	.146	.208	.246	.229	.142	.036
	14	.000	.000	.000	.000	.000	.000	.000	.000	.000	.001	.002	.006	.015	.035	.073	.134	.211	.277	.275	.146
	15	.000	.000	.000	.000	.000	.000	.000	.000	.000	.000	.000	.001	.003	.009	.023	.053	.113	.210	.329	.371
	16	.000	.000	.000	.000	.000	.000	.000	.000	.000	.000	.000	.000	.000	.001	.003	.010	.028	.074	.185	.440
20	0	.818	.358	.122	.039	.012	.003	.001	.000	.000	.000	.000	.000	.000	.000	.000	.000	.000	.000	.000	.000
	1	.165	.377	.270	.137	.058	.021	.007	.002	.000	.000	.000	.000	.000	.000	.000	.000	.000	.000	.000	.000
	2	.016	.189	.285	.229	.137	.067	.028	.010	.003	.001	.000	.000	.000	.000	.000	.000	.000	.000	.000	.000
	3	.001	.060	.190	.243	.205	.134	.072	.032	.012	.004	.001	.000	.000	.000	.000	.000	.000	.000	.000	.000
	4	.000	.013	.090	.182	.218	.190	.130	.074	.035	.014	.005	.001	.000	.000	.000	.000	.000	.000	.000	.000
	5	.000	.002	.032	.103	.175	.202	.179	.127	.075	.036	.015	.005	.001	.000	.000	.000	.000	.000	.000	.000
	6	.000	.000	.009	.045	.109	.169	.192	.171	.124	.075	.036	.015	.005	.001	.000	.000	.000	.000	.000	.000
	7	.000	.000	.002	.016	.055	.112	.164	.184	.166	.122	.074	.037	.015	.005	.001	.000	.000	.000	.000	.000
	8	.000	.000	.000	.005	.022	.061	.114	.161	.180	.162	.120	.073	.035	.014	.004	.001	.000	.000	.000	.000
	9	.000	.000	.000	.001	.007	.027	.065	.116	.160	.177	.160	.119	.071	.034	.012	.003	.000	.000	.000	.000
	10	.000	.000	.000	.000	.002	.010	.031	.069	.117	.159	.176	.159	.117	.069	.031	.010	.002	.000	.000	.000
	11	.000	.000	.000	.000	.000	.003	.012	.034	.071	.119	.160	.177	.160	.116	.065	.027	.007	.001	.000	.000
	12	.000	.000	.000	.000	.000	.001	.004	.014	.035	.073	.120	.162	.180	.161	.114	.061	.022	.005	.000	.000
	13	.000	.000	.000	.000	.000	.000	.001	.005	.015	.037	.074	.122	.166	.184	.164	.112	.055	.016	.002	.000
	14	.000	.000	.000	.000	.000	.000	.000	.001	.005	.015	.037	.075	.124	.171	.192	.169	.109	.045	.009	.000
	15	.000	.000	.000	.000	.000	.000	.000	.000	.001	.005	.015	.036	.075	.127	.179	.202	.175	.103	.032	.002
	16	.000	.000	.000	.000	.000	.000	.000	.000	.000	.001	.005	.014	.035	.074	.130	.190	.218	.182	.090	.013
	17	.000	.000	.000	.000	.000	.000	.000	.000	.000	.000	.001	.004	.012	.032	.072	.134	.205	.243	.190	.060
	18	.000	.000	.000	.000	.000	.000	.000	.000	.000	.000	.000	.001	.003	.010	.028	.067	.137	.229	.285	.189
	19	.000	.000	.000	.000	.000	.000	.000	.000	.000	.000	.000	.000	.000	.002	.007	.021	.058	.137	.270	.377
	20	.000	.000	.000	.000	.000	.000	.000	.000	.000	.000	.000	.000	.000	.000	.001	.003	.012	.039	.122	.358

TABLE 4 Poisson Probability Distribution

For a given value of λ, entry indicates the probability of obtaining a specified value of *r*.

r	λ = .1	.2	.3	.4	.5	.6	.7	.8	.9	1.0
0	.9048	.8187	.7408	.6703	.6065	.5488	.4966	.4493	.4066	.3679
1	.0905	.1637	.2222	.2681	.3033	.3293	.3476	.3595	.3659	.3679
2	.0045	.0164	.0333	.0536	.0758	.0988	.1217	.1438	.1647	.1839
3	.0002	.0011	.0033	.0072	.0126	.0198	.0284	.0383	.0494	.0613
4	.0000	.0001	.0003	.0007	.0016	.0030	.0050	.0077	.0111	.0153
5	.0000	.0000	.0000	.0001	.0002	.0004	.0007	.0012	.0020	.0031
6	.0000	.0000	.0000	.0000	.0000	.0000	.0001	.0002	.0003	.0005
7	.0000	.0000	.0000	.0000	.0000	.0000	.0000	.0000	.0000	.0001

r	λ = 1.1	1.2	1.3	1.4	1.5	1.6	1.7	1.8	1.9	2.0
0	.3329	.3012	.2725	.2466	.2231	.2019	.1827	.1653	.1496	.1353
1	.3662	.3614	.3543	.3452	.3347	.3230	.3106	.2975	.2842	.2707
2	.2014	.2169	.2303	.2417	.2510	.2584	.2640	.2678	.2700	.2707
3	.0738	.0867	.0998	.1128	.1255	.1378	.1496	.1607	.1710	.1804
4	.0203	.0260	.0324	.0395	.0471	.0551	.0636	.0723	.0812	.0902
5	.0045	.0062	.0084	.0111	.0141	.0176	.0216	.0260	.0309	.0361
6	.0008	.0012	.0018	.0026	.0035	.0047	.0061	.0078	.0098	.0120
7	.0001	.0002	.0003	.0005	.0008	.0011	.0015	.0020	.0027	.0034
8	.0000	.0000	.0001	.0001	.0001	.0002	.0003	.0005	.0006	.0009
9	.0000	.0000	.0000	.0000	.0000	.0000	.0001	.0001	.0001	.0002

r	λ = 2.1	2.2	2.3	2.4	2.5	2.6	2.7	2.8	2.9	3.0
0	.1225	.1108	.1003	.0907	.0821	.0743	.0672	.0608	.0550	.0498
1	.2572	.2438	.2306	.2177	.2052	.1931	.1815	.1703	.1596	.1494
2	.2700	.2681	.2652	.2613	.2565	.2510	.2450	.2384	.2314	.2240
3	.1890	.1966	.2033	.2090	.2138	.2176	.2205	.2225	.2237	.2240
4	.0992	.1082	.1169	.1254	.1336	.1414	.1488	.1557	.1622	.1680
5	.0417	.0476	.0538	.0602	.0668	.0735	.0804	.0872	.0940	.1008
6	.0146	.0174	.0206	.0241	.0278	.0319	.0362	.0407	.0455	.0504
7	.0044	.0055	.0068	.0083	.0099	.0118	.0139	.0163	.0188	.0216
8	.0011	.0015	.0019	.0025	.0031	.0038	.0047	.0057	.0068	.0081
9	.0003	.0004	.0005	.0007	.0009	.0011	.0014	.0018	.0022	.0027
10	.0001	.0001	.0001	.0002	.0002	.0003	.0004	.0005	.0006	.0008
11	.0000	.0000	.0000	.0000	.0000	.0001	.0001	.0001	.0002	.0002
12	.0000	.0000	.0000	.0000	.0000	.0000	.0000	.0000	.0000	.0001

TABLE 4 *continued*

	λ									
r	3.1	3.2	3.3	3.4	3.5	3.6	3.7	3.8	3.9	4.0
0	.0450	.0408	.0369	.0334	.0302	.0273	.0247	.0224	.0202	.0183
1	.1397	.1304	.1217	.1135	.1057	.0984	.0915	.0850	.0789	.0733
2	.2165	.2087	.2008	.1929	.1850	.1771	.1692	.1615	.1539	.1465
3	.2237	.2226	.2209	.2186	.2158	.2125	.2087	.2046	.2001	.1954
4	.1734	.1781	.1823	.1858	.1888	.1912	.1931	.1944	.1951	.1954
5	.1075	.1140	.1203	.1264	.1322	.1377	.1429	.1477	.1522	.1563
6	.0555	.0608	.0662	.0716	.0771	.0826	.0881	.0936	.0989	.1042
7	.0246	.0278	.0312	.0348	.0385	.0425	.0466	.0508	.0551	.0595
8	.0095	.0111	.0129	.0148	.0169	.0191	.0215	.0241	.0269	.0298
9	.0033	.0040	.0047	.0056	.0066	.0076	.0089	.0102	.0116	.0132
10	.0010	.0013	.0016	.0019	.0023	.0028	.0033	.0039	.0045	.0053
11	.0003	.0004	.0005	.0006	.0007	.0009	.0011	.0013	.0016	.0019
12	.0001	.0001	.0001	.0002	.0002	.0003	.0003	.0004	.0005	.0006
13	.0000	.0000	.0000	.0000	.0001	.0001	.0001	.0001	.0002	.0002
14	.0000	.0000	.0000	.0000	.0000	.0000	.0000	.0000	.0000	.0001

	λ									
r	4.1	4.2	4.3	4.4	4.5	4.6	4.7	4.8	4.9	5.0
0	.0166	.0150	.0136	.0123	.0111	.0101	.0091	.0082	.0074	.0067
1	.0679	.0630	.0583	.0540	.0500	.0462	.0427	.0395	.0365	.0337
2	.1393	.1323	.1254	.1188	.1125	.1063	.1005	.0948	.0894	.0842
3	.1904	.1852	.1798	.1743	.1687	.1631	.1574	.1517	.1460	.1404
4	.1951	.1944	.1933	.1917	.1898	.1875	.1849	.1820	.1789	.1755
5	.1600	.1633	.1662	.1687	.1708	.1725	.1738	.1747	.1753	.1755
6	.1093	.1143	.1191	.1237	.1281	.1323	.1362	.1398	.1432	.1462
7	.0640	.1686	.0732	.0778	.0824	.0869	.0914	.0959	.1002	.1044
8	.0328	.0360	.0393	.0428	.0463	.0500	.0537	.0575	.0614	.0653
9	.0150	.0168	.0188	.0209	.0232	.0255	.0280	.0307	.0334	.0363
10	.0061	.0071	.0081	.0092	.0104	.0118	.0132	.0147	.0164	.0181
11	.0026	.0027	.0032	.0037	.0043	.0049	.0056	.0064	.0073	.0082
12	.0008	.0009	.0011	.0014	.0016	.0019	.0022	.0026	.0030	.0034
13	.0002	.0003	.0004	.0005	.0006	.0007	.0008	.0009	.0011	.0013
14	.0001	.0001	.0001	.0001	.0002	.0002	.0003	.0003	.0004	.0005
15	.0000	.0000	.0000	.0000	.0001	.0001	.0001	.0001	.0001	.0002

TABLE 4 *continued*

	λ									
r	5.1	5.2	5.3	5.4	5.5	5.6	5.7	5.8	5.9	6.0
0	.0061	.0055	.0050	.0045	.0041	.0037	.0033	.0030	.0027	.0025
1	.0311	.0287	.0265	.0244	.0225	.0207	.0191	.0176	.0162	.0149
2	.0793	.0746	.0701	.0659	.0618	.0580	.0544	.0509	.0477	.0446
3	.1348	.1293	.1239	.1185	.1133	.1082	.1033	.0985	.0938	.0892
4	.1719	.1681	.1641	.1600	.1558	.1515	.1472	.1428	.1383	.1339
5	.1753	.1748	.1740	.1728	.1714	.1697	.1678	.1656	.1632	.1606
6	.1490	.1515	.1537	.1555	.1571	.1584	.1594	.1601	.1605	.1606
7	.1086	.1125	.1163	.1200	.1234	.1267	.1298	.1326	.1353	.1377
8	.0692	.0731	.0771	.0810	.0849	.0887	.0925	.0962	.0998	.1033
9	.0392	.0423	.0454	.0486	.0519	.0552	.0586	.0620	.0654	.0688
10	.0200	.0220	.0241	.0262	.0285	.0309	.0334	.0359	.0386	.0413
11	.0093	.0104	.0116	.0129	.0143	.0157	.0173	.0190	.0207	.0225
12	.0039	.0045	.0051	.0058	.0065	.0073	.0082	.0092	.0102	.0113
13	.0015	.0018	.0021	.0024	.0028	.0032	.0036	.0041	.0046	.0052
14	.0006	.0007	.0008	.0009	.0011	.0013	.0015	.0017	.0019	.0022
15	.0002	.0002	.0003	.0003	.0004	.0005	.0006	.0007	.0008	.0009
16	.0001	.0001	.0001	.0001	.0001	.0002	.0002	.0002	.0003	.0003
17	.0000	.0000	.0000	.0000	.0000	.0000	.0001	.0001	.0001	.0001

	λ									
r	6.1	6.2	6.3	6.4	6.5	6.6	6.7	6.8	6.9	7.0
0	.0022	.0020	.0018	.0017	.0015	.0014	.0012	.0011	.0010	.0009
1	.0137	.0126	.0116	.0106	.0098	.0090	.0082	.0076	.0070	.0064
2	.0417	.0390	.0364	.0340	.0318	.0296	.0276	.0258	.0240	.0223
3	.0848	.0806	.0765	.0726	.0688	.0652	.0617	.0584	.0552	.0521
4	.1294	.1249	.1205	.1162	.1118	.1076	.1034	.0992	.0952	.0912
5	.1579	.1549	.1519	.1487	.1454	.1420	.1385	.1349	.1314	.1277
6	.1605	.0601	.1595	.1586	.1575	.1562	.1546	.1529	.1511	.1490
7	.1399	.1418	.1435	.1450	.1462	.1472	.1480	.1486	.1489	.1490
8	.1066	.1099	.1130	.1160	.1188	.1215	.1240	.1263	.1284	.1304
9	.0723	.0757	.0791	.0825	.0858	.0891	.0923	.0954	.0985	.1014
10	.0441	.0469	.0498	.0528	.0558	.0588	.0618	.0649	.0679	.0710
11	.0245	.0265	.0285	.0307	.0330	.0353	.0377	.0401	.0426	.0452
12	.0124	.0137	.0150	.0164	.0179	.0194	.0210	.0227	.0245	.0264
13	.0058	.0065	.0073	.0081	.0089	.0098	.0108	.0119	.0130	.0142
14	.0025	.0029	.0033	.0037	.0041	.0046	.0052	.0058	.0064	.0071
15	.0010	.0012	.0014	.0016	.0018	.0020	.0023	.0026	.0029	.0033
16	.0004	.0005	.0005	.0006	.0007	.0008	.0010	.0011	.0013	.0014
17	.0001	.0002	.0002	.0002	.0003	.0003	.0004	.0004	.0005	.0006
18	.0000	.0001	.0001	.0001	.0001	.0001	.0001	.0002	.0002	.0002
19	.0000	.0000	.0000	.0000	.0000	.0000	.0000	.0001	.0001	.0001

TABLE 4 *continued*

	λ									
r	7.1	7.2	7.3	7.4	7.5	7.6	7.7	7.8	7.9	8.0
0	.0008	.0007	.0007	.0006	.0006	.0005	.0005	.0004	.0004	.0003
1	.0059	.0054	.0049	.0045	.0041	.0038	.0035	.0032	.0029	.0027
2	.0208	.0194	.0180	.0167	.0156	.0145	.0134	.0125	.0116	.0107
3	.0492	.0464	.0438	.0413	.0389	.0366	.0345	.0324	.0305	.0286
4	.0874	.0836	.0799	.0764	.0729	.0696	.0663	.0632	.0602	.0573
5	.1241	.1204	.1167	.1130	.1094	.1057	.1021	.0986	.0951	.0916
6	.1468	.1445	.1420	.1394	.1367	.1339	.1311	.1282	.1252	.1221
7	.1489	.1486	.1481	.1474	.1465	.1454	.1442	.1428	.1413	.1396
8	.1321	.1337	.1351	.1363	.1373	.1382	.1388	.1392	.1395	.1396
9	.1042	.1070	.1096	.1121	.1144	.1167	.1187	.1207	.1224	.1241
10	.0740	.0770	.0800	.0829	.0858	.0887	.0914	.0941	.0967	.0993
11	.0478	.0504	.0531	.0558	.0585	.0613	.0640	.0667	.0695	.0722
12	.0283	.0303	.0323	.0344	.0366	.0388	.0411	.0434	.0457	.0481
13	.0154	.0168	.0181	.0196	.0211	.0227	.0243	.0260	.0278	.0296
14	.0078	.0086	.0095	.0104	.0113	.0123	.0134	.0145	.0157	.0169
15	.0037	.0041	.0046	.0051	.0057	.0062	.0069	.0075	.0083	.0090
16	.0016	.0019	.0021	.0024	.0026	.0030	.0033	.0037	.0041	.0045
17	.0007	.0008	.0009	.0010	.0012	.0013	.0015	.0017	.0019	.0021
18	.0003	.0003	.0004	.0004	.0005	.0006	.0006	.0007	.0008	.0009
19	.0001	.0001	.0001	.0002	.0002	.0002	.0003	.0003	.0003	.0004
20	.0000	.0000	.0001	.0001	.0001	.0001	.0001	.0001	.0001	.0002
21	.0000	.0000	.0000	.0000	.0000	.0000	.0000	.0000	.0001	.0001

TABLE 4 *continued*

	λ									
r	8.1	8.2	8.3	8.4	8.5	8.6	8.7	8.8	8.9	9.0
0	.0003	.0003	.0002	.0002	.0002	.0002	.0002	.0002	.0001	.0001
1	.0025	.0023	.0021	.0019	.0017	.0016	.0014	.0013	.0012	.0011
2	.0100	.0092	.0086	.0079	.0074	.0068	.0063	.0058	.0054	.0050
3	.0269	.0252	.0237	.0222	.0208	.0195	.0183	.0171	.0160	.0150
4	.0544	.0517	.0491	.0466	.0443	.0420	.0398	.0377	.0357	.0337
5	.0882	.0849	.0816	.0784	.0752	.0722	.0692	.0663	.0635	.0607
6	.1191	.1160	.1128	.1097	.1066	.1034	.1003	.0972	.0941	.0911
7	.1378	.1358	.1338	.1317	.1294	.1271	.1247	.1222	.1197	.1171
8	.1395	.1392	.1388	.1382	.1375	.1366	.1356	.1344	.1332	.1318
9	.1256	.1269	.1280	.1290	.1299	.1306	.1311	.1315	.1317	.1318
10	.1017	.1040	.1063	.1084	.1104	.1123	.1140	.1157	.1172	.1186
11	.0749	.0776	.0802	.0828	.0853	.0878	.0902	.0925	.0948	.0970
12	.0505	.0530	.0555	.0579	.0604	.0629	.0654	.0679	.0703	.0728
13	.0315	.0334	.0354	.0374	.0395	.0416	.0438	.0459	.0481	.0504
14	.0182	.0196	.0210	.0225	.0240	.0256	.0272	.0289	.0306	.0324
15	.0098	.0107	.0116	.0126	.0136	.0147	.0158	.0169	.0182	.0194
16	.0050	.0055	.0060	.0066	.0072	.0079	.0086	.0093	.0101	.0109
17	.0024	.0026	.0029	.0033	.0036	.0040	.0044	.0048	.0053	.0058
18	.0011	.0012	.0014	.0015	.0017	.0019	.0021	.0024	.0026	.0029
19	.0005	.0005	.0006	.0007	.0008	.0009	.0010	.0011	.0012	.0014
20	.0002	.0002	.0002	.0003	.0003	.0004	.0004	.0005	.0005	.0006
21	.0001	.0001	.0001	.0001	.0001	.0002	.0002	.0002	.0002	.0003
22	.0000	.0000	.0000	.0000	.0001	.0001	.0001	.0001	.0001	.0001

TABLE 4 *continued*

	λ									
r	9.1	9.2	9.3	9.4	9.5	9.6	9.7	9.8	9.9	10
0	.0001	.0001	.0001	.0001	.0001	.0001	.0001	.0001	.0001	.0000
1	.0010	.0009	.0009	.0008	.0007	.0007	.0006	.0005	.0005	.0005
2	.0046	.0043	.0040	.0037	.0034	.0031	.0029	.0027	.0025	.0023
3	.0140	.0131	.0123	.0115	.0107	.0100	.0093	.0087	.0081	.0076
4	.0319	.0302	.0285	.0269	.0254	.0240	.0226	.0213	.0201	.0189
5	.0581	.0555	.0530	.0506	.0483	.0460	.0439	.0418	.0398	.0378
6	.0881	.0851	.0822	.0793	.0764	.0736	.0709	.0682	.0656	.0631
7	.1145	.1118	.1091	.1064	.1037	.1010	.0982	.0955	.0928	.0901
8	.1302	.1286	.1269	.1251	.1232	.1212	.1191	.1170	.1148	.1126
9	.1317	.1315	.1311	.1306	.1300	.1293	.1284	.1274	.1263	.1251
10	.1198	.1210	.1219	.1228	.1235	.1241	.1245	.1249	.1250	.1251
11	.0991	.1012	.1031	.1049	.1067	.1083	.1098	.1112	.1125	.1137
12	.0752	.0776	.0799	.0822	.0844	.0866	.0888	.0908	.0928	.0948
13	.0526	.0549	.0572	.0594	.0617	.0640	.0662	.0685	.0707	.0729
14	.0342	.0361	.0380	.0399	.0419	.0439	.0459	.0479	.0500	.0521
15	.0208	.0221	.0235	.0250	.0265	.0281	.0297	.0313	.0330	.0347
16	.0118	.0127	.0137	.0147	.0157	.0168	.0180	.0192	.0204	.0217
17	.0063	.0069	.0075	.0081	.0088	.0095	.0103	.0111	.0119	.0128
18	.0032	.0035	.0039	.0042	.0046	.0051	.0055	.0060	.0065	.0071
19	.0015	.0017	.0019	.0021	.0023	.0026	.0028	.0031	.0034	.0037
20	.0007	.0008	.0009	.0010	.0011	.0012	.0014	.0015	.0017	.0019
21	.0003	.0003	.0004	.0004	.0005	.0006	.0006	.0007	.0008	.0009
22	.0001	.0001	.0002	.0002	.0002	.0002	.0003	.0003	.0004	.0004
23	.0000	.0001	.0001	.0001	.0001	.0001	.0001	.0001	.0002	.0002
24	.0000	.0000	.0000	.0000	.0000	.0000	.0000	.0001	.0001	.0001

TABLE 4 *continued*

	λ									
r	11	12	13	14	15	16	17	18	19	20
0	.0000	.0000	.0000	.0000	.0000	.0000	.0000	.0000	.0000	.0000
1	.0002	.0001	.0000	.0000	.0000	.0000	.0000	.0000	.0000	.0000
2	.0010	.0004	.0002	.0001	.0000	.0000	.0000	.0000	.0000	.0000
3	.0037	.0018	.0008	.0004	.0002	.0001	.0000	.0000	.0000	.0000
4	.0102	.0053	.0027	.0013	.0006	.0003	.0001	.0001	.0000	.0000
5	.0224	.0127	.0070	.0037	.0019	.0010	.0005	.0002	.0001	.0001
6	.0411	.0255	.0152	.0087	.0048	.0026	.0014	.0007	.0004	.0002
7	.0646	.0437	.0281	.0174	.0104	.0060	.0034	.0018	.0010	.0005
8	.0888	.0655	.0457	.0304	.0194	.0120	.0072	.0042	.0024	.0013
9	.1085	.0874	.0661	.0473	.0324	.0213	.0135	.0083	.0050	.0029
10	.1194	.1048	.0859	.0663	.0486	.0341	.0230	.0150	.0095	.0058
11	.1194	.1144	.1015	.0844	.0663	.0496	.0355	.0245	.0164	.0106
12	.1094	.1144	.1099	.0984	.0829	.0661	.0504	.0368	.0259	.0176
13	.0926	.1056	.1099	.1060	.0956	.0814	.0658	.0509	.0378	.0271
14	.0728	.0905	.1021	.1060	.1024	.0930	.0800	.0655	.0514	.0387
15	.0534	.0724	.0885	.0989	.1024	.0992	.0906	.0786	.0650	.0516
16	.0367	.0543	.0719	.0866	.0960	.0992	.0963	.0884	.0772	.0646
17	.0237	.0383	.0550	.0713	.0847	.0934	.0963	.0936	.0863	.0760
18	.0145	.0256	.0397	.0554	.0706	.0830	.0909	.0936	.0911	.0844
19	.0084	.0161	.0272	.0409	.0557	.0699	.0814	.0887	.0911	.0888
20	.0046	.0097	.0177	.0286	.0418	.0559	.0692	.0798	.0866	.0888
21	.0024	.0055	.0109	.0191	.0299	.0426	.0560	.0684	.0783	.0846
22	.0012	.0030	.0065	.0121	.0204	.0310	.0433	.0560	.0676	.0769
23	.0006	.0016	.0037	.0074	.0133	.0216	.0320	.0438	.0559	.0669
24	.0003	.0008	.0020	.0043	.0083	.0144	.0226	.0328	.0442	.0557
25	.0001	.0004	.0010	.0024	.0050	.0092	.0154	.0237	.0336	.0446
26	.0000	.0002	.0005	.0013	.0029	.0057	.0101	.0164	.0246	.0343
27	.0000	.0001	.0002	.0007	.0016	.0034	.0063	.0109	.0173	.0254
28	.0000	.0000	.0001	.0003	.0009	.0019	.0038	.0070	.0117	.0181
29	.0000	.0000	.0001	.0002	.0004	.0011	.0023	.0044	.0077	.0125
30	.0000	.0000	.0000	.0001	.0002	.0006	.0013	.0026	.0049	.0083
31	.0000	.0000	.0000	.0000	.0001	.0003	.0007	.0015	.0030	.0054
32	.0000	.0000	.0000	.0000	.0001	.0001	.0004	.0009	.0018	.0034
33	.0000	.0000	.0000	.0000	.0000	.0001	.0002	.0005	.0010	.0020
34	.0000	.0000	.0000	.0000	.0000	.0000	.0001	.0002	.0006	.0012
35	.0000	.0000	.0000	.0000	.0000	.0000	.0000	.0001	.0003	.0007
36	.0000	.0000	.0000	.0000	.0000	.0000	.0000	.0001	.0002	.0004
37	.0000	.0000	.0000	.0000	.0000	.0000	.0000	.0000	.0001	.0002
38	.0000	.0000	.0000	.0000	.0000	.0000	.0000	.0000	.0000	.0001
39	.0000	.0000	.0000	.0000	.0000	.0000	.0000	.0000	.0000	0001

Source: Extracted from William H. Beyer (ed.), *CRC Basic Statistical Tables* (Cleveland, Ohio: The Chemical Rebber Co. 1971).

TABLE 5 Areas of a Standard Normal Distribution

(a) Table of Areas to the Left of z

z	.00	.01	.02	.03	.04	.05	.06	.07	.08	.09
−3.4	.0003	.0003	.0003	.0003	.0003	.0003	.0003	.0003	.0003	.0002
−3.3	.0005	.0005	.0005	.0004	.0004	.0004	.0004	.0004	.0004	.0003
−3.2	.0007	.0007	.0006	.0006	.0006	.0006	.0006	.0005	.0005	.0005
−3.1	.0010	.0009	.0009	.0009	.0008	.0008	.0008	.0008	.0007	.0007
−3.0	.0013	.0013	.0013	.0012	.0012	.0011	.0011	.0011	.0010	.0010
−2.9	.0019	.0018	.0018	.0017	.0016	.0016	.0015	.0015	.0014	.0014
−2.8	.0026	.0025	.0024	.0023	.0023	.0022	.0021	.0021	.0020	.0019
−2.7	.0035	.0034	.0033	.0032	.0031	.0030	.0029	.0028	.0027	.0026
−2.6	.0047	.0045	.0044	.0043	.0041	.0040	.0039	.0038	.0037	.0036
−2.5	.0062	.0060	.0059	.0057	.0055	.0054	.0052	.0051	.0049	.0048
−2.4	.0082	.0080	.0078	.0075	.0073	.0071	.0069	.0068	.0066	.0064
−2.3	.0107	.0104	.0102	.0099	.0096	.0094	.0091	.0089	.0087	.0084
−2.2	.0139	.0136	.0132	.0129	.0125	.0122	.0119	.0116	.0113	.0110
−2.1	.0179	.0174	.0170	.0166	.0162	.0158	.0154	.0150	.0146	.0143
−2.0	.0228	.0222	.0217	.0212	.0207	.0202	.0197	.0192	.0188	.0183
−1.9	.0287	.0281	.0274	.0268	.0262	.0256	.0250	.0244	.0239	.0233
−1.8	.0359	.0351	.0344	.0336	.0329	.0322	.0314	.0307	.0301	.0294
−1.7	.0446	.0436	.0427	.0418	.0409	.0401	.0392	.0384	.0375	.0367
−1.6	.0548	.0537	.0526	.0516	.0505	.0495	.0485	.0475	.0465	.0455
−1.5	.0668	.0655	.0643	.0630	.0618	.0606	.0594	.0582	.0571	.0559
−1.4	.0808	.0793	.0778	.0764	.0749	.0735	.0721	.0708	.0694	.0681
−1.3	.0968	.0951	.0934	.0918	.0901	.0885	.0869	.0853	.0838	.0823
−1.2	.1151	.1131	.1112	.1093	.1075	.1056	.1038	.1020	.1003	.0985
−1.1	.1357	.1335	.1314	.1292	.1271	.1251	.1230	.1210	.1190	.1170
−1.0	.1587	.1562	.1539	.1515	.1492	.1469	.1446	.1423	.1401	.1379
−0.9	.1841	.1814	.1788	.1762	.1736	.1711	.1685	.1660	.1635	.1611
−0.8	.2119	.2090	.2061	.2033	.2005	.1977	.1949	.1922	.1894	.1867
−0.7	.2420	.2389	.2358	.2327	.2296	.2266	.2236	.2206	.2177	.2148
−0.6	.2743	.2709	.2676	.2643	.2611	.2578	.2546	.2514	.2483	.2451
−0.5	.3085	.3050	.3015	.2981	.2946	.2912	.2877	.2843	.2810	.2776
−0.4	.3446	.3409	.3372	.3336	.3300	.3264	.3228	.3192	.3156	.3121
−0.3	.3821	.3783	.3745	.3707	.3669	.3632	.3594	.3557	.3520	.3483
−0.2	.4207	.4168	.4129	.4090	.4052	.4013	.3974	.3936	.3897	.3859
−0.1	.4602	.4562	.4522	.4483	.4443	.4404	.4364	.4325	.4286	.4247
−0.0	.5000	.4960	.4920	.4880	.4840	.4801	.4761	.4721	.4681	.4641

For values of z less than −3.49, use 0.000 to approximate the area.

TABLE 5(a) *continued*

z	.00	.01	.02	.03	.04	.05	.06	.07	.08	.09
0.0	.5000	.5040	.5080	.5120	.5160	.5199	.5239	.5279	.5319	.5359
0.1	.5398	.5438	.5478	.5517	.5557	.5596	.5636	.5675	.5714	.5753
0.2	.5793	.5832	.5871	.5910	.5948	.5987	.6026	.6064	.6103	.6141
0.3	.6179	.6217	.6255	.6293	.6331	.6368	.6406	.6443	.6480	.6517
0.4	.6554	.6591	.6628	.6664	.6700	.6736	.6772	.6808	.6844	.6879
0.5	.6915	.6950	.6985	.7019	.7054	.7088	.7123	.7157	.7190	.7224
0.6	.7257	.7291	.7324	.7357	.7389	.7422	.7454	.7486	.7517	.7549
0.7	.7580	.7611	.7642	.7673	.7704	.7734	.7764	.7794	.7823	.7852
0.8	.7881	.7910	.7939	.7967	.7995	.8023	.8051	.8078	.8106	.8133
0.9	.8159	.8186	.8212	.8238	.8264	.8289	.8315	.8340	.8365	.8389
1.0	.8413	.8438	.8461	.8485	.8508	.8531	.8554	.8577	.8599	.8621
1.1	.8643	.8665	.8686	.8708	.8729	.8749	.8770	.8790	.8810	.8830
1.2	.8849	.8869	.8888	.8907	.8925	.8944	.8962	.8980	.8997	.9015
1.3	.9032	.9049	.9066	.9082	.9099	.9115	.9131	.9147	.9162	.9177
1.4	.9192	.9207	.9222	.9236	.9251	.9265	.9279	.9292	.9306	.9319
1.5	.9332	.9345	.9357	.9370	.9382	.9394	.9406	.9418	.9429	.9441
1.6	.9452	.9463	.9474	.9484	.9495	.9505	.9515	.9525	.9535	.9545
1.7	.9554	.9564	.9573	.9582	.9591	.9599	.9608	.9616	.9625	.9633
1.8	.9641	.9649	.9656	.9664	.9671	.9678	.9686	.9693	.9699	.9706
1.9	.9713	.9719	.9726	.9732	.9738	.9744	.9750	.9756	.9761	.9767
2.0	.9772	.9778	.9783	.9788	.9793	.9798	.9803	.9808	.9812	.9817
2.1	.9821	.9826	.9830	.9834	.9838	.9842	.9846	.9850	.9854	.9857
2.2	.9861	.9864	.9868	.9871	.9875	.9878	.9881	.9884	.9887	.9890
2.3	.9893	.9896	.9898	.9901	.9904	.9906	.9909	.9911	.9913	.9916
2.4	.9918	.9920	.9922	.9925	.9927	.9929	.9931	.9932	.9934	.9936
2.5	.9938	.9940	.9941	.9943	.9945	.9946	.9948	.9949	.9951	.9952
2.6	.9953	.9955	.9956	.9957	.9959	.9960	.9961	.9962	.9963	.9964
2.7	.9965	.9966	.9967	.9968	.9969	.9970	.9971	.9972	.9973	.9974
2.8	.9974	.9975	.9976	.9977	.9977	.9978	.9979	.9979	.9980	.9981
2.9	.9981	.9982	.9982	.9983	.9984	.9984	.9985	.9985	.9986	.9986
3.0	.9987	.9987	.9987	.9988	.9988	.9989	.9989	.9989	.9990	.9990
3.1	.9990	.9991	.9991	.9991	.9992	.9992	.9992	.9992	.9993	.9993
3.2	.9993	.9993	.9994	.9994	.9994	.9994	.9994	.9995	.9995	.9995
3.3	.9995	.9995	.9995	.9996	.9996	.9996	.9996	.9996	.9996	.9997
3.4	.9997	.9997	.9997	.9997	.9997	.9997	.9997	.9997	.9997	.9998

For *z* values greater than 3.49, use 1.000 to approximate the area.

TABLE 5 *continued*

(b) Confidence Interval, Critical Values z_c

Level of Confidence c	Critical Value z_c
0.75, or 75%	1.15
0.80, or 80%	1.28
0.85, or 85%	1.44
0.90, or 95%	1.645
0.95, or 95%	1.96
0.98, or 98%	2.33
0.99, or 99%	2.58

TABLE 5 *continued*

(c) Hypothesis Testing, Critical Values z_0

Level of Significance	$\alpha = 0.05$	$\alpha = 0.01$
Critical value z_0 for a left-tailed test	−1.645	−2.33
Critical value z_0 for a right-tailed test	1.645	2.33
Critical value $\pm z_0$ for a two-tailed test	±1.96	±2.58

TABLE 6 Student's *t* Distribution

Student's *t* values generated by Minitab Version 9.2

d.f. \ c	0.750	0.800	0.850	0.900	0.950	0.980	0.990
α'	0.125	0.100	0.075	0.050	0.025	0.010	0.005
α''	0.250	0.200	0.150	0.100	0.050	0.020	0.010
1	2.414	3.078	4.165	6.314	12.706	31.821	63.657
2	1.604	1.886	2.282	2.290	4.303	6.965	9.925
3	1.423	1.638	1.924	2.353	3.182	4.541	5.841
4	1.344	1.533	1.778	2.132	2.776	3.747	4.604
5	1.301	1.476	1.699	2.015	2.571	3.365	4.032
6	1.273	1.440	1.650	1.943	2.447	3.143	3.707
7	1.254	1.415	1.617	1.895	2.365	2.998	3.499
8	1.240	1.397	1.592	1.860	2.306	2.896	3.355
9	1.230	1.383	1.574	1.833	2.262	2.821	3.250
10	1.221	1.372	1.559	1.812	2.228	2.764	3.169
11	1.214	1.363	1.548	1.796	2.201	2.718	3.106
12	1.209	1.356	1.538	1.782	2.179	2.681	3.055
13	1.204	1.350	1.530	1.771	2.160	2.650	3.012
14	1.200	1.345	1.523	1.761	2.145	2.624	2.977
15	1.197	1.341	1.517	1.753	2.131	2.602	2.947
16	1.194	1.337	1.512	1.746	2.120	2.583	2.921
17	1.191	1.333	1.508	1.740	2.110	2.567	2.898
18	1.189	1.330	1.504	1.734	2.101	2.552	2.878
19	1.187	1.328	1.500	1.729	2.093	2.539	2.861
20	1.185	1.325	1.497	1.725	2.086	2.528	2.845
21	1.183	1.323	1.494	1.721	2.080	2.518	2.831
22	1.182	1.321	1.492	1.717	2.074	2.508	2.819
23	1.180	1.319	1.489	1.714	2.069	2.500	2.807
24	1.179	1.318	1.487	1.711	2.064	2.492	2.797
25	1.178	1.316	1.485	1.708	2.060	2.485	2.787
26	1.177	1.315	1.483	1.706	2.056	2.479	2.779
27	1.176	1.314	1.482	1.703	2.052	2.473	2.771
28	1.175	1.313	1.480	1.701	2.048	2.467	2.763
29	1.174	1.311	1.479	1.699	2.045	2.462	2.756
30	1.173	1.310	1.477	1.697	2.042	2.457	2.750
35	1.170	1.306	1.472	1.690	2.030	2.438	2.724
40	1.167	1.303	1.468	1.684	2.021	2.423	2.704
45	1.165	1.301	1.465	1.679	2.014	2.412	2.690
50	1.164	1.299	1.462	1.676	2.009	2.403	2.678
55	1.163	1.297	1.460	1.673	2.004	2.396	2.668
60	1.162	1.296	1.458	1.671	2.000	2.390	2.660
90	1.158	1.291	1.452	1.662	1.987	2.369	2.632
120	1.156	1.289	1.449	1.658	1.980	2.358	2.617
∞	1.150	1.282	1.440	1.645	1.960	2.326	2.576

TABLE 7 The χ^2 Distribution

d.f. \ α	.995	.990	.975	.950	.900	.100	.050	.025	.010	.005
1	0.0^4393	0.0^3157	0.0^3982	0.0^2393	0.0158	2.71	3.84	5.02	6.63	7.88
2	0.0100	0.0201	0.0506	0.103	0.211	4.61	5.99	7.38	9.21	10.60
3	0.072	0.115	0.216	0.352	0.584	6.25	7.81	9.35	11.34	12.84
4	0.207	0.297	0.484	0.711	1.064	7.78	9.49	11.14	13.28	14.86
5	0.412	0.554	0.831	1.145	1.61	9.24	11.07	12.83	15.09	16.75
6	0.676	0.872	1.24	1.64	2.20	10.64	12.59	14.45	16.81	18.55
7	0.989	1.24	1.69	2.17	2.83	12.02	14.07	16.01	18.48	20.28
8	1.34	1.65	2.18	2.73	3.49	13.36	15.51	17.53	20.09	21.96
9	1.73	2.09	2.70	3.33	4.17	14.68	16.92	19.02	21.67	23.59
10	2.16	2.56	3.25	3.94	4.87	15.99	18.31	20.48	23.21	25.19
11	2.60	3.05	3.82	4.57	5.58	17.28	19.68	21.92	24.72	26.76
12	3.07	3.57	4.40	5.23	6.30	18.55	21.03	23.34	26.22	28.30
13	3.57	4.11	5.01	5.89	7.04	19.81	22.36	24.74	27.69	29.82
14	4.07	4.66	5.63	6.57	7.79	21.06	23.68	26.12	29.14	31.32
15	4.60	5.23	6.26	7.26	8.55	22.31	25.00	27.49	30.58	32.80
16	5.14	5.81	6.91	7.96	9.31	23.54	26.30	28.85	32.00	34.27
17	5.70	6.41	7.56	8.67	10.09	24.77	27.59	30.19	33.41	35.72
18	6.26	7.01	8.23	9.39	10.86	25.99	28.87	31.53	34.81	37.16
19	6.84	7.63	8.91	10.12	11.65	27.20	30.14	32.85	36.19	38.58
20	7.43	8.26	8.59	10.85	12.44	28.41	31.41	34.17	37.57	40.00
21	8.03	8.90	10.28	11.59	13.24	29.62	32.67	35.48	38.93	41.40
22	8.64	9.54	10.98	12.34	14.04	30.81	33.92	36.78	40.29	42.80
23	9.26	10.20	11.69	13.09	14.85	32.01	35.17	38.08	41.64	44.18
24	9.89	10.86	12.40	13.85	15.66	33.20	36.42	39.36	42.98	45.56
25	10.52	11.52	13.12	14.61	16.47	34.38	37.65	40.65	44.31	46.93
26	11.16	12.20	13.84	15.38	17.29	35.56	38.89	41.92	45.64	48.29
27	11.81	12.88	14.57	16.15	18.11	36.74	40.11	43.19	46.96	49.64
28	12.46	13.56	15.31	16.93	18.94	37.92	41.34	44.46	48.28	50.99
29	13.21	14.26	16.05	17.71	19.77	39.09	42.56	45.72	49.59	52.34
30	13.79	14.95	16.79	18.49	20.60	40.26	43.77	46.98	50.89	53.67
40	20.71	22.16	24.43	26.51	29.05	51.80	55.76	59.34	63.69	66.77
50	27.99	29.71	32.36	34.76	37.69	63.17	67.50	71.42	76.15	79.49
60	35.53	37.48	40.48	43.19	46.46	74.40	79.08	83.30	88.38	91.95
70	43.28	45.44	48.76	51.74	55.33	85.53	90.53	95.02	100.4	104.2
80	51.17	53.54	57.15	60.39	64.28	96.58	101.9	106.6	112.3	116.3
90	59.20	61.75	65.65	69.13	73.29	107.6	113.1	118.1	124.1	128.3
100	67.33	70.06	74.22	77.93	82.36	118.5	124.3	129.6	135.8	140.2

Source: From H. L. Herter, *Biometrika*, June 1964. Printed by permission of Biometrika Trustees.

TABLE 8 The *F* Distribution

Degrees of Freedom for Denominator	α	Degrees of Freedom for Numerator								
		1	2	3	4	5	6	7	8	9
1	.050	161.45	199.50	215.71	224.58	230.16	233.99	236.77	238.88	240.54
1	.025	647.79	799.50	864.16	899.58	921.85	937.11	948.22	956.66	963.28
1	.010	4052.2	4999.5	5403.4	5624.6	5763.6	5859.0	5928.4	5981.1	6022.5
2	.050	18.51	19.00	19.16	19.25	19.30	19.33	19.35	19.37	19.38
2	.025	38.51	39.00	39.17	39.25	39.30	39.33	39.36	39.37	39.39
2	.010	98.50	99.00	99.17	99.25	99.30	99.33	99.36	99.37	99.39
3	.050	10.13	9.55	9.28	9.12	9.01	8.94	8.89	8.85	8.81
3	.025	17.44	16.04	15.44	15.10	14.88	14.73	14.62	14.54	14.47
3	.010	34.12	30.82	29.46	28.71	28.24	27.91	27.67	27.49	27.35
4	.050	7.71	6.94	6.59	6.39	6.26	6.16	6.09	6.04	6.00
4	.025	12.22	10.65	9.98	9.60	9.36	9.20	9.07	8.98	8.90
4	.010	21.20	18.00	16.69	15.98	15.52	15.21	14.98	14.80	14.66
5	.050	6.61	5.79	5.41	5.19	5.05	4.95	4.88	4.82	4.77
5	.025	10.01	8.43	7.76	7.39	7.15	6.98	6.85	6.76	6.68
5	.010	16.26	13.27	12.06	11.39	10.97	10.67	10.46	10.29	10.16
6	.050	5.99	5.14	4.76	4.53	4.39	4.28	4.21	4.15	4.10
6	.025	8.81	7.26	6.60	6.23	5.99	5.82	5.70	5.60	5.52
6	.010	13.75	10.92	9.78	9.15	8.75	8.47	8.26	8.10	7.98
7	.050	5.59	4.74	4.35	4.12	3.97	3.87	3.79	3.73	3.68
7	.025	8.07	6.54	5.89	5.52	5.29	5.12	4.99	4.90	4.82
7	.010	12.25	9.55	8.45	7.85	7.46	7.19	6.99	6.84	6.72
8	.050	5.32	4.46	4.07	3.84	3.69	3.58	3.50	3.44	3.39
8	.025	7.57	6.06	5.42	5.05	4.82	4.65	5.53	4.43	4.36
8	.010	11.26	8.65	7.59	7.01	6.63	6.37	6.18	6.03	5.91
9	.050	5.12	4.26	3.86	3.63	3.48	3.37	3.29	3.23	3.18
9	.025	7.21	5.71	5.08	4.72	4.48	4.32	4.20	4.10	4.03
9	.010	10.56	8.02	6.99	6.42	6.06	5.80	5.61	5.47	5.35
10	.050	4.96	4.10	3.71	3.48	3.33	3.22	3.14	3.07	3.02
10	.025	6.94	5.46	4.83	4.47	4.24	4.07	3.95	3.85	3.78
10	.010	10.04	7.56	6.55	5.99	5.64	5.39	5.20	5.06	4.94
11	.050	4.84	3.98	3.59	3.36	3.20	3.09	3.01	2.95	2.90
11	.025	6.72	5.26	4.63	4.28	4.04	3.88	3.76	3.66	3.59
11	.010	9.65	7.21	6.22	5.67	5.32	5.07	4.89	4.74	4.63
12	.050	4.75	3.89	3.49	3.26	3.11	3.00	2.91	2.85	2.80
12	.025	6.55	5.10	4.47	4.12	3.89	3.73	3.61	3.51	3.44
12	.010	9.33	6.93	5.95	5.41	5.06	4.82	4.64	4.50	4.39

TABLE 8 *continued*

Degrees of Freedom for Numerator										
10	12	15	20	25	30	40	50	60	120	1000
241.88	243.91	245.95	248.01	249.26	250.10	251.14	251.77	252.20	253.25	254.19
968.63	976.71	984.87	993.10	998.08	1001.4	1005.6	1008.1	1009.8	1014.0	1017.7
6055.8	6106.3	6157.3	6208.7	6239.8	6260.6	6286.8	6302.5	6313.0	6339.4	6362.7
19.40	19.41	19.43	19.45	19.46	19.46	19.47	19.48	19.48	19.49	19.49
39.40	39.41	39.43	39.45	39.46	39.46	39.47	39.48	39.48	39.49	39.50
99.40	99.42	99.43	99.45	99.46	99.47	99.47	99.48	99.48	99.49	99.50
8.79	8.74	8.70	8.66	8.63	8.62	8.59	8.58	8.57	8.55	8.53
14.42	14.34	14.25	14.17	14.12	14.08	14.04	14.01	13.99	13.95	13.91
27.23	27.05	26.87	26.69	26.58	26.50	26.41	26.35	26.32	26.22	26.14
5.96	5.91	5.86	5.80	5.77	5.75	5.72	5.70	5.69	5.66	5.63
8.84	8.75	8.66	8.56	8.580	8.46	8.41	8.38	8.36	8.31	8.26
14.55	14.37	14.20	14.02	13.91	13.84	13.75	13.69	13.65	13.56	13.47
4.74	4.68	4.62	4.56	4.52	4.50	4.46	4.44	4.43	4.40	4.37
6.62	6.52	6.43	6.33	6.27	6.23	6.18	6.14	6.12	6.07	6.02
10.05	9.89	9.72	9.55	9.45	9.38	9.29	9.24	9.20	9.11	9.03
4.06	4.00	3.94	3.87	3.83	3.81	3.77	3.75	3.74	3.70	3.67
5.46	5.37	5.27	5.17	5.11	5.07	5.01	4.98	4.96	4.90	4.86
7.87	7.72	7.56	7.40	7.30	7.23	7.14	7.09	7.06	6.97	6.89
3.64	3.57	3.51	3.44	3.40	3.38	3.34	3.32	3.30	3.27	3.23
4.76	4.67	4.57	4.47	4.40	4.36	4.31	4.28	4.25	4.20	4.15
6.62	6.47	6.31	6.16	6.06	5.99	5.91	5.86	5.82	5.74	5.66
3.35	3.28	3.22	3.15	3.11	3.08	3.04	3.02	3.01	2.97	2.93
4.30	4.20	4.10	4.00	3.94	3.89	3.84	3.81	3.78	3.73	3.68
5.81	5.67	5.52	5.36	5.26	5.20	5.12	5.07	5.03	4.95	4.87
3.14	3.07	3.01	2.94	2.89	2.86	2.83	2.80	2.79	2.75	2.71
3.96	3.87	3.77	3.67	3.60	3.56	3.51	3.47	3.45	3.39	3.34
5.26	5.11	4.96	4.81	4.71	4.65	4.57	4.52	4.48	4.40	4.32
2.98	2.91	2.85	2.77	2.73	2.70	2.66	2.64	2.62	2.58	2.54
3.72	3.62	3.52	3.42	3.35	3.31	3.26	3.22	3.20	3.14	3.09
4.85	4.71	4.56	4.41	4.31	4.25	4.17	4.12	4.08	4.00	3.92
2.85	2.79	2.72	2.65	2.60	2.57	2.53	2.51	2.49	2.45	2.41
3.53	3.43	3.33	3.23	3.16	3.12	3.06	3.03	3.00	2.94	2.89
4.54	4.40	4.25	4.10	4.01	3.94	3.86	3.81	3.78	3.69	3.61
2.75	2.69	2.62	2.54	2.50	2.47	2.43	2.40	2.38	2.34	2.30
3.37	3.28	3.18	3.07	3.01	2.96	2.91	2.87	2.85	2.79	2.73
4.30	4.16	4.01	3.86	3.76	3.70	3.62	3.57	3.54	3.45	3.37

TABLE 8 *continued*

Degrees of Freedom for Denominator	α	Degrees of Freedom for Numerator								
		1	2	3	4	5	6	7	8	9
13	.050	4.67	3.81	3.41	3.18	3.03	2.92	2.83	2.77	2.71
13	.025	6.41	4.97	4.35	4.00	3.77	3.60	3.48	3.39	3.31
13	.010	9.07	6.70	5.74	5.21	4.86	4.62	4.44	4.30	4.19
14	.050	4.60	3.74	3.34	3.11	2.96	2.85	2.76	2.70	2.65
14	.025	6.30	4.86	4.24	3.89	3.66	3.50	3.38	3.29	3.21
14	.010	8.86	6.51	5.56	5.04	4.69	4.46	4.28	4.14	4.03
15	.050	4.54	3.68	3.29	3.06	2.90	2.79	2.71	2.64	2.59
15	.025	6.20	4.77	4.15	3.80	3.58	3.41	3.29	3.20	3.12
15	.010	8.68	6.36	5.42	4.89	4.56	4.32	4.14	4.00	3.89
16	.050	4.49	3.63	3.24	3.01	2.85	2.74	2.66	2.59	2.54
16	.025	6.12	4.69	4.08	3.73	3.50	3.34	3.22	3.12	3.05
16	.010	8.53	6.12	5.29	4.77	4.44	4.20	4.03	3.89	3.78
17	.050	4.45	3.59	3.20	2.96	2.81	2.70	2.61	2.55	2.49
17	.025	6.04	4.62	4.01	3.66	3.44	3.28	3.16	3.06	2.98
17	.010	8.40	6.11	5.19	4.67	4.34	4.10	3.93	3.79	3.68
18	.050	4.41	3.55	3.16	2.93	2.77	2.66	5.58	2.51	2.46
18	.025	5.98	4.56	3.95	3.61	3.38	3.22	3.10	3.01	2.93
18	.010	8.29	6.01	5.09	4.58	4.25	4.01	3.84	3.71	3.60
19	.050	4.38	3.52	3.13	2.90	2.74	2.63	2.54	2.48	2.42
19	.025	5.92	4.51	3.90	3.56	3.33	3.17	3.05	2.96	2.88
19	.010	8.18	5.93	5.01	4.50	4.17	3.94	3.77	3.63	3.52
20	.050	4.35	3.49	3.10	2.87	2.71	2.60	2.51	2.45	2.39
20	.025	5.87	4.46	3.86	3.51	3.29	3.13	3.01	2.91	2.84
20	.010	8.10	5.85	4.94	4.43	4.10	3.87	3.70	3.56	3.46
21	.050	4.32	3.47	3.07	2.84	2.68	2.57	2.49	2.42	2.37
21	.025	5.83	4.42	3.82	3.48	3.25	3.09	2.97	2.87	2.80
21	.010	8.02	5.78	4.87	4.37	4.04	3.81	3.64	3.51	3.40
22	.050	4.30	3.44	3.05	2.82	2.66	2.55	2.46	2.40	2.34
22	.025	5.79	4.38	3.78	3.44	3.22	3.05	2.93	2.84	2.76
22	.010	7.95	5.72	4.82	4.31	3.99	3.76	3.59	3.45	3.35
23	.050	4.28	3.42	3.03	2.80	2.64	2.53	2.44	2.37	2.32
23	.025	5.75	4.35	3.75	3.41	3.18	3.02	2.90	2.81	2.73
23	.010	7.88	5.66	4.76	4.26	3.94	3.71	3.54	3.41	3.30
24	.050	4.26	3.40	3.01	2.78	2.62	2.51	2.42	2.36	2.30
24	.025	5.72	4.32	3.72	3.38	3.15	2.99	2.87	2.78	2.70
24	.010	7.82	5.61	4.72	4.22	3.90	3.67	3.50	3.36	3.26

TABLE 8 *continued*

Degrees of Freedom for Numerator										
10	12	15	20	25	30	40	50	60	120	1000
2.67	2.60	2.53	2.46	2.41	2.38	2.34	2.31	2.30	2.25	2.21
3.25	3.15	3.05	2.95	2.88	2.84	2.78	2.74	2.72	2.66	2.60
4.10	3.96	3.82	3.66	3.57	3.51	3.43	3.38	3.34	3.25	3.18
2.60	2.53	2.46	2.39	2.34	2.31	2.27	2.24	2.22	2.18	2.14
3.15	3.05	2.95	2.84	2.78	2.73	2.67	2.64	2.61	2.55	2.50
3.94	3.80	3.66	3.51	3.41	3.35	3.27	3.22	3.18	3.09	3.02
2.54	2.48	2.40	2.33	2.28	2.25	2.20	2.18	2.16	2.11	2.07
3.06	2.96	2.86	2.76	2.69	2.64	2.59	2.55	2.52	2.46	2.40
3.80	3.67	3.52	3.37	3.28	3.21	3.13	3.08	3.05	2.96	2.88
2.49	2.42	2.35	2.28	2.23	2.19	2.15	2.12	2.11	2.06	2.02
2.99	2.89	2.79	2.68	2.61	2.57	2.51	2.47	2.45	2.38	2.32
3.69	3.55	3.41	3.26	3.16	3.10	3.02	2.97	2.93	2.84	2.76
2.45	2.38	2.31	2.23	2.18	2.15	2.10	2.08	2.06	2.01	1.97
2.92	2.82	2.72	2.62	2.55	2.50	2.44	2.41	2.38	2.32	2.26
3.59	3.46	3.31	3.16	3.07	3.00	2.92	2.87	2.83	2.75	2.66
2.41	2.34	2.27	2.19	2.14	2.11	2.06	2.04	2.02	1.97	1.92
2.87	2.77	2.67	2.56	2.49	2.44	2.38	2.35	2.32	2.26	2.20
3.51	3.37	3.23	3.08	2.98	2.92	2.84	2.78	2.75	2.66	2.58
2.38	2.31	2.23	2.16	2.11	2.07	2.03	2.00	1.98	1.93	1.88
2.82	2.72	2.62	2.51	2.44	2.39	2.33	2.30	2.27	2.20	2.14
3.43	3.30	3.15	3.00	2.91	2.84	2.76	2.71	2.67	2.58	2.50
2.35	2.28	2.20	2.12	2.07	2.04	1.99	1.97	1.95	1.90	1.85
2.77	2.68	2.57	2.46	2.40	2.35	2.29	2.25	2.22	2.16	2.09
3.37	3.23	3.09	2.94	2.84	2.78	2.69	2.64	2.61	2.52	2.43
2.32	2.25	2.18	2.10	2.05	2.01	1.96	1.94	1.92	1.87	1.82
2.73	2.64	2.53	2.42	2.36	2.31	2.25	2.24	2.18	2.11	2.05
3.31	3.17	3.03	2.88	2.79	2.72	2.64	2.58	2.55	2.46	2.37
2.30	2.23	2.15	2.07	2.02	1.98	1.94	1.91	1.89	1.84	1.79
2.70	2.60	2.50	2.39	2.32	2.27	2.24	2.17	2.14	2.08	2.01
3.26	3.12	2.98	2.83	2.73	2.67	2.58	2.53	2.50	2.40	2.32
2.27	2.20	2.13	2.05	2.00	1.96	1.91	1.88	1.86	1.81	1.76
2.67	2.57	2.47	2.36	2.29	2.24	2.18	2.14	2.11	2.04	1.98
3.21	3.07	2.93	2.78	2.69	2.62	2.54	2.48	2.45	2.35	2.27
2.25	2.18	2.11	2.03	1.97	1.94	1.89	1.86	1.84	1.79	1.74
2.64	2.54	2.44	2.33	2.26	2.21	2.15	2.11	2.08	2.01	1.94
3.17	3.03	2.89	2.74	2.64	2.58	2.49	2.44	2.40	2.31	2.22

TABLE 8 *continued*

Degrees of Freedom for Denominator	α	Degrees of Freedom for Numerator								
		1	2	3	4	5	6	7	8	9
25	.050	4.24	3.39	2.99	2.76	2.60	2.49	2.40	2.34	2.28
25	.025	5.69	4.29	3.69	3.35	3.13	2.97	2.85	2.75	2.68
25	.010	7.77	5.57	4.68	4.18	3.85	3.63	3.46	3.32	3.22
26	.050	4.23	3.37	2.98	2.74	2.59	2.47	2.39	2.32	2.27
26	.025	5.66	4.27	3.67	3.33	3.10	2.94	2.82	2.73	2.65
26	.010	7.72	2.53	4.64	4.14	3.82	3.59	3.42	3.29	3.18
27	.050	4.21	3.35	2.96	2.73	2.57	3.46	2.37	2.31	2.25
27	.025	5.63	4.24	3.65	3.31	3.08	2.92	2.80	2.71	2.63
27	.010	7.68	5.49	4.60	4.11	3.78	3.56	3.39	3.26	3.15
28	.050	4.20	3.34	2.95	2.71	2.56	2.45	2.36	2.29	2.24
28	.025	5.61	4.22	3.63	3.29	3.06	2.90	2.78	2.69	2.61
28	.010	7.64	5.45	4.57	4.07	3.75	3.53	3.36	3.23	3.12
29	.050	4.18	3.33	2.93	2.70	2.55	2.43	2.35	2.28	2.22
29	.025	5.59	4.20	3.61	3.27	3.04	2.88	2.76	2.67	2.59
29	.010	7.60	5.42	4.54	4.04	3.73	3.50	3.33	3.20	3.09
30	.050	4.17	3.32	2.92	2.69	5.53	2.42	2.33	2.27	2.21
30	.025	5.57	4.18	3.59	3.25	3.03	2.87	2.75	2.65	2.57
30	.010	7.56	5.39	4.51	4.02	3.70	3.47	3.30	3.17	3.07
40	.050	4.08	3.23	2.84	2.61	2.45	2.34	2.25	2.18	2.12
40	.025	5.42	4.05	3.46	3.13	2.90	2.74	2.62	2.53	2.45
40	.010	7.31	5.18	4.31	3.83	3.51	3.29	3.12	3.99	2.89
50	.050	4.03	3.18	2.79	2.56	2.40	2.29	2.20	2.13	2.07
50	.025	5.34	3.97	3.39	3.05	2.83	2.67	2.55	2.46	2.38
50	.010	7.17	5.16	4.20	3.72	3.41	3.19	3.02	2.89	2.78
60	.050	4.00	3.15	2.76	2.53	2.37	2.25	2.17	2.10	2.04
60	.025	5.29	3.93	3.34	3.01	2.79	2.63	2.51	2.41	2.33
60	.010	7.08	4.98	4.13	3.65	3.34	3.12	2.95	2.82	2.72
100	.050	3.94	3.09	2.70	2.46	2.31	2.19	2.10	2.03	1.97
100	.025	5.18	3.83	3.25	2.92	2.70	2.54	2.42	2.32	2.24
100	.010	6.90	4.82	3.98	3.51	3.21	2.99	2.82	2.69	2.59
200	.050	3.89	3.04	2.65	2.42	2.26	2.14	2.06	1.98	1.93
200	.025	5.10	3.76	3.18	2.85	2.63	2.47	2.35	2.26	2.18
200	.010	6.76	4.71	3.88	3.41	3.11	2.89	2.73	2.60	2.50
1000	.050	3.85	3.00	2.61	2.38	2.22	2.11	2.02	1.95	1.89
1000	.025	5.04	3.70	3.13	2.80	2.58	2.42	2.30	2.20	2.13
1000	.010	6.66	4.63	3.80	3.34	3.04	2.82	2.66	2.53	2.43

Source: From *Biometrika Tables for Statisticians, Vol. 1,* by permission of the Biometrika Trustees.

TABLE 8 *continued*

Degrees of Freedom for Numerator										
10	12	15	20	25	30	40	50	60	120	1000
2.24	2.16	2.09	2.01	1.96	1.92	1.87	1.84	1.82	1.77	1.72
2.61	2.51	2.41	2.30	2.23	2.18	2.12	2.08	2.05	1.98	1.91
3.13	2.99	2.85	2.70	2.60	2.54	2.45	2.40	2.36	2.27	2.18
2.22	2.15	2.07	1.99	1.94	1.90	1.85	1.82	1.80	1.75	1.70
2.59	2.49	2.39	2.28	2.21	2.16	2.09	2.05	2.03	1.95	1.89
3.09	2.96	2.81	2.66	2.57	2.50	2.42	2.36	2.33	2.23	2.14
2.20	2.13	2.06	1.97	1.92	1.88	1.84	1.81	1.79	1.73	1.68
2.57	2.47	2.36	2.25	2.18	2.13	2.07	2.03	2.00	1.93	1.86
3.06	2.93	2.78	2.63	5.54	2.47	2.38	2.33	2.29	2.20	2.11
2.19	2.12	2.04	1.96	1.91	1.87	1.82	1.79	1.44	1.71	1.66
2.55	2.45	2.34	2.23	2.16	2.11	2.05	2.01	1.98	1.91	1.84
3.03	2.90	2.75	2.60	2.51	2.44	2.35	2.30	2.26	2.17	2.08
2.18	2.10	2.03	1.94	1.89	1.85	1.81	1.77	1.75	1.70	1.65
2.53	2.43	2.32	2.21	2.14	2.09	2.03	1.99	1.96	1.89	1.82
3.00	2.87	2.73	2.57	2.48	2.41	2.33	2.27	2.23	2.14	2.05
2.16	2.09	2.01	1.93	1.88	1.84	1.79	1.76	1.74	1.68	1.63
2.51	2.41	2.31	2.20	2.12	2.07	2.01	1.97	1.94	1.87	1.80
2.98	2.84	2.70	2.55	2.45	2.39	2.30	2.25	2.21	2.11	2.02
2.08	2.00	1.92	1.84	1.78	1.74	1.69	1.66	1.64	1.58	1.52
2.39	2.29	2.18	2.07	1.99	1.94	1.88	1.83	1.80	1.72	1.65
2.80	2.66	2.52	2.37	2.27	2.20	2.11	2.06	2.02	1.92	1.82
2.03	1.95	1.87	1.78	1.73	1.69	1.63	1.60	1.58	1.51	1.45
2.32	2.22	2.11	1.99	1.92	1.87	1.80	1.75	1.72	1.64	1.56
2.70	2.56	2.42	2.27	2.17	2.10	2.01	1.95	1.91	1.80	1.70
1.99	1.92	1.84	1.75	1.69	1.65	1.59	1.56	1.53	1.47	1.40
2.27	2.17	2.06	1.94	1.87	1.82	1.74	1.70	1.67	1.58	1.49
2.63	2.50	2.35	2.20	2.10	2.03	1.94	1.88	1.84	1.73	1.62
1.93	1.85	1.77	1.68	1.62	1.57	1.52	1.48	1.45	1.38	1.30
2.18	2.08	1.97	1.85	1.77	1.71	1.64	1.59	1.56	1.46	1.36
2.50	2.37	2.22	2.07	1.97	1.89	1.80	1.74	1.69	1.57	1.45
1.88	1.80	1.72	1.62	1.56	1.52	1.46	1.41	1.39	1.30	1.21
2.11	2.01	1.90	1.78	1.70	1.64	1.56	1.51	1.47	1.37	1.25
2.41	2.27	2.46	1.97	1.87	1.79	1.69	1.63	1.58	1.45	1.30
1.84	1.76	1.68	1.58	1.52	1.47	1.41	1.36	1.33	1.24	1.11
2.06	1.96	1.85	1.72	1.64	1.58	1.50	1.45	1.41	1.29	1.13
2.34	2.20	2.06	1.90	1.79	1.72	1.61	1.54	1.50	1.35	1.16

Chapter 9
Sample Test Statistics for Tests of Hypotheses

for $\mu(n \geq 30)$ $\quad z = \dfrac{\overline{x} - \mu}{\sigma / \sqrt{n}}$

for $\mu(n < 30); d.f. = n-1$ $\quad t = \dfrac{\overline{x} - \mu}{s / \sqrt{n}}$

for p $\quad z = \dfrac{\hat{p} - p}{\sqrt{pq/n}}$ where $q = 1 - p$

for paired differences d $\quad t = \dfrac{\overline{d} - \mu_d}{s_d / \sqrt{n}}$ with $d.f. = n-1$

difference of means large sample $\quad z = \dfrac{(\overline{x}_1 - \overline{x}_2) - (\mu_1 - \mu_2)}{\sqrt{\dfrac{\sigma_1^2}{n_1} + \dfrac{\sigma_2^2}{n_2}}}$

difference of means small sample with $\sigma_1 \approx \sigma_2; d.f. = n_1 + n_2 - 2$

$$t = \frac{(\overline{x}_1 - \overline{x}_2) - (\mu_1 - \mu_2)}{s\sqrt{\dfrac{1}{n_1} + \dfrac{1}{n_2}}} \text{ where } s = \sqrt{\frac{(n_1 - 1)s_1^2 + (n_2 - 1)s_2^2}{n_1 + n_2 - 2}}$$

difference of proportions $\quad z = \dfrac{\hat{p}_1 - \hat{p}_2}{\sqrt{\dfrac{\hat{p}\hat{q}}{n_1} + \dfrac{\hat{p}\hat{q}}{n_2}}}$ where $\hat{p} = \dfrac{r_1 + r_2}{n_1 + n_2}$; $\hat{q} = 1 - \hat{p}$; $\hat{p}_1 = r_1 / n_1$; $\hat{p}_2 = r_2 / n_2$

Chapter 10
Regression and Correlation

In all these formulas $SS_x = \Sigma x^2 - \dfrac{(\Sigma x)^2}{n}$, $SS_y = \Sigma y^2 - \dfrac{(\Sigma y)^2}{n}$, $SS_{xy} = \Sigma xy - \dfrac{(\Sigma x)(\Sigma y)}{n}$

Least squares line $y = a + bx$ where $b = \dfrac{SS_{xy}}{SS_x}$ and $a = \overline{y} - b\overline{x}$

Standard error of estimate $\quad S_e = \sqrt{\dfrac{SS_y - bSS_{xy}}{n-2}}$ where $b = \dfrac{SS_{xy}}{SS_x}$

Pearson product moment correlation coefficient $\quad r = \dfrac{SS_{xy}}{\sqrt{SS_x SS_y}}$

Coefficient of determination $= r^2$

Confidence interval for y $\quad y_p - E < y < y_p + E$ where y_p is the predicted y value for x

$E = t_c S_e \sqrt{1 + \frac{1}{n} + \ldots}$ with $d.f. = n-2$

Sample test statistic fc ... $= \dfrac{r\sqrt{n-2}}{\sqrt{1-r^2}}$ $\quad d.f. = n-2$

Sample test statistic f ... $= \dfrac{b - \beta}{S_e / \sqrt{SS_x}}$ $\quad d.f. = n-2$

Confidence interval ... β $\quad b - t_c \dfrac{S_e}{\sqrt{SS_x}} < \beta < b + t_c \dfrac{S_e}{\sqrt{SS_x}}$ $\quad d.f. = n-2$

Chapter 11

$$\chi_2 = \Sigma\frac{(O-E)^2}{E} \quad \text{where } E = \frac{(\text{row total})(\text{column total})}{\text{sample size}}$$

Tests of Independence $d.f. = (R-1)(C-1)$

Goodness of fit $d.f. = (\text{number of entries})-1$

Confidence Interval for σ^2; $d.f. = n-1$ $\frac{(n-1)s^2}{\chi_U^2} < \sigma^2 < \frac{(n-1)s^2}{\chi_L^2}$

Sample test statistic for H_0: $\sigma^2 = k$; $d.f. = n-1$ $\chi^2 = \frac{(n-1)s^2}{\sigma^2}$

Testing Two Variances

Sample test statistic $F = \frac{s_1^2}{s_2^2}$ where $s_1^2 \geq s_2^2$ $d.f._N = n_1 - 1$; $d.f._D = n_2 - 1$

ANOVA

k = number of groups; N = total sample size

$$SS_{TOT} = \Sigma x_{TOT}^2 - \frac{(\Sigma x_{TOT})^2}{N};\ SS_{BET} = \sum_{all\ groups}\left(\frac{(\Sigma x_i)^2}{n_i}\right) - \frac{(\Sigma x_{TOT})^2}{N};\ SS_W = \sum_{all\ groups}\left(\Sigma x_i^2 - \frac{(\Sigma x_i)^2}{n_i}\right)$$

$$SS_{TOT} = SS_{BET} + SS_W;\ MS_{BET} = \frac{SS_{BET}}{d.f._{BET}} \text{ where } d.f._{BET} = k-1;\ MS_W = \frac{SS_W}{d.f._W} \text{ where } d.f._W = N-k;$$

$$F = \frac{MS_{BET}}{MS_W} \text{ where } d.f. \text{ numerator } = d.f._{BET} = k-1;\ d.f. \text{ denominator } = d.f._W = N-k$$

Two-Way ANOVA

r = number of rows; c = number of columns

Row factor F: $\frac{MS \text{ row factor}}{MS \text{ error}}$; Column factor F: $\frac{MS \text{ column factor}}{MS \text{ error}}$; Interaction F: $\frac{MS \text{ interaction}}{MS \text{ error}}$

with degrees of freedom for

row factor = $r - 1$; interaction = $(r - 1)(c - 1)$; column factor = $c - 1$; error = $rc(n - 1)$

Chapter 12

Sample test statistic for x = proportion of plus signs to all signs ($n \geq 12$) $z = \frac{x-0.5}{\sqrt{0.25/n}}$

Sample test statistic for R = sum of ranks

$$z = \frac{R-\mu_R}{\sigma_R} \text{ where } \mu_R = \frac{n_1(n_1+n_2+1)}{2} \text{ and } \sigma_R = \sqrt{\frac{n_1 n_2 (n_1+n_2+1)}{12}}$$

Spearman rank correlation coefficient $r_s = 1 - \frac{6\Sigma d^2}{n(n^2-1)}$ where $d = x - y$

Part IV

Sample Chapter Tests with Answers

CHAPTER 1 TEST
FORM A

1. The Colorado State Legislature wants to estimate the length of time it takes a resident of Colorado to earn a Bachelor's degree from a state college or university. A random sample of 265 recent in-state graduates were surveyed.

(a) Identify the variable. **1. (a)** ____________________

(b) Is the variable quantitative or qualitative? **(b)** ____________________

(c) What is the implied population? **(c)** ____________________

2. For the information in parts **(a)** through **(g)** below, list the highest level of measurement as ratio, interval, ordinal, or nominal and explain your choice.

A student advising file contains the following information.

(a) Name of student **2. (a)** ____________________

(b) Student I.D. number **(b)** ____________________

(c) Cumulative grade point average **(c)** ____________________

(d) Dates of awards (scholarships, dean's list, ...) **(d)** ____________________

(e) Declared major or undecided if no major declared **(e)** ____________________

(f) A number code representing class standing:
1 = Freshman, 2 = Sophomore, 3 = Junior,
4 = Senior, 5 = Graduate student **(f)** ____________________

(g) Entrance exam rating for competency in English:
Excellent, Satisfactory, Unsatisfactory **(g)** ____________________

3. Categorize the style of gathering data (sampling, experiment, simulation, census) described in each of the following situations.

(a) Look at all the apartments in a complex and determine the monthly rent charged for each unit. **3. (a)** ____________________

(b) Give one group of students a flu vaccination and compare the number of times these students are sick during the semester with students in a group who did not receive the vaccination. **(b)** ____________________

(c) Select a sample of students and determine the percentage who are taking mathematics this semester. **(c)** ____________________

(d) Use a computer program to show the effects on traffic flow when the timing of stop lights is changed. **(d)** ____________________

CHAPTER 1, FORM A, PAGE 2

4. Write a brief essay in which you describe what is meant by an experiment. Given an example of a situation in which data is gathered by means of an experiment. How is gathering data from an experiment different from using a sample from a specified population?

4. ______________________

5. Consider the experiment of rolling a single die. Describe how you would use a random number table to simulate the outcomes of rolling a single die. Using the following row of random numbers from the table, find the first five outcomes.

36017 98590 64180 72315 39710

5. ______________________

6. Identify each of the following samples by naming the sampling technique used (cluster, convenience, simple random, stratified, systematic).

(a) Measure the length of time every fifth person coming into a bank waits for teller service over a period of two days.

6. (a) ______________________

(b) Take a sample of five Zip codes from the Chicago metropolitan region and use all the elementary schools from each of the Zip code regions. Determine the number of students enrolled in first grade in each of the schools selected.

(b) ______________________

(c) Divide the users of the computer online service Internet into different age groups and then select a random sample from each age group to survey about the amount of time they are connected to Internet each month.

(c) ______________________

(d) Survey five friends regarding their opinion of the student cafeteria.

(d) ______________________

(e) Pick a random sample of students enrolled at your college and determine the number of credit hours they have each accumulated toward their degree program.

(e) ______________________

CHAPTER 1 TEST
FORM B

1. A book store wants to estimate the proportion of its customers who buy murder mysteries. A random sample of 76 customers are observed at the checkout counter and the number purchasing murder mysteries is recorded.

(a) Identify the variable. **1. (a)** ________________

(b) Is the variable quantitative or qualitative? **(b)** ________________

(c) What is the implied population? **(c)** ________________

2. For the information in parts **(a)** through **(e)** below, list the highest level of measurement as ratio, interval, ordinal, or nominal and explain your choice.

A restaurant manager is developing a clientele profile. Some of the information for the profile follows:

(a) Gender of diners **2. (a)** ________________

(b) Size of groups dining together **(b)** ________________

(c) Time of day the last diner of the evening departs **(c)** ________________

(d) Age grouping: young, middle age, senior **(d)** ________________

(e) Length of time a diner waits for a table. **(e)** ________________

3. Categorize the style of gathering data (sampling, experiment, simulation, census) for the following situations.

(a) Consider all the students enrolled at your college this semester and report the age of each student. **3. (a)** ________________

(b) Select a sample of new F10 pickup trucks and count the number of manufacturer defects in each of the trucks. **(b)** ________________

(c) Use computer graphics to determine the flight path of a golf ball when the position of the hand on the golf club is changed. **(c)** ________________

(d) Teach one section of English composition using a specific word processing package and teach another without using any computerized word processing. Count the number of grammar errors made by students in each section on a final draft of a 20 page term paper. **(d)** ________________

CHAPTER 1, FORM B, PAGE 2

4. Write a brief essay in which you discuss some of the aspects surveys. Give specific examples to illustrate your main points.

4. ______________________

5. A business employs 736 people. Describe how you could get a random sample of size 30 to survey regarding desire for professional training opportunities. Identify the first 5 to be included in the sample using the following random number sequence.

62283 14130 55790 40133 47596 17654

5. ______________________

6. To determine monthly rental prices of apartment units in the San Francisco area, samples were constructed in the following ways. Categorize (cluster, convenience, simple random, stratified, systematic) each sampling technique described.

(a) Number all the units in the area and use a random number table to select the apartments to include in the sample.

6. (a) ______________________

(b) Divide the apartment units according to number of bedrooms and then sample from each of the groups.

(b) ______________________

(c) Select 5 Zip codes at random and include every apartment unit in the selected Zip codes.

(c) ______________________

(d) Look in the newspaper and consider the first sample of apartment units that list rent per month.

(d) ______________________

(e) Call every 50th apartment complex listed in the yellow pages and record the rent of the unit with unit number closest to 200.

(e) ______________________

CHAPTER 1 TEST FORM C

Write the letter of the response that best answers each problem.

1. A consumer research company wants to estimate the average cost of an airline ticket for a round trip within the continental United States. A random sample of 50 airfares was gathered giving an average price of $438. Identify the variable. **1.** ________

(a) Random sample of 50 airfares (b) Airline fare

(c) Consumer research company (d) Quantitative (e) $438

2. For the information in parts A. through E., choose the highest level of measurement (or cannot determine):

(a) Ratio (b) Interval

(c) Ordinal (d) Nominal (e) Cannot determine

A. Temperature of refrigerators **2. A.** ________

B. Horsepower of racecar engines **B.** ________

C. Marital status of school board members **C.** ________

D. Ratings of television programs (poor, fair, good, excellent) **D.** ________

E. Ages of children enrolled in a daycare **E.** ________

3. Categorize the style of gathering data described in each of the following situations:

(a) Sampling (b) Experiment

(c) Simulation (d) Census (e) Cannot determine

A. Give one group of people a diet supplement and another a placebo. After both groups have been on the same meal program for one month, compare the weight losses of the two groups. **3. A.** ________

B. Use a computer program to show the effects on airline traffic flow where air traffic controllers change methods. **B.** ________

C. Select a sample of consumers and determine the percentage who own cellular phones. **C.** ________

D. Determine the annual income for all employees in a company. **D.** ________

CHAPTER 1, FORM C, PAGE 2

4. Consider the following study:

Students in a limnology class took water samples from a lake to determine the temperature at different depths. Which of the following techniques for gathering data do you think was used? **4.** ________

(a) Double-blind experiment (b) Experiment

(c) Analysis of variance (d) Placebo effect (e) Observational study

5. When using a random-number table to get a list of nine random numbers from 57 to 634, you would use groups of **5.** ________

(a) 9 digits. (b) 2 digits.

(c) 1 digit. (d) 3 digits. (e) 2 digits and then 3 digits.

6. Identify each of the following samples by naming the sampling technique used.

(a) Cluster (b) Convenience

(c) Simple random (d) Stratified (e) Systematic

A. Every tenth customer entering a health club is asked to select his or her preferred method of exercise. **6. A.** ________

B. Divide the subscribers of a magazine into three different income categories and then select a random sample from each category to survey about their favorite feature. **B.** ________

C. Take a sample of six Zip codes from the Minneapolis metropolitan region and use all the car dealerships in the selected areas. Determine the number of new cars sold each month at each dealership. **C.** ________

D. Use a random number table to select a sample of books and determine the number of pages in each book. **D.** ________

E. Determine the annual salary of each of the nurses that are on duty at the time you chose to interview at the hospital. **E.** ________

CHAPTER 2 TEST
FORM A

1. The Dean's Office at Hendrix College gave the following information about numbers of majors in different academic areas: Humanities, 372; Natural Science, 415; Social Science, 511; Business Administration, 619; Philosophy, 196. Make a Pareto chart representing this information.

1.

2. Professor Hill in the Music Department kept a list of the number of students visiting his office each week for two semesters (30 weeks). The results were

15	23	17	13	3	9	7	6	8	11
16	32	27	4	20	3	28	5	6	11
20	12	8	10	25	10	8	15	11	9

(a) Make a frequency table with five classes, showing class boundaries, class midpoints, frequencies, relative frequencies, and cumulative frequencies.

2. (a)

(b) Make a frequency histogram with five classes.

(b)

CHAPTER 2, FORM A, PAGE 2

(c) Make a relative frequency histogram with five classes.

(c)

(d) Make an ogive with five classes.

(d)

3. Jim is a taxi driver who keeps a record of his meter readings. The results for the past twenty meter readings (rounded to the nearest dollar) are given below.

15	7	9	21	19	17	8	35	22	33
46	5	24	37	51	49	57	42	12	16

Make a stem-and-leaf display of the data.

3. ________________

4. The Air Pollution Index in Denver for each day of the second week of February is shown below.

1.7 2.4 5.3 4.1 3.2 2.0 2.5

Make a time plot for these data.

4.

CHAPTER 2, FORM A, PAGE 3

5. A survey of 100 students was taken to see how they preferred to study. The survey showed that 38 students liked it quiet, 20 students liked the television on, 34 students liked the stereo on, and 8 students liked white noise such as in a lunch room. Make a circle graph to display this information.

5.

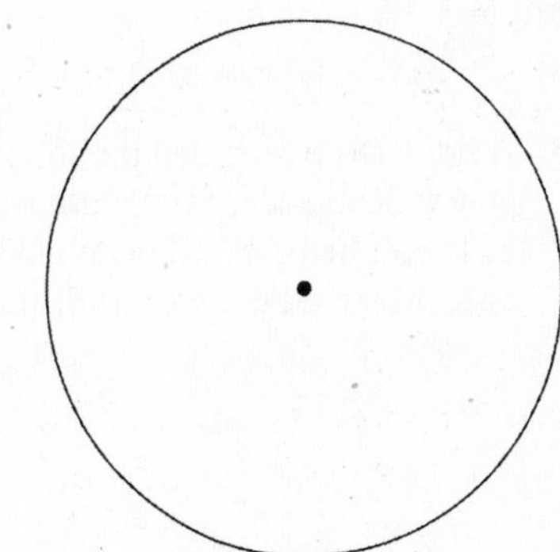

6. Of all the shoppers at a supermarket on a given day, it was determined that 71% were women under age 60, 20% were women 60 years or older, 7% were men under age 60 and 2% were men 60 years or older. Make a pie chart of this information.

6.

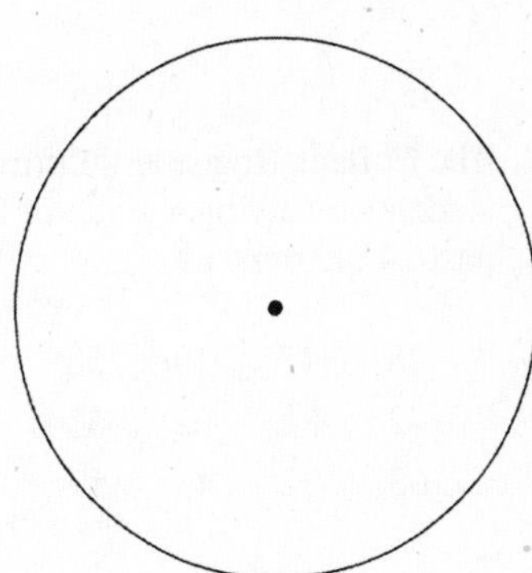

7. Make a dotplot for the data in Problem 2 regarding the number of students visiting the office. Compare the dotplot to the histogram in Problem 2.

7.

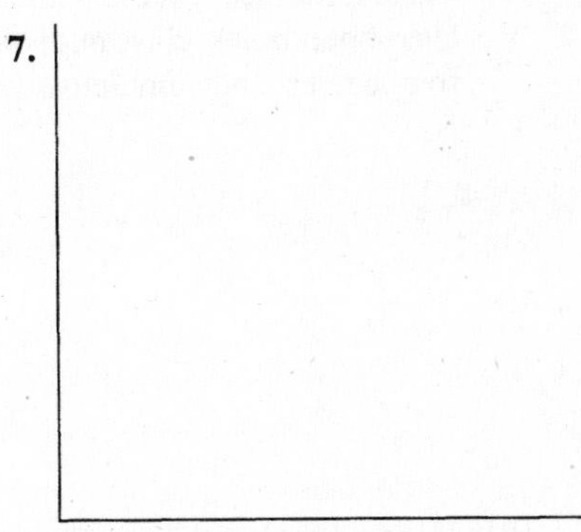

8. A sample of 20 motorists was taken from a freeway where the speed limit was 65 mph. A dotplot of their speeds is shown below. How many motorists were speeding?

8. 

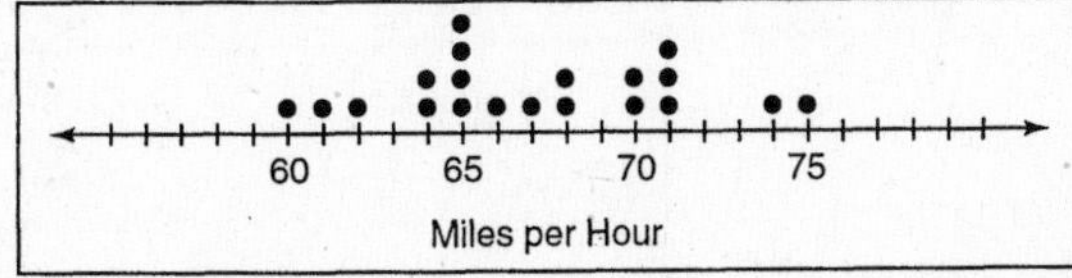

9. Following is a list of ages of participants entered in a 5K fun run. Make a stem-and-leaf display for these data and describe the distributions.

24	31	8	29	36	55	42	40	22	19	24
43	38	18	32	50	10	28	35	25	28	47

9. ______________________

CHAPTER 2 TEST FORM B

1. A book store recorded the following sales last month by genre: Romance, 519; Murder Mystery, 732; Biography, 211; Self help, 819; Travel guide, 143; Children's books, 643. Make a Pareto chart displaying this information.

1.

2. The College Registrar's Office recorded the number of students receiving a grade of Incomplete. Results for the past 24 quarters are

28	47	19	58	63	77	53	39	93	35
42	81	62	67	71	59	48	56	75	48
63	32	46	57						

(a) Make a frequency table with five classes, showing class boundaries, class midpoints, frequencies, relative frequencies, and cumulative frequencies.

2. (a)

(b) Make a frequency histogram with five classes.

(b)

CHAPTER 2, FORM B, PAGE 2

(c) Make a relative frequency histogram with five classes. **(c)**

(d) Make an ogive with five classes. **(d)**

3. The Humanities Division recorded the number of students signed up for the Study Abroad Program each quarter. The results are

58	26	21	29	33	47	42	38	44	56
52	64	68	59	63	36	34	45	51	50

Make a stem-and-leaf display of the data. **3.** ____________________

4. The Air Pollution Index in Denver for each day of the second week of February is shown below. **4.**

Week	1	2	3	4	5	6
Price (S)	289	291	298	305	311	322

Week	7	8	9	10	11	12
Price (S)	316	300	290	299	291	288

Make a time plot for these data.

CHAPTER 2, FORM B, PAGE 3

5. A college senior class has 5000 students. Their graduation forms have their chosen major. There are 800 who chose social science, 400 who chose science, 1100 who chose humanities, 1400 who chose computer-related majors, 900 who chose engineering, and 400 who have yet to fill their major. Make a circle graph to display this information.

5.

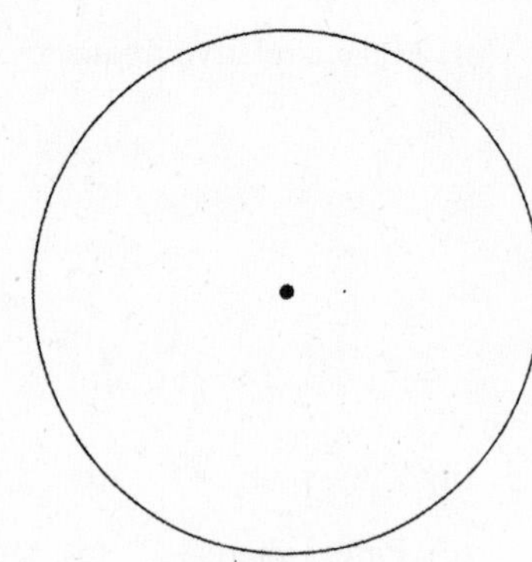

6. The school administration would like to know who is taking the city bus to school. A survey showed that the buses held 61% freshman, 25% sophomores, 12% juniors, and 2% seniors. Make a pie chart of this information.

6.

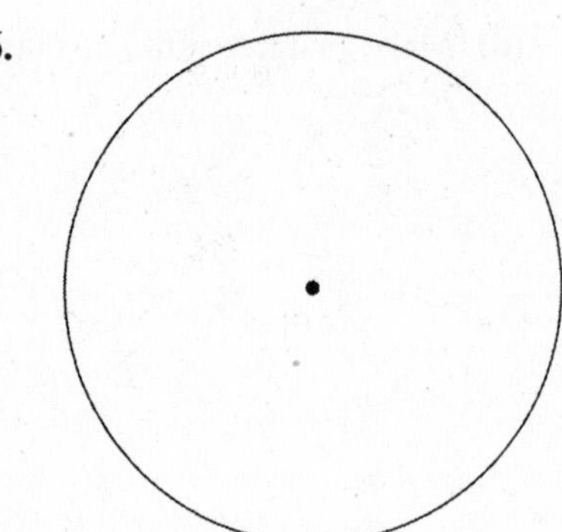

7. Make a dotplot for the data in Problem 2 regarding the number of students receiving a grade of Incomplete. Compare the dotplot to the histogram of Problem 2.

7.

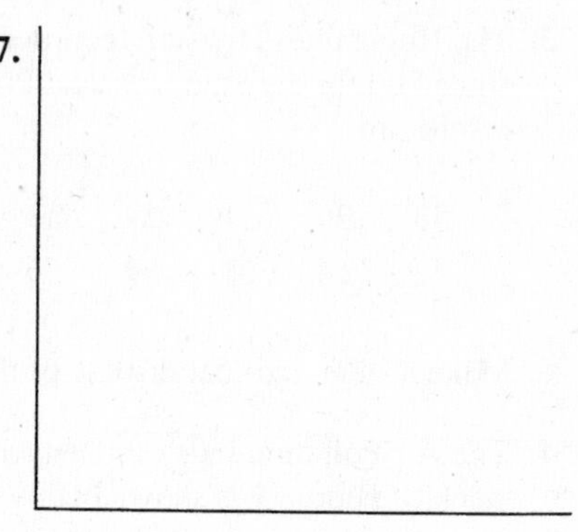

8. A sample of 15 days was selected from the summer season. A dotplot of the daily high temperature is shown here. How many days were colder than 70°F?

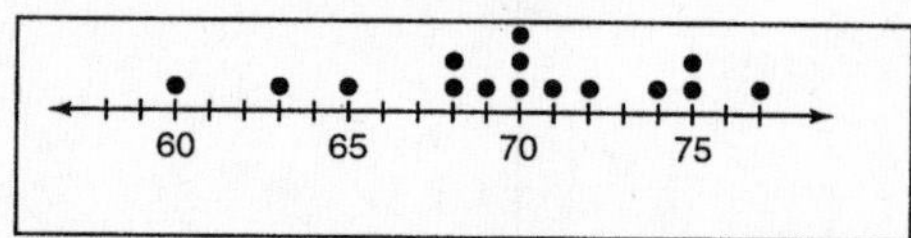

8. ______________________

9. Following is a list of diameters (in mm) of holes produced by an assembly line machine. Make a stem-and-leaf display for these data and describe the distribution.

2.3	3.7	1.2	3.6	2.4	2.6	3.7	0.9
1.8	2.5	2.5	3.0	2.8	1.7	3.1	4.1

9. ______________________

CHAPTER 2 TEST
FORM C

Write the letter of the response that best answers each problem.

1. __________ identify the frequency of events or categories in decreasing order of frequency of occurrence. **1.** __________

(a) Time plots (b) Bar graphs
(c) Pareto charts (d) Ogives (e) Circle graphs

2. __________ are useful for quantitative or qualitative data. With qualitative date, the frequency or percentage of occurrence can be displayed. With quantitative data, the measurement itself can be displayed. Watch that the measurement scale is consistent or that a jump scale squiggle is used. **2.** __________

(a) Time plots (b) Bar graphs
(c) Pareto charts (d) Ogives (e) Circle graphs

3. __________ display how a *total* is dispersed into several categories. This graph is very appropriate for qualitative data, or any data where percentage of occurrence makes sense. **3.** __________

(a) Time plots (b) Bar graphs
(c) Pareto charts (d) Ogives (e) Circle graphs

4. __________ display how data change over time. It is best if the units of time are consistent in a given plot. **4.** __________

(a) Time plots (b) Bar graphs
(c) Pareto charts (d) Ogives (e) Circle graphs

5. __________ display cumulative frequencies. They are especially useful for quickly determining the number of data values above or below a specified level. **5.** __________

(a) Time plots (b) Bar graphs
(c) Pareto charts (d) Ogives (e) Circle graphs

CHAPTER 2, FORM C, PAGE 2

6. A survey of 500 teenagers was taken to see which sport was their favorite to watch on television. The pie chart below displays the results. Choose the correct data (numbers of teenagers) from which the pie chart was constructed. **6.** 

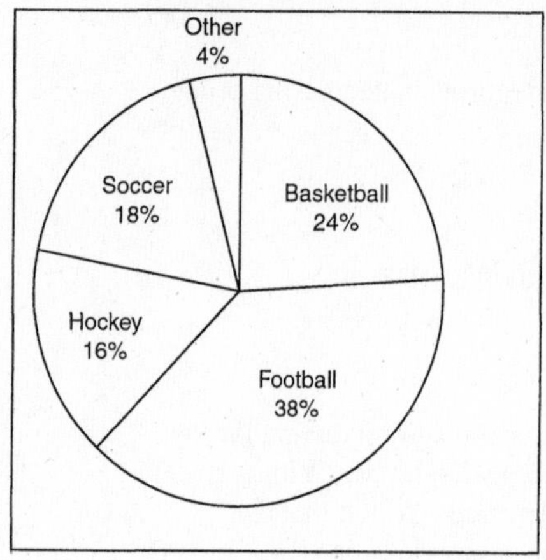

(a) Basketball, 190; football, 120; hockey, 90; soccer, 80; other, 20

(b) Basketball, 120; football, 190, hockey, 90; soccer, 80; other, 20

(c) Basketball, 20; football, 90, hockey, 80; soccer, 190; other, 120

(d) Basketball, 240; football, 380, hockey, 160; soccer, 180; other, 40

(e) Basketball, 120; football, 190, hockey, 80; soccer, 90; other, 20

7. Following is a histogram displaying the test scores for students in a statistics class.

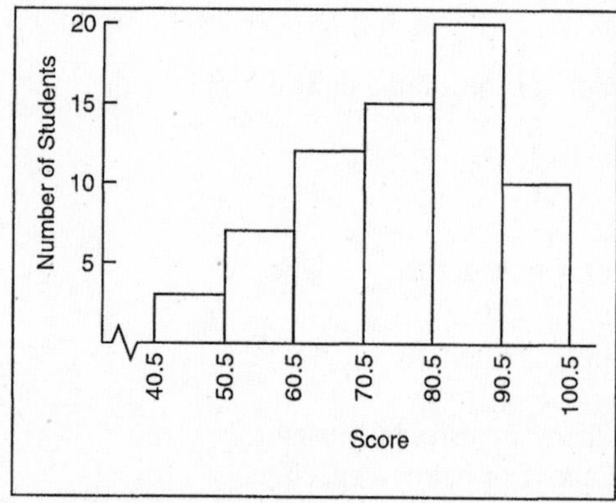

Categorize the distribution shape as **7.** ________

(a) Uniform (b) Symmetric

(c) Bimodal (d) Skewed left (e) Skewed right

CHAPTER 2, FORM C, PAGE 3

8. A sample of 12 children was taken from a daycare. A dotplot of the average number of hours of daily television viewing is shown here.

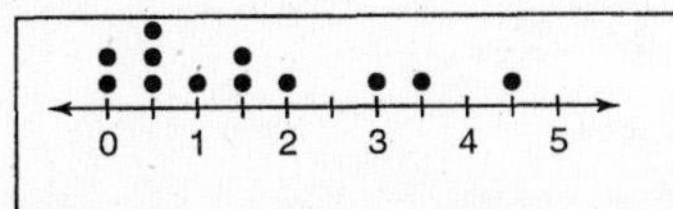

How many children watch television more than 3 hours per day?

8. 

(a) 2 (b) 3

(c) 9 (d) 10 (e) Cannot determine

9. Following is a list of prices (to the nearest dollar) for college textbooks. Make a stem-and-leaf display for these data.

9. ________

2.3	3.7	1.2	3.6	2.4	2.6	3.7	0.9
1.8	2.5	2.5	3.0	2.8	1.7	3.1	4.1

(a)

Stem	Leaves
0	2 2 3
1	2 7 8
2	4 4 7 9
3	1 2 5 8
4	2 4

(b)

Stem	Leaves
10	2 7 8
20	0 0 4 4 7 9
30	0 1 2 5 8
40	2 4

(c)

Stem	Leaves
0	9
1	2 7 8
2	3 4 5 5 6 8
3	0 1 6 7 7
4	1

(d)

Stem	Leaves
1	2 7 8
2	0 4 4 7 9
3	0 1 2 5 8
4	2 4

(e)

12 17 18
20 20 24 24 27 29
30 31 32 35 38
42 44

CHAPTER 3 TEST FORM A

1. A random sample of 18 airline carry-on luggage bags gave the following weights (rounded to the nearest pound).

12	25	10	38	12	19	8	12	17
41	7	22	10	19	12	16	5	14

Find the mean, median, and mode of these weights. **1.** ________________

2. Find the mean and the 5% trimmed mean for the following annual salaries (in thousands) of employees in a small company. Which is most representative of the average annual salary? Why? **2.** ________________

38.5	31.0	29.8	37.4	40.1	35.1	41.5	12.6	39.7	28.4
34.2	38.6	187.4	40.6	39.7	31.0	29.8	42.0	30.8	35.5

3. A random sample of 7 Northern Pike from Taltson Lake (Canada) gave the following lengths rounded to the nearest inch.

21 27 46 35 41 36 25

(a) Find the range. **3. (a)** ________________

(b) Find the sample mean. **(b)** ________________

(c) Find the sample variance. **(c)** ________________

(d) Find the sample standard deviation. **(d)** ________________

4. A random sample of receipts for individuals eating at the Terrace Restaurant showed the sample mean to be $\bar{x}$ = \$10.38 with sample standard deviation s = \$2.17.

(a) Compute the coefficient of variation for this data. **4. (a)** ________________

(b) Use Chevyshev's Theorem to find the smallest interval centered on the mean in which we can expect at least 75% of the data to fall. **(b)** ________________

CHAPTER 3, FORM A, PAGE 2

5. A random sample of 330 adults were asked the maximal amount (dollars) they would spend on a ticket to a top rated performance. The results follow where x is the cost and f is the number of people who would spend that maximal amount.

x	20	30	40	50	60
f	62	83	120	40	25

(a) Compute the sample mean. 5. (a) ______

(b) Compute the sample variance. (b) ______

(c) Compute the sample standard deviation. (c) ______

6. A random sample of 27 skiers at Vail, Colorado gave their ages. The results were

18	25	32	16	41	52	29	58	23
62	47	56	19	22	38	15	46	33
49	52	37	26	72	44	19	24	29

(a) Give the five number summary including the low value Q_1, median, Q_3 and high value. 6. (a) ______

(b) Make a box-and-whisker plot for the given data. (b)

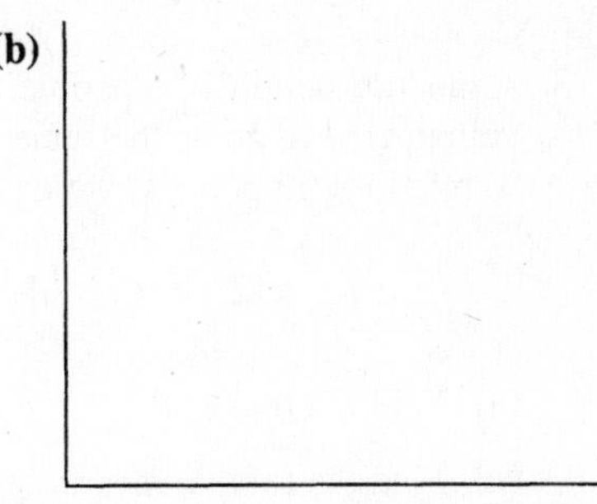

(c) Find the interquartile range. (c) ______

7. In Biology 340, weights are assigned to required activities as follows:

project, 25%; exam 1, 15%; exam 2, 15%; exam 3, 15%; final exam, 30%

Each activity is graded on a 100 point scale. Gary earned 75 points on the project, 85 points on exam 1, 95 points on exam 2, 90 points on exam 3, and 88 points on the final exam. Compute his overall weighted average in the Biology 340 class. 7. ______

8. Lifestyles Weight-loss Clinic gave the following information about the distribution of its clients. Estimate the weighted average of the weight (in pounds) of a client. 8. ______

Weight (lb)	130–149	150–169	170–189	190–209
Clients	11%	48%	32%	7%

9. Sophia took a test and scored in the 79th percentile. What percentage of the scores were at or below her score? What percentage were above? 9. ______

CHAPTER 3 TEST
FORM B

1. A veterinarian in a small animal clinic had the following record of life spans of Golden Retrievers (to the nearest year).

9	12	15	11	8	10	7	5	11	14
13	6	11	16	11	14	11	4	12	11

Find the mean, median, and mode for this data. **1.** ____________

2. Find the mean and the 10% trimmed mean for the following annual snowfalls (in inches) for a city in northern Wisconsin. Which is most representative of the average annual snowfall? Why? **2.** ____________

24 37 28 13 38 29 112 21 40 36

3. A random sample of 6 people, each 20 pounds overweight, volunteered to go on the same diet. After 3 months, their weight loss (in pounds) were

12 5 14 19 15 8

(a) Find the range. **3. (a)** ____________

(b) Find the sample mean. **(b)** ____________

(c) Find the sample variance. **(c)** ____________

(d) Find the sample standard deviation. **(d)** ____________

4. A large sample of Northern Pike caught at Taltson Lake (Canada) showed that the average length was $\overline{x} = 32.5$ inches with sample standard deviation $s = 8.6$ inches.

(a) Compute the coefficient of variation for this data. **4. (a)** ____________

(b) Use Chevyshev's Theorem to find an interval centered on the mean in which we can expect at least 75% of the data to fall. **(b)** ____________

CHAPTER 3, FORM B, PAGE 2

5. A random sample of 146 students in Chemistry 215 gave the following grade information (A = 4.0, B = 3.0, C = 2.0, D = 1.0, and F = 0). In the following table x = grade and f = number of students receiving this grade.

x	0	1	2	3	4
f	8	14	62	43	19

(a) Find the sample mean. **5. (a)** ______________

(b) Find the sample variance. **(b)** ______________

(c) Find the sample standard deviation. **(c)** ______________

6. A random sample of 24 professors at Montana State University gave the following ages (years).

29	32	56	61	27	43	38	65
36	47	41	68	59	40	33	35
44	39	28	46	42	62	58	45

(a) Give the five number summary including the low value Q_1, median, Q_3 and high value. **6. (a)** ______________

(b) Make a box-and-whisker plot for the given data. **(b)**

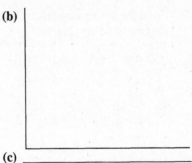

(c) Find the interquartile range. **(c)** ______________

7. A teacher evaluation rating system uses the following items and weights:

Availability of professor outside of class, 10%; Clarity of presentation, 25%
Respectful of student ideas, 20%; Grades fairly, 15%; Knowledge of the field, 30%

Each item is rated on a 100 point scale. Dr. Gill was evaluated by her Sociology 350 class and received the following ratings: Availability, 65; Clarity, 85; Respects students, 90; Grades fairly, 70; Knowledge, 95. Compute a weighted average to determine Dr. Gills overall teacher rating. **7.** ______________

8. Famous Framing gave the following information about the distribution of costs and sales. Estimate the weighted average of the cost (in dollars) of a sale. **8.** ______________

Cost ($)	10–26	27–43	44–60	61–77	78–94
Sales	2%	15%	48%	23%	12%

9. Tyler took a test and scored in the 81st percentile. What percent of scores were above his score? What percent were at or below his score? **9.** ______________

CHAPTER 3 TEST
FORM C

Write the letter of the response that best answers each problem.

1. The durations of a random sample of 16 commercials are below (in seconds). Find the mean, median, and mode of these durations. **1.** ________

30	12	26	7	14	35	20	30
55	8	35	18	42	15	30	10

(a) Mean = 24.19, median = 30, mode = 23

(b) Mean = 20.13, median = 21, mode = 35

(c) Mean = 24.19, median = 23, mode = 30

(d) Mean = 20, median = 24.19, mode = 30

(e) Mean = 30, median = 20, mode = 22.13

2. Find the 5% trimmed mean for the following heights of fruit trees (in feet) in Gordy's Farm Market. **2.** ________

5.2	6.5	7.4	8.0	9.1	7.6	5.4	3.1	4.7	15.0
4.1	3.7	7.4	6.9	5.5	4.0	3.9	5.2	5.8	7.2
8.2	4.9	7.3	6.1	7.2	6.5	3.4	8.6	4.7	5.8
1.3	6.0	5.8	4.3	5.4	6.5	7.6	9.0	6.7	13.4

(a) 6.05 ft (b) 6.27 ft

(c) 5.80 ft (d) 6.16 ft (e) 6.36 ft

3. A random sample of 9 Walleye Pike from Salty Lake gave the following weights rounded to the nearest pound.

3 4 11 6 5 7 6 2 4

A. Find the range. **3. A.** ________

(a) 4 (b) 5 (c) 7 (d) 8 (e) 9

B. Find the sample mean. **B.** ________

(a) 5.33 (b) 9 (c) 7 (d) 2.65 (e) 5

CHAPTER 3, FORM C, PAGE 2

C. Find the sample variance. **C.** ________

(a) 2.65 (b) 5 (c) 7 (d) 5.33 (e) 6.22

D. Find the sample standard deviation. **D.** ________

(a) 5.33 (b) 7 (c) 2.49 (d) 2.65 (e) 6.22

4. A random sample of 30 receipts for individuals shopping at the Community Drug Store showed the sample mean to be $\overline{x}$ = \$28.19 with sample standard deviation s = \$4.06.

A. Compute the coefficient of variation for this data. **4. A.** ________

(a) 6.94% (b) 14.4% (c) 694% (d) 4.32% (e) 0.48%

B. Use Chevyshev's Theorem to find the smallest interval centered on the mean in which we can expect at least 88.9% of the data to fall. **B.** ________

(a) 16.01 to 40.37 (b) 24.13 to 28.19

(c) 20.07 to 36.31 (d) 11.95 to 44.43 (e) 24.13 to 32.25

5. A random sample of 210 high school students were asked how many hours per week they spent studying at home. The results follow where x is the hours and f is the number of students who spend that amount of time.

x	3	5	7	9	11
f	30	45	70	55	10

A. Compute the sample mean. **5. A.** ________

(a) 0.025 (b) 40.29 (c) 6.71 (d) 0.149 (e) 6

B. Compute the sample variance. **B.** ________

(a) 4.871 (b) 2.212 (c) 199 (d) 210 (e) 4.894

C. Compute the sample variance. **C.** ________

(a) 4.894 (b) 4.871 (c) 2.207 (d) 2.212 (e) 14.11

CHAPTER 3, FORM C, PAGE 3

6. What are the numbers used in making a box-and-whisker plot? **6.** ________

(a) Low value, Q_1, mean, Q_3, high value

(b) Low value, Q_1, median, Q_3, high value

(c) s, mean, s^2, interquartile range

(d) Q_1, Q_2, Q_3

(e) Low value, interquartile range, high value

7. In Chemistry 400, weights are assigned to required activities as follows:

class participation, 15%; exam 1, 20%; exam 2, 20%;
exam 3, 20%; laboratory 25%

Each activity is graded on a 100 point scale. Mary earned 70 points on class participation, 80 points on exam 1, 64 points on exam 2, 77 points on exam 3, and 96 points on laboratory. Compute her overall weighted average in the Chemistry 400 class. **7.** ________

(a) 78.7 (b) 77.4

(c) 100 (d) 78.2 (e) Cannot determine

8. Calico Corner gave the following information about the distribution of cost and sales. Estimate the weighted average of the cost (in dollars) of a sale. **8.** ________

Cost ($)	20–29	30–39	40–49	50–59
Sales	64%	23%	10%	3%

(a) 80.44 (b) 29.2

(c) 29.7 (d) 30.2 (e) Cannot determine

9. Luke took a test and scored in the 88th percentile. What percentage of the scores were above his score? **9.** ________

(a) 87% (b) 13% (c) 89% (d) 88% (e) 12%

CHAPTER 4 TEST FORM A

1. A random sample of 317 new Smile Bright electric toothbrushes showed 19 were defective.

(a) How would you estimate the probability that a new Smile Bright electric toothbrush is defective? What is your estimate?

1. (a) ____________

(b) What is your estimate for the probability that a Smile Bright electric toothbrush is not defective?

(b) ____________

(c) Either an electric toothbrush is defective or not. What is the sample space in this problem. Do the probabilities assigned to the sample space add up to one?

(c) ____________

2. If you roll a single fair die and count the number of dots on top, what is the probability of getting a number less than 3 on a single throw?

2. ____________

3. You roll two fair dice, a blue one and a yellow one.

(a) Find *P*(even number on the blue die and 3 on the yellow die).

3. (a) ____________

(b) Find *P*(3 on the blue die and even number on the yellow die).

(b) ____________

(c) Find *P*(even number on the blue die and 3 on the yellow die) or *P*(3 on the blue die and even number on the yellow die).

(c) ____________

4. An urn contains 12 balls identical in every respect except color. There are 3 red balls, 7 green balls, and 2 blue balls.

(a) You draw two balls from the urn, but replace the first ball before drawing the second. Find the probability that the first ball is red and the second is green.

4. (a) ____________

(b) Repeat part (a), but do not replace the first ball before drawing the second.

(b) ____________

5. Robert is applying for a bank loan to open up a pizza franchise. He must complete a written application, and then be interviewed by bank officers. Past records for this bank show that the probability of being approved in the written part is 0.63. Then the probability of being approved by the interview committee is 0.85, given the candidate has been approved on the written application. What is the probability Robert is approved on both the written application and the interview?

5. ____________

CHAPTER 4, FORM A, PAGE 2

6. A hair salon did a survey of 360 customers regarding satisfaction with service and type of customer. A walk-in customer is one who has seen no ads and not been referred. The other customers either saw a TV ad or were referred to the salon (but not both). The results follow.

	Walk-In	TV Ad	Referred	Total
Not Satisfied	21	9	5	35
Neutral	18	25	37	80
Satisfied	36	43	59	138
Very Satisfied	28	31	48	107
Total	103	108	149	360

Assume the sample represents the entire population of customers. Find the probability that a customer is

(a) Not satisfied **6. (a)** ____________

(b) Not satisfied and walk-in **(b)** ____________

(c) Not satisfied, given referred **(c)** ____________

(d) Very satisfied **(d)** ____________

(e) Very satisfied, given referred **(e)** ____________

(f) Very satisfied and TV ad **(f)** ____________

(g) Are the events satisfied and referred independent or not? Explain your answer. **(g)** ____________

7. A computer package sale comes with two different choices of printers and four different choices of monitors. If a store wants to display each package combination that is for sale, how many packages must be displayed? Make a tree diagram showing the outcomes for selecting printer and monitor. **7.** ____________

8. In how many ways can the 40 members of a 4H club select a president, a vice-president, a secretary, and a treasurer? **8.** ____________

9. In how many different ways can a person choose three movies to see in a theater playing 11 movies. **9.** ____________

CHAPTER 4 TEST
FORM B

1. A Student Council is made up of 4 women and 6 men. One of the women is president of the Council. A member of the council is selected at random to report to the Dean of Student Life.

(a) What is the probability a woman is selected? **1. (a)** ________

(b) What is the probability a man is selected? **(b)** ________

(c) What is the probability that the president of the Student Council is selected? **(c)** ________

2. If you roll a single fair die and count the number of dots on top, what is the probability of getting a number greater than 2 on a single throw? **2.** ________

3. You roll two fair dice, a white one and a red one.

(a) Find *P*(5 or 6 on the white die and odd number on the red die). **3. (a)** ________

(b) Find *P*(odd number on the white die and 5 or 6 on the red die). **(b)** ________

(c) Find *P*(5 or 6 on the white die and odd number on the red die)or *P*(odd number on the white die and 5 or 6 on the red die). **(c)** ________

4. An urn contains 17 balls identical in every respect except color. There are 6 red balls, 8 green balls, and 3 blue balls.

(a) You draw two balls from the urn, but replace the first ball before drawing the second. Find the probability that the first ball is red and the second ball is green. **4. (a)** ________

(b) Repeat part (a), but do not replace the first ball before drawing the second. **(b)** ________

5. The Dean of Hinsdale College found that 12% of the female students are majoring in Computer Science. If 64% of the students at Hinsdale are women, what is the probability that a student chosen at random will be a woman majoring in Computer Science? **5.** ________

CHAPTER 4, FORM B, PAGE 2

6. The Committee on Student Life did a survey of 417 students regarding satisfaction with Student Government and class standing. The results follow:

	Freshman	Sophomore	Junior	Senior	Total
Not Satisfied	17	19	23	12	71
Neutral	61	35	32	38	166
Satisfied	23	49	43	65	180
Total	101	103	98	115	417

Assume the sample represents the entire population of students. Find the probability that a student selected at random is

(a) Satisfied (with Student Government) **6. (a)** ______

(b) Satisfied, given the student is a Senior **(b)** ______

(c) Neutral **(c)** ______

(d) Neutral and Freshman **(d)** ______

(e) Neutral, given the student is a Freshman **(e)** ______

(f) Senior, given satisfied **(f)** ______

(g) Are the events, Freshman and neutral independent or not? Explain. **(g)** ______

7. There are 3 different routes that Alexander can walk from home to the post office and 2 different routes that he can walk from the post office to the bank. How many different routes can Alexander walk from home to the bank? Make a tree diagram showing the outcomes for selecting the routes. **7.** ______

8. A fishing camp has 16 clients. Each cabin at the camp will accommodate 5 fishermen. In how many different ways can the first cabin be filled with clients? **8.** ______

9. In how many different ways can a committee of four be selected from the 24 parents attending a school board meeting? **9.** ______

CHAPTER 4 TEST
FORM C

Write the letter of the response that best answers each problem.

1. A random sample of 420 new Ford trucks showed that 105 required repairs within the first warranty year.

A. What is the estimate for the probability that a new Ford truck will need repairs within the first warranty year? **1. A.** ________

(a) 105 (b) 0.75 (c) 315 (d) 0.25 (e) 0.20

B. What is the estimate for the probability that a new Ford truck will not need repairs within the first warranty year? **B.** ________

(a) 105 (b) 0.75 (c) 315 (d) 0.25 (e) 0.80

2. If you roll a single fair die and count the number of dots on top, what is the probability of getting an even number or a 5 on a single throw? **2.** ________

(a) $\frac{2}{3}$ (b) $\frac{1}{2}+\frac{1}{6}$ (c) $\frac{1}{12}$ (d) $\frac{5}{6}$ (e) $\frac{1}{3}$

3. You roll two fair dice, a white one and a green one.

A. Find P(number greater than 2 on the white die and 4 on the green die). **3. A.** ________

(a) $\frac{5}{6}$ (b) $\frac{5}{36}$ (c) $\frac{1}{9}$ (d) $\frac{1}{2}$ (e) $\frac{2}{9}$

B. Find P(4 on the white die and number greater than 2 on the green die). **B.** ________

(a) $\frac{2}{9}$ (b) $\frac{1}{2}$ (c) $\frac{5}{6}$ (d) $\frac{5}{36}$ (e) $\frac{1}{9}$

C. Find P(number greater than 2 on the white die and 4 on the green die) or P(4 on the white die and number greater than 2 on the green die). **C.** ________

(a) 1 (b) $\frac{2}{9}$ (c) $\frac{5}{18}$ (d) $\frac{1}{81}$ (e) $\frac{25}{36}$

CHAPTER 4, FORM C, PAGE 2

4. An urn contains 8 balls identical in every aspect except color. There is 1 red ball, 2 green balls, and 5 blue balls.

A. You draw two balls from the urn, but replace the first ball before drawing the second. Find the probability that the first ball is blue and the second is green. **4. A.** ________

(a) $\frac{5}{32}$ (b) $\frac{7}{8}$ (c) $\frac{51}{56}$ (d) $\frac{5}{28}$ (e) $\frac{3}{4}$

B. Repeat part A, but do not replace the first ball before drawing the second. **B.** ________

(a) $\frac{5}{32}$ (b) $\frac{7}{8}$ (c) $\frac{51}{56}$ (d) $\frac{5}{28}$ (e) $\frac{3}{4}$

5. The athletic coach found that 31% of the basketball players have an A average in school. If 2% of the students at the school are basketball players, what is the probability that a student chosen at random will be a basketball player with an A average? **5.** ________

(a) 62% (b) 0.62% (c) 6.45% (d) 0.0645% (e) 0.0062%

6. A hospital administration did a survey of patients regarding satisfaction with care and type of surgery. The results follow:

	Heart	Hip	Knee	Total
Not Satisfied	7	12	2	21
Neutral	15	38	10	63
Satisfied	32	16	25	73
Very Satisfied	4	22	23	49
Total	58	88	60	206

Assume the sample represents the entire population of patients. Find the probability that a patient selected at random is

A. Satisfied **6. A.** ________

(a) $\frac{32}{206}$ (b) 73 (c) $\frac{122}{206}$ (d) 122 (e) $\frac{73}{206}$

CHAPTER 4, FORM C, PAGE 3

B. Very satisfied and had knee surgery **B.** ________

(a) $\frac{109}{206}$ (b) $\frac{11}{206}$ (c) $\frac{23}{206}$ (d) $\frac{23}{60}$ (e) $\frac{23}{60}+\frac{23}{49}$

C. Neutral, given had hip surgery **C.** ________

(a) $\frac{38}{88}$ (b) $\frac{88}{206}$ (c) $\frac{38}{206}$ (d) $\frac{38}{63}$ (e) $\frac{63}{88}$

D. A knee surgery patient **D.** ________

(a) 60 (b) 206 (c) $\frac{146}{206}$ (d) $\frac{60}{206}$ (e) $\frac{2}{206}$

E. Satisfied given had heart surgery. **E.** ________

(a) $\frac{73}{206}$ (b) $\frac{58}{73}$ (c) $\frac{32}{58}$ (d) $\frac{32}{206}$ (e) $\frac{32}{73}$

F. Not satisfied and had heart surgery. **F.** ________

(a) $\frac{7}{58}$ (b) $\frac{7}{206}$ (c) $\frac{7}{21}$ (d) $\frac{21}{206}$ (e) $\frac{58}{206}$

7. George has 4 ties, 3 shirts, and 2 pairs of pants. How many different outfits can he wear if he chooses one tie, one shirt and one pair of pants for each outfit? **7.** ________

(a) 288 (b) 12 (c) 9 (d) 24 (e) 10

8. In how many ways can 12 athletes be awarded a first-place medal, a second-place medal, and a third-place medal? **8.** ________

(a) 33 (b) 220 (c) 6 (d) 1728 (e) 1320

9. In how many different ways can a student choose 3 out of 8 problems to complete on a take-home exam? **9.** ________

(a) 56 (b) 336 (c) 21 (d) 3.5 (e) 3

CHAPTER 5 TEST FORM A

1. Sam is a representative who sells large appliances such as refrigerators, stoves, and so forth. Let x = number of appliances Sam sells on a given day. Let f = frequency (number of days) with which he sells x appliances. For a random sample of 240 days, Sam had the following sales record.

x	0	1	2	3	4	5	6	7
f	9	72	63	41	28	14	8	5

Assume the sales record is representative of the population of all sales day.

(a) Use the relative frequency to find $P(x)$ for $x = 0$ to 7.

(b) Use a histogram to graph the probability distribution of part (a).

(c) Compute the probability that x is between 2 and 5 (including 2 and 5).

(d) Compute the probability that x is less than 3.

(e) Compute the expected value of the x distribution.

(f) Compute the standard deviation of the x distribution.

1. (a) ______________

(b)

(c) ______________

(d) ______________

(e) ______________

(f) ______________

2. The director of a health club conducted a survey and found that 23% of members used only the pool for workouts. Based on this information, what is the probability that for a random sample of 10 members, 4 used only the pool for workouts?

2. ______________

3. Of those mountain climbers who attempt Mt. McKinley (Denali), only 65% reach the summit. In a random sample of 16 mountain climbers who are going to attempt Mt. McKinley, what is the probability of each of the following?

(a) All 16 reach the summit.

(b) At least 10 reach the summit.

(c) No more than 12 reach the summit.

(d) From 9 to 12 reach the summit, including 9 and 12.

3. (a) ______________

(b) ______________

(c) ______________

(d) ______________

CHAPTER 5, FORM A, PAGE 2

4. A coach found that about 12% of all hockey games end in overtime. What is the expected number of games ending in overtime if a random sample of 50 hockey games are played?

4. ____________________

5. The probability that a truck will be going over the speed limit on I-80 between Cheyenne and Rock Springs, Wyoming is about 75%. Suppose a random sample of 5 trucks on this stretch of I-80 are observed.

(a) Make a histogram showing the probability that $r = 0, 1, 2, 3, 4, 5$ trucks going over the speed limit.

5. (a)

(b) Find the mean μ of this probability distribution.

(b) ____________________

(c) Find the standard deviation of the probability distribution.

(c) ____________________

6. Records show that the probability of catching a Northern Pike over 40 inches at Taltson Lake (Canada) is about 15% for each full day a person spends fishing. What is the minimal number of days a person must fish to be at least 83.3% sure of catching one or more Northern Pike over 40 inches?

6. ____________________

7. We are interested in when the first six will occur for repeated rolls of a balanced die. What is the population mean for this geometric distribution (i.e., the expected number of rolls for the first 6 to occur)?

7. ____________________

CHAPTER 5, FORM A, PAGE 3

8. The probability that an airplane is more than 45 minutes late on arrival is about 15%. Let $n = 1, 2, 3, \ldots$ represent the number of times a person travels on an airplane until the first time the plane is more than 45 minutes late.

(a) Write a brief but complete discussion in which you explain why the Geometric distribution would be appropriate. Write out a formula for the probability distribution of the random variable n.

8. (a) ______________

(b) What is the probability that the 3rd time a person flies, he or she is on a flight that is more than 45 minutes ?

(b) ______________

(c) What is the probability that more than three flights are required before a plane is more than 45 minutes late?

(c) ______________

9. Suppose the average number of customers entering a store in a 20 minute period is 6 customers. The store wants a probability distribution for the number of people entering the store each 20 minutes.

(a) Write a brief but complete discussion in which you explain why the Poisson approximation to the binomial would be appropriate. Are the assumptions satisfied? What is λ? Write out a formula for the probability distribution of r.

9. (a) ______________

(b) What is the probability that exactly 3 customers enter the store during a 20 minute period?

(b) ______________

(c) What is the probability that more than 3 customers enter the store during a 20 minute period?

(c) ______________

10. The probability a new medication will cause a bad side effect is 0.03. The new medication has been given to 150 volunteers. Let r be the random variable representing the number of people who have a bad side effect.

(a) Write a brief but complete discussion in which you explain why the Poisson approximation to the binomial would be appropriate. Are the assumptions satisfied? What is λ? Write out a formula for the probability distribution of r.

10. (a) ______________

(b) Compute the probability that exactly 3 people from the sample of 150 volunteers will have a bad side effect from the medication.

(b) ______________

(c) Compute the probability that more than 3 people out of the sample of 150 volunteers will have a bad side effect from the medication?

(c) ______________

CHAPTER 5 TEST
FORM B

1. An aptitude test was given to a random sample of 228 people intending to become Data Entry Clerks. The results are shown below where x is the score on a 10 point scale, and f is the frequency of people with this score.

x	1	2	3	4	5	6	7	8	9	10
f	9	21	46	51	42	18	12	10	8	5

Assume the above data represents the entire population of people intending to become Data Entry Clerks.

(a) Use the relative frequencies to find $P(x)$ for $x = 1$ to 10. **1. (a)** ______________

(b) Use a histogram to graph the probability distribution of part (a). **(b)**

(c) To be accepted into a training program, students must have a score of 4 or higher. What is the probability an applicant selected at random will have this score? **(c)** ______________

(d) To receive a tuition scholarship a student needs a score of 8 or higher. What is the probability an applicant selected at random will have such a score? **(d)** ______________

(e) Compute the expected value of the x distribution. **(e)** ______________

(f) Compute the standard deviation of the x distribution. **(f)** ______________

2. The management of a restaurant conducted a survey and found that 28 of the customers preferred to sit in the smoking section. Based on this information, what is the probability that for a random sample of 12 customers, 3 preferred the smoking section? **2.** ______________

3. Of all college freshmen who try out for the track team, the coach will only accept 30%. If 15 freshmen try out for the track team, what is the probability that

(a) all 15 are accepted? **3. (a)** ______________

(b) at least 8 are accepted? **(b)** ______________

(c) no more than 4 are accepted? **(c)** ______________

CHAPTER 5, FORM B, PAGE 2

(d) between 5 and 10 are accepted (including 5 and 10)? **(d)** ____________

4. The president of a bank approves 68% of all new applications. What is the expected number of approvals if a random sample of 75 loan applications are chosen? **4.** ____________

5. The probability that a vehicle will change lanes while making a turn is 55%. Suppose a random sample of 7 vehicles are observed making turns at a busy intersection.

(a) Make a histogram showing the probability that $r = 0, 1, 2, 3, 4, 5, 6, 7$ vehicles will make a land change while turning. **5. (a)**

(b) Find the expected value μ of this probability distribution. **(b)** ____________

(c) Find the standard deviation of this probability distribution. **(c)** ____________

6. Past records show that the probability of catching a Lake Trout over 15 pounds at Talston Lake (Canada) us about 20% for each full day a person spends fishing. What is the minimal number of days a person must fish to be at least 89.3% sure of catching one or more Lake Trout over 15 pounds? **6.** ____________

7. We are interested in when the first odd number will occur for repeated rolls of a balanced die. What is the population mean for this geometric distribution (i.e., the expected number of rolls for the first odd number to occur)? **7.** ____________

CHAPTER 5, FORM B, PAGE 3

8. Past records at an appliance store show that about 60% of the customers who look at appliances will buy one. Let $n = 1, 2, 3, \ldots$ represent the number of customers a sales clerk must help until the first sale of the day.

(a) Write a brief but complete discussion in which you explain why the Geometric distribution would apply in this context. Write out a formula for the probability distribution of the random variable n. **8. (a)** __________

(b) Compute $P(n = 4)$. **(b)** __________

(c) Compute $P(n \geq 3)$. **(c)** __________

9. At Community Hospital maternity ward, babies arrive at an average of 8 babies per hour. The hospital staff wants a probability distribution for the number of babies arriving each hour.

(a) Write a brief but complete discussion in which you explain why the Poisson distribution would be appropriate. What is λ? Write out a formula for the probability distribution. **9. (a)** __________

(b) What is the probability exactly 7 babies are born during the next hour? **(b)** __________

(c) What is the probability that fewer than 3 babies are born during the next hour? **(c)** __________

10. As a telecommunications satellite goes over the horizon, stored messages are relayed to the next satellite which is still in position. However, the probability is 0.01 that an interruption will occur, and the relay transmission will be lost. Out of 200 such relays, let r be the random variable that represent the number of transmissions that are lost.

(a) Write a brief but complete discussion in which you explain why the Poisson approximation to the binomial would be appropriate. Are the assumptions satisfied? What is λ? Write out a formula for the probability distribution of r. **10. (a)** __________

(b) Compute the probability that exactly two transmissions are lost. **(b)** __________

(c) Compute the probability that more than two transmissions are lost. **(c)** __________

CHAPTER 5 TEST FORM C

Write the letter of the response that best answers each problem.

1. The following data are based on a survey taken by a consumer research firm. In this table x = number of televisions in household and % = percentages of U.S. households.

x	0	1	2	3	4	5 or more
%	3%	11%	28%	39%	12%	7%

A. What is the probability that a household selected at random has less than 3 televisions? **1. A.** ________

(a) 0.81 (b) 0.39 (c) 0.42 (d) 0.58 (e) 0.19

B. What is the probability that a household selected at random has more than 4 televisions? **B.** ________

(a) 0.7 (b) 0.19 (c) 0.81 (d) 0.93 (e) 0.07

C. Compute the expected value of the x distribution (round televisions of 5 or more to 5). **C.** ________

(a) 15 (b) 2.67 (c) 1.28 (d) 1.13 (e) 3.1

D. Compute the standard deviation of the x distribution (round televisions of 5 or more to 5). **D.** ________

(a) 15 (b) 2.67 (c) 1.28 (d) 1.13 (e) 3.1

2. A meteorologist found from the past year's records that it rained 17% of the days. Based on this information, what is the probability that for a random sample of 15 days, it rained 3 of those days? **2.** ________

(a) 0.17 (b) 0.67 (c) 0.28 (d) 0.13 (e) 0.22

3. Of those people who lose weight on a diet, 90% gain all the weight back. In a random sample of 12 dieters who have lost weight, what is the probability of each of the following.

A. All 12 gain the weight back? **3. A.** ________

(a) 0.90 (b) 0.282 (c) 0.540 (d) 0.142 (e) 10.8%

B. At least 9 gain the weight back? **B.** ________

(a) 0.974 (b) 0.026 (c) 0.889 (d) 1.33% (e) 0.997

C. No more than 6 gain the weight back? **C.** ________

(a) 0.004 (b) 1.000 (c) 0.999 (d) 0.000 (e) 0.531

D. From 8 to 10 gain the weight back, including 8 and 10. **D.** ________

(a) 0.085 (b) 1.17% (c) 0.336 (d) 0.387 (e) 0.118

CHAPTER 5, FORM C, PAGE 2

4. The manager of a supermarket found that 72% of the shoppers who taste a free sample of a food item will buy the item. What is the expected number of shoppers that will buy the item if a random sample of 50 shoppers taste a free sample? **4.** ________

(a) 10 (b) 36 (c) 3 (d) 72 (e) 50

5. The probability that merchandise stolen from a store will be recovered is 15%. Suppose a random sample of 8 stores, from which merchandise has been stolen, is chosen.

A. Find the mean μ of this probability distribution. **5. A.** ________

(a) 1.02 (b) 1.07 (c) 1.01 (d) 1.14 (e) 1.2

B. Find the standard deviation of the probability distribution. **B.** ________

(a) 1.02 (b) 1.07 (c) 1.01 (d) 1.14 (e) 1.2

6. Records show that the probability of seeing a hawk migrating on a day in September is about 35%. What is the minimal number of days a person must watch to be at least 96.8% sure of seeing one or more hawks migrating? **6.** ________

(a) 5 (b) 6 (c) 7 (d) 8 (e) 9

7. We are interested in when the first six will occur for repeated rolls of a balanced die. What is the population mean for this geometric distribution (i.e., the expected number of rolls for the first 6 to occur)? **7.** ________

(a) 6 (b) $\frac{1}{6}$ (c) 7 (d) 8 (e) 9

8. Rita is studying to be a real estate agent. About 61% of all people who take the licensing exam pass. Let $n = 1, 2, 3, \ldots$ represent the number of times a person takes the exam until the first pass.

A. What is the formula for the probability distribution of the random variable n. **8. A.** ________

(a) $P(n) = (0.61)^n(0.39)^{n-1}$ (b) $P(n) = 0.39(0.61)^{n-1}$

(c) $P(n) = 0.61(0.39)^{n-1}$ (d) $P(n) = (0.61)^{n-1}(0.39)^n$ (e) $P(n) = (0.39)^n$

B. What is the probability that Rita needs three attempts to pass the exam? **B.** ________

(a) 0.227 (b) 0.036 (c) 0.145 (d) 0.093 (e) 0.059

C. What is the probability that Rita needs more than three attempts to pass the exam? **C.** ________

(a) 0.941 (b) 0.059 (c) 0.152 (d) 0.023 (e) 0.907

CHAPTER 5, FORM C, PAGE 3

9. Suppose the average number of customers calling a technical support number in a 10-minute period is 7 customers. The company wants a probability distribution for the number of people calling each 10 minutes.

A. What is the formula for the Poisson probability distribution? **9. A.** ________

(a) $P(r)=\frac{e^{7}7^{r}}{r!}$ (b) $P(r)=\frac{e^{-7}r!}{7^{r}}$

(c) $P(r)=\frac{e^{7}r!}{7^{r}}$ (d) $P(r)=\frac{7^{r}r!}{e^{7}}$ (e) $P(r)=\frac{e^{-7}7^{r}}{r!}$

B. What is the probability that exactly 4 customers call the support number during a 10 minute period? **B.** ________

(a) 0.0912 (b) 0.9088 (c) 0.0521 (d) 0.1729 (e) 0.5714

C. What is the probability that more than 4 customers call the support number during a 10 minute period? **C.** ________

(a) 0.1729 (b) 0.8271 (c) 0.0817 (d) 0.9183 (e) 0.9088

10. The probability that a manufactured part at a plant is defective is 0.02. The plant has manufactured 300 parts. Let r be the random variable representing the number of defective parts.

A. What is the formula for the Poisson approximation to the binomial probability distribution of r? **10. A.** ________

(a) $P(r)=\frac{e^{0.02}(300)^{r}}{r!}$ (b) $P(r)=\frac{e^{6}6^{r}}{r!}$

(c) $P(r)=\frac{e^{-0.02}0.02^{r}}{r!}$ (d) $P(r)=\frac{e^{-6}6^{r}}{r!}$ (e) $P(r)=\frac{e^{-6}r!}{6^{r}}$

B. What is the probability that exactly 5 parts are defective? **B.** ________

(a) 0.0268 (b) 0.9732 (c) 0.8394 (d) 0.0000 (e) 0.1606

C. What is the probability that fewer than 2 parts are defective? **C.** ________

(a) 0.0620 (b) 0.9380 (c) 0.9826 (d) 0.0174 (e) 0.9999

CHAPTER 6 TEST
FORM A

1. Each of the following curves fails to be a normal curve. Give reasons why these curves are not normal curves.

(a) 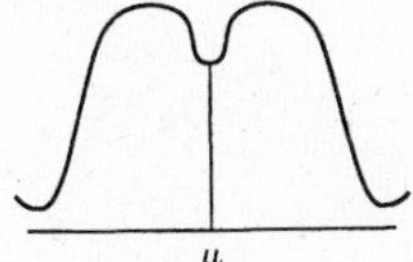

(a) ________________

(b) 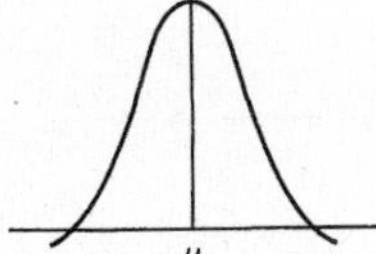

(b) ________________

2. According to the Empirical rule, for a distribution that is symmetrical and bell-shaped (in particular, for a normal distribution) approximately _______ of the data values will lie within three standard deviations on each side of the mean.

2. ________________

3. Assuming that the heights of boys in a high school basketball tournament are normally distributed, with mean 70 in. and standard deviation 2.5 in., how many boys in a group of 40 in the tournament will be taller than 75 inches?

3. ________________

4. Let x be a random variable that represents the length of time it takes a student to complete Dr. Gill's Chemistry Lab Project. From long experience, it is known that x has a normal distribution with mean $\mu = 3.6$ hours and standard deviation $\sigma = 0.5$ hour.

Convert each of the following x intervals to standard z intervals.

(a) $x \geq 4.5$

(b) $3 \leq x \leq 4$

(c) $x \leq 2.5$

4. (a) ________________

(b) ________________

(c) ________________

Convert each of the following z intervals to raw score x intervals.

(d) $z \leq -1$

(e) $1 \leq z \leq 2$

(f) $z \geq 1.5$

(d) ________________

(e) ________________

(f) ________________

CHAPTER 6, FORM A, PAGE 2

5. John and Joel are salesmen in different districts. In John's district, the long term mean sales is \$17,319 each month with standard deviation \$684. In Joel's district, the long term mean sales is \$21,971 each month with standard deviation \$495. Assume that sales in both districts follow a normal distribution.

(a) Last month John sold \$19,214 whereas Joel sold \$22,718 worth of merchandise. Relative to the buying habits of customers in each district, does this mean Joel is a better salesman? Explain.

5. (a) ____________________

(b) Convert Joel's sales last month to a standard z score, and do the same for John's sales last month. Then locate both z scores under a standard normal curve. Who do you think is the better salesman? Explain your answer.

(b) ____________________

6. The length of time to complete a door assembly on an automobile factory assembly line is normally distributed with mean $\mu = 6.7$ minutes and standard deviation $\sigma = 2.2$ minutes. For a door selected at random, what is the probability the assembly line time will be

(a) 5 minutes or less?

6. (a) ____________________

(b) 10 minutes or more?

(b) ____________________

(c) between 5 and 10 minutes?

(c) ____________________

7. From long experience, it is known that the time it takes to do an oil change and lubrication job on a vehicle has a normal distribution with mean $\mu = 17.8$ minutes and standard deviation $\sigma = 5.2$ minutes. An auto service shop will give a free lube job to any customer who must wait beyond the guaranteed time to complete the work. If the shop does not want to give more than 1% of its customers a free lube job, how long should the guarantee be (round to the nearest minute).

7. ____________________

CHAPTER 6, FORM A, PAGE 3

8. You are examining a quality control chart regarding the number of employees absent each shift from a large manufacturing plant. The plant is staffed so that operations are still efficient when the average number of employees absent each shift is $\mu = 15.7$ with standard deviation $\sigma = 3.5$. For the most recent 12 shifts, the number of absent employees were

Shift	1	2	3	4	5	6	7	8	9	10	11	12
#	6	10	7	16	19	18	17	21	22	18	16	19

(a) Make a control chart showing the number of employees absent during the 12-day period.

8. (a)

(b) Are there any periods during which the number absent is out of control? Identify the out of control periods according to Type I, Type II, Type III out of control signals.

(b) ______________

9. Medical treatment will cure about 87% of all people who suffer from a certain eye disorder. Suppose a large medical clinic treats 57 people with this disorder. Let r be a random variable that represents the number of people that will recover. The clinic wants a probability distribution for r.

(a) Write a brief but complete description in which you explain why the normal approximation to the binomial would apply. Are the assumptions satisfied? Explain.

9. (a) ______________

(b) Estimate $P(r \leq 47)$.

(b) ______________

(c) Estimate $P(47 \leq r \leq 55)$.

(c) ______________

CHAPTER 6 TEST FORM B

1. Each of the following curves fails to be a normal curve. Give reasons why these curves are not normal curves.

(a)

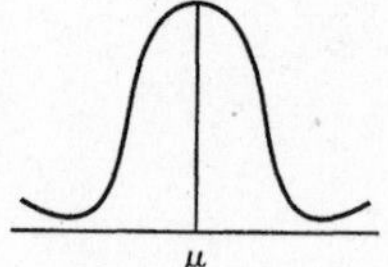

1. (a) ____________________

(b)

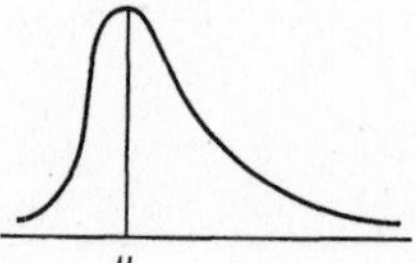

(b) ____________________

2. According to the Empirical rule, for a distribution that is symmetrical and bell-shaped (in particular, for a normal distribution) approximately _______ of the data values will lie within one standard deviation on each side of the mean.

2. ____________________

3. Assuming that the weights of newborn babies at a certain hospital are normally distributed with mean 6.5 pounds and standard deviation 1.2 pounds, how many babies in a group of 80 babies from this hospital will weigh more than 8.9 pounds?

3. ____________________

4. Let x be a random variable that represents the length of time it takes a student to write a term paper for Dr. Adam's Sociology class. After interviewing many students, it was found that x has an approximately normal distribution with mean $\mu = 6.8$ hours and standard deviation $\sigma = 2.1$ hours.

Convert each of the following x intervals to standardized z units.

(a) $x \le 7.5$

(b) $5 \le x \le 8$

(c) $x \ge 4$

4. (a) ____________________

(b) ____________________

(c) ____________________

Convert each of the following z intervals to raw score x intervals.

(d) $z \ge -2$

(e) $0 \le z \le 2$

(f) $z \le 3$

(d) ____________________

(e) ____________________

(f) ____________________

CHAPTER 6, FORM B, PAGE 2

5. Operating temperatures of two models of portable electric generators follow a normal distribution. For generator I, the mean temperature is $\mu_1 = 148°F$ with standard deviation $\sigma_1 = 25°F$. For generator II, the mean temperature is $\mu_2 = 143°F$ with standard deviation $\sigma_2 = 8°F$. At peak power demand, generator I was operating at 166°F, and generator II was operating at 165°F.

(a) At peak power output, both generators are operating at about the same temperature. Relative to the operating characteristics, is one a lot hotter than the other? Explain.

5. (a) ____________________

(b) Convert the peak power temperature for each generator to standard *z* units. Then locate both *z* scores under a standard normal curve. Could one generator be near a melt down? Which one? Explain your answer.

(b) ____________________

6. Weights of a certain model of fully loaded gravel trucks follow a normal distribution with mean $\mu = 6.4$ tons and standard deviation $\sigma = 0.3$ tons. What is the probability that a fully loaded truck of this model is

(a) less than 6 tons?

(b) more than 7 tons?

(c) between 6 and 7 tons?

6. (a) ____________________

(b) ____________________

(c) ____________________

7. Quality control studies for Speedy Jet Computer Printers show the lifetime of the printer follows a normal distribution with mean $\mu = 4$ years and standard deviation $\sigma = 0.78$ years. The company will replace any printer that fails during the guarantee period. How long should Speedy Jet printers be guaranteed if the company wishes to replace no more than 10% of the printers?

7. ____________________

CHAPTER 6, FORM B, PAGE 3

8. A toll free computer software support service for a spreadsheet program has established target length of time for each customer help phone call. The calls are targeted to have mean duration of 12 minutes with standard deviation 3 minutes. For one help technician the most recent 10 calls had the following duration.

Call #	1	2	3	4	5	6	7	8	9	10
Length	15	25	10	9	20	19	11	5	4	8

(a) Make a control chart showing the number of calls.

8. (a)

(b) Are there any periods during which the length of calls are out of control? Identify the out of control periods according to Type I, Type II, Type III out of control signals.

(b) ________________

9. Psychology 231 can be taken as a correspondence course on a Pass/Fail basis. Long experience with this course shows that about 71% of the students pass. This semester 88 students are taking Psychology 231 by correspondence. Let r be a random variable that represents the number that will pass. The Psychology Department wants a probability distribution for r.

(a) Write a brief but complete description in which you explain why the normal approximation to the binomial would apply. Are the assumptions satisfied? Explain.

9. (a) ________________

(b) Estimate $P(r \geq 60)$.

(b) ________________

(c) Estimate $P(60 \leq r \leq 70)$.

(c) ________________

CHAPTER 6 TEST
FORM C

Write the letter of the response that best answers each problem.

1. Which of the following curves is a normal curve? **1.** ________

(a)
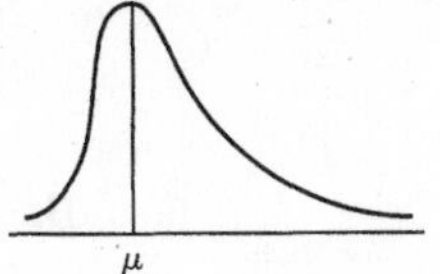

(b)
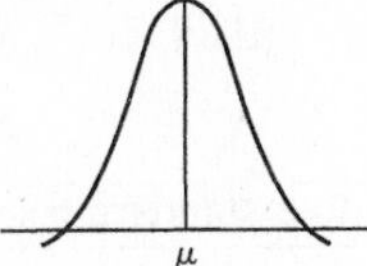

(c)
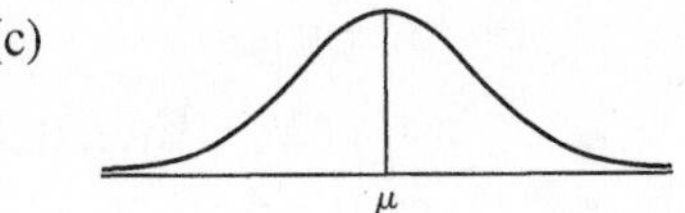

(d)
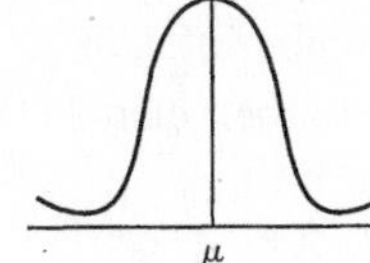

(e)
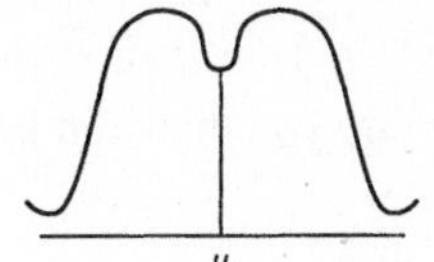

2. According to the Empirical rule, for a distribution that is symmetrical and bell-shaped (in particular, for a normal distribution) approximately ______ of the data values will lie within two standard deviations on each side of the mean. **2.** ________

(a) 75% (b) 95% (c) 68% (d) 88.9% (e) 99.7%

3. The delivery time for a package sent within the United States is normally distributed with mean of 4 days and standard deviation of approximately 1 day. If 300 packages are being sent, how many packages will arrive in less than 3 days? **3.** ________

(a) 8 (b) 96 (c) 102 (d) 198 (e) 48

4. Let x be a random variable that represents the length of time it takes a student to complete a take-home exam in Dr. Larson's psychology class. After interviewing many students, it was found that x has an approximately normal distribution with mean $\mu = 5.2$ hours and standard deviation $\sigma = 1.8$ hours.

A. Convert the x interval $x \geq 9.7$ to a standard z interval. **4. A.** ________

(a) $z \leq 2.5$ (b) $z \geq -2.5$

(c) $z \geq 4.5$ (d) $z \geq 2.5$ (e) $z \leq -2.5$

B. Convert the z interval $-1.5 \leq z \leq 1$ to a raw score x interval. **B.** ________

(a) $2.5 \leq x \leq 7$ (b) $3.44 \leq x \leq 6.66$

(c) $3.7 \leq x \leq 12.2$ (d) $-7 \leq x \leq 2.5$ (e) $-3.7 \leq x \leq -2.3$

CHAPTER 6, FORM C, PAGE 2

5. Maria and Zoe are taking Biology 105, but are in different classes. Maria's class has an average of 78% with a standard deviation of 5% on the midterm while Zoe's class has an average of 83% with a standard deviation of 12%. Assume that scores in both classes follow a normal distribution.

A. Convert Maria's midterm score of 84 to a standard z score. **5. A.** ________

(a) 0.083 (b) 0.5 (c) 0.2 (d) 1.2 (e) 6

B. Convert Zoe's midterm score of 89 to a standard z score. **B.** ________

(a) 1.2 (b) 0.5 (c) 6 (d) 0.917 (e) 2.2

C. Who do you think did better relative to their class? **C.** ________

(a) Maria (b) Zoe

(c) They performed the same (d) Neither (e) Cannot determine

6. The lifetime of a SuperTough AAA battery is normally distributed with mean $\mu = 28.5$ hours and standard deviation $\sigma = 5.3$ hours. For a battery selected at random, what is the probability that the lifetime will be

A. 25 hours or less? **6. A.** ________

(a) 0.7454 (b) 0.6604 (c) 0.2546 (d) 0.3396 (e) 0.9999

B. 34 hours or more? **B.** ________

(a) 0.8485 (b) 0.1515 (c) 1.038 (d) 0.8508 (e) 0.1492

C. between 25 hours and 34 hours? **C.** ________

(a) 0.4038 (b) 0.5962 (c) 0.1054 (d) 0.8946 (e) 2/736

7. Quality control studies for Dependable Dishwashers show the lifetime of a dishwasher follows a normal distribution with mean $\mu = 8$ years and standard deviation $\sigma = 1.2$ years. The company will replace any dishwasher that fails during the guarantee period. How long should the company's dishwashers be guaranteed if the company wishes to replace no more than 2% of the dishwashers? **7.** ________

(a) 0.16 year (b) 0.13 year

(c) 5.5 years (d) 10.5 years (e) 2.5 years

CHAPTER 6, FORM C, PAGE 3

8. When evaluating a control chart, which of the following is not a warning signal that a random variable x is out of control? **8.** ________

(a) A run of nine consecutive points on one side of the center line (the line at target value μ).

(b) One point falls beyond the 3σ level.

(c) Two points fall beyond the 3σ level.

(d) At least two points lie beyond the 2σ level on the same side of the center line.

(e) At least two of three consecutive points lie beyond the 2σ level on the same side of the center line.

9. Records show that 29% of all payments to a mail-order company are submitted after the due date. Suppose 50 payments are submitted this week. Let r be a random variable that represents the number of payments that are late. Use the normal approximation to the binomial to estimate

A. $P(r \geq 20)$ **9. A.** ________

(a) 0.0307 (b) 0.0594 (c) 0.9406 (d) 0.9564 (e) 0.0436

B. $P(20 \leq r \leq 25)$ **B.** ________

(a) 0.0591 (b) 0.0585 (c) 0.0431 (d) 0.0304 (e) 0.0298

CHAPTER 7 TEST
FORM A

1. Write a brief but complete discussion of each of the following topics:

population, parameter, sample, sampling distribution,

statistical inference using sampling distributions.

In each case be sure to give a complete and accurate definition of the terms. Illustrate your discussion using examples from everyday life.

1. ______________________

2. The diameters of oranges from a Florida orchard are normally distributed with mean $\mu = 3.2$ inches and standard deviation $\sigma = 1.1$ inches. A packing supplier is designing special occasion presentation boxes of oranges and needs to know the average diameter for a random sample of 8 oranges. What is the probability that the mean diameter $\overline{x}$ for these oranges is

(a) smaller than 3 inches?

(b) longer than 4 inches?

(c) between 3 and 4 inches?

2. (a) ______________________

(b) ______________________

(c) ______________________

3. The manufacturer of a new compact car claims the miles per gallon (mpg) for the gasoline consumption is mound shaped and symmetric with mean $\mu = 25.9$ mph and standard deviation $\sigma = 9.5$ mph. If 30 such cars are tested, what is the probability the average mph $\overline{x}$ is

(a) less than 23 mph?

(b) more than 28 mph?

(c) between 23 and 28 mpg?

3. (a) ______________________

(b) ______________________

(c) ______________________

CHAPTER 7, FORM A, PAGE 2

4. About 68% of the students at Fairview Community College favor a new policy regarding parking on campus. Suppose we are interested in the proportion of 45 students in a mathematics class who favor the policy.

(a) Is the normal approximation to the proportion $\hat{p} = r / n$ valid? Explain.

4. (a) ______________________

(b) What is the probability that the proportion of the class who favor the policy is at least one half?

(b) ______________________

(c) What is the probability that the proportion of the class who favor the policy is no more than two thirds?

(c) ______________________

5. Statistics 101 fills up to its maximum of 45 students each semester. The instructor would like a control chart for the proportion of freshmen in the course each semester for the past 12 semesters.

Shift	1	2	3	4	5	6	7	8	9	10	11	12
#	9	8	12	7	6	10	13	10	11	9	15	11
$\hat{p} = r/45$	0.20	0.18	0.27	0.16	0.13	0.22	0.29	0.22	0.24	0.20	0.33	0.24

(a) Use the above information to make a P-chart.

5. (a)

(b) List any out-of-control signals by type (I, II, or III).

(b) ______________________

CHAPTER 7 TEST FORM B

1. Write a brief but complete discussion in which you cover the following topics: What is the mean $\mu_{\bar{x}}$ and standard deviation $\sigma_{\bar{x}}$ of the $\bar{x}$ distribution based on a sample size n? Be sure to give appropriate formulas in your discussion. How do you find a standard z score corresponding to $\bar{x}$? State the Central Limit Theorem, and the general conditions under which it can be used. Illustrate your discussion using examples from everyday life.

1. ______________________

2. Chemists use pH to measure the acidity/alkaline nature of compounds. A large vat of mixed commercial chemicals is supposed to have a mean pH $\mu = 6.3$ with a standard deviation $\sigma = 1.9$. Assume a normal distribution for pH values. If a random sample of ten readings in the vat is taken and the mean pH $\bar{x}$ is computed, find each of the following.

(a) $P(5.2 \le \bar{x})$ — **2. (a)** ______________________

(b) $P(\bar{x} \le 7.1)$ — **(b)** ______________________

(c) $P(5.2 \le \bar{x} \le 7.1)$ — **(c)** ______________________

3. Fire department response time is the length of time it takes a fire truck to arrive at the scene of a fire starting from the time the call was given to the truck. Response time for the Castle Wood Fire Department follows a mound shaped and symmetric distribution. The response time has mean $\mu = 8.8$ minutes with standard deviation $\sigma = 2.1$ minutes. If a random sample of 32 response times is taken and the mean response time $\bar{x}$ is computed, find each of the following.

(a) $P(8 \le \bar{x})$ — **3. (a)** ______________________

(b) $P(\bar{x} \le 9)$ — **(b)** ______________________

(c) $P(8 \le \bar{x} \le 9)$ — **(c)** ______________________

CHAPTER 7, FORM B, PAGE 2

4. Studies show that 24% of all students at Richardson Technical College smoke. Suppose we are interested in the proportion of the 70 students in the lunchroom cafeteria that smoke.

(a) Is the normal approximation to the proportion $\hat{p} = r / n$ valid? Explain. **4. (a)** ____________________

(b) What is the probability that the proportion of those in the cafeteria who smoke is at least one third? **(b)** ____________________

(c) What is the probability that the proportion of those in the cafeteria who smoke is no more than 20%? **(c)** ____________________

5. The quality control engineer monitors the number of defective units in a shipment of manufactured units. She would like to make a control chart for the proportion of defective units in each shipment of 150 units for the past 10 shipments.

Shipment	1	2	3	4	5	6	7	8	9	10
r = no. of defectives	7	13	12	25	13	10	12	12	9	14
$\hat{p} = r/150$	0.05	0.09	0.08	0.17	0.09	0.07	0.08	0.08	0.06	0.09

(a) Use the above information to make a P-chart. **5. (a)**

(b) List any out-of-control signals by type (I, II, or III). **(b)** ____________________

CHAPTER 7 TEST FORM C

Write the letter of the response that best answers each problem.

1. Complete the following definitions

A. A __________ is a numerical descriptive measure of a sample. **1. A.** __________

(a) parameter (b) population

(c) statistic (d) statistical inference (e) probability sampling distribution

B. A __________ is a subset of measurements from the population. **B.** __________

(a) proportion (b) sample

(c) estimate (d) statistic (e) parameter

C. A __________ is a numerical descriptive measure of a population. **C.** __________

(a) parameter (b) central limit theorem

(c) statistic (d) statistical inference (e) probability sampling distribution

D. A __________ can be thought of as a set of measurements (or counts), either existing or conceptual. **D.** __________

(a) population (b) statistic

(c) estimate (d) sample (e) parameter

2. The weights of envelopes sent from an insurance office are normally distributed with mean $\mu = 12$ ounces and standard deviation $\sigma = 3.7$ ounces. The mail room clerk would like to know the average weight of 20 envelopes. What is the probability that the mean weight $\bar{x}$ is

A. lighter than 10 ounces? **2. A.** __________

(a) 0.0351 (b) 0.0078 (c) 0.2946 (d) 0.4922 (e) 0.9922

B. heavier than 13 ounces? **B.** __________

(a) 0.6064 (b) 0.3936 (c) 0.8869 (d) 0.1131 (e) 0.2743

C. between 10 and 13 ounces? **C.** __________

(a) 0.9636 (b) 0.3118 (c) 0.8791 (d) 0.1209 (e) 0.1053

CHAPTER 7, FORM C, PAGE 2

3. The manufacturer of a coffee dispensing machine claims the ounces per cup is mound shaped and symmetric with mean $\mu = 7$ ounces and standard deviation $\sigma = 0.8$ ounce. If 40 cups of coffee are measured, what is the probability that the average ounces per cup $\overline{x}$ is

A. less than 6.8 ounces? **3. A.** ________

(a) 0.0571 (b) 0.9429 (c) 0.1170 (d) 0.4013 (e) 0.5987

B. more than 7.4 ounces? **B.** ________

(a) 0.0028 (b) 0.9992 (c) 0.6915 (d) 0.0008 (e) 0.3085

C. between 6.8 and 7.4 ounces? **B.** ________

(a) 0.0579 (b) 0.2902 (c) 0.9760 (d) 0.0563 (e) 0.9421

4. According to the school board, 48% of all the voters in the district support the referendum. Suppose a principal is interested in the proportion who support the referendum in a group of 38 parents. Approximate $\hat{p}$ by a normal distribution.

A. What are the values of n and p? **4. A.** ________

(a) $n = 48, p = 0.38$ (b) $n = 38, p = 0.48$

(c) $n = 38, p = 0.52$ (d) $n = 0.48, p = 0.52$ (e) Cannot determine

B. What is the probability that the proportion of the group who support the referendum is at least two thirds? **B.** ________

(a) 0.0162 (b) 0.5675 (c) 0.0107 (d) 0.9838 (e) 0.9893

C. What is the probability that the proportion of the group who support the referendum is no more than 30%? $P(\hat{p} \leq 30)$ **C.** ________

(a) 0.5636 (b) 0.0125 (c) 0.0197 (d) 0.9868 (e) 0.0132

CHAPTER 7, FORM C, PAGE 3

5. Answer the following questions regarding control charts.

A. A control chart for proportions is often called **5. A.** __________

(a) $\overline{X}$-Chart (b) *R*-Chart
(c) Dotplot (d) *P*-Chart (e) Unnecessary

B. We use a chart as in (A) when we are examining __________ data. **B.** __________

(a) size (b) non-random
(c) quantitative (d) interval (e) qualitative

C. Determining whether the following control chart warns that the random variable is out of control. If so, which type of out-of-control signal is present. **C.** 

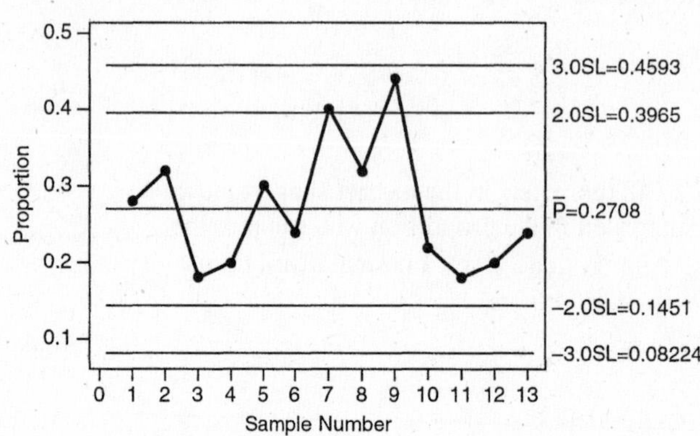

(a) Type I out-of-control signal (b) Type II out-of-control signal
(c) Type III out-of-control signal (d) Type IV out-of-control signal
(e) No out-of-control signal

CHAPTER 8 TEST
FORM A

1. As part of an Environmental Studies class project, students measured the circumferences of a random sample of 45 Blue Spruce trees near Brainard Lake, Colorado. The sample mean circumference was $\bar{x} = 29.8$ inches with sample deviation $s = 7.2$ inches. Find a 95% confidence interval for the population mean circumference of all Blue Spruce trees near this lake. Write a brief explanation of the meaning of the confidence interval in the context of this problem.

1. ______________________

2. Collette is self-employed, selling stamps at home parties. She wants to estimate the average amount a client spends at each party. A random sample of 35 clients' receipts gave a mean of $\bar{x} = \$34.70$ with standard deviation $s = \$4.85$.

(a) Find a 90% confidence interval for the average amount spent by all clients.

2. (a) ______________________

(b) For a party with 35 clients, use part (a) to estimate a range of dollar values for Collette's total sales at that party.

(b) ______________________

3. How long does it take to commute from home to work? It depends on several factors including route, traffic, and time of departure. The data below are results (in minutes) from a random sample of 8 trips. Use these data to create a 95% confidence interval for the population mean time of the commute.

27 38 30 42 24 37 30 39

3. ______________________

4. A random sample of 19 Rainbow Trout caught at Brainard Lake, Colorado had mean length $\bar{x} = 11.9$ inches with sample standard deviation $s = 2.8$ inches. Find a 99% confidence interval for the population mean length of all Rainbow Trout in this lake. Write a brief explanation of the meaning of the confidence interval in the context of this problem.

4. ______________________

CHAPTER 8, FORM A, PAGE 2

5. A random sample of 78 students were interviewed and 59 said they would vote for Jennifer McNamara as student body president.

(a) Let p represent the proportion of all students at this college who will vote for Jennifer. Find a point estimate $\hat{p}$ for p.

5. (a) ______________

(b) Find a 90% confidence interval for p.

(b) ______________

(c) What assumptions are required for the calculation of part (b)? Do you think these assumptions are satisfied? Explain.

(c) ______________

(d) How many more students should be included in the sample to be 90% sure that a point estimate $\hat{p}$ will be within a distance of 0.05 from p.

(d) ______________

6. A random sample of 53 students were asked for the number of semester hours they are taking this semester. The sample standard deviation was found to be $s = 4.7$ semester hours. How many <u>more</u> students should be included in the sample to be 99% sure the sample mean $\bar{x}$ is within one semester hour of the population mean μ for all students at this college?

6. ______________

7. What percentage of college students own cellular phones? Let p be the proportion of college students who own cellular phones.

(a) If no preliminary study is made to estimate p, how large a sample is needed to be 90% sure that a point estimate $\hat{p}$ will be within a distance of 0.08 from p.

7. (a) ______________

(b) A preliminary study shows that approximately 38% of college students own cellular phones. Answer part (a) using this estimate for p.

(b) ______________

CHAPTER 8, FORM A, PAGE 3

8. How long do new batteries last on a camping trip? A random sample of $n_1 = 42$ small camp flashlights were installed with brand I batteries and left on until the batteries failed. The sample mean lifetime was $\bar{x}_1 = 9.8$ hours with sample standard deviation $s_1 = 2.2$ hours. Another random sample of $n_2 = 38$ small flashlights of the same model were installed with brand II batteries and left on until the batteries failed. The sample mean of lifetimes was $\bar{x}_2 = 8.1$ hours with sample standard deviation $s_2 = 3.5$ hours.

(a) Find a 90% confidence interval for the population difference $\mu_1 - \mu_2$ of lifetimes for these batteries.

8. (a) ____________________

(b) Does the confidence interval of part (a) contain all positive, all negative, or both positive and negative numbers? What does this tell you about the mean life of battery I compared to battery II?

(b) ____________________

9. Two pain relief drugs are being considered. A random sample of 8 doses of the first drug showed that the average amount of time required before the drug was absorbed into the blood stream was $\bar{x}_1 = 24$ minutes with standard deviation $s_1 = 4$ minutes. For the second drug, a random sample of 10 doses showed the average time required for absorption was $\bar{x}_2 = 29$ minutes with standard deviation $s_2 = 3.9$ minutes. Assume the absorption times follow a normal distribution. Find a 90% confidence interval for the difference in average absorption time for the two drugs. Does it appear that one drug is absorbed faster than the other (at the 90% level)? Explain.

9. ____________________

10. A random sample of 83 investment portfolios managed by Kendra showed that 62 of them met the targeted annual percent growth. A random sample of 112 portfolios managed by Lisa showed that 87 met the targeted annual percent growth. Find a 99% confidence interval for the difference in the proportion of the portfolios meeting target goals managed by Kendra compared to those managed by Lisa. Is there a difference in the proportions at the 99% confidence level? Explain.

10. ____________________

CHAPTER 8 TEST
FORM B

1. A random sample of 14 evenings (6 PM to 9PM) at the O'Sullivan household showed the family received an average of $\bar{x} = 5.2$ solicitation phone calls each evening. The sample standard deviation was $s = 1.9$. Find a 96% confidence interval for the population mean number of solicitation calls this family receives each night. Write a brief explanation of the meaning of the confidence interval in the context of this problem.

1. ______________________

2. Jordan is the manager of a used book store. He wants to estimate the average amount a customer spends per visit. A random sample of 80 customers' receipts gave a mean of $\bar{x}$ = \$6.90 with standard deviation s = \$2.45.

(a) Find a 90% confidence interval for the average amount spent by all customers.

2. (a) ______________________

(b) For a day when the book store had 80 customers, use part (a) to estimate a range of dollar values for the total income on that day.

(b) ______________________

3. Mr. Crandall has assigned a term paper due at the end of the semester. He would like to know the average length of the paper. The data below are the numbers of typed pages from a random sample of 10 term papers. Use these data to create a 95% confidence interval for the population mean length of all term papers for his class.

14	20	25	10	16
8	15	12	18	9

3. ______________________

4. Computer Depot is a large store that sells and repairs computers. A random sample of 110 computer repair jobs took technicians an average of $\bar{x} = 93.2$ minutes per computer. The sample standard deviation was $s = 16.9$ minutes. Find a 99% confidence interval for the population mean time μ for computer repairs. Write a brief explanation of the meaning of the confidence interval in the context of this problem.

4. ______________________

CHAPTER 8, FORM B, PAGE 2

5. A random sample of 56 credit card holders showed that 41 regularly paid their credit card bills on time.

(a) Let p represent the proportion of all people who regularly paid their credit card bills on time. Find a point estimate $\hat{p}$ for p. **5. (a)** ____________

(b) Find a 95% confidence interval for p. **(b)** ____________

(c) What assumptions are required for the calculations of part (b)? Do you think these assumptions are satisfied? Explain. **(c)** ____________

(d) How many more credit card holders should be included in the sample to be 95% sure that a point estimate $\hat{p}$ will be within a distance of 0.05 from p? **(d)** ____________

6. Allen is an appliance salesman who works on commission. A random sample of 39 days showed that the sample standard deviation value of sales was $s = \$215$. How many more days should be included in the sample to be 95% sure the population mean μ is within \$50 of the sample mean $\bar{x}$? **6.** ____________

7. What percentage of male athletes wear contact lenses during performances? Let p be the proportion of male athletes who wear contact lenses.

(a) If you have no preliminary estimate for p, how many male athletes should you include in a random sample to be 90% sure that the point estimate $\hat{p}$ will be within a distance of 0.05 from p. **7. (a)** ____________

(b) Studies show that approximately 19% of male athletes wear contact lenses during performances. Answer part (a) using this estimate for p. **(b)** ____________

CHAPTER 8, FORM B, PAGE 3

8. At a large office supply store, the daily sales of two similar brand-name laser printers are being compared. A random sample of 16 days showed that Brand I had mean daily sales $\bar{x}_1 = \$2464$ with standard deviation $s_1 = \$529$. A random sample of 19 days showed that Brand II had mean daily sales $\bar{x}_2 = \$2285$ with sample standard deviation $s_2 = 612$. Assume sales follow an approximately normal distribution.

(a) Find a 90% confidence interval for the population mean difference in sales $\mu_1 - \mu_2$. **8. (a)** ____________________

(b) Does the confidence interval of part (a) contain all positive, all negative, or both positive and negative numbers? What does this tell you about the mean sales of one printer compared to that of the other? **(b)** ____________________

9. A production manager is studying the effect of overtime on different shifts. On Shift I at least half of the workers were on overtime. A random sample of 245 items from the assembly line showed that 24 were defective. Shift II had no overtime workers. A random sample of 258 items from the assembly line showed that 11 had defects.

(a) Find a 90% confidence interval for the population proportion difference $p_1 - p_2$ of defective items for Shift I versus Shift II. **9. (a)** ____________________

(b) What assumptions are required for the calculation of part (a)? Do you think these assumptions are satisfied? Explain. **(b)** ____________________

(c) Does the confidence interval of part (a) contain all positive, all negative, or both positive and negative numbers? What does this tell you about the population proportion of defects for Shift I compared to Shift II? **(c)** ____________________

10. Red Stone Tires has developed a new tread which they claim reduces stopping distance on wet pavement. A random sample of 56 test drives with cars using tires with tread type I (old design) showed that the average stopping distance on wet pavement was $\bar{x}_1 = 183$ feet with sample standard deviation $s_1 = 49$ feet. A random sample of 61 test drives conducted under similar conditions, but with cars using tires with tread type II (new tread) showed that the average stopping distance was $\bar{x}_2 = 152$ feet with sample standard deviation $s_2 = 53$ feet.

(a) Find a 90% confidence interval for the population mean difference $\mu_1 - \mu_2$ of stopping distances for the two types of tire tread. **10. (a)** ____________________

(b) Does the confidence interval of part (a) contain all positive, all negative, or both positive and negative numbers? What does this tell you about the mean stopping distance using tires with the new tread design compared to that using tires with the old tread design? **(b)** ____________________

CHAPTER 8 TEST
FORM C

Write the letter of the response that best answers each problem.

1. As part of a real estate company's study, the selling prices of 50 homes in a particular neighborhood were gathered. The sample mean price was $\bar{x}$ = $234,000 with sample standard deviation s = $28,500. Find a 95% confidence interval for the population mean selling price of all homes in this neighborhood. **1.** ________

(a) $229,969 to $238,031 (b) $226,100 to $241,900

(c) $227,370 to $240,630 (d) $223,601 to $244,399

(e) $232,883 to $235,117

2. Latasha is a waitress at Seventh Heaven Hamburgers. She wants to estimate the average amount each group at a table leaves for a tip. A random sample of 42 groups gave a mean of $\bar{x}$ = $7.30 with standard deviation s = $2.92.

A. Find a 90% confidence interval for the average amount left by all groups. **2. A.** ________

(a) $7.19 to $7.41 (b) $6.14 to $8.46

(c) $6.56 to $8.04 (d) $2.50 to $12.10 (e) $6.42 to $8.18

B. For a double-shift with 42 groups, use part A to estimate a range of dollar values for Latasha's total sales for that double-shift. **B.** ________

(a) $301.98 to $311.22 (b) $269.64 to $343.56

(c) $257.88 to $355.32 (d) $105.00 to $508.20 (e) $275.52 to $337.68

3. How healthy are the employees at Direct Marketing Industry? A random sample of 12 employees was taken and the number of days each was absent for sickness was recorded (during a one-year period). Use these data to create a 95% confidence interval for the population mean days absent for sickness.

2	5	3	7	10	0
6	8	5	11	3	1

3. ________

(a) 2.87 days to 7.29 days (b) 3.28 days to 6.89 days

(c) 3.11 days to 7.05 days (d) 2.77 days to 7.39 days

(e) 2.87 days to 7.29 days

CHAPTER 8, FORM C, PAGE 2

4. Denise is a professional swimmer who trains, in part, by running. She would like to estimate the average number of miles she runs in each week. For a random sample of 20 weeks, the mean is $\overline{x}$ = 17.5 miles with standard deviation s = 3.8 miles. Find a 995 confidence interval for the population mean number of weekly miles Denise runs. **4.** ________

(a) 15.01 miles to 19.99 miles (b) 15.07 miles to 19.93 miles

(c) 15.34 miles to 19.66 miles (d) 15.31 miles to 19.69 miles

(e) 15.08 miles to 19.92 miles

5. A random sample of 84 shoppers were interviewed and 51 said they prefer to shop alone rather than with someone such as friends or family.

A. Let p represent the proportion of all shoppers at this mall who would prefer to shop alone. Find a point estimate $\hat{p}$ for p. **5. A.** ________

(a) 0.393 (b) 51 (c) 84 (d) 0.607 (e) 0.5

B. Find a 90% confidence interval for p. **B.** ________

(a) 0.519 to 0.695 (b) 0.517 to 0.697

(c) −0.20 to 1.41 (d) 0.503 to 0.711 (e) 0.305 to 0.481

C. How many more students should be included in the sample to be 90% sure that a point estimate $\hat{p}$ will be within a distance of 0.05 from p. **C.** ________

(a) 271 (b) 187 (c) 259 (d) 283 (e) 175

6. A random sample of 61 students were asked how much they spent for classroom textbooks this semester. The sample standard deviation was found to be s = \$28.70. How many more students should be included in the sample to be 99% sure the sample mean $\overline{x}$ is within \$7 of the population mean μ for all students at this college? **6.** ________

(a) 0 (b) 65 (c) 51 (d) 4 (e) 112

CHAPTER 8, FORM C, PAGE 3

7. What percentage of college students are attending a college in the state where they grew up? Let p be the proportion of college students from the same state as that in which the college resides.

A. If no preliminary study is made to estimate p, how large a sample is needed to be 90% sure that a point estimate $\hat{p}$ will be within a distance of 0.07 from p? **7. A.** ______

(a) 139 (b) 196 (c) 340 (d) 6 (e) 138

B. A preliminary study shows that approximately 71% of college students grew up in the same state as that in which the college resides. Answer part A using this estimate for p. **B.** ______

(a) 280 (b) 113 (c) 139 (d) 114 (e) 162

8. Is there a difference in the total scores for women's and men's basketball games? A random sample of $n_1 = 55$ women's games had a mean winning score of $\bar{x}_1 = 78$ with standard deviation $s_1 = 10$. Another random sample of $n_2 = 60$ men's games had a mean winning score of $\bar{x}_2 = 90$ with standard deviation $s_2 = 16$. Find a 95% confidence interval for the population difference $\mu_1 - \mu_2$. **8.** ______

(a) −13.3 to −10.7 (b) −16.8 to −7.2

(c) −16.1 to −7.9 (d) −18.4 to −5.6 (e) −38.2 to 14.2

9. Two growth hormones are being considered. A random sample of 10 rats were given the first hormone and their average weight gain was $\bar{x}_1 = 2.3$ pounds with standard deviation $s_1 = 0.4$ pound. For the second hormone, a random sample of 15 rats showed their average weight gain to be $\bar{x}_2 = 1.9$ pounds with standard deviation $s_2 = 0.2$ pound. Assume the weight gains follow a normal distribution. Find a 90% confidence interval for the difference in average weight gains for the two growth hormones. **9.** ______

(a) 0.20 lb to 0.60 lb (b) 0.17 lb to 0.63 lb

(c) 0.24 lb to 0.56 lb (d) 0.175 lb to 0.625 lb (e) 0.19 lb to 0.61 lb

10. A random sample of 47 manuscripts typed by Katlyn showed that 13 of them had errors. A random sample of 85 manuscripts typed by Dara shows that 31 of them had errors. Find a 99% confidence interval for the difference in the proportion of the manuscripts with errors typed by Katlyn compared to those typed by Dara. **10.** ______

(a) −0.323 to 0.146 (b) −0.252 to 0.076

(c) −0.887 to 0.711 (d) −0.304 to 0.128 (e) −0.256 to 0.295

CHAPTER 9 TEST FORM A

For each of the following problems, please provide the requested information.

(a) State the null and alternate hypotheses. Will we use a left-tailed, right-tailed, or two-tailed test? What is the level of significance?

(b) Identify the sampling distribution to be used: the standard normal or the Student's t. Find the critical value(s).

(c) Sketch the critical region and show the critical value(s) on the sketch.

(d) Compute the z or t value of the sample test statistic and show it's location on the sketch of part (c).

(e) Find the P value or an interval containing the P value for the sample test statistic.

(f) Based on your answers for parts (a) to (e), shall we reject or fail to reject the null hypothesis. Explain your conclusion in the context of the problem.

1. A large furniture store has begun a new ad campaign on local television. Before the campaign, the long term average daily sales were $24,819. A random sample of 40 days during the new ad campaign gave a sample mean daily sale of $\overline{x}$ = $25,910 with sample standard deviation s = $1917. Does this indicate that the population mean daily sales is now more than $24,819? Use a 1% level of significance.

1. (a) ____________

(b) ____________

(c)

(d) ____________

(e) ____________

(f) ____________

CHAPTER 9, FORM A, PAGE 2

2. A new bus route has been established between downtown Denver and Englewood, a suburb of Denver. Dan has taken the bus to work for many years. For the old bus route, he knows from long experience that the mean waiting time between buses at his stop was $\mu = 18.3$ minutes. However, a random sample of 5 waiting times between buses using the new route had mean $\bar{x} = 15.1$ minutes with sample standard deviation $s = 6.2$ minutes. Does this indicate that the population mean waiting time for the new route is different from what it used to be? Use $\alpha = 0.05$.

2. (a) ____________________

(b) ____________________

(c)

(d) ____________________

(e) ____________________

(f) ____________________

3. The State Fish and Game Division claims that 75% of the fish in Homestead Creek are Rainbow Trout. However, the local fishing club caught (and released) 189 fish one weekend, and found that 125 were Rainbow Trout. The other fish were Brook Trout, Brown Trout, and so on. Does this indicate that the percentage of Rainbow Trout in Homestead Creek is less than 75%? Use $\alpha = 0.01$.

3. (a) ____________________

(b) ____________________

(c)

(d) ____________________

(e) ____________________

(f) ____________________

CHAPTER 9, FORM A, PAGE 3

4. A telemarketer is trying two different sales pitches to sell a carpet cleaning service. For Sales Pitch I, 175 people were contacted by phone and 62 of these people bought the cleaning service. For Sales Pitch II, 154 people were contacted by phone and 45 of these people bought the cleaning service. Does this indicate that there is any difference in the population proportions of people who will buy the cleaning service, depending on which sales pitch is used? Use $\alpha = 0.05$

4. (a) ____________________

(b) ____________________

(c)

(d) ____________________

(e) ____________________

(f) ____________________

5. A systems specialist has studied the work-flow of clerks all doing the same inventory work. Based on this study, she designed a new work-flow layout for the inventory system. To compare average production for the old and new methods, a random sample of six clerks was used. The average production rate (number of inventory items processed per shift) for each clerk was measured both before and after the new system was introduced. The results are shown below. Test the claim that the new system increases the mean number of items process per shift. Use $\alpha = 0.05$.

Clerk	1	2	3	4	5	6
B: Old	116	108	93	88	119	111
A: New	123	114	112	82	127	122

5. (a) ____________________

(b) ____________________

(c)

(d) ____________________

(e) ____________________

(f) ____________________

CHAPTER 9, FORM A, PAGE 4

6. How productive are employees? One way to answer this question is to study annual company profits per employee. Let x_1 represent annual profits per employee in computer stores in St. Louis. A random sample of $n_1 = 11$ computer stores gave a sample mean of $\overline{x}_1 = 25.2$ thousand dollars profit per employee with sample standard deviation $s_1 = 8.4$ thousand dollars. Another random sample of $n_2 = 9$ building supply stores in St. Louis gave a sample mean $\overline{x}_2 = 19.9$ thousand dollars per employee with sample standard deviation $s_2 = 7.6$ thousand dollars. Does this indicate that in St. Louis, computer stores tend to have higher mean profits per employee? Use $\alpha = 0.01$

6. (a) ________________

(b) ________________

(c)

(d) ________________

(e) ________________

(f) ________________

7. How big are tomatoes? Some say that depends on the growing conditions. A random sample of $n_1 = 89$ organically grown tomatoes had sample mean weight $\overline{x}_1 = 3.8$ ounces with sample standard deviation $s_1 = 0.9$ ounces. Another random sample of $n_2 = 75$ tomatoes that were not organically grown had sample mean weight $\overline{x}_2 = 4.1$ ounces with sample standard deviation $s_2 = 1.5$ ounces. Does this indicate a difference either way between population mean weights of organically grown tomatoes compared to those not organically grown? Use a 5% level of significance.

7. (a) ________________

(b) ________________

(c)

(d) ________________

(e) ________________

(f) ________________

CHAPTER 9, FORM A, PAGE 5

8. How tall are college hockey players? The average height has been 68.3 inches. A random sample of 55 hockey players gave a mean height of 69.1 inches with sample standard deviation $s = 1.6$ inches. Does this indicate that the population mean height is different from 68.3 inches? Use 5% level of significance.

8. (a) ____________________

(b) ____________________

(c)

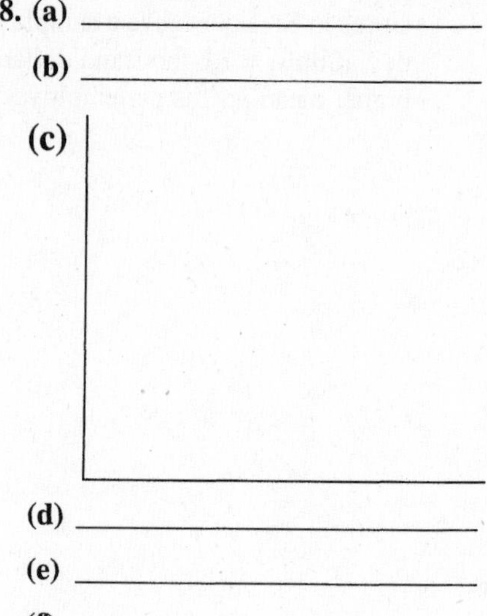

(d) ____________________

(e) ____________________

(f) ____________________

9. How long does it take to have food delivered? A Chinese restaurant advertises that delivery will be no more than 30 minutes. A random sample of delivery times (in minutes) is shown below. Based on this sample, is the delivery time greater than 30 minutes? Use a 5% level of significance. Assume that the distribution of times is normal.

32	28	21	39	30	27	29
39	32	28	42	25	26	30

9. (a) ____________________

(b) ____________________

(c)

(d) ____________________

(e) ____________________

(f) ____________________

CHAPTER 9, FORM A, PAGE 6

10. A music teacher knows from past records that 60% of students taking summer lessons play the piano. The instructor believes this proportion may have dropped due to the popularity of wind and brass instruments. A random sample of 80 students yielded 43 piano players. Test the instructor's claim at $\alpha = 0.05$.

10. (a) ________________

(b) ________________

(c)

(d) ________________

(e) ________________

(f) ________________

CHAPTER 9 TEST
FORM B

For each of the following problems, please provide the requested information.

(a) State the null and alternate hypotheses. Will we use a left-tailed, right-tailed, or two-tailed test? What is the level of significance?

(b) Identify the sampling distribution to be used: the standard normal or the Student's t. Find the critical value(s).

(c) Sketch the critical region and show the critical value(s) on the sketch.

(d) Compute the z or t value of the sample test statistic and show it's location on the sketch of part (c).

(e) Find the P value or an interval containing the P value for the sample test statistic.

(f) Based on your answers for parts (a) to (e), shall we reject or fail to reject the null hypothesis. Explain your conclusion in the context of the problem.

1. Long term experience showed that after a type of eye surgery it took a mean of $\mu = 5.3$ days recovery time in a hospital. However, a random sample of 32 patients with this type of eye surgery, were recently treated as outpatients during the recovery. The sample mean recovery time was $\bar{x} = 4.2$ days with sample standard deviation $s = 1.9$ days. Does this indicate that the mean recovery time for outpatients is less than the time for those recovering in the hospital? Use a 1% level of significance.

1. (a) ____________________

(b) ____________________

(c)

(d) ____________________

(e) ____________________

(f) ____________________

CHAPTER 9, FORM B, PAGE 2

2. Recently the national average yield on municipal bonds has been $\mu = 4.19\%$. A random sample of 16 Arizona municipal bonds gave an average yield of 5.11% with sample standard deviation $s = 1.15\%$. Does this indicate that the population mean yield for all Arizona municipal bonds is greater than the national average? Use a 5% level of significance.

2. (a) ______________________

(b) ______________________

(c)

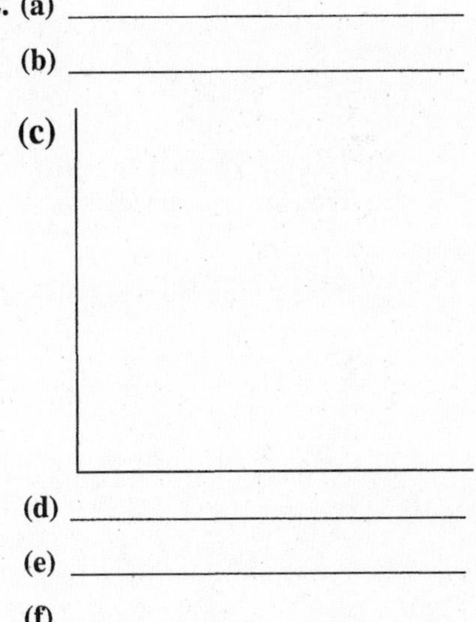

(d) ______________________

(e) ______________________

(f) ______________________

3. At a local four-year college, 37% of the student-body are freshmen. A random sample of 42 student names taken from the Dean's Honor List over the past several semesters showed that 17 were freshmen. Does this indicate the population proportion of freshmen on the Dean's Honor List is different from 37%? Use a 1% level of significance.

3. (a) ______________________

(b) ______________________

(c)

(d) ______________________

(e) ______________________

(f) ______________________

CHAPTER 9, FORM B, PAGE 3

4. In a random sample of 62 students, 34 said they would vote for Jennifer as student body president. In another random sample of 77 students, 48 said they would vote for Kevin as student body president. Does this indicate that in the population of all students, Kevin has a higher proportion of votes? Use $\alpha = 0.05$

4. (a) ______________

(b) ______________

(c)

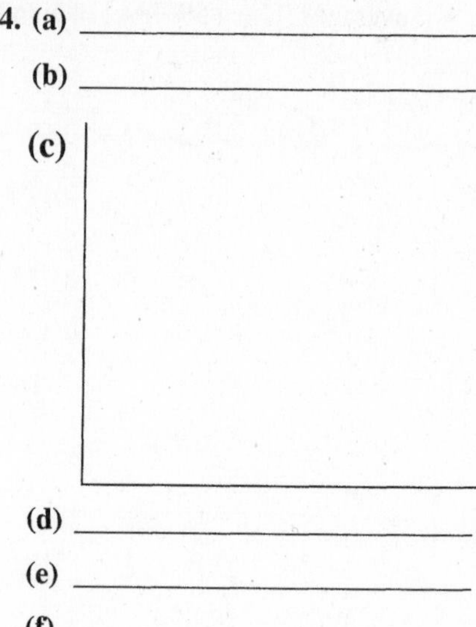

(d) ______________

(e) ______________

(f) ______________

5. Five members of the college track team in Denver (elevation 5200 ft) went up to Leadville (elevation 10,152 ft) for a track meet. The times in minutes for these team members to run two miles at each location are shown below.

Team Member	1	2	3	4	5
Denver	10.7	9.1	11.4	9.7	9.2
Leadville	11.5	10.6	11.0	11.2	10.3

Assume the team members constitute a random sample of track team members. Use a 5% level of significance to test the claim that the times were longer at the higher elevation.

5. (a) ______________

(b) ______________

(c)

(d) ______________

(e) ______________

(f) ______________

CHAPTER 9, FORM B, PAGE 4

6. Two models of a popular pick-up truck are tested for miles per gallon (mpg) gasoline consumption. The Pacer model was tested using a random sample of $n_1 = 9$ trucks and the sample mean was $\bar{x}_1 = 27.3$ mpg with sample standard deviation $s_1 = 6.2$ mpg. The Road Runner model was tested using a random sample of $n_2 = 14$ trucks. The sample mean was $\bar{x}_2 = 22.5$ mpg with sample standard deviation $s_2 = 6.8$ mpg. Does this indicate that the population mean gasoline consumption for the Pacer is higher than that of the Road Runner? Use $\alpha = 0.01$

6. (a) __________

(b) __________

(c)

(d) __________

(e) __________

(f) __________

7. Students at the college agricultural research station are studying egg production of range free chickens compared to caged chickens. During a one week period, a random sample of $n_1 = 93$ range free hens produced an average of $\bar{x}_1 = 11.2$ eggs with sample standard deviation $s_1 = 4.4$ eggs. For the same period, another random sample of $n_2 = 87$ caged hens produced a sample average of $\bar{x}_2 = 8.5$ eggs per hen with sample standard deviation $s_2 = 5.7$. Does this indicate the population mean egg production for range free hens is higher? Use a 5% level of significance.

7. (a) __________

(b) __________

(c)

(d) __________

(e) __________

(f) __________

CHAPTER 9, FORM B, PAGE 5

8. How long does it take juniors to complete a standardized exam? The long-term average is 2.8 hours. A random sample of 43 juniors gave a sample mean of $\overline{x} = 2.5$ hours with standard deviation $s = 0.8$ hour. Does this indicate that the population mean time is different from 2.8 hours? Use 5% level of significance.

8. (a) ____________________

(b) ____________________

(c)

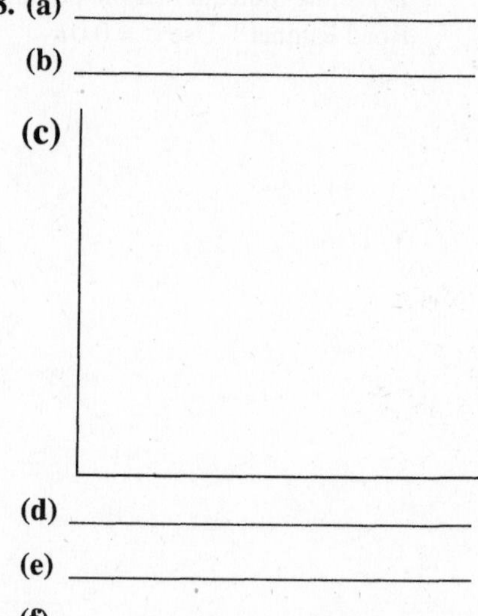

(d) ____________________

(e) ____________________

(f) ____________________

9. How old are the customers? The owner of a comedy club has based business decisions on the average of customers historically being 30 years. A random sample of customers' ages (in years) is shown below. Based on this sample, is the average age more than 30 years? Use a 5% level of significance. Assume that the distribution of ages is normal.

37	30	26	35	45	42	51	40
43	27	39	38	46	21	28	20

9. (a) ____________________

(b) ____________________

(c)

(d) ____________________

(e) ____________________

(f) ____________________

CHAPTER 9, FORM B, PAGE 6

10. The Department of Transportation in a particular city knows from past records that 27% of workers in the downtown district use the subway system each day to commute to or from work. The department suspects this proportion has increased due to decreased parking spaces in the downtown district. A random sample of 130 workers in the downtown district showed 49 used the subway daily. Test the departments' suspicion at the 5% level of significance.

10. (a) ____________

(b) ____________

(c)

(d) ____________

(e) ____________

(f) ____________

CHAPTER 9 TEST
FORM C

Write the letter of the response that best answers each problem.

1. A small electronics store has begun to advertise in the local newspaper. Before advertising, the long term average weekly sales were $9820. A random sample of 50 weeks while the newspaper ads were running gave a sample mean weekly sale of $\overline{x}$ = $10,960 with the sample standard deviation s = $1580. Does this indicate that the population mean weekly sales is now more than $9820? Test at the 5% level of significance.

A. State the null and alternate hypotheses. **1. A.** ________

(a) H_0: $\mu = 9820$; H_1: $\mu < 9820$ (b) H_0: $\mu = 9820$; H_1: $\mu > 9820$

(c) H_0: $\overline{x} = 10{,}960$; H_1: $\overline{x} > 10{,}960$ (d) H_0: $\mu = 10{,}960$; H_1: $\mu > 10{,}960$

(e) H_0: $\mu > 9820$; H_1: $\mu = 9820$

B. Find the critical value(s). **B.** ________

(a) $z_0 = 2.33$ (b) $z_0 = 1.96$

(c) $t_0 = -1.96$ (d) $z_0 = 1.645$ (e) $t_0 = -1.96$

C. Compute the z or t value of the sample test statistic. **C.** ________

(a) $z = 5.10$ (b) $z = 0.10$

(c) $t = 0.72$ (d) $z = -5.10$ (e) $t = -0.10$

D. Find the P value or an interval containing the P value for the sample test statistic. **D.** ________

(a) P value = 0.236 (b) P value = 0.460

(c) P value < 0.0001 (d) P value > 0.0001 (e) Cannot determine

E. Based on your answers for parts A–D, what is your conclusion? **E.** ________

(a) Do not reject H_0 (b) Reject H_0 (c) Cannot determine

(d) The population mean weekly sales is less than $9820.

(e) The population mean weekly sales is more than $10,960.

CHAPTER 9, FORM C, PAGE 2

2. The average annual salary of employees at Wintertime Sports was \$28,750 last year. This year the company opened another store. Suppose a random sample of 18 employees gave an average annual salary of $\overline{x}$ = \$25,810 with sample standard deviation s = \$4230. Use a 1% level of significance to test the claim that the average annual salary for all employees is different from last year's average salary. Assume salaries are normally distributed.

A. State the null and alternate hypotheses. **2. A.** ________

(a) H_0: $\mu = 28{,}750$; H_1: $\mu < 28{,}750$ (b) H_0: $\mu = 25{,}810$; H_1: $\mu \neq 25{,}810$

(c) H_0: $\mu_1 = \mu_2$; H_1: $\mu_1 \neq \mu_2$ (d) H_0: $\overline{x} = 25{,}810$; H_1: $\overline{x} \neq 25{,}810$

(e) H_0: $\mu = 28{,}750$; H_1: $\mu \neq 28{,}750$

B. Find the critical value(s). **B.** ________

(a) $t_0 = 2.58$ (b) $t_0 = \pm 1.96$

(c) $t_0 = \pm 2.567$ (d) $t_0 = \pm 2.898$ (e) $z_0 = -2.567$

C. Compute the z or t value of the sample test statistic. **C.** ________

(a) $t = -2.95$ (b) $z = -2.95$

(c) $t = -2.87$ (d) $z = -12.51$ (e) $t = 2.95$

D. Find the P value or an interval containing the P value for the sample test statistic. **D.** ________

(a) Cannot determine (b) $0.01 < P$ value < 0.02

(c) P value < 0.010 (d) P value > 0.010 (e) P value < 0.005

E. Based on your answers for parts A–D, what is your conclusion? **E.** ________

(a) Do not reject H_0 (b) Reject H_0 (c) Cannot determine

(d) The average salary is less than \$25,810.

(e) The average salary is different from \$10,960.

CHAPTER 9, FORM C, PAGE 3

3. The owner of Prices Limited claims that 75% of all the items in the store are less than \$5. Suppose that you check a random sample of 146 items in the store and find that 105 have prices less than \$5. Does this indicate that the items in the store costing less than \$5 is different from 75%? Use $\alpha = 0.01$.

A. State the null and alternate hypotheses. **1. A.** __________

(a) H_0: $p_1 = p_2$; H_1: $p_1 \neq p_2$ (b) H_0: $p = 5$; H_1: $p \neq 5$

(c) H_0: $\hat{p} = 0.75$; H_1: $\hat{p} \neq 0.75$ (d) H_0: $p = 0.75$; H_1: $p \neq 0.75$

(e) H_0: $\hat{p} = 0.72$; H_1: $\hat{p} \neq 0.72$

B. Find the critical value(s). **B.** __________

(a) $z_0 = \pm 2.58$ (b) $z_0 = -2.33$

(c) $z_0 = \pm 1.96$ (d) $t_0 = -1.645$ (e) $t_0 = \pm 2.58$

C. Compute the z or t value of the sample test statistic. **C.** __________

(a) $t = -0.86$ (b) $t = -0.73$

(c) $z = -0.73$ (d) $z = 0.86$ (e) $z = -0.86$

D. Find the P value or an interval containing the P value for the sample test statistic. **D.** __________

(a) P value = 0.2327 (b) P value = 0.0975

(c) P value = 0.3898 (d) P value = 0.1949 (e) P value = 0.8051

E. Based on your answers for parts A–D, what is your conclusion? **E.** __________

(a) Do not reject H_0 (b) Reject H_0 (c) Cannot determine

(d) The items in the store cost less than \$5.

(e) The items in the store do not cost less than \$5.

CHAPTER 9, FORM C, PAGE 4

4. A random sample of 257 dog owners was taken 10 years ago, and it was found that 146 owned more than one dog (Sample 1). Recently, a random sample of 380 dog owners showed that 200 owned more than one dog (Sample 2). Do these data indicate that the proportion of dog owners owning more than one dog has decreased? Use a 5% level of significance.

A. State the null and alternate hypotheses. **4. A.** ________

(a) H_0: $\hat{p}_1 = \hat{p}_2$; H_1: $\hat{p}_1 > \hat{p}_2$ (b) H_0: $p_1 = p_2$; H_1: $p_1 < p_2$

(c) H_0: $p_1 = \frac{146}{257} = 0.57$; H_1: $p_1 < 0.57$ (d) H_0: $p_1 = p_2$; H_1: $p_1 \neq p_2$

(e) H_0: $p_1 = p_2$; H_1: $p_1 > p_2$

B. Find the critical value(s). **B.** ________

(a) $t_0 = \pm 1.96$ (b) $z_0 = 2.33$

(c) $t_0 = -1.645$ (d) $z_0 = 1.645$ (e) $z_0 = \pm 1.96$

C. Compute the z or t value of the sample test statistic. **C.** ________

(a) $z = 0.04$ (b) $z = 1.04$

(c) $z = 0.08$ (d) $t = -0.08$ (e) $t = 1.04$

D. Find the P value or an interval containing the P value for the sample test statistic. **D.** ________

(a) P value = 0.8508 (b) P value = 0.4681

(c) P value = 0.2984 (d) P value = 0.4840 (e) P value = 0.1492

E. Based on your answers for parts A–D, what is your conclusion? **E.** ________

(a) Do not reject H_0 (b) Reject H_0 (c) Cannot determine

(d) More people own dogs.

(e) Less people own dogs.

CHAPTER 9, FORM C, PAGE 5

5. Seven manufacturing companies agreed to implement a time management program in hopes of improving productivity. The average times, in minutes, it took the companies to produce the same quantity and kind of part are listed below. Does this information indicate the program decreased production time? Assume normal population distributions. Use $\alpha = 0.05$.

Company	1	2	3	4	5	6	7
Before program (1)	75	112	89	95	80	105	110
After program (2)	70	110	88	100	80	100	99

A. State the null and alternate hypotheses. **5. A.** ________

(a) H_0: $\mu_1 = \mu_2$; H_1: $\mu_1 > \mu_2$ (b) H_0: $\mu_d = 0$; H_1: $\mu_d \neq 0$

(c) H_0: $\mu_1 = \mu_2$; H_1: $\mu_1 < \mu_2$ (d) H_0: $\mu_d = 0$; H_1: $\mu_d > 0$

(e) H_0: $\mu = 0$; H_1: $\mu < 0$

B. Find the critical value(s). **B.** ________

(a) $t_0 = 2.447$ (b) $t_0 = 1.782$

(c) $t_0 = 1.895$ (d) $z_0 = 1.645$ (e) $t_0 = 1.943$

C. Compute the z or t value of the sample test statistic. **C.** ________

(a) $t = 0$ (b) $z = 0.36$

(c) $t = 1.44$ (d) $t = 0.36$ (e) $z = -1.44$

D. Find the P value or an interval containing the P value for the sample test statistic. **D.** ________

(a) P value = 0.1498 (b) P value = 0.10

(c) P value = 0.0749 (d) P value > 0.250 (e) Cannot determine

E. Based on your answers for parts A–D, what is your conclusion? **E.** ________

(a) Do not reject H_0 (b) Reject H_0 (c) Cannot determine

(d) All manufacturing companies should implement the program.

(e) Some manufacturing companies should implement the program.

CHAPTER 9, FORM C, PAGE 6

6. An independent rating service is trying to determine which of two film developing ships has quicker service. Over a period of 12 randomly selected times, the average waiting period to develop a 24-exposure roll sold at Shop 1 is 58 minutes with standard deviation 3.5 minutes. The average waiting period at Shop 2 to develop a 24-exposure roll over a period of 8 randomly selected times is 53 minutes with standard deviation 4.9 minutes. Using a 1% level of significance, can we say there is a difference in the average waiting time at Shop 1 and Shop 2?

A. State the null and alternate hypotheses. **6. A.** ________

(a) H_0: $\overline{x}_1 = \overline{x}_2$; H_1: $\overline{x}_1 \neq \overline{x}_2$ (b) H_0: $\mu_1 = \mu_2$; H_1: $\mu_1 \neq \mu_2$

(c) H_0: $\mu_1 = \mu_2$; H_1: $\mu_1 > \mu_2$ (d) H_0: $\mu = 58$; H_1: $\mu \neq 58$

(e) H_0: $\mu_d > 0$; H_1: $\mu_d \neq 0$

B. Find the critical value(s). **B.** ________

(a) $t_0 = \pm 2.878$ (b) $z_0 = \pm 2.56$

(c) $z_0 = \pm 1.96$ (d) $t_0 = 2.552$ (e) $t_0 = 2.878$

C. Compute the z or t value of the sample test statistic. **C.** ________

(a) $z = 2.67$ (b) $t = 2.49$

(c) $t_0 = \pm 2.67$ (d) $z = 2.49$ (e) $t = 2.67$

D. Find the P value or an interval containing the P value for the sample test statistic. **D.** ________

(a) $0.010 < P$ value < 0.025 (b) $0.02 < P$ value < 0.05

(c) Cannot determine (d) $0.01 < P$ value < 0.02 (e) $0.005 < P$ value < 0.010

E. Based on your answers for parts A–D, what is your conclusion? **E.** ________

(a) Do not reject H_0 (b) Reject H_0 (c) Cannot determine

(d) It takes about an hour to develop film.

(e) Shop 1 takes longer than Shop 2.

CHAPTER 9, FORM C, PAGE 7

7. The personnel manager of a large retail clothing store suspects a difference in the mean amount of break time taken by workers during the weekday shifts compared to that of the weekend shifts. It is suspected that the weekday workers take longer breaks on the average. A random sample of 46 weekday workers had a mean $\bar{x}_1 = 53$ minutes of break time per 8-hour shift with standard deviation $s_1 = 7.3$ minutes. A random sample of 40 weekend workers had a mean $\bar{x}_2 = 47$ minutes with standard deviation $s_2 = 9.1$ minutes. Test the manager's suspicion at the 5% level of significance.

A. State the null and alternate hypotheses. **7. A.** ________

(a) H_0: $\mu_1 = \mu_2$; H_1: $\mu_1 < \mu_2$ (b) H_0: $\mu_1 = \mu_2$; H_1: $\mu_1 > \mu_2$

(c) H_0: $\mu_1 = \mu_2$; H_1: $\mu_1 \neq \mu_2$ (d) H_0: $\bar{x}_1 = \bar{x}_2$; H_1: $\bar{x}_1 > \bar{x}_2$

(e) H_0: $\mu_d = 0$; H_1: $\mu_d > 0$

B. Find the critical value(s). **B.** ________

(a) $t_0 = 1.645$ (b) $t_0 = \pm 1.96$

(c) $z_0 = 1.645$ (d) $z_0 = 3.34$ (e) $z_0 = 2.33$

C. Compute the z or t value of the sample test statistic. **C.** ________

(a) $t = 3.34$ (b) $t = 0.73$

(c) $z = 0.73$ (d) $z = 1.645$ (e) $z = 3.34$

D. Find the P value or an interval containing the P value for the sample test statistic. **D.** ________

(a) Cannot determine (b) P value = 0.0495

(c) P value = 0.0008 (d) P value = 0.0004 (e) P value = 0.2327

E. Based on your answers for parts A–D, what is your conclusion? **E.** ________

(a) Do not reject H_0 (b) Reject H_0 (c) Cannot determine

(d) All weekend workers take shorter breaks.

(e) Some weekend workers take shorter breaks.

CHAPTER 9, FORM C, PAGE 8

8. A machine in the lodge at a ski resort dispenses a hot chocolate drink. The average cup of hot hocolate is supposed to contain 7.75 ounces. A random sample of 68 cups of hot chocolate form this machine show the average content to be 7.62 ounces with a standard deviation of 0.6 ounces. Do you think the machine is out of adjustment and the average amount of hot chocolate is less than it is supped to be? Use a 5% level of significance.

A. State the null and alternate hypotheses. **8. A.** __________

(a) H_0: $\mu_1 = \mu_2$; H_1: $\mu_1 < \mu_2$ (b) H_0: $\mu = 7.75$; H_1: $\mu \neq 7.75$

(c) H_0: $\overline{x} = 7.62$; H_1: $\overline{x} < 7.62$ (d) H_0: $\mu > 7.62$; H_1: $\mu = 7.62$

(e) H_0: $\mu = 7.75$; H_1: $\mu < 7.75$

B. Find the critical value(s). **B.** __________

(a) $z_0 = -1.645$ (b) $z_0 = \pm 2.58$

(c) $z_0 = \pm 1.96$ (d) $z_0 = 1.645$ (e) $t_0 = -1.645$

C. Compute the z or t value of the sample test statistic. **C.** __________

(a) $z = -14.73$ (b) $z = -1.645$

(c) $z = -1.79$ (d) $t = -0.03$ (e) $z = -0.03$

D. Find the P value or an interval containing the P value for the sample test statistic. **D.** __________

(a) P value = 0.0734 (b) P value = 0.4880

(c) P value = 0.4880 (d) P value = 0.0367 (e) P value = 0.9633

E. Based on your answers for parts A–D, what is your conclusion? **E.** __________

(a) Do not reject H_0 (b) Reject H_0 (c) Cannot determine

(d) The cup will be over full.

(e) The machine is working fine.

CHAPTER 9, FORM C, PAGE 9

9. The average number of miles on vehicles traded in at Smith Brothers Motors is 64,000. Smith Brothers Motors has started a new deal offering lower financing charges. They are interested in whether the average mileage on trade-in vehicles has decreased. Test using $\alpha = 0.01$ and the results (in thousands) from a random sample printed below (taken after the deal started). Assume mileage is normally distributed.

39	47	62	110	58
90	50	99	41	28

A. State the null and alternate hypotheses. **9. A.** ________

(a) H_0: $\overline{x} = 62{,}400$; H_1: $\overline{x} \neq 62{,}400$ (b) H_0: $\overline{x} = 64{,}000$; H_1: $\overline{x} > 64{,}000$

(c) H_0: $\mu_d = 64{,}000$; H_1: $\mu_d < 64{,}000$ (d) H_0: $\mu = 64{,}000$; H_1: $\mu < 64{,}000$

(e) H_0: $\mu > 64{,}000$; H_1: $\mu > 64{,}000$

B. Find the critical value(s). **B.** ________

(a) $t_0 = 2.821$ (b) $z_0 = -2.33$

(c) $t_0 = -2.821$ (d) $t_0 = -3.250$ (e) $t_0 = -2.764$

C. Compute the z or t value of the sample test statistic. **C.** ________

(a) $t = -0.52$ (b) $t = -0.18$

(c) $t = -0.17$ (d) $t = -0.02$ (e) $z = -0.58$

D. Find the P value or an interval containing the P value for the sample test statistic. **D.** ________

(a) Cannot determine (b) P value = 0.4286

(c) P value = 0.4325 (d) P value > 0.250 (e) P value > 0.125

E. Based on your answers for parts A–D, what is your conclusion? **E.** ________

(a) Do not reject H_0 (b) Reject H_0 (c) Cannot determine

(d) People are trading in more vehicles.

(e) People are trading in fewer vehicles.

CHAPTER 9, FORM C, PAGE 10

10. Results from previous studies showed 79% of all high school seniors from a certain city plan to attend college after graduation. A random sample of 200 high school seniors from this city showed 162 plan to attend college. Does this indicate that the percentage has increased from that of previous studies? Test at 5% level of significance.

A. State the null and alternate hypotheses. **10. A.** ________

(a) H_0: $\mu = 0.79$; H_1: $\mu > 0.79$ (b) H_0: $p = 0.79$; H_1: $p \neq 0.79$

(c) H_0: $p = 0.79$; H_1: $p > 0.79$ (d) H_0: $\hat{p} = 0.81$; H_1: $\hat{p} \neq 0.81$

(e) H_0: $\hat{p} = 0.79$; H_1: $\hat{p} > 0.79$

B. Find the critical value(s). **B.** ________

(a) $z_0 = 1.645$ (b) $t_0 = 2.33$

(c) $z_0 = 2.33$ (d) $t_0 = \pm 2.58$ (e) $z_0 = \pm 1.96$

C. Compute the z or t value of the sample test statistic. **C.** ________

(a) $z = 0.72$ (b) $t = 1.645$

(c) $z = 0.62$ (d) $z = 1.645$ (e) $z = 0.69$

D. Find the P value or an interval containing the P value for the sample test statistic. **D.** ________

(a) P value = 0.2676 (b) P value = 0.7642

(c) P value > 0.05 (d) P value = 0.2451 (e) P value = 0.2358

E. Based on your answers for parts A–D, what is your conclusion? **E.** ________

(a) Do not reject H_0 (b) Reject H_0 (c) Cannot determine

(d) More seniors are going to college.

(e) Less seniors are going to college.

CHAPTER 10 TEST
FORM A

For the given data, solve the following problems.

Taltson Lake is in the Canadian Northwest Territories. This lake has many Northern Pike. The following data was obtained by two fishermen visiting the lake. Let x = length of a Northern Pike in inches and let y = weight in pounds.

x (inches)	20	24	36	41	46
y (pounds)	2	4	12	15	20

1. Draw a scatter diagram. Using the scatter diagram (no calculations) would you estimate the linear correlation coefficient to be positive, close to zero, or negative? Explain your answer.

1.

2. For the given data compute each of the following.

(a) $\overline{x}$ and $\overline{y}$ **2. (a)** ______

(b) SS_x, SS_y, SS_{xy} **(b)** ______

(c) The slope b and y intercept a of the least squares line; write out the equation for the least squares line. **(c)** ______

(d) Graph the least squares line on your scatter plot of problem 1. **(d)** ______

3. Compute the sample correlation coefficient r. Compute the coefficient of determination. Give a brief explanation of the meaning of the correlation coefficient and the coefficient of determination in the context of this problem. **3.** ______

4. Compute the standard error of estimate S_e. **4.** ______

5. If a 32 inch Northern Pike is caught, what is the weight in pounds as predicted by the least squares line? **5.** ______

6. Find a 90% confidence interval for your prediction of Problem 5. **6.** ______

7. Using the sample correlation coefficient r computed in Problem 3, test whether or not the population correlation coefficient p is different from zero. Use $\alpha = 0.01$. Is r significant in this problem? Explain. **7.** ______

CHAPTER 10, FORM A, PAGE 2

For the given data, solve the following problems.

A marketing analyst is studying the relationship between x = amount spent on television advertising and y = increase in sales. The following data represents a random sample from the study.

x ($ thousands)	15	28	19	47	10	92
y ($ thousands)	340	260	152	413	130	855

8. Draw a scatter diagram. Using the scatter diagram (no calculations) would you estimate the linear correlation coefficient to be positive, close to zero, or negative? Explain your answer.

8.

9. For the given data compute each of the following.

(a) $\bar{x}$ and $\bar{y}$ **9. (a)** ______

(b) SS_x, SS_y, SS_{xy} **(b)** ______

(c) The slope b and y intercept a of the least squares line; write out the equation for the least squares line. **(c)** ______

(d) Graph the least squares line on your scatter plot of problem 8. **(d)** ______

10. Compute the sample correlation coefficient r. Compute the coefficient of determination. Give a brief explanation of the meaning of the correlation coefficient and the coefficient of determination in the context of this problem. **10.** ______

11. Compute the standard error of estimate S_e. **11.** ______

12. Suppose that the amount spent on advertising is $37,000. What does the least-squares line predict for the increase in sales? **12.** ______

13. Find a 95% confidence interval for your prediction of Problem 12. **13.** ______

14. Using the sample correlation coefficient r computed in Problem 10, test whether or not the population correlation coefficient p is positive. Use $\alpha = 0.05$. Is r significant in this problem? Explain. **14.** ______

CHAPTER 10 TEST FORM B

For the given data, solve the following problems.

Do higher paid chief executive officers (CEO's) control bigger companies? Let us study x = annual CEO salary ($ millions) and y = annual company revenue ($ billions). The following data are based on information from *Forbes* magazine and represents a sample of top US executives.

x ($ millions)	0.8	1.0	1.1	1.7	2.3
y ($ billions)	14	11	19	20	25

1. Draw a scatter diagram. Using the scatter diagram (no calculations) would you estimate the linear correlation coefficient to be positive, close to zero, or negative? Explain your answer.

1.

2. For the given data compute each of the following.

(a) $\overline{x}$ and $\overline{y}$

(b) SS_x, SS_y, SS_{xy}

(c) The slope b and y intercept a of the least squares line; write out the equation for the least squares line.

(d) Graph the least squares line on your scatter plot of problem 1.

2. (a) ______________________

(b) ______________________

(c) ______________________

(d) ______________________

3. Compute the sample correlation coefficient r. Compute the coefficient of determination. Give a brief explanation of the meaning of the correlation coefficient and the coefficient of determination in the context of this problem.

3. ______________________

4. Compute the standard error of estimate S_e.

4. ______________________

5. If a CEO has an annual salary of 1.5 million, what is his or her annual company revenue as predicted by the least squares line?

5. ______________________

6. Find a 90% confidence interval for your prediction of Problem 5.

6. ______________________

7. Using the sample correlation coefficient r computed in Problem 3, test whether or not the population correlation coefficient p is different from zero. Use $\alpha = 0.01$. Is r significant in this problem? Explain.

7. ______________________

CHAPTER 10, FORM B, PAGE 2

For the given data, solve the following problems.

An accountant for a small manufacturing plant collected the following random sample to study the relationship between x = the cost to make a particular item and y = the selling price.

x ($)	26	50	47	23	52	71
y ($)	78	132	128	70	152	198

8. Draw a scatter diagram. Using the scatter diagram (no calculations) would you estimate the linear correlation coefficient to be positive, close to zero, or negative? Explain your answer.

8.

9. For the given data compute each of the following.

(a) $\overline{x}$ and $\overline{y}$

(b) SS_x, SS_y, SS_{xy}

(c) The slope b and y intercept a of the least squares line; write out the equation for the least squares line.

(d) Graph the least squares line on your scatter plot of problem 8.

9. (a) ______________

(b) ______________

(c) ______________

(d) ______________

10. Compute the sample correlation coefficient r. Compute the coefficient of determination. Give a brief explanation of the meaning of the correlation coefficient and the coefficient of determination in the context of this problem.

10. ______________

11. Compute the standard error of estimate S_e.

11. ______________

12. Suppose that the cost to make a particular item is $35. What does the least-squares line predict for the selling price?

12. ______________

13. Find a 95% confidence interval for your prediction of Problem 12.

13. ______________

14. Using the sample correlation coefficient r computed in Problem 10, test whether or not the population correlation coefficient p is positive. Use $\alpha = 0.05$. Is r significant in this problem? Explain.

14. ______________

CHAPTER 10 TEST
FORM C

Write the letter of the response that best answers each problem.

Does the weight of a vehicle affect the gas mileage? The following random sample was collected where x = weight of a vehicle in hundreds of pounds and y = miles per gallon.

x (lb hundreds)	26	35	29	39	20
y (mpg)	22.0	16.1	18.8	15.7	23.4

1. Based on a scatter diagram, would you estimate the linear correlation coefficient to be **1.** ________

(a) close to −1 (b) closer to 0 and negative
(c) close to 1 (d) closer to 0 and positive (e) Cannot determine

2. What is the equation for the least squares line? **2.** ________

(a) $y = -32.55x + 0.448$ (b) $y = -32.55x - 0.448$
(c) $y = -32.55x + 0.448$ (d) $y = -0.448x + 32.55$ (e) $y = 0.448x - 32.55$

3. Compute the coefficient of determination. **3.** ________

(a) −0.941 (b) 0.941
(c) −0.970 (d) 0.970 (e) 0.965

4. Compute the standard error of estimate S_e. **4.** ________

(a) 0.965 (b) −0.970
(c) 0.941 (d) 1.975 (e) 0.065

5. If a vehicle weighs 2200 pounds, what does the least-squares line predict for the miles per gallon? **5.** ________

(a) 22.7 (b) 66.0
(c) 42.4 (d) 22.0 (e) Cannot determine

CHAPTER 10, FORM C, PAGE 2

6. Find a 90% confidence interval for your prediction of Problem 5. **6.** ________

(a) 21.1 mpg $\leq y \leq$ 24.3 mpg (b) 19.5 mpg $\leq y \leq$ 25.9 mpg

(c) 19.9 mpg $\leq y \leq$ 25.5 mpg (d) 19.0 mpg $\leq y \leq$ 26.4 mpg

(e) 20.6 mpg $\leq y \leq$ 24.8 mpg

7. Using the sample correlation coefficient r, test whether or not the population correlation coefficient p is different from zero. Use $\alpha = 0.01$. Is r significant in this problem? Explain. **7.** ________

(a) Do not reject H_0; r is not significant (b) Reject H_0; r is significant

(c) Do not reject H_0; r is significant (d) Reject H_0; r is not significant

(e) Cannot determine

Write the letter of the response that best answers each problem.

A graduate school committee is studying the relationship between x = an applicants' undergraduate grade point average and y = the applicants' score on the graduate entrance exam. The following random sample was collected to study this relationship.

x (GPA)	3.2	3.9	4.0	3.4	3.7	3.0
y (score)	725	788	775	647	800	672

8. Based on a scatter diagram, would you estimate the linear correlation coefficient to be **8.** ________

(a) close to -1 (b) closer to 0 and negative

(c) close to 1 (d) closer to 0 and positive (e) Cannot determine

9. What is the equation for the least squares line? **9.** ________

(a) $y = -123.03x + 299.8$ (b) $y = 123.03x - 299.8$

(c) $y = 299.8x + 123.03$ (d) $y = -299.8x + 123.03$ (e) $y = 123.03x + 299.8$

CHAPTER 10, FORM C, PAGE 3

10. Compute the sample correlation coefficient. **10.** ________

(a) 0.587 (b) −0.766

(c) 0.875 (d) 0.766 (e) −0.586

11. Compute the standard error of estimate S_e. **11.** ________

(a) 45.93 (b) 0.766

(c) 183.2 (d) 51.6 (e) 0.587

12. If a student has a grade point average of 3.5, what does the least-squares line predict for the score on the graduate entrance exam? **12.** ________

(a) 926.3 (b) 3.5

(c) 730.4 (d) 130.8 (e) 1172.3

13. Find a 95% confidence interval for your prediction of Problem 12. **13.** ________

(a) $690.3 \le y \le 770.5$ (b) $678.1 \le y \le 782.7$

(c) $624.6 \le y \le 836.2$ (d) $629.3 \le y \le 831.5$

(e) $592.6 \le y \le 868.2$

14. Using the sample correlation coefficient r, test whether or not the population correlation coefficient p is positive. Use $\alpha = 0.05$. Is r significant in this problem? Explain. **14.** ________

(a) Do not reject H_0; r is significant (b) Do not reject H_0; r is not significant

(c) Reject H_0; r is significant (d) Reject H_0; r is significant

(e) Cannot determine

CHAPTER 11 TEST FORM A

1. Are teacher evaluations independent of grades? After midterm, a random sample of 284 students were asked to evaluate teacher performance. The students were also asked to supply their midterm grade in the course being evaluated. In this study, only students with a passing grade (A, B, or C) were included in the summary table.

	Mid Term Grade			
Teacher Evaluation	A	B	C	Row Total
Positive	53	33	18	104
Neutral	25	46	29	100
Negative	14	22	44	80
Column Total	92	101	91	284

Use a 5% level of significance to test the claim that teacher evaluations are independent of midterm grades. **1.** ______________________

2. How old are college students? The national age distributions for college students is shown below.

National Age Distribution for College Students

Age	Under 26	26–35	36–45	46–55	Over 55
Clients	39%	25%	16%	12%	8%

The Western Association of Mountain Colleges took a random sample of 212 students and obtained the following sample distribution.

Sample Distribution, Western Association of Mountain Colleges

Age	Under 26	26–35	36–45	46–55	Over 55
Number of Students	65	73	41	21	12

Is the sample age distribution for the Western Association of Mountain Colleges a good fit to the national distribution? Use $\alpha = 0.05$. **2.** ______________________

3. If we have a normal population with variance σ^2 and a random sample of n measurements taken from this population, what probability distribution do we use to test claims about the variance? **3.** ______________________

CHAPTER 11, FORM A, PAGE 2

4. A technician tested 25 motors for toy electric trains and found the sample standard deviation of electrical current to be $s = 4.9$ amperes.

(a) Find a 95% confidence interval for σ, the population standard deviation of electric current in all such toy trains. **4. (a)** ____________

(b) If the manufacturer specifies that $\sigma = 4.1$ amperes, does the sample data indicate that σ is larger than 4.1? Use a 1% level of significance. **(b)** ____________

5. Two methods of manufacturing large roller bearings are under study. For Method I, a random sample of $n_1 = 16$ bearings had sample standard deviation of diameters $s_1 = 2.9$ mm. For Method II, a random sample of 18 bearings had sample standard deviation of diameters $s_2 = 1.2$ mm. Assume the diameters follow a normal distribution. Test the claim that $\sigma_1^2 > \sigma_2^2$ using a 1% level of significance. **5.** ____________

6. Sasha has decided to buy one of four different cars. She is interested in whether there is a difference in the gas mileage of the cars. In a study, miles per gallon were obtained for a random sample for each of the four cars. The results of a one-way ANOVA test are summarized below.

ANOVA for mpg

Source	*SS*	*d.f.*	*MS*
Between Groups	65.43	3	21.81
Within Groups	216.29	24	9.01
Number of Students	281.71	27	

Use a 5% level of significance to test whether there is a difference among the population means. **6.** ____________

7. A study to determine if management style affects the number of sick leave days taken by employees in a department was conducted. Three departments with the same number of employees were studied. The management style used in one department was top down with employees having little input into decisions; in another department, quality control experts made recommendations; in the last department the management gathered input informally from the employees. The total number of sick leave days taken per month by all of the employees in the department was recorded. For a random sample of 3 months, the numbers follow:

Top Down Management:	19	34	28
Quality Teams:	16	21	15
Informal Input:	15	12	14

Use a one-way ANOVA to test if the mean number of sick leave days for departments managed in the various styles are different. Use $\alpha = 0.05$. **7.** ____________

CHAPTER 11, FORM A, PAGE 3

8. Will students perform better if they can choose the section of a course in which they enroll? Does the class status of the student make a difference? A researcher is studying this question. Four blocks of students are formed according to class status: freshman, sophomore, junior, senior. Each of the students must enroll in the course Spanish I. The researcher selects a random sample of 10 students from each of the blocks and allows them to enroll in the section of their choice. Another random sample of 10 students from each block are assigned a section of Spanish I. At the end of the semester, all students take the same final exam. The researcher records the scores and compares the scores for all the students participating in the study.

(a) Draw a flowchart showing the design of this experiment. **8. (a)** ______________________

(b) Does the design fit the model for a two-way ANOVA randomized block design? Explain. **(b)** ______________________

9. James drives to work each morning during rush-hour. Does commute time depend on route? Does it depend on time of departure? In a study, the times (in minutes) were gathered for random samples. There were four different routes and three different departure times. The results of a two-way ANOVA test are summarized below.

ANOVA

Source	*SS*	*d.f.*	*MS*
Route	613.4	3	204.5
Departure Time	19.1	2	9.5
Interaction	357.2	6	59.5
Error	982.7	24	40.9
Total	1972.4	35	

(a) Test to see if there is any evidence of interaction between the two factors at a level of significance of 0.01. **9. (a)** ______________________

(b) If there is no evidence of interaction, test to see if there is a difference in mean time based on route. Use $\alpha = 0.01$. **(b)** ______________________

(c) If there is no evidence of interaction, test to see if there is a difference in mean time based on departure time. Use $\alpha = 0.01$. **(c)** ______________________

CHAPTER 11 TEST FORM B

1. Is the choice of college major independent of grade average? A random sample of 445 students were surveyed by the Registrar's Office regarding major field of study and grade average. In this study, only students with passing grades (A, B, or C) were included in the survey. Grade averages were rounded to the nearest letter grade (e.g. 3.6 grade point average was rounded to 4.0 or A).

	Grade Average			
Major	A	B	C	Row Total
Science	38	49	63	150
Business	41	42	59	142
Humanities	32	53	68	153
Column Total	111	144	190	445

Use a 1% level of significance to test the claim that choice of major field is independent of grade average.

1. ____________________

2. The Fish and Game Department in Wisconsin stocked a new lake with the following distribution of game fish.

Initial Stocking Distribution

Fish	Pike	Trout	Perch	Bass	Bluegill
Percent	10%	15%	20%	25%	30%

After six years a random sample of 197 fish from the lake were netted, identified, and released. The sample distribution is shown next.

Sample Distribution after Six Years

Fish	Pike	Trout	Perch	Bass	Bluegill
Number	52	15	33	55	42

Is the sample distribution of fish in the lake after six years a good fit to the initial stocking distribution? Use a 5% level of significance.

2. ____________________

3. If we have two normal populations with equal variances and random samples n_1 and n_2 are taken from these populations, what probability distribution do we use to test claims about the variances?

3. ____________________

CHAPTER 11, FORM B, PAGE 2

4. An automobile service station times the Quick Lube service for a random sample of 22 customers. The sample standard deviation of times was $s = 6.8$ minutes.

(a) Find a 90% confidence interval for σ, the population standard deviation of Quick Lube times. **4. (a)** ____________________

(b) The service manager specifies that σ be 6.0 minutes. Does the sample data indicate that σ is different from 6.0? Use a 1% level of significance. **(b)** ____________________

5. A large national chain of department stores has two basic inventories. Variation of cash flow for the two types of inventories is under study. A random sample of $n_1 = 9$ stores with Inventory I had sample standard deviation of daily cash flow $s_1 = \$3115$. Another random sample of $n_2 = 11$ stores with Inventory II had sample standard deviation of daily cash flow $s_2 = \$2719$. Assume daily cash flow follows a normal distribution. Test the claim that the population variances of two inventories are different. Use a 5% level of significance. **5.** ____________________

6. Elizabeth watches the sodium content of foods because she has high blood pressure. The sodium content was measured for random samples from each of four different brands of tuna. The results of a one-way ANOVA test are summarized below.

ANOVA for sodium content

Source	*SS*	*d.f.*	*MS*
Between Groups	11,786	3	3929
Within Groups	17,979	20	899
Total	29,766	23	

Use a 5% level of significance to test whether there is a difference among the population means. **6.** ____________________

7. A study of depression and exercise was conducted. Three groups were used: those in a designed exercise program; a group that is sedentary; and a group of runners. A depression rating (higher scores meaning more depression) was given to the participants in each group. Small random samples from each group provided the following data on the depression rating.

Treatment Group:	63	58	61
Sedentary Group:	71	64	68
Runners:	49	52	47

Use a one-way ANOVA to test if the mean depression ratings for the three groups are different. Use $\alpha = 0.05$. **7.** ____________________

CHAPTER 11, FORM B, PAGE 3

8. A study was conducted to measure sales volume of a grocery store item. The study looked at sales volume for the product placed in 3 different shelf locations: eye level, low, special display. In addition, the study looked at sales volume for the item when it was advertised in two different ways: on TV or with newspaper coupons. A two-way ANOVA test was used to determine if there was any difference in mean sales volume according to shelf location or advertising method.

(a) List the factors and the levels of each factor for this study. **8. (a)** ____________________

(b) Explain what it means to have interaction between the factors. State the null and the alternate hypotheses used to test for interaction. **(b)** ____________________

9. A travel agent primarily reserves flights with four major airlines. The agent would like to know if the price depends on the airline or if the price depends on the destination. In a study, the prices were gathered for random samples. There were four different airlines and four different destinations. The results of a two-way ANOVA test are summarized below.

ANOVA

Source	*SS*	*d.f.*	*MS*
Airline	19,080	3	6,360
Destination	326,793	2	163,397
Interaction	49,168	6	8,195
Error	230,050	24	9,585
Total	625,091	35	

(a) Test to see if there is any evidence of interaction between the two factors at a level of significance of 0.05. **9. (a)** ____________________

(b) If there is no evidence of interaction, test to see if there is a difference in mean price based on airline. Use α - 0.05. **(b)** ____________________

(c) If there is no evidence of interaction, test to see if there is a difference in mean price based on destination. Use $\alpha = 0.05$. **(c)** ____________________

CHAPTER 11 TEST
FORM C

Write the letter of the response that best answers each problem.

1. A market research study was conducted to compare three different brands of antiperspirant. The results of the study are summarized below. Use a 5% level of significant to test the claim that opinion is independent of brank.

	Brand			
Opinion	A	B	C	Total
Excellent	29	37	50	116
Satisfactory	83	65	43	191
Unsatisfactory	18	9	6	33
Total	130	111	99	340

A. State the null and alternate hypotheses. **1. A.** ________

(a) H_0: Opinion and brand are dependent; H_1: Opinion and brand are independent

(b) H_0: $\mu_A = \mu_B = \mu_C$; H_1: Not all μ_1, μ_2, μ_3, are equal.

(c) H_0: Opinion and brand are independent; H_1: Opinion and brand are dependent

(d) H_0: $\sigma_1^2 = \sigma_2^2$; H_1: $\mu_1 = \mu_2$

(e) H_0: The distributions are normal; H_1: The distributions are not normal

B. What is the critical value (or critical values)? **B.** ________

(a) $\chi^2_{0.05} = 0.711$ (b) $\chi^2_{0.05} = 16.92$

(c) $z_0 = 1.645$ (d) $\chi^2_{0.05} = 9.49$ (e) $F_0 = 19.00$

C. What is the value of the sample test statistic? **C.** ________

(a) $\chi^2 = 19.00$ (b) $\chi^2 = 9.49$

(c) $t = 0.25$ (d) $F = 0.10$ (e) $\chi^2 = 21.4$

D. What is your conclusion? **D.** ________

(a) Reject H_0 (b) Do not reject H_0 (c) Cannot determine

(d) Brand A is the best.

(e) All of the brands work equally well.

CHAPTER 11, FORM C, PAGE 2

2. How much do second graders weigh? A county hospital found the weight distribution shown below.

Hospital Weight Distribution

Weight (lb)	Under 45	45–59	60–74	75–89	Over 89
Percent	7%	21%	41%	19%	12%

An elementary school within the county took a random sample of 125 second graders and obtained the following sample distribution.

Sample Distribution, Elementary School

Weight (lb)	Under 45	45–59	60–74	75–89	Over 89
Number of Second Graders	6	29	50	30	10

Is the sample weight distribution for the elementary school a good fit to the hospital distribution? Use $\alpha = 0.05$.

A. State the null and alternate hypotheses. **2. A.** ________

(a) H_0: $\mu_1 = \mu_2 = \mu_3 = \mu_4 = \mu_5$; H_1: Not all μ_1, μ_2, μ_3, are equal.

(b) H_0: Weight and percent are independent; H_1: Weight and percent are dependent

(c) H_0: $\sigma_1^2 = \sigma_2^2$; H_1: $\mu_1 = \mu_2$

(d) H_0: The distributions are the same; H_1: The distributions are different.

(e) H_0: The distributions are the same; H_1: The distributions for elementary school are higher.

B. What is the critical value (or critical values)? **B.** ________

(a) $\chi^2_{0.05} = 9.49$ (b) $\chi^2_{0.05} = 11.07$

(c) $\chi^2_{0.05} = 0.711$ (d) $\chi^2_{0.05} = 1.145$ (e) $t_0 = 2.776$

C. What is the value of the sample test statistic? **C.** ________

(a) $\chi^2 = 11.07$ (b) $\chi^2 = 5.35$

(c) $\chi^2 = 4.49$ (d) $t = 7.27$ (e) $\chi^2 = 9.49$

D. What is your conclusion? **D.** ________

(a) Reject H_0 (b) Do not reject H_0 (c) Cannot determine

(d) The elementary school has heavier second graders.

(e) The means are the same.

CHAPTER 11, FORM C, PAGE 3

3. Find the χ^2 value for each situation.

A. 1% of the area under the curve is to the right of χ^2 when *d.f.* = 18. **3. A.** __________

(a) 33.41 (b) 7.01 (c) 37.16 (d) 6.41 (e) 34.81

B. 5% of the area under the curve is to the left of χ^2 when *d.f.* = 15. **B.** __________

(a) 6.57 (b) 25.00 (c) 7.26 (d) 23.00 (e) 6.26

C. 5% of the area under the curve is to the right of χ^2 when $n = 20$. **B.** __________

(a) 10.12 (b) 31.41 (c) 32.85 (d) 30.14 (e) 10.85

4. A salesperson tested 30 sport utility vehicles for gas mileage (in miles per gallon) and found the sample standard deviation to be $s = 4.7$ mpg.

A. Find a 95% confidence interval for σ^2, the population variance of mileage for all such sport utility vehicles. **4. A.** __________

(a) $14.01 < \sigma^2 < 39.91$ (b) $15.05 < \sigma^2 < 36.17$

(c) $2.98 < \sigma^2 < 8.49$ (d) $14.49 < \sigma^2 < 41.29$ (e) $13.64 < \sigma^2 < 36.65$

B. If the manufacturer specifies that $\sigma = 4.0$ mpg, does the sample data indicate that σ is larger than 4.0? Use $\alpha = 0.01$ and compute the critical value and the value of the sample test statistic. **B.** __________

(a) $\chi^2_{0.01} = 40.04, \chi^2 = 49.59$ (b) $\chi^2_{0.01} = 14.26, \chi^2 = 40.04$

(c) $\chi^2_{0.01} = 52.34, \chi^2 = 41.42$ (d) $\chi^2_{0.01} = 50.89, \chi^2 = 41.42$

(e) $\chi^2_{0.01} = 49.59, \chi^2 = 40.04$

C. What is your conclusion for the test in Part B? **C.** __________

(a) There is sufficient evidence to conclude that the standard deviation is larger than 4.0 mpg.

(b) The distributions are different.

(c) The variances are unequal.

(d) The mpg for the sample is larger than 4.0 mpg.

(e) There is insufficient evidence to conclude that the standard deviation is larger than 4.0 mpg.

CHAPTER 11, FORM C, PAGE 4

5. Two printing machines are under study. For Machine I, a random sample of $n_1 = 10$ newspapers had a sample standard deviation of time $s_1 = 1.4$ minute. For Machine II, a random sample of $n_2 = 12$ newspapers had a sample standard deviation of $s_2 = 0.8$ minutes. Assume the times follow a normal distribution. Test the claim that $\sigma_1^2 > \sigma_2^2$ using a 1% level of significance.

A. State the null and alternate hypotheses. **5. A.** ____________

(a) H_0: $\sigma_1^2 > \sigma_2^2$; H_1: $\sigma_1^2 = \sigma_2^2$ (b) H_0: $\sigma^2 = 0$; H_1: $\sigma^2 > 0$

(c) H_0: $\sigma_1^2 = \sigma_2^2$; H_1: $\sigma_1^2 \neq \sigma_2^2$ (d) H_0: $\sigma_1^2 = \sigma_2^2$; H_1: $\sigma_1^2 < \sigma_2^2$

(e) H_0: $\sigma_1^2 = \sigma_2^2$; H_1: $\sigma_1^2 > \sigma_2^2$

B. What is the critical value (or critical values)? **B.** ____________

(a) $F_{0.01} = 4.71$ (b) $t_0 = 2.845$

(c) $z_0 = -2.33$ (d) $F_{0.01} = 2.90$ (e) $F_{0.01} = 4.63$

C. What is the value of the sample test statistic? **C.** ____________

(a) $F = 0.33$ (b) $F = 1.75$

(c) $F = 3.06$ (d) $t = 3.06$ (e) $F = 0.57$

D. What is your conclusion? **D.** ____________

(a) Reject H_0 (b) Do not reject H_0 (c) Cannot determine

(d) The variances are different.

(e) The distributions are different.

6. Do cough medicines differ in the length of time of relief? The hours of relief was recorded for random samples of volunteers from each of four different brands of cough medicine. The results of ANOVA test are summarized below.

ANOVA

Source	*SS*	*d.f.*	*MS*
Between Groups	6.17	3	2.056
Within Groups	27.26	28	0.974
Total	33.43	31	

Use a 5% level of significance to test whether there is a difference among the population means.

CHAPTER 11, FORM C, PAGE 5

A. What are the null and alternate hypotheses? **6. A.** ________

(a) H_0: $\mu_1 = \mu_2 = \mu_3 = \mu_4$; H_1: Not all of the means are equal.

(b) H_0: $\mu_1 = \mu_2 = \mu_3 = \mu_4$; H_1: $\mu_1 > \mu_2 > \mu_3 > \mu_4$

(c) H_0: $\mu_1 = \mu_2 = \mu_3$; H_1: Not all of the means are equal.

(d) H_0: $\sigma_1^2 = \sigma_2^2 = \sigma_3^2 = \sigma_4^2$; H_1: $\sigma_1^2 \neq \sigma_2^2 \neq \sigma_3^2 \neq \sigma_4^2$

(e) H_0: $\mu_1 \neq \mu_2 \neq \mu_3 \neq \mu_4$; H_1: $\mu_1 = \mu_2 = \mu_3 = \mu_4$

B. What is the critical value? **B.** ________

(a) $F_{0.05} = 8.62$ (b) $F_{0.05} = 2.92$

(c) $x^2_{0.05} = 7.81$ (d) $F_{0.05} = 2.95$ (e) $\chi^2_{0.05} = 0.352$

C. What is the value of the sample test statistic? **C.** ________

(a) $F = 6.85$ (b) $F = 2.056$

(c) $F = 0.974$ (d) $F = 0.035$ (e) $F = 2.11$

D. What is your conclusion? **D.** ________

(a) Reject H_0 (b) Do not reject H_0 (c) Cannot determine

(d) The distributions are the same.

(e) The variances are unequal.

7. An ornithologist is studying the length (in seconds) of bird calls. Random samples from three different breeds yielded the following results.

Breed 1	2.3	1.9	2.1
Breed 2	0.8	1.2	1.1
Breed 3	2.0	1.4	1.7

Use one-way ANOVA to test if the mean call length differs for the three breeds. Use $\alpha = 0.05$.

CHAPTER 11, FORM C, PAGE 6

A. What are the null and alternate hypotheses? **7. A.** ________

(a) H_0: $\mu_1 \neq \mu_2 \neq \mu_3$; H_1: $\mu_1 = \mu_2 = \mu_3$

(b) H_0: $\sigma_1^2 = \sigma_2^2 = \sigma_3^2$; H_1: $\sigma_1^2 \neq \sigma_2^2 \neq \sigma_3^2$

(c) H_0: $\mu_1 = \mu_2 = \mu_3$; H_1: Not all of μ_1, μ_2, μ_3 are equal.

(d) H_0: $\mu_1 \neq \mu_2 \neq \mu_3$; H_1: $\mu_1 > \mu_2 > \mu_3$

(e) H_0: The distributions are the same; H_1: The distributions are not the same.

B. What is the critical value? **B.** ________

(a) $F_{0.05} = 8.62$ (b) $F_{0.05} = 2.92$

(c) $F_{0.05} = 7.81$ (d) $F_{0.05}^2 = 5.14$ (e) $\chi_{0.05}^2 = 12.59$

C. What is the value of the sample test statistic? **C.** ________

(a) $F = 0.09$ (b) $F = 19.33$

(c) $\chi^2 = 15.08$ (d) $F = 15.08$ (e) $F = 5.14$

D. What is your conclusion? **D.** ________

(a) Reject H_0 (b) Do not reject H_0 (c) Cannot determine

(d) The distributions are the same.

(e) The variances are the same.

8. When performing a two-way ANOVA test, which of the following is not a required assumption? **8.** ________

(a) There are the same number of measurements in each cell.

(b) The measurements in each cell of a two-way ANOVA model are assumed to come from distributions with approximately the same variance.

(c) There are the same number of levels for each factor.

(d) The measurements in each cell come from independent random samples.

(e) The measurements in each cell of a two-way ANOVA model are assumed to be drawn from a population with a normal distribution.

CHAPTER 11, FORM C, PAGE 7

9. Are differences in test scores due to schools or are they due to exam forms? Three different, although supposedly equivalent, forms of a standardized achievement exam were given to a random sample of students in each of four different schools. Their scores were recorded. The results of a two-way ANOVA test are summarized below.

ANOVA

Source	*SS*	*d.f.*	*MS*
Exam Form	3532	2	1766
School	749	3	250
Interaction	768	6	128
Error	4917	24	205
Total	9965	35	

A. When conducting a test to see if there is evidence of interaction between the factors, what are the critical *F* values and the value of the test statistic? Use $\alpha = 0.05$.

9. A. ________

(a) $F_{0.05} = 3.40$; $F = 8.61$ (b) $F_{0.05} = 3.01$; $F = 1.22$

(c) $F_{0.05} = 2.51$; $F = 0.62$ (d) $F_{0.05} = 2.38$; $F = 0.62$

(e) $F_{0.05} = 2.51$; $F = 8.62$

B. What is your conclusion from the test in Part A?

B. ________

(a) Do not reject H_0; There is evidence of interaction.

(b) Do not reject H_0; There is no evidence of interaction.

(c) Reject H_0; There is evidence of interaction.

(d) Reject H_0; There is no evidence of interaction.

(e) Cannot determine.

C. Assume that there is no evidence of interaction between the factors. When conducting a test to see if there is a difference in mean scores based on an exam form, what are the critical *F* value and the value of the test statistic? Use $\alpha = 0.05$.

C. ________

(a) $F_{0.05} = 3.40$; $F = 8.61$ (b) $F_{0.05} = 2.51$; $F = 1.22$

(c) $F_{0.05} = 8.61$; $F = 3.40$ (d) $F_{0.05} = 1.22$; $F = 3.40$

(e) $F_{0.05} = 3.01$; $F = 8.61$

CHAPTER 11, FORM C, PAGE 8

D. Assume that there is no evidence of interaction between the factors. When conducting a test to see if there is a difference in mean scores based on school, what are the critical F value and the value of the test statistic? Use $\alpha = 0.05$.

D. __________

(a) $F_{0.05} = 3.40$; $F = 8.62$

(b) $F_{0.05} = 3.01$; $F = 0.62$

(c) $F_{0.05} = 2.51$; $F = 1.22$

(d) $F_{0.05} = 3.01$ $F = 1.22$

(e) $F_{0.05} = 1.22$; $F = 3.01$

E. What are your conclusions from the tests in Part C and D?

E. __________

(a) Cannot determine.

(b) Do not reject H_0 from C; Do not reject H_0 from D.

(c) Do not reject H_0 from C; Reject H_0 from D.

(d) Reject H_0 from C; Reject H_0 from D.

(e) Reject H_0 from C; Do not reject H_0 from D.

CHAPTER 12 TEST FORM A

1. The shift managers believe delivery trucks could be loaded in less time. A training program was implemented to help the employees be more efficient. The data below represent the times, in minutes, that each of 16 employees required to load the same truck before and after the program. Use a 0.05 level of significance to test the claim that the times are smaller after the program.

1. ____________________

Employee	After	Before
1	39	42
2	47	38
3	40	45
4	50	57
5	31	37
6	28	30
7	41	41
8	47	45
9	35	38
10	50	50
11	67	62
12	50	59
13	39	57
14	38	38
15	45	47
16	56	55

2. The management of a large retail store did a study of sales in different departments last year and this year and ranked the departments by sales volume (with lowest rank meaning highest sales). The data follow.

Department	1	2	3	4	5	6	7	8
Last Year Rank	1	7	4	5	3	2	6	8
This Year Rank	1	6	5	7	2	3	4	8

Test the claim at the 0.01 level of significance that there is a monotone relation either way between last year's and this year's performance.

2. ____________________

CHAPTER 12, FORM A, PAGE 2

3. A workshop on harmony in the work place was given to a randomly selected group of employees. Another group did not participate in the workshop. A test measuring sensitivity to other viewpoints was given to both groups with higher scores indicating more sensitivity. The results follow.

Workshop Participant	73	81	91	56	78	83	52	92
Non-Workshop	85	70	74	55	90	48	75	86

Test the claim at the 5% level of significance that there is a difference either way in the average sensitivity score for the two groups.

3. ______________________

4. A high school science teacher decided to give a series of lectures on current events. To determine if the lectures had any effect on student awareness of current events, an exam was given to the class before the lectures, and a similar exam was given after the lectures. The scores follow. Use a 0.05 level of significance to test the claim that the lectures mad no difference against the claim that the lectures did make some difference (either up or down).

Student	After Lectures	Before Lectures
1	107	111
2	115	110
3	120	93
4	78	75
5	83	88
6	56	56
7	71	75
8	89	73
9	77	83
10	44	40
11	119	115
12	130	101
13	91	110

4. ______________________

5. Describe when the sign test is used.

5. ______________________

CHAPTER 12 TEST
FORM B

1. A design specialist believes she has developed a new computer keyboard that is more comfortable and more efficient to use than a standard keyboard. The times for 14 different people were recorded for a manuscript typed on the standard keyboard and a similar manuscript typed on the new keyboard. Use a 0.05 level of significance to test the claim that the times are less for the new keyboard. **1.** ____________________

Typist	New	Standard
1	30	28
2	35	37
3	20	29
4	39	32
5	47	40
6	31	31
7	30	39
8	41	44
9	45	50
10	36	36
11	38	31
12	40	45
13	21	30
14	30	37

2. Professor Smith gives a midterm and final exam. For a random sample of ten students, the class rank on the two exams follow, with a lower rank number meaning a higher score.

Student	1	2	3	4	5	6	7	8	9	10
Midterm	5	3	1	7	10	2	8	4	6	9
Final	9	4	5	7	8	3	6	1	2	10

Test the claim that there is a monotone increasing relation between the ranks of the two exams. Use a 5% level of significance. **2.** ____________________

CHAPTER 12, FORM B, PAGE 2

3. A random sample of households with an income level below \$30,000 were asked to record the number of hours per week someone in the household was watching TV. A random sample of households with income level at or above \$30,000 were asked to record the same information. The results follow.

Less than \$30,000	100	40	35	70	80	90	15	75
\$30,000 or more	85	62	41	37	45	91	30	10

Test the claim at the 5% level of significance that there is a difference either way in the average number of hours households in the two income categories watch TV. **3.** ______________

4. A self confidence inventory instrument was administered to a group of students before and after a self confidence training workshop. The scores follow with a higher score indicating more self confidence.

Student	1	2	3	4	5	6	7	8	9	10	11	12	13	14
Before	35	42	37	45	43	47	33	37	35	32	41	40	39	42
After	40	38	37	43	45	46	41	40	36	45	44	45	38	39

Use a 5% level of significance to test the hypothesis that the mean scores were higher after the workshop. **4.** ______________

5. Describe when the rank-sum test (also called the Mann-Whitney test) is used. **5.** ______________

CHAPTER 12 TEST
FORM C

Write the letter of the response that best answers each problem.

1. A study group is interested in whether environment improves test scores. An exam was given to 15 students in a standard (old) classroom and a similar exam was given in a new testing area. The standard classrooms provided a small desk for each student and was lit by overhead fluorescent lights. The new testing area was twice the size of the standard classroom, provided a table for each student, and was lit by natural sunlight from large windows. Use a 0.05 level of significance to test the claim that scores are higher in the new testing area.

Student	New	Old
1	90	87
2	85	80
3	93	93
4	74	76
5	81	80
6	76	65
7	90	79
8	95	95
9	100	98
10	76	70
11	67	69
12	88	92
13	79	70
14	80	66
15	93	90

A. What are the null and alternate hypotheses? **1. A.** ________

(a) H_0: $\mu_{new} = \mu_{old}$; H_1: $\mu_{new} \neq \mu_{old}$

(b) H_0: $\mu_{new} = \mu_{old}$; H_1: $\mu_{new} < \mu_{old}$

(c) H_0: The distributions are the same; H_1: The distribution for new is higher.

(d) H_0: The distributions are the same; H_1: The distributions are different.

(e) H_0: $\rho_s = 0$; H_1: $\rho_s > 0$

B. What is the critical value (or critical values)? **B.** ________

(a) $t_0 = 1.645$ (b) $z_0 = \pm 1.96$

(c) $z_0 = 2.33$ (d) $z_0 = \pm 2.58$ (e) $z_0 = 1.645$

CHAPTER 12, FORM C, PAGE 2

C. Calculate the z value of the sample test statistic. **C.** ________

(a) $z = 1.29$ (b) $z = 2.09$

(c) $z = \frac{10}{13} \approx 0.77$ (d) $z = 1.94$ (e) $z = \frac{10}{15} \approx 0.67$

D. What is your conclusion? **D.** ________

(a) Reject H_0 (b) Do not reject H_0 (c) Cannot determine

(d) The distributions are the same.

(e) Testing in the new environment is difficult.

2. The management of a pharmaceutical company compiled the sales volume for 9 employees last year and this year. Listed below are the ranks of the employees by sales volume (with lowest rank meaning highest sales). Test the claim at the 0.01 level of significance that there is a monotone relation either way between last year's and this year's sales.

Salesperson	1	2	3	4	5	6	7	8	9
Last Year Rank	8	2	5	1	6	3	9	4	7
This Year Rank	8	1	7	3	5	2	9	4	6

A. What are the null and alternate hypotheses? **2. A.** ________

(a) H_0: The distributions are the same; H_1: The distributions are different.

(b) H_0: $\rho_s = 0$; H_1: $\rho_s \neq 0$

(c) H_0: TheThere is no monotone relation; H_1: There is a monotone-increasing relation

(d) H_0: $\mu_1 = \mu_2$; H_1: $\mu_1 \, ? \, \mu_2$

(e) H_0: $\rho_s = 0$; H_1: $\rho_s > 0$

B. What is the critical value (or critical values)? **B.** ________

(a) ±2.896 (b) 0.881

(c) 0.834 (d) ±0.834 (e) 3.355

CHAPTER 12, FORM C, PAGE 3

C. Calculate the observed value of the sample test statistic. **C.** ________

(a) $r_s = 0.834$ (b) $r_s = 0.881$

(c) $z = 2.33$ (d) $t = \frac{2}{3} \approx 0.67$ (e) $r_s = 0.900$

D. What is your conclusion? **D.** ________

(a) Reject H_0 (b) Do not reject H_0 (c) Cannot determine

(d) The distributions are the same.

(e) The salespeople are doing a great job.

3. A mathematics teacher teaches multiplication using two different methods. Two groups of eight students were taught a list of multiplication equations using the two different methods, one method for each group. The time required to learn the list using each method is shown below (in minutes). Use a 0.05 level of significance to test the claim that there is no difference in learning times.

Method 1	43	39	47	56	35	52	90	74
Method 2	71	48	59	88	30	69	28	60

A. What are the null and alternate hypotheses? **3. A.** ________

(a) H_0: $\rho_s = 0$; H_1: $\rho_s \neq 0$

(b) H_0: $\mu_d = 0$; H_1: $\mu_d \neq 0$

(c) H_0: $\mu_1 = \mu_2$; H_1: $\mu_1 > \mu_2$

(d) H_0: Distributions are the same; H_1: Distributions are different.

(e) H_0: Distributions are the same; H_1: Distributions for Method 1 is lower.

B. What is the critical value (or critical values)? **B.** ________

(a) $z_0 = 1.96$ (b) $t_0 = \pm 2.145$

(c) $z_0 = \pm 1.96$ (d) $z_0 = \pm 2.58$ (e) $t_0 = 1.76$

CHAPTER 12, FORM C, PAGE 4

C. Calculate the z value of the sample test statistic. **C.** ________

(a) $z = -0.315$ (b) $t = -0.22$

(c) $z = -0.22$ (d) $z = \pm 1.96$ (e) $t = -0.20$

D. What is your conclusion? **D.** ________

(a) Reject H_0 (b) Do not reject H_0 (c) Cannot determine

(d) The distributions are different.

(e) The means are different.

4. A diet pill is being tested for its effectiveness on weight loss. Eight volunteers were weighed before they started taking the pill and after six weeks of taking the pill. They were asked to not change any behavior such as eating or exercise. Use a 1% level of significance to test the hypothesis that the mean weights were lower after taking the pill.

Volunteer	1	2	3	4	5	6	7	8	9	10	11	12	13	14	15
Before Weight	178	194	156	207	215	169	188	195	183	170	165	182	195	194	203
After Weight	180	190	158	198	203	159	188	200	179	172	165	174	188	198	191

A. What are the null and alternate hypotheses? **4. A.** ________

(a) H_0: $\mu_B = \mu_A$; H_1: $\mu_B < \mu_A$

(b) H_0: Distributions are the same; H_1: Distributions are different.

(c) H_0: $\rho_s = 0$; H_1: $\rho_s > 0$

(d) H_0: $\mu_B = \mu_A$; H_1: $\mu_B \neq \mu_A$

(e) H_0: Distributions are the same; H_1: Distribution after pill is lower.

B. What is the critical value (or critical values)? **B.** ________

(a) $z_0 = -1.645$ (b) $z_0 = \pm 2.58$

(c) $z_0 = 2.58$ (d) $z_0 = -2.33$ (e) $z_0 = \pm 1.96$

CHAPTER 12, FORM C, PAGE 5

C. Calculate the z value of the sample test statistic. **C.** ________

(a) $z = -2.33$ (b) $z = \frac{5}{13} \approx 0.38$
(c) $z = -0.83$ (d) $z = \frac{8}{13} \approx 0.62$ (e) $z = 0$

D. What is your conclusion? **D.** ________

(a) Reject H_0 (b) Do not reject H_0 (c) Cannot determine
(d) The diet pill is effective.
(e) Most of the volunteers lost weight.

5. Choose the test appropriate for each situation. We cannot make assumptions about the population distribution(s).

A. We would like to test data given in ranked form. **5. A.** ________

(a) T test (b) Rank-sum test
(c) Sign test (d) Chi-square test (e) Spearman rank correlation test

B. We would like to test paired data values coming from dependent samples. **B.** ________

(a) T test (b) Rank-sum test
(c) Sign test (d) Chi-square test (e) Spearman rank correlation test

C. We would like to test the difference between sample means coming from independent random samples from two populations. **C.** ________

(a) T test (b) Rank-sum test
(c) Sign test (d) Chi-square test (e) Spearman rank correlation test

Answers to Sample Chapter Tests

CHAPTER 1 FORM A

1. (a) Length of time to earn a Bachelor's degree.

(b) Quantitative

(c) Length of time it took each of the Colorado residents who earned (or will earn) a Bachelor's degree to complete the degree program.

2. Explanations will vary.

(a) Nominal

(b) Nominal

(c) Ratio

(d) Interval

(e) Nominal

(f) Ordinal

(g) Ordinal

3. (a) Census

(b) Experiment

(c) Sampling

(d) Simulation

4. Answers will vary.

5. The outcomes are the number of dots on the face, 1 through 6. Consider single digits in the random number table. Select a starting place at random. Record the first five digits you encounter that are between (and including) 1 and 6. The first five outcomes are

3 6 1 5 6

6. (a) Systematic

(b) Cluster

(c) Stratified

(d) Convenience

(e) Simple random

CHAPTER 1 FORM B

1. (a) Observed book purchase (mystery or not a mystery).

(b) Quantitative

(c) Observed book purchase (mystery or not a mystery)
of all current customers of the bookstore.

2. Explanations will vary.

(a) Nominal

(b) Ratio

(c) Interval

(d) Ordinal

(e) Ratio

3. (a) Census

(b) Sampling

(c) Simulation

(d) Experiment

4. Answers will vary.

5. Assign each of the 736 employees a distinct number between 1 and 736. Select a starting place in the random number table at random. Use groups of three digits. Use the first 30 distinct groups of three digits that correspond to employees numbers.

622 413 055 401 334

6. (a) Simple random

(b) Stratified

(c) Cluster

(d) Convenience

(e) Systematic

CHAPTER 1
FORM C

1. (b)

2. A. (b)

B. (a)

C. (d)

D. (c)

E. (a)

3. A. (b)

B. (c)

C. (a)

D. (d)

4. (e)

5. (d)

6. A. (e)

B. (d)

C. (a)

D. (c)

E. (b)

CHAPTER 2
FORM A

1.

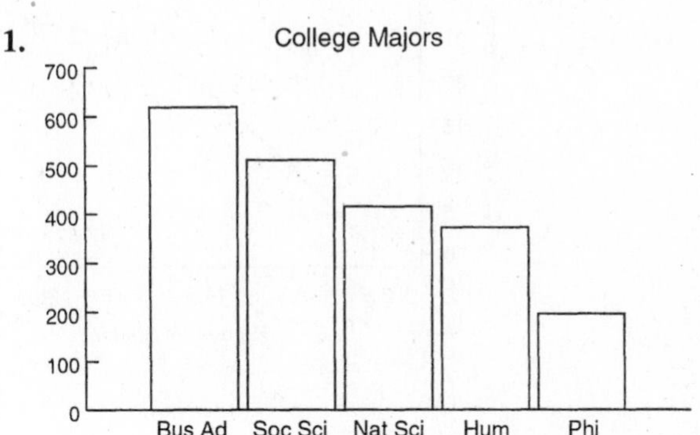

2. (a) The Class Width is 6

Frequency and Relative Frequency Table				
Class Boundaries	Freq.	Rel. Frequency	Class Midpoint	Cum. Freq.
2.5 – 8.5	10	0.3333	5.5	10
8.5 – 14.5	9	0.3000	11.5	19
14.5 – 20.5	6	0.2000	17.5	25
20.5 – 26.5	2	0.0667	23.5	27
26.5 – 32.5	3	0.1000	29.5	30

(b)

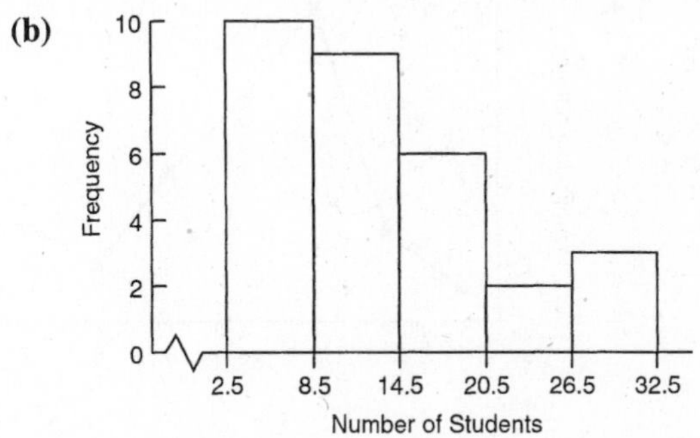

(c)

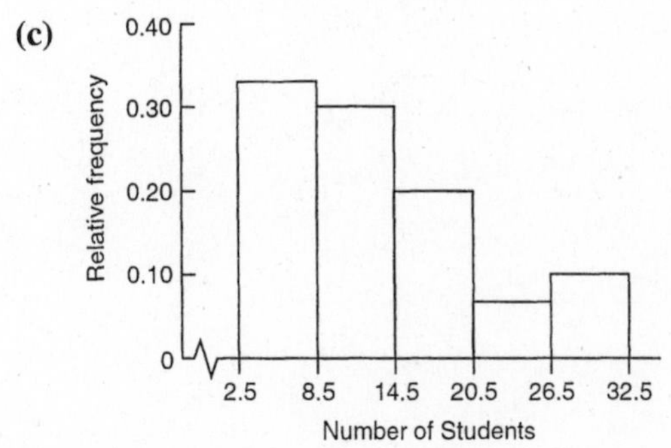

CHAPTER 2, FORM A, PAGE 2

(d)

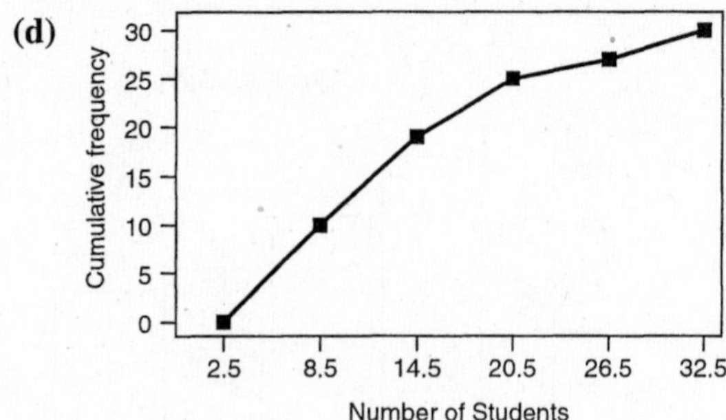

3. 0 | 5 = $5

0	5 7 8 9
1	2 5 6 7 9
2	1 2 4
3	3 5 7
4	2 6 9
5	1 7

4.

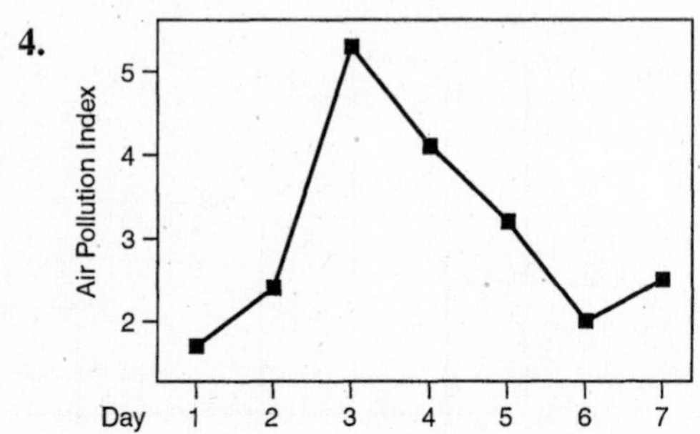

5.

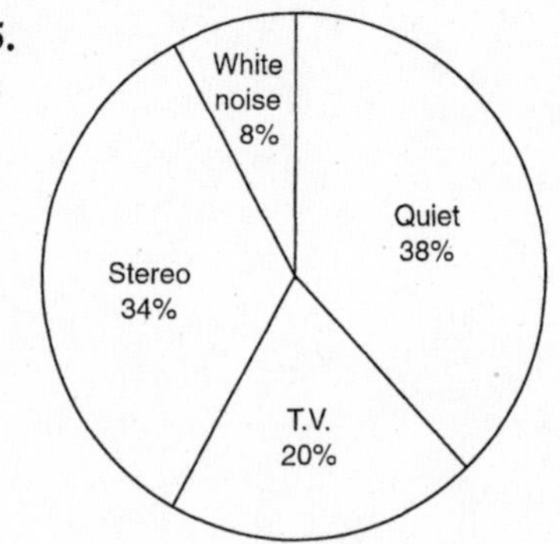

6.

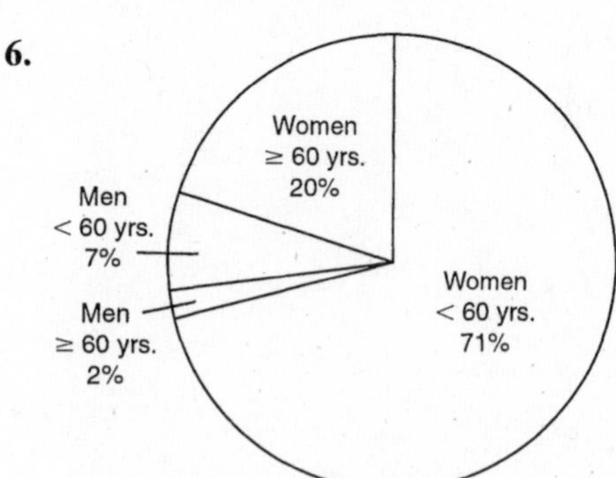

7.

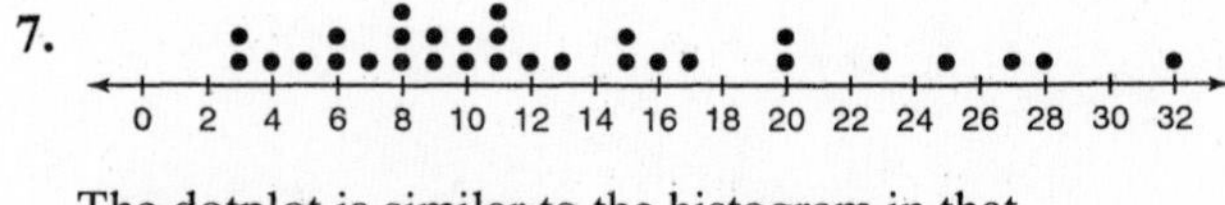

The dotplot is similar to the histogram in that most data values fall below 20.5. However, the dotplot has more detail, i.e., each data value can be seen in the dotplot.

8. 11 motorists

9. 3 | 1 = 31 years old

0	8
1	0 8 9
2	2 4 4 5 8 8 9
3	1 2 5 6 8
4	0 2 3 7
5	0 5

The distribution is fairly symmetrical.

CHAPTER 2
FORM B

1.

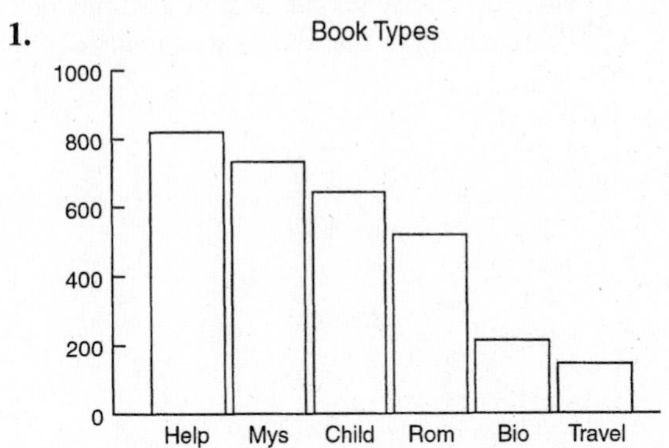

2. (a) The Class Width is 15

Frequency and Relative Frequency Table				
Class Boundaries	Freq.	Rel. Frequency	Class Midpoint	Cum. Freq.
18.5 – 33.5	3	0.1250	26	3
33.5 – 48.5	7	0.2917	41	10
48.5 – 63.5	8	0.3333	56	18
63.5 – 78.5	4	0.1667	71	22
78.5 – 93.5	2	0.0833	86	24

(b)

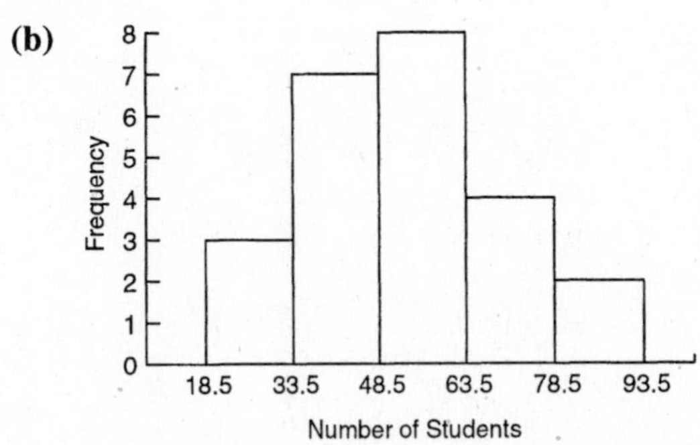

(c)

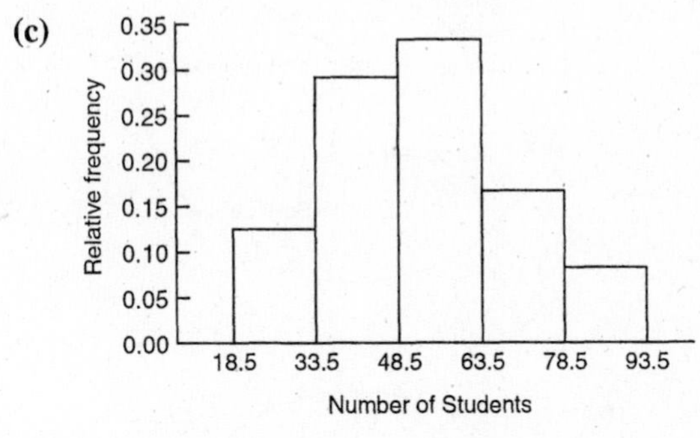

(d)

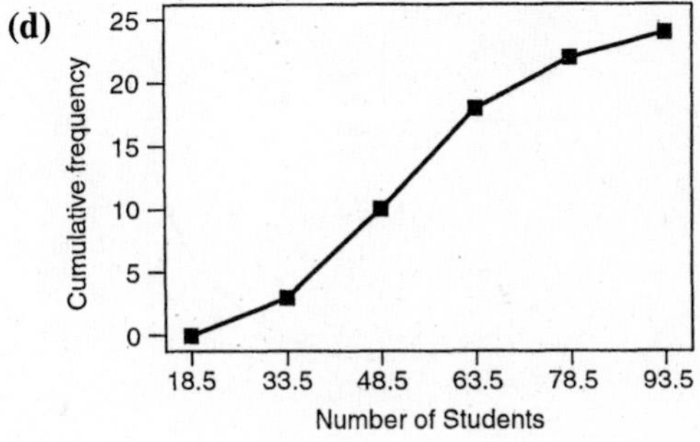

3. 2 | 1 = 21 students

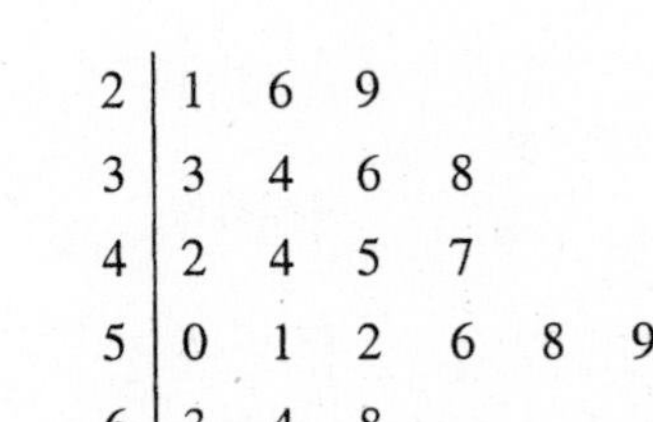

2	1 6 9
3	3 4 6 8
4	2 4 5 7
5	0 1 2 6 8 9
6	3 4 8

4.

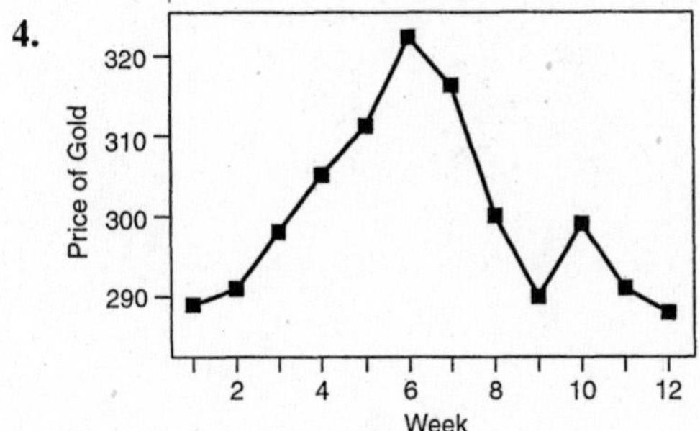

CHAPTER 2, FORM B, PAGE 2

5.

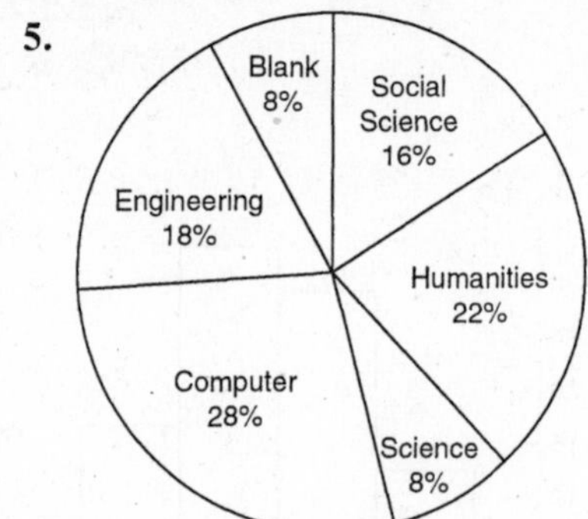

6.

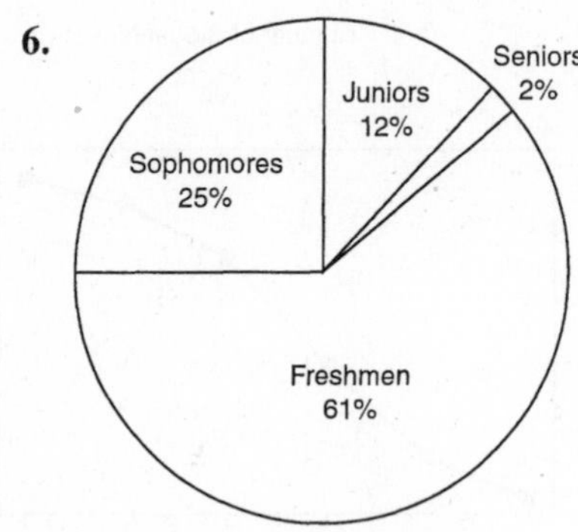

7.

20 30 40 50 60 70 80 90

The dotplot is similar to the histogram in that most data values fall in the middle (mound-shaped). However, the dotplot has more detail, i.e., each data value can be seen in the dotplot.

8. 6 days

9. 1 | 7 = 1.7 mm

0	9
1	2 7 8
2	3 4 5 5 6 8
3	0 1 6 7 7
4	1

The distribution is fairly symmetrical.

CHAPTER 2
FORM C

1. (c)

2. (e)

3. (b)

4. (a)

5. (d)

6. (e)

7. (d)

8. (a)

9. (c)

CHAPTER 3 FORM A

1. $\bar{x} = 16.61$; median = 13; mode = 12

2. \$42,185; \$35,761; The trimmed mean because it does not include the extreme values. Note that all the salaries are below \$42,185 except one.

3. (a) Range = 25
   (b) $\bar{x} = 33$
   (c) $s^2 = 81.67$
   (d) $s = 9.04$

4. (a) $CV = 21\%$
   (b) 6.04 to 14.72

5. (a) $\bar{x} = 36.45$
   (b) $s^2 = 130.55$
   (c) $s = 11.43$

6. (a) Low value = 15; $Q_1 = 23$; median = 33; $Q_3 = 49$; High value = 72
   (b)

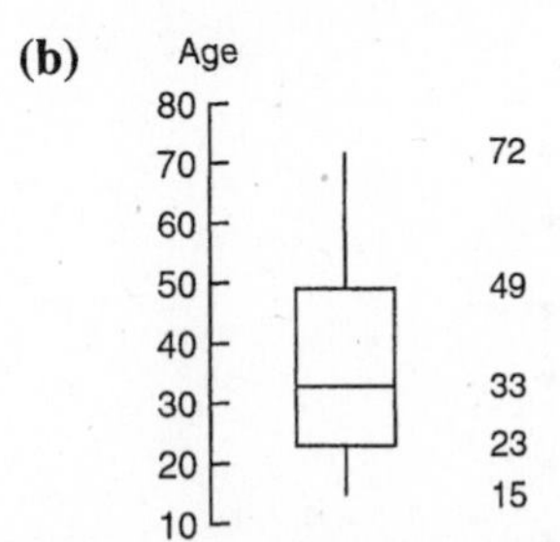

   (c) Interquartile range = 26

7. Weighted average = 85.65

8. 163.31 lb

9. 79% below; 21% above

CHAPTER 3 FORM B

1. $\bar{x} = 10.55$; median = 11; mode = 11

2. 37.8 in.; 31.63 in.; The trimmed mean because it does not include the extreme values. Note that all but 3 values are below 37.8 in.

3. (a) Range = 14
   (b) $\bar{x} = 12.17$
   (c) $s^2 = 25.37$
   (d) $s = 5.04$

4. (a) $CV = 26.5\%$
   (b) 15.3 to 49.7

5. (a) $\bar{x} = 2.35$
   (b) $s^2 = 1.02$
   (c) $s = 1.007$

6. (a) Low value = 27; $Q_1 = 35.5$; median = 42.5; $Q_3 = 57$; High value = 68
   (b)

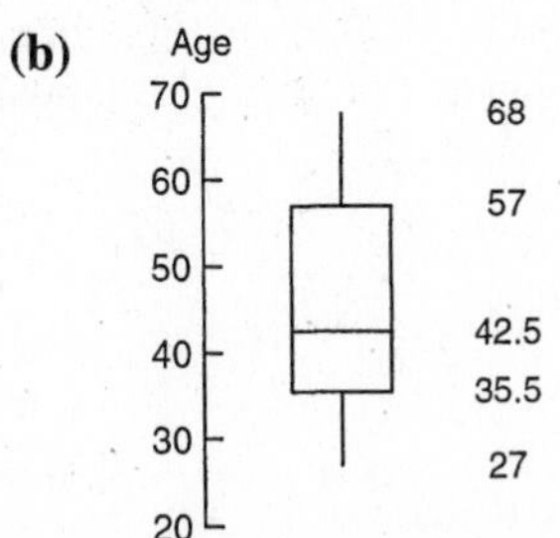

   (c) Interquartile range = 21.5

7. Weighted average = 84.75

8. \$56.76

9. 19% above; 81% below

CHAPTER 3 FORM C

1. (c)

2. (d)

3. A. (e)
   B. (a)
   C. (c)
   D. (d)

4. A. (b)
   B. (a)

5. A. (c)
   B. (e)
   C. (d)

6. (b)

7. (a)

8. (c)

9. (e)

CHAPTER 4 FORM A

1. (a) Relative frequency; 19/317 = 0.0599 or 5.99%

(b) 1 – 0.599 = 0.9401 or about 94%

(c) Defective, not defective; the probabilities add up to one.

2. 1/3

3. (a) 1/12 **(b)** 1/12 **(c)** 1/6

4. (a) With replacement, *P*(Red first *and* Green second) = (3/12)(7/12) = 7/48 or 0.146

(b) Without replacement, *P*(Red first *and* Green second) = (3/12)(7/11) = 21/132 or 0.159

5. *P*(Approval on written *and* interview) = *P*(written)*P*(interview, *given* written) = (0.63)(0.85) = 0.536 or about 53.6%

6. (a) 35/360 **(b)** 21/360

(c) 5/149 **(d)** 107/360

(e) 48/149 **(f)** 31/360

(g) No; *P*(referred) = 149/360 is not equal to *P*(referred, given satisfied) = 59/138.

7. 8;

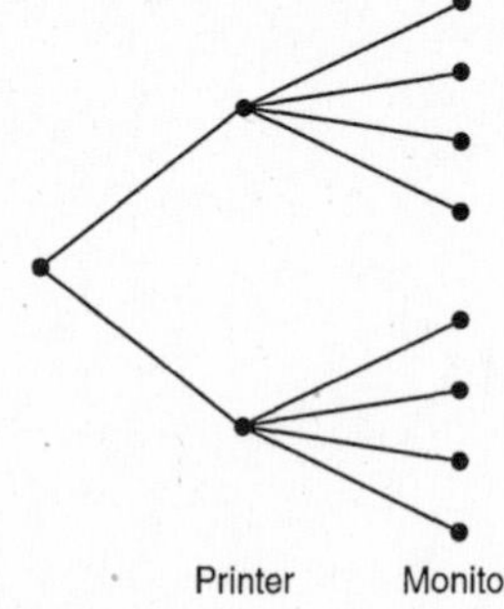

8. 40•39•38•37 = 2,193,360

9. $C_{11,3} = 165$

CHAPTER 4 FORM B

1. (a) *P*(woman) = 4/10 = 0.4 or 40%

(b) *P*(man) = 6/10 = 0.6 or 60%

(c) *P*(President) = 1/10 = 0.1 or 10%

2. 2/3

3. (a) 1/6 **(b)** 1/6 **(c)** 1/3

4. (a) With replacement, *P*(Red first *and* Green second) = (6/17)(8/17) = 0.166 or 16.6%

(b) Without replacement, *P*(Red first *and* Green second) = (6/17)(8/16) = 0.176 or 17.6%

5. *P*(woman *and* computer science major) = *P*(woman)*P*(computer science major *given woman*) = (0.64)(0.12) = 0.077 or about 7.7%

6. (a) 180/417 **(b)** 65/115

(c) 166/417 **(d)** 61/417

(e) 61/101 **(f)** 65/180

(g) No; *P*(neutral) = 166/417 is not equal to *P*(neutral, given freshman) = 61/101

7. 6;

Home

Post Office Bank

8. 16•15•14•13•12 = 524,160

9. $C_{24,4} = 10,626$

CHAPTER 4 FORM C

1. A. (d)
B. (b)

2. (a)

3. A. (c)
B. (e)
C. (b)

4. A. (a)
B. (d)

5. (b)

6. A. (e)
B. (c)
C. (a)
D. (d)
E. (c)
F. (b)

7. (d)

8. (e)

9. (a)

CHAPTER 5
FORM A

1. (a) These results are rounded to three digits.
$P(0) = 0.038$; $P(1) = 0.300$; $P(2) = 0.263$;
$P(3) = 0.171$; $P(4) = 0.117$; $P(5) = 0.058$;
$P(6) = 0.033$; $P(7) = 0.021$

(b)

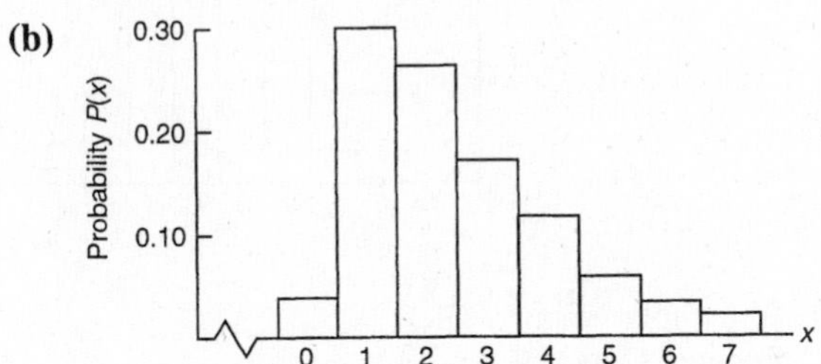

(c) $P(2 \le x \le 5) = 0.609$

(d) $P(x < 3) = 0.601$

(e) $\mu = 2.44$

(f) $\sigma = 1.57$

2. $P(4) = C_{10,4}(0.23)^4(0.77)^6 = 0.12$

3. $n = 16$; $p = 0.65$;
Success = reach summit

(a) $P(r = 16) = 0.001$

(b) $P(r \ge 10) = 0.688$

(c) $P(r \le 12) = 0.866$

(d) $P(9 \le r \le 12) = 0.706$

4. 6

5. (a)

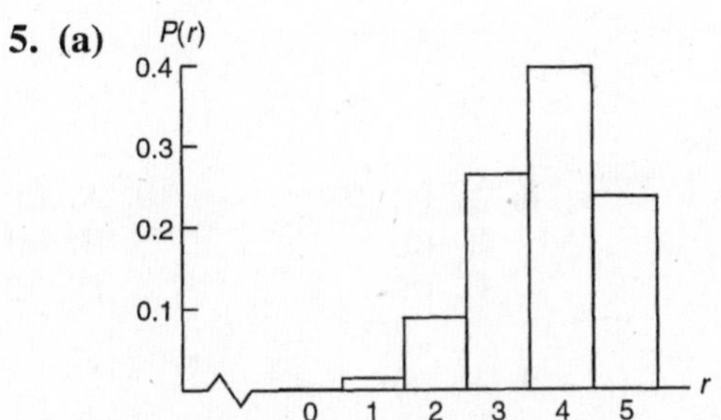

(b) $\mu = 3.75$

(c) $\sigma = 0.968$

6. $n = 11$ is the minimal number.

7. 6

8. (a) Essay; $P(n) = 0.15(0.85)^{n-1}$

(b) $P(n = 3) = 0.108$

(c) $P(n > 3) = 0.614$

9. (a) Essay; $\lambda = 6$;
$P(r) = (e^{-6}6^r)/r!$

(b) $P(r = 3) = 0.0892$

(c) $P(r > 3) = 0.8488$

10. (a) Essay; $\lambda = 4.5$;
$P(r) = (e^{-4.5}4.5^r)/r!$

(b) $(r = 3) = 0.1687$

(c) $P(r > 3) = 0.6577$

CHAPTER 5
FORM B

1. **(a)** Values are rounded to three digits.
$P(1) = 0.066$; $P(2) = 0.092$; $P(3) = 0.202$; $P(4) = 0.224$; $P(5) = 0.184$; $P(6) = 0.079$; $P(7) = 0.053$; $P(8) = 0.044$; $P(9) = 0.035$; $P(10) = 0.022$

(b)

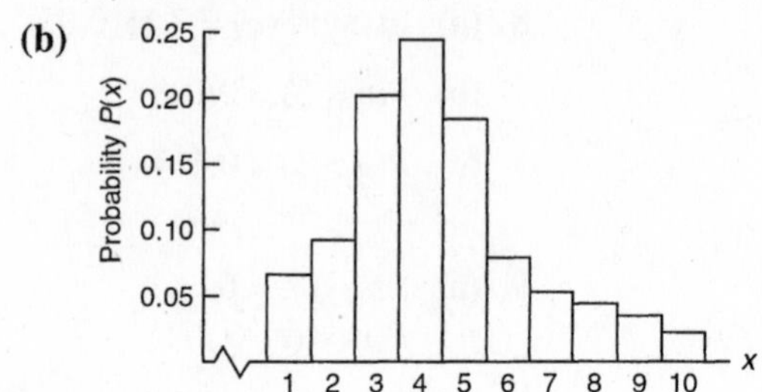

(c) 0.641

(d) 0.101

(e) $\mu = 4.40$

(f) $\sigma = 2.08$

2. $P(3) = C_{12,3}(0.28)^3(0.72)^9 = 0.25$

3. Success = accept; $p = 0.30$; $n = 55$;

(a) $P(r = 15) = 0.000$ (to three digits)

(b) $P(r \geq 8) = 0.051$

(c) $P(r \leq 4) = 0.517$

(d) $P(5 \leq r \leq 10) = 0.484$

4. 51

5. **(a)**

(b) $\mu = 3.85$

(c) $\sigma = 1.32$

6. $n = 10$ is the smallest number.

7. 2

8. **(a)** $P(n) = 0.60(0.40)^{n-1}$

(b) $P(n = 4) = 0.0384$

(c) $P(n \geq 3) = 0.16$

9. **(a)** Essay; $\lambda = 8$;
$P(r) = (e^{-8}8^r)/r!$

(b) 0.1396

(c) $P(r < 3) = 0.0137$

10. **(a)** Essay; $\lambda = 2$;
$P(r) = (e^{-2}2^r)/r!$

(b) $P(r = 2) = 0.2707$

(c) $P(r > 2) = 0.3233$

CHAPTER 5
FORM C

1. **A.** (c) **B.** (e) **C.** (b) **D.** (d)

2. (e)

3. **A.** (b) **B.** (a) **C.** (d) **D.** (c)

4. (b)

5. **A.** (e) **B.** (c)

6. (d)

7. (a)

8. **A.** (c) **B.** (d) **C.** (b)

9. **A.** (e) **B.** (a) **C.** (b)

10. **A.** (d) **B.** (e) **C.** (d)

CHAPTER 6
FORM A

1. (a) A normal curve is bell-shaped with one peak. Because this curve has two peaks, it is not *normal.*

(b) A normal curve gets closer and closer to the horizontal axis, but it never touches it or crosses it.

2. 99.7%

3. 1

4. (a) $z \geq 1.8$

(b) $-1.2 \leq z \leq 0.8$

(c) $z \leq -2.2$

(d) $x \leq 3.1$

(e) $4.1 \leq x \leq 4.6$

(f) $x \geq 4.35$

5. (a) No, look at z values

(b) For Joel, $z = 1.51$. For John, $z = 2.77$. Relative to the district, John is a better salesman.

6. (a) $P(x \leq 5) = P(z \leq -0.77) = 0.2206$

(b) $P(x \geq 10) = P(z \geq 1.5) = 0.0668$

(c) $P(5 \leq x \leq 10)$
$= P(-0.77 \leq z \leq 1.5)$
$= 0.7126$

7. 29.92 minutes or 30 minutes

8. (a)

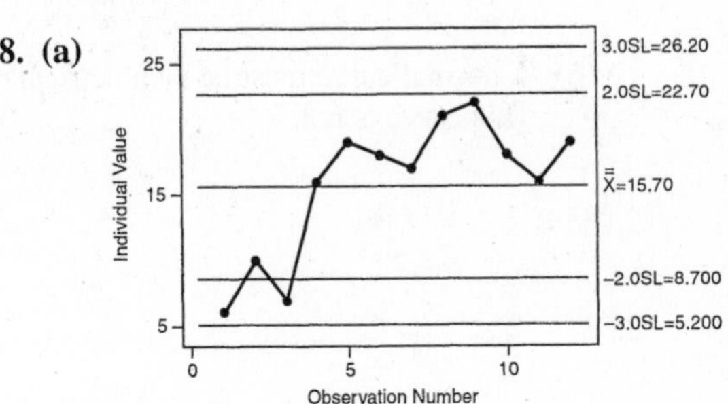

(b) Yes;
Type III for days 1 to 3;
Type II for days 4 thru 12

9. (a) *Essay*

(b) $P(r \leq 47)$
$= P(x \leq 47.5)$
$= P(z \leq -0.82)$
$= 0.2061$

(c) $P(47 \leq r \leq 55)$
$= P(46.5 \leq x \leq 55.5)$
$= P(-1.22 \leq z \leq 2.33)$
$= 0.8789$

CHAPTER 6
FORM B

1. **(a)** The tails of a normal curve must get closer and closer to the x-axis. In this curve the tails are going away from the x-axis.

   (b) A normal curve must be symmetrical. This curve is not.

2. 68%

3. 2

4. **(a)** $z \le 0.33$

   (b) $-0.86 \le z \le 0.57$

   (c) $z \ge -1.33$

   (d) $x \ge 2.6$

   (e) $6.8 \le x \le 11$

   (f) $x \le 13.1$

5. **(a)** Generator II is hotter; see the z values

   (b) $z = 0.72$ for Generator I; $z = 2.75$ for Generator II
   Generator II could be near a melt down since it is hotter.

6. **(a)** $P(x < 6) = P(z < -1.33) = 0.0918$

   (b) $P(x > 7) = P(z > 2.00) = 0.0228$

   (c) $P(6 \le x \le 7) = P(-1.33 \le z \le 2.00) = 0.8854$

7. $z = 3$ years

8. **(a)**

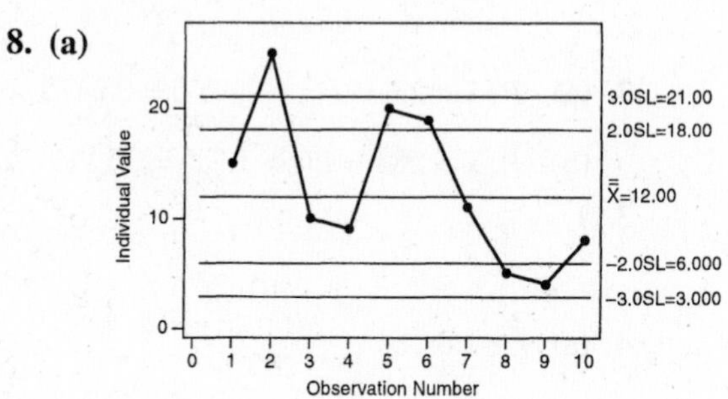

   (b) Type I, day 2; Type III for days 5–6 and 8–10.

9. **(a)** Essay

   (b) $P(r \ge 60) = P(x \ge 59.5) = P(z \ge -0.70) = 0.7580$

   (c) $P(60 \le r \le 70) = P(59.5 \le x \le 70.5) = P(-0.70 \le z \le 1.88) = 0.7279$

CHAPTER 6
FORM C

1. (c)

2. (b)

3. (e)

4. **A.** (d)
   B. (a)

5. **A.** (d)
   B. (b)
   C. (a)

6. **A.** (c)
   B. (e)
   C. (b)

7. (c)

8. (d)

9. **A.** (b)
   B. (a)

CHAPTER 7 FORM A

1. Essay

2. (a) $P(\bar{x} < 3) = P(z < -0.51) = 0.3050$

(b) $P(\bar{x} > 4) = P(z > 2.06) = 0.0197$

(c) $P(3 \le \bar{x} \le 4) = P(-0.51 \le z \le 2.06)$
$= 0.6753$

3. (a) $P(\bar{x} < 23) = P(z < -1.67) = 0.0475$

(b) $P(\bar{x} > 28) = P(z > 1.21) = 0.1131$

(c) $P(23 \le \bar{x} \le 28) = P(-1.67 \le z \le 1.21)$
$= 0.8394$

4. (a) Yes; $np > 5$; $nq > 5$

(b) $P(\hat{p} \ge 0.5) = P(x \ge 0.489)$
$= P(z \ge -2.75)$
$= 0.997$

(c) $P(\hat{p} \le 0.667) = P(x \le 0.678)$
$= P(z \le -0.03)$
$= 0.4880$

5. (a)

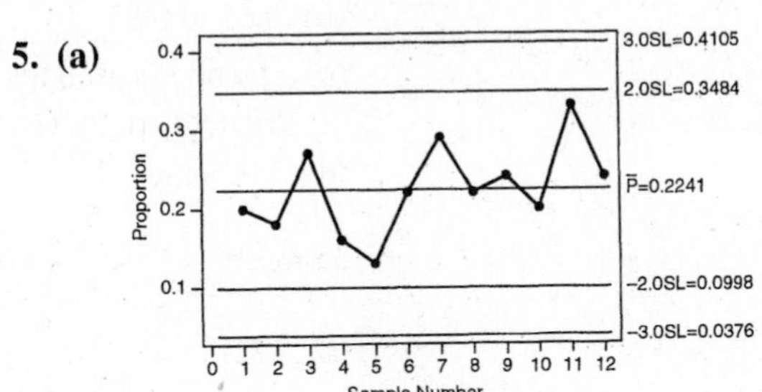

(b) No out-of-control signals.

CHAPTER 7 FORM B

1. Essay

2. (a) $P(5.2 \le \bar{x}) = P(-1.83 \le z) = 0.9664$

(b) $P(\bar{x} \le 7.1) = P(z \le 1.33) = 0.9082$

(c) $P(5.2 \le \bar{x} \le 7.1) = P(-1.83 \le z \le 1.33)$
$= 0.8746$

3. (a) $P(8 \le \bar{x}) = P(-2.15 \le z) = 0.9842$

(b) $P(\bar{x} \le 9) = P(z \le 0.54) = 0.7054$

(c) $P(8 \le \bar{x} \le 9) = P(-2.15 \le z \le 0.54)$
$= 0.6896$

4. (a) Yes; $np > 5$; $nq > 5$

(b) $P(\hat{p} \ge 0.333) = P(x \ge 0.326)$
$= P(z \ge 1.69)$
$= 0.0455$

(c) $P(\hat{p} \le 0.2) = P(x \le 0.207)$
$= P(z \le -0.64)$
$= 0.2611$

5. (a)

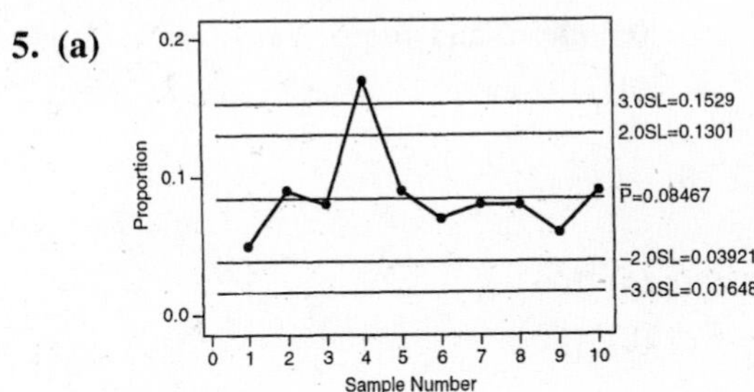

(b) Signal I: One point lies outside 3σ limit (4th shipment)

CHAPTER 7 FORM C

1. A. (c)
B. (b)
C. (a)
D. (a)

2. A. (b)
B. (d)
C. (c)

3. A. (a)
B. (d)
C. (e)

4. A. (b)
B. (a)
C. (c)

5. A. (d)
B. (e)
C. (c)

CHAPTER 8 FORM A

1. 27.70 to 31.90 inches
We are 95% confident that the mean circumference of all Blue Spruce trees near this lake will lie between 27.70 and 31.90 inches.

2. **(a)** \$33.35 to \$36.05
(b) \$1167.25 to \$1261.75

3. $\bar{x} = 33.38$, $s = 6.46$, $t = 2.365$,
27.98 to 38.78 minutes

4. 10.05 to 13.75 inches; use $t = 2.878$
We are 99% confident that the mean length of Rainbow Trout is between 10.05 and 13.75 minutes.

5. **(a)** $\hat{p} = 59/78 \approx 0.756$
(b) 0.68 to 0.84
(c) $np > 5$ and $nq > 5$; Yes
(d) 122 more

6. 94 more

7. **(a)** 106
(b) 100

8. **(a)** 0.61 to 2.79 for $\mu_1 - \mu_2$
(b) Since the interval contains all positive numbers, it seems that Battery I has a longer population mean life time.

9. $s = 3.94$; interval from -8.26 to -1.74 for $\mu_1 - \mu_2$; Since the interval contains numbers that are all negative it appears that the population mean duration of the first drug is less than that of the second.

10. $\hat{p}_1 = 62/83$ for Kendra; $\hat{p}_2 = 87/112$ for Lisa; interval from -0.19 to 0.13 for $p_1 - p_2$. Since the interval contains both positive and negative values, there is no evidence of a difference in population proportions of successful portfolios managed by Kendra compared to those managed by Lisa.

CHAPTER 8 FORM B

1. 4.10 to 6.30 calls; use $t = 2.160$
We are 96% confident that the mean number of solicitation calls this family receives each night is between 4.10 and 6.30 calls.

2. **(a)** \$6.45 to \$7.35
(b) \$516 to \$588

3. $\bar{x} = 14.7$, $s = 5.31$, $t = 2.262$,
10.90 to 18.50 pages

4. 89.0 to 97.4 minutes
We are 99% confident that mean time for computer repairs is between 89.0 and 97.4 minutes.

5. **(a)** $\hat{p} = 41/56$ or 0.732
(b) 0.62 to 0.85
(c) np and nq are both greater than 5; Yes
(d) 246 more

6. 33 more

7. **(a)** 271
(b) 167

8. **(a)** $s = 575.75$; -151.6 to 509.62 dollars for $\mu_1 - \mu_2$
(b) Since the interval contains both positive and negative values, it does not appear that the population mean daily sales of the printers differ.

9. (a) $\hat{p}_1 = 0.098$;
$\hat{p}_2 = 0.043$; 0.018 to 0.093 for $p_1 - p_2$.

(b) n_1p_1, n_1q_1, n_2p_2, n_2q_2 are all greater than 5; Yes

(c) The interval contains all positive values and shows that at the 90% confidence level, the population proportion of defects is greater on Shift I.

10. (a) 15.5 to 46.5 for $\mu_1 - \mu_2$

(b) The interval contains values that are all positive. At the 90% confidence level, the population mean stopping distance of the old tread design is greater than that for the new.

CHAPTER 8 FORM C

1. (b)

2. A. (c)
B. (e)

3. (a)

4. (b)

5. A. (d)
B. (a)
C. (e)

6. (c)

7. A. (a)
B. (d)

8. (b)

9. (e)

10. (d)

CHAPTER 9
FORM A

1. (a) H_0: $\mu = 24{,}819$;
H_1: $\mu > 24{,}819$; right-tailed; $\alpha = 0.01$

(b) standard normal; $z_0 = 2.33$

(c)

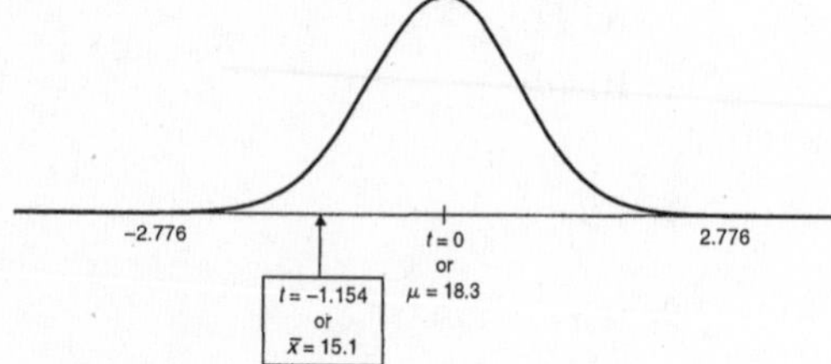

(d) $\bar{x} = 25{,}910$ corresponds to $z = 3.60$

(e) P value = 0.0002

(f) Reject H_0. There is evidence that the population mean daily sales is greater.

2. (a) H_0: $\mu = 18.3$; H_1: $\mu \neq 18.3$; two-tailed; $\alpha = 0.05$

(b) Student's t; $t_0 = \pm 2.776$; $d.f. = 4$

(c)

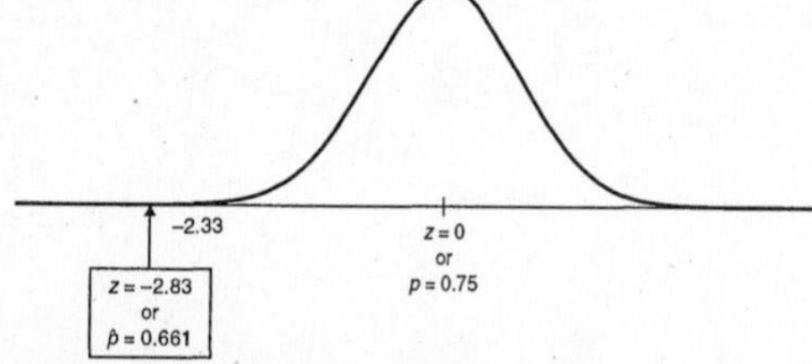

(d) $\bar{x} = 15.1$ corresponds to $t = -1.154$

(e) P value > 0.250

(f) Do not reject H_0. There is not enough evidence to conclude that the waiting times are different.

3. (a) H_0: $p = 0.75$; H_1: $p < 0.75$; left-tailed; $\alpha = 0.01$

(b) standard normal; $z_0 = -2.33$

(c)

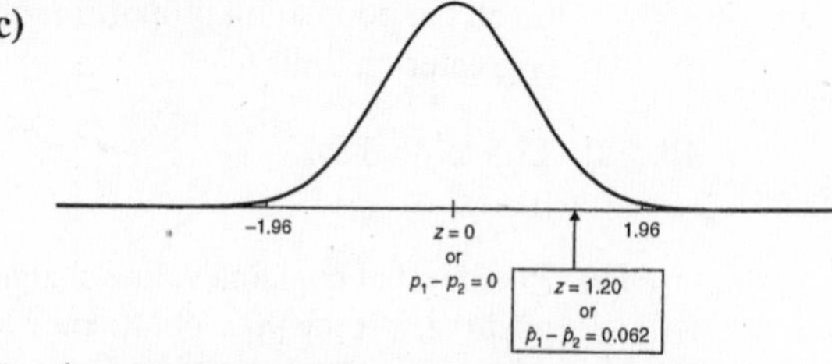

(d) $\hat{p} = 125/189 = 0.661$ corresponds to $z = -2.83$

(e) P value = 0.0023

(f) Reject H_0. There is evidence that the proportion of Rainbow Trout is less than 75%.

4. (a) H_0: $p_1 = p_2$; H_1: $p_1 \neq p_2$; two-tailed; $\alpha = 0.05$

(b) standard normal; $z_0 = \pm 1.96$

(c)

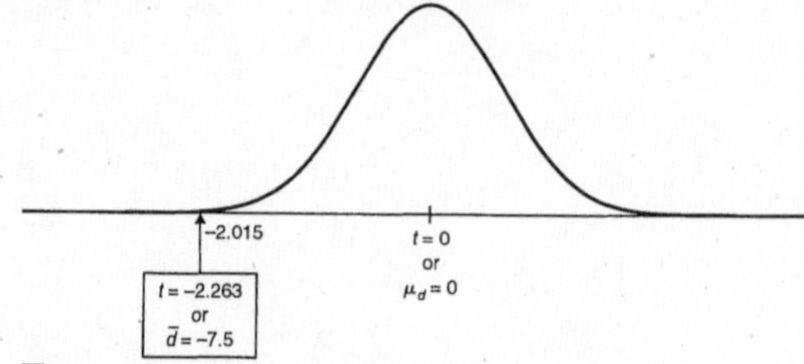

(d) $\hat{p}_1 = 62/175 = 0.354$; $\hat{p}_2 = 45/154 = 0.292$; $\hat{p}_1 - \hat{p}_2 = 0.062$ corresponds to $z = 1.20$

(e) P value = 0.2302

(f) Do not reject H_0. There is not enough evidence to conclude that there is difference in population proportions of success between the two different sales pitches.

5. (a) H_0: $\mu_d = 0$; H_1: $\mu_d < 0$; left-tailed; $\alpha = 0.05$

(b) Student's t; $d.f. = 5$; $t_0 = -2.015$

(c)

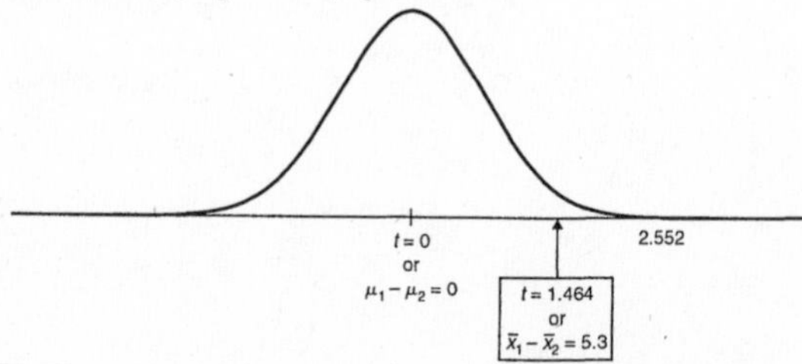

(d) $\bar{d} = -7.5$ corresponds to $t = -2.263$

(e) $0.025 < P$ value < 0.050

(f) Reject H_0. There is evidence to conclude that the new process increases the mean number of items processed per shift.

6. (a) H_0: $\mu_1 = \mu_2$; H_1: $\mu_1 > \mu_2$; right-tailed; $\alpha = 0.01$

(b) Student's t; $d.f. = 18$; $t_0 = 2.552$

(c)

t = 0
or
$\mu_1 - \mu_2 = 0$
2.552
t = 1.464
or
$\bar{x}_1 - \bar{x}_2 = 5.3$

(d) $\overline{x}_1 - \overline{x}_2 = 5.3$ corresponds to $t = 1.464$

(e) $0.075 < P$ value < 0.10

(f) Do not reject H_0. There is not sufficient evidence to show that the population mean profit per employee in computer stores is higher than those for building supply stores.

7. (a) H_0: $\mu_1 = \mu_2$; H_1: $\mu_1 \neq \mu_2$; two-tailed; $\alpha = 0.05$

(b) standard normal; $z_0 = \pm 1.96$

(c)

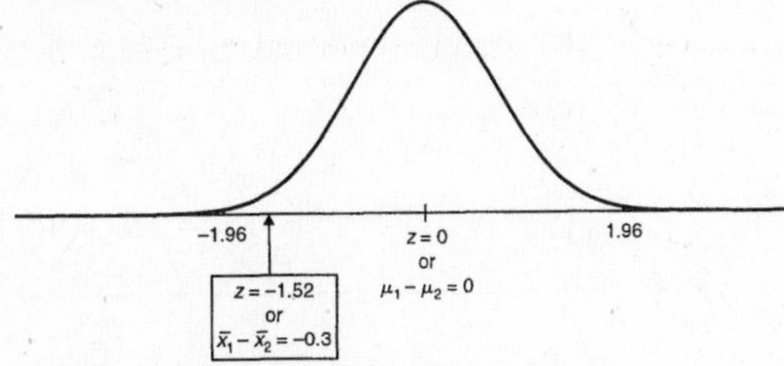

(d) $\overline{x}_1 - \overline{x}_2 = -0.3$ corresponds to $z = -1.52$

(e) P value $= 0.1286$

(f) Do not reject H_0. There is not enough evidence to say that the mean weight of tomatoes grown organically is different than that of other tomatoes.

8. (a) H_0: $\mu = 68.3$; H_1: $\mu \neq 68.3$; two-tailed; $\alpha = 0.05$

(b) standard normal; $z_0 = \pm 1.96$

(c)

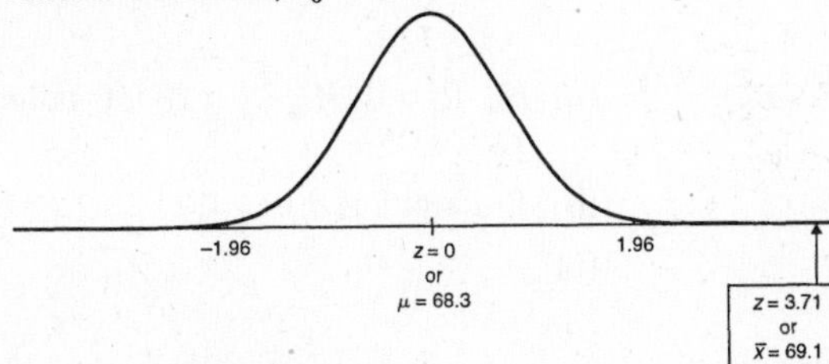

(d) $\overline{x} = 69.1$ corresponds to $z = 3.71$

(e) P value < 0.0001

(f) Reject H_0. There is evidence that the population mean height is different from 68.3 inches.

9. (a) H_0: $\mu = 30$; H_1: $\mu > 30$; right-tailed; $\alpha = 0.05$

(b) Student's t; $t_0 = 1.771$; $d.f. = 13$

(c)

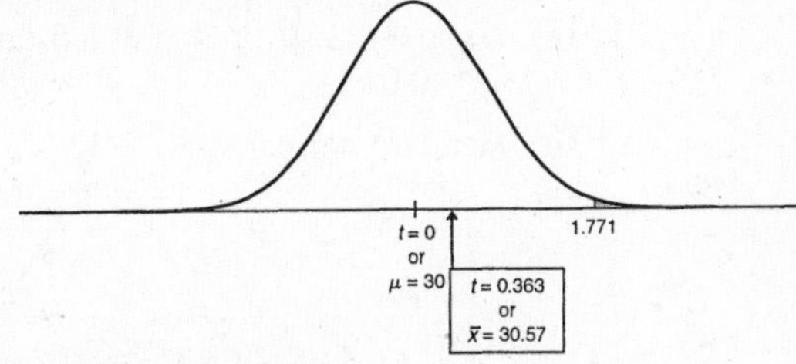

(d) $\overline{x} = 30.57$ corresponds to $t = 0.363$

(e) P value > 0.25

(f) Do not reject H_0. There is not enough evidence to conclude that the delivery time is greater than 30 min.

10. (a) H_0: $p = 0.6$; H_1: $p < 0.6$; left-tailed; $\alpha = 0.05$

(b) standard normal; $z_0 = -1.645$

(c)

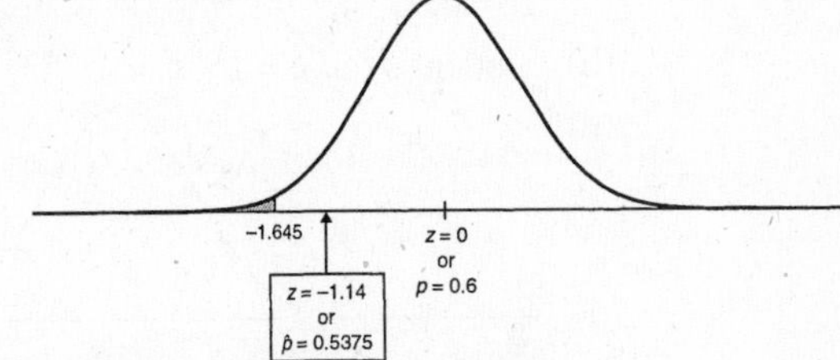

(d) $\hat{p} = 43/80 = 0.5375$ corresponds to $z = -1.14$

(e) P value $= 0.1271$

(f) Do not reject H_0. There is not enough evidence to conclude that the proportion is less than 60%.

CHAPTER 9
FORM B

1. (a) H_0: $\mu = 5.3$; H_1: $\mu < 5.3$; left-tailed; $\alpha = 0.01$

   (b) standard normal; $z_0 = -2.33$

   (c)

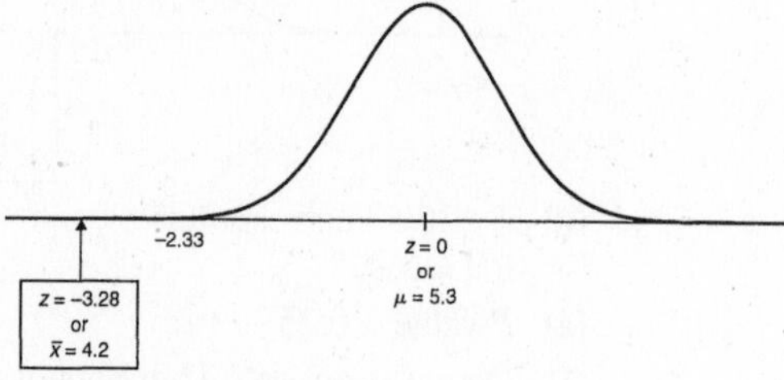

   (d) $\bar{x} = 4.2$ corresponds to $z = -3.28$

   (e) P value $= 0.0005$

   (f) Reject H_0. There is evidence that the average recovery time is less as an outpatient.

2. (a) H_0: $\mu = 4.19$; H_1: $\mu > 4.19$; right-tailed; $\alpha = 0.05$

   (b) Student's t; $d.f. = 15$; $t_0 = 1.753$

   (c)

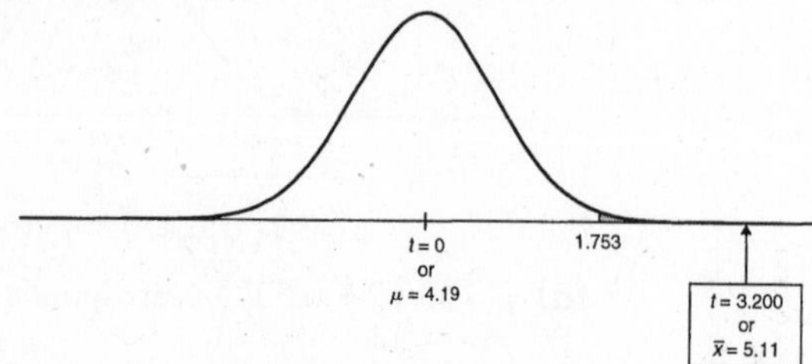

   (d) $\bar{x} = 5.11$ corresponds to $t = 3.200$

   (e) P value < 0.005

   (f) Reject H_0. There is evidence that the average yield of Arizona municipal bonds is higher than the national average yield.

3. (a) H_0: $p = 0.37$; H_1: $p \neq 0.37$; two-tailed; $\alpha = 0.01$

   (b) standard normal; $z_0 = \pm 2.576$

   (c)

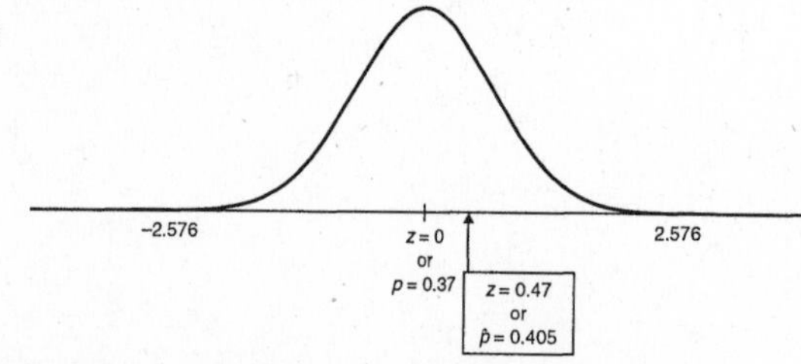

   (d) $\hat{p} = 17/42 = 0.405$ corresponds to $z = 0.47$

   (e) P value $= 0.6384$

   (f) Do not reject H_0. There is not evidence to conclude that the proportion of freshmen on the Dean's List is different from that in the college.

4. (a) H_0: $p_1 = p_2$; H_1: $p_1 < p_2$; left-tailed; $\alpha = 0.05$

   (b) standard normal; $z_0 = -1.645$

   (c)

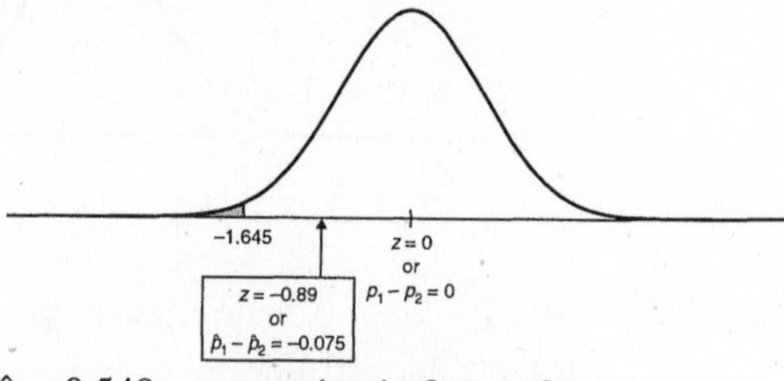

   (d) $\hat{p}_1 = 0.548$ = proportion in favor of Jennifer; $\hat{p}_2 = 0.623$ = proportion in favor of Kevin; $\hat{p}_1 - \hat{p}_2 = -0.075$ corresponds to $z = -0.89$

   (e) P value $= 0.1867$

   (f) Do not reject H_0. There is not enough evidence to say that the proportion who plan to vote for Kevin is higher.

5. (a) H_0: $\mu_d = 0$; H_1: $\mu_d < 0$; left-tailed; $\alpha = 0.05$

   (b) Student's t; $d.f. = 4$; $t_0 = -2.132$

   (c)

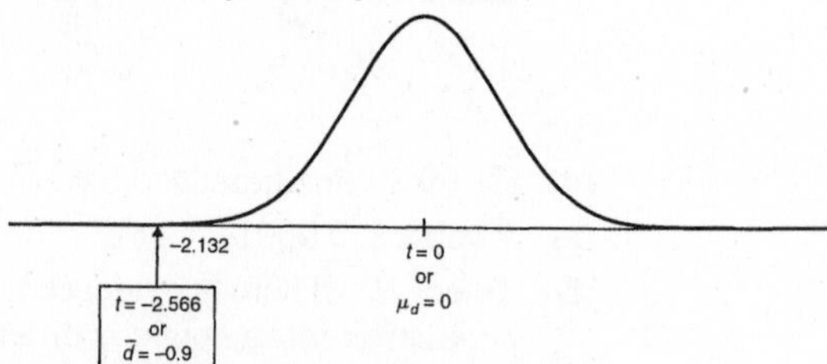

   (d) $\bar{d} = -0.9$ corresponds to $t = -2.566$

   (e) $0.025 < P$ value < 0.050

   (f) Reject H_0. There is evidence that the average time for runners at higher elevation is longer.

6. **(a)** H_0: $\mu_1 = \mu_2$; H_1: $\mu_1 > \mu_2$; right-tailed; $\alpha = 0.01$

(b) Student's t; $d.f. = 21$; $t_0 = 2.518$

(c)

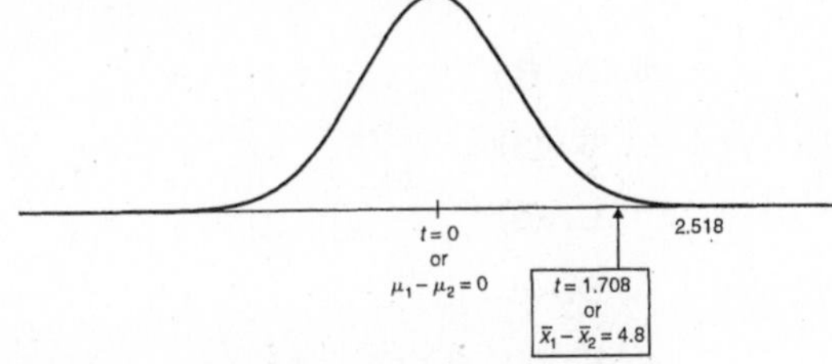

(d) $\bar{x}_1 - \bar{x}_2 = 4.8$ corresponds to $t = 1.708$

(e) $0.05 < P$ value < 0.075

(f) Do not reject H_0. There is not enough evidence to conclude that the average mileage for the Pacer is greater.

7. **(a)** H_0: $\mu_1 = \mu_2$; H_1: $\mu_1 > \mu_2$; right-tailed; $\alpha = 0.05$

(b) standard normal; $z_0 = 1.645$

(c)

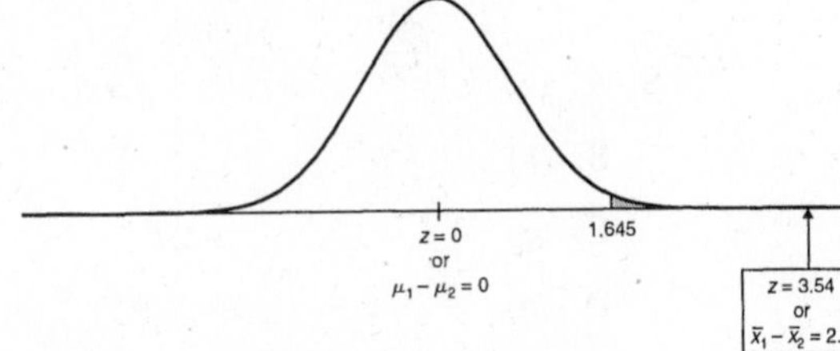

(d) $\bar{x}_1 - \bar{x}_2 = 2.7$ corresponds to $z = 3.54$

(e) P value $= 0.0002$

(f) Reject H_0. The evidence indicates that the average egg production of range free chickens is higher.

8. **(a)** H_0: $\mu = 2.8$; H_1: $\mu \neq 2.8$; two-tailed; $\alpha = 0.05$

(b) standard normal; $z_0 = \pm 1.96$

(c)

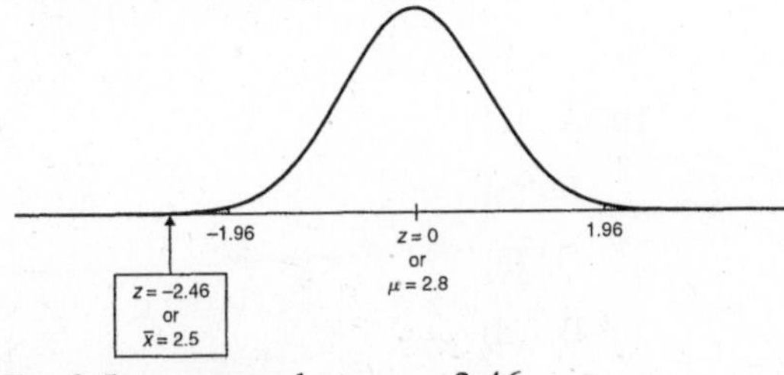

(d) $\bar{x} = 2.5$ corresponds to $z = -2.46$

(e) P value $= 0.0138$

(f) Reject H_0. There is evidence that the population mean time is different from 2.8 hours.

9. **(a)** H_0: $\mu = 30$; H_1: $\mu > 30$; right-tailed; $\alpha = 0.05$

(b) Student's t; $t_0 = 1.753$; $d.f. = 15$

(c)

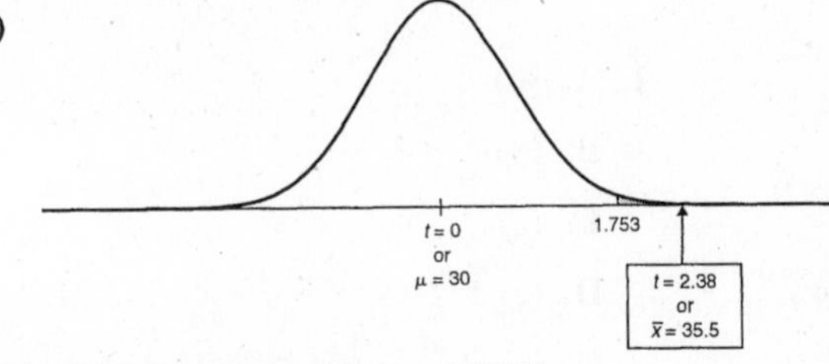

(d) $\bar{x} = 35.5$ corresponds to $t = 2.38$

(e) $0.01 < P$ value > 0.025

(f) Reject H_0. There is evidence that the average age is greater than 30 years.

10. **(a)** H_0: $p = 0.27$; H_1: $p > 0.27$; right-tailed; $\alpha = 0.05$

(b) standard normal; $z_0 = 1.645$

(c)

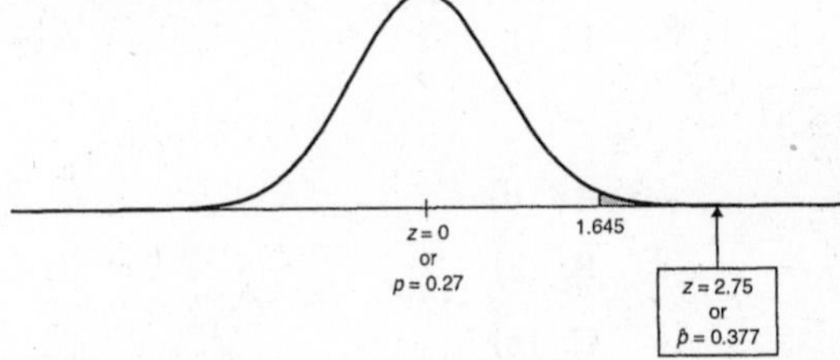

(d) $\hat{p} = 49/130 = 0.377$ corresponds to $z = 2.75$

(e) P value $= 0.003$

(f) Reject H_0. There is sufficient evidence to conclude that the proportion is greater than 27%.

CHAPTER 9
FORM C

1. **A.** (b)
   B. (d)
   C. (a)
   D. (c)
   E. (b)

2. **A.** (e)
   B. (d)
   C. (a)
   D. (c)
   E. (b)

3. **A.** (d)
   B. (a)
   C. (e)
   D. (c)
   E. (a)

4. **A.** (e)
   B. (d)
   C. (b)
   D. (e)
   E. (a)

5. **A.** (d)
   B. (e)
   C. (c)
   D. (b)
   E. (a)

6. **A.** (b)
   B. (a)
   C. (e)
   D. (d)
   E. (a)

7. **A.** (b)
   B. (c)
   C. (e)
   D. (d)
   E. (b)

8. **A.** (e)
   B. (a)
   C. (c)
   D. (d)
   E. (b)

9. **A.** (d)
   B. (c)
   C. (b)
   D. (e)
   E. (a)

10. **A.** (c)
    B. (a)
    C. (e)
    D. (d)
    E. (a)

CHAPTER 10
FORM A

1. Length of Northern Pike x versus Weight y

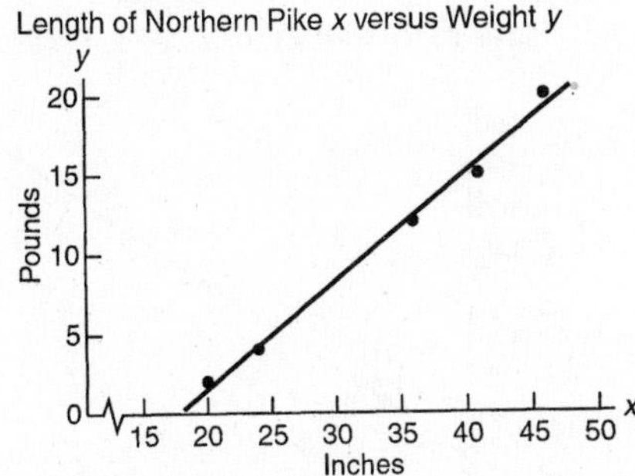

The linear correlation coefficient appears to be positive.

2. **(a)** $\overline{x} = 33.4$; $\overline{y} = 10.6$

(b) $SS_x = 491.2$; $SS_y = 227.2$; $SS_{xy} = 332.8$

(c) $b = 0.6775$; $a = -12.029$;
$y = 0.6775x - 12.029$

(d) See line on the graph of Problem 1.

3. $r = 0.996$; $r^2 = 0.992$; 99.2% of the variation in y can be explained by the least squares line using x as the predicting variable.

4. $S_e = 0.757$

5. For $x = 32$ inches, $y = 9.65$ pounds

6. $7.70 \le y \le 11.61$ pounds

7. H_0: $\rho = 0$; H_1: $\rho \ne 0$; $t_0 = \pm 5.841$;
sample $t = 19.31$; Reject H_0; There is evidence that the population correlation coefficient is not equal to 0. r is significant.

8. Advertising Cost x versus Increase in Sales y

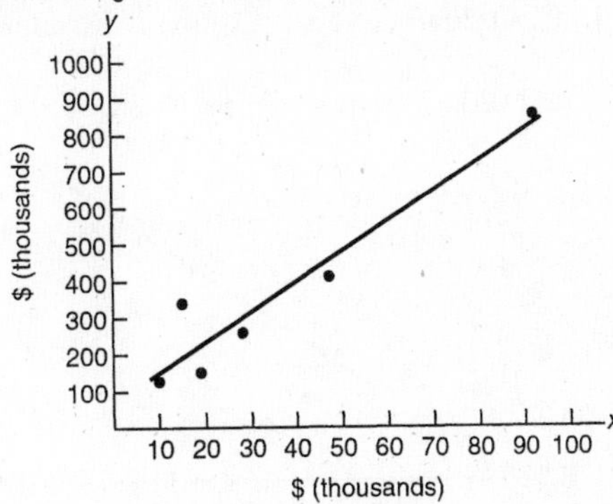

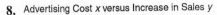

The linear correlation coefficient appears to be positive.

9. **(a)** $\overline{x} = 35.17$; $\overline{y} = 358.33$

(b) $SS_x = 4722.83$; $SS_y = 381.33$;
$SS_{xy} = 39{,}030.67$

(c) $b = 8.264$; $a = 67.71$; $y = 8.26x + 67.7$

(d) See line on the graph of Problem 8.

10. $r = 0.954$; $r^2 = 0.910$; 91.0% of the variation in y can be explained by the least squares line using x as the predicting variable.

11. $S_e = 89.19$

12. For $x = 37$ (or \$37,000),
$y = 373.5$ (or \$373,500)

13. $\$105{,}900 \le y \le \$641{,}100$

14. H_0: $\rho = 0$; H_1: $\rho > 0$; $t_0 = 2.132$;
sample $t = 6.37$; Reject H_0; There is sufficient evidence that the population correlation coefficient is positive. r is significant.

CHAPTER 10
FORM B

1. CEO salary x versus Company Revenue y

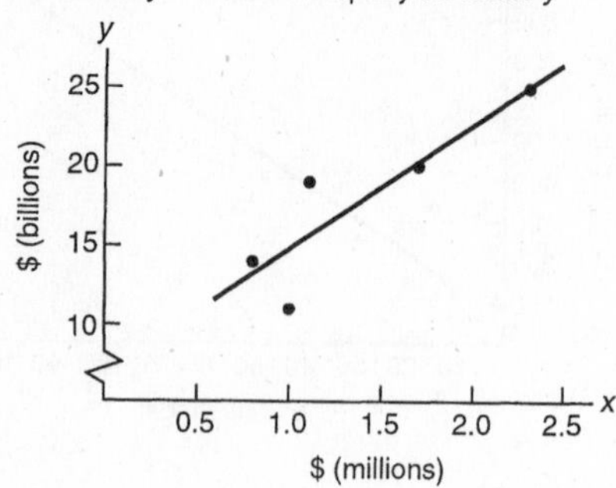

The linear correlation coefficient appears to be positive.

2. (a) $\bar{x} = 1.38$; $\bar{y} = 17.8$

   (b) $SS_x = 1.508$; $SS_y = 118.8$; $SS_{xy} = 11.78$

   (c) $b = 7.81$; $a = 7.02$;
   $y = 7.81x + 7.02$

   (d) See the line on the graph in Problem 1.

3. $r = 0.880$; $r^2 = 0.775$; 77.5% of the variation in y can be explained by the least squares line using x as the predicting variable.

4. $S_e = 2.988$

5. For a CEO salary of 1.5 million dollars, we predict an annual company revenue of 18.74 billion dollars.

6. $11.01 \le y \le 26.47$ billion dollars for company revenue

7. H_0: $\rho = 0$; H_1: $\rho \ne 0$; $t_0 = 5.841$; sample statistic $t = 3.21$; Do not reject H_0; The sample statistic is not significant. We do not have evidence of correlation between CEO salary and company revenue at the 1% level of significance. r is not significant.

8. Manufacturing Cost x versus Selling Price y

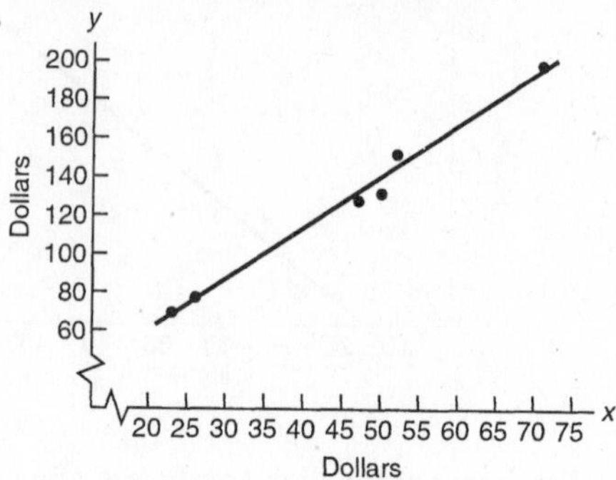

The linear correlation coefficient appears to be positive.

9. (a) $\bar{x} = 44.83$; $\bar{y} = 126.33$

   (b) $SS_x = 1598.83$; $SS_y = 11{,}339.33$;
   $SS_{xy} = 4232.33$

   (c) $b = 2.6471$; $a = 7.653$; $y = 2.65x + 7.65$

   (d) See line on the graph of Problem 8.

10. $r = 0.994$; $r^2 = 0.988$; 98.8% of the variation in y can be explained by the least squares line using x as the predicting variable.

11. $S_e = 5.826$

12. For $x = \$35$, $y = \$100.30$

13. $\$82.38 \le y \le \$118.22$

14. H_0: $\rho = 0$; H_1: $\rho > 0$; $t_0 = 2.132$; sample $t =$ 18.17; Reject H_0; There is evidence that the population correlation coefficient is positive. r is significant.

CHAPTER 10
FORM C

1. (a)	3. (b)	5. (a)	7. (b)	9. (e)	11. (a)	13. (e)
2. (d)	4. (a)	6. (c)	8. (c)	10. (d)	12. (c)	14. (b)

CHAPTER 11
FORM A

1. H_0: Teacher evaluations are independent of midterm grades;
H_1: Teacher evaluations are not independent of midterm grades; $\chi^2 = 43.68$; $\chi^2_{0.05} = 9.49$;
Reject H_0. There is evidence to say that at the 5% level of significance teacher evaluations are not independent of midterm grades.

2. H_0: The distribution of ages of college students is the same in the Western Association as in the nation.
H_1: The distribution of ages of college students is different in the Western Association than it is in the nation. $\chi^2 = 15.03$; $\chi^2_{0.05} = 9.49$;
Reject H_0. There is evidence that the distribution of ages is different.

3. Chi-square distribution

4. **(a)** $3.83 \le \sigma \le 6.82$

(b) H_0: $\sigma = 4.1$; H_1: $\sigma > 4.1$; $\chi^2_{0.01} = 42.98$; $\chi^2 = 34.28$; Do not reject H_0. There is not enough evidence to reject $\sigma = 4.1$.

5. H_0: $\sigma_1^2 = \sigma_2^2$; H_1: $\sigma_1^2 > \sigma_2^2$; $d.f._N = 15$; $d.f._D = 17$; critical value is 3.31; sample $F = 5.84$; Reject H_0.
There is evidence that the variance of diameters in Method I is greater.

6. H_0: $\mu_1 = \mu_2 = \mu_3 = \mu_4$; H_1: Not all means are equal; $F_{0.05} = 3.01$; sample $F = 2.42$;
Do not reject H_0. The means do not seem to be different among the groups.

7. H_0: all the means are equal; H_1: not all the means are equal;
$SS_{BET} = 284.67$; $SS_W = 139.33$; $SS_{TOT} = 424$; $d.f._{BET} = 2$; $d.f._W = 6$; $d.f._{TOT} = 8$;
$MS_{BET} = 142.33$; $MS_W = 23.22$; $F_{0.05} = 5.14$; Sample $F = 6.13$;
Reject H_0. There is evidence that the means among the departments are different.

8. **(a)**

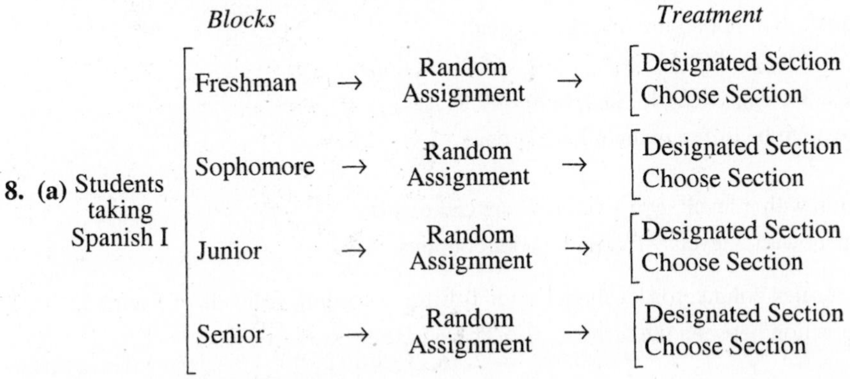

	Blocks				*Treatment*
Students taking Spanish I	Freshman	→	Random Assignment	→	Designated Section Choose Section
	Sophomore	→	Random Assignment	→	Designated Section Choose Section
	Junior	→	Random Assignment	→	Designated Section Choose Section
	Senior	→	Random Assignment	→	Designated Section Choose Section

(b) Yes, because you are arranging data into similar groups (or blocks) and then assigning the different treatments.

9. **(a)** H_0: No interaction between factors; H_1: Some interaction between factors;
$F_{0.01} = 3.67$; $F_{\text{interaction}} = 1.45$; Do not reject H_0; There is no evidence of interaction.

(b) H_0: No difference in mean time based on route;
H_1: At least two routes have different population mean times. $F_{0.01} = 4.72$; $F_{\text{route}} = 5.00$; Reject H_0.

(c) H_0: No difference in mean time based on departure time;
H_1: At least two departure times have different population mean times;
$F_{0.01} = 5.61$; $F_{\text{departure}} = 0.23$; Do not reject H_0.

CHAPTER 11
FORM B

1. H_0: The choice of college major is independent of grade average.
   H_1: The choice of college major is not independent of college average.
   $\chi^2_{0.05} = 13.28$; $\chi^2 = 2.64$;
   Do not reject H_0. There is not enough evidence to conclude that college major is not independent of grade average.

2. H_0: The distribution of fish fits the initial stocking distribution.
   H_1: The distribution of fish after six years does not fit the initial stocking distribution.
   $\chi^2_{0.05} = 9.49$; $\chi^2 = 66.78$;
   Reject H_0. There is enough evidence to conclude that the fish distribution has changed.

3. F distribution

4. **(a)** $5.45 \leq \sigma \leq 9.15$

   (b) H_0: $\sigma = 6$; H_1: $\sigma \neq 6$; critical values are 8.03 and 41.40. $\chi^2 = 26.97$;
   Do not reject H_0. There is not enough evidence to conclude that the standard deviation is different from 6.

5. H_0: $\sigma_1^2 = \sigma_2^2$; H_1: $\sigma_1^2 \neq \sigma_2^2$; $d.f._N = 8$; $d.f._D = 10$; use $\alpha = 0.025$ to find the critical value of 3.85; Sample F = 1.31; Do not reject H_0. There is not sufficient evidence to conclude that the variances of the two inventories are different.

6. H_0: $\mu_1 = \mu_2 = \mu_3 = \mu_4$; H_1: Not all means are equal; $F_{0.05} = 3.10$; Sample $F = 4.37$; Reject H_0. The means are not all equal.

7. H_0: all the means are equal; H_1: not all the means are equal;
   $SS_{BET} = 513.56$; $SS_W = 50$; $SS_{TOT} = 563.56$; $d.f._{BET} = 2$; $d.f._W = 6$; $d.f._{TOT} = 8$;
   $MS_{BET} = 256.78$; $MS_W = 8.33$; $F_{0.05} = 5.14$; Sample $F = 30.81$;
   Reject H_0. The means seem to be different among the groups.

8. **(a)** Factor 1 shelf location with 3 level: eye level, low, special display
   Factor 2 advertisement with 2 levels: TV, newspaper coupons

   (b) There is interaction if sales volume for levels in Factor 1 differ according to levels of Factor 2.
   H_0: There is no interaction between the factors; H_1: There is some interaction.

9. **(a)** H_0: No interaction between factors; H_1: Some interaction between factors;
   $F_{0.05} = 2.51$; $F_{\text{interaction}} = 0.85$; Do not reject H_0; There is no evidence of interaction.

   (b) H_0: No difference in mean price based on airline;
   H_1: At least two airlines have different population mean prices;
   $F_{0.05} = 3.01$; $F_{\text{airline}} = 0.66$; Do not reject H_0.

   (c) H_0: No difference in mean price based on destination;
   H_1: At least two destinations have different mean prices;
   $F_{0.05} = 3.40$; $F_{\text{destination}} = 17.05$; Reject H_0.

CHAPTER 11
FORM C

1. **A.** (c)
   B. (d)
   C. (e)
   D. (a)

2. **A.** (d)
   B. (a)
   C. (c)
   D. (b)

3. **A.** (e)
   B. (c)
   C. (d)

4. **A.** (a)
   B. (e)
   C. (e)

5. **A.** (e)
   B. (e)
   C. (c)
   D. (b)

6. **A.** (a)
   B. (d)
   C. (e)
   D. (b)

7. **A.** (c)
   B. (d)
   C. (d)
   D. (a)

8. (c)

9. **A.** (c)
   B. (b)
   C. (a)
   D. (d)
   E. (e)

CHAPTER 12 FORM A

1. H_0: Distributions are the same; H_1: Distribution after program is lower; one-tailed; $z_0 = -1.645$; $z = -1.39$ for $x = 4/13$. Do not reject H_0. The program did not seem to make a difference.

2. H_0: $\rho_s = 0$; H_1: $\rho_s \neq 0$; critical value = 0.881; Since the sample test statistic $r_s = 0.857$ does not fall in the critical region, we fail to reject H_0. There does not seem to be a monotone relation.

3. H_0: Workshop makes no difference; H_1: Workshop makes a difference; $z_0 = \pm 1.96$; $\mu_R = 68$; $\sigma_R = 9.522$; R(workshop participants) = 73 corresponds to $z = 0.525$; Since the sample test statistic does not fall in the critical region, we fail to reject H_0. The workshop does not seem to make a difference.

4. H_0: Distributions are the same; H_1: Distributions are different; two-tailed; $z_0 = \pm 1.96$; The sample proportion of plus signs $x = 7/12$ corresponds to $z = 0.577$. Since the sample test statistic does not fall in the critical region, we fail to reject H_0. There appears to be no difference in the scores after the lectures.

5. The sign that is used when we have paired data values coming from dependent samples as in "before-and-after" studies. It can be used when assumptions about normal populations are not satisfied or when assumptions about equal population variances are not satisfied.

CHAPTER 12 FORM B

1. H_0: Distributions are the same; H_1: Distribution for new is lower; one-tailed; $z_0 = -1.645$; $z = -1.15$ for $x = 4/12$. Do not reject H_0. The new keyboard did not seem to make a difference.

2. H_0: $\rho_s = 0$; H_1: $\rho_s \neq 0$; critical value = 0.648; Since the sample test statistic $r_s = 0.588$ does not fall in the critical region, we do not reject H_0. There does not seem to be a monotone increasing relation between midterm and final exam scores.

3. H_0: Income level makes no difference; H_1: Income level makes a difference; $z_0 = \pm 1.96$; $\mu_R = 68$; $\sigma_R = 9.522$; R(less than \$30,000) = 75 corresponds to $z = 0.735$; Since the sample test statistic does not fall in the critical region, we fail to reject H_0. Income level does not seem to make a difference.

4. H_0: Distributions are the same; H_1: Distribution after workshop is higher; one-tailed; $z_0 = 1.645$; The sample proportion of plus signs $x = 8/13 \approx 0.62$ corresponds to $z = 0.83$. Since the sample test statistic does not fall in the critical region, we fail to reject H_0.

5. The rank-sum test is used when independent random samples are drawn from two populations and the difference between sample means is tested. It can be used when assumptions about normal populations are not satisfied or when assumptions about population variances are not satisfied.

CHAPTER 12 FORM C

1. **A.** (c)
   B. (e)
   C. (d)
   D. (a)

2. **A.** (b)
   B. (c)
   C. (e)
   D. (a)

3. **A.** (d)
   B. (c)
   C. (a)
   D. (b)

4. **A.** (e)
   B. (d)
   C. (c)
   D. (b)

5. **A.** (e)
   B. (c)
   C. (b)

Part V

Complete Solutions

Chapter 1 Getting Started

Section 1.1

1. **(a)** The variable is the response regarding frequency of eating at fast-food restaurants.

(b) The variable is qualitative. The categories are the number of times one eats in fast-food restaurants.

(c) The implied population is responses for all adults in the U.S.

2. **(a)** The variable is the miles per gallon.

(b) The variable is quantitative because arithmetic operations can be applied the mpg values.

(c) The implied population is gasoline mileage for <u>all</u> new 2001 cars.

3. **(a)** The variable is student fees.

(b) The variable is quantitative because arithmetic operations can be applied to the fee values.

(c) The implied population is student fees at all colleges and universities in the U.S.

4. **(a)** The variable is the shelf life.

(b) The variable is quantitative because arithmetic operations can be applied to the shelf life values.

(c) The implied population is the shelf life of <u>all</u> Healthy Crunch granola bars.

5. **(a)** The variable is the time interval between check arrival and clearance.

(b) The variable is quantitative because arithmetic operations can be applied to the time intervals.

(c) The implied population is the time interval between check arrival and clearance for <u>all</u> companies in the five-state region.

6. Form B would be better. Statistical methods can be applied to the ordinal data obtained from Form B, but not to the answers obtained from Form A.

7. **(a)** *Length of time to complete an exam* is a ratio level of measurement. The data may be arranged in order, differences and ratios are meaningful, and a time of 0 is the starting point for all measurements.

(b) *Time of first class* is an interval level of measurement. The data may be arranged in order and differences are meaningful.

(c) *Class categories* is a nominal level of measurement. The data consists of names only.

(d) *Course evaluation scale* is an ordinal level of measurement. The data may be arranged in order.

(e) *Score on last exam* is a ratio level of measurement. The data may be arranged in order, differences and ratios are meaningful, and a score of 0 is the starting point for all measurements.

(f) *Age of student* is a ratio level of measurement. The data may be arranged in order, differences and ratios are meaningful, and an age of 0 is the starting point for all measurements.

8. **(a)** *Salesperson's performance* is an ordinal level of measurement. The data may be arranged in order.

(b) *Price of company's stock* is a ratio level of measurement. The data may be arranged in order, differences and ratios are meaningful, and a price of 0 is the starting point for all measurements.

(c) *Names of new products* is a nominal level of measurement. The data consist of names only.

(d) *Room temperature* is an interval level of measurement. The data may be arranged in order and differences are meaningful.

(e) *Gross income* is a ratio level of measurement. The data may be arranged in order, differences and ratios are meaningful, and an income of 0 is the starting point for all measurements.

(f) *Color of packaging* is a nominal level of measurement. The data consist of names only.

9. **(a)** *Species of fish* is a nominal level of measurement. Data consist of names only.

(b) *Cost of rod and reel* is a ratio level of measurement. The data may be arranged in order, differences and ratios are meaningful, and a cost of 0 is the starting point for all measurements.

(c) *Time of return home* is an interval level of measurement. The data may be arranged in order and differences are meaningful.

(d) *Guidebook rating* is an ordinal level of measurement. Data may be arranged in order.

(e) *Number of fish* caught is a ratio level of measurement. The data may be arranged in order, differences and ratios are meaningful, and 0 fish caught is the starting point for all measurements.

(f) *Temperature of the water* is an interval level of measurement. The data may be arranged in order and differences are meaningful.

Section 1.2

1. Essay

2. Answers vary. Use groups of 3 digits.

3. Answers vary. Use groups of 4 digits.

4. Answers vary. Use groups of 3 digits.

5. **(a)** Assign a distinct number to each subject. Then use a random number table. Group assignment methods vary.

(b) Repeat part (a) for 22 subjects.

(c) Answers vary.

6. Answers vary. Use single digits with odd corresponding to heads and even to tails.

7. **(a)** Yes, it is appropriate that the same number appears more than once because the outcome of a die roll can repeat. The outcome of the 4th roll is 2.

(b) No, we do not expect the same sequence because the process is random.

8. Answers vary. Use groups of 3 digits.

9. **(a)** Reasons may vary. For instance, the first four students may make a special effort to get to class on time.

(b) Reasons may vary. For instance, four students who come in late might all be nursing students enrolled in an anatomy and physiology class that meets the hour before in a far-away building. They may be more motivated than other students to complete a degree requirement.

(c) Reasons may vary. For instance, four students sitting in the back row might be less inclined to participate in class discussions.

(d) Reasons may vary. For instance, the tallest students might all be male.

10. In all cases, assign distinct numbers to the items, and use a random-number table.

11. In all cases, assign distinct numbers to the items, and use a random-number table.

12. Answers vary. Use single digits with even corresponding to true and odd corresponding to false.

13. Answers vary. Use single digits with correct answer placed in corresponding position.

14. (a) This technique is stratified sampling. The population was divided into strata (4 categories of length of hospital stay), then a simple random sample was drawn from each stratum.

(b) This technique is simple random sampling. Every sample of size n from the population has an equal chance of being selected and every member of the population has an equal chance of being included in the sample.

(c) This technique is cluster sampling. There are 5 geographic regions and a random sample of hospitals is selected from each region. Then, for each selected hospital, all patients on the discharge list are surveyed to create the patient satisfaction profiles. Within each hospital, the degree of satisfaction varies patient to patient. The sampling units (the hospitals) are clusters of individuals who will be studied.

(d) This technique is systematic sampling. Every k^{th} element is included in the sample.

(e) This technique is convenience sampling. This technique uses results or data that are conveniently and readily obtained.

15. (a) This technique is simple random sampling. Every sample of size n from the population has an equal chance of being selected and every member of the population has an equal chance of being included in the sample.

(b) This technique is cluster sampling. The state, Hawaii, is divided into regions using, say, the first 3 digits of the Zip code. Within each region a random sample of 10 Zip code areas is selected using, say, all 5 digits of the Zip code. Then, within each selected Zip codes, all businesses are surveyed. The sampling units, defined by 5 digit Zip codes, are clusters of businesses, and within each selected Zip code, the benefits package the businesses offer their employees differs business to business.

(c) This technique is convenience sampling. This technique uses results or data that are conveniently and readily obtained.

(d) This technique is systematic sampling. Every k^{th} element is included in the sample.

(e) This technique is stratified sampling. The population was divided into strata (10 business types), then a simple random sample was drawn from each stratum.

Section 1.3

1. (a) This is an observational study because observations and measurements of individuals are conducted in a way that doesn't change the response or the variable being measured.

(b) This is an experiment because a treatment is deliberately imposed on the individuals in order to observe a possible change in the response or variable being measured.

(c) This is an experiment because a treatment is deliberately imposed on the individuals in order to observe a possible change in the response or variable being measured.

(d) This is an observational study because observations and measurements of individuals are conducted in a way that doesn't change the response or the variable being measured.

2. (a) A census was used because data for all the games were used.

(b) An experiment was used. A treatment is deliberately imposed on the individuals in order to observe change in the response or variable being measured.

(c) A simulation was used because computer imaging of runners was used.

(d) Sampling was used because measurements from a representative part of the population were used.

3. (a) Sampling was used because measurements from a representative part of the population were used.

(b) A simulation was used because computer programs that mimic actual flight were used.

(c) A census was used because data for all scores are available.

(d) An experiment was used. A treatment is deliberately imposed on the individuals in order to observe change in the response or variable being measured.

4. (a) No, "over the last few years" could mean the last three years to some and the last five years to others, etc.; answers vary.

(b) Yes. The response to doubling fines would be affected by whether the responder had ever run a stop sign.

(c) Answers vary.

5. (a) Use random selection to pick 10 calves to inoculate. Then test all calves to see if there is a difference in resistance to infection between the two groups. There is no placebo being used.

(b) Use random selection to pick 9 schools to visit. Then survey all the schools to see if there is a difference in views between the two groups. There is no placebo being used.

(c) Use random selection to pick 40 volunteers for skin patch with drug. Then survey all volunteers to see if a difference exists between the two groups. A placebo for the remaining 35 volunteers in the second group is used.

6. (a) Use random selection to pick 25 cars for high-temperature bond tires. Then examine tires of all the cars to see if a difference exists between the two groups. This is a double-blind experiment because neither the individuals in the study nor the observers know which subjects are receiving the new tires.

(b) Use random selection to pick 10 bags. Then send all bags through the security check. This is not a double-blind experiment because the agent carrying the bag knows whether or not the bag contains a weapon.

(c) Use random selection to pick 35 patients for new eye drops. Then measure eye pressure for all patients to see if a difference exists between the two groups. This is a double-blind experiment because neither the patients nor the doctors know which subjects are receiving the new drops.

Chapter 1 Review

1. Answers vary.

2. The implied population is the opinions of all the listeners. The variable is the opinion of a caller. There is probably bias in the selection of the sample because those with the strongest opinions are most likely to call in.

3. Essay

4. Name, social security number, color of hair and eyes, address, phone number, place of birth, and college major are all nominal because the data consist of names or qualities only. Letter grade on test is ordinal because the data may be arranged in order. Year of birth is interval because the data may be arranged in order and differences are meaningful. Height, age, and distance from home to college are ratio because the data may be arranged in order, differences and ratios are meaningful, and 0 is the starting point for all measurements.

5. In the random number table use groups of 2 digits. Select the first six distinct groups of 2 digits that fall in the range from 01 to 42. Choices vary according to the starting place in the random number table.

6. (a) Cluster sampling was used because a random sample of 10 telephone prefixes was selected and all households in the selected prefixes were included in the sample.

(b) Convenience sampling was used because it uses results or data that are conveniently and readily obtained.

(c) Systematic sampling was used because every k^{th} element is included in the sample.

(d) Random sampling was used because every sample of size 30 from the population has an equal chance of being selected and every member of the population has an equal chance of being included.

(e) Stratified sampling was used because the population was divided into strata (three age categories), then a simple random sample was drawn from each stratum.

7. (a) This is an observational study because observations and measurements of individuals are conducted in a way that doesn't change the response or the variable being measured.

(b) This is an experiment because a treatment is deliberately imposed on the individuals in order to observe a possible change in the response or variable being measured.

8. (a) Use random selection to pick half to solicit by mail. Then compute the percentage of donors in each group. Compare the results. No placebo was used.

(b) Use random selection to pick 43 volunteers to be given whitening gel. Evaluate tooth whiteness for all participants. Compare the results. A placebo was used with the remaining 42 in the second group. The experiment could be double-blind if the observers did not know which subjects were receiving the tooth whitening chemicals.

9. This is a good problem for class discussion. Some items such as age and grade point average might be sensitive information. You could ask the class to design a data form that can be filled out anonymously. Other issues to discuss involve the accuracy and honesty of the responses.

10. Students may easily spend several hours at this Web site.

Chapter 2 Organizing Data

Section 2.1

1. Highest Level of Education and Average Annual Household Income (in thousands of dollars)

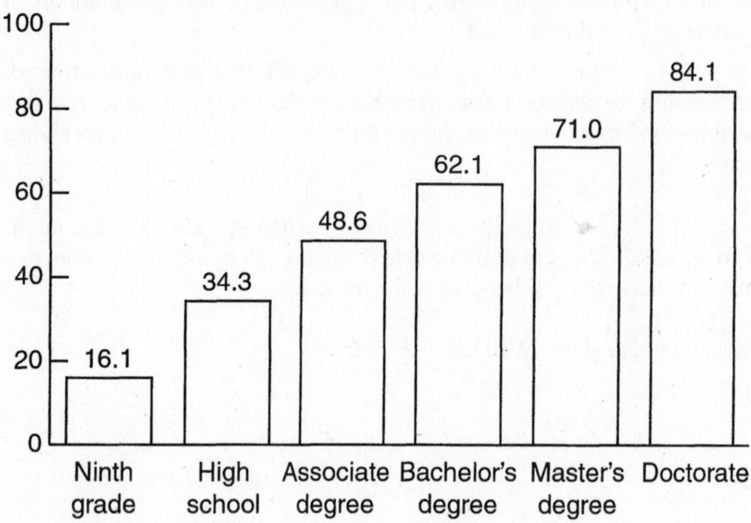

2. Annual Number of Deaths from Injuries per 100,000 Children (Ages 1 to 14)

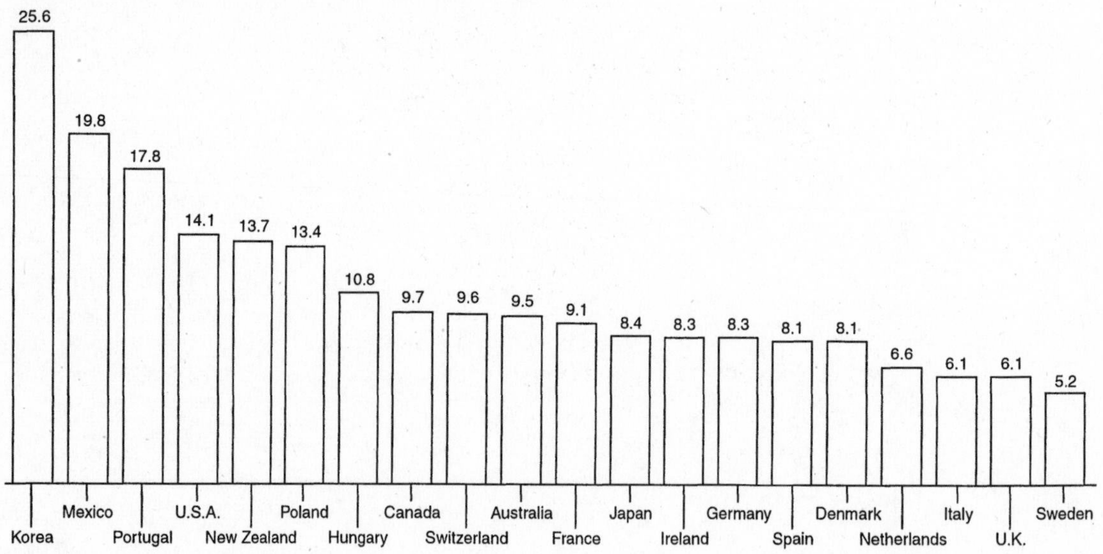

3. Number of People Who Died in a Calendar Year from Listed Causes—Pareto Chart

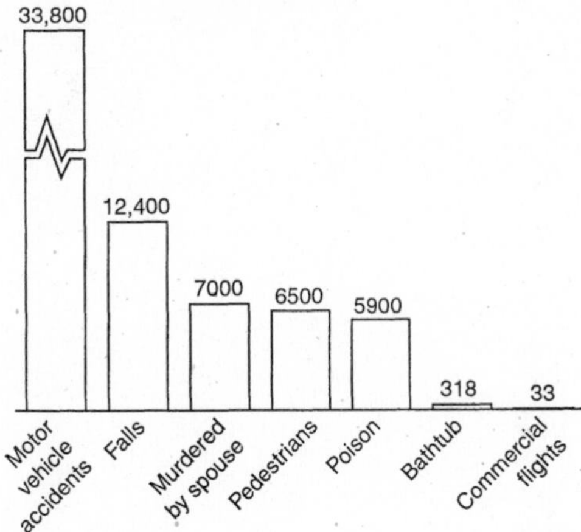

4. (a) Since 88% of those surveyed cited internal problems, 100% – 88% = 12% cited external factors as the leading cause of business failure. Among the internal causes, 88% – 13% – 13% – 18% – 29% = 15% must have listed various other internal factors for the leading cause of business failure.

Causes for Business Failure—Pareto Chart

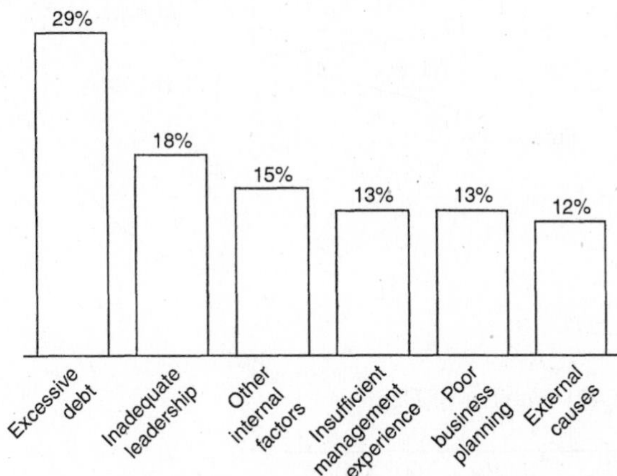

(b) As shown in part (a), 15% of those interviewed cited other internal factors as the leading cause of business failure. Excessive debt was the most commonly cited (internal and overall) cause for business failure.

Cause of Business Failure	Percentage	Frequency
Insufficient management experiences	13%	13% × 1300 = 169
Poor business planning	13%	13% × 1300 = 169
Inadequate leadership	18%	18% × 1300 = 234
Excessive debt	29%	29% × 1300 = 377
Other internal factors	15%	15% × 1300 = 195
External factors	12%	12% × 1300 = 156
Total	100%	1300

5.

Hiding place	Percentage	Number of Degrees
In the closet	68%	68% × 360° ≈ 245°
Under the bed	23%	23% × 360° ≈ 83°
In the bathtub	6%	6% × 360° ≈ 22°
In the freezer	3%	3% × 360° ≈ 11°
Total	100%	361°*

*Total does not add to 360° due to rounding.

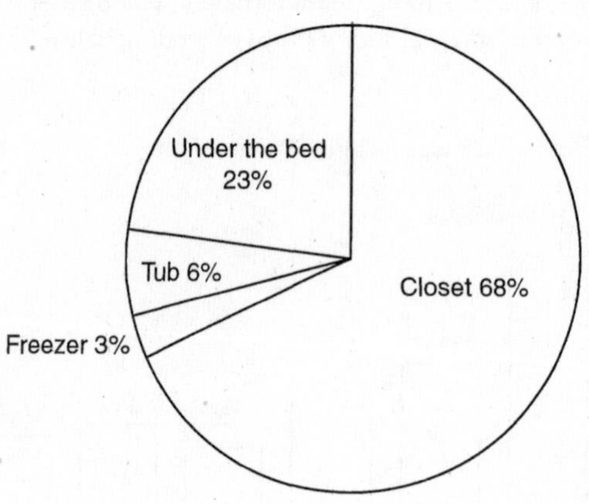

6.

Meal	Percentage	Number of Degrees
Lunch	48.9%	48.9% × 360° ≈ 176°
Breakfast	7.7%	7.7% × 360° ≈ 28°
Dinner	31.6%	31.6% × 360° ≈ 114°
Snack	10.0%	10.0% × 360° = 36°
Don't know	1.8%	1.8% × 360° ≈ 6°
Total	100.0%	360°

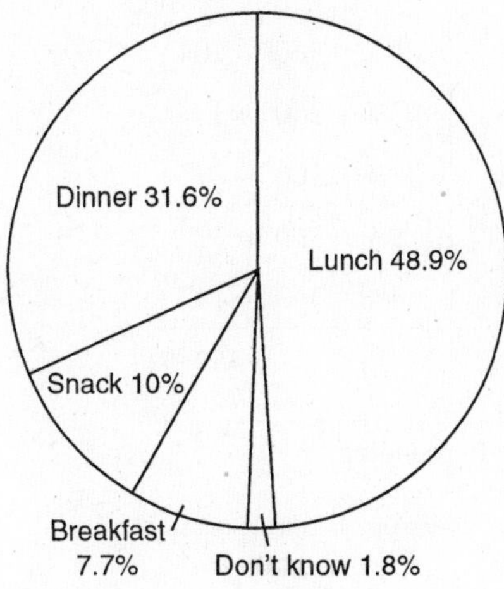

7. Professional Activity	Percentage	Number of Degrees
Teaching	51%	$51\% \times 360° \approx 184°$
Research	16%	$16\% \times 360° \approx 58°$
Professional growth	5%	$5\% \times 360° = 18°$
Community service	11%	$11\% \times 360° \approx 40°$
Service to the college	11%	$11\% \times 360° \approx 40°$
Consulting outside the college	6%	$6\% \times 360° \approx 22°$
Total	100%	362°*

* Total does not add to 360° due to rounding.

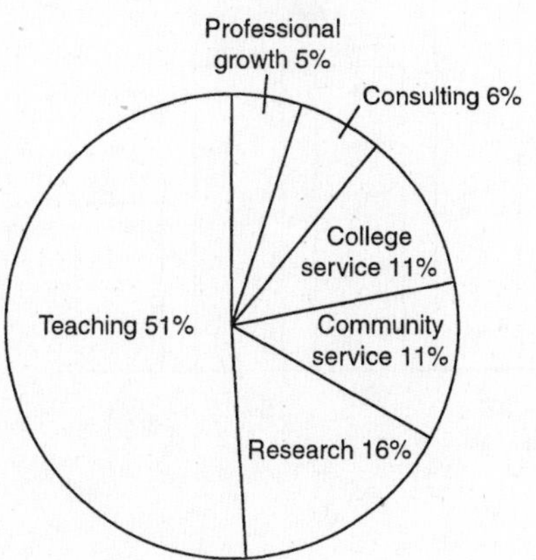

8.

Age	Percentage	Number of Degrees
Under 35 years	8%	$8\% \times 360° \approx 29°$
35–44 years	29%	$29\% \times 360° \approx 104°$
45–54 years	37%	$37\% \times 360° \approx 133°$
55–59 years	13%	$13\% \times 360° \approx 47°$
60–64 years	9%	$9\% \times 360° \approx 32°$
65 years and over	4%	$4\% \times 360° \approx 14°$
Total	100%	359°*

*Total does not add to 360° due to rounding.

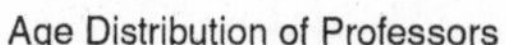

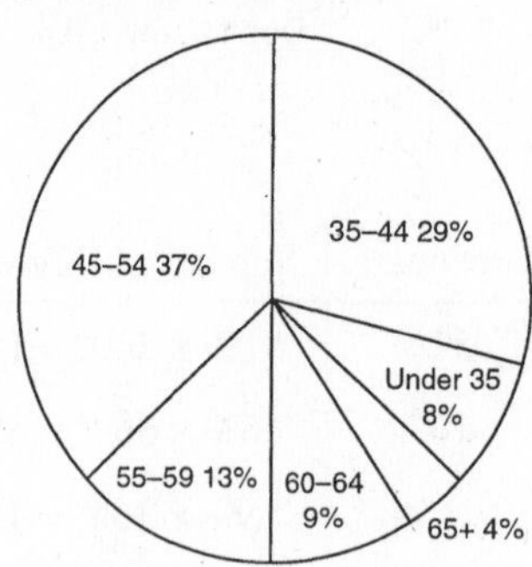

9. Percentage of Households with Telephone Gadgets

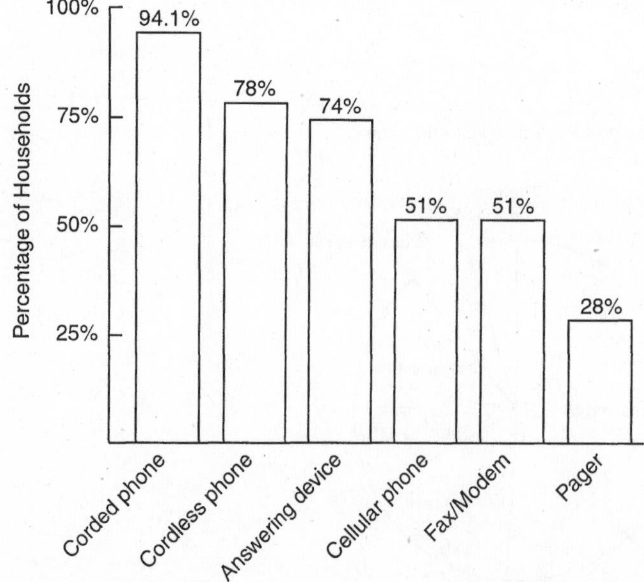

No. Since household can report having more than one telephone gadget, the percentages will not add to 100%.

10. The following Pareto Chart shows the percentage of drivers for each stated complaint.

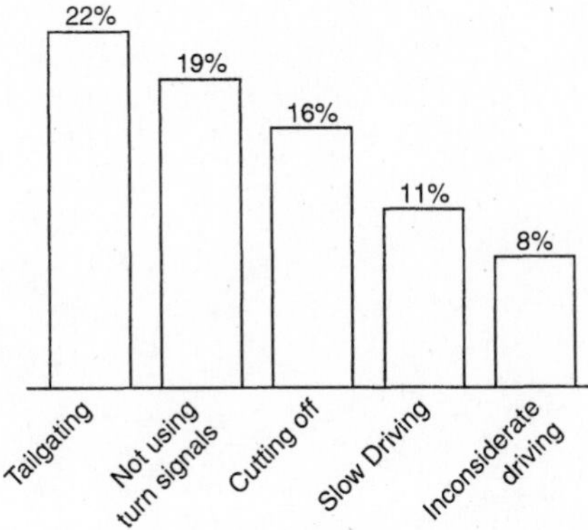

By subtraction, 100% – 22% – 19% – 16% – 11% – 8% = 24% of the respondents citied other bad habits.

Bad Habit	Percentage	Frequency
Tailgating	22%	$22\% \times 500 = 110$
Not using turn signals	19%	$19\% \times 500 = 95$
Cutting off other drivers	16%	$16\% \times 500 = 80$
Driving too slowly	11%	$11\% \times 500 = 55$
Being inconsiderate	8%	$8\% \times 500 = 40$
Other	24%	$24\% \times 500 = 120$
Total	100%	500

As reported, the percentages add to 76%, not the 100% needed for a circle graph. However, if there was only one response per person, knowing that the company surveyed 500 drivers tells us that 120 drivers, or 24%, had other bad driving complaints. Using this fact, a circle graph could be used.

11.

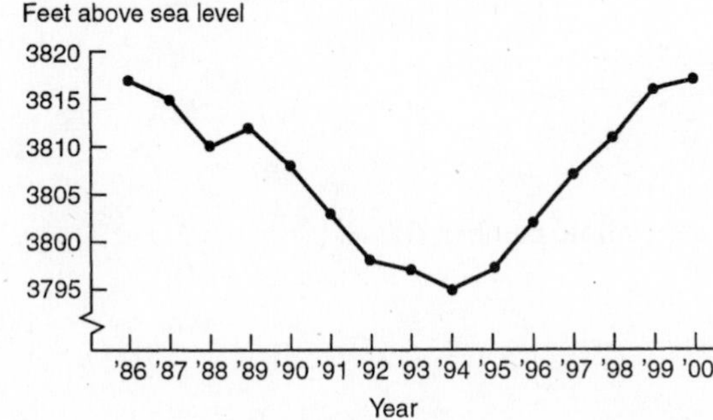

12.

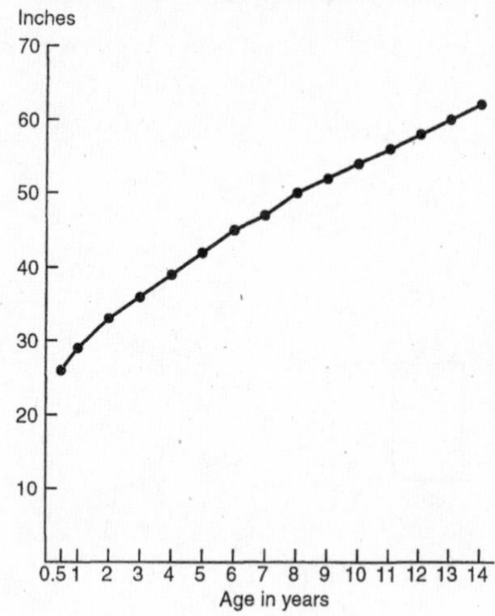

13. Both stocks ended down for the one-year period. Coca-Cola ranged from a high of about \$64 to a low of about \$42.50. McDonald's ranged from a high of about \$37 to a low of about \$25.McDonald's attained its high during the first week and was never as high again. From the high of the first week to the high of the last week shown, we can calculate the approximate percentage change in price by finding the difference in the high values and dividing that by the 6/9/00 high. Thus, Coca-Cola declined $\frac{54-47}{54} \approx 13\%$ while McDonald's declined $\frac{36-29}{36} \approx 19\%$.

Append: Volatility is shown by the moving average lines: the smoother the line, the less volatile the stock price. The 200-day moving average will always be smoother than the 50-day moving average, and it is less sensitive than the 50-day moving average to abrupt changes. Coke's 200-day moving average does not yet register the steep drop in price during the February to April period. Both moving average lines are smoother for McDonald's indicating its price is less volatile.

Both McDonald's and Coca-Cola's week-to-week-patterns are similar, rising and dropping over approximately the same periods. This, coupled with the DJIA's increase of 2.3% over the same year, may reflect some factor affecting the fast food/soft drink sector that does not impact the market as a whole. For example, a rise in gasoline prices would depress the fast food and soft drink sectors as well as the overall market, by increasing the cost of transporting food and reducing disposable income overall. Impacted sectors would become less profitable, and their stock values would decrease.

Section 2.2

1. (a) largest data value = 360

smallest data value = 236

number of classes specified = 5

class width $= \frac{360-236}{5} = 24.8$, increased to next whole number, 25

(b) The lower class limit of the first class in the smallest value, 236.

The lower class limit of the next class is the previous class's lower class limit plus the class width; for the second class, this is 236 + 25 = 261.

The upper class limit is one value less than lower class limit of the next class; for the first class, the upper class limit is 261 − 1 = 260.

The class boundaries are the halfway points between (i.e., the average of) the (adjacent) upper class limit of one class and the lower class limit of the next class. The lower class boundary of the first class is the lower class limit minus one-half unit. The upper class boundary for the last class is the upper class limit plus one-half unit. For the first class, the class boundaries are $236 - \frac{1}{2} = 235.5$ and $\frac{260+261}{2} = 260.5$. For the last class, the class boundaries are $\frac{335+336}{2} = 335.5$ and $360 + \frac{1}{2} = 360.5$.

The class mark or midpoint is the average of the class limits for that class. For the first class, the midpoint is $\frac{236+260}{2} = 248$.

The class frequency is the number of data values that belong to that class; call this value f.

The relative frequency of a class is the class frequency, f, divided by the total number of data values, i.e., the overall sample size, n.

For the first class, $f = 4$, $n = 57$, and the relative frequency is $f/n = \frac{4}{57} \approx 0.07$.

The cumulative frequency of a class is the sum of the frequencies for all previous classes, plus the frequency of that class. For the first and second classes, the class cumulative frequencies are 4 and 4 + 9 = 13, respectively.

Class Limits	Boundaries	Midpoint	Frequency	Relative Frequency	Cumulative Frequency
236–260	235.5–260.5	248	4	0.07	4
261–285	260.5–285.5	273	9	0.16	13
286–310	285.5–310.5	298	25	0.44	38
311–335	310.5–335.5	323	16	0.28	54
336–360	335.5–360.5	348	3	0.05	57

(c) The histogram plots the class frequencies on the y-axis and the class boundaries on the x-axis. Since adjacent classes share boundary values, the bars touch each other. [Alternatively, the bars may be centered over the class marks (midpoints).]

(d) A frequency polygon connects the midpoints of each class (shown as a dot in the middle of the top of the histogram bar) with line segments. Place a dot on the x-axis one class width below the midpoint of the first class, and place another dot on the x-axis one class width above the last class's midpoint. Connect these dots to the adjacent midpoint dots with line segments.

(e) The relative frequency histogram is exactly the same shape as the frequency histogram, but the vertical scale is relative frequency, f/n, instead of actual frequency, f.

The following figure shows the histogram, frequency polygon, and relative-frequency histogram for (c), (d), and (e) above, overlaying one another. (Note that two vertical scales are shown.)

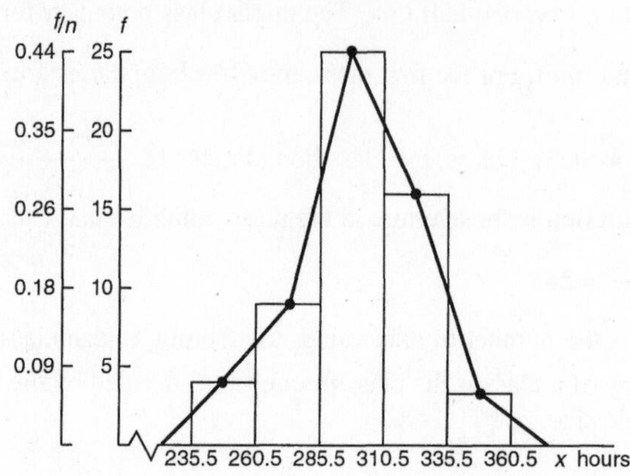

(f) To create the ogive, place a dot on the x-axis at the lower class boundary of the first class and then, for each class, place a dot above the upper class boundary value at the height of the cumulative frequency for the class. Connect the dots with line segments.

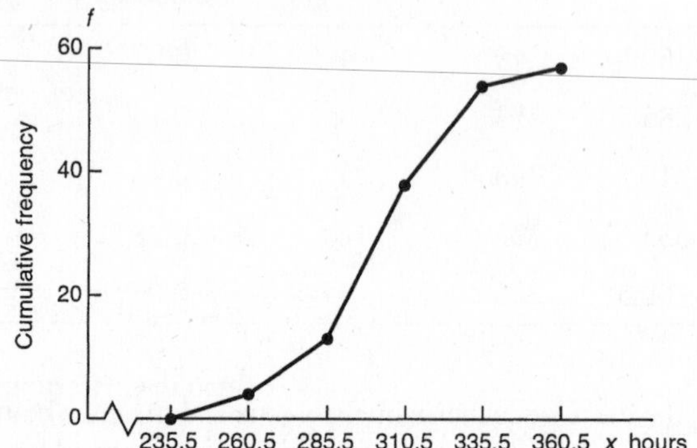

2. (a) largest data value = 65

smallest data value = 20

number of classes specified = 5

class width $= \dfrac{65-20}{5} = 9$, increased to next whole number, 10

(b) The lower class limit of the first class in the smallest value, 20.

The lower class limit of the next class is the previous class's lower class limit plus the class width; for the second class, this is 20 + 10 = 30.

The upper class limit is one value less than lower class limit of the next class; for the first class, the upper class limit is 30 – 1 = 29.

The class boundaries are the halfway points between (i.e., the average of) the (adjacent) upper class limit of one class and the lower class limit of the next class. The lower class boundary of the first class is the lower class limit minus one-half unit. The upper class boundary for the last class is the upper class limit plus one-half unit. For the first class, the class boundaries are $20-\frac{1}{2}=19.5$ and $\frac{29+30}{2}=29.5$. For the last class, the class boundaries are $\frac{59+60}{2}=59.5$ and $69+\frac{1}{2}=69.5$.

The class mark or midpoint is the average of the class limits for that class. For the first class, the midpoint is $\frac{20+29}{2}=24.5$.

The class frequency is the number of data values that belong to that class; call this value f.

The relative frequency of a class is the class frequency, f, divided by the total number of data values, i.e., the overall sample size, n.

For the first class, $f = 3$, $n = 35$, and the relative frequency is $f/n = 3/35 \approx 0.0857$.

The cumulative frequency of a class is the sum of the frequencies for all previous classes, plus the frequency of that class. For the first and second classes, the class cumulative frequencies are 3 and 3 + 6 = 9, respectively.

Percent Difficult Ski Terrain

Class Limits	Class Boundaries	Midpoint	Frequency	Relative Frequency	Cumulative Frequency
20–29	19.5–29.5	24.5	3	0.0857	3
30–39	29.5–39.5	34.5	6	0.1714	9
40–49	39.5–49.5	44.5	13	0.3714	22
50–59	49.5–59.5	54.5	9	0.2571	31
60–69	59.5–69.5	64.5	4	0.1143	35

(c) The histogram plots the class frequencies on the y-axis and the class boundaries on the x-axis. Since adjacent classes share boundary values, the bars touch each other. [Alternatively, the bars may be centered over the class marks (midpoints).]

(d) A frequency polygon connects the midpoints of each class (shown as a dot in the middle of the top of the histogram bar) with line segments. Place a dot on the x-axis one class width below the midpoint of the first class, and place another dot on the x-axis one class width above the last class's midpoint. Connect these dots to the adjacent midpoint dots with line segments.

(e) The relative frequency histogram is exactly the same shape as the frequency histogram, but the vertical scale is relative frequency, f/n, instead of actual frequency, f.

The following figure shows the histogram, frequency polygon, and relative-frequency histogram for (c), (d), and (e) above, overlaying one another. (Note that two vertical scales are shown.)

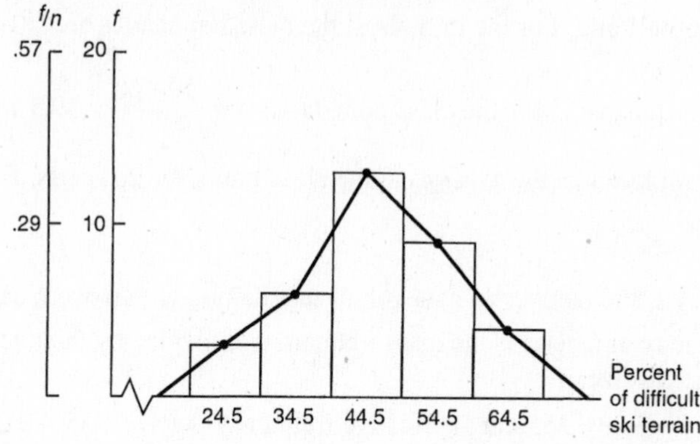

(f) To create the ogive, place a dot on the x-axis at the lower class boundary of the first class and then, for each class, place a dot above the upper class boundary value at the height of the cumulative frequency for the class. Connect the dots with line segments.

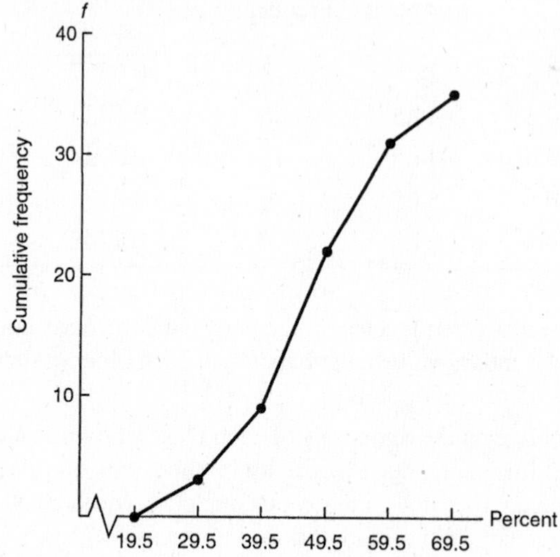

3. (a) largest data value = 53

smallest data value = 5

number of classes specified = 7

class width $= \frac{53-5}{7} \approx 6.86$, increased to next whole number, 7

(b) The lower class limit of the first class in the smallest value, 5.

The lower class limit of the next class is the previous class's lower class limit plus the class width; for the second class, this is 5 + 7 = 12.

The upper class limit is one value less than lower class limit of the next class; for the first class, the upper class limit is 12 – 1 = 11.

The class boundaries are the halfway points between (i.e., the average of) the (adjacent) upper class limit of one class and the lower class limit of the next class. The lower class boundary of the first class is the lower class limit minus one-half unit. The upper class boundary for the last class is the upper class limit plus one-half unit. For the first class, the class boundaries are $5-\frac{1}{2}=4.5$ and $\frac{11+12}{2}=11.5$. For the last class, the class boundaries are $\frac{46+47}{2}=46.5$ and $53+\frac{1}{2}=53.5$.

The class mark or midpoint is the average of the class limits for that class. For the first class, the midpoint is $\frac{5+11}{2}=8$.

The class frequency is the number of data values that belong to that class; call this value f.

The relative frequency of a class is the class frequency, f, divided by the total number of data values, i.e., the overall sample size, n.

For the first class, $f = 4$, $n = 50$, and the relative frequency is $f/n = 4/50 \approx 0.08$.

The cumulative frequency of a class is the sum of the frequencies for all previous classes, plus the frequency of that class. For the first and second classes, the class cumulative frequencies are 4 and 4 + 7 = 11, respectively.

Class Limits	Class Boundaries	Midpoint	Frequency	Relative Frequency	Cumulative Frequency
5–11	4.5–11.5	8	4	0.08	4
12–18	11.5–18.5	15	7	0.14	11
19–25	18.5–25.5	22	12	0.24	22
26–32	25.5–32.5	29	12	0.24	35
33–39	32.5–39.5	36	12	0.24	47
40–46	39.5–46.5	43	2	0.04	49
47–53	46.5–53.5	50	1	0.02	50

(c) The histogram plots the class frequencies on the y-axis and the class boundaries on the x-axis. Since adjacent classes share boundary values, the bars touch each other. [Alternatively, the bars may be centered over the class marks (midpoints).]

(d) A frequency polygon connects the midpoints of each class (shown as a dot in the middle of the top of the histogram bar) with line segments. Place a dot on the x-axis one class width below the midpoint of the first class, and place another dot on the x-axis one class width above the last class's midpoint. Connect these dots to the adjacent midpoint dots with line segments.

(e) The relative frequency histogram is exactly the same shape as the frequency histogram, but the vertical scale is relative frequency, f/n, instead of actual frequency, f.

The following figure shows the histogram, frequency polygon, and relative-frequency histogram for (c), (d), and (e) above, overlaying one another. (Note that two vertical scales are shown.)

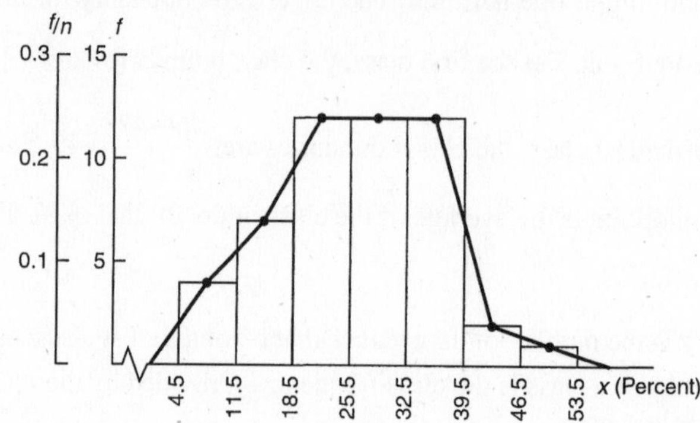

(f) To create the ogive, place a dot on the x-axis at the lower class boundary of the first class and then, for each class, place a dot above the upper class boundary value at the height of the cumulative frequency for the class. Connect the dots with line segments.

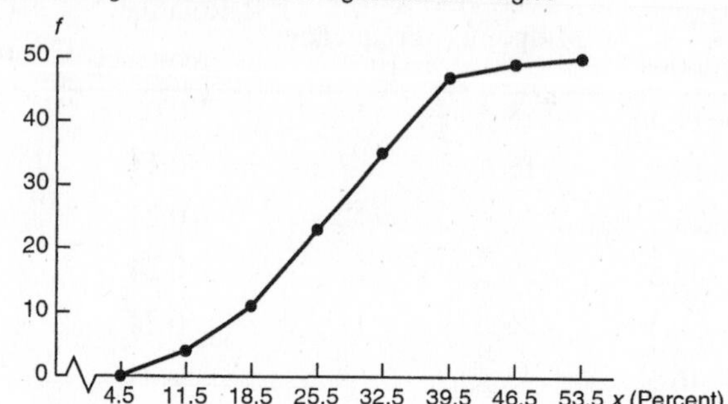

4. (a) largest data value = 75

smallest data value = 5

number of classes specified = 5

class width $= \dfrac{75-5}{5} = 14$, increased to next whole number, 15

(b) The lower class limit of the first class in the smallest value, 5.

The lower class limit of the next class is the previous class's lower class limit plus the class width; for the second class, this is 5 + 15 = 20.

The upper class limit is one value less than lower class limit of the next class; for the first class, the upper class limit is 20 – 1 = 19.

The class boundaries are the halfway points between (i.e., the average of) the (adjacent) upper class limit of one class and the lower class limit of the next class. The lower class boundary of the first class is the lower class limit minus one-half unit. The upper class boundary for the last class is the upper class limit plus one-half unit. For the first class, the class boundaries are $5-\frac{1}{2}=4.5$ and $\frac{19+20}{2}=19.5$. For the last class, the class boundaries are $\frac{64+65}{2}=64.5$ and $79+\frac{1}{2}=79.5$.

The class mark or midpoint is the average of the class limits for that class. For the first class, the midpoint is $\frac{5+19}{2}=12$.

The class frequency is the number of data values that belong to that class; call this value f.

The relative frequency of a class is the class frequency, f, divided by the total number of data values, i.e., the overall sample size, n.

For the first class, $f = 21$, $n = 63$, and the relative frequency is $f/n = 21/63 \approx 0.3333$.

The cumulative frequency of a class is the sum of the frequencies for all previous classes, plus the frequency of that class. For the first and second classes, the class cumulative frequencies are 21 and 21 + 35 = 56, respectively.

Fast-Food Franchise Fees (in thousands)

Class Limits	Class Boundaries	Midpoint	Frequency	Relative Frequency	Cumulative Frequency
5–19	4.5–19.5	12	21	0.3333	21
20–34	19.5–34.5	27	35	0.5556	56
35–49	34.5–49.5	42	5	0.0794	61
50–64	49.5–64.5	57	1	0.0159	62
65–79	64.5–79.5	72	1	0.0159	63

(c) The histogram plots the class frequencies on the y-axis and the class boundaries on the x-axis. Since adjacent classes share boundary values, the bars touch each other. [Alternatively, the bars may be centered over the class marks (midpoints).]

(d) A frequency polygon connects the midpoints of each class (shown as a dot in the middle of the top of the histogram bar) with line segments. Place a dot on the x-axis one class width below the midpoint of the first class, and place another dot on the x-axis one class width above the last class's midpoint. Connect these dots to the adjacent midpoint dots with line segments.

(e) The relative frequency histogram is exactly the same shape as the frequency histogram, but the vertical scale is relative frequency, f/n, instead of actual frequency, f.

The following figure shows the histogram, frequency polygon, and relative-frequency histogram for (c), (d), and (e) above, overlaying one another. (Note that two vertical scales are shown.)

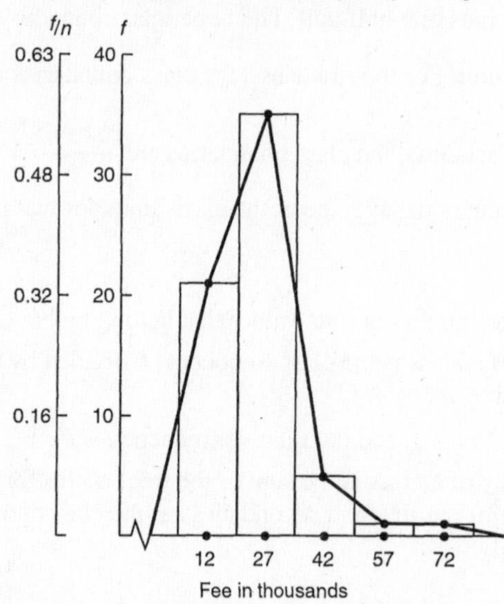

(f) To create the ogive, place a dot on the x-axis at the lower class boundary of the first class and then, for each class, place a dot above the upper class boundary value at the height of the cumulative frequency for the class. Connect the dots with line segments.

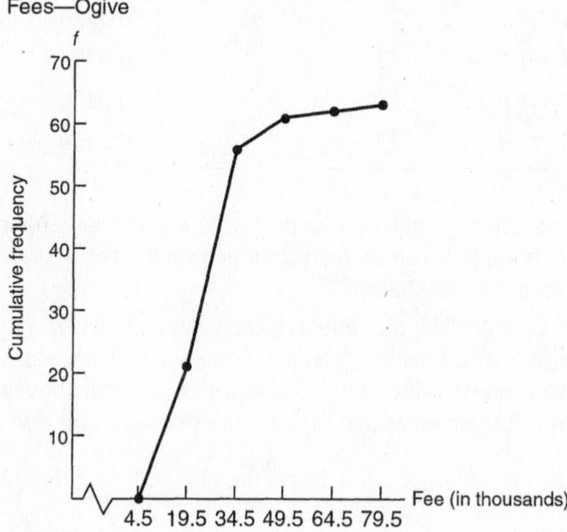

5. (a) largest data value = 102

smallest data value = 18

number of classes specified = 5

class width $= \dfrac{102-18}{5} = 16.8$, increased to next whole number, 17

(b) The lower class limit of the first class in the smallest value, 18.

The lower class limit of the next class is the previous class's lower class limit plus the class width; for the second class, this is 18 + 17 = 35.

The upper class limit is one value less than lower class limit of the next class; for the first class, the upper class limit is 35 – 1 = 34.

The class boundaries are the halfway points between (i.e., the average of) the (adjacent) upper class limit of one class and the lower class limit of the next class. The lower class boundary of the first class is the lower class limit minus one-half unit. The upper class boundary for the last class is the upper class limit plus one-half unit. For the first class, the class boundaries are $18-\frac{1}{2}=17.5$ and $\frac{34+35}{2}=34.5$. For the last class, the class boundaries are $\frac{85+86}{2}=85.5$ and $102+\frac{1}{2}=102.5$.

The class mark or midpoint is the average of the class limits for that class. For the first class, the midpoint is $\frac{18+34}{2}=26$.

The class frequency is the number of data values that belong to that class; call this value f.

The relative frequency of a class is the class frequency, f, divided by the total number of data values, i.e., the overall sample size, n.

For the first class, $f = 1$, $n = 35$, and the relative frequency is $f/n = 1/35 \approx 0.03$.

The cumulative frequency of a class is the sum of the frequencies for all previous classes, plus the frequency of that class. For the first and second classes, the class cumulative frequencies are 1 and 1 + 2 = 3, respectively.

Number of Room Calls per Night

Class Limits	Class Boundaries	Midpoint	Frequency	Relative Frequency	Cumulative Frequency
18–34	17.5–34.5	26	1	0.03	1
35–51	34.5–51.5	43	2	0.06	3
52–68	51.5–68.5	60	5	0.14	8
69–85	68.5–85.5	77	15	0.43	23
86–102	85.5–102.5	94	12	0.34	35

(c) The histogram plots the class frequencies on the y-axis and the class boundaries on the x-axis. Since adjacent classes share boundary values, the bars touch each other. [Alternatively, the bars may be centered over the class marks (midpoints).]

(d) A frequency polygon connects the midpoints of each class (shown as a dot in the middle of the top of the histogram bar) with line segments. Place a dot on the x-axis one class width below the midpoint of the first class, and place another dot on the x-axis one class width above the last class's midpoint. Connect these dots to the adjacent midpoint dots with line segments.

(e) The relative frequency histogram is exactly the same shape as the frequency histogram, but the vertical scale is relative frequency, *f/n*, instead of actual frequency, *f*.

The following figure shows the histogram, frequency polygon, and relative-frequency histogram for (c), (d), and (e) above, overlaying one another. (Note that two vertical scales are shown.)

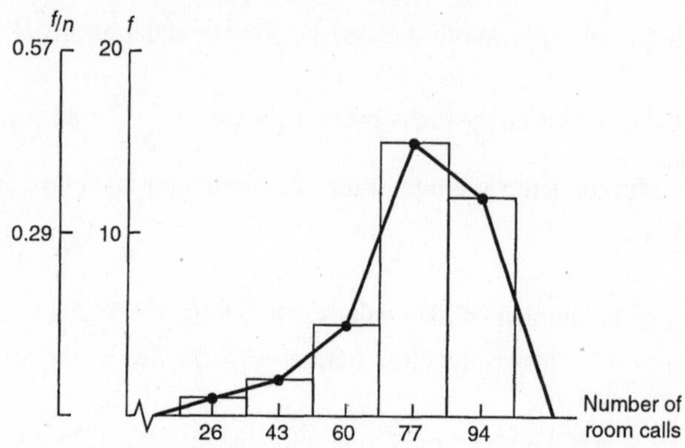

(f) To create the ogive, place a dot on the x-axis at the lower class boundary of the first class and then, for each class, place a dot above the upper class boundary value at the height of the cumulative frequency for the class. Connect the dots with line segments.

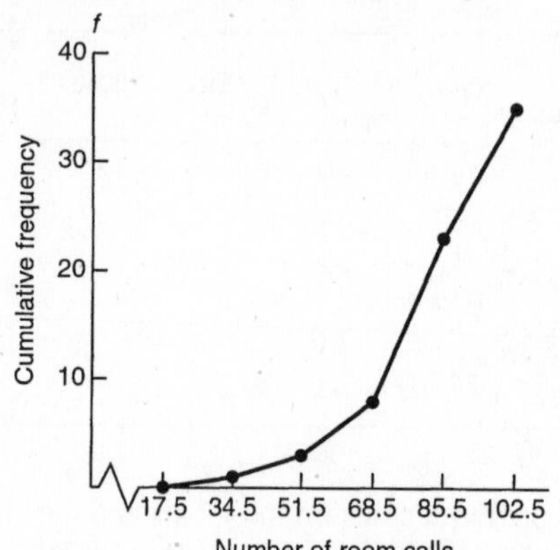

6. (a) largest data value = 43

smallest data value = 0

number of classes specified = 8

class width $= \dfrac{43-0}{8} = 5.375$, increased to next whole number, 6

(b) The lower class limit of the first class in the smallest value, 0.

The lower class limit of the next class is the previous class's lower class limit plus the class width; for the second class, this is $0 + 6 = 6$.

The upper class limit is one value less than lower class limit of the next class; for the first class, the upper class limit is $6 - 1 = 5$.

The class boundaries are the halfway points between (i.e., the average of) the (adjacent) upper class limit of one class and the lower class limit of the next class. The lower class boundary of the first class is the lower class limit minus one-half unit. The upper class boundary for the last class is the upper class limit plus one-half unit. For the first class, the class boundaries are $0-\frac{1}{2}=-0.5$ and $\frac{5+6}{2}=5.5$.

For the last class, the class boundaries are $\frac{41+42}{2}=41.5$ and $47+\frac{1}{2}=47.5$.

The class mark or midpoint is the average of the class limits for that class. For the first class, the midpoint is $\frac{0+5}{2}=2.5$.

The class frequency is the number of data values that belong to that class; call this value f.

The relative frequency of a class is the class frequency, f, divided by the total number of data values, i.e., the overall sample size, n.

For the first class, $f = 13$, $n = 55$, and the relative frequency is $f/n = 13/55 \approx 0.24$.

The cumulative frequency of a class is the sum of the frequencies for all previous classes, plus the frequency of that class. For the first and second classes, the class cumulative frequencies are 13 and $13 + 15 = 28$, respectively.

Words of Three Syllables or More

Class Limits	Class Boundaries	Midpoint	Frequency	Relative Frequency	Cumulative Frequency
0–5	0.5–5.5	2.5	13	0.24	13
6–11	5.5–11.5	8.5	15	0.27	28
12–17	11.5–17.5	14.5	11	0.20	39
18–23	17.5–23.5	20.5	3	0.05	42
24–29	23.5–29.5	26.5	6	0.11	48
30–35	29.5–35.5	32.5	4	0.07	52
36–41	35.5–41.5	38.5	2	0.04	54
42–47	41.5–47.5	44.5	1	0.02	55

(c) The histogram plots the class frequencies on the y-axis and the class boundaries on the x-axis. Since adjacent classes share boundary values, the bars touch each other. [Alternatively, the bars may be centered over the class marks (midpoints).]

(d) A frequency polygon connects the midpoints of each class (shown as a dot in the middle of the top of the histogram bar) with line segments. Place a dot on the x-axis one class width below the midpoint of the first class, and place another dot on the x-axis one class width above the last class's midpoint. Connect these dots to the adjacent midpoint dots with line segments.

(e) The relative frequency histogram is exactly the same shape as the frequency histogram, but the vertical scale is relative frequency, f/n, instead of actual frequency, f.

The following figure shows the histogram, frequency polygon, and relative-frequency histogram for (c), (d), and (e) above, overlaying one another. (Note that two vertical scales are shown.)

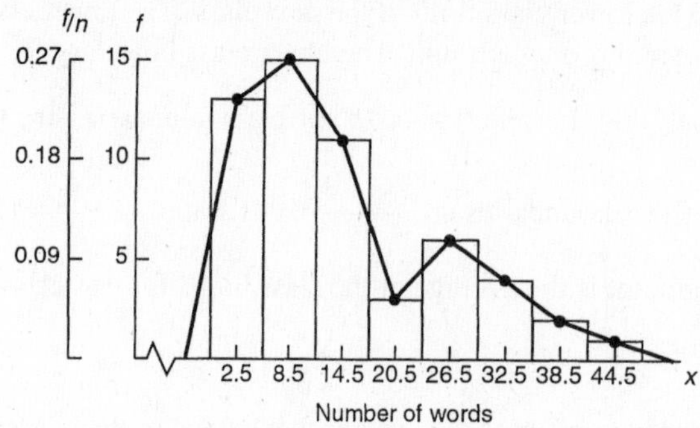

(f) To create the ogive, place a dot on the x-axis at the lower class boundary of the first class and then, for each class, place a dot above the upper class boundary value at the height of the cumulative frequency for the class. Connect the dots with line segments.

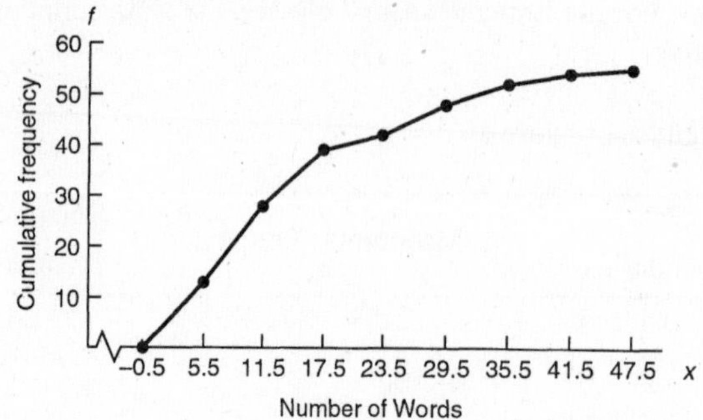

7. (a) The class midpoint is the average of the class limits for that class.

Class Midpoints: 34.5; 44.5; 54.5; 64.5; 74.5; 84.5.

(b) The frequency polygon connects to the x-axis one class width below the smallest midpoint and one class width above the largest midpoint; here the class width is 10, so we have points on the x-axis at $34.5 - 10 = 24.5$ and $84.5 + 10 = 94.5$.

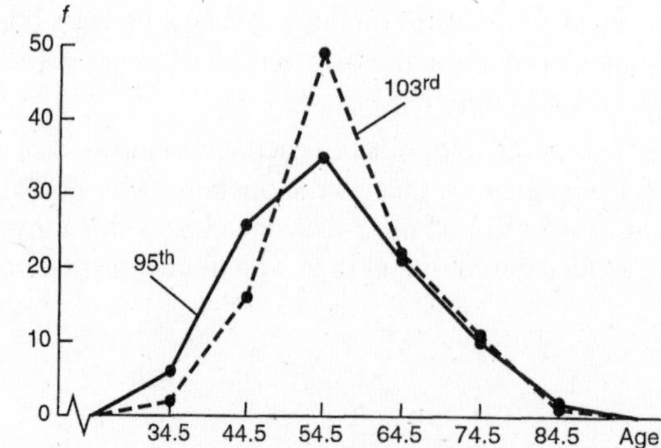

(c) The two polygons have the same general shape, but the dashed polygon is shifted slightly to the right (older ages), so, in general, the members of the 103rd Congress are older.

8. (a) The class midpoint is the average of the class limits for that class.

Class Midpoints: 34.5; 44.5; 54.5; 64.5; 74.5; 84.5.

(b) The frequency polygon connects to the x-axis one class width below the smallest midpoint and one class width above the largest midpoint; here the class width is 10, so we have points on the x-axis at $34.5 - 10 = 24.5$ and $84.5 + 10 = 94.5$.

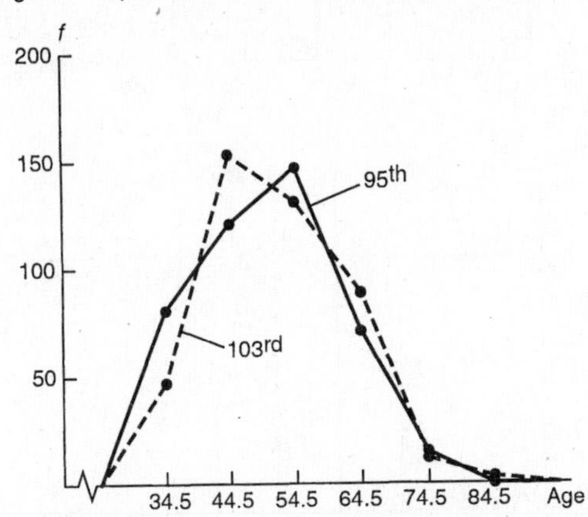

(c) The age distribution shapes are similar. The 95th Congress members of the House have more people in their 30s and (to a lesser extent) 50s, but fewer in their 40s and (to a lesser extent) 60s. There is essentially no difference in frequencies for members over 70.

9. (a)

	Largest value	Smallest value	Class width
Food Companies	11	−3	$\frac{11-(-3)}{5} = 2.8$; use 3
Electronic Companies	16	−6	$\frac{16-(-6)}{5} = 4.4$; use 5

Profit as Percent of Sales—Food Companies

Class	Frequency	Midpoint
−3 to −1	2	−2
0–2	16	1
3–5	10	4
6–8	9	7
9–11	2	10

Profit as Percent of Sales—Electronic Companies

Class	Frequency	Midpoint
−6 to −2	3	−4
−1 to 3	13	1
4–8	20	6
9–13	7	11
14–18	1	16

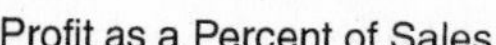

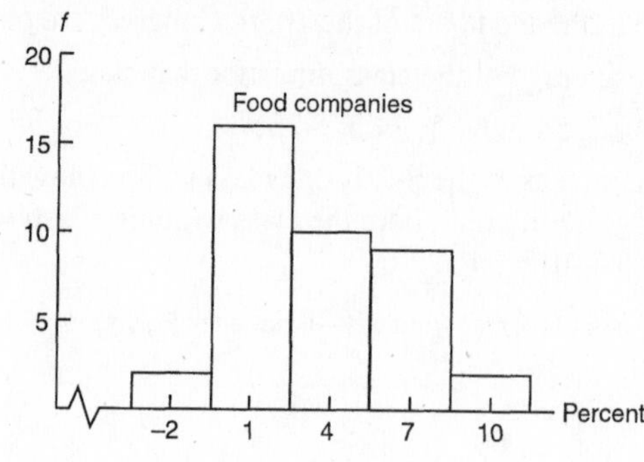

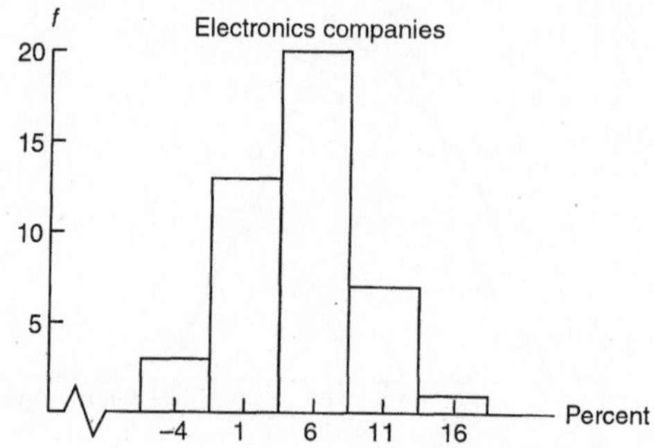

(b) Because the classes and class widths are different for the two company types, it is difficult to compare profits as a percentage of sales. We can notice that for the electronic companies the 16 profits as a percentage of sales extends as high as 18, while for the food companies the highest profit as a percentage of sales is 11. On the other hand, some of the electronic companies also have greater losses than the food companies. Had we made the class limits the same for both company types and overlaid the histograms, it would be easier to compare the data.

10. (a)

	Largest value	Smallest value	Class width
Miami Dolphins	295	175	$\frac{295-175}{6}=20$; use 21
San Diego Charges	310	119	$\frac{310-119}{6}\approx 31.8$; use 32

Weights of Football Players:
Miami Dolphins

Class	Midpoint	Frequency
175–195	185	13
196–216	206	7
217–237	227	19
238–258	248	8
259–279	269	11
280–300	290	12

San Diego Chargers

Class	Midpoint	Frequency
119–150	134.5	1
151–182	166.5	4
183–214	198.5	27
215–246	230.5	15
247–278	262.5	14
279–310	294.5	11

Weights of Football Players—Miami Dolphins

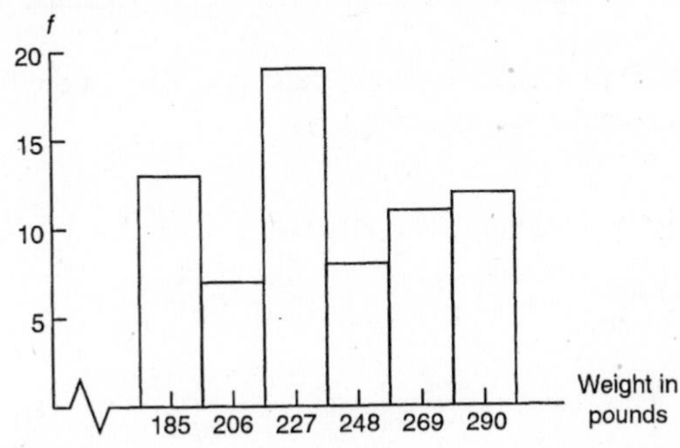

Weights of Football Players—San Diego Chargers

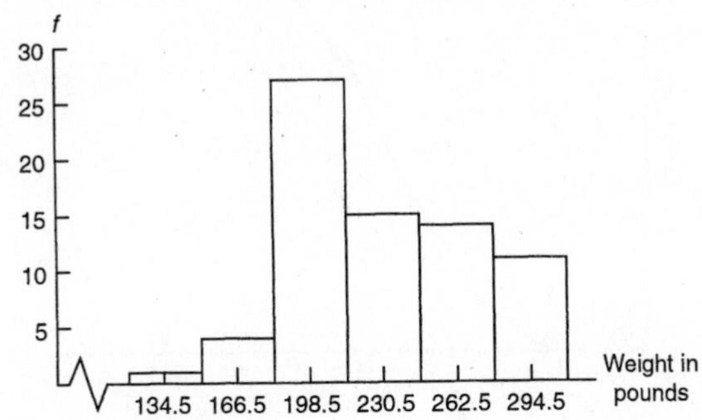

(b) Because the class widths are different, it is difficult to compare the histograms. However, San Diego has 4 players who are smaller than the smallest Miami player, and 4 players who are larger than the largest player.

It would be easier to compare the teams' weights if the histograms had common classes and were overlaid.

11. (a) Since ogives show the cumulative frequency at the upper class boundary, and begin at the point with (x, y) coordinates (lower class boundary of the first class, 0), the numbers on the x-axis are class boundaries. Recall that class boundary values are not values the data can attain. Thus the point marked 85 over the x-value 7.15 means that 85 winning times were less than or equal to 7.15 and, since 7.15 is not a possible data value, 85 winning times were less than 7.15 (i.e., less than 2 minutes 7.15 seconds), Eighty-five of 101 times are less than 7.15, or $\frac{85}{101} \approx 84.2\%$.

(b) Subtract the cumulative frequency at or below 5.15 seconds from the cumulative frequency at or below 11.15 seconds (which includes all the values at or below 5.15 seconds) to get the number of winning times between 5.15 and 11.15 seconds/over two minutes): $100 - 75 = 25$, or $\frac{25}{101} \approx 24.8\%$.

12. (a) Since the values at the edges of the bars on the histogram are shown, these are class boundaries.

Class	Frequency	Cumulative Frequency
390.5–490.5	6	6
490.5–590.5	11	17
590.5–690.5	15	32
690.5–790.5	10	42
790.5–890.5	6	48
890.5–990.5	1	49
990.5–1090.5	2	51

Begin the ogive at (390.5, 0) (i.e., at the lower class boundary of the first class) and plot the values (upper class boundary, cumulative frequency).

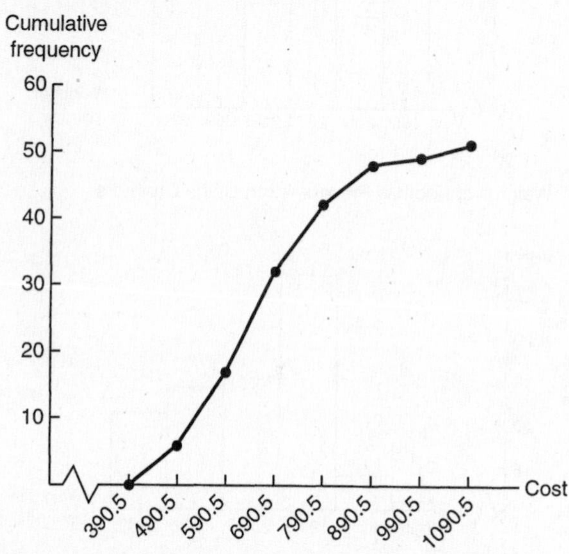

(b) From the ogive point (690.5, 32), (or the table above) we have that 32 of the "51 states" (states plus D.C.) have an average cost per day per patient less than $690.50.

13. (a) Uniform is rectangular, symmetric looks like mirror images on each side of the middle, bimodal has two modes (peaks), and skewed distributions have long tails on one side, and are skewed in the direction of the tail ("skew, few"). (Note that uniform distributions are also symmetric, but "uniform" is more descriptive.)

(a) skewed left; (b) uniform, (c) symmetric, (d) bimodal, (e) skewed right.

(b) Answers vary. Students would probably like (a) since there are many high scores and few low scores. Students would probably dislike (e) since there are few high scores but lots of lows scores. (b) is designed to give approximately the same number of As, Bs, etc. (d) has more Bs and Ds, say. (c) is the way many tests are designed: As and Fs for the exceptionally high and low scores with most students receiving Cs.

14. (a) Uniform is rectangular, symmetric looks like mirror images on each side of the middle, bimodal has two modes (peaks), and skewed distributions have long tails on one side, and are skewed in the direction of the tail ("skew, few"). (Note that uniform distributions are also symmetric, but "uniform" is more descriptive.)

(a) uniform, (b) skewed right, (c) bimodal, (d) bimodal, (e) symmetric. [Note that (c) has a major and a minor mode. "Tails" in a distribution's shape "tail off," i.e., get thinner, and do not have "bumps" in them as (c) does.]

(b) Answers vary. Ads should target the largest number of potential buyers, so ads should be aimed at the income levels with the greatest concentration (frequency) of households.

(c) Answers vary. Since warranty/registration cards are returned voluntarily, the income data are most likely not representative of the buying public in general, and probably are not even representative of those buying the specific product. Also, people tend to inflate their income levels on most forms, except those sent to the IRS.

15. (a) $2.71 \times 100 = 271$, $1.62 \times 100 = 162, \ldots, 0.70 \times 100 = 70$.

(b) largest value = 282, smallest value = 46

class width $= \dfrac{282 - 46}{6} \approx 39.3$; use 40

Class Limits	Class Boundaries	Midpoint	Frequency
46–85	45.5–85.5	65.5	4
86–125	85.5–125.5	105.5	5
126–165	125.5–165.5	145.5	10
166–205	165.5–205.5	185.5	5
206–245	205.5–245.5	225.5	5
246–285	245.5–285.5	265.5	3

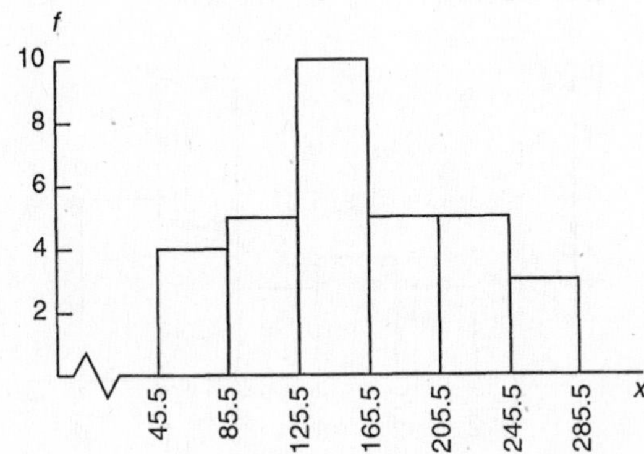

(c) class width is $\frac{40}{100} = 0.40$

Class Limits	Class Boundaries	Midpoint	Frequency
0.46–0.85	0.455–0.855	0. 655	4
0.86–1.25	0.855–1.255	1.055	5
1.26–1.65	1.255–1.655	1.455	10
1.66–2.05	1.655–2.055	1.855	5
2.06–2.45	2.055–2.455	2.255	5
2.46–2.85	2.455–2.855	2.655	3

16. (a) $0.194 \times 1000 = 194, 0.258 \times 1000 = 258, \ldots, 0.200 \times 1000 = 200.$

(b) largest value = 317, smallest value = 107

class width = $\frac{317-107}{5} = 42$, use 43

Class Limits	Class Boundaries	Midpoint	Frequency
107–149	106.5–149.5	128	3
150–192	149.5–192.5	171	4
193–235	192.5–235.5	214	3
236–278	235.5–278.5	257	10
279–321	278.5–321.5	300	6

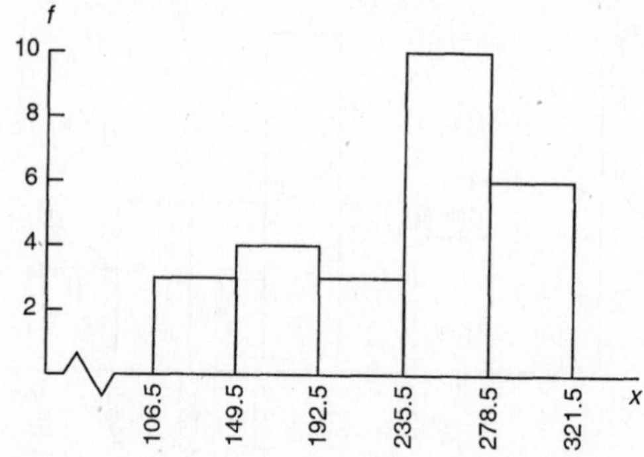

(c) class width = $\frac{43}{1000} = 0.043$

Class Limits	Class Boundaries	Midpoint	Frequency
0.107–0.149	0.1065–0.1495	0.128	3
0.150–0.192	0.1495–0.1925	0.171	4
0.193–0.235	0.1925–0.2355	0.214	3
0.236–0.278	0.2355–0.2785	0.257	10
0.279–0.321	0.2785–0.3215	0.300	6

17. (a) There is one dot below 600, so 1 state has 600 or fewer licensed drivers per 1000 residents.

(b) 5 values are close to 800; $\frac{5}{51} \approx 0.0980 \approx 9.8\%$

(c) 9 values below 650
37 values between 650 and 750
5 values above 750
From either the counts or the dotplot, the interval from 650 to 750 licensed drivers per 1000 residents has the most "states."

18. The dotplot shows some of the characteristics of the histogram such as more dot density from, say 280 to 340, corresponding roughly to the histogram bars of heights 25 and 16.
However, they are somewhat difficult to compare since the dotplot can be thought of as a histogram with one value, the class mark, i.e., the data value, per class.
Because the definitions of the classes and, therefore, the class widths, differ, it is difficult to compare the two figures.

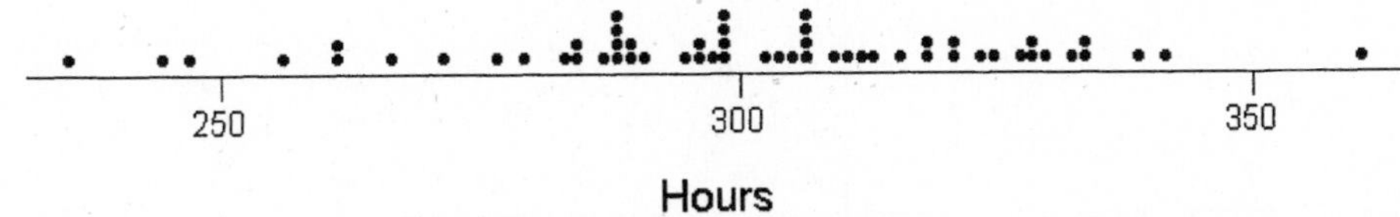

19. The dotplot shows some of the characteristics of the histogram, such as the concentration of most of the data from, say, 20 to 40; this corresponds roughly to the 3 histogram bars of height 12. There are more data (dots) below 20 than above 40, which corresponds to the histogram bars of heights 4 and 7, and the bars of heights 2 and 1, respectively.

However, they are somewhat difficult to compare since the dotplot can be thought of as a histogram with one value, the class mark, i.e., the data value, per class.

Because the definitions of the classes and, therefore, the class widths, differ, it is difficult to compare the two figures.

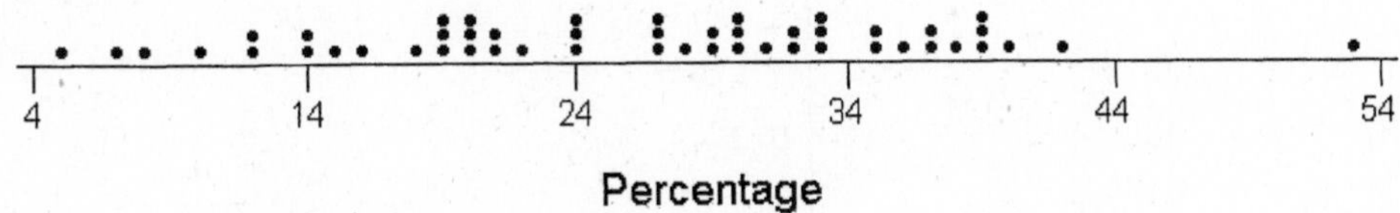

Section 2.3

1. (a) The smallest value is 47 and the largest is 97, so we need stems 4, 5, 6, 7, 8, and 9. Use the tens digit as the stem and the ones digit as the leaf.

Longevity of Cowboys

4	7 = 47 years
4	7
5	2 7 8 8
6	1 6 6 8 8
7	0 2 2 3 3 5 6 7
8	4 4 4 5 6 6 7 9
9	0 1 1 2 3 7

(b) Yes, certainly these cowboys lived long lives, as evidenced by the high frequency of leaves for stems 7, 8, and 9 (i.e., 70-, 80-, and 90-year olds).

2. The largest value is 91 (percent of wetlands lost) and the smallest value is 9 (percent), which is coded as 09. We need stems 0 to 9. Use the tens digit as the stem and the ones digit as the leaf. The percentages are concentrated from 20 to 50 percent. The distribution is asymmetrical but not skewed because of the "bump" in the 80s. If we smoothed the shape, we might consider this bimodal. There is a gap showing none of the lower 48 states has lost from 10 to 19% of its wetlands.

Percent of Wetlands Lost

4	0 = 40%
0	9
1	
2	0 3 4 7 7 8
3	0 1 3 5 5 5 6 7 8 8 9
4	2 2 6 6 6 8 9 9
5	0 0 0 2 2 4 6 6 9 9
6	0 7
7	2 3 4
8	1 5 7 7 9
9	0 1

3. The longest average length of stay is 11.1 days in North Dakota and the shortest is 5.2 days in Utah. We need stems from 5 to 11. Use the digit(s) to the left of the decimal point as the stem, and the digit to the right as the leaf.

Average Length of Hospital Stay

5	2 = 5.2 days
5	2 3 5 5 6 7
6	0 2 4 6 6 7 7 8 8 8 8 9 9
7	0 0 0 0 0 0 1 1 1 2 2 2 3 3 3 3 4 4 5 5 6 6 8
8	4 5 7
9	4 6 9
10	0 3
11	1

The distribution is skewed right.

4. Number of Hospitals per State

0	8 = 8 hospitals		
0	8	15	
1	1 2 5 6 9	16	2
2	1 7 7	17	5
3	5 7 8	18	
4	1 2 7	19	3
5	1 2 3 9	20	9
6	1 6 8	21	
7	1	22	7
8	8	23	1 6
9	0 2 6 8		
10	1 2 7	42	1
11	3 3 7 9	43	
12	2 3 9	44	0
13	3 3 6		
14	8		

Texas and California have the highest number of hospitals, 421 and 440, respectively. Both states have large populations and large areas. The four largest states by area are Alaska, Texas, California, and Montana; however, both Alaska and Montana have small populations, but the population tends to cluster at their largest cities, thus reducing the number of hospitals needed.

5. **(a)** The longest time during 1961–1980 is 23 minutes (i.e., 2:23) and the shortest time is 9 minutes (2:09). We need stems 0, 1, and 2, which we'll write as 0*, 0•, 1*, 1•, 2*, and 2•. (We can eliminate 0* since no time was 2:04 or less and 2• because no winning time was 2:25 or more. We'll use the tens digit as the stem and the ones digit as the leaf, placing leaves 0, 1, 2, 3, and 4 on the "* stem" and leaves 5, 6, 7, 8, and 9 on the "• stem."

Minutes Beyond 2 Hours (1961-1980)

0	9 = 9 minutes past 2 hours
0•	9 9
1*	0 0 2 3 3
1•	5 5 6 6 7 8 8 9
2*	0 2 3 3

(b) The longest time during the period 1981–2000 was 14 (2:14), and the shortest was 7 (2:07), so we'll need stems 0• and 1* only.

Minutes Beyond 2 Hours (1981-2000)

0	7 = 7 minutes past 2 hours
0•	7 7 7 8 8 8 8 9 9 9 9 9 9 9 9
1*	0 0 1 1 4

(c) In more recent times, the winning times have been closer to 2 hours, with all 20 times between 7 and 14 minutes over two hours. In the earlier period, more than half the times (12 or 20) were more than 2 hours and 14 minutes.

6. (a) The largest (worst) score in the first round was 75; the smallest (best) score was 65. We need stems 6• and both 7* and 7•; leaves 0 to 4 go on the "* stem" and leaves 5–9 belong on the "• stem."

First Round Scores

6	5 = score of 65
6•	5 6 7 7
7*	0 1 1 1 1 1 1 1 1 1 1 2 2 2 3 3 3 3 4 4 4
7•	5 5 5 5 5 5 5

(b) the largest score in the fourth round was 74 and the smallest was 68. Here we need stems 6• and 7*, we don't need 7• because no scores were over 74.

Fourth Round Scores

6	8 = score of 68
6•	8 9 9 9 9 9
7*	0 0 0 0 1 1 1 1 1 1 1 1 2 2 2 2 2 2 2 3 3 3 3 3 4 4 4

(c) Scores are lower in the fourth round. In the first round both the low and high scores were more extreme than in the fourth round.

7. The largest value is 1.808 arc seconds per century; the smallest is 0.008. These values would be coded as 18|08 and 00|08, respectively. We need stems 00 to 18.

Angular Momentum of Stars

00	14 = 0.014 arc sec/century
00	08 14 38 42 50 57
01	73
02	16 19 51
03	51 69
04	30
05	
06	23 67
07	59 88
08	88
09	
10	24 57
11	69 69
12	60 60
13	
14	38
15	
16	16 60
17	
18	08

There are no large gaps, but 4 small gaps. Interestingly, gaps at 05, 09, and 13 are 4 stem units apart, as in the gap from 13 to 17, except that the gap at 15 falls between 13 and 17. This might indicate a cycle. The *midrange** is the average of the largest and smallest values; here, $\frac{0.008+1.808}{2} = 0.908$. If this value had occurred in the data, it would be shown as 09|08. In a sense, this value locates the "middle" of the data. We can see that more of the data (18/28, or approximately 64%) occurs below the midrange than above it (where 10/28 ≈ 36% of the data are located).

*The midrange is often calculated in Exploratory Data Analysis (EDA), which is discussed in the next chapter. It is also used in nonparametrics, which is the topic of Chapter 12.

8. The largest value in the data is 67.0×10^{-26} watts per square meter per hertz and the smallest value is 9.0 (i.e., 09.0). We need stems ranging from 0 to 6, and we will use the ones digit and the number after the decimal point to create 2 digit leaves.

Radio Brightness

0	90 = 09.0 units
0	90 90 94 95 95 95 98
1	05 10 15 15 15 25 25 35 36 37 65 65 65
2	00 00 80
3	
4	40 40 40 40
5	
6	70

The measurement 67.0 is unusually bright. Values which are extremely large or extremely small, relative to the rest of the data, are called *outliers*. These are discussed in Chapter 3.

9. The largest value in the data is 29.8 mg. Of tar per cigarette smoked, and the smallest value is 1.0. We will need stems from 1 to 29, and we will use the numbers to the right of the decimal point as the leaves.

Milligrams of Tar per Cigarette

1	0 = 1.0 mg tar
1	0
2	
3	
4	1 5
5	
6	
7	3 8
8	0 6 8
9	0
10	
11	4
12	0 4 8
13	7
14	1 5 9
15	0 1 2 8
16	0 6
17	0
29	8

10. The largest value in the data set is 23.5 mg Carbon monoxide per cigarette smoked, and the smallest is 1.5. We need stems from 1 to 23, and we'll use the numbers to the right of the decimal point as leaves.

Milligrams of Carbon Monoxide

1	5 = 1.5 mg CO
1	5
2	
3	
4	9
5	4
6	
7	
8	5
9	0 5
10	0 2 2 6
11	
12	3 6
13	0 6 9
14	4 9
15	0 4 9
16	3 6
17	5
18	5
23	5

11. The largest value in the data set is 2.03 mg nicotine per cigarette smoked. The smallest value is 0.13. We will need stems 0*, 0•, 1*, 1•, and 2*. Leaves 0 to 4 belong on the * stems and leaves 5 to 9 belong on the • stems. We will use the number to the left of the decimal point as the stem and the first number to the right of the decimal point as the leaf. The number 2 places to the right of the decimal point (the hundredths digit) will be truncated (chopped off; <u>not</u> rounded off).

Milligrams of Nicotine per Cigarette

0	1 = 0.1 milligram
0*	1 4 4
0•	5 6 6 6 7 7 7 8 8 9 9 9
1*	0 0 0 0 0 0 0 1 2
1•	
2*	0

12. (a) For Site I, read the values in Figure 2-27 from the center (stem) to the left to find the least depth is 25 cm and the greatest depth is 110 cm. For Site II, read the values from the center (stem) to the right to find the least depth is 20 cm and the greatest depth is 125 cm.

(b) The Site I depth distribution is, smoothed out, fairly symmetrical around approximately 70 cm. Site II, however, is fairly uniform in shape except that it has a huge gap with no artifacts from about 70 to 100 cm.

(c) It would appear that Site II was probably unoccupied during the time period associated with 70 cm to 100 cm.

13. (a) Average salaries in California range from \$49,000 to \$126,000. Salaries in New York range from \$45,000 to \$120,000.

(b) New York has a greater number of average salaries in the \$60,000 than California, but California has more average salaries than New York in the \$70,000 range.

(c) The California data appear to be similar in shape to the New York data, but California's distribution has been shifted up approximately \$10,000. It is also heavier in the upper tail and shows no gap in average salaries, unlike New York which has no salaries in the \$110,000 range. California has higher average salaries.

Chapter 2 Review

1. Figure 2-1 (a) (in the text) is essentially a bar graph with a "horizontal" axis showing years and a "vertical" axis showing miles per gallon. However, in depicting the data as a highway and showing it in perspective, the ability to correctly compare bar heights visually has been lost. For example, determining what would appear to be the bar heights by measuring from the white line on the road to the edge of the road along a line drawn from the year to its mpg value, we get the bar height for 1983 to be approximately 7/8 inch and the bar height for 1985 to be approximately 1 3/8 inches (i.e., 11/8 inches). Taking the ratio of the given bar heights, we see that the bar for 1985 should be $\frac{27.5}{26} \approx 1.06$ times the length of the 1983 bar.

However, the measurements show a ratio of $\frac{\frac{11}{8}}{\frac{7}{8}} = \frac{11}{7} \approx 1.60$, i.e., the 1985 bar is (visually) 1.6 times the length of the 1983 bar. Also, the years are evenly spaced numerically, but the figure shows the more recent years to be more widely spaced due to the use of perspective.

Figure 2-1(b) is a time plot, showing the years on the x-axis and miles per gallon on the y-axis. Everything is to scale and not distorted visually by the use of perspective. It is easy to see the mpg standards for each year, and you can also see how fuel economy standards for new cars have changed over the eight years shown (i.e., a steep increase in the early years and a leveling off in the later years).

2. (a) By reading the y-coordinate of the dot associated with the year, we estimate the 1980 prison population at approximately 140 prisoners per 100,000, and the 1997 population at approximately 440 prisoners per 100,000 people

(b) The number of inmates per 100,000 increased.

(c) The population 266,574,000 is 2,665.74 × 100,000, and 444 per 100,000 is $\frac{444}{100{,}000}$.

So $\frac{444}{100{,}000} \times (2{,}665.74 \times 100{,}000) \approx 1{,}183{,}589$ prisoners.

The projected 2020 population is 323,724,000, or 3,237.24 × 100,000.

So $\frac{444}{100{,}000} \times (3{,}237.24 \times 100{,}000) \approx 1{,}437{,}335$ prisoners.

3.

Most Difficult Task	Percentage	Degrees
IRS jargon	43%	$0.43 \times 360° \approx 155°$
Deductions	28%	$0.28 \times 360° \approx 101°$
Right form	10%	$0.10 \times 360° = 36°$
Calculations	8%	$0.08 \times 360° \approx 29°$
Don't know	10%	$0.10 \times 360° = 36°$

Note: Degrees do not total 360° due to rounding.

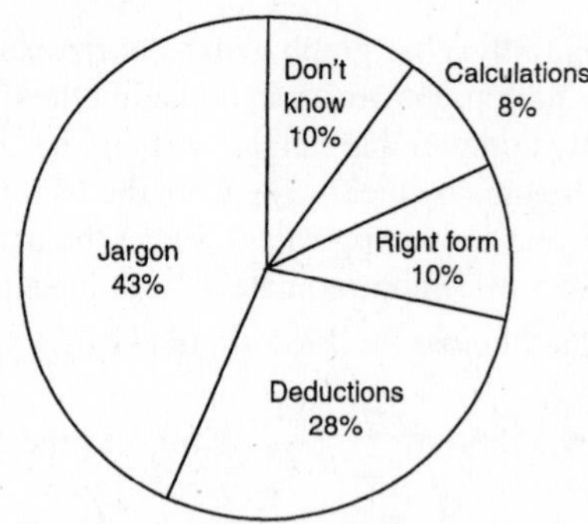

4. **(a)** Since the ages are two digit numbers, use the tens digit as the stem and the ones digit as the leaf.

Age of DUI Arrests

1	6 = 16 years
1	6 8
2	0 1 1 2 2 2 3 4 4 5 6 6 6 7 7 7 9
3	0 0 1 1 2 3 4 4 5 5 6 7 8 9
4	0 0 1 3 5 6 7 7 9 9
5	1 3 5 6 8
6	3 4

(b) The largest age is 64 and the smallest is 16, so the class with for 7 classes is $\frac{64-16}{7} \approx 6.86$; use 7. The lower class limit for the first class is 16; the lower class limit for the second class is $16 + 7 = 23$. The total number of data points is 50, so calculate the relative frequency by dividing the class frequency by 50.

Age Distribution of DUI Arrests

Class Limits	Class Boundaries	Midpoint	Frequency	Relative Frequency	Cumulative Frequency
16–22	15.5–22.5	19	8	0.16	8
23–29	22.5–29.5	26	11	0.22	19
30–36	29.5–36.5	33	11	0.22	30
37–43	36.5–43.5	40	7	0.14	37
44–50	43.5–50.5	47	6	0.12	43
51–57	50.5–57.5	54	4	0.08	47
58–64	57.5–64.5	61	3	0.06	50

The class boundaries are the average of the upper class limit of the next class. The midpoint is the average of the class limits for that class.

(c) The class boundaries are shown in (b).

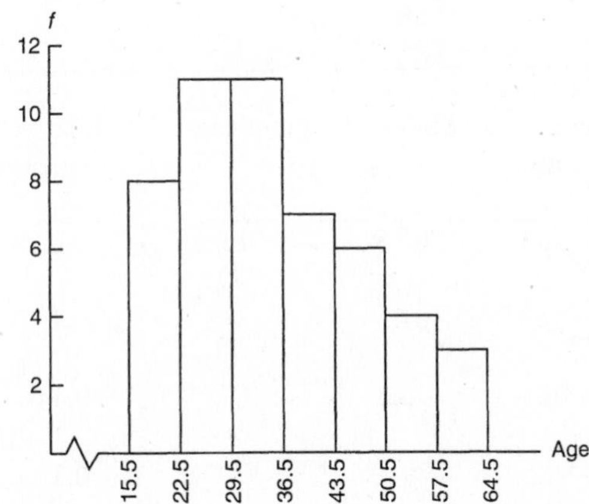

(d) The ogive plots the cumulative frequency up to the upper class boundary value.

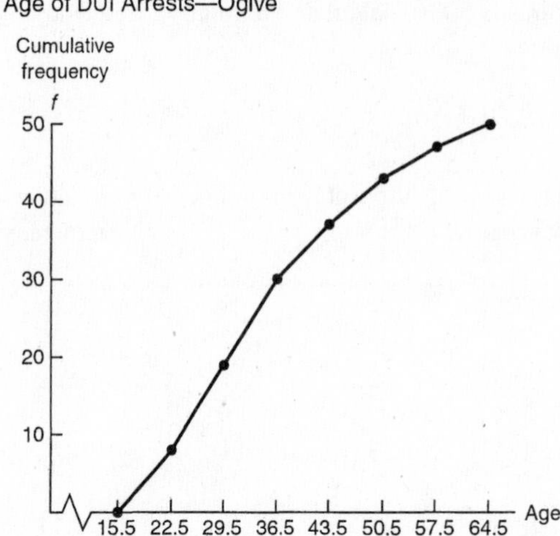

By reading the y-axis value for the dot over the upper boundary 29.5, we see that 19 of 50, or $\frac{19}{50} = 38\%$ of the drivers were 29 years or younger when arrested.

5. (a) The largest value is 96 mg of glucose per 100 ml of blood, and the smallest value is 59. For 7 classes we need a class width of $\frac{96-59}{7} \approx 5.3$; use 6. The lower class limit of the first class is 59, and the lower class limit of the second class is $59 + 6 = 65$.

The class boundaries are the average of the upper class limit of one class and the lower class limit of the next higher class. The midpoint is the average of the class limits for that class. There are 53 data values total so the relative frequency is the class frequency divided by 53.

Class Limits	Class Boundaries	Midpoint	Frequency	Relative Frequency	Cumulative Frequency
59–64	58.5–64.5	61.5	1	0.02	1
65–70	64.5–70.5	67.5	7	0.13	8
71–76	70.5–76.5	73.5	6	0.11	14
77–82	76.5–82.5	79.5	13	0.25	27
83–88	82.5–88.5	85.5	18	0.34	45
89–94	88.5–94.5	91.5	7	0.13	52
95–100	94.5–100.5	97.5	1	0.02	53

(b) The histogram shows the bars centered over the midpoints of each class.

(c) The frequency polygon begins on the x-axis at the point one class width below the first class midpoint: $61.5 - 6 = 55.5$. It connects this point and the other midpoints with line segments. It ends on the x-axis one class width above the last class midpoint: $97.5 + 6 = 103.5$.

(d) The frequency histogram and the relative frequency histogram are the same except in the latter, the vertical scale is relative frequency, not frequency.

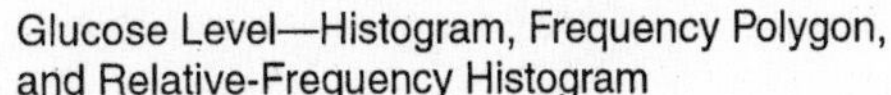

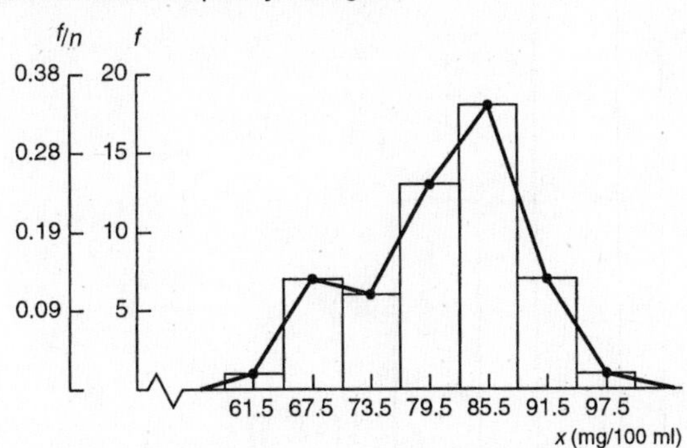

(e) The ogive begins on the x-axis at the lower class boundary and connects dots placed at (x, y) coordinates (upper class boundary, cumulative frequency).

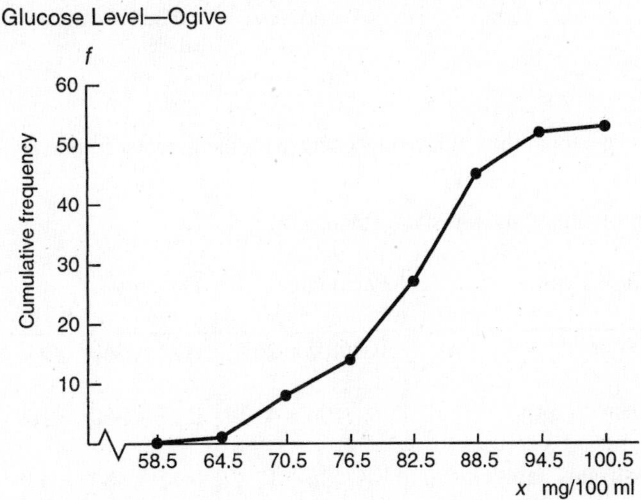

6. (a) A pareto chart is similar to a bar chart, except the bars are in decreasing order by frequency.

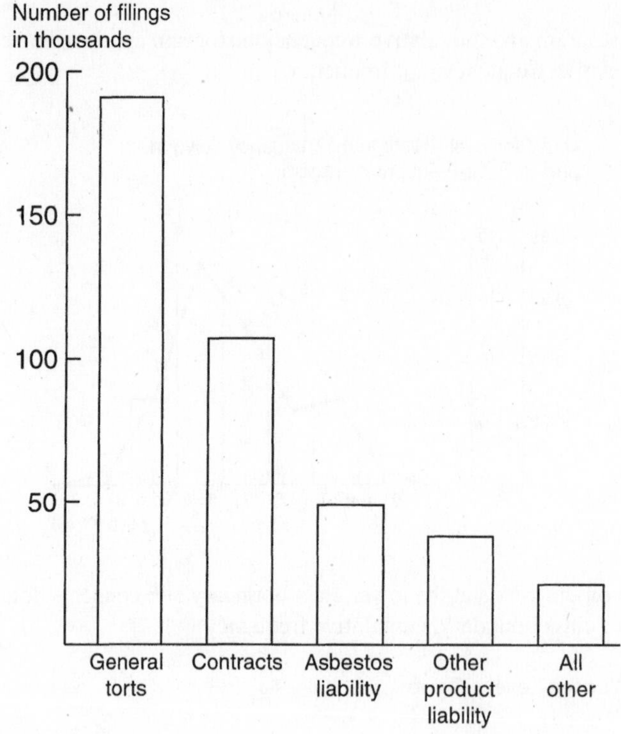

The general torts (personal injury) lawsuits occur with the greatest frequency.

(b) The total number of filings shown is 406 (thousand).

Case Type	Percentage	Degrees
Contracts	$107/406 \approx 26\%$	$0.26 \times 360° \approx 94°$
General torts	$191/406 \approx 47\%$	$0.47 \times 360° \approx 169°$
Asbestos liability	$49/406 \approx 12\%$	$0.12 \times 360° \approx 43°$
Other product liability	$38/406 \approx 9\%$	$0.09 \times 360° \approx 32°$
All other	$21/406 \approx 5\%$	$0.05 \times 360° = 18°$

Note: Percentages do not add to 100% due to rounding. Similarly, the degrees do not add to 360° due to rounding.

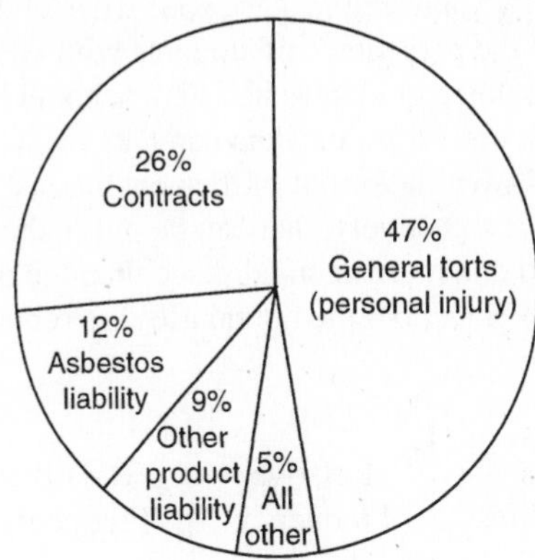

7. **(a)** To determine the decade which contained the most samples, count both rows (if shown) of leaves; recall leaves 0–4 belong on the first line and 5–9 belong on the second line when two lines per stem are used. The greatest number of leaves is found on stem 124, i.e., the 1240s (the 40s decade in the 1200s), with 40 samples.

   (b) The number of samples with tree ring dates 1200 A.D. to 1239 A.D. is 28 + 3 + 19 + 25 = 75.

   (c) The dates of the longest interval with no sample values are 1204 through 1211 A.D. This might mean that for these eight years, the pueblo was unoccupied (thus no new or repaired structures) or that the population remained stable (no new structures needed) or that, say, weather conditions were favorable these years so existing structures didn't need repair. If relatively few new structures were built or repaired during this period, their tree rings might have been missed during sample selection.

8. **(a)** It has a long tail on the left, so it is skewed left.

   (b) The class width is the difference between any two adjacent midpoints. Here, for example, the class width is 4 – 3.5 = 0.5 grade points. The average of any two adjacent midpoints is the boundary value between the two midpoints classes*. So, for midpoints 1 and 1.5, the boundary value is $1+\frac{1.5}{26}=1.25$.

   The difference between any two adjacent boundary values is also the class width, so the other class boundary values within the histogram are 1.25 + 0.5 = 1.75, 1.75 + 0.5 = 2.25, 2.25 + 0.5 = 2.75, 2.75 + 0.5 = 3.25, and 3.25 + 0.5 = 3.75; 3.75 is the lower class boundary for the class, so its upper class boundary is 3.75 + 0.5 = 4.25. Similarly, the upper class boundary of the first class was 1.25, so its lower class boundary is 1.25 – 0.5 = 0.75. The class boundaries are, therefore, 0.75, 1.25, 1.75, 2.25, 2.75, 3.25, 3.75 and 4.25 (from left to right).

   *Recall that the average of a and b is $\frac{a+b}{2}$ which is also the value halfway between a and b.

(c) The relative frequencies are *f/n*, so if we multiply this decimal value by 100, we have the relative frequency expressed as a percent. The relative frequencies, expressed as percents, are 1%, 1%, 2%, 8%, 17%, 27%, and 44%, from left to right. The GPA of 3.25 is a boundary value, so to find the percentage of college graduates who had high school GPAs less than 3.25 is the sum of the relative frequency percentages for bars at or below 3.25: 1% + 1% + 2% + 8% + 17% = 29%. A high school GPA of 3.75 is the next boundary value above 3.25, so if we take the percentage of students with GPAs less 3.25 (29%), and add the percentage of students with GPAs between 3.25 and 3.75 (27%), we find 29% + 27% = 56% of college graduates had high school GPAs of less than 3.75. (Recall that, technically, boundary values are not values the data can take on. They are values between the upper class limit of one class and the lower class limit of the next class, and the class limits specify the largest and smallest data values, respectively, that can be put in those classes. Traditionally, the boundary values are specified to one more decimal place than the data, and that is the case here: the data are reported to one decimal place, but the boundaries are reported to two decimal places.)

Class Midpoints	Class Boundaries	Relative Frequency	Relative Frequency	Cumulative Relative Frequency (%)
1	0.75–1.25	0.01	1%	1%
1.5	1.25–1.75	0.01	1%	2%
2	1.75–2.25	0.02	2%	4%
2.5	2.25–2.75	0.08	8%	12%
3	2.75–3.25	0.17	17%	29%
3.5	3.25–3.75	0.27	27%	56%
4	3.75–4.25	0.44	44%	100%

9. (a) The age group that is most frequently in the hospital has the highest frequency and, therefore, the highest relative frequency: the age group with boundaries 64.5 and 84.5, enclosing ages 65 to 84.

(b)

Class Limits	Class Boundaries	Relative Frequency	Relative Frequency	Cumulative Relative Frequency (%)
5–24	4.5–24.5	0.16	16%	16%
25–44	24.5–44.5	0.28	28%	44%
45–64	44.5–64.5	0.21	21%	65%
65–84	64.5–84.5	0.35	35%	100%

The percentage of patients older than 44, i.e., from 45 to 84, is 21% + 35% = 56%.

(c) The percentage of patients 44 or younger is 16% + 28% = 44%.

10.(a) The largest value is 93 years of age, and the smallest value is 34 years of age (probably Bill Gates of Microsoft). We will need stems from 3 to 9. Use the tens digit as the stem and the ones digit as the leaf.

Ages of Wealthy

3	4 = 34 years old
3	4
4	0 0 0 1 3 7 8 8 8
5	0 2 2 2 2 3 3 3 3 4 6 6 7 7 8 9
6	0 0 1 3 4 5 5 6 6 6 6 6 7 7 8 8
7	0 0 0 1 1 2 3 3 3 4 5 6 6 7 7 7 9
8	2 2 3 3 8
9	3

(b) The class width for 7 class is $\frac{93-34}{7} \approx 8.4$; use 9. The first class' lower limit is 34 and the second class' lower limit is 34 + 9 = 43. The boundary value between them is $\frac{34+43}{2} = 38.5$.

Class Limits	Class Boundaries	Frequency	Cumulative Frequency
34-42	33.5-42.5	5	5
43-51	42.5-51.5	6	11
52-60	51.5-60.5	17	28
61-69	60.5-69.5	14	42
70-78	69.5-78.5	16	58
79-87	78.5-87.5	5	63
88-96	87.5-96.5	2	65

Age Distribution of Billionaires—Histogram

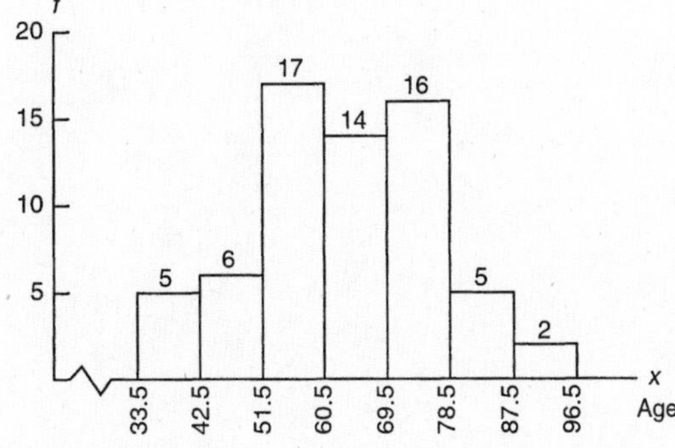

Smoothed, the histogram would be fairly symmetrical.

(c) The ogive connects dots placed over the upper boundary values at the height of the cumulative frequency at those values. It begins with a dot on the x-axis at the lower class boundary of the first class.

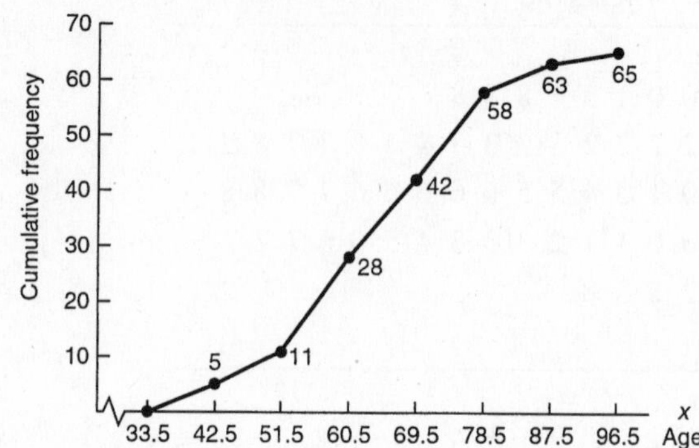

The number of multi billionaires 51 years old or younger in the cumulative frequency at boundary value 51.5 (which is 11). The percentage of such persons is $11/65 \approx 17\%$ (where 65 is the total number of ages given in the data).

Chapter 3 Averages and Variation

Section 3.1

1. Mean $= \bar{x} = \frac{\Sigma x}{n} = \frac{156+161+152+\cdots+157}{12}$

$= \frac{1876}{12}$

$= 156.33$

The mean is 156.33.

Organize the data from smallest to largest.

144	148	152	153	156	157
157	157	161	161	162	168

To find the median, add the two middle values and divide by 2 since there is an even number of values.

$$\text{Median} = \frac{157+157}{2} = 157$$

The median is 157.

The mode is 157 because it is the value that occurs most frequently.

A gardener in Colorado should look at seed and plant descriptions to determine if the plant can thrive and mature in the designated number of frost-free days. The mean, median, and mode are all close. About half the locations have 157 or fewer frost-free days.

2. Mean $= \bar{x} = \frac{\Sigma x}{n} = \frac{11+29+54+\cdots+46}{12}$

$= \frac{542}{12}$

$= 45.17$

The mean is 45.17.

Organize the data from smallest to largest.

11	29	41	46	46	46
47	49	54	54	59	60

To find the median, add the two middle values and divide by 2 since there is an even number of values.

$$\text{Median} = \frac{46+47}{2} = 46.5$$

The median is 46.5.

The mode is 46 because it is the value that occurs most frequently.

3. Mean $= \bar{x} = \frac{\Sigma x}{n} = \frac{146+152+168+\cdots+144}{14}$

$= \frac{2342}{14}$

$= 167.3$

The mean is 167.3°F.

Organize the data from smallest to largest.

144	146	152	152	165	168	168
174	178	178	178	179	180	180

To find the median, add the two middle values and divide by 2 since there is an even number of values.

$$\text{Median} = \frac{168+174}{2} = 171$$

The median is 171° F.

The mode is 178° F because it is the value that occurs most frequently.

4. Mean $= \bar{x} = \frac{\Sigma x}{n} = \frac{13+10+7+\cdots+8}{18}$

$= \frac{111}{18}$

$= 6.2$

The mean is 6.2.

Organize the data from smallest to largest.

2	2	2	3	3	4	4	4	5
7	7	7	7	8	8	10	13	15

To find the median, add the two middle values and divide by 2 since there is an even number of values.

$$\text{Median} = \frac{5+7}{2} = 6$$

The median is 6.

The mode is 7 because it is the value that occurs most frequently.

5. First organize the data from smallest to largest. Then compute the mean, median, and mode.

(a) Upper Canyon

1	1	1	2	3	3	3	3	4	6	9

Mean $= \bar{x} = \frac{\Sigma x}{n} = \frac{36}{11} \approx 3.27$

Median = 3 (middle value)

Mode = 3 (occurs most frequently)

(b) Lower Canyon

0	0	1	1	1	1	2	2	3	6	7	8	13	14

$$\text{Mean} = \bar{x} = \frac{\Sigma x}{n} = \frac{59}{14} \approx 4.21$$

$$\text{Median} = \frac{2+2}{2} = 2$$

Mode = 1 (occurs most frequently)

(c) The mean for the Lower Canyon is greater than that of the Upper Canyon. However, the median and mode for the Lower Canyon are less than those of the Upper Canyon.

(d) 5% of 14 is 0.7 which rounds to 1. So, eliminate one data value from the bottom of the list and one from the top. Then compute the mean of the remaining 12 values.

$$5\% \text{ trimmed mean} = \frac{\Sigma x}{n} = \frac{45}{12} = 3.75$$

Now this value is closer to the Upper Canyon mean.

6. (a) First arrange the data from smallest to largest. Then compute the mean, median, and mode.

$$\text{Mean} = \bar{x} = \frac{\Sigma x}{n} = \frac{1050}{40} \approx 26.3$$

The mean is 26.3 yr.

$$\text{Median} = \frac{25+26}{2} = 25.5$$

The median is 25.5 yr.

Mode = 25

The mode is 25 yr.

(b) The median may represent the age most accurately. The answers are very close.

7. (a) $\text{Mean} = \bar{x} = \frac{\Sigma x}{n} = \frac{93+80+15+\cdots+13}{12}$

$$= \frac{346}{12}$$

$$\approx 28.83$$

The mean is 28.83 thousand dollars.

(b) $\text{Median} = \frac{18+19}{2} = 18.5$

The median is 18.5 thousand dollars.

The median best describes the salary of the majority of employees, since the mean is influenced by the high salaries of the president and vice president.

(c) $\text{Mean} = \bar{x} = \frac{\Sigma x}{n} = \frac{15+25+14+\cdots+13}{10}$

$= \frac{173}{10}$

$= 17.3$

The mean is 17.3 thousand dollars.

$\text{Median} = \frac{16+18}{2} = 17$

The median is 17 thousand dollars.

(d) Without the salaries for the two executives, the mean and the median are closer, and both reflect the salary of most of the other workers more accurately. The mean changed quite a bit, while the median did not, a difference that indicates that the mean is more sensitive to the absence or presence of extreme values.

8. (a) $\text{Mean} = \bar{x} = \frac{\Sigma x}{n} = \frac{9+6+10+\cdots+8}{10} = \frac{74}{10} = 7.4$

$\text{Median} = \frac{8+8}{2} = 8$

Mode = 8 (occurs most frequently)

(b) $\text{Mean} = \bar{x} = \frac{\Sigma x}{n} = \frac{74+36+51+30}{13} = \frac{191}{13} \approx 14.69$

Median = 8 (middle value)

Mode = 8 (occurs most frequently)

(c) The mean is most affected by extreme values.

9. (a) $\text{Mean} = \bar{x} = \frac{\Sigma x}{n} = \frac{15+12+\cdots+15}{7} = \frac{102}{7} \approx 14.57$

Median = 15 (middle value)

Mode = 15 (occurs most frequently)

(b) $\text{Mean} = \bar{x} = \frac{\Sigma x}{n} = \frac{102+57+62}{9} = \frac{221}{9} \approx 24.56$

Median = 15 (middle value)

Mode = 15 (occurs most frequently)

(c) The mean is most affected by extreme values.

10. (a) $\text{Mean} = \bar{x} = \frac{\Sigma x}{n} = \frac{5.2+3.3+\cdots+1.8}{7} = \frac{21.6}{7} \approx 3.09$

Median = 2.9 (middle value)

Mode = 3.3 (occurs most frequently)

(b) Mean $= \overline{x} = \frac{\Sigma x}{n} = \frac{41.9 + 7.7 + \cdots + 5.1}{8} = \frac{88.2}{8} = 11.025$

Median $= \frac{6.6 + 6.9}{2} = 6.75$

Mode = 6.6 (occurs most frequently)

Data with first time omitted:

Mean $= \overline{x} = \frac{\Sigma x}{n} = \frac{46.3}{7} \approx 6.61$

Median = 6.6 (middle value)

Mode = 6.6 (occurs most frequently)

The mean is very sensitive to extreme values.

11. (a) Mean $= \overline{x} = \frac{\Sigma x}{n} = \frac{2723}{20} = 136.15$

The mean is \$136.15.

The median is \$66.50.

The mode is \$60.

(b) 5% of 20 is 1. Eliminate one data value from the bottom and one from the top of the ordered data. In this case eliminate \$40 and \$500.

Mean $= \overline{x} = \frac{\Sigma x}{n} = \frac{2183}{18} \approx 121.28$

The 5% trimmed mean is \$121.28.

Yes, the trimmed mean more accurately reflects the general level of the daily rental cost, but is still higher than the median.

(c) Median. The low and high prices would be helpful also.

12. (a) Since this data is at the ratio level of measurement, the mean, median, and mode (if it exists) can be used to summarize the data.

(b) Since this data is at the nominal level of measurement, only the mode (if it exists) can be used to summarize the data.

(c) Since this data is at the ratio level of measurement, the mean, median, and mode (if it exists) can be used to summarize the data.

13. (a) Since this data is at the nominal level of measurement, only the mode (if it exists) can be used to summarize the data.

(b) Since this data is at the ratio level of measurement, the mean, median, and mode (if it exists) can be used to summarize the data.

(c) The mode can be used (if it exists). If a 24-hour clock is used, then the data is at the ratio level of measurement, so the mean and median may be used as well.

14. Discussion question.

15. (a) If the largest data value is *replaced* by a larger value, the mean will increase because the sum of the data values will increase, but the number of them will remain the same. The median will not change. The same value will still be in the eighth position when the data are ordered.

(b) If the largest value is replaced by a value that is smaller (but still higher than the median), the mean will decrease because the sum of the data values will decrease. The median will not change. The same value will be in the eighth position in increasing order.

(c) If the largest value is replaced by a value that is smaller than the median, the mean will decrease because the sum of the data values will decrease. The median also will decrease because the former value in the eighth position will move to the ninth position in increasing order. The median will be the new value in the eighth position.

16. Answers may vary. Some examples are

(a) 1 2 2 2 3

(b) 1 2 2 2 13

(c) 1 1 5 5 5

(d) 1 2 4 5 5

(e) −2 −1 0 1 2

17. Answers will vary according to data collected.

Section 3.2

1. (a) Range = largest value − smallest value
$= 58 - 4 = 54$

The range is 54 deer/km².

$$\bar{x} = \frac{\Sigma x}{n} = \frac{251}{12} \approx 20.9$$

The sample mean is 20.9 deer/km².

$$s^2 = \frac{\Sigma(x-\bar{x})^2}{n-1} = \frac{2474.9}{11} \approx 225.0$$

The sample variance is 225.0.

$$s = \sqrt{s^2} = \sqrt{225.0} = 15.0$$

The sample standard deviation is 15.0 deer/km².

(b) $CV = \frac{s}{\bar{x}} \cdot 100 = \frac{15.0}{20.9} \cdot 100 \approx 71.8\%$

s is 71.8% of $\bar{x}$.

Since the standard deviation is about 71.8% of the mean, there is considerable variation in the distribution of deer from one part of the park to another.

2. (a) Range = largest value − smallest value
$= 78.6 - 17.8 = 60.8$

The range is 60.8%.

$$\bar{x} = \frac{\Sigma x}{n} = \frac{540.8}{10} \approx 54.1$$

The mean is 54.1%.

(b) $s^2 = \dfrac{\Sigma(x-\overline{x})^2}{n-1} = \dfrac{3400}{9} \approx 377.78$

The sample variance is 377.78.

$$s = \sqrt{s^2} = \sqrt{377.78} \approx 19.44$$

The standard deviation is 19.44%.

(c) $CV = \dfrac{s}{\overline{x}} \cdot 100 = \dfrac{19.44}{54.1} \cdot 100 \approx 35.9\%$

s is 35.9% of $\overline{x}$.

3. (a) Range $= 90.3 - 12.7 = 77.6$

The range is 77.6%.

$$\overline{x} = \frac{\Sigma x}{n} = \frac{556.7}{10} \approx 55.7$$

The mean is 55.7%.

(b) $s^2 = \dfrac{\Sigma(x-\overline{x})^2}{n-1} = \dfrac{4833}{9} \approx 537$

The sample variance is 537.

$$s = \sqrt{s^2} = \sqrt{537} \approx 23.17$$

The standard deviation is 23.17%.

(c) $CV = \dfrac{s}{\overline{x}} \cdot 100 = \dfrac{23.17}{55.7} \cdot 100 \approx 41.6\%$

s is 41.6% of $\overline{x}$.

This *CV* is larger than the *CV* for geese. So, nesting success rates for ducks have greater relative variability.

4. (a) Range $= 14.1 - 6.8 = 7.3$

$$\overline{x} = \frac{\Sigma x}{n} = \frac{63.7}{7} = 9.1$$

$$s^2 = \frac{\Sigma(x-\overline{x})^2}{n-1} = \frac{53.28}{6} = 8.88$$

$$s = \sqrt{s^2} = \sqrt{8.88} \approx 2.98$$

$$CV = \frac{s}{\overline{x}} \cdot 100 = \frac{2.98}{9.1} \cdot 100 = 32.7\%$$

(b) Range $= 31.0 - 19.1 = 11.9$

$$\bar{x} = \frac{\Sigma x}{n} = \frac{182.9}{7} = 26.1$$

$$s^2 = \frac{\Sigma(x-\bar{x})^2}{n-1} = \frac{118.71}{6} \approx 19.79$$

$$s = \sqrt{s^2} = \sqrt{19.79} \approx 4.45$$

$$CV = \frac{s}{\bar{x}} \cdot 100 = \frac{4.45}{26.1} \cdot 100 = 17.0\%$$

(c) More relatively consistent productivity at a higher average level.

5. (a)

$$\text{Pax } CV = \frac{s}{\bar{x}} \cdot 100 = \frac{11.56}{11.69} \cdot 100 \approx 98.9\%$$

$$\text{Vanguard } CV = \frac{s}{\bar{x}} \cdot 100 = \frac{12.50}{5.61} \cdot 100 \approx 222.8\%$$

Pax World Balanced seems less risky.

(b) Pax: $\bar{x} - 2s = 11.69 - 2(11.56) = -11.43$

$\bar{x} + 2s = 11.69 + 2(11.56) = 34.81$

At least 75% of the data fall in the interval –11.43% to 34.81%.

Vanguard: $\bar{x} - 2s = 5.61 - 2(12.50) = -19.39$

$\bar{x} + 2s = 5.61 + 2(12.50) = 30.61$

At least 75% of the data fall in the interval –19.39% to 30.61%.

The performance range for Pax seems better than for Vanguard (based on these historical data).

6. (a)-(c) Students verify results.

(d) The 3-year moving average has a much lower standard deviation.

7. (a) $\bar{x} - 2s = 11.01 - 2(2.17) = 6.67$

$\bar{x} + 2s = 11.01 + 2(2.17) = 15.35$

We expect at least 75% of the cycles to fall in the interval 6.67 years to 15.35 years.

(b) $\bar{x} - 4s = 11.01 - 4(2.17) = 2.33$

$\bar{x} + 4s = 11.01 + 4(2.17) = 19.69$

We expect at least 93.8% of the cycles to fall in the interval 2.33 years to 19.69 years.

8. (a) Results round to answers given.

(b) $\bar{x} - 2s = 730 - 2(172) = 386$

$\bar{x} + 2s = 730 + 2(172) = 1074$

We expect at least 75% of the years to have between 386 and 1074 tornados.

(c) $\bar{x} - 3s = 730 - 3(172) = 214$

$\bar{x} + 3s = 730 + 3(172) = 1246$

We expect at least 88.9% of the years to have between 214 and 1246 tornados.

9. **(a)** Range $= 956 - 219 = 737$

$$\bar{x} = \frac{\Sigma x}{n} = \frac{3968}{7} \approx 566.9$$

(b) $$s^2 = \frac{\Sigma(x-\bar{x})^2}{n-1} = \frac{427{,}213}{6} \approx 71{,}202$$

$$s = \sqrt{s^2} = \sqrt{71{,}202} \approx 266.8$$

(c) $$CV = \frac{s}{\bar{x}} \cdot 100 = \frac{266.8}{566.9} \cdot 100 = 47.1\%$$

s is 47.1% of $\bar{x}$.

(d) $\bar{x} - 2s = 566.9 - 2(266.8) \approx 33$

$\bar{x} + 2s = 566.9 + 2(266.8) \approx 1100$

We expect at least 75% of the artifact counts for all such excavation sites to fall in the interval 33 to 1100.

10. $\bar{x} = 4.0$, $s = 1.2$ for indulgences.

$\bar{x} - 2s = 4.0 - 2(1.2) = 1.6$

$\bar{x} + 2s = 4.0 + 2(1.2) = 6.4$

We would expect at least 75% of the *P*s to fall in the interval 1.6% to 6.4%.

11. $\bar{x} = 9.3$, $s = 2.6$ for domestic routine.

$\bar{x} - 2s = 9.3 - 2(2.6) = 4.1$

$\bar{x} + 2s = 9.3 + 2(2.6) = 14.5$

We would expect at least 75% of the percentages of domestic routine artifacts at different sites to fall in the interval 4.1% to 14.5%.

12. $\bar{x} = 0.4$, $s = 0.1$ for arms.

$\bar{x} - 2s = 0.4 - 2(0.1) = 0.2$

$\bar{x} + 2s = 0.4 + 2(0.1) = 0.6$

We would expect at least 75% of the percentages of arms artifacts at different sites to fall in the interval 0.2% to 0.6%.

13. Construction artifacts have the largest mean and the smallest *CV*. Therefore, construction artifacts have the highest average and lowest relative standard deviation.

14. The mean for arms artifacts is twice that of stable artifacts.

15. **(a)** Students verify results.

(b) Wal-Mart $CV = \frac{s}{\bar{x}} \cdot 100 = \frac{1.06}{52.03} \cdot 100 \approx 2\%$

Disney $CV = \frac{s}{\bar{x}} \cdot 100 = \frac{0.98}{32.23} \cdot 100 \approx 3\%$

Yes, since the CV's are approximately equal, they appear to be equally attractive.

(c) Wal-Mart:

$\overline{x}-3s = 52.03-3(1.06) = 48.85$

$\overline{x}+3s = 52.03+3(1.06) = 55.21$

Disney:

$\overline{x}-3s = 32.23-3(0.98) = 29.29$

$\overline{x}+3s = 32.23+3(0.98) = 35.17$

The support is $48.85 and resistance is $55.21 for Wal-Mart.
The support is $29.29 and the resistance is $35.17 for Disney.

16. $CV = \frac{s}{\overline{x}} \cdot 100$

$\frac{\overline{x} \cdot CV}{100} = s$

$s = \frac{\overline{x} \cdot CV}{100}$

$s = \frac{2.2(1.5)}{100}$

$s = 0.033$

17. Answers vary.

Section 3.3

1.

Class	f	x	xf	$x-\overline{x}$	$(x-\overline{x})^2$	$(x-\overline{x})^2 f$
21–30	260	25.5	6630	–10.3	106.09	27,583.4
31–40	348	35.5	12,354	–0.3	0.09	31.3
41 and over	287	45.5	13,058.5	9.7	94.09	27,003.8
	$n = \Sigma f = 895$		$\Sigma xf = 32{,}042.5$			$\Sigma(x-\overline{x})^2 f = 54{,}619$

$\overline{x} = \frac{\Sigma xf}{n} = \frac{32{,}042.5}{895} \approx 35.80$

$s^2 = \frac{\Sigma(x-\overline{x})^2 \cdot f}{n-1} = \frac{54{,}619}{894} \approx 61.1$

$s = \sqrt{61.1} \approx 7.82$

2.

Class	f	x	xf	$x-\overline{x}$	$(x-\overline{x})^2$	$(x-\overline{x})^2 f$
1–10	34	5.5	187	–10.6	112.36	3820.24
11–20	18	15.5	279	–0.6	0.36	6.48
21–30	17	25.5	433.5	9.4	88.36	1502.12
31 and over	11	35.5	390.5	19.4	376.36	4139.96
	$n = \Sigma f = 80$		$\Sigma xf = 1290$			$\Sigma(x-\overline{x})^2 f = 9468.8$

$$\overline{x} = \frac{\Sigma xf}{n} = \frac{1290}{80} \approx 16.1$$

$$s^2 = \frac{\Sigma(x-\overline{x})^2 f}{n-1} = \frac{9468.8}{79} \approx 119.9$$

$$s = \sqrt{119.9} \approx 10.95$$

3.

Class	f	x	xf	$x-\overline{x}$	$(x-\overline{x})^2$	$(x-\overline{x})^2 f$
8.6–12.5	15	10.55	158.25	–5.05	25.502	382.537
12.6–16.5	20	14.55	291.00	–1.05	1.102	22.050
16.6–20.5	5	18.55	92.75	2.95	8.703	43.513
20.6–24.5	7	22.55	157.85	6.95	48.303	338.118
24.6–28.5	3	26.55	79.65	10.95	119.903	359.708
	$n = \Sigma f = 50$		$\Sigma xf = 779.5$			$\Sigma(x-\overline{x})^2 f = 1145.9$

$$\overline{x} = \frac{\Sigma xf}{n} = \frac{779.5}{50} \approx 15.6$$

$$s^2 = \frac{\Sigma(x-\overline{x})^2 f}{n-1} = \frac{1145.9}{49} \approx 23.4$$

$$s = \sqrt{23.4} \approx 4.8$$

4.

Class	f	x	xf	$x-\overline{x}$	$(x-\overline{x})^2$	$(x-\overline{x})^2 f$
12–14	1	13	13	–7.35	54.0225	54.023
15–17	3	16	48	–4.35	18.9225	56.768
18–20	8	19	152	–1.35	1.8225	14.580
21–23	2	22	44	1.65	2.7225	5.445
24–26	6	25	150	4.65	21.6225	129.735
	$n = \Sigma f = 20$		$\Sigma xf = 407$			$\Sigma(x-\overline{x})^2 f = 260.55$

$$\overline{x} = \frac{\Sigma xf}{n} = \frac{407}{20} = 20.35$$

$$s = \sqrt{\frac{\Sigma(x-\overline{x})^2 f}{n-1}} = \sqrt{\frac{260.55}{19}} \approx 3.703$$

$$CV = \frac{s}{\overline{x}} \cdot 100 = \frac{3.703}{20.35} \cdot 100 = 18.2\%$$

5.

Class	f	x	xf	$x-\overline{x}$	$(x-\overline{x})^2$	$(x-\overline{x})^2 f$
18–24	78	21.0	1638.0	–18.12	328.33	25610.1
25–34	75	29.5	2212.5	–9.62	92.54	6940.8
35–44	48	39.5	1896.0	0.38	0.14	6.9
45–54	33	49.5	1633.5	10.38	107.74	3555.6
55–64	33	59.5	1963.5	20.38	415.34	13706.4
65–80	33	72.5	2392.5	33.38	1114.22	36769.4
	$n = \Sigma f = 300$		$\Sigma xf = 11,736$			$\Sigma(x-\overline{x})^2 f = 86,589$

$$\bar{x} = \frac{\Sigma xf}{n} = \frac{11,736}{300} = 39.12$$

$$s = \sqrt{\frac{\Sigma(x-\bar{x})^2 f}{n-1}} = \sqrt{\frac{86,589}{299}} \approx 17.02$$

$$CV = \frac{s}{\bar{x}} \cdot 100 = \frac{17.02}{39.12} \cdot 100 \approx 43.5\%$$

6. Men:

Class	f	x	xf	$x-\bar{x}$	$(x-\bar{x})^2$	$(x-\bar{x})^2 f$
0–24	560	12	6720	–15	225	126000
25–49	320	37	11840	10	100	32000
50–74	80	62	4960	35	1225	98000
75–99	40	87	3480	60	3600	144000
	$n = \Sigma f = 1000$		$\Sigma xf = 27,000$			$\Sigma(x-\bar{x})^2 f = 400,000$

$$\bar{x} = \frac{\Sigma xf}{n} = \frac{27,000}{1000} = 27$$

$$s = \sqrt{\frac{\Sigma(x-\bar{x})^2 f}{n-1}} = \sqrt{\frac{400,000}{999}} \approx 20.01$$

$$CV = \frac{s}{\bar{x}} \cdot 100 = \frac{20.01}{27} \cdot 100 \approx 74.1\%$$

Women:

Class	f	x	xf	$x-\bar{x}$	$(x-\bar{x})^2$	$(x-\bar{x})^2 f$
0–24	800	12	9600	–6	36	28800
25–49	170	37	6290	19	361	61370
50–74	20	62	1240	44	1936	38720
75–99	10	87	870	69	4761	47610
	$n = \Sigma f = 1000$		$\Sigma xf = 18,000$			$\Sigma(x-\bar{x})^2 f = 176,500$

$$\bar{x} = \frac{\Sigma xf}{n} = \frac{18,000}{1000} = 18$$

$$s = \sqrt{\frac{\Sigma(x-\bar{x})^2 f}{n-1}} = \sqrt{\frac{176,500}{999}} \approx 13.29$$

$$CV = \frac{s}{\bar{x}} \cdot 100 = \frac{13.29}{18} \cdot 100 \approx 73.8\%$$

7.

x	f	xf	x^2f
3.5	2	7	24.5
4.5	2	9	40.5
5.5	4	22	121.0
6.5	22	143	929.5
7.5	64	480	3600.0
8.5	90	765	6502.5
9.5	14	133	1263.5
10.5	2	21	220.5
	$\Sigma f = 200$	$\Sigma xf = 1580$	$\Sigma x^2 f = 12{,}702$

$$\bar{x} = \frac{\Sigma xf}{n} = \frac{1580}{200} = 7.9$$

$$SS_x = \Sigma x^2 f - \frac{(\Sigma xf)^2}{n} = 12{,}702 - \frac{(1580)^2}{200} = 220$$

$$s = \sqrt{\frac{SS_x}{n-1}} = \sqrt{\frac{220}{199}} \approx 1.05$$

$$CV = \frac{s}{\bar{x}} \cdot 100 = \frac{1.05}{7.9} \cdot 100 \approx 13.29\%$$

8.

x	f	xf	x^2f
1	15	15	15
2	15	30	60
3	7	21	63
4	9	36	144
5	13	65	325
6	13	78	468
7	9	63	441
8	8	64	512
9	9	81	729
	$\Sigma f = 98$	$\Sigma xf = 453$	$\Sigma x^2 f = 2757$

$$\bar{x} = \frac{\Sigma xf}{n} = \frac{453}{98} \approx 4.6$$

$$SS_x = \Sigma x^2 f - \frac{(\Sigma xf)^2}{n} = 2757 - \frac{(453)^2}{98} \approx 663.03$$

$$s^2 = \frac{SS_x}{n-1} = \frac{663.03}{97} \approx 6.8$$

$$s = \sqrt{6.8} \approx 2.6$$

9. (a)

x	f	xf	x^2f
1	3	3	3
2	7	14	28
3	6	18	54
4	5	20	80
5	4	20	100
6	2	12	72
7	0	0	0
8	1	8	64
9	2	18	162
10	1	10	100
	$\Sigma f = 31$	$\Sigma xf = 123$	$\Sigma x^2 f = 663$

$$\overline{x} = \frac{\Sigma xf}{n} = \frac{123}{31} \approx 3.97$$

$$SS_x = \Sigma x^2 f - \frac{(\Sigma xf)^2}{n} = 663 - \frac{(123)^2}{31} \approx 175$$

$$s = \sqrt{\frac{SS_x}{n-1}} = \sqrt{\frac{175}{30}} \approx 2.415$$

(b) The results are the same.

10.

x	f	xf	x^2f
35.4	79	2796.6	99000
23.0	565	12995.0	298885
29.4	136	3998.4	117553
38.3	103	3944.9	151090
61.5	400	24600.0	1512900
	$\Sigma f = 1283$	$\Sigma xf = 48,335$	$\Sigma x^2 f = 2,179,427$

$$\overline{x} = \frac{\Sigma xf}{n} = \frac{48,335}{1283} \approx 37.7$$

$$SS_x = \Sigma x^2 f - \frac{(\Sigma xf)^2}{n} = 2,179,427 - \frac{(48,335)^2}{1283} \approx 358,482.2$$

$$s^2 = \frac{SS_x}{n-1} = \frac{358,482.2}{1282} \approx 279.6$$

$$s = \sqrt{279.6} \approx 16.7$$

(Calculations may vary slightly due to rounding.)

11.

x	f	xf	$x^2 f$
2.8	145	406.0	1136.8
6.3	270	1701.0	10716.3
1.8	224	403.2	725.8
4.8	271	1300.8	6243.8
3.0	67	201.0	603.0
	$\Sigma f = 977$	$\Sigma xf = 4012$	$\Sigma x^2 f = 19{,}426$

$$\overline{x} = \frac{\Sigma xf}{n} = \frac{4012}{977} \approx 4.11$$

$$SS_x = \Sigma x^2 f - \frac{(\Sigma xf)^2}{n} = 19{,}426 - \frac{(4012)^2}{977} \approx 2951$$

$$s^2 = \frac{SS_x}{n-1} = \frac{2951}{976} \approx 3.02$$

$$s = \sqrt{3.02} \approx 1.74$$

12.

x	f	xf	$x^2 f$
1.3	75	97.5	126.8
8.7	190	1653.0	14381.1
11.3	80	904.0	10215.2
5.9	51	300.9	1775.3
3.3	181	597.3	1971.1
	$\Sigma f = 577$	$\Sigma xf = 3552.7$	$\Sigma x^2 f = 28{,}469$

$$\overline{x} = \frac{\Sigma xf}{n} = \frac{3552.7}{577} \approx 6.16$$

$$SS_x = \Sigma x^2 f - \frac{(\Sigma xf)^2}{n} = 28{,}469 - \frac{(3552.7)^2}{577} \approx 6594$$

$$s^2 = \frac{SS_x}{n-1} = \frac{6594}{576} \approx 11.45$$

$$s = \sqrt{11.45} \approx 3.38$$

13. Weighted average $= \dfrac{\Sigma xw}{\Sigma w}$

$$= \frac{92(0.25)+81(0.225)+93(0.225)+85(0.30)}{1}$$

$$= 87.65$$

14. $$\text{Weighted average} = \frac{\sum xw}{\sum w} = \frac{92(0.25)+81(0.25)+93(0.25)+85(0.25)}{1} = 87.75$$

The weighted average here is slightly greater than that in Problem 13. Since the weights are the same, we could have computed the mean of the four scores directly.

15. $$\text{Weighted average} = \frac{\sum xw}{\sum w} = \frac{9(2)+7(3)+6(1)+10(4)}{2+3+1+4} = \frac{85}{10} = 8.5$$

16. (a) $$\text{Weighted average} = \frac{\sum xw}{\sum w} = \frac{9(5)+7(2)+6(1)+8(3)}{5+2+1+3} = \frac{89}{11} \approx 8.09$$

(b) $$\text{Weighted average} = \frac{\sum xw}{\sum w} = \frac{8(5)+9(2)+5(1)+9(3)}{5+2+1+3} = \frac{90}{11} \approx 8.18$$

This athlete has the higher average rating.

17. Use the midpoints of the classes for x.

$$\text{Weighted average} = \frac{\sum xw}{\sum w} = \frac{7(0.15)+11(0.39)+14(0.27)+16.5(0.19)}{0.15+0.39+0.27+0.19} \approx 12.26$$

The weighted average is 12.26 lb.

18. Use the midpoints of the classes for x.

(a) $$\text{Weighted average} = \frac{\sum xw}{\sum w} = \frac{3.5(0.26)+8(0.40)+13(0.34)}{1} = 8.53$$

(b) $$\text{Weighted average} = \frac{\sum xw}{\sum w} = \frac{3.5(0.26)+8(0.40)+15.5(0.34)}{1} = 9.38$$

(c) Weighted average is sensitive to extreme values.

(d) Answers vary.

Section 3.4

1. 82% or more of the scores were at or below her score. 100% −82% = 18% or less of the scores were above her score. Note: This answer is correct, but it relies on a more precise definition than that given in the text on page 124. An adequate answer, matching the definition in the text would be: 82% of the scores were at or below her score, and (100 − 82)% = 18% of the scores were at or above her score.

2. The upper quartile is the 75th percentile. Therefore, the minimal percentile rank must be the 75th.

3. No, the score 82 might have a percentile rank less than 70.

4. Timothy performed better because a percentile rank of 72 is greater than a percentile rank of 70.

5. Order the data from smallest to largest.

Lowest value = 0.52
Highest value = 1.92

There are 16 data values.

$$\text{Median} = \frac{0.85+0.90}{2} = 0.875$$

There are 8 values less than 0.875 and 8 values greater than 0.875.

$$Q_1 = \frac{0.72+0.75}{2} = 0.735$$

$$Q_3 = \frac{1.15+1.50}{2} = 1.325$$

$$IQR = Q_3 - Q_1 = 1.325 - 0.735 = 0.59$$

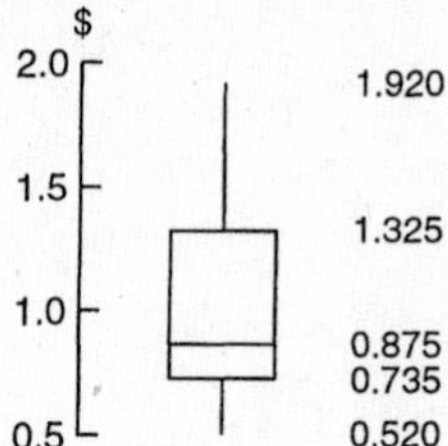

6. Order the data from smallest to largest.

Lowest value = 275
Highest value = 393

There are 16 data values.

$$\text{Median} = \frac{333+337}{2} = 335$$

There are 8 values less than 335 and 8 values greater than 335.

$$Q_1 = \frac{316+322}{2} = 319$$

$$Q_3 = \frac{353+357}{2} = 355$$

$$IQR = Q_3 - Q_1 = 355 - 319 = 36$$

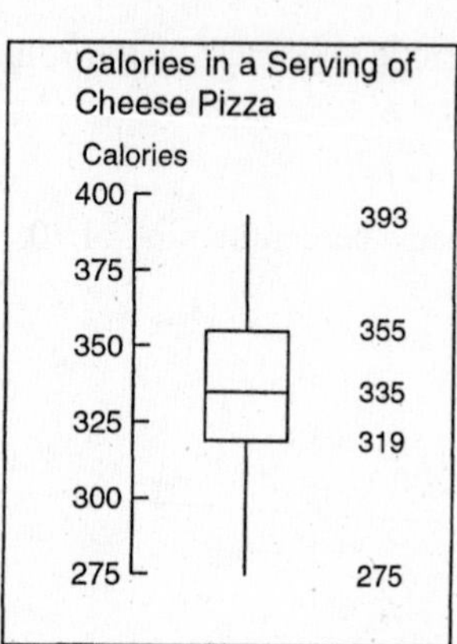

7. Order the data from smallest to largest.

Lowest value = 2
Highest value = 42

There are 20 data values.

$$\text{Median} = \frac{23+23}{2} = 23$$

There are 10 values less than the Q_2 position and 10 values greater than the Q_2 position.

$$Q_1 = \frac{8+11}{2} = 9.5$$

$$Q_3 = \frac{28+29}{2} = 28.5$$

$$IQR = Q_3 - Q_1 = 28.5 - 9.5 = 19$$

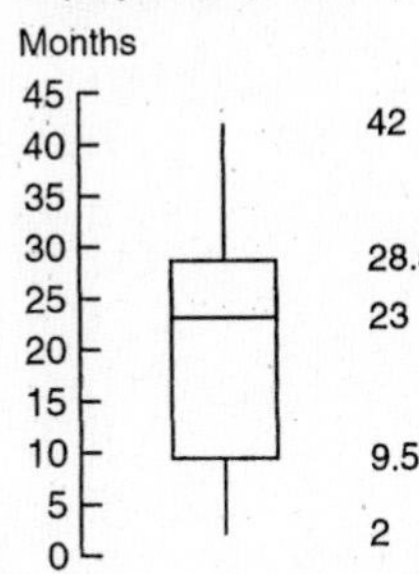

8. (a) Order the data from smallest to largest.

Lowest value = 3
Highest value = 72

There are 20 data values.

$$\text{Median} = \frac{22+24}{2} = 23$$

There are 10 values less than the median and 10 values greater than the median.

$$Q_1 = \frac{15+17}{2} = 16$$

$$Q_3 = \frac{29+31}{2} = 30$$

$$IQR = Q_3 - Q_1 = 30 - 16 = 14$$

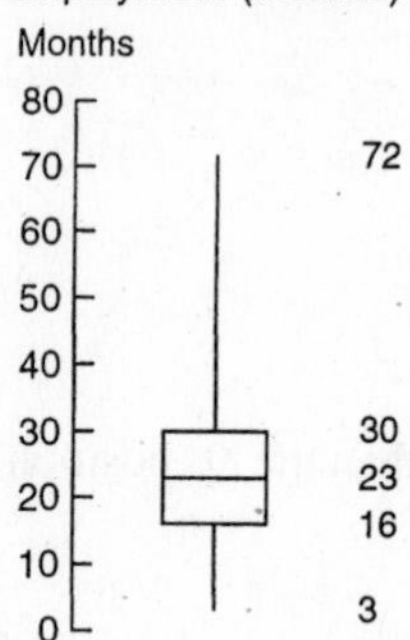

(b) The medians are the same (23) and the *IQR*'s are similar. However, the distances from Q_1 to the minimum value and from Q_3 to the maximum value are greater here than in Problem 7.

9. Order each set of data from smallest to largest.

Suburban

Lowest value = 808
Highest value = 1292

$$\text{Median} = \frac{992 + 1170}{2} = 1081$$

There are five values above and five values below the median.

$$Q_1 = 972$$
$$Q_3 = 1216$$
$$IQR = 1216 - 972 = 244$$

Urban

Lowest value = 1768
Highest value = 2910

$$\text{Median} = \frac{2107 + 2356}{2} = 2231.5$$

There are five values above and five values below the median.

$$Q_1 = 1968$$
$$Q_3 = 2674$$
$$IQR = 2674 - 1968 = 706$$

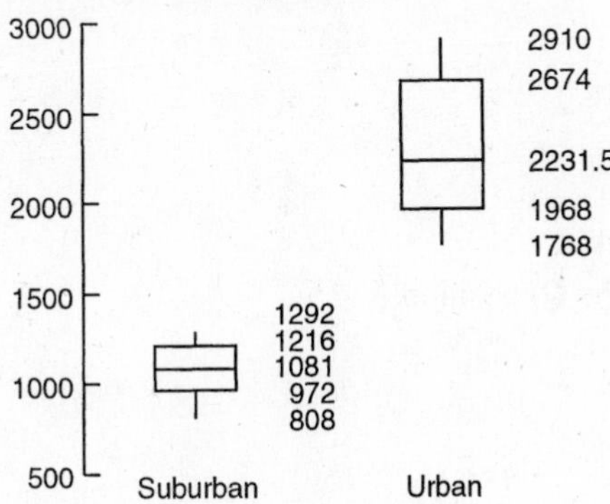

The entire box-and-whisker plot for urban is above that for suburban. Even the highest value for suburban is less than the lowest value for urban. The suburban data is less variable than that of urban data.

10. (a) Order the data from smallest to largest.

Lowest value = 5
Highest value = 15

There are 50 data values.

$$\text{Median} = \frac{10+10}{2} = 10$$

There are 25 values above and 25 values below the Q_2 position.

$$Q_1 = 9$$
$$Q_3 = 12$$
$$IQR = 12 - 9 = 3$$

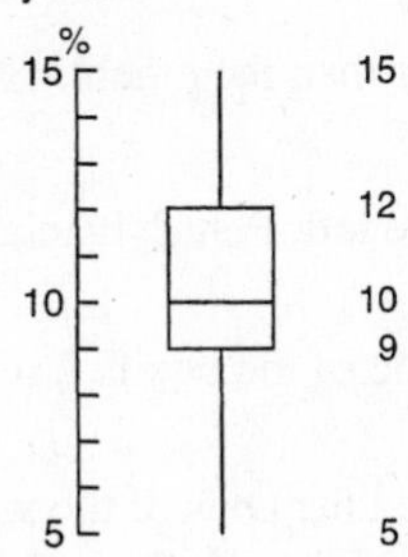

(b) 7% is in the 1st quartile, since it is below Q_1.

11. (a) Order the data from smallest to largest.

Lowest value = 17
Highest value = 38

There are 50 data values.

$$\text{Median} = \frac{24+24}{2} = 24$$

There are 25 values above and 25 values below the Q_2 position.

$$Q_1 = 22$$
$$Q_3 = 27$$
$$IQR = 27 - 22 = 5$$

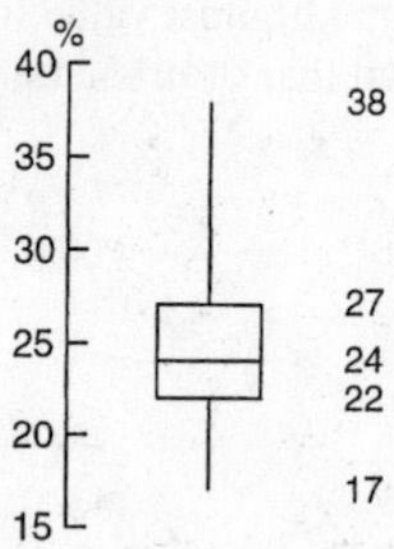

(b) 26% is in the 3rd quartile, since it is between the median and Q_3.

12. (a) Yes; the data above the median has more spread.

(b) Coca-Cola; the difference between the highest value and lowest value is greatest.

(c) Coca-Cola; the distribution has the most spread.

(d) McDonalds; McDonalds; the line representing the median is at a negative value which means more weekly declines than weekly increases.

(e) Disney; the sizes of the percentage increases are smaller than the others.

(f) Coca-Cola; Coca-Cola; the percentage decreases of this stock are larger than the others.

13. (a) California has the lowest premium since its left whisker is farthest to the left. Pennsylvania has the highest premium since its right whisker is farthest to the right.

(b) Pennsylvania has the highest median premium since its line in the middle of the box is farthest to the right.

(c) California has the smallest range of premiums since the distance between the ends of the whiskers is the smallest. Texas has the smallest interquartile range since the distance between the ends of the boxes is the smallest.

(d) Based on the answers to (a)-(c) above, we can determine that part (a) of Figure 3-13 is for Texas, part (b) of Figure 3-13 is for Pennsylvania, and part (c) of Figure 3-13 is for California.

14. **(a)** Order the data from smallest to largest.

Lowest value = 4
Highest value = 80

There are 24 data values.

$$\text{Median} = \frac{65+66}{2} = 65.5$$

There are 12 values above and 12 values below the median.

$$Q_1 = \frac{61+62}{2} = 61.5$$

$$Q_3 = \frac{71+72}{2} = 71.5$$

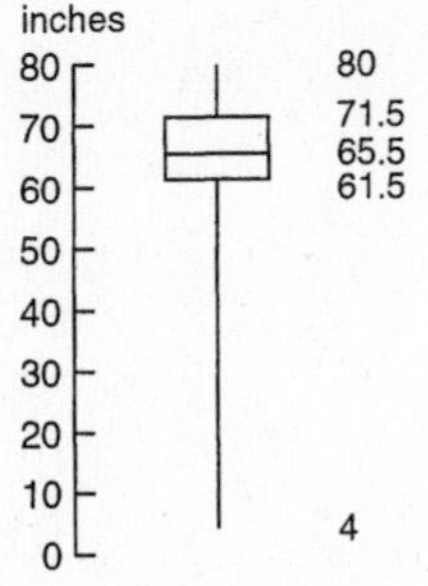

(b) $IQR = Q_3 - Q_1 = 71.5 - 61.5 = 10$

(c) $1.5(10) = 15$
Lower limit: $Q_1 - 1.5(IQR) = 61.5 - 15 = 46.5$
Upper limit: $Q_3 + 1.5(IQR) = 71.5 + 15 = 86.5$

(d) Yes, the value 4 is below the lower limit and so is an outlier; it is probably an error. Our guess is that one of the students is 4 feet tall and listed height in feet instead of inches. There are no values above the upper limit.

15. **(a)** Assistant had the smallest median percentage salary increase since the bar in the middle of the box is the lowest. Associate had the single highest salary increase since it has the highest asterisk.

(b) Instructor had the largest spread between the first and third quartiles since the distance between the ends of the box is greatest.

(c) Assistant had the smallest spread for the lower 50% of the percentage salary increases since the distance between the bar in the box and the maximum value is the smallest.

(d) Professor had the most symmetric percentage salary increases because there are no outliers and the bar representing the median is close to the center of the box.
Yes, if the outliers for the associate professors were omitted, that distribution would appear to be symmetric.

(e) Associate professor:

$$IQR = 5.075 - 2.350 = 2.725$$
$$Q_3 + 1.5(IQR) = 5.075 + 1.5(2.725) \approx 9.16$$

Yes, since 17.7 is greater than 9.16, there is at least one outlier.

Instructor:

$$IQR = 5.800 - 2.850 = 2.950$$
$$Q_3 + 1.5(IQR) = 5.800 + 1.5(2.950) \approx 10.23$$

Yes, since 13.4 is greater than 10.23, there is at least one outlier.

Chapter 3 Review

1. (a) $\bar{x} = \frac{\Sigma x}{n} = \frac{876}{8} = 109.5$

$$s = \sqrt{\frac{\Sigma(x-\bar{x})^2}{n-1}} = \sqrt{\frac{7044}{7}} = \sqrt{1006.3} \approx 31.7$$

$$CV = \frac{s}{\bar{x}} \cdot 100 = \frac{31.7}{109.5} \cdot 100 \approx 28.9\%$$

range = maximum value − minimum value
= 142 − 73 = 69

(b) $\bar{x} = \frac{\Sigma x}{n} = \frac{881}{8} = 110.125$

$$s = \sqrt{\frac{\Sigma(x-\bar{x})^2}{n-1}} = \sqrt{\frac{358.87}{7}} \approx 7.2$$

$$CV = \frac{s}{\bar{x}} \cdot 100 = \frac{7.2}{110.125} \cdot 100 \approx 6.5\%$$

range = maximum value − minimum value
= 120 − 100 = 20

(c) The means are about the same. The first distribution has greater spread. The standard deviation, *CV,* and range for the first set of measurements are greater than those for the second set of measurements.

2. (a) Mean $= \bar{x} = \frac{\Sigma x}{n} = \frac{1.9 + 2.8 + \cdots + 7.2}{8}$

$$= \frac{36.2}{8}$$

$$= 4.525$$

Order the data from smallest to largest.

1.9 1.9 2.8 3.9 4.2 5.7 7.2 8.6

Median $= \frac{3.9 + 4.2}{2} = 4.05$

The mode is 1.9 because it is the value that occurs most frequently.

(b) $s = \sqrt{\frac{\Sigma(x-\bar{x})^2}{n-1}} = \sqrt{\frac{42.395}{7}} \approx 2.46$

$CV = \frac{s}{\bar{x}} \cdot 100 = \frac{2.46}{4.525} \cdot 100 \approx 54.4\%$

Range $= 8.6 - 1.9 = 6.7$

3. (a) Order the data from smallest to largest.

Lowest value = 31
Highest value = 68

There are 60 data values.

$$\text{Median} = \frac{45+45}{2} = 45$$

There are 30 values above and 30 values below the Q_2 position.

$$Q_1 = \frac{40+40}{2} = 40$$

$$Q_3 = \frac{52+53}{2} = 52.5$$

$$IQR = 52.5 - 40 = 12.5$$

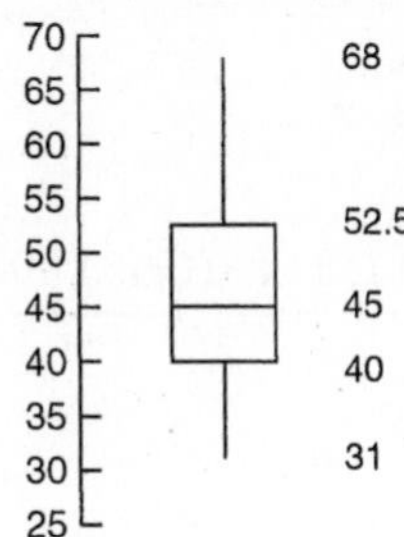

(b) Class width = 8

Class	x Midpoint	f	xf	$x^2 f$
31–38	34.5	11	379.5	13,092.8
39–46	42.5	24	1020	43,350.0
47–54	50.5	15	757.5	38,253.8
55–62	58.5	7	409.5	23,955.8
63–70	66.5	3	199.5	13,266.8
		$n = \Sigma f = 60$	$\Sigma xf = 2766$	$\Sigma x^2 f = 131,919$

$$\bar{x} = \frac{\Sigma xf}{n} = \frac{2766}{60} = 46.1$$

$$SS_x = \Sigma x^2 f - \frac{(\Sigma xf)^2}{n} = 131{,}919 - \frac{(2766)^2}{60} = 4406.4$$

$$s = \sqrt{\frac{SS_x}{n-1}} = \sqrt{\frac{4406.4}{59}} \approx 8.64$$

$\bar{x} - 2s = 46.1 - 2(8.64) = 28.82$
$\bar{x} + 2s = 46.1 + 2(8.64) = 63.38$

We expect at least 75% of the data to fall in the interval 28.82 to 63.38.

(c) $\bar{x} = 46.15,\ s \approx 8.63$

4. (a) Weighted average $= \dfrac{\Sigma xw}{\Sigma w}$

$$= \frac{92(0.05)+73(0.08)+81(0.08)+85(0.15)+87(0.15)+83(0.15)+90(0.34)}{0.05+0.08+0.08+0.15+0.15+0.15+0.34}$$

$$= \frac{85.77}{1}$$

$$= 85.77$$

(b) Weighted average $= \dfrac{\Sigma xw}{\Sigma w}$

$$= \frac{20(0.05)+73(0.08)+81(0.08)+85(0.15)+87(0.15)+83(0.15)+90(0.34)}{1}$$

$$= 82.17$$

5. Mean weight $= \dfrac{2500}{16} = 156.25$

The mean weight is 156.25 lb.

6.

x	f	xf	$x^2 f$
17	6	102	1734
32	20	640	20,480
47	52	2444	114,868
62	16	992	61,504
	$\Sigma f = 94$	$\Sigma xf = 4178$	$\Sigma x^2 f = 198{,}586$

$$\bar{x} = \frac{\sum xf}{n} = \frac{4178}{94} \approx 44.4$$

The mean is 44.4 in.

$$SS_x = \sum x^2 f - \frac{(\sum xf)^2}{n} = 198{,}586 - \frac{(4178)^2}{94} \approx 12{,}887$$

$$s = \sqrt{\frac{SS_x}{n-1}} = \sqrt{\frac{12{,}887}{93}} \approx 11.8$$

The standard deviation is 11.8 in.

7. **(a)** Mean $= \bar{x} = \frac{\sum x}{n} = \frac{10.1 + 6.2 + \cdots + 5.7}{6} = \frac{47}{6} \approx 7.83$

$$s = \sqrt{\frac{\sum(x-\bar{x})^2}{n-1}} = \sqrt{\frac{26.913}{5}} \approx 2.32$$

$$CV = \frac{s}{\bar{x}} \cdot 100 = \frac{2.32}{7.83} \cdot 100 \approx 29.6\%$$

Range = largest value − smallest value
$= 10.1 - 5.3 = 4.8$

(b) Mean $= \bar{x} = \frac{\sum x}{n} = \frac{10.2 + 9.7 + \cdots + 10.1}{6} = \frac{59.7}{6} = 9.95$

$$s = \sqrt{\frac{\sum(x-\bar{x})^2}{n-1}} = \sqrt{\frac{0.415}{5}} \approx 0.29$$

$$CV = \frac{s}{\bar{x}} \cdot 100 = \frac{0.29}{9.95} \cdot 100 \approx 2.9\%$$

Range = largest value − smallest value
$= 10.3 - 9.6 = 0.7$

(c) Second line has more consistent performance as reflected by the smaller standard deviation, *CV*, and range.

8. Order the data from smallest to largest.

Lowest value = 45
Highest value = 109

There are 70 data values.

$$\text{Median} = \frac{80 + 80}{2} = 80$$

There are 35 values above and 35 values below the Q_2 position.

$Q_1 = 71$

$Q_3 = 84$

$IQR = 84 - 71 = 13$

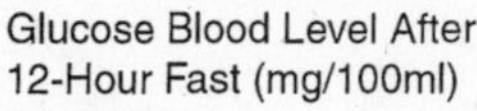

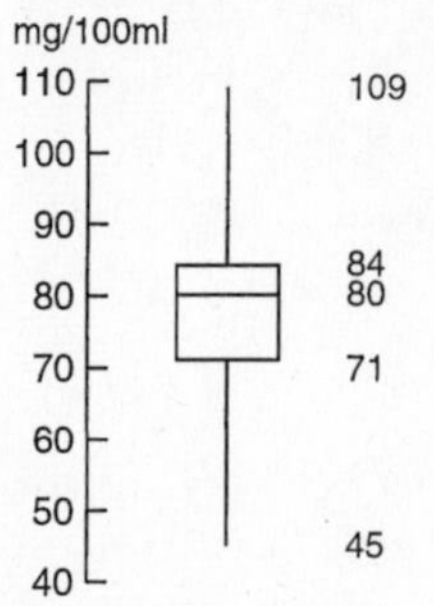

9. (a)

x	f	xf	$x^2 f$
50	3	150	7500
61	7	427	26047
72	22	1584	114048
83	26	2158	179114
94	9	846	79524
105	3	315	33075
	$n = \Sigma f = 70$	$\Sigma xf = 5480$	$\Sigma x^2 f = 439{,}308$

$$\overline{x} = \frac{\Sigma xf}{n} = \frac{5480}{70} \approx 78.3$$

$$SS_x = \Sigma x^2 f - \frac{(\Sigma xf)^2}{n} = 439{,}308 - \frac{(5480)^2}{70} \approx 10302.3$$

$$s^2 = \frac{SS_x}{n-1} = \frac{10302.3}{69} \approx 149$$

$$s = \sqrt{s^2} = \sqrt{149} \approx 12.2$$

$$CV = \frac{s}{\overline{x}} \cdot 100 = \frac{12.2}{78.3} \cdot 100 \approx 15.6\%$$

(b) $\overline{x} - 2s = 78.3 - 2(12.2) = 53.9$
$\overline{x} + 2s = 78.3 + 2(12.2) = 102.7$

We expect at least 75% of the glucose blood level measurements to fall in the interval 53.9 to 102.7.

10.

x	f	xf	$x^2 f$
4.6	304	1398.4	6432.64
12.0	52	624.0	7488.00
2.6	39	101.4	263.64
4.1	319	1307.9	5362.39
3.9	77	300.3	1171.17
	$\Sigma f = 791$	$\Sigma xf = 3732$	$\Sigma x^2 f = 20{,}718$

$$\overline{x} = \frac{\Sigma xf}{n} = \frac{3732}{791} \approx 4.7$$

$$SS_x = \Sigma x^2 f - \frac{(\Sigma xf)^2}{n} = 20{,}718 - \frac{(3732)^2}{791} \approx 3110$$

$$s^2 = \frac{SS_x}{n-1} = \frac{3110}{790} \approx 3.94$$

$$s = \sqrt{3.94} = 1.98$$

11. Weighted average $= \dfrac{\Sigma xw}{\Sigma w}$

$$= \frac{5(2)+8(3)+7(3)+9(5)+7(3)}{2+3+3+5+3}$$

$$= \frac{121}{16}$$

$$\approx 7.56$$

12. (a) Order the data from smallest to largest.

Lowest value = 6
Highest value = 16

There are 50 data values.

$$\text{Median} = \frac{11+11}{2} = 11$$

There are 25 values above and 25 values below the Q_2 position.

$$Q_1 = 10$$
$$Q_3 = 13$$
$$IQR = Q_3 - Q_1 = 13 - 10 = 3$$

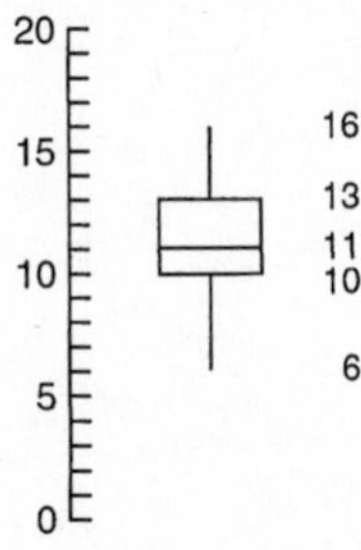

(b)

Class	x Midpoint	f	xf	$x^2 f$
6–8	7	4	28	196
9–11	10	24	240	2400
12–14	13	15	195	2535
15–17	16	7	112	1792
		$n = \Sigma f = 50$	$\Sigma xf = 575$	$\Sigma x^2 f = 6923$

$$\bar{x} = \frac{\Sigma xf}{n} = \frac{575}{50} = 11.5$$

$$SS_x = \Sigma x^2 f - \frac{(\Sigma xf)^2}{n} = 6923 - \frac{(575)^2}{50} = 310.5$$

$$s = \sqrt{\frac{SS_x}{n-1}} = \sqrt{\frac{310.5}{49}} \approx 2.52$$

$$\bar{x} - 2s = 11.5 - 2(2.52) = 6.46$$
$$\bar{x} + 2s = 11.5 + 2(2.52) = 16.54$$

We expect at least 75% of the data to fall in the interval 6.46 to 16.54.

(c) $\bar{x} \approx 11.48$; $s \approx 2.44$

13. (a) It is possible for the range and the standard deviation to be the same. For instance, for data values that are all the same, such as 1, 1, 1, 1, 1, the range and standard deviation are both 0.

(b) It is possible for the mean, median, and mode to be all the same. For instance, the data set 1, 2, 3, 3, 3, 4, 5 has mean, median, and mode all equal to 3. The averages can all be different, as in the data set 1, 2, 3, 3. In this case, the mean is 2.25, the median is 2.5, and the mode is 3.

Chapter 4 Elementary Probability Theory

Section 4.1

1. Answers vary. Probability is a number between 0 and 1, inclusive, that expresses the likelihood that a specific event will occur. Three ways to find or assign a probability to an event are (1) through intuition (subjective probability), (2) by considering the long-term relative frequency of recurrence of an event in repeated independent trials (empirical probability), and (3) by computing the ratio of the number of favorable outcomes to the total number of possible outcomes, assuming all outcomes are equally likely (classical probability).

2. Answers vary. Probability in business: market research; in medicine: drug tests to determine if a new drug is more effective than the standard treatment; in social science: determining which characteristics to use in creating a profile to detect terrorists; in natural sciences: predicting the likely path and location of landfall for a hurricane.
Statistics is the science of collecting, analyzing, and interpreting quantitative data in such a way that the reliability of the conclusions based on the data can be evaluated objectively. Probability is used in determining the reliability of the results.

3. These are not probabilities: (b) because it is greater than 1, (d) because it is less than zero (negative), (h) 150% = 1.50, because it is greater than 1.

4. Remember $0 \le \text{probability of an event} \le 1$

(a) $-0.41 < 0$

(b) $1.21 > 1$

(c) $120\% = 1.2 > 1$

(d) yes, $0 \le 0.56 \le 1$

5. Answers vary. The result is a sample, although not necessarily a good one, showing the relative frequency of people able to wiggle their ears.

6. Answers vary. The results are one example (not necessarily a good one) of the relative frequency of occurrence of raising one eyebrow.

7. (a) $P(\text{no similar preferences}) = P(0) = \frac{15}{375}$, $P(1) = \frac{71}{375}$, $P(2) = \frac{124}{375}$, $P(3) = \frac{131}{375}$, $P(4) = \frac{34}{375}$

(b) $\frac{15+71+124+131+34}{375} = \frac{375}{375} = 1$, yes
Personality types were classified into 4 main preferences; all possible numbers of shared preferences were considered. The sample space is 0, 1, 2, 3, and 4 shared preferences.

8. (a) $P(\text{couple not engaged}) = \frac{200}{1000} = 0.20$, $P(\text{dated less than 1 year}) = \frac{240}{1000} = 0.24$, $P(\text{dated 1 to 2 years}) = \frac{210}{1000} = 0.21$, $P(\text{dated more than 2 years}) = \frac{350}{1000} = 0.35$, based on the number of "favorable outcomes divided by the total number of outcomes (1000 couples' engagement status)

(b) $\frac{200+240+210+350}{1000} = \frac{1000}{1000} = 1$, yes
They should add to 1 because all possible outcomes were considered. The sample space is never engaged, engaged less than 1 year, engaged 1 to 2 years, engaged more than 2 years.

9. (a) Note: "includes the left limit but not the right limit" means 6 A.M. $\le$ time $t <$ noon, noon $\le t <$ 6 P.M., 6 P.M. $\le t <$ midnight, midnight $\le t <$ 6 A.M. P(best idea 6 A.M.–12 noon) $= \frac{290}{966} \approx 0.30$; P(best idea 12 noon–6 P.M.) $= \frac{135}{966} \approx 0.14$; P(best idea 6 P.M.–12 midnight) $\frac{319}{966} \approx 0.33$; P(best idea from 12 midnight to 6 A.M.) $= \frac{222}{966} \approx 0.23$.

(b) The probabilities add up to 1. They should add up to 1 provided that the intervals do not overlap and each inventor chose only one interval. The sample space is the set of four time intervals.

10. (a) The sample space would be 1, 2, 3, 4, 5, 6 dots. If the die is fair, all outcomes would be equally likely.

(b) $P(1) = P(2) = P(3) = P(4) = P(5) = P(6) = \frac{1}{6}$ because the die faces are equally likely and there are 6 outcomes. The probabilities should and do add to 1 $\left(\frac{1}{6}+\frac{1}{6}+\frac{1}{6}+\frac{1}{6}+\frac{1}{6}+\frac{1}{6}=\frac{6}{6}=1\right)$ because all possible outcomes have been considered.

(c) P(number of dots < 5) = P(1 *or* 2 *or* 3 *or* 4 dots) = $P(1) + P(2) + P(3) + P(4) = \frac{1}{6}+\frac{1}{6}+\frac{1}{6}+\frac{1}{6}$ $= \frac{4}{6} = \frac{2}{3}$ or P(dots < 5) = 1 – P(5 *or* 6 dots) $= 1 - \frac{1}{3} = \frac{2}{3}$ (The applicable probability rule used here will be discussed in the next section of the text; rely on your common sense for now.)

(d) Complementary event rule: $P(A) = 1 - P(not\ A)$
P(5 *or* 6 dots) = 1 – P(1 *or* 2 *or* 3 *or* 4 dots) $\frac{2}{3} = \frac{1}{3}$, or P(5 *or* 6) = $P(5) + P(6) = \frac{1}{6}+\frac{1}{6}=\frac{2}{6}=\frac{1}{3}$

11. (a) Since the responses of all 1000 people surveyed have been accounted for (770 + 160 + 70 = 1000), the 3 responses describe the sample space. P(left alone) $= \frac{770}{1000} = 0.77$, P(waited on) $= \frac{160}{1000} = 0.16$,
P(treated differently) $= \frac{70}{1000} = 0.07$
$0.77 + 0.16 + 0.07 = 1$
The probabilities do add to 1, which they should, because they are the sum of probabilities of all possible outcomes in the sample space.

(b) Complementary events: $P(not\ A) = 1 - P(A)$:
P(do not want to be left alone) = 1 – P(left alone) = 1 – 0.77 = 0.23
P(do not want to be waited on) = 1 – P(waited on) = 1 – 0.16 = 0.84

12. (a) $P(\text{germinate}) = \frac{\text{number germinated}}{\text{number planted}} = \frac{2430}{3000} = 0.81$

(b) $P(\text{not germinate}) = \frac{3000-2430}{3000} = \frac{570}{3000} = 0.19$

(c) The sample space is 2 outcomes, germinate and not germinate.
P(germinate) + P(not germinate) = 0.81 + 0.19 = 1
The probabilities of all the outcomes in the sample space should and do sum to 1.

(d) no; P(germinate) = 0.81, P(not germinate) = 0.19
If they were equally likely, each would have probability $\frac{1}{2} = 0.5$.

13. (a) Given: odds in favor of A are $n{:}m$ $\left(\text{i.e., } \frac{n}{m}\right)$.

Show $P(A) = \frac{n}{m+n}$

Proof: odds in favor of A are $\frac{P(A)}{P(not\ A)}$ by definition

$$P(not\ A) = 1 - P(A) \quad \text{complementary events}$$

$$\frac{n}{m} = \frac{P(A)}{P(not\ A)} = \frac{P(A)}{1-P(A)} \quad \text{substitution}$$

$$n[1-P(A)] = m[P(A)] \quad \text{cross multiply}$$

$$n - n[P(A)] = m[P(A)]$$

$$n = n[P(A)] + m[P(A)]$$

$$n = (n+m)[P(A)]$$

So $\frac{n}{n+m} = P(A)$ as was to be shown.

(b) Odds of a successful call = odds of sale are 2 to 15. 2 to 15 can be written as 2:15 or $\frac{2}{15}$ then from part (a): if the odds in favor of a sale are 2:15 (let $n = 2$, $m = 15$) then $P(\text{sale}) = \frac{n}{n+m} = \frac{2}{2+15}$ $= \frac{2}{17} \approx 0.118$.

(c) Odds of free throw are 3 to 5, i.e., 3:5
Let $n = 3$ and $m = 5$ here then from part (a):
$P(\text{free throw}) = \frac{n}{n+m} = \frac{3}{3+5} = \frac{3}{8} = 0.375$.

14. (a) Given: odds against W are $a{:}b$ $\left(\text{or } \frac{a}{b}\right)$

Show: $P(not\ W) = \frac{a}{a+b}$

Proof: odds against W are $\frac{P(not\ W)}{P(W)}$ by definition

$$P(W) = 1 - P(not\ W) \quad \text{complementary events}$$

$$\frac{P(not\ W)}{P(W)} = \frac{a}{b} \quad \text{substitution}$$

$$\frac{P(not\ W)}{1-P(not\ W)} = \frac{a}{b} \quad \text{substitution}$$

$$b[P(not\ W)] = a[1 - P(not\ W)] \quad \text{cross multiply}$$

$$b[P(not\ W)] = a - a[P(not\ W)]$$

$$b[P(not\ W)] + a[P(not\ W)] = a$$

$$(a+b)[P(not\ W)] = a$$

$$P(not\ W) = \frac{a}{a+b}$$

$P(not\ W) = \frac{a}{a+b}$ as was to be shown.

(b) Point Given's betting odds is 9:5. Betting odds are based on the probability that the horse does not win, so odds against PG winning is $\frac{P(\text{not } PG \text{ wins})}{P(PG \text{ wins})}$.

Let $a = 9$ and $b = 5$ in part (a) formula. From part (a), $P(\text{not } PG \text{ wins}) = \frac{a}{a+b} = \frac{9}{9+5} = \frac{9}{14}$, but event *not PG* wins is the same as *PG* loses, so $P(\text{Point Given loses}) = \frac{9}{14} \approx 0.64$ and $P(PG \text{ wins the race})$ $= 1 - \frac{9}{14} = \frac{5}{14} \approx 0.36.$

(c) Betting odds for Monarchos is 6:1. Betting odds are based on the probability that the horse does not win, i.e., the horse loses.
Let W be the event that Monarchos wins. From part (a), if the events against W are given as a:b, the $P(\text{not } W) = \frac{a}{a+b}$. Let $a = 6$ and $b = 1$ in part (a) formula so

$$P(\text{not } W) = \frac{6}{6+1} = \frac{6}{7}$$

$$P(\text{not } W) = P(\text{Monarchos loses}) = \frac{6}{7} \approx 0.86$$

$$P(\text{Monarchos wins}) = P(W) = 1 - P(\text{not } W) = 1 - \frac{6}{7} = \frac{1}{7} \approx 0.14.$$

(d) Invisible Ink was given betting odds of 30 to 1, i.e., odds against Invisible Ink winning were $\frac{30}{1}$. Let W denote the event Invisible Ink wins. Let $a = 30$, $b = 1$ in formula from part (a). Then, from part (a), $P(\text{not } W) = \frac{a}{a+b}$, $P(\text{not Invisible Ink wins}) = \frac{30}{30+1} = \frac{30}{31}$, i.e.,

$$P(\text{Invisible Ink loses}) = \frac{30}{31} \approx 0.97$$

$$P(\text{Invisible Ink wins}) = 1 - P(\text{Invisible Ink loses}) = 1 - \frac{30}{31} - \frac{1}{31} \approx 0.03.$$

15. Make a table showing the information known about the 127 people who walked by the store: [Example 6 in Section 4.2 uses this technique.]

	Buy	Did not buy	Row Total
Came into the store	25	58 – 25 = 33	58
Did not come in	0	69	127 – 58 = 69
Column Total	25	102	127

If 58 came in, 69 didn't; 25 of the 58 bought something, so 33 came in but didn't buy anything. Those who did not come in, couldn't buy anything. The row entries must sum to the row totals; the column entries must sum to the column totals; and the row totals, as well as the column totals, must sum to the overall total, i.e., the 127 people who walked by the store. Also, the four inner cells must sum to the overall total: 25 + 33 + 0 + 69 = 127.

This kind of problem relies on formula (2), $P(\text{event } A) = \frac{\text{number outcomes favorable to } A}{\text{total number of outcomes}}$. The "trick" is to decide what belongs in the denominator *first*. If the denominator is a row total, stay in that row. If the denominator is a column total, stay in that column. If the denominator is the overall total, the numerator can be a row total, a column total, or the number in any one of the four "cells" inside the table.

(a) total outcomes: people walking by, overall total, 127
favorable outcomes: enter the store, row total, 58 (that's all we know about them)

$$P(A) = \frac{58}{127} \approx 0.46$$

(b) total outcomes: people who walk into the store, row total 58
favorable outcomes: staying in the row, those who buy: 25

$$P(A) = \frac{25}{58} \approx 0.43$$

(c) total outcomes: people walking by, overall total 127
favorable outcomes: people coming in *and* buying, the cell at the *intersection* of the "coming in" row and the "buying" column (the upper left corner), 25 (Recall from set theory that "and" means both things happen, that the two sets *intersect*: >)

$$P(A) = \frac{25}{127} \approx 0.20$$

(d) total outcomes: people coming into the store, row total, 58
favorable outcomes: staying in the row, those who do not buy, 33

$$P(A) = \frac{33}{58} \approx 0.57$$

$$\left(\text{alternate method: this is the complement to (b): } P(A) = 1 - \frac{25}{58} = \frac{33}{58} \approx 0.57\right)$$

Section 4.2

1. (a) Orange and blue are mutually exclusive because each M&M candy is only 1 color.
$P(\text{orange } or \text{ blue}) = P(\text{orange}) + P(\text{blue}) = 10\% + 10\% = 20\%$

(b) Yellow and red are mutually exclusive, again, because each candy is only one color, and if the candy is yellow, it can't be red, too.
$P(\text{yellow } or \text{ red}) = P(\text{yellow}) + P(\text{red}) = 20\% + 20\% = 40\%$

(c) It is faster here to use the complementary event rule than to add up the probabilities of all the colors except brown.
$P(not \text{ brown}) = 1 - P(\text{brown}) = 1 - 0.30 = 0.70$, or 70%

2. (a) Orange and blue are mutually exclusive because each M&M candy is only 1 color.
$P(\text{orange } or \text{ blue}) = P(\text{orange}) + P(\text{blue}) = 10\% + 20\% = 30\%$

(b) Yes, mutually exclusive colors
$P(\text{yellow } or \text{ red}) = P(\text{yellow}) + P(\text{red}) = 20\% + 20\% = 40\%$

(c) $P(not \text{ brown}) = 1 - P(\text{brown}) = 1 - 0.20 = 0.80 = 80\%$
Since the color distributions differ for plain and peanut M&Ms (see brown and blue percentages), if the answers were the same, it would only be by coincidence.

3. (a) Mutually exclusive. Notice the color orange is not available in almond M&Ms.
$P(\text{orange } or \text{ blue}) = P(\text{orange}) + P(\text{blue}) = 0\% + 20\% = 20\%$

(b) Mutually exclusive: $P(\text{yellow } or \text{ red}) = P(\text{yellow}) + P(\text{red}) = 20\% + 20\% = 40\%$

(c) $P(not \text{ brown}) = 1 - P(\text{brown}) = 1 - 0.20 = 0.80 = 80\%$
Since the color distributions differ for plain and almond M&Ms, if the answers were the same, it would only be by coincidence.

4. The total number of arches tabled is 288. Arch heights are mutually exclusive because if the height is 12 feet, it can't be 42 feet as well.

(a) $P(3 \text{ to } 9) = \dfrac{111}{288}$

(b) $P(30 \text{ or taller}) = P(30 \text{ to } 49) + P(50 \text{ to } 74) + P(75 \text{ and higher}) = \frac{30}{288} + \frac{33}{288} + \frac{18}{288} = \frac{81}{288}$

(c) $P(3 \text{ to } 49) = P(3-9) + P(10-29) + P(30-49) = \frac{111}{288} + \frac{96}{288} + \frac{30}{288} = \frac{237}{288}$

(d) $P(10 \text{ to } 74) = P(10-29) + P(30-49) + P(50-74) = \frac{96}{288} + \frac{30}{288} + \frac{33}{288} = \frac{159}{288}$

(e) $P(75 \text{ or taller}) = \frac{18}{288}$

Hint for Problems 5–8: Refer to Figure 4–1 if necessary. (Without loss of generality, let the red die be the first die and the green die be the second die in Figure 4–1.) Think of the outcomes as an (x, y) ordered pair. Then, without loss of generality, (1, 6) means 1 on the red die and 6 on the green die. (We are "ordering" the dice for convenience only – which is first and which is second have no bearing on this problem.) The only important fact is that they are distinguishable outcomes, so that (1 on red, 2 on green) is different from (2 on red, 1 on green).

5. **(a)** Yes, the outcome of the red die does not influence the outcome of the green die.

(b) $P(5 \text{ on green } and \text{ 3 on red}) = P(5 \text{ on green}) \cdot P(3 \text{ on red}) = \left(\frac{1}{6}\right)\left(\frac{1}{6}\right) = \frac{1}{36} \approx 0.028$ because they are independent.

(c) $P(3 \text{ on green } and \text{ 5 on red}) = P(3 \text{ on green}) \cdot P(5 \text{ on red}) = \left(\frac{1}{6}\right)\left(\frac{1}{6}\right) = \frac{1}{36} \approx 0.028$

(d) $P[(5 \text{ on green } and \text{ 3 on red}) \text{ or } (3 \text{ on green } and \text{ 5 on red})]$
$= P(5 \text{ on green } and \text{ 3 on red}) + P(3 \text{ on green } and \text{ 5 on red})]$
$= \frac{1}{36} + \frac{1}{36} = \frac{2}{36} = \frac{1}{18} \approx 0.056$ [because they are mutually exclusive outcomes]

6. **(a)** Yes, the outcome of the red die does not influence the outcome of the green die.

(b) $P(1 \text{ on green } and \text{ 2 on red}) = P(1 \text{ on green}) \cdot P(2 \text{ on red}) = \left(\frac{1}{6}\right)\left(\frac{1}{6}\right) = \frac{1}{36}$

(c) $P(2 \text{ on green } and \text{ 1 on red}) = P(2 \text{ on green}) \cdot P(1 \text{ on red}) = \left(\frac{1}{6}\right)\left(\frac{1}{6}\right) = \frac{1}{36}$

(d) $P[(1 \text{ on green } and \text{ 2 on red}) \text{ or } (2 \text{ on green } and \text{ 1 on red})]$
$= P(1 \text{ on green } and \text{ 2 on red}) + P(2 \text{ on green } and \text{ 1 on red})]$
$= \frac{1}{36} + \frac{1}{36} = \frac{2}{36} = \frac{1}{18}$ [because they are mutually exclusive outcomes]

7. **(a)** $1 + 5 = 6, 2 + 4 = 6, 3 + 3 = 6, 4 + 2 = 6, 5 + 1 = 6$
$P(\text{sum} = 6) = P[(1, 5) \text{ or } (2, 4) \text{ or } (3 \text{ on red, } 3 \text{ on green}) \text{ or } (4, 2) \text{ or } (5, 1)]$
$= P(1, 5) + P(2, 4) + P(3, 3) + P(4, 2) + P(5, 1)$
since the (red, green) outcomes are mutually exclusive
$= \left(\frac{1}{6}\right)\left(\frac{1}{6}\right) + \left(\frac{1}{6}\right)\left(\frac{1}{6}\right) + \left(\frac{1}{6}\right)\left(\frac{1}{6}\right) + \left(\frac{1}{6}\right)\left(\frac{1}{6}\right) + \left(\frac{1}{6}\right)\left(\frac{1}{6}\right)$
because the red die outcome is independent of the green die outcome
$= \frac{1}{36} + \frac{1}{36} + \frac{1}{36} + \frac{1}{36} + \frac{1}{36} = \frac{5}{36}$

(b) $1 + 3 = 4, 2 + 2 = 4, 3 + 1 = 4$

$P(\text{sum is } 4) = P[(1, 3) \text{ or } (2, 2) \text{ or } (3, 1)]$

$= P(1, 3) + P(2, 2) + P(3, 1)$

because the (red, green) outcomes are mutually exclusive

$= \left(\frac{1}{6}\right)\left(\frac{1}{6}\right) + \left(\frac{1}{6}\right)\left(\frac{1}{6}\right) + \left(\frac{1}{6}\right)\left(\frac{1}{6}\right)$

because the red die outcome is independent of the green die outcome

$= \frac{1}{36} + \frac{1}{36} + \frac{1}{36} = \frac{3}{36} = \frac{1}{12}$

(c) Since a sum of six can't simultaneously be a sum of 4, these are mutually exclusive events;

$P(\text{sum of } 6 \text{ or } 4) = P(\text{sum of } 6) + P(\text{sum of } 4) = \frac{5}{36} + \frac{3}{36} = \frac{8}{36} = \frac{2}{9}$

8. (a) $1 + 6 = 7, 2 + 5 = 7, 3 + 4 = 7, 4 + 3 = 7, 5 + 2 = 7, 6 + 1 = 7$

$P(\text{sum is } 7) = P[(1, 6) \text{ or } (2, 5) \text{ or } (3, 4) \text{ or } (4, 3) \text{ or } (5, 2) \text{ or } (6, 1)]$

$= P(1, 6) + P(2, 5) + P(3, 4) + P(4, 3) + P(5, 2) + P(6, 1)$

because the (red, green) outcomes are mutually exclusive

$= \left(\frac{1}{6}\right)\left(\frac{1}{6}\right) + \left(\frac{1}{6}\right)\left(\frac{1}{6}\right) + \left(\frac{1}{6}\right)\left(\frac{1}{6}\right) + \left(\frac{1}{6}\right)\left(\frac{1}{6}\right) + \left(\frac{1}{6}\right)\left(\frac{1}{6}\right) + \left(\frac{1}{6}\right)\left(\frac{1}{6}\right)$

because the red die outcome is independent of the green die outcome

$= \frac{1}{36} + \frac{1}{36} + \frac{1}{36} + \frac{1}{36} + \frac{1}{36} + \frac{1}{36} = \frac{6}{36} = \frac{1}{6}$

(b) $5 + 6 = 11, 6 + 5 = 11$

$P(\text{sum is } 11) = P[(5, 6) \text{ or } (6, 5)]$

$= P(5, 6) + P(6, 5)$

because the (red, green) outcomes are mutually exclusive

$= \left(\frac{1}{6}\right)\left(\frac{1}{6}\right) + \left(\frac{1}{6}\right)\left(\frac{1}{6}\right)$

because the red die outcome is independent of the green die outcome

$= \frac{1}{36} + \frac{1}{36} = \frac{2}{36} = \frac{1}{18}$

(c) Since a sum of can't be both 7 and 11, they are mutually exclusive

$P(\text{sum is } 7 \text{ or } 11) = P(\text{sum is } 7) + P(\text{sum is } 11) = \frac{6}{36} + \frac{2}{36} = \frac{8}{36} = \frac{2}{9}$

9. (a) No, the key idea here is "without replacement," which means the draws are dependent, because the outcome of the second card drawn depends on what the first card drawn was. Let the card draws be represented by an (x, y) ordered pair. For example, (K, 6) means the first card drawn was a king and the second card drawn was a 6. Here the order of the cards is important.

(b) $P(\text{ace on 1st } \textit{and} \text{ king on second}) = P(\text{ace, king}) = \left(\frac{4}{52}\right)\left(\frac{4}{51}\right) = \frac{16}{2652} = \frac{4}{663}$

There are 4 aces and 4 kings in the deck. Once the first card is drawn and not replaced, there are only 51 cards left to draw from, but all the kings are still there.

(c) $P(\text{king, ace}) = \left(\frac{4}{52}\right)\left(\frac{4}{51}\right) = \frac{16}{2652} = \frac{4}{663}$

There are 4 kings and 4 aces in the deck. Once the first card is drawn and not replaced, there are only 51 cards left to draw from, but all the aces are still there.

(d) $P(\text{ace } \textit{and} \text{ king in either order})$
$= P[(\text{ace, king}) \textit{ or } (\text{king, ace})]$
$= P(\text{ace, king}) + P(\text{king, ace})$ because these two outcomes are mutually exclusive
$= \frac{16}{2652} + \frac{16}{2652} = \frac{32}{2652} = \frac{8}{663}$

10. (a) No, the key idea here is "without replacement," which means the draws are dependent, because the outcome of the second card drawn depends on what the first card was. Let the card draws be represented by an (x, y) ordered pair. For example, (K, 6) means the first card drawn was a king and the second card drawn was a 6. Here the order of the cards *is* important.

(b) $P(3, 10) = P[(3 \text{ on 1st}) \textit{ and } (10 \text{ on 2nd, } \textit{given} \text{ 3 on 1st})]$
$= P(3 \text{ on 1st}) \cdot P(10 \text{ on 2nd, } \textit{given} \text{ 3 on 1st})$
$= \left(\frac{4}{52}\right)\left(\frac{4}{51}\right) = \frac{16}{2652} = \frac{4}{663} \approx 0.006$

(c) $P(10, 3) = P[(10 \text{ on 1st}) \textit{ and } (3 \text{ on 2nd, } \textit{given} \text{ 10 on 1st})]$
$= P(10 \text{ on 1st}) \cdot P(3 \text{ on 2nd, } \textit{given} \text{ 10 on 1st})$
$= \left(\frac{4}{52}\right)\left(\frac{4}{51}\right) = \frac{16}{2652} = \frac{4}{663} \approx 0.006$

(d) $P[(3, 10) \textit{ or } (10, 3)] = P(3, 10) + P(10, 3)$ since these 2 outcomes are mutually exclusive
$= \frac{4}{663} + \frac{4}{663} = \frac{8}{663} \approx 0.012$

11. (a) Yes; the key idea here is "with replacement." When the first card drawn is replaced, the sample space is the same when the second card is drawn as it was when the first card was drawn and the second card is in no way influenced by the outcome of the first draw; in fact, it is possible to draw the same card twice. Let the card draws be represented by an (x, y) ordered pair; for example (K, 6) means a king was drawn first, replaced, and then the second card, a "6," was drawn independently of the first.

(b) $P(A, K) = P(A) \cdot P(K)$ because they are independent
$= \left(\frac{4}{52}\right)\left(\frac{4}{52}\right) = \frac{16}{2704} = \frac{1}{169}$

(c) $P(K, A) = P(K) \cdot P(A)$ because they are independent
$= \left(\frac{4}{52}\right)\left(\frac{4}{52}\right) = \frac{16}{2704} = \frac{1}{169}$

(d) $P[(A, K) \textit{ or } (K, A)] = P(A, K) + P(K, A)$ since the 2 outcomes are mutually exclusive when we consider the order
$= \frac{1}{169} + \frac{1}{169} = \frac{2}{169}$

12. (a) Yes; the key idea here is "with replacement." When the first card drawn is replaced, the sample space is the same when the second card is drawn as it was when the first card was drawn and the second card is in no way influenced by the outcome of the first draw; in fact, it is possible to draw the same card twice. Let the card draws be represented by an (x, y) ordered pair; for example (K, 6) means a king was drawn first, replaced, and then the second card, a "6," was drawn independently of the first.

(b) $P(3, 10) = P(3) \cdot P(10)$ because draws are independent
$= \left(\frac{4}{52}\right)\left(\frac{4}{52}\right) = \frac{16}{2704} = \frac{1}{169} \approx 0.0059$

(c) $P(10, 3) = P(10) \cdot P(3)$ because of independence
$= \left(\frac{4}{52}\right)\left(\frac{4}{52}\right) = \frac{16}{2704} = \frac{1}{169} \approx 0.0059$

(d) $P[(3, 10)\ or\ (10, 3)] = P(3, 10) + P(10, 3)$ because these outcomes are mutually exclusive

$$= \frac{1}{169} + \frac{1}{169} = \frac{2}{169} \approx 0.0118$$

13. **(a)** $P(6\ or\ \text{older}) = P[(6 \text{ to } 9)\ or\ (10 \text{ to } 12)\ or\ (13 \text{ and over})]$

$= P(6-9) + P(10-12) + P(13+)$ because they are mutually exclusive age groups - no child is both 7 and 11 years old.

$= 27\% + 14\% + 22\% = 63\% = 0.63$

(b) $P(12 \text{ or younger}) = 1 - P(13 \text{ and over}) = 1 - 0.22 = 0.78$

(c) $P(\text{between 6 and 12}) = P[(6 \text{ to } 9)\ or\ (10 \text{ to } 12)]$

$= P(6 \text{ to } 9) + P(10 \text{ to } 12)$ because the age groups are mutually exclusive

$= 27\% + 14\% = 41\% = 0.41$

(d) $P(\text{between 3 and 9}) = P[(3 \text{ to } 5)\ or\ (6 \text{ to } 9)]$

$= P(3 \text{ to } 5) + P(6 \text{ to } 9)$ because age categories are mutually exclusive

$= 22\% + 27\% = 49\% = 0.49$

Answers vary; however, category 10–12 years covers only 3 years while 13 and over covers many more years and many more people, including adults who buy toys for themselves.

14. What we know: $P(\text{seniors get flu}) = 0.14$,
$P(\text{younger people get flu}) = 0.24$
$P(\text{senior}) = 0.125$
Let S denote seniors, so *not* S denotes younger people. Let F denote flu and *not* F denote did not get the flu. So $P(\text{F}, given\ \text{S}) = 0.14$, $P(\text{F}, given\ not\ \text{S}) = 0.24$ and $P(\text{S}) = 0.125$ so $P(not\ \text{S}) = 1 - 0.125 = 0.875$. Note the phrases 14% <u>of</u> seniors, i.e., they were already seniors, so this is a given condition; and 24% <u>of</u> people under 65, i.e., these people were already under 65, so under 65 (younger) is a given condition

(a) $P(\text{person is senior } and \text{ will get flu}) = P(\text{S}\ and\ \text{F})$

$= P(\text{S}) \cdot P(\text{F},\ given\ \text{S}) = (0.125)(0.14) = 0.0175$

conditional probability rule

(b) $P(\text{person is } not \text{ senior } and \text{ will get flu}) = P[(not\ \text{S})\ and\ \text{F}]$

$= P(not\ \text{S}) \cdot P(\text{F},\ given\ not\ \text{S}) = 0.875(0.24) = 0.21$

(c) Here, $P(\text{S}) = 0.95$ so $P(not\ \text{S}) = 1 - 0.95 = 0.05$
(a) $P(\text{S}\ and\ \text{F}) = P(\text{S}) \cdot P(\text{F}, given\ \text{S}) = (0.95)(0.14) = 0.133$
(b) $P(not\ \text{S}\ and\ \text{F}) = P(not\ \text{S}) \cdot P(\text{F}, given\ not\ \text{S}) = (0.05)(0.24) = 0.012$

(d) Here, $P(\text{S}) = P(not\ \text{S}) = 0.50$
(a) $P(\text{S}\ and\ \text{F}) = P(\text{S}) \cdot P(\text{F}, given\ \text{S}) = 0.50(0.14) = 0.07$
(b) $P(not\ \text{S}\ and\ \text{F}) = P(not\ \text{S}) \cdot P(\text{F}, given\ not\ \text{S}) = 0.50(0.24) = 0.12$

15. What we know: $P(\text{polygraph says "lying" when person is lying}) = 72\%$
$P(\text{polygraph says "lying" when person is not lying}) = 7\%$
Let L denote that the polygraph results show lying and *not* L denote that the polygraph results show the person is not lying. Let T denote that the person is telling the truth and let *not* T denote that the person is not telling the truth, so $P(\text{L}, given\ not\ \text{T}) = 72\%$
$P(\text{L}, given\ \text{T}) = 7\%$.
We are told whether the person is telling the truth or not; what we know is what the polygraph results are, given the case where the person tells the truth, and given the situation where the person is not telling the truth.

(a) $P(\text{T}) = 0.90$ so $P(not\ \text{T}) = 0.10$
$P(\text{polygraph says lying and person tells truth})$
$= \text{P}(\text{L}\ and\ \text{T}) = P(\text{T}) \cdot P(\text{L},\ given\ \text{T})$
$= (0.90)(0.07) = 0.063 = 6.3\%$

(b) $P(not\ \text{T}) = 0.10$ so $P(\text{T}) = 0.90$
P(polygraph says lying and person is not telling the truth)
$= P(\text{L}\ and\ not\ \text{T}) = P(not\ \text{T}) \cdot P(\text{L},\ given\ not\ \text{T})$
$= (0.10)(0.72) = 0.072 = 7.2\%$

(c) $P(\text{T}) = P(not\ \text{T}) = 0.50$
(a) $P(\text{L}\ and\ \text{T}) = P(\text{T}) \cdot P(\text{L},\ given\ \text{T})$
$= (0.50)(0.07) = 0.035 = 3.5\%$
(b) $P(\text{L}\ and\ not\ \text{T}) = P(not\ \text{T}) \cdot P(\text{L},\ given\ not\ \text{T})$
$= (0.50)(0.72) = 0.36 = 36\%$

(d) $P(\text{T}) = 0.15$ so $P(not\ \text{T}) = 1 - P(\text{T}) = 1 - 0.15 = 0.85$
(a) $P(\text{L}\ and\ \text{T}) = P(\text{T}) \cdot P(\text{L},\ given\ \text{T})$
$= (0.15)(0.07) = 0.0105 = 1.05\%$
(b) $P(\text{L}\ and\ not\ \text{T}) = P(not\ \text{T}) \cdot P(\text{L},\ given\ not\ \text{T})$
$= (0.85)(0.72) = 0.612 = 61.2\%$

16. What we know: P(polygraph says "lying" when person is lying) = 72%
P(polygraph says "lying" when person is not lying) = 7%
Let L denote that the polygraph results show lying and *not* L denote that the polygraph results show the person is not lying. Let T denote that the person is telling the truth and let *not* T denote that the person is not telling the truth, so $P(\text{L},\ given\ not\ \text{T}) = 72\%$
$P(\text{L},\ given\ \text{T}) = 7\%$
We are told whether the person is telling the truth or not; what we know is what the polygraph results are, given the case where the person tells the truth, and given the situation where the person is not telling the truth.

(a) P(polygraph reports "lying") = $P(\text{L}) = 30\%$
We want to find P(person is lying) = $P(not\ \text{T})$
There are two possibilities when the polygraph says the person is lying: either the polygraph is right, or the polygraph is wrong. If the polygraph is right, the polygraph results show "lying" and the person is not telling the truth, i.e., $P(\text{L}\ and\ not\ \text{T})$. If the polygraph is wrong, then the polygraph results show "lying" but, in fact, the person is telling the truth, i.e., $P(\text{L}\ and\ \text{T})$. (This is the basic "trick" to this problem, and the idea comes directly from set theory.)

So $P(\text{L}) = P(\text{L}\ and\ not\ \text{T}) + P(\text{L}\ and\ \text{T})$
$= [P(not\ \text{T}) \cdot P(\text{L},\ given\ not\ \text{T})] + [P(\text{T}) \cdot P(\text{L},\ given\ \text{T})]$
using conditional probability rules
$= [P(not\ \text{T}) \cdot P(\text{L},\ given\ not\ \text{T})] + \{[1 - P(not\ \text{T})] \cdot P(\text{L},\ given\ \text{T})\}$
using the complementary event rule to rewrite $P(\text{T})$ as $1 - P(not\ \text{T})$
$0.30 = [P(not\ \text{T})] \cdot (0.72)] + [(1 - P(not\ \text{T})] \cdot (0.07)$
substituting in the known values as given in # 15, and as given above
$= (0.72) \cdot P(not\ \text{T}) + [0.07 - (0.07) \cdot P(not\ \text{T})]$
$0.30 - 0.07 = (0.72) \cdot P(not\ \text{T}) - (0.07) \cdot P(not\ \text{T})$
$0.23 = P(not\ \text{T})(0.72 - 0.07) = P(not\ \text{T})(0.65)$
$\frac{0.23}{0.65} = P(not\ \text{T})$, or $P(not\ \text{T}) \approx 0.354 = 35.4\%$

(b) Here, $P(\text{L}) = 70\% = 0.70$
This is the same as (a) except for the new $P(\text{L})$. Starting from the step in (a) just before we substituted in the numerical values we knew:

$$P(\text{L}) = [P(not\ \text{T}) \cdot P(\text{L},\ given\ not\ \text{T})] + \{[1 - P(not\ \text{T})] \cdot P(\text{L},\ given\ \text{T})\}$$
$$0.70 = P(not\ \text{T}) \cdot (0.72) + [1 - P(not\ \text{T})] \cdot (0.07)$$
$$0.70 = (0.72) \cdot P(not\ \text{T}) + [0.07 - 0.07 \cdot P(not\ \text{T})]$$
$$0.70 - 0.07 = (0.72 - 0.07) \cdot P(not\ \text{T})$$
$$0.63 = 0.65P(not\ \text{T})$$
so $P(not\ \text{T}) = \dfrac{0.63}{0.65} \approx 0.969 = 96.9\%.$

17. Let E denote eyeglasses, C denote contact lenses, W denote women, and M denote men. Then we have $P(\text{E}) = 56\%$, $P(\text{C}) = 3.6\%$, $P(\text{W},\ given\ \text{E}) = 55.4\%$, $P(\text{M},\ given\ \text{E}) = 44.6\%$, $P(\text{W},\ given\ \text{C}) = 63.1\%$, $P(\text{M},\ given\ \text{C}) = 36.9\%$, and $P(\text{E}\ and\ \text{C}) = 0$.

(a) $P(\text{W}\ and\ \text{E}) = P(\text{E}) \cdot P(\text{W},\ given\ \text{E})$
using a conditional probability rule
$= (0.56)(0.554) \approx 0.310$

(b) $P(\text{M}\ and\ \text{E}) = P(\text{E}) \cdot P(\text{M},\ given\ \text{E})$
$= (0.56)(0.446) \approx 0.250$

(c) $P(\text{W}\ and\ \text{C}) = P(\text{C}) \cdot P(\text{W},\ given\ \text{C})$
$= (0.036)(0.631) \approx 0.023$

(d) $P(\text{M}\ and\ \text{C}) = P(\text{C}) \cdot P(\text{M},\ given\ \text{C})$
$= (0.036)(0.369) \approx 0.013$

(e) $P(\text{none of the above}) = 1 - [P(\text{W}\ and\ \text{E}) + P(\text{M}\ and\ \text{E}) + P(\text{W}\ and\ \text{C}) + P(\text{M}\ and\ \text{C})]$
$= 1 - [0.310 + 0.250 + 0.023 + 0.013]$
$= 1 - 0.596 = 0.404$

18. $P(\$0) = 0.275$, $P(\text{less than }\$200) = 0.096$, $P(\$200 - \$599) = 0.135$, $P(\$600 - \$999) = 0.021$, $P(\$1000\text{ or more}) = 0.262$, $P(\text{don't know}) = 0.211$

$P(\$600\text{ or more}) = P[(\$600 - \$999)\ or\ (\$1000\text{ or more})]$
$= P(\$600 - \$999) + P(\$1000\text{ or more})$
since mutually exclusive price ranger
$= 0.021 + 0.262 = 0.283$

$P(\text{no more than }\$199) = P[(\$0)\ or\ (\text{less than }\$200)]$
$= 0.275 + 0.096$
assuming "less than \$200" means \$1 to \$199 so that this category does not overlap with those who said \$0
$= 0.371$

19. We have $P(A) = \dfrac{580}{1160}$, $P(Pa) = \dfrac{580}{1160} = P(not\ A)$, $P(S) = \dfrac{686}{1160}$, $P(N) = \dfrac{474}{1160} = P(not\ S)$

(a) $P(S) = \dfrac{686}{1160}$

$P(S,\ given\ A) = \dfrac{270}{580}$ (*given A* means stay in the *A*, aggressive row)

$P(S,\ given\ Pa) = \dfrac{416}{580}$ (staying in row *Pa*)

(b) $P(S) = \dfrac{686}{1160} = \dfrac{343}{580}$

$P(S,\ given\ Pa) = \dfrac{416}{580}$

They are not independent since the probabilities are not the same.

(c) $P(A\ and\ S) = P(A) \cdot P(S,\ given\ A)$

$$= \left(\frac{580}{1160}\right)\left(\frac{270}{580}\right) = \frac{270}{1160}$$

$P(Pa\ and\ S) = P(Pa) \cdot P(S,\ given\ Pa)$

$$= \left(\frac{580}{1160}\right)\left(\frac{416}{580}\right) = \frac{416}{1160}$$

(d) $P(N) = \frac{474}{1160}$

$P(N,\ given\ A) = \frac{310}{580}$ (stay in the *A* row)

(e) $P(N) = \frac{474}{1160} = \frac{237}{580}$

$P(N,\ given\ A) = \frac{310}{580}$

Since the probabilities are not the same, *N* and *A* are not independent.

(f) $P(A\ or\ S) = P(A) + P(S) - P(A\ and\ S)$

$$= \frac{580}{1160} + \frac{686}{1160} - \frac{270}{1160} = \frac{996}{1160}$$

20. (a) $P(+,\ given$ condition present$) = \frac{110}{130}$ (stay in "condition present" row)

(b) $P(-,\ given$ condition present$) = \frac{20}{130}$ (stay in "condition present" row)

[(a) and (b) are complementary events]

(c) $P(-,\ given$ condition absent$) = \frac{50}{70}$ (stay in the row or column of the "*given*")

(d) $P(+,\ given$ condition absent$) = \frac{20}{70}$

(e) $P($condition present *and* $+) = P($condition present$) \cdot P(+,\ given$ condition present$)$

$$= \left(\frac{130}{200}\right)\left(\frac{110}{130}\right) = \frac{110}{200}$$

(f) $P($condition present *and* $-) = P($condition present$) \cdot P(-,\ given$ condition present$)$

$$= \left(\frac{130}{200}\right)\left(\frac{20}{130}\right) = \frac{20}{200}$$

21. Let C denote the condition is present, and *not* C denote the condition is absent.

(a) $P(+,\ given\ \text{C}) = \frac{72}{154}$ (stay in C column)

(b) $P(-,\ given\ \text{C}) = \frac{82}{154}$ (stay in C column)

(c) $P(-,\ given\ not\ \text{C}) = \frac{79}{116}$ (stay in *not* C column)

(d) $P(+,\ given\ not\ \text{C}) = \frac{37}{116}$ (stay in *not* C column)

(e) $P(\text{C}\ and\ +) = P(\text{C}) \cdot P(+,\ given\ \text{C}) = \left(\frac{154}{270}\right)\left(\frac{72}{154}\right) = \frac{72}{270}$

(f) $P(\text{C}\ and\ -) = P(\text{C}) \cdot P(-,\ given\ \text{C}) = \left(\frac{154}{270}\right)\left(\frac{82}{154}\right) = \frac{82}{270}$

22. First determine the denominator. If it is a row or column total, the numerator will be in the body (inside) of the table in that same row or column. If the denominator is the grand total the numerator can be one or more row totals, one or more column totals, or a body-of-the-table cell entry. A cell entry is usually indicated when the problem mentions both a row category and a column category, in which case the desired cell is the one where the row and column intersect.

(a) customer at random, denominator is grand total, 2008; loyal 10–14 years, numerator is column total, 291; $\frac{291}{2008}$

(b) given: customer is from the East, so denominator is row total, 452; loyal 10–14 years: the cell entry in that row, 77; $\frac{77}{452}$

(c) no qualifiers on the customers, so denominator is grand total, 2008; at least 10 years: need entry for 10–14 years and 15+ years, so numerator is the sum of these 2 column totals, 291 + 535 = 826; $\frac{826}{2008}$

(d) given: from the West means the denominator is the West row total, 373; loyal at least 10 years means we sum the numbers in the West row for 10–14 and 15+ years, 45 + 86 = 131; $\frac{131}{373}$

(e) given: loyal less than 1 year means the denominator is column total, 157; from the West means the numerator is the cell entry for West in that column, 41; $\frac{41}{157}$

(f) given: loyal < 1 year, so denominator is 157; from South, so numerator is at the intersection of the < 1 year column and the South row, 53; $\frac{53}{157}$

(g) given: East, so denominator is 452; loyal 1+ years: either add up all the entries except < 1 year in the East row, or use the complementary event rule (less work!);

$$P(\text{loyal } 1+ \text{ years, } given \text{ East}) = 1 - P(\text{loyal} < 1 \text{ year, } given \text{ East})$$
$$= 1 - \frac{32}{452} = \frac{420}{452}$$

(h) given: West, so denominator is West row total, 373; loyal 1+ years is either the sum of all the West row entries except < 1 year, or apply the complementary event rule in the probability calculation;

$$P(\text{loyal } 1+ \text{ years, } given \text{ West}) = 1 - P(\text{loyal} < 1 \text{ year, } given \text{ West})$$
$$= 1 - \frac{41}{373} = \frac{332}{373}$$

(i) $P(\text{East}) = \frac{452}{2008} \approx 0.2251$

$P(\text{loyal 15+ years}) = \frac{535}{2008} \approx 0.2664$

$P(\text{East, } given \text{ 15+ years}) = \frac{118}{535} \approx 0.2206$

$P(\text{loyal 15+ years, } given \text{ East}) = \frac{118}{452} \approx 0.2611$

If they are independent, $P(\text{East}) = P(\text{East, } given \text{ 15+ years})$ but $0.2251 \neq 0.2206$, and if they are independent, $P(\text{loyal 15+ years}) = P(\text{loyal 15+ years, } given \text{ East})$ but $0.2664 \neq 0.2611$, so they aren't independent. (If you use decimal approximations, and the 2 probabilities are quite close, it's time to reduce fractions or use the least common denominator to get an accurate comparison.)

Note: independence is symmetric, i.e., if A is independent of B, then B is independent of A; this means you don't have to do *both* independence checks; one is sufficient.

23. First determine the denominator. If it is a row or column total, the numerator will be in the body (inside) of the table in that same row or column. If the denominator is the grand total the numerator can be one or more row totals, one or more column totals, or a body-of-the-table cell entry. A cell entry is usually indicated when the problem mentions both a row category and a column category, in which case the desired cell is the one where the row and column intersect.

(a) $P(2+) = 1 - P(<2) = 1 - P(1 \text{ visit}) = 1 - \frac{962}{1894} = \frac{932}{1894}$

There is no additional information about the customer, so the denominator is the grand total.

(b) $P(2+, \textit{given } 25\text{–}39 \text{ years old}) = 1 - P(<2, \textit{given } 25\text{–}39) = 1 - \frac{386}{739} = \frac{353}{739}$

The customer's age is given, so the denominator is the 25–39 row total, and the numerator is determined by the numbers in that row, using the complimentary rule for probabilities.

(c)
$$\begin{aligned} P(>3 \text{ visits}) &= P(4 \textit{ or } 5 \textit{ or } 6 \text{ or more visits}) \\ &= P(4) + P(5) + P(6+) \\ &= \frac{66}{1894} + \frac{44}{1894} + \frac{32}{1894} = \frac{142}{1894} \end{aligned}$$

There is no qualifier on the customer, so we use the grand total, 1894, as the denominator.

(d)
$$\begin{aligned} P(>3, \textit{given} \text{ age } 65+) &= 1 - P(\le 3, \textit{given } 65+) \\ &= 1 - P[(1, 2, \textit{or } 3 \text{ visits}), \textit{given } 65+] \\ &= 1 - [P(1 \text{ visit}, \textit{given } 65+) + P(2 \text{ visits}, \textit{given } 65+) + P(3 \text{ visits}, \textit{given } 65+)] \\ &= 1 - \left(\frac{115}{224} + \frac{69}{224} + \frac{18}{224}\right) = 1 - \frac{202}{224} = \frac{22}{224} \end{aligned}$$

Alternately, this can be solved without the complementary event rule:

$$\begin{aligned} P(>3 \text{ visits}, \textit{given } 65 \text{ or older}) &= P(4 \textit{ or } 5 \textit{ or } 6 \text{ or more visits}, \textit{given } 65+) \\ &= P(4, \textit{given } 65+) + P(5, \textit{given } 65+) + P(6 \text{ or more}, \textit{given } 65+) \\ &= \frac{12}{224} + \frac{7}{224} + \frac{3}{224} = \frac{22}{224} \end{aligned}$$

Here, the complementary event rule has no advantage, work-wise, over the regular method.

(e)
$$\begin{aligned} P(40 \text{ or older}) &= P(40\text{–}49 \textit{ or } 50\text{–}64 \textit{ or } 65+) \\ &= P(40\text{–}49) + P(50\text{–}64) + P(65+) \\ &= \frac{434}{1894} + \frac{349}{1894} + \frac{224}{1894} = \frac{1007}{1894} \end{aligned}$$

(f)
$$\begin{aligned} P(40 \text{ or older}, \textit{given } 4 \text{ visits}) &= P(40\text{–}49 \textit{ or } 50\text{–}64 \textit{ or } 65+ \text{or over}, \textit{given } 4 \text{ visits}) \\ &= P(40\text{–}49, \textit{given } 4) + P(50\text{–}64, \textit{given } 4) + P(65+, \textit{given } 4) \\ &= \frac{13}{66} + \frac{14}{66} + \frac{12}{66} = \frac{39}{66} \end{aligned}$$

The given 4 visits means the denominator is the 4 visit column total, and the numerator is composed from numbers in that column.

(g) $P(25\text{–}39 \text{ years old}) = \frac{739}{1894} \approx 0.3902$

$P(\text{visits more than once a week}) = 1 - P(\text{visits once}) = 1 - \frac{962}{1894} = \frac{932}{1894} \approx 0.4921$

$P(\text{visits} > 1, \textit{given } 25\text{–}39) = 1 - P(1 \text{ visit}, \textit{given } 25\text{–}39) = 1 - \frac{386}{739} = \frac{353}{739} \approx 0.4777$

25–39 years old is independent of more than 1 visit if $P(>1 \text{ visit}) = P(>1 \text{ visit}, \textit{given} \text{ age } 25\text{–}39)$ but $0.4921 \ne 0.4777$ so they are not independent.

24. P(female) = 85% so P(male) = 15%
P(BSN, *given* female) = 70%
P(BSN, *given* male) = 90%
70% of females, 90% of males are conditions further defining a randomly selected student, so gender is the "given…"

(a) P(BSN, *given* F) = 70% = 0.70

(b) P(BSN *and* F) = P(F) · P(BSN, *given* F) = (0.85)(0.70) = 0.595 conditional probability rule

(c) P(BSN, *given* M) = 90% = 0.90

(d) P(BSN *and* M) = P(M) · P(BSN, *given* M) = (0.15)(0.90) = 0.135

(e) Of the graduates, some are female and some are male, so if we add the numbers of male graduates and female graduates, we will have all the graduates.

$$
\begin{aligned}
P(\text{BSN}) &= P[\text{BSN and } (\text{M } or \text{ F})] \\
&= P[(\text{BSN and M}) \; or \; (\text{BSN and F})] \\
&= P(\text{BSN and M}) + P(\text{BSN and F})
\end{aligned}
$$

We can use the mutually exclusive addition rule here because no graduating student is both male and female; these are disjoint conditions.

$$
\begin{aligned}
&= 0.135 + 0.595 \quad \text{from (b) and (d)} \\
&= 0.730
\end{aligned}
$$

(Refer to the hint in 16(a) above which uses the same method.)
A and (B *or* C) = (A and B) *or* (A and C) is the distribution law of "and" over "or." Recall the distributive law for multiplication over addition gives us, for example,
5(6 + 7) = 5(6) + 5(7) = 30 + 35 = 65
The word "and" in mathematics is translated as "multiply" in algebra, and as "intersection" in set theory. "Or" is translated as "add" in algebra, and as "union" in set theory.

(f) If all incoming freshmen nursing students from the overall samples space, the phrase "(given) female" describes only part of the sample space. The "given" restricts the sample space *for this problem*, (a) P(BSN, given F), to females only.

Consider the following 4 graphs. Figure A shows 100 squares partitioned into one group of 85 squares and one group of 15 squares, 85% women and 15% men, overall.

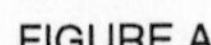

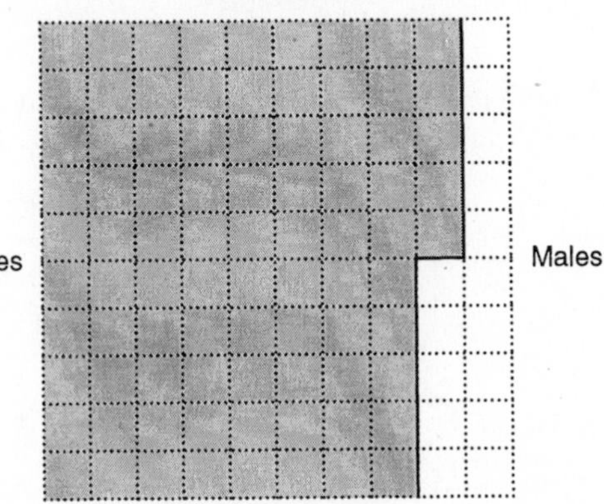

Figure B shows the same 100 squares with 73 squares total shaded, i.e., 73% of students overall will graduate [see part (e)].

FIGURE B

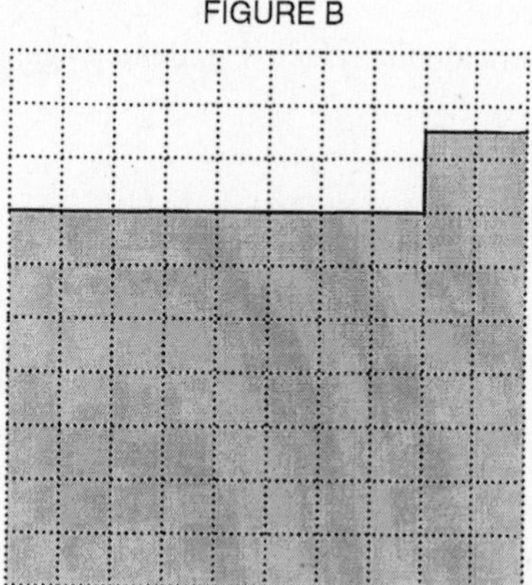

Graduates

Figure C shows the graduation squares overlaying the female squares, with their 59.5 squares in common shaded, showing those who are graduates and females among the 100 squares overall [part (b)].

FIGURE C

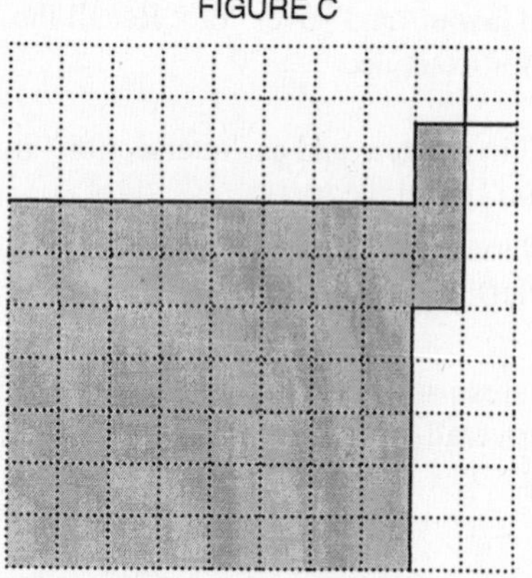

Figure D shows the same 59.5 squares shaded as a part of the 85 shaded female squares, showing $\frac{59.5}{85} = 70\%$ of the females graduating.

FIGURE D

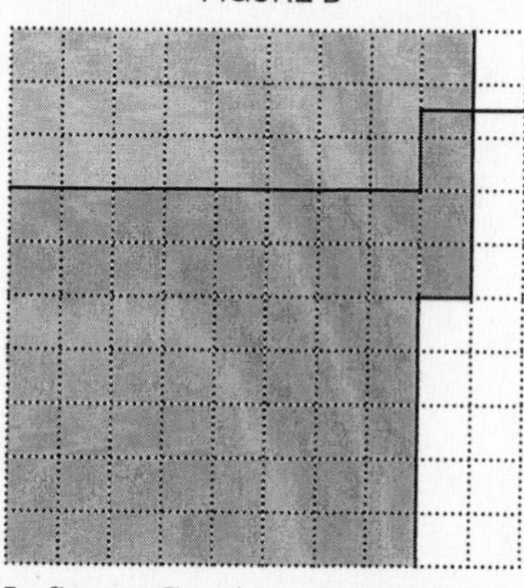

In figures C and D we are looking at the same 59.5 squares, describing the same students, but in C we compare them to all 100 squares, and in D, we compare them only to the 85 female squares.

Formula (2) on page 151 shows the probability for equally likely outcomes:

$$P(\text{event}) = \frac{\text{number of favorable outcomes}}{\text{total number of outcomes}}$$

The phrases "will graduate and is female" and "will graduate, given female" *do* describe the same students represented by the 59.5 squares. This is the number of favorable outcomes (squares), i.e., the numerator of the probability calculation in parts (a) and (b).

However, the denominator changes depending on the context; in part (b), it is the 100 students (squares) overall, but in part (a), you are given 85 females (squares) as the total number of outcomes.

Thus, although part (a) and part (b) refer to the same students, the probabilities differ because the total number of outcomes being considered in part (a) is different from the total number of outcomes being considered in part (b).

(In part (a), each of the 85 squares is equally likely to be chosen, and in part (b), each of the 100 squares is equally likely to be chosen as the incoming freshman nursing student selected at random.)

25. Given: Let A be the event that a new store grosses > \$940,000 in year 1; then not A is the event the new store grosses ≤ \$940,000 the first year.
Let B be the event that the store grosses > \$940,000 in the second year; then not B is the event the store grosses ≤ \$940,000 in the second year of operation.

2 year results	Translations
A and B	profitable both years
A and *not* B	profitable first but not second year
not A and B	profitable second but not first year
not A and *not* B	not profitable either year

P(A) = 65% (show profit in first year)
P(*not* A) = 35%
P(B) = 71% (show profit in second year)
P(*not* B) = 29%
P(close) = P(*not* A and *not* B)
P(B, *given* A) = 87%

(a) P(A) = 65% = 0.65 (from the given)

(b) P(B) = 71% = 0.71 (from the given)

(c) P(B, *given* A) = 87% = 0.87 (from the given)

(d) P(A *and* B) = P(A) · P(B, *given* A) = (0.65)(0.87) = 0.5655 ≈ 0.57 (conditional probability rule)

(e) P(A *or* B) = P(A) + P(B) – P(A and B) = 0.65 + 0.71 – 0.57 = 0.79 (addition rule)

(f) P(not closed) = P(show a profit in year 1 or year 2 or both) (same question as (e))
P(closed) = 1 – P(not closed) = 1 – 0.79 = 0.21 (complimentary event rule)

26. Known: Let A be the event the client relapses in phase I.
Let B be the event the client relapses in phase II.
Let C be the event that the client has no relapse in phase I, i.e., C = *not* A.
Let D be the event that the client has no relapse in phase II, i.e., D = *not* B.
P(A) = 0.27 so P(*not* A) = P(C) = 1 – 0.27 = 0.73
P(B) = 0.23 so P(*not* B) = P(D) = 1 – 0.23 = 0.77
P(*not* B, *given not* A) = 0.95 = P(D, *given* C) = 0.95
P(B, *given* A) = 0.70

Possible outcomes	Translation
A, B	relapse in I, relapse in II
not A, B (= C, B)	no relapse in I, relapse in II
A, *not* B (= A, D)	relapse in I, no relapse in II
not A, *not* B (= C, D)	no relapse in I no relapse in II

(a) $P(A) = 0.27$, $P(B) = 0.23$, $P(C) = 0.73$, $P(D) = 0.77$ (from the given)

(b) $P(B, \textit{given } A) = 0.70$, $P(D, \textit{given } C) = 0.95$ (from the given)

(c) $P(A \textit{ and } B) = P(A) \cdot P(B, \textit{given } A)$
$= (0.27)(0.70) = 0.189$ (conditional probability rule)
$P(C \textit{ and } D) = P(C) \cdot P(D, \textit{given } C)$
$= (0.73)(0.95) = 0.6935 \approx 0.69$

(d) $P(A \textit{ or } B) = P(A) + P(B) - P(A \text{ and } B)$ (general addition rule)
$= 0.27 + 0.23 - 0.189 = 0.311 \approx 0.31$

(e) $P(C \textit{ and } D) = 0.69$ [from (c)]

(f) $P(A \textit{ and } B) = 0.189$ [from (c)]

(g) translate as "inclusive or," i.e., as "or both"
$P(A \textit{ or } B) = 0.31$ [from (d)]

27. Let TB denote that the person has tuberculosis, so *not* TB denotes that the person does not have tuberculosis.
Let + indicate the test for tuberculosis indicates the presence of the disease, so – indicates that the test for tuberculosis shows no disease.
Given: $P(+, \textit{given } TB) = 0.82$ (sensitivity of the test)
$P(+, \textit{given not } TB) = 0.09$ (false-positive rate)
$P(TB) = 0.04$

(a) $P(TB \textit{ and } +) = P(TB) \cdot P(+, \textit{given } TB)$ (by the conditional probability rule)
$= (0.04)(0.82) = 0.0328 \approx 0.033$ (predictive value of the test)

(b) $P(\textit{not } TB) = 1 - P(TB)$ (complementary events)
$= 1 - 0.04 = 0.96$

(c) $P(\textit{not } TB \textit{ and } +) = P(\textit{not } TB) \cdot P(+, \textit{given not } TB)$ (conditional probability rule and (b))
$= (0.96)(0.09) = 0.0864 \approx 0.086$

(Note: refer to #20 above to see terminology.)

Section 4.3

1. (a) Outcomes for Tossing a Coin Three Times

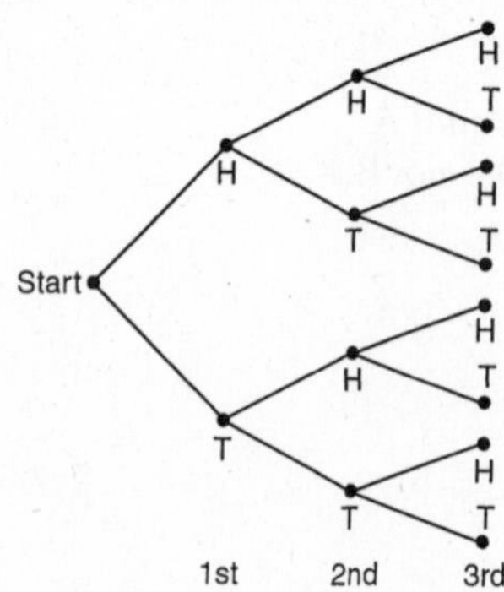

(b) HHT, HTH, THH: 3

(c) 8 possible outcomes, 3 with exactly 2 Hs: $\frac{3}{8}$

2. (a) Outcomes of Tossing a Coin and Throwing a Die

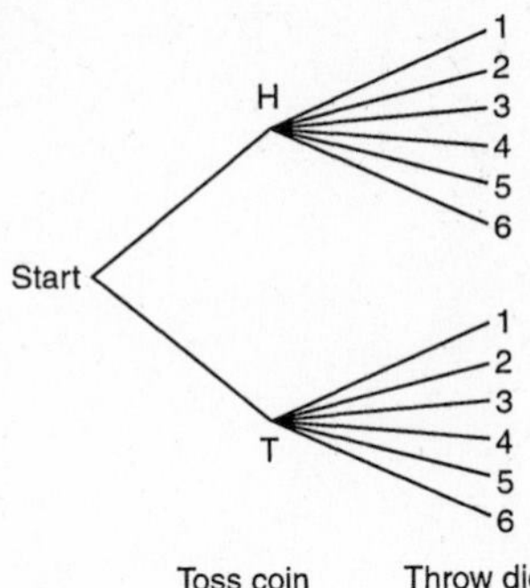

(b) outcomes with H and > 4
H5, H6:2

(c) 12 outcomes, two with H and > 4: $\frac{2}{12} = \frac{1}{6}$

3. (a) Outcomes for Drawing Two Balls (without replacement)

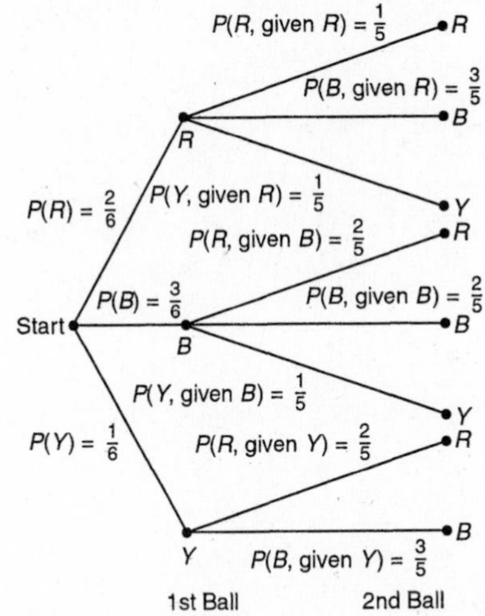

Because we drew without replacement the number of available balls drops to 5 and one of the colors drops by 1. Note that if the yellow ball is drawn first, there are only two possibilities for the second draw: red and blue; the yellow balls are exhausted.

(b) $P(R, R) = \left(\frac{2}{6}\right)\left(\frac{1}{5}\right) = \frac{2}{30} = \frac{1}{15}$

$P(R, B) = \left(\frac{2}{6}\right)\left(\frac{3}{5}\right) = \frac{6}{30} = \frac{1}{5}$

$P(R, Y) = \left(\frac{2}{6}\right)\left(\frac{1}{5}\right) = \frac{2}{30} = \frac{1}{15}$

$P(B, R) = \left(\frac{3}{6}\right)\left(\frac{2}{5}\right) = \frac{6}{30} = \frac{1}{5}$

$P(B, B) = \left(\frac{3}{6}\right)\left(\frac{2}{5}\right) = \frac{6}{30} = \frac{1}{5}$

$P(B, Y) = \left(\frac{3}{6}\right)\left(\frac{1}{5}\right) = \frac{3}{30} = \frac{1}{10}$

$P(Y, R) = \left(\frac{1}{6}\right)\left(\frac{2}{5}\right) = \frac{2}{30} = \frac{1}{15}$

$P(Y, B) = \left(\frac{1}{6}\right)\left(\frac{3}{5}\right) = \frac{3}{30} = \frac{1}{10}$

where $P(x, y)$ is the probability the first ball is color x, and the second ball is color y. Multiply the branch probability values along each branch from start to finish. Observe the sum of the probabilities is 1.

4. (a) Outcomes for Drawing Two Balls with Replacement

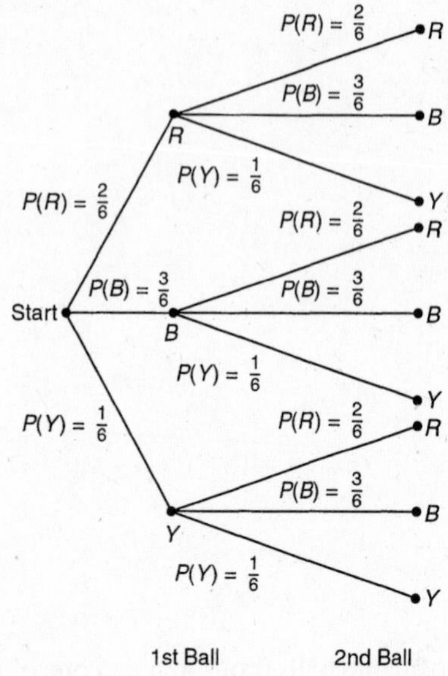

Because the draws are with replacement, $P(R)$ stays at $\frac{2}{6}$, $P(B) = \frac{3}{6}$, and $P(Y) = \frac{1}{6}$ for each draw.

(b) Using $P(x, y)$ to denote the probability of x on the first draw and y on the second:

$$P(R, R) = \left(\frac{2}{6}\right)\left(\frac{2}{6}\right) = \frac{4}{36} = \frac{1}{9}$$

$$P(R, B) = \left(\frac{2}{6}\right)\left(\frac{3}{6}\right) = \frac{6}{36} = \frac{1}{6}$$

$$P(R, Y) = \left(\frac{2}{6}\right)\left(\frac{1}{6}\right) = \frac{2}{36} = \frac{1}{18}$$

$$P(B, R) = \left(\frac{3}{6}\right)\left(\frac{2}{6}\right) = \frac{6}{36} = \frac{1}{6}$$

$$P(B, B) = \left(\frac{3}{6}\right)\left(\frac{3}{6}\right) = \frac{9}{36} = \frac{1}{4}$$

$$P(B, Y) = \left(\frac{3}{6}\right)\left(\frac{1}{6}\right) = \frac{3}{36} = \frac{1}{12}$$

$$P(Y, R) = \left(\frac{1}{6}\right)\left(\frac{2}{6}\right) = \frac{2}{36} = \frac{1}{18}$$

$$P(Y, B) = \left(\frac{1}{6}\right)\left(\frac{3}{6}\right) = \frac{3}{36} = \frac{1}{12}$$

$$P(Y, Y) = \left(\frac{1}{6}\right)\left(\frac{1}{6}\right) = \frac{1}{36}$$

Multiplying the probabilities along each branch.

5. (a) Choices for Three True/False Questions

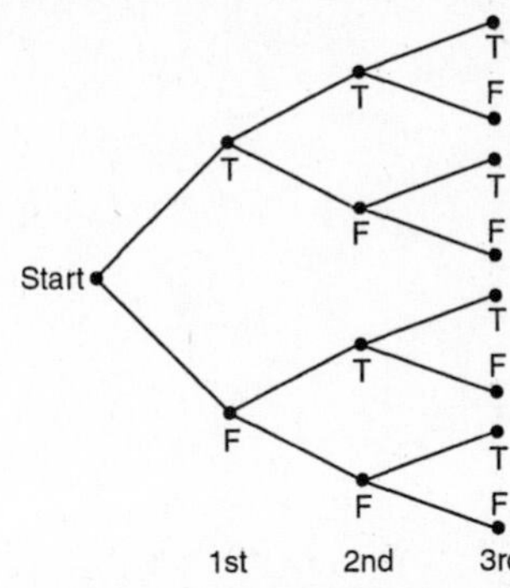

The tree diagram looks exactly like that of problem 1, because each event has 2 outcomes, and the events are independent, so possible outcomes for the second event are the same as for the first event.

(b) $P(\text{3 correct responses}) = \left(\frac{1}{2}\right)\left(\frac{1}{2}\right)\left(\frac{1}{2}\right) = \left(\frac{1}{2}\right)^3 = \frac{1}{8}$

6. (a) Outcomes of Three Multiple-Choice Questions

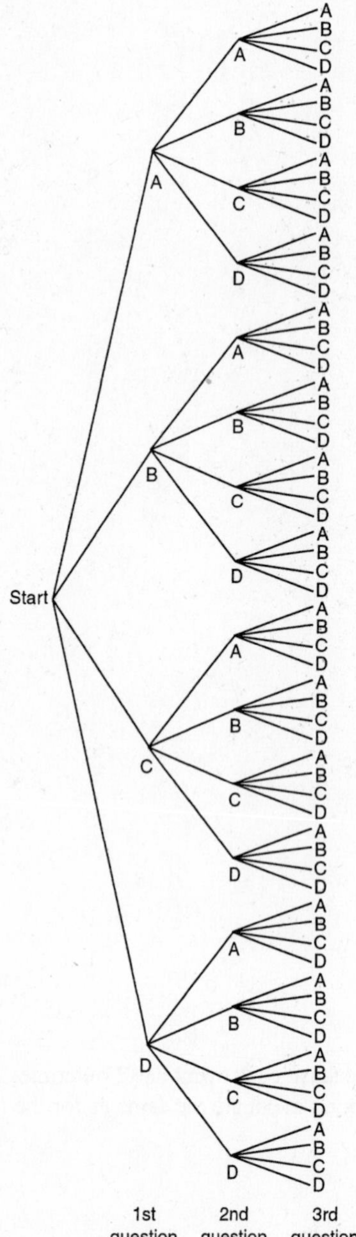

This is a gaudier version of problems 1 and 5 where there are 3 questions, but now there are 4 responses (A, B, C, D) for each question at each step.

(b) If the outcomes are equally likely, then $P(\text{all 3 correct}) = \left(\frac{1}{4}\right)\left(\frac{1}{4}\right)\left(\frac{1}{4}\right) = \frac{1}{64}$.

7. 4 wire choices for the first leaves 3 wire choices for the second, 2 for the third, and only 1 wire choice for the fourth wire connection: $4 \cdot 3 \cdot 2 \cdot 1 = 4! = 24$.

8. 4 choices for his first stop, 3 for the second, 2 for the third, and only 1 city for his (last) fourth stop: $4 \cdot 3 \cdot 2 \cdot 1 = 4! = 24$. This problem is identical to problem 7 except wires were changed to cities.

9. (a) Choose 1 card from each deck. The number of pairs (one card from the first deck and one card from the second) is $52 \cdot 52 = 52^2 = 2704$.

(b) There are 4 kings in the first deck and four in the second, so $4 \cdot 4 = 16$.

(c) There are 16 ways to draw a king from each deck, and 2704 ways to draw a card from each deck, so $\frac{16}{2704} = \frac{1}{169} \approx 0.006$.

10. (a) The die rolls are independent, so multiply the 6 ways the first die can land by the 6 ways the second die can land: $6 \cdot 6 = 36$.

(b) Even numbers are 2, 4, and 6, three possibilities per die, so $3 \cdot 3 = 9$.

(c) $P(\text{even, even}) = \frac{9}{36} = \frac{1}{4} = 0.25$

using $P(\text{event}) = \dfrac{\text{number of favorable outcomes}}{\text{total number of outcomes}}$

11. There are 4 fertilizers to choose from, and 3 temperature zones to choose from for each fertilizer, and 3 possible water treatments for every fertilizer-temperature zone combination: $4 \cdot 3 \cdot 3 = 36$.

12. There are 3 possible sandwiches to choose from, and for each, 4 possible salads, and for each sandwich-salad combination, there are also 5 desserts to choose from: $3 \cdot 4 \cdot 5 = 60$.

Problems 13, 14, 15, and 16 deal with permutations, $P_{n,r} = \dfrac{n!}{(n-r)!}$. This counts the number of ways r objects can be selected from n when the order of the result is important. For example, if we choose two people from a group, the first of which is to be the group's chair, and the second, the assistant chair, then (John, Mary) is distinct from (Mary, John).

13. $P_{5,2}: n = 5,\ r = 2$

$$P_{5,2} = \frac{5!}{(5-2)!} = \frac{5 \cdot 4 \cdot 3 \cdot 2 \cdot 1}{3!} = 20$$

14. $P_{8,3}: n = 8,\ r = 3$

$$P_{8,3} = \frac{8!}{(8-3)!} = \frac{8 \cdot 7 \cdot 6 \cdot 5 \cdot 4 \cdot 3 \cdot 2 \cdot 1}{5!} = \frac{8 \cdot 7 \cdot 6 \cdot 5!}{5!} = 336$$

15. $P_{7,7}: n = r = 7$

$$P_{7,7} = \frac{7!}{(7-7)!} = \frac{7!}{0!} = 7! = 5040 \text{ (recall } 0! = 1)$$

In general, $P_{n,n} = \dfrac{n!}{(n-n)!} = \dfrac{n!}{0!} = \dfrac{n!}{1} = n!$.

16. $P_{9,9}: n = r = 9$

$$P_{9,9} = \frac{9!}{(9-9)!} = \frac{9!}{0!} = \frac{9!}{1} = 362{,}880$$

In general, $P_{n,n} = \dfrac{n!}{(n-n)!} = \dfrac{n!}{0!} = \dfrac{n!}{1} = n!$.

Problems 17, 18, 19, and 20 deal with combination, $C_{n,r} = \frac{n!}{r!(n-r)!}$. This counts the number of ways r items can be selected from among n items when the order of the result doesn't matter. For example, when choosing two people from an office to pick up coffee and doughnuts, (John, Mary) is the same as (Mary, John) – both get to carry the goodies back to the office.

17. $C_{5,2}$: $n = 5$, $r = 2$

$$C_{5,2} = \frac{5!}{2!(5-2)!} = \frac{5!}{2!3!} = \frac{5 \cdot 4 \cdot 3 \cdot 2 \cdot 1}{2 \cdot 1 \cdot 3 \cdot 2 \cdot 1} = \frac{20}{2} = 10$$

18. $C_{8,3}$: $n = 8$, $r = 3$

$$C_{8,3} = \frac{8!}{3!(8-3)!} = \frac{8!}{3!5!} = \frac{8 \cdot 7 \cdot 6 \cdot 5!}{3 \cdot 2 \cdot 1 \cdot 5!} = 56$$

19. $C_{7,7}$: $n = r = 7$

$$C_{7,7} = \frac{7!}{7!(7-7)!} = \frac{7!}{7!0!} = \frac{7!}{7!(1)} = 1 \text{ (recall } 0! = 1)$$

In general, $C_{n,n} = \frac{n!}{n!(n-n)!} = \frac{n!}{n!0!} = \frac{n!}{n!(1)} = 1$. There is only 1 way to choose all n objects without regard to order.

20. $C_{8,8}$: $n = r = 8$

$$P_{9,9} = \frac{8!}{8!(8-8)!} = \frac{8!}{8!0!} = \frac{8!}{8!(1)} = 1 \text{ (recall } 0! = 1)$$

In general, $C_{n,n} = \frac{n!}{n!(n-n)!} = \frac{n!}{n!0!} = \frac{n!}{n!(1)} = 1$. There is only 1 way to choose all n objects without regard to order.

21. Since the order matters (first is day supervisor, second is night supervisor, and third is coordinator), this is a permutation of 15 nurse candidates to fill 3 positions.

$$P_{15,3} = \frac{15!}{(15-3)!} = \frac{15!}{12!} = \frac{15 \cdot 14 \cdot 13 \cdot 12!}{12!} = 2730$$

22. Order matters here, since the order of the finalists selected determines who gets what amount of money.

$$P_{10,3} = \frac{10!}{(10-3)!} = \frac{10!}{7!} = \frac{10 \cdot 9 \cdot 8 \cdot 7!}{7!} = 720$$

23. **(a)** Think of this as 2 urns, the first having 8 red balls numbered 1 to 8, indicating the word to be defined, and the second urn containing 8 blue balls numbered 1 to 8, representing the possible definitions. Draw 1 ball from each urn without replacement. The (red number, blue number) pair indicates which word is "matched" with which definition–maybe correctly matched, maybe not. Here, (red 4, blue 6) is different from (red 6, blue 4)

$n = r = 8$

$$P_{8,8} = \frac{8!}{(8-8)!} = \frac{8!}{0!} = \frac{8!}{1} = 40,320$$

(b) This is the same as part (a), except we throw 3 definitions out; 3 words will be left with no definition.

$$P_{8,5} = \frac{8!}{(8-5)!} = \frac{8!}{3!} = \frac{40,320}{6} = 6720$$

24. Order of the books matter: history, art, fiction, ... is distinct from fiction, art, history, ...

$$P_{6,6} = \frac{6!}{(6-6)!} = \frac{6!}{0!} = \frac{6!}{1} = 720$$

25. Order matters because the resulting sequence determines who wins first place, who wins second place, and who wins third place.

$$P_{5,3} = \frac{5!}{(5-3)!} = \frac{5!}{2!} = \frac{120}{2} = 60$$

26. The order of the software packages selected doesn't matter, since all three are going home with the customer. (Assume the software packages are of equal interest to the customer.)

$$C_{10,3} = \frac{10!}{3!(10-3)!} = \frac{10!}{3!7!} = \frac{10 \cdot 9 \cdot 8 \cdot 7!}{3!7!} = \frac{720}{6} = 120$$

27. The order of trainee selection doesn't matter, since they are all going to be trained the same.

$$C_{15,5} = \frac{15!}{5!(15-5)!} = \frac{15!}{5!10!} = \frac{15 \cdot 14 \cdot 13 \cdot 12 \cdot 11 \cdot 10!}{5!10!} = \frac{15 \cdot 14 \cdot 13 \cdot 12 \cdot 11}{5 \cdot 4 \cdot 3 \cdot 2 \cdot 1} = 3003$$

28. It doesn't matter in which order the professor grades the problems, the 5 selected problems all get graded.

(a) $C_{12,5} = \frac{12!}{5!(12-5)!} = \frac{12!}{5!7!} = \frac{12 \cdot 11 \cdot 10 \cdot 9 \cdot 8 \cdot 7!}{5!7!} = \frac{12 \cdot 11 \cdot 10 \cdot 9 \cdot 8}{5 \cdot 4 \cdot 3 \cdot 2 \cdot 1} = 792$

(b) Jerry must have the very same 5 problems as the professor selected to grade, so

$P(\text{Jerry chose the right problems}) = \frac{1}{792} \approx 0.001$. (Jerry is pushing his luck.)

(c) Silvia did seven problems, which have $C_{7,5}$ subsets of 5 problems which would be among 792 subsets of 5 the professor selected from.

$$C_{7,5} = \frac{7!}{5!(7-5)!} = \frac{7!}{5!2!} = \frac{7 \cdot 6 \cdot 5!}{5!2!} = \frac{7 \cdot 6}{2 \cdot 1} = \frac{42}{2} = 21$$

$P(\text{Silvia lucked out}) = \frac{21}{792} \approx 0.027$

(Silvia is pushing her luck, too, but she increased her chances by a factor of 21, compared to Jerry, just by doing two more problems. Now, if these two had just done all the problems, or even split them half and half, ...)

29. (a) Six applicants are selected from among 12 without regard to order.

$$C_{12,6} = \frac{12!}{6!6!} = \frac{479{,}001{,}600}{(720)^2} = 924$$

(b) There are 7 women and 5 men. This problem really asks, in how many ways can 6 women be selected from among 7, and zero men be selected from 5?

$$(C_{7,6})(C_{5,0}) = \left(\frac{7!}{6!(7-6)!}\right)\left(\frac{5!}{0!(5-0)!}\right) = \frac{7!}{6!1!} \cdot \frac{5!}{0!5!} = 7$$

Since the zero men are "selected" be default, all positions being filled. This problem reduces to, in how many ways can 6 applicants be selected from 7 women?

(c) $P(\text{event A}) = \frac{\text{number of favorable outcomes}}{\text{total number of outcomes}}$

$P(\text{all hired are women}) = \frac{7}{924} = \frac{1}{132} \approx 0.008$

30. It doesn't matter in which order you or the state select the 6 numbers each. It only matters that you and the state pick the *same* six numbers. While you spend your zillion dollars, you can always reorder your numbers if you want to.

(a) $C_{42,6} = \frac{42!}{6!(42-6)!} = \frac{42!}{6!36!} = \frac{42 \cdot 41 \cdot 40 \cdot 39 \cdot 38 \cdot 37 \cdot 36!}{6!36!} = \frac{3,776,965,920}{720} = 5,245,786$

(Most calculators will handle numbers through 69! But if you hate to see numbers like 1.771×10^{98}, cancel out the common factorial factors, such as 36! here.)

(b) This problem asks, what is the chance you choose the very same 6 numbers the state chose.

$P(\text{winning ticket}) = \frac{1}{5,245,786} \approx 0.000000191$

(c) What is the chance one of your 10 tickets is the winning ticket? (We'll assume each ticket is different from the other 9 you have, but, it really doesn't matter much …)

$P(\text{win}) = \frac{10}{5,245,786} = \frac{5}{2,622,893} \approx 0.0000019$

Chapter 4 Review

1. $P(\text{asked}) = 24\% = 0.24$

$P(\text{received, } given \text{ asked}) = 45\% = 0.45$

$P(\text{asked } and \text{ received}) = P(\text{asked}) \cdot P(\text{received, } given \text{ asked}) = (0.24)(0.45) = 0.108 = 10.8\%$

2. $P(\text{asked}) = 20\% = 0.20$

$P(\text{received, } given \text{ asked}) = 59\% = 0.59$

$P(\text{asked } and \text{ received}) = P(\text{asked}) \cdot P(\text{received, } given \text{ asked}) = (0.20)(0.59) = 0.118 = 11.8\%$

3. (a) If the first card is replaced before the second is chosen (sampling with replacement), they are independent. If the sampling is without replacements they are dependent.

(b) $P(\text{heart}) = \frac{13}{52} = \frac{1}{4}$

with replacement, independent

$P(\text{H on both}) = \left(\frac{1}{4}\right)\left(\frac{1}{4}\right) = \frac{1}{16} = 0.0625 \approx 0.063$

(c) without replacement, dependent

$P(\text{H on first } and \text{ H on second}) = \frac{13}{52} \cdot \frac{12}{51} = \frac{156}{2652} \approx 0.059$

4. (a) There are 11 other outcomes besides 3H. The sample space is the 12 outcomes shown.

1H 1T
2H 2T
(3H) 3T
4H 4T
5H 5T
6H 6T

(b) Yes; the die and the coin are independent. Each outcome has probability $\left(\frac{1}{6}\right)\left(\frac{1}{2}\right) = \frac{1}{12}$.

(c) $P(\text{H } and \text{ number} < 3) = P[\text{H } and \text{ } (1 \text{ } or \text{ } 2)] = P(\text{1H } or \text{ 2H}) = P(\text{1H}) + P(\text{2H}) = \frac{1}{12} + \frac{1}{12} = \frac{2}{12} = \frac{1}{6} \approx 0.167$

5. (a) Throw a large number of similar thumbtacks, or one thumbtack a large number of times, and record the frequency of occurrence of the various outcomes. Assume the thumbtack falls either flat side down (i.e., point up), or tilted (with the point down, resting on the edge of the flat side). (We will

assume these are the only two ways the tack can land.) To estimate the probability the tack lands on its flat side with the point up, find the relative frequency of this occurrence, dividing the number of times this occurred by the total number of thumbtack tosses.

(b) The sample space is the two outcomes flat side down (point up) and tilted (point down).

(c) $P(\text{flat side down, point up}) = \frac{340}{500} = 0.68$

$P(\text{tilted, point down}) = 1 - 0.68 = 0.32$

6. (a) $P(N) = \frac{470}{1000} = 0.470$

$P(M) = \frac{390}{1000} = 0.390$

$P(S) = \frac{140}{1000} = 0.140$

(b) $P(N, \textit{given } W) = \frac{420}{500} = 0.840$

$P(S, \textit{given } W) = \frac{20}{500} = 0.040$

(c) $P(N, \textit{given } A) = \frac{50}{500} = 0.100$

$P(S, \textit{given } A) = \frac{120}{500} = 0.240$

(d) $P(N \textit{ and } W) = P(W) \cdot P(N, \textit{ given } W)$

$= \left(\frac{500}{1000}\right)(0.840) = 0.420$

$P(M \textit{ and } W) = P(W) \cdot P(M, \textit{ given } W)$

$= \left(\frac{500}{1000}\right)\left(\frac{60}{500}\right) = 0.060$

(e) $P(N \textit{ or } M) = P(N) + P(M)$ if mutually exclusive

$= \left(\frac{470}{1000}\right) + \left(\frac{390}{1000}\right) = \frac{860}{1000} = 0.860$

They are mutually exclusive because the reactions are defined into 3 distinct, mutually exclusive categories, a reaction can't be both mild and non-existent.

(f) If N and W were independent, $P(N \text{ and } W) = P(N) \cdot P(W) = (0.470)(0.500) = 0.235$. However, from (d), we have $P(N \text{ and } W) = 0.420$. They are not independent.

7. (a) possible values for x, the sum of the two dice faces, is 2, 3, 4, 5, 6, 7, 8, 9, 10, 11, and 12

(b) 2:1 and 1
3:1 and 2, or 2 and 1
4:1 and 3, 2 and 2, 3 and 1
5:1 and 4, 2 and 3, 3 and 2, 4 and 1
6:1 and 5, 2 and 4, 3 and 3, 4 and 2, 5 and 1
7:1 and 6, 2 and 5, 3 and 4, 4 and 3, 5 and 2, 6 and 1
8:2 and 6, 3 and 5, 4 and 4, 5 and 3, 6 and 2
9:3 and 6, 4 and 5, 5 and 4, 6 and 3
10:4 and 6, 5 and 5, 6 and 4
11:5 and 6, 6 and 5
12:6 and 6

x	$P(x)$
2	$\frac{1}{36} \approx 0.028$
3	$\frac{2}{36} \approx 0.056$
4	$\frac{3}{36} \approx 0.083$
5	$\frac{4}{36} \approx 0.111$
6	$\frac{5}{36} \approx 0.139$
7	$\frac{6}{36} \approx 0.167$
8	$\frac{5}{36} \approx 0.139$
9	$\frac{4}{36} \approx 0.111$
10	$\frac{3}{36} \approx 0.083$
11	$\frac{2}{36} \approx 0.056$
12	$\frac{1}{36} \approx 0.028$

Where there are (6)(6) = 36 possible, equally likely outcomes (the sums, however, are not equally likely).

8. P(pass 101) = 0.77
P(pass 102, *given* pass 101) = 0.90
P(pass 101 *and* pass 102) = P(pass 101) · P(pass 102, *given* pass 101) = 0.77(0.90) = 0.693

9. $C_{8,2} = \frac{8!}{2!6!} = \frac{8 \cdot 7 \cdot 6!}{(2 \cdot 1)6!} = \frac{56}{2} = 28$

10. **(a)** $P_{7,2} = \frac{7!}{(7-2)!} = \frac{7!}{5!} = 7(6) = 42$

(b) $C_{7,2} = \frac{7!}{2!5!} = \frac{7 \cdot 6}{2} = 21$

(c) $P_{3,3} = \frac{3!}{(3-3)!} = \frac{3!}{0!} = 6$

(d) $C_{4,4} = \frac{4!}{4!(4-4)!} = \frac{4!}{4!0!} = 1$

11. $3 \cdot 2 \cdot 1 = 6$

12. Ways to Satisfy Literature, Social Science, and Philosophy Requirements

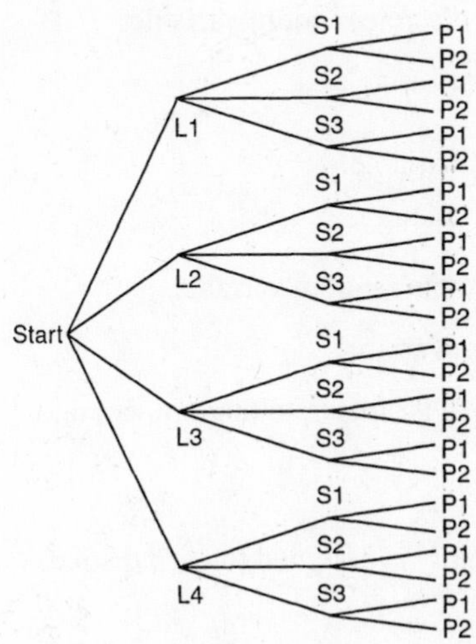

Let Li, $i = 1, \cdots, 4$ denote the 4 literature courses.
Let Si, $i = 1, 2, 3$ denote the 3 social science courses.
Let Pi, $i = 1, 2$ denote the 2 philosophy courses.
There are $4 \cdot 3 \cdot 2 = 24$ possible course combinations.

13. 5 multiple choice questions, each with 4 possible answers (A, B, C, or D), so 4 answers for first question; and for each of those, 4 answers for the second question; and for each of those, 4 answers for the third question; and for each of those, 4 answers for the fifth question. There are $4 \cdot 4 \cdot 4 \cdot 4 \cdot 4 = 4^5 = 1024$ possible sequences, such as A, D, B, B, C or C, B, A, D, D, etc.

$P(\text{getting the correct sequence}) = \frac{1}{1024} \approx 0.00098$

14. Two possible outcomes per coin toss; 6 tosses to get a sequence such as THTHHT
$2 \cdot 2 \cdot 2 \cdot 2 \cdot 2 \cdot 2 = 2^6 = 64$ possible sequences.

15. 10 possible numbers per turn of dial; 3 dial turns
$10 \cdot 10 \cdot 10 = 1000$ possible combinations

16. The combination uses the three numbers 2, 9, and 5, in some sequence.

The number of sequences is $P_{3,3} = \frac{3!}{(3-3)!} = \frac{3 \cdot 2 \cdot 1}{0!} = 6.$

They are 2, 9, 5   9, 2, 5   5, 2, 9   2, 5, 9   9, 5, 2   5, 9, 2
Since all three numbers must be used, think of it as drawing without replacement from an urn containing the numbers 2, 9, and 5.

Chapter 5 The Binomial Probability Distribution and Related Topics

Section 5.1

1. **(a)** The number of traffic fatalities can be only a whole number. This is a discrete random variable.

   (b) Distance can assume any value, so this is a continuous random variable.

   (c) Time can take on any value, so this is a continuous random variable.

   (d) The number of ships can be only a whole number. This is a discrete random variable.

   (e) Weight can assume any value, so this is a continuous random variable.

2. **(a)** Speed can assume any value, so this is a continuous random variable.

   (b) Age can take on any value, so this is a continuous random variable.

   (c) Number of books can be only a whole number. This is a discrete random variable.

   (d) Weight can assume any value, so this is a continuous random variable.

   (e) Number of lightning strikes can be only a whole number. This is a discrete random variable.

3. **(a)** $\Sigma P(x) = 0.25 + 0.60 + 0.15 = 1.00$

   Yes, this is a valid probability distribution because a probability is assigned to each distinct value of the random variable and the sum of these probabilities is 1.

   (b) $\Sigma P(x) = 0.25 + 0.60 + 0.20 = 1.05$

   No, this is not a probability distribution because the probabilities total to more than 1.

4. **(a)** $\Sigma P(x) = 0.07 + 0.44 + 0.24 + 0.4 + 0.11 = 1.00$

   Yes, this is a valid probability distribution because the events are distinct and the probabilities total to 1.

   (b)

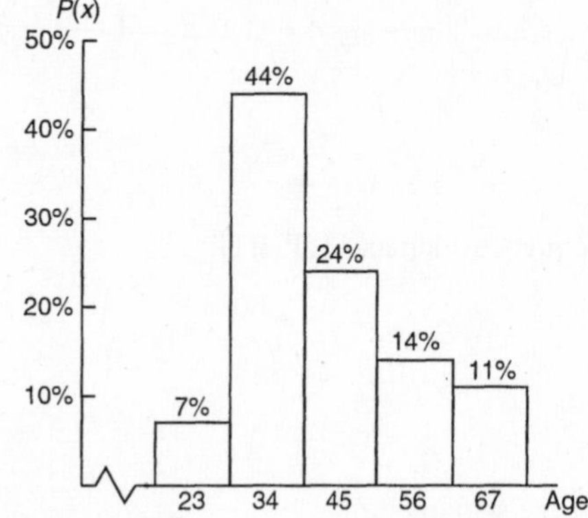

   (c) $\mu = \Sigma xP(x)$

$= 23(0.07) + 34(0.44) + 45(0.24) + 56(0.14) + 67(0.11)$

$= 42.58$

(d) $\sigma = \sqrt{\Sigma (x-\mu)^2 P(x)}$

$= \sqrt{(-19.58)^2 (0.07) + (-8.58)^2 (0.44) + (2.42)^2 (0.24) + (13.42)^2 (0.14) + (24.42)^2 (0.11)}$

$= \sqrt{151.44}$

≈ 12.31

5. (a) $\Sigma P(x) = 0.21 + 0.14 + 0.22 + 0.15 + 0.20 + 0.08 = 1.00$

Yes, this is a valid probability distribution because the events are distinct and the probabilities total to 1.

(b) Income Distribution ($1000)

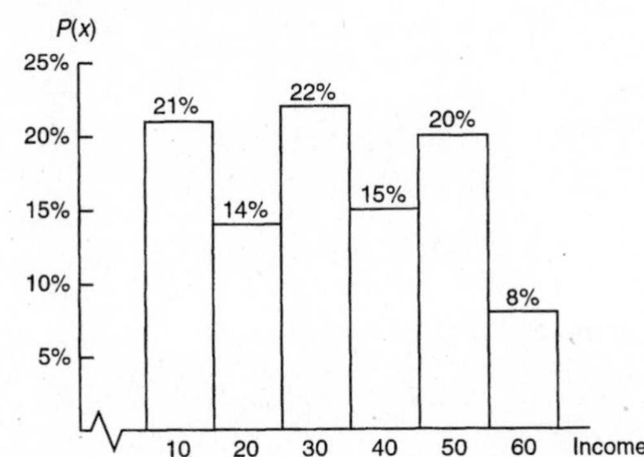

(c) $\mu = \Sigma x P(x)$

$= 10(0.21) + 20(0.14) + 30(0.22) + 40(0.15) + 50(0.20) + 60(0.08)$

$= 32.3$

(d) $\sigma = \sqrt{\Sigma (x-\mu)^2 P(x)}$

$= \sqrt{(-22.3)^2 (0.21) + (-12.3)^2 (0.14) + (-2.3)^2 (0.22) + (7.7)^2 (0.15) + (17.7)^2 (0.20) + (27.7)^2 (0.08)}$

$= \sqrt{259.71}$

≈ 16.12

6. (a) 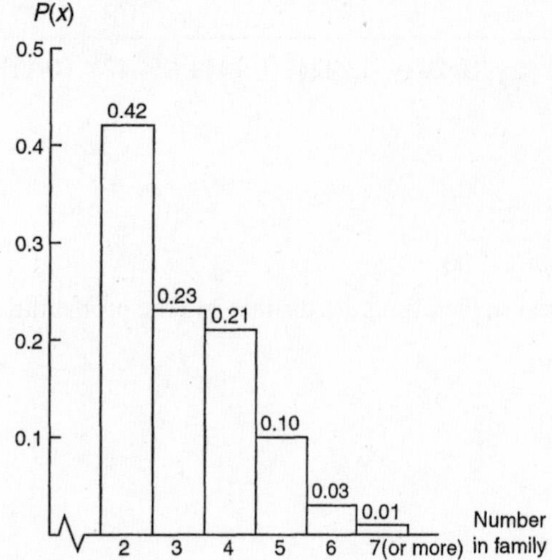

(b) $P(2) = 0.42$

(c) $P(\text{more than } 3) = P(4, 5, 6, 7 \text{ or more})$

$$= P(4) + P(5) + P(6) + P(7 \text{ or more})$$
$$= 0.21 + 0.10 + 0.03 + 0.01$$
$$= 0.35$$

(d) $\mu = \Sigma x P(x)$

$$= 2(0.42) + 3(0.23) + 4(0.21) + 5(0.10) + 6(0.03) + 7(0.01)$$
$$= 3.12$$

(e) $\sigma = \sqrt{\Sigma (x - \mu)^2 P(x)}$

$$= \sqrt{(-1.12)^2 (0.42) + (-0.12)^2 (0.23) + (0.88)^2 (0.21) + (1.88)^2 (0.10) + (2.88)^2 (0.03) + (3.88)^2 (0.01)}$$
$$= \sqrt{1.4456}$$
$$\approx 1.20$$

7. (a)

x	f	Relative Frequency	$P(x)$
36	6	6/208	0.029
37	10	10/208	0.048
38	11	11/208	0.053
39	20	20/208	0.096
40	26	26/208	0.125
41	32	32/208	0.154
42	34	34/208	0.163
43	28	28/208	0.135
44	25	25/208	0.120
45	16	16/208	0.077

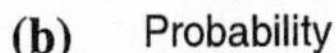

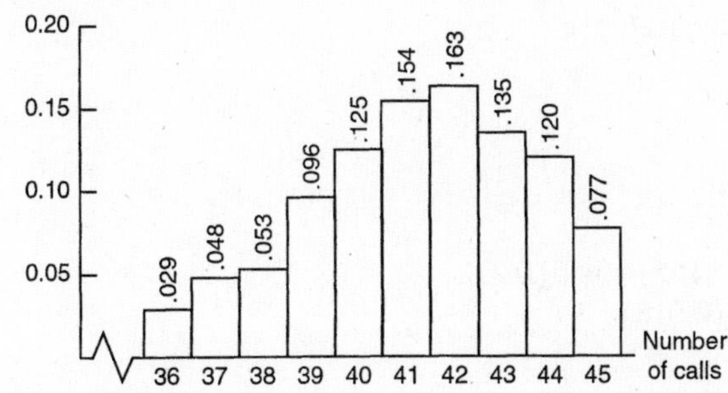

(c) $P(39,40,41,42,43) = P(39)+P(40)+P(41)+P(42)+P(43)$
$= 0.096+0.125+0.154+0.163+0.135$
$= 0.673$

(d) $P(36,37,38,39,40) = P(36)+P(37)+P(38)+P(39)+P(40)$
$= 0.029+0.048+0.053+0.096+0.125$
$= 0.351$

(e) $\mu = \Sigma xP(x)$
$= 36(0.029)+37(0.048)+38(0.053)+39(0.096)+40(0.125)+41(0.154)$
$+42(0.163)+43(0.135)+44(0.120)+45(0.077)$
$= 41.288$

(f) $\sigma = \sqrt{\Sigma(x-\mu)^2 P(x)}$

$$= \sqrt{\begin{array}{l}(-5.288)^2(0.029)+(-4.288)^2(0.048)+(-3.288)^2(0.053)+(-2.288)^2(0.096)+(-1.288)^2(0.125)\\+(-0.288)^2(0.154)+(0.712)^2(0.163)+(1.712)^2(0.135)+(2.712)^2(0.120)+(3.712)^2(0.077)\end{array}}$$

$= \sqrt{5.411}$

≈ 2.326

8. (a) $\Sigma P(x) = 0.057+0.097+0.195+0.292+0.250+0.091+0.018$
$= 1.000$

Yes, this is a valid probability distribution because the outcomes are distinct and the probabilities total to 1.

(b)

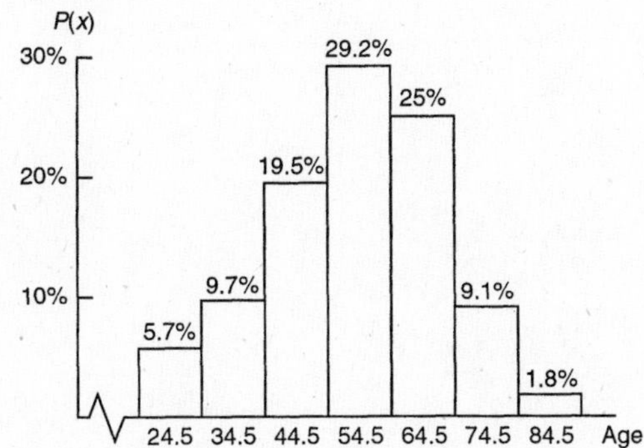

(c) $P(60 \text{ years of age or older}) = P(64.5) + P(74.5) + P(84.5)$

$$= 0.250 + 0.091 + 0.018$$
$$= 0.359$$

The probability is 35.9%.

(d) $\mu = \Sigma xP(x)$

$$= 24.5(0.057) + 34.5(0.097) + 44.5(0.195) + 54.5(0.292) + 64.5(0.250) + 74.5(0.091) + 84.5(0.018)$$
$$= 53.76$$

(e) $\sigma = \sqrt{\Sigma(x-\mu)^2 P(x)}$

$$= \sqrt{(-29.26)^2(0.057) + (-19.26)^2(0.097) + (-9.26)^2(0.195) + (0.74)^2(0.292) + (10.74)^2(0.250) + (20.74)^2(0.091) + (30.74)^2(0.018)}$$
$$= \sqrt{186.65}$$
$$\approx 13.66$$

9. (a) Number of Fish Caught in a 6-Hour Period at Pyramid Lake, Nevada

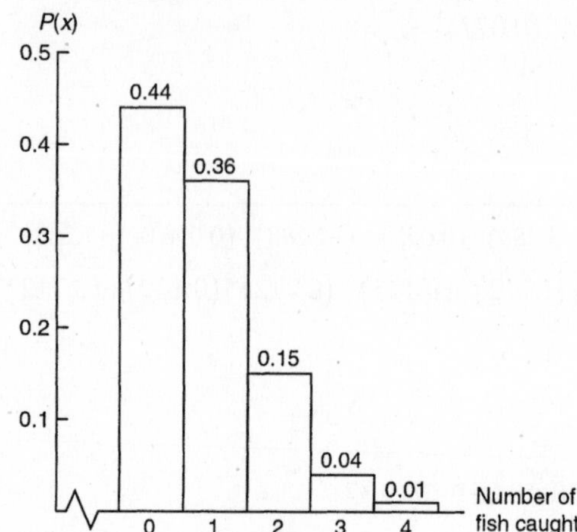

(b) $P(1 \text{ or more}) = 1 - P(0)$

$$= 1 - 0.44$$
$$= 0.56$$

(c) $P(2 \text{ or more}) = P(2) + P(3) + P(4 \text{ or more})$

$$= 0.15 + 0.04 + 0.01$$
$$= 0.20$$

(d) $\mu = \Sigma xP(x)$

$$= 0(0.44) + 1(0.36) + 2(0.15) + 3(0.04) + 4(0.01)$$
$$= 0.82$$

(e) $\sigma = \sqrt{\Sigma (x-\mu)^2 P(x)}$

$= \sqrt{(-0.82)^2 (0.44) + (0.18)^2 (0.36) + (1.18)^2 (0.15) + (2.18)^2 (0.04) + (3.18)^2 (0.01)}$

$= \sqrt{0.8076}$

≈ 0.899

10. $\Sigma P(x) \neq 1.000$ due to rounding

(a) $P(1 \text{ or more}) = 1 - P(0)$

$= 1 - 0.237$

$= 0.763$

This is the complement of the probability that none of the parolees will be repeat offenders.

(b) $P(2 \text{ or more}) = P(2) + P(3) + P(4) + P(5)$

$= 0.264 + 0.088 + 0.015 + 0.001$

$= 0.368$

(c) $P(4 \text{ or more}) = P(4) + P(5)$

$= 0.015 + 0.001$

$= 0.016$

(d) $\mu = \Sigma x P(x)$

$= 0(0.237) + 1(0.396) + 2(0.264) + 3(0.088) + 4(0.015) + 5(0.001)$

$= 1.253$

(e) $\sigma = \sqrt{\Sigma (x-\mu)^2 P(x)}$

$$= \sqrt{\begin{aligned}&(-1.253)^2 (0.237) + (-0.253)^2 (0.396) + (0.747)^2 (0.264) + (1.747)^2 (0.088) \\ &+ (2.747)^2 (0.015) + (3.747)^2 (0.001)\end{aligned}}$$

$= \sqrt{0.941}$

≈ 0.97

11. (a) $P(\text{win}) = \dfrac{15}{719} \approx 0.021$

$P(\text{not win}) = \dfrac{719 - 15}{719} = \dfrac{704}{719} \approx 0.979$

(b) Expected earnings $= (\text{value of dinner})(\text{probability of winning})$

$= \$35\left(\dfrac{15}{719}\right)$

$\approx \$0.73$

Lisa's expected earnings are \$0.73.

contribution $= \$15 - \$0.73 = \$14.27$

Lisa effectively contributed \$14.27 to the hiking club.

12. (a) $P(\text{win}) = \dfrac{6}{2852} \approx 0.0021$

$P(\text{not win}) = \dfrac{2852-6}{2852} = \dfrac{2846}{2852} \approx 0.9979$

(b) $\text{Expected earnings} = (\text{value of cruise})(\text{probability of winning})$
$\approx \$2000(0.0021)$
$\approx \$4.20$

Kevin spent 6($5) = $30 for the tickets. His expected earnings are less than the amount he paid.

$\text{contribution} = \$30 - \$4.20 = \$25.80$

Kevin effectively contributed $25.80 to the homeless center.

13. (a) $P(60 \text{ years}) = 0.01191$

Expected loss = $\$50{,}000(0.01191) = \$595.50$

The expected loss for Big Rock Insurance is $595.50.

(b)

Probability	Expected Loss
$P(61) = 0.01292$	$\$50{,}000(0.01292) = \$646$
$P(62) = 0.01396$	$\$50{,}000(0.01396) = \$698$
$P(63) = 0.01503$	$\$50{,}000(0.01503) = \$751.50$
$P(64) = 0.01613$	$\$50{,}000(0.01613) = \$806.50$

$\text{Expected loss} = \$595.50 + \$646 + \$698 + \$751.50 + \$806.50$
$= \$3497.50$

The total expected loss is $3497.50.

(c) $\$3497.50 + \$700 = \$4197.50$

They should charge $4197.50.

(d) $\$5000 - \$3497.50 = \$1502.50$

They can expect to make $1502.50.

Comment: losses are usually denoted by negative numbers such as –$50,000.

14. (a) $P(60 \text{ years}) = 0.00756$

Expected loss = $\$50{,}000(0.00756) = \$378$

The expected loss for Big Rock Insurance is $378.

(b)

Probability	Expected Loss
$P(61) = 0.00825$	$\$50{,}000(0.00825) = \$412.50$
$P(62) = 0.00896$	$\$50{,}000(0.00896) = \$448$
$P(63) = 0.00965$	$\$50{,}000(0.00965) = \$482.50$
$P(64) = 0.01035$	$\$50{,}000(0.01035) = \$517.50$

$\text{expected loss} = \$378 + \$412.50 + \$448 + \$482.50 + \$517.50$
$= \$2238.50$

The total expected loss is $2238.50.

(c) $\$2238.50 + \$700 = \$2938.50$
They should charge \$2938.50.

(d) $\$5000 - \$2238.50 = \$2761.50$
They can expect to make \$2761.50.

15. (a) $W = x_1 - x_2;\ a = 1,\ b = -1$

$$\mu_W = \mu_1 - \mu_2 = 115 - 100 = 15$$
$$\sigma_W^2 = 1^2\sigma_1^2 + (-1)^2\sigma_2^2 = 12^2 + 8^2 = 208$$
$$\sigma_W = \sqrt{\sigma_W^2} = \sqrt{208} \approx 14.4$$

(b) $W = 0.5x_1 + 0.5x_2;\ a = 0.5,\ b = 0.5$

$$\mu_W = 0.5\mu_1 + 0.5\mu_2 = 0.5(115) + 0.5(100) = 107.5$$
$$\sigma_W^2 = (0.5)^2\sigma_1^2 + (0.5)^2\sigma_2^2 = 0.25(12)^2 + 0.25(8)^2 = 52$$
$$\sigma_W = \sqrt{\sigma_W^2} = \sqrt{52} \approx 7.2$$

(c) $L = 0.8x_1 - 2;\ a = -2,\ b = 0.8$

$$\mu_L = -2 + 0.8\mu_1 = -2 + 0.8(115) = 90$$
$$\sigma_L^2 = (0.8)^2\sigma_1^2 = 0.64(12)^2 = 92.16$$
$$\sigma_L = \sqrt{\sigma_L^2} = \sqrt{92.16} = 9.6$$

(d) $L = 0.95x_2 - 5;\ a = -5,\ b = 0.95$

$$\mu_L = -5 + 0.95\mu_2 = -5 + 0.95(100) = 90$$
$$\sigma_L^2 = (0.95)^2\sigma_2^2 = 0.9025(8)^2 = 57.76$$
$$\sigma_L = \sqrt{\sigma_L^2} = \sqrt{57.76} = 7.6$$

16. (a) $W = x_1 + x_2;\ a = 1,\ b = 1$

$$\mu_W = \mu_1 + \mu_2 = 28.1 + 90.5 = 118.6 \text{ minutes}$$
$$\sigma_W^2 = \sigma_1^2 + \sigma_2^2 = (8.2)^2 + (15.2)^2 = 298.28$$
$$\sigma_W = \sqrt{\sigma_W^2} = \sqrt{298.28} \approx 17.27 \text{ minutes}$$

(b) $W = 1.50x_1 + 2.75x_2;\ a = 1.50,\ b = 2.75$

$$\mu_W = 1.50\mu_1 + 2.75\mu_2 = 1.50(28.1) + 2.75(90.5) \approx \$291.03$$
$$\sigma_W^2 = (1.50)^2\sigma_1^2 + (2.75)^2\sigma_2^2 = 2.25(8.2)^2 + 7.5625(15.2)^2 = 1898.53$$
$$\sigma_W = \sqrt{\sigma_W^2} = \sqrt{1898.53} \approx \$43.57$$

(c) $L = 1.5x_1 + 50;\ a = 50,\ b = 1.5$

$$\mu_L = 50 + 1.5\mu_1 = 50 + 1.5(28.1) = \$92.15$$
$$\sigma_L^2 = (1.5)^2\sigma_1^2 = 2.25(8.2)^2 = 151.29$$
$$\sigma_L = \sqrt{\sigma_L^2} = \sqrt{151.29} = \$12.30$$

17. **(a)** $W = 0.5x_1 + 0.5x_2$; $a = 0.5$, $b = 0.5$

$\mu_W = 0.5\mu_1 + 0.5\mu_2 = 0.5(50.2) + 0.5(50.2) = 50.2$

$\sigma_W^2 = 0.5^2\sigma_1^2 + 0.5^2\sigma_2^2 = 0.5^2(11.5)^2 + 0.5^2(11.5)^2 = 66.125$

$\sigma_W = \sqrt{\sigma_W^2} = \sqrt{66.125} \approx 8.13$

(b) Single policy (x_1): $\mu_1 = 50.2$

Two policies (W): $\mu_W \approx 50.2$

The means are the same.

(c) Single policy (x_1): $\sigma_1 = 11.5$

Two policies (W): $\sigma_W \approx 8.13$

The standard deviation for two policies is smaller.

(d) Yes, the risk decreases by a factor of $\frac{1}{\sqrt{n}}$ because $\sigma_W = \frac{1}{\sqrt{n}}\sigma$.

Section 5.2

1. A trial is one flip of a fair quarter. Success = head. Failure = tail.

$n = 3$, $p = 0.5$, $q = 1 - 0.5 = 0.5$

(a) $P(3) = C_{3,3}(0.5)^3(0.5)^{3-3}$

$= 1(0.5)^3(0.5)^0$

$= 0.125$

To find this value in Table 3 of Appendix II, use the group in which $n = 3$, the column headed by $p = 0.5$, and the row headed by $r = 3$.

(b) $P(2) = C_{3,2}(0.5)^2(0.5)^{3-2}$

$= 3(0.5)^2(0.5)^1$

$= 0.375$

To find this value in Table 3 of Appendix II, use the group in which $n = 3$, the column headed by $p = 0.5$, and the row headed by $r = 2$.

(c) $P(r \geq 2) = P(2) + P(3)$

$= 0.125 + 0.375$

$= 0.5$

(d) The probability of getting exactly three tails is the same as getting exactly zero heads.

$P(0) = C_{3,0}(0.5)^0(0.5)^{3-0}$

$= 1(0.5)^0(0.5)^3$

$= 0.125$

To find this value in Table 3 of Appendix II, use the group in which $n = 3$, the column headed by $p = 0.5$, and the row headed by $r = 0$.

The results from Table 3 of Appendix II are the same.

In the problems that follow, there are often other ways the solve the problems than those shown. As long as you get the same answer, your method is probably correct.

2. A trial is answering a question on the quiz. Success = correct answer. Failure = incorrect answer.

$n = 10,\ p = \frac{1}{5} = 0.2,\ q = 1 - 0.2 = 0.8$

(a) $P(10) = C_{10,10}(0.2)^{10}(0.8)^{10-10}$

$= 1(0.2)^{10}(0.8)^{0}$

$= 0.000$ (to three digits)

(b) 10 incorrect is the same as 0 correct.

$P(0) = C_{10,0}(0.2)^{0}(0.8)^{10-0}$

$= 1(0.2)^{0}(0.8)^{10}$

$= 0.107$

(c) First method:

$P(r \geq 1) = P(1) + P(2) + P(3) + P(4) + P(5) + P(6) + P(7) + P(8) + P(9) + P(10)$

$= 0.268 + 0.302 + 0.201 + 0.088 + 0.026 + 0.006 + 0.001 + 0.000 + 0.000 + 0.000$

$= 0.892$

Second method:

$P(r \geq 1) = 1 - P(0)$

$= 1 - 0.107$

$= 0.893$

The two results should be equal, but because of rounding error, they differ slightly.

(d) $P(r \geq 5) = P(5) + P(6) + P(7) + P(8) + P(9) + P(10)$

$= 0.026 + 0.006 + 0.001 + 0.000 + 0.000 + 0.000$

$= 0.033$

3. (a) A trial is a man's response to the question, "Would you marry the same woman again?" Success = a positive response. Failure = a negative response.

$n = 10,\ p = 0.80,\ q = 1 - 0.80 = 0.20$

Using values in Table 3 of Appendix II:

$P(r \geq 7) = P(7) + P(8) + P(9) + P(10)$

$= 0.201 + 0.302 + 0.268 + 0.107$

$= 0.878$

$P(r \text{ is less than half of } 10) = P(r < 5)$

$= P(0) + P(1) + P(2) + P(3) + P(4)$

$= 0.000 + 0.000 + 0.000 + 0.001 + 0.006$

$= 0.007$

(b) A trial is a woman's response to the question, "Would you marry the same man again?"
Success = a positive response. Failure = a negative response.
$n = 10,\ p = 0.5,\ q = 1 - 0.5 = 0.5$
Using values in Table 3 of Appendix II:

$$P(r \geq 7) = P(7) + P(8) + P(9) + P(10)$$
$$= 0.117 + 0.044 + 0.010 + 0.001$$
$$= 0.172$$

$$P(r < 5) = P(0) + P(1) + P(2) + P(3) + P(4)$$
$$= 0.001 + 0.010 + 0.044 + 0.117 + 0.205$$
$$= 0.377$$

4. A trial is a one-time fling. Success = has done a one-time fling. Failure = has not done a one-time fling.
$n = 7,\ p = 0.10,\ q = 1 - 0.10 = 0.90$

(a) $P(0) = C_{7,0}(0.10)^0(0.90)^{7-0}$
$$= 1(0.10)^0(0.90)^7$$
$$= 0.478$$

(b) $P(r \geq 1) = 1 - P(0)$
$$= 1 - 0.478$$
$$= 0.522$$

(c) $P(r \leq 2) = P(0) + P(1) + P(2)$
$$= 0.478 + 0.372 + 0.124$$
$$= 0.974$$

5. A trial consists of a woman's response regarding her mother-in-law. Success = dislike. Failure = like.
$n = 6,\ p = 0.90,\ q = 1 - 0.90 = 0.10$

(a) $P(6) = C_{6,6}(0.90)^6(0.10)^{6-6}$
$$= 1(0.90)^6(0.10)^0$$
$$= 0.531$$

(b) $P(0) = C_{6,0}(0.90)^0(0.10)^{6-0}$
$$= 1(0.90)^0(0.10)^6$$
$$\approx 0.000 \text{ (to 3 digits)}$$

(c) $P(r \geq 4) = P(4) + P(5) + P(6)$
$$= 0.098 + 0.354 + 0.531$$
$$= 0.983$$

(d) $P(r \le 3) = 1 - P(r \ge 4)$
$\approx 1 - 0.983$
$= 0.017$

From the table:
$P(r \le 3) = P(0) + P(1) + P(2) + P(3)$
$= 0.000 + 0.000 + 0.001 + 0.015$
$= 0.016$

6. A trial is how a businessman wears a tie. Success = too tight. Failure = not too tight.
$n = 20,\ p = 0.10,\ q = 1 - 0.10 = 0.90$

(a) $P(r \ge 1) = 1 - P(r = 0)$
$= 1 - 0.122$
$= 0.878$

(b) $P(r > 2) = 1 - P(r \le 2)$
$= 1 - [P(r = 0) + P(r = 1) + P(r = 2)]$
$= 1 - P(r = 0) - P(r = 1) - P(r = 2)$
$= [1 - P(r = 0)] - P(r = 1) - P(r = 2)$
$= P(r \ge 1) - P(r = 1) - P(r = 2)$
$= 0.878 - 0.270 - 0.285$ using (a)
$= 0.323$

(c) $P(r = 0) = 0.122$

(d) At least 18 are not too tight is the same as at most 2 are too tight. (To see this, note that at least 18 failures is the same as 18 or 19 or 20 failures, which is 2, 1, or 0 successes. i.e., at most 2 successes.)
$P(r \le 2) = 1 - P(r > 2)$
$= 1 - 0.323$ using (b)
$= 0.677$

7. A trial consists of taking a polygraph examination. Success = pass. Failure = fail.
$n = 9,\ p = 0.85,\ q = 1 - 0.85 = 0.15$

(a) $P(9) = 0.232$

(b) $P(r \ge 5) = P(5) + P(6) + P(7) + P(8) + P(9)$
$= 0.028 + 0.107 + 0.260 + 0.368 + 0.232$
$= 0.995$

(c) $P(r \le 4) = 1 - P(r \ge 5)$
$= 1 - 0.995$
$= 0.005$

From the table:
$P(r \le 4) = P(0) + P(1) + P(2) + P(3) + P(4)$
$= 0.000 + 0.000 + 0.000 + 0.001 + 0.005$
$= 0.006$

The two results should be equal, but because of rounding error, they differ slightly.

(d) All students fail is the same as no students pass.
$P(0) = 0.000$ (to 3 digits)

8. A trial is asking a person if he/she has a cellular phone. Success = has a cellular phone. Failure = does not have a cellular phone.
$n = 11,\ p = 0.35,\ q = 1 - p = 0.65$

(a) $P(11) = 0.000$ (to 3 digits)

(b) $P(r > 4) = P(r \ge 5)$
$= P(5) + P(6) + P(7) + P(8) + P(9) + P(10) + P(11)$
$= 0.183 + 0.099 + 0.038 + 0.010 + 0.002 + 0.000 + 0.000$
$= 0.332$

(c) Fewer than 5 do not have a cellular phone is the same as more than 6 have a cellular phone.
$P(r > 6) = P(7) + P(8) + P(9) + P(10) + P(11)$
$= 0.038 + 0.010 + 0.002 + 0.000 + 0.000$
$= 0.050$

(d) More than 7 do not have a cellular phone is the same as fewer than 4 have a cellular phone.
$P(r < 4) = P(0) + P(1) + P(2) + P(3)$
$= 0.009 + 0.052 + 0.140 + 0.225$
$= 0.426$

9. A trial consists of checking the gross receipts of the Green Parrot Italian Restaurant for one business day. Success = gross is over \$2200. Failure = gross is at or below \$2200.
$p = 0.85,\ q = 1 - 0.85 = 0.15$

(a) $n = 7$
$P(r \ge 5) = P(5) + P(6) + P(7)$
$= 0.210 + 0.396 + 0.321$
$= 0.927$

(b) $n = 10$
$P(r \ge 5) = P(5) + P(6) + P(7) + P(8) + P(9) + P(10)$
$= 0.008 + 0.040 + 0.130 + 0.276 + 0.347 + 0.197$
$= 0.998$

(c) $n = 5$

$$P(r < 3) = P(0) + P(1) + P(2)$$
$$= 0.000 + 0.002 + 0.024$$
$$= 0.026$$

(d) $n = 10$

$$P(r < 7) = P(0) + P(1) + P(2) + P(3) + P(4) + P(5) + P(6)$$
$$= 0.000 + 0.000 + 0.000 + 0.000 + 0.001 + 0.008 + 0.040$$
$$= 0.049$$

(e) $n = 7$

$$P(r < 3) = P(0) + P(1) + P(2)$$
$$= 0.000 + 0.000 + 0.001$$
$$= 0.001$$

Yes. If p were really 0.85, then the event of a 7-day period with gross income exceeding \$2200 fewer than 3 days would be very rare. If it happened again, we would suspect that $p = 0.85$ is too high.

10. A trial consists of checking the gross receipts of the store for one business day. Success = gross over \$850. Failure = gross is at or below \$850. $p = 0.6$, $q = 1 - p = 0.4$

(a) $n = 5$

$$P(r \geq 3) = P(3) + P(4) + P(5)$$
$$= 0.346 + 0.259 + 0.078$$
$$= 0.683$$

(b) $n = 10$

$$P(r \geq 6) = P(6) + P(7) + P(8) + P(9) + P(10)$$
$$= 0.251 + 0.215 + 0.121 + 0.040 + 0.006$$
$$= 0.633$$

(c) $n = 10$

$$P(r < 5) = P(0) + P(1) + P(2) + P(3) + P(4)$$
$$= 0.000 + 0.002 + 0.011 + 0.042 + 0.111$$
$$= 0.166$$

(d) $n = 20$

$$P(r < 6) = P(0) + P(1) + P(2) + P(3) + P(4) + P(5)$$
$$= 0.000 + 0.000 + 0.000 + 0.000 + 0.000 + 0.001$$
$$= 0.001$$

Yes. If p were really 0.60, then the event of a 20-day period with gross income exceeding \$850 fewer than 6 days would be very rare. If it happened again, we would suspect that $p = 0.60$ is too high.

(e) $n = 20$

$$P(r > 17) = P(18) + P(19) + P(20)$$
$$= 0.003 + 0.000 + 0.000$$
$$= 0.003$$

Yes. If p were really 0.60, then the event of a 20-day period with gross income exceeding \$850 more than 17 days would be very rare. If it happened again, we would suspect that $p = 0.60$ is too low.

11. A trial is catching and releasing a pike. Success = pike dies. Failure = pike lives.

$n = 16,\ p = 0.05,\ q = 1 - 0.05 = 0.95$

(a) $P(0) = 0.440$

(b) $P(r < 3) = P(0) + P(1) + P(2)$
$= 0.440 + 0.371 + 0.146$
$= 0.957$

(c) All of the fish lived is the same as none of the fish died.
$P(0) = 0.440$

(d) More than 14 fish lived is the same as less than 2 fish died.
$P(r < 2) = P(0) + P(1)$
$= 0.440 + 0.371$
$= 0.811$

12. A trial is tasting coffee. Success = choose Tasty Bean. Failure = do not choose Tasty Bean.

$n = 4,\ p = \frac{1}{5} = 0.2,\ q = 1 - 0.2 = 0.8$

(a) $P(4) = 0.002$

(b) $P(0) = 0.410$

(c) $P(r \geq 3) = P(3) + P(4)$
$= 0.026 + 0.002$
$= 0.028$

13. (a) A trial consists of using the Meyers-Briggs instrument to determine if a person in marketing is an extrovert. Success = extrovert. Failure = not extrovert.

$n = 15,\ p = 0.75,\ q = 1 - 0.75 = 0.25$

$P(r \geq 10) = P(10) + P(11) + P(12) + P(13) + P(14) + P(15)$
$= 0.165 + 0.225 + 0.225 + 0.156 + 0.067 + 0.013$
$= 0.851$

$P(r \geq 5) = P(5) + P(6) + P(7) + P(8) + P(9) + P(r \geq 10)$
$= 0.001 + 0.003 + 0.013 + 0.039 + 0.092 + 0.851$
$= 0.999$

$P(15) = 0.013$

(b) A trial consists of using the Meyers-Briggs instrument to determine if a computer programmer is an introvert. Success = introvert. Failure = not introvert.

$n = 5,\ p = 0.60,\ q = 1 - 0.60 = 0.40$

$$P(0) = 0.010$$

$$\begin{aligned} P(r \ge 3) &= P(3) + P(4) + P(5) \\ &= 0.346 + 0.259 + 0.078 \\ &= 0.683 \end{aligned}$$

$$P(5) = 0.078$$

14. A trial consists of a man's response regarding welcoming a woman taking the initiative in asking for a date. Success = yes. Failure = no.

$n = 20,\ p = 0.70,\ q = 1 - 0.70 = 0.30$

(a) $$\begin{aligned} P(r \ge 18) &= P(18) + P(19) + P(20) \\ &= 0.028 + 0.007 + 0.001 \\ &= 0.036 \end{aligned}$$

(b) $$\begin{aligned} P(r < 3) &= P(0) + P(1) + P(2) \\ &= 0.000 + 0.000 + 0.000 \\ &= 0.000 \text{ (to 3 digits)} \end{aligned}$$

(c) $P(0) = 0.000$ (to 3 digits)

(d) At least 5 say no is the same as at most 15 say yes.

$$\begin{aligned} P(r \le 15) &= 1 - P(r \ge 16) \\ &= 1 - [P(16) + P(17) + P(18) + P(19) + P(20)] \\ &= 1 - (0.130 + 0.072 + 0.028 + 0.007 + 0.001) \\ &= 1 - 0.238 \\ &= 0.762 \end{aligned}$$

15. A trial is checking the development of hypertension in patients with diabetes. Success = yes. Failure = no.

$n = 10,\ p = 0.40,\ q = 1 - 0.40 = 0.60$

(a) $P(0) = 0.006$

(b) $$\begin{aligned} P(r < 5) &= P(0) + P(1) + P(2) + P(3) + P(4) \\ &= 0.006 + 0.040 + 0.121 + 0.215 + 0.251 \\ &= 0.633 \end{aligned}$$

A trial is checking the development of an eye disease in patients with diabetes. Success = yes. Failure = no.

$n = 10,\ p = 0.30,\ q = 1 - 0.30 = 0.70$

(c) $$\begin{aligned} P(r \le 2) &= P(0) + P(1) + P(2) \\ &= 0.028 + 0.121 + 0.233 \\ &= 0.382 \end{aligned}$$

(d) At least 6 will never develop a related eye disease is the same as at most 4 will never develop a related eye disease.

$$\begin{aligned} P(r \le 4) &= P(0)+P(1)+P(2)+P(3)+P(4) \\ &= 0.028+0.121+0.233+0.267+0.200 \\ &= 0.849 \end{aligned}$$

16. A trial consists of the response of adults regarding their concern that employers are monitoring phone calls. Success = yes. Failure = no.

$p = 0.37,\ q = 1-0.37 = 0.63$

(a) $n = 5$

$$\begin{aligned} P(0) &= C_{5,0}(0.37)^0(0.63)^{5-0} \\ &= 1(0.37)^0(0.63)^5 \\ &\approx 0.099 \end{aligned}$$

(b) $n = 5$

$$\begin{aligned} P(5) &= C_{5,5}(0.37)^5(0.63)^{5-5} \\ &= 1(0.37)^5(0.63)^0 \\ &\approx 0.007 \end{aligned}$$

(c) $n = 5$

$$\begin{aligned} P(3) &= C_{5,3}(0.37)^3(0.63)^{5-3} \\ &= 10(0.37)^3(0.63)^2 \\ &\approx 0.201 \end{aligned}$$

17. A trial consists of the response of adults regarding their concern that Social Security numbers are used for general identification. Success = concerned that SS numbers are being used for identification. Failure = not concerned that SS numbers are being used for identification.

$n = 8,\ p = 0.53,\ q = 1-0.53 = 0.47$

(a) $P(r \le 5) = P(0)+P(1)+P(2)+P(3)+P(4)+P(5)$

$$\begin{aligned} &= 0.002381+0.021481+0.084781+0.191208+0.269521+0.243143 \\ &= 0.812515 \end{aligned}$$

$P(r \le 5) = 0.81251$ from the cumulative probability is the same, truncated to 5 digits.

(b) $P(r > 5) = P(6)+P(7)+P(8)$

$$\begin{aligned} &= 0.137091+0.044169+0.006726 \\ &= 0.187486 \end{aligned}$$

$$\begin{aligned} P(r > 5) &= 1 - P(r \le 5) \\ &= 1-0.81251 \\ &= 0.18749 \end{aligned}$$

Yes, this is the same result rounded to 5 digits.

18. A trial consists of determining the sex of a wolf. Success = male. Failure = female.

(a) $n = 12,\ p = 0.55,\ q = 0.45$

$$\begin{aligned} P(r \geq 6) &= P(6) + P(7) + P(8) + P(9) + P(10) + P(11) + P(12) \\ &= 0.212 + 0.223 + 0.170 + 0.092 + 0.034 + 0.008 + 0.001 \\ &= 0.740 \end{aligned}$$

Six or more female is the same as six or fewer male.

$$\begin{aligned} P(r \leq 6) &= P(0) + P(1) + P(2) + P(3) + P(4) + P(5) + P(6) \\ &= 0.000 + 0.001 + 0.007 + 0.028 + 0.076 + 0.149 + 0.212 \\ &= 0.473 \end{aligned}$$

Fewer than 4 female is the same as more than 8 male.

$$\begin{aligned} P(r > 8) &= P(9) + P(10) + P(11) + P(12) \\ &= 0.092 + 0.034 + 0.008 + 0.001 \\ &= 0.135 \end{aligned}$$

(b) $n = 12,\ p = 0.70,\ q = 0.30$

$$\begin{aligned} P(r \geq 6) &= P(6) + P(7) + P(8) + P(9) + P(10) + P(11) + P(12) \\ &= 0.079 + 0.158 + 0.231 + 0.240 + 0.168 + 0.071 + 0.014 \\ &= 0.961 \end{aligned}$$

$$\begin{aligned} P(r \leq 6) &= P(0) + P(1) + P(2) + P(3) + P(4) + P(5) + P(6) \\ &= 0.000 + 0.000 + 0.000 + 0.001 + 0.008 + 0.029 + 0.079 \\ &= 0.117 \end{aligned}$$

$$\begin{aligned} P(r > 8) &= P(9) + P(10) + P(11) + P(12) \\ &= 0.240 + 0.168 + 0.071 + 0.014 \\ &= 0.493 \end{aligned}$$

19. A trial consists of determining the kind of stone in a chipped stone tool.

(a) $n = 11$; Success = obsidian. Failure = not obsidian.

$p = 0.15,\ q = 1 - 0.15 = 0.85$

$$\begin{aligned} P(r \geq 3) &= 1 - P(r \leq 2) \\ &= 1 - [P(0) + P(1) + P(2)] \\ &= 1 - (0.167 + 0.325 + 0.287) \\ &= 1 - 0.779 \\ &= 0.221 \end{aligned}$$

(b) $n = 5$; Success = basalt. Failure = not basalt.

$p = 0.55,\ q = 1 - 0.55 = 0.45$

$$\begin{aligned} P(r \geq 2) &= P(2) + P(3) + P(4) + P(5) \\ &= 0.276 + 0.337 + 0.206 + 0.050 \\ &= 0.869 \end{aligned}$$

(c) $n = 10$; Success = neither obsidian nor basalt. Failure = either obsidian or basalt. The two outcomes, tool is obsidian or tool is basalt, are mutually exclusive. Therefore, *P*(obsidian *or* basalt) = 0.55 + 0.15 = 0.70. *P*(neither obsidian nor basalt) = 1 − 0.70 = 0.30. Therefore, $p = 0.30$, $q = 1 - 0.30 = 0.70$.

$$\begin{aligned} P(r \geq 4) &= P(4)+P(5)+P(6)+P(7)+P(8)+P(9)+P(10) \\ &= 0.200+0.103+0.037+0.009+0.001+0.000+0.000 \\ &= 0.350 \end{aligned}$$

Note that the phrase "neither obsidian nor basalt" is the English translation of the math phrase "not (obsidian or basalt)" and therefore, it describes the complement of the event "obsidian or basalt." Using $P(\bar{A}) = 1 - P(A)$, we get p = *P*(Success) = 0.30.

20. A trial consists of an office visit.

(a) Success = visitor age is under 15 years old.
Failure = visitor age is 15 years old or older.

$n = 8,\ p = 0.20,\ q = 1 - 0.20 = 0.80$

$$\begin{aligned} P(r \geq 4) &= P(4)+P(5)+P(6)+P(7)+P(8) \\ &= 0.046+0.009+0.001+0.000+0.000 \\ &= 0.056 \end{aligned}$$

(b) Success = visitor age is 65 years old or older.
Failure = visitor age is under 65 years old.

$n = 8,\ p = 0.25,\ q = 1 - 0.25 = 0.75$

$$\begin{aligned} P(2 \leq r \leq 5) &= P(2)+P(3)+P(4)+P(5) \\ &= 0.311+0.208+0.087+0.023 \\ &= 0.629 \end{aligned}$$

(c) Success = visitor age is 45 years old or older.
Failure = visitor age is less than 65 years old.

$n = 8,\ p = 0.20+0.25 = 0.45,\ q = 1 - 0.45 = 0.55$

$$\begin{aligned} P(2 \leq r \leq 5) &= P(2)+P(3)+P(4)+P(5) \\ &= 0.157+0.257+0.263+0.172 \\ &= 0.849 \end{aligned}$$

(d) Success = visitor age is under 25 years old.
Failure = visitor age is 25 years old or older.

$n = 8,\ p = 0.20+0.10 = 0.30,\ q = 1 - 0.30 = 0.70$

$P(8) = 0.000$ (to 3 digits)

(e) Success = visitor age is 15 years old or older.
Failure = visitor age is under 15 years old.

$n = 8,\ p = 0.10+0.25+0.20+0.25 = 0.80,\ q = 0.20$

$P(8) = 0.168$

21. **(a)** $p = 0.30,\ P(3) = 0.132$
$p = 0.70,\ P(2) = 0.132$
They are the same.

(b) $p = 0.30, P(r \geq 3) = 0.132 + 0.028 + 0.002 = 0.162$
$p = 0.70, P(r \leq 2) = 0.002 + 0.028 + 0.132 = 0.162$
They are the same.

(c) $p = 0.30, P(4) = 0.028$
$p = 0.70, P(1) = 0.028$
$r = 1$

(d) The column headed by $p = 0.80$ is symmetrical with the one headed by $p = 0.20$.

22. $n = 3, p = 0.0228, q = 1 - p = 0.9772$

(a) $P(2) = C_{3,2}p^2q^{3-2} = 3(0.0228)^2(0.9772)^1 = 0.00152$

(b) $P(3) = C_{3,3}p^3q^{3-3} = 1(0.0228)^3(0.9772)^0 = 0.00001$

(c) $P(2 \text{ or } 3) = P(2) + P(3) = 0.00153$

Section 5.3

1. (a) Binomial Distribution
The distribution is symmetrical.

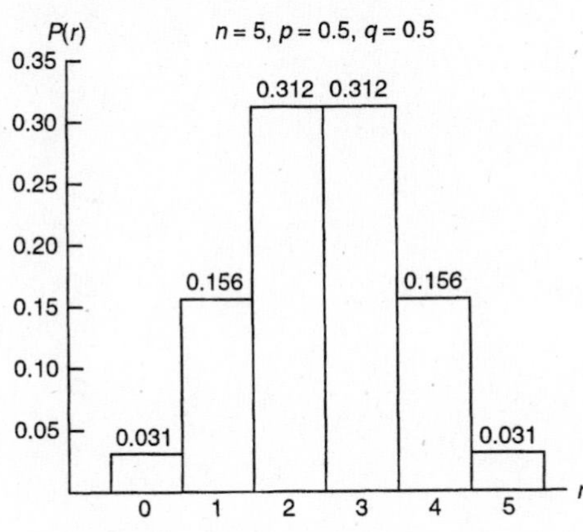

(b) Binomial Distribution
The distribution is skewed right.

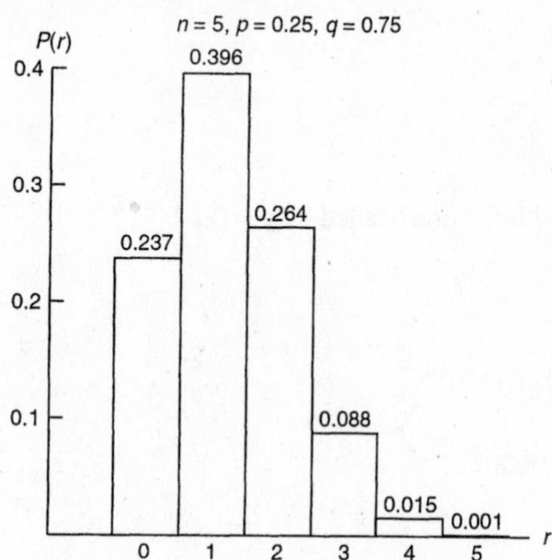

(c) Binomial Distribution
The distribution is skewed left.

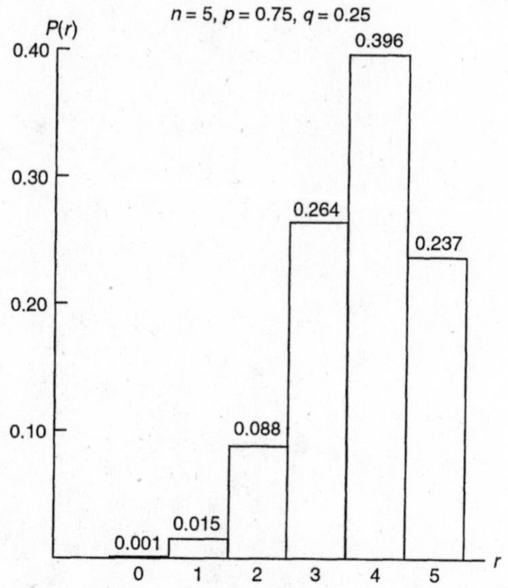

(d) The distributions are mirror images of one another.

(e) The distribution would be skewed left for $p = 0.73$ because the more likely number of successes are to the right of the middle.

2. **(a)** $p = 0.30$ goes with graph II since it is slightly skewed right.

(b) $p = 0.50$ goes with graph I since it is symmetrical.

(c) $p = 0.65$ goes with graph III since it is slightly skewed left.

(d) $p = 0.90$ goes with graph IV since it is drastically skewed left.

(e) The graph is more symmetrical when p is close to 0.5. The graph is skewed left when p is close to 1 and skewed right when p is close to 0.

3. The probabilities can be taken directly from Table 3 in Appendix II.

(a) $n = 10,\ p = 0.80$

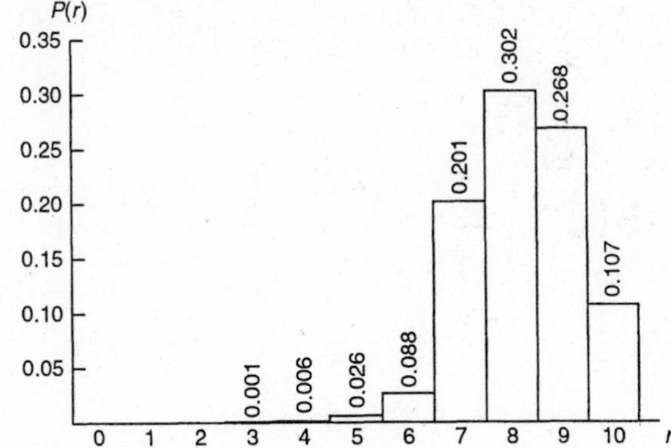

$$\mu = np = 10(0.8) = 8$$
$$\sigma = \sqrt{npq} = \sqrt{10(0.8)(0.2)} \approx 1.26$$

(b) $n = 10,\ p = 0.5$

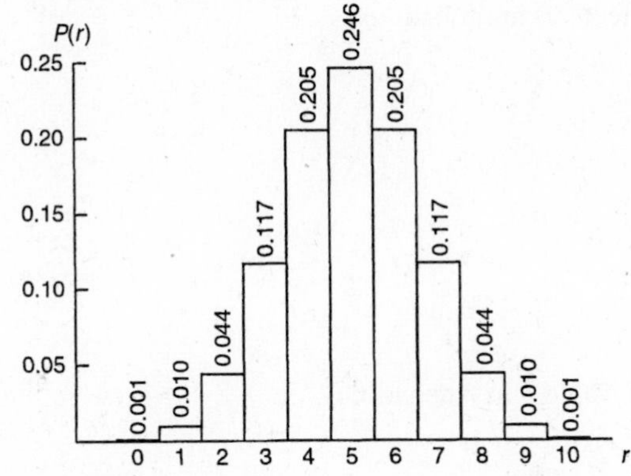

$$\mu = np = 10(0.5) = 5$$
$$\sigma = \sqrt{npq} = \sqrt{10(0.5)(0.5)} \approx 1.58$$

(c) Yes; since the graph in part (a) is skewed left, it supports the claim that more households buy film that have children under 2 years than households that have no children under 21 years.

4. (a) $n = 8,\ p = 0.01$

The probabilities can be taken directly from Table 3 in Appendix II.

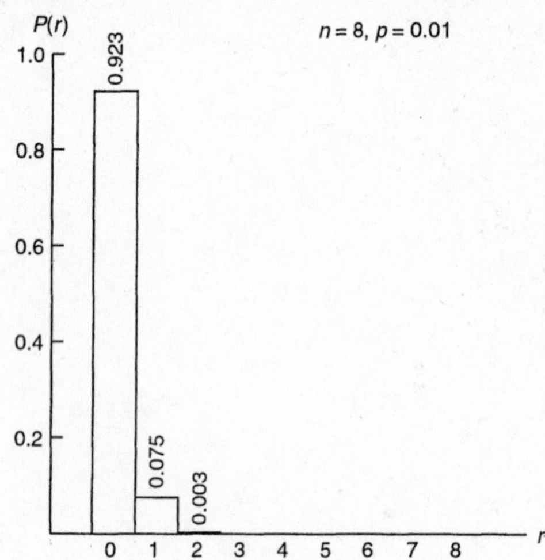

(b) $\mu = np = 8(0.01) = 0.08$

The expected number of defective syringes the inspector will find is 0.08.

(c) The batch will be accepted if less than 2 defectives are found.

$$\begin{aligned} P(r < 2) &= P(0) + P(1) \\ &= 0.923 + 0.075 \\ &= 0.998 \end{aligned}$$

(d) $\sigma = \sqrt{npq} = \sqrt{8(0.01)(0.99)} \approx 0.281$

5. (a) $n = 6,\ p = 0.70$

The probabilities can be taken directly from Table 3 in Appendix II.

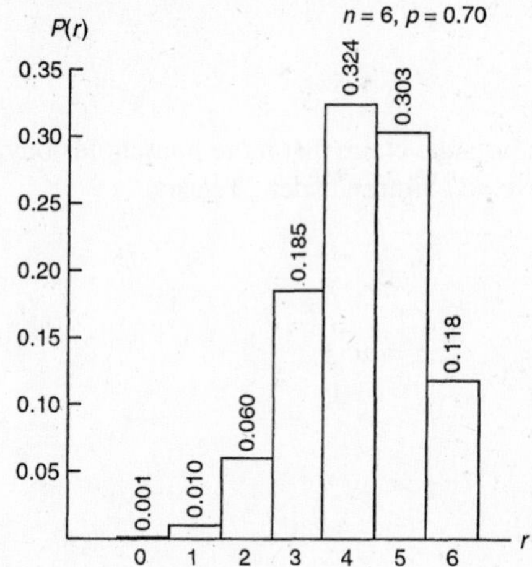

(b) $\mu = np = 6(0.70) = 4.2$

$$\sigma = \sqrt{npq} = \sqrt{6(0.70)(0.30)} \approx 1.122$$

The expected number of friends for whom addresses will be found is 4.2.

(c) Find n such that $P(r \geq 2) = 0.97$.

Try $n = 5$.

$$\begin{aligned} P(r \geq 2) &= P(2) + P(3) + P(4) + P(5) \\ &= 0.132 + 0.309 + 0.360 + 0.168 \\ &= 0.969 \\ &\approx 0.97 \end{aligned}$$

You would have to submit 5 names to be 97% sure that at least two addresses will be found.

If you solve this problem as

$$\begin{aligned} P(r \geq 2) &= 1 - P(r < 2) \\ &= 1 - [P(r = 0) + P(r = 1)] \\ &= 1 - 0.002 - 0.028 = 0.97, \end{aligned}$$

the answers differ due to rounding error in the table.

6. (a) $n = 5,\ p = 0.85$

The probabilities can be taken directly from Table 3 in Appendix II.

Binomial Distribution for Number of Automobile Damage Claims by People Under Age 25

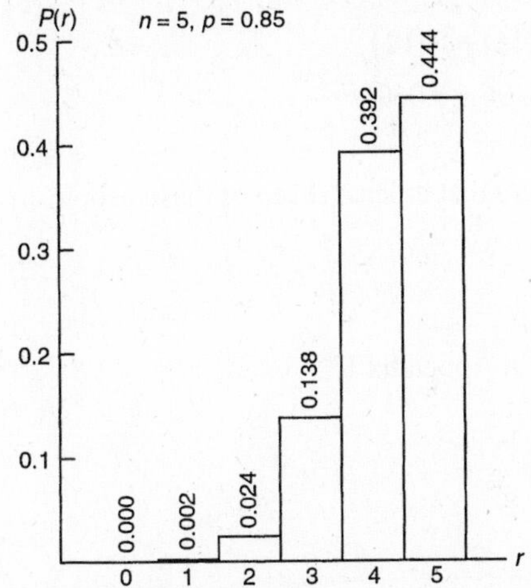

(b) $\mu = np = 5(0.85) = 4.25$

$$\sigma = \sqrt{npq} = \sqrt{5(0.85)(0.15)} \approx 0.798$$

For samples of size 5, the expected number of claims made by people under 25 years of age is about 4.

7. (a) $n = 7,\ p = 0.20$

The probabilities can be taken directly from Table 3 in Appendix II.

Binomial Distribution for Number of Illiterate People

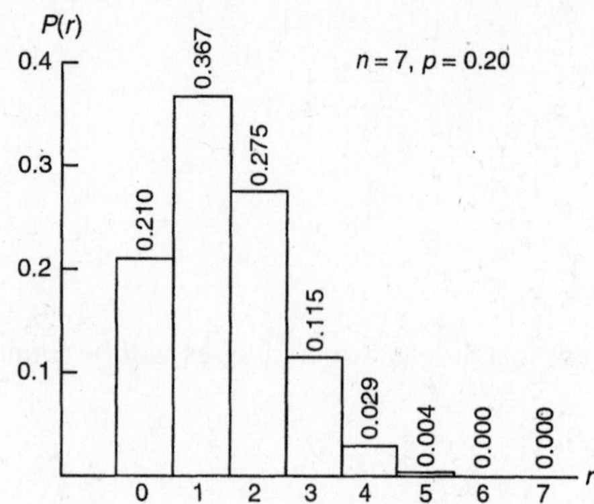

(b) $\mu = np = 7(0.20) = 1.4$

$$\sigma = \sqrt{npq} = \sqrt{7(0.20)(0.80)} \approx 1.058$$

The expected number of people in this sample who are illiterate is 1.4.

(c) Let success = literate and $p = 0.80$.
Find n such that

$$P(r \geq 7) = 0.98.$$

Try $n = 12$.

$$P(r \geq 7) = P(7) + P(8) + P(9) + P(10) + P(11) + P(12)$$
$$= 0.053 + 0.133 + 0.236 + 0.283 + 0.206 + 0.069$$
$$= 0.98$$

You would need to interview 12 people to be 98% sure that at least seven of these people are not illiterate.

8. (a) $n = 12,\ p = 0.35$

The probabilities can be taken directly from Table 3 in Appendix II.

Drivers Who Tailgate

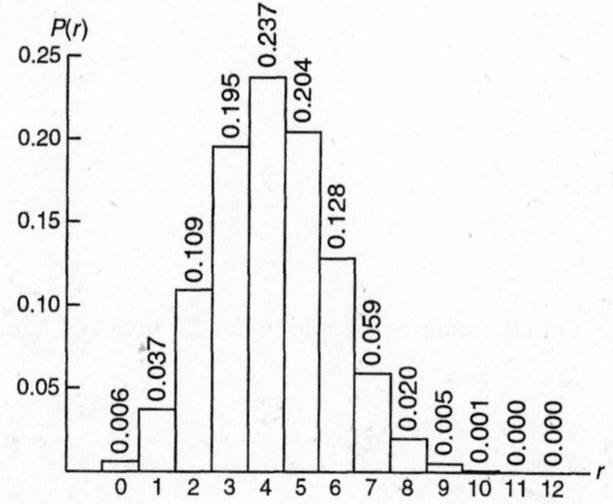

(b) $\mu = np = 12(0.35) = 4.2$

The expected number of vehicles out of 12 that will tailgate is 4.2.

(c) $\sigma = \sqrt{npq} = \sqrt{12(0.35)(0.65)} \approx 1.65$

9. (a) $n = 8,\ p = 0.25$

The probabilities can be taken directly from Table 3 in Appendix II.

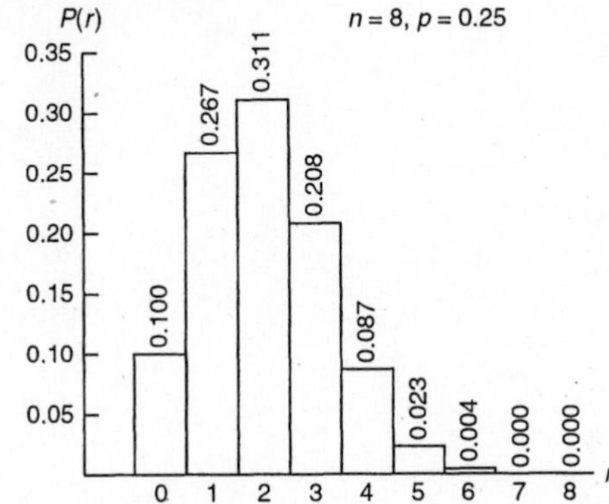

(b) $\mu = np = 8(0.25) = 2$

$$\sigma = \sqrt{npq} = \sqrt{8(0.25)(0.75)} \approx 1.225$$

The expected number of people in this sample who believe the product is improved is 1.4.

(c) Find n such that

$$P(r \geq 1) = 0.99.$$

Try $n = 16$.

$$P(r \geq 1) = 1 - P(0)$$
$$= 1 - 0.01$$
$$= 0.99$$

Sixteen people are needed in the marketing study to be 99% sure that at least one person believes the product to be improved.

10. (a) From Table 3 in Appendix II and $n = 9$, $p = 85$.

r	0	1	2	3	4	5	6	7	8	9
$P(r)$	0.000	0.000	0.000	0.001	0.005	0.028	0.107	0.260	0.368	0.232

(b) Binomial Distribution for Number of Hot Spots that are Forest Fires

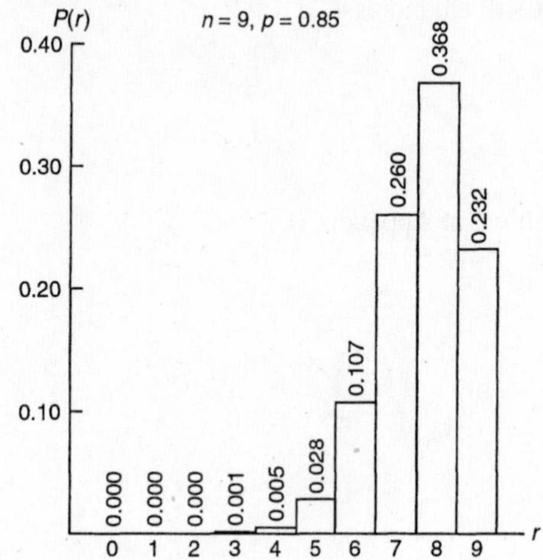

(c) $\mu = np = 9(0.85) = 7.65$

The expected number of real forest fires is 7.65.

(d) $\sigma = \sqrt{npq} = \sqrt{9(0.85)(0.15)} \approx 1.071$

(e) Find n such that

$$P(r \geq 1) = 0.999.$$

Try $n = 4$.

$$P(r \geq 1) = 1 - P(r = 0)$$
$$= 1 - 0.001$$
$$= 0.999$$

The satellite must report 4 hot spots to be 99.9% sure of at least one real forest fire.

11. $p = 0.40$

Find n such that

$$P(r \geq 5) = 0.95.$$

Try $n = 20$.

$$P(r \geq 5) = 1 - [P(0) + P(1) + P(2) + P(3) + P(4)]$$
$$= 1 - (0.000 + 0.000 + 0.003 + 0.012 + 0.035)$$
$$= 1 - 0.05$$
$$= 0.95$$

He must make 20 sales calls to be 95% sure of meeting the quota.

12. $p = 0.55$

Find n such that

$$P(r \geq 4) = 0.964.$$

Try $n = 12$.

$$\begin{aligned} P(r \geq 4) &= 1 - [P(0) + P(1) + P(2) + P(3)] \\ &= 1 - (0.000 + 0.001 + 0.007 + 0.028) \\ &= 1 - 0.036 \\ &= 0.964 \end{aligned}$$

She must make 12 phone calls to be 96.4% sure of meeting the quota.

13. $p = 0.10$

Find n such that

$$P(r \geq 1) = 0.90$$

From a calculator or a computer, we determine $n = 22$ gives $P(r \geq 1) = 0.9015$.

14. **(a)** $p = 0.40, n = 7$

$$\begin{aligned} P(r \geq 1) &= 1 - P(0) \\ &= 1 - 0.028 \\ &= 0.972 \end{aligned}$$

(b) $\mu = np = 7(0.40) = 2.8$

The expected number of these seven drivers who will warn oncoming traffic is 2.8.

$$\sigma = \sqrt{npq} = \sqrt{7(0.40)(0.60)} \approx 1.30$$

(c) Find n such that

$$P(r \geq 1) = 0.998.$$

Try $n = 12$.

$$\begin{aligned} P(r \geq 1) &= 1 - P(0) \\ &= 1 - 0.002 \\ &= 0.998 \end{aligned}$$

Twelve cars would need to go by the speed trap to be 99.8% sure that at least one driver will warn others.

15. **(a)** Since success = not a repeat offender, then $p = 0.75$.

From Table 3 in Appendix II and $n = 4$, $p = 0.75$.

r	0	1	2	3	4
$P(r)$	0.004	0.047	0.211	0.422	0.316

(b) Binomial Distribution for Number of Parolees Who Do Not Become Repeat Offenders

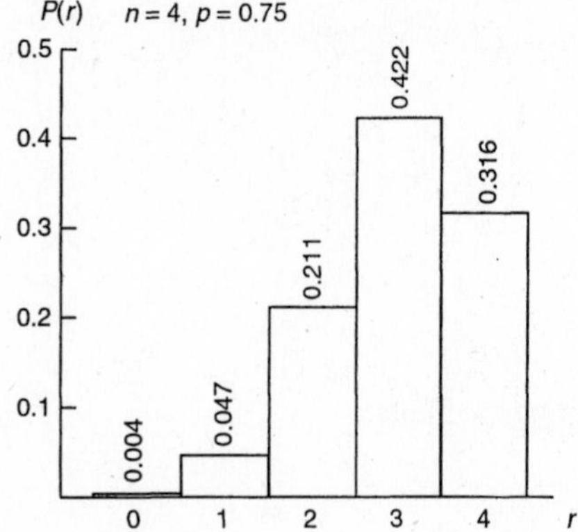

(c) $\mu = np = 4(0.75) = 3$

The expected number of parolees in Alice's group who will not be repeat offenders is 3.

$$\sigma = \sqrt{npq} = \sqrt{4(0.75)(0.25)} \approx 0.866$$

(d) Find n such that

$$P(r \geq 3) = 0.98.$$

Try $n = 7$.

$$\begin{aligned} P(r \geq 3) &= P(3) + P(4) + P(5) + P(6) + P(7) \\ &= 0.058 + 0.173 + 0.311 + 0.311 + 0.133 \\ &= 0.986 \end{aligned}$$

This is slightly higher than needed, but $n = 6$ yields $P(r \geq 3) = 0.963$.

Alice should have a group of 7 to be about 98% sure three or more will not become repeat offenders.

16. (a) $p = 0.65$

Find n such that

$$P(r \geq 1) = 0.98.$$

Try $n = 4$.

$$\begin{aligned} P(r \geq 1) &= 1 - P(0) \\ &= 1 - 0.015 \\ &= 0.985 \end{aligned}$$

Four stations are required to be 98% certain that an enemy plane flying over will be detected by at least one station.

(b) $n = 4, p = 0.65$

$$\mu = np = 4(0.65) = 2.6$$

If four stations are in use, 2.6 is the expected number of stations that will detect an enemy plane.

17. (a) Let success = available, then $p = 0.75$, $n = 12$.

$$P(12) = 0.032$$

(b) Let success = not available, then $p = 0.25$, $n = 12$.

$$P(r \geq 6) = P(6) + P(7) + P(8) + P(9) + P(10) + P(11) + P(12)$$
$$= 0.040 + 0.011 + 0.002 + 0.000 + 0.000 + 0.000 + 0.000$$
$$= 0.053$$

(c) $n = 12$, $p = 0.75$

$$\mu = np = 12(0.75) = 9$$

The expected number of those available to serve on the jury is 9.

$$\sigma = \sqrt{npq} = \sqrt{12(0.75)(0.25)} = 1.5$$

(d) $p = 0.75$

Find n such that

$$P(r \geq 12) = 0.959.$$

Try $n = 20$.

$$P(r \geq 12) = P(12) + P(13) + P(14) + P(15) + P(16) + P(17) + P(18) + P(19) + P(20)$$
$$= 0.061 + 0.112 + 0.169 + 0.202 + 0.190 + 0.134 + 0.067 + 0.021 + 0.003$$
$$= 0.959$$

The jury commissioner must contact 20 people to be 95.9% sure of finding at least 12 people who available to serve.

18. **(a)** Let success = emergency, then $p = 0.15$, $n = 4$.

$$P(4) = 0.001$$

(b) Let success = not emergency, then $p = 0.85$, $n = 4$.

$$P(r \geq 3) = P(3) + P(4)$$
$$= 0.368 + 0.522$$
$$= 0.890$$

(c) $p = 0.15$

Find n such that

$$P(r \geq 1) = 0.96.$$

Try $n = 20$.

$$P(r \geq 1) = 1 - P(0)$$
$$= 1 - 0.039$$
$$= 0.961$$

The operators need to answer 20 calls to be 96% (or more) sure that at least one call was in fact an emergency.

19. Let success = case solved, then $p = 0.2$, $n = 6$.

(a) $P(0) = 0.262$

(b) $P(r \geq 1) = 1 - P(0)$

$$= 1 - 0.262$$
$$= 0.738$$

(c) $\mu = np = 6(0.20) = 1.2$

The expected number of crimes that will be solved is 1.2.

$$\sigma = \sqrt{npq} = \sqrt{6(0.20)(0.80)} \approx 0.98$$

(d) Find n such that

$$P(r \geq 1) = 0.90.$$

Try $n = 11$.

$$\begin{aligned} P(r \geq 1) &= 1 - P(0) \\ &= 1 - 0.086 \\ &= 0.914 \end{aligned}$$

[Note: For $n = 10$, $P(r \geq 1) = 0.893$.]

The police must investigate 11 property crimes before they can be at least 90% sure of solving one or more cases.

20. (a) $p = 0.55$

Find n such that

$$P(r \geq 1) = 0.99.$$

Try $n = 6$.

$$\begin{aligned} P(r \geq 1) &= 1 - P(0) \\ &= 1 - 0.008 \\ &= 0.992 \end{aligned}$$

Six alarms should be used to be 99% certain that a burglar trying to enter is detected by at least one alarm.

(b) $n = 9$, $p = 0.55$

$$\mu = np = 9(0.55) = 4.95$$

The expected number of alarms that would detect a burglar is about 5.

21. (a) Japan: $n = 7, p = 0.95$

$$P(7) = 0.698$$

United States: $n = 7, p = 0.60$

$$P(7) = 0.028$$

(b) Japan: $n = 7, p = 0.95$

$$\mu = np = 7(0.95) = 6.65$$

$$\sigma = \sqrt{npq} = \sqrt{7(0.95)(0.05)} \approx 0.58$$

United States: $n = 7, p = 0.60$

$$\mu = np = 7(0.60) = 4.2$$

$$\sigma = \sqrt{npq} = \sqrt{7(0.60)(0.40)} \approx 1.30$$

The expected number of verdicts in Japan is 6.65 and in the United States is 4.2.

(c) United States: $p = 0.60$

Find n such that

$$P(r \geq 2) = 0.99.$$

Try $n = 8$.

$$\begin{aligned} P(r \geq 2) &= 1 - [P(0) + P(1)] \\ &= 1 - (0.001 + 0.008) \\ &= 0.991 \end{aligned}$$

Japan: $p = 0.95$

Find n such that

$$P(r \geq 2) = 0.99.$$

Try $n = 3$.

$$\begin{aligned} P(r \geq 2) &= P(2) + P(3) \\ &= 0.135 + 0.857 \\ &= 0.992 \end{aligned}$$

Cover 8 trials in the U.S. and 3 trials in Japan.

22. $n = 6,\ p = 0.45$

(a) $P(6) = 0.008$

(b) $P(0) = 0.028$

(c) $$\begin{aligned} P(r \geq 2) &= P(2) + P(3) + P(4) + P(5) + P(6) \\ &= 0.278 + 0.303 + 0.186 + 0.061 + 0.008 \\ &= 0.836 \end{aligned}$$

(d) $\mu = np = 6(0.45) = 2.7$

The expected number is 2.7.

$$\sigma = \sqrt{npq} = \sqrt{6(0.45)(0.55)} \approx 1.219$$

(e) Find n such that

$$P(r \geq 3) = 0.90.$$

Try $n = 10$.

$$\begin{aligned} P(r \geq 3) &= 1 - [P(0) + P(1) + P(2)] \\ &= 1 - (0.003 + 0.021 + 0.076) \\ &= 1 - 0.100 \\ &= 0.900 \end{aligned}$$

You need to interview 10 professors to be at least 90% sure of filling the quota.

23. (a) $p = 0.40$

Find n such that

$$P(r \ge 1) = 0.99.$$

Try $n = 9$.

$$\begin{aligned} P(r \ge 1) &= 1 - P(0) \\ &= 1 - 0.010 \\ &= 0.990 \end{aligned}$$

The owner must answer 9 inquiries to be 99% sure of renting at least one room.

(b) $n = 25, p = 0.40$

$\mu = np = 25(0.40) = 10$

The expected number is 10 room rentals.

Section 5.4

1. (a) Geometric probability distribution, $p = 0.77$.

$$P(n) = p(1-p)^{n-1}$$
$$P(n) = (0.77)(0.23)^{n-1}$$

(b) $$\begin{aligned} P(1) &= (0.77)(0.23)^{1-1} \\ &= (0.77)(0.23)^0 \\ &= 0.77 \end{aligned}$$

(c) $$\begin{aligned} P(2) &= (0.77)(0.23)^{2-1} \\ &= (0.77)(0.23)^1 \\ &= 0.1771 \end{aligned}$$

(d) $$\begin{aligned} P(3 \text{ or more tries}) &= 1 - P(1) - P(2) \\ &= 1 - 0.77 - 0.1771 \\ &= 0.0529 \end{aligned}$$

(e) $\mu = \frac{1}{p} = \frac{1}{0.77} \approx 1.29$

The expected number is 1 attempt.

2. (a) Geometric probability distribution, $p = 0.57$.

$$P(n) = p(1-p)^{n-1}$$
$$P(n) = (0.57)(0.43)^{n-1}$$

(b) $$\begin{aligned} P(2) &= (0.57)(0.43)^{2-1} \\ &= (0.57)(0.43)^1 \\ &= 0.2451 \end{aligned}$$

(c) $P(3) = (0.57)(0.43)^{3-1}$
$= (0.57)(0.43)^2$
≈ 0.1054

(d) $P(\text{more than 3 attempts}) = 1 - P(1) - P(2) - P(3)$
$= 1 - 0.57 - 0.2451 - 0.1054$
$= 0.0795$

(e) $\mu = \frac{1}{p} = \frac{1}{0.57} \approx 1.75$
The expected number is 2 attempts.

3. (a) Geometric probability distribution, $p = 0.05$.
$P(n) = p(1-p)^{n-1}$
$P(n) = (0.05)(0.95)^{n-1}$

(b) $P(5) = (0.05)(0.95)^{5-1}$
$= (0.05)(0.95)^4$
≈ 0.0407

(c) $P(10) = (0.05)(0.95)^{10-1}$
$= (0.05)(0.95)^9$
≈ 0.0315

(d) $P(\text{more than } 3) = 1 - P(1) - P(2) - P(3)$
$= 1 - 0.05 - (0.05)(0.95) - (0.05)(0.95)^2$
$= 1 - 0.05 - 0.0475 - 0.0451$
$= 0.8574$

(e) $\mu = \frac{1}{p} = \frac{1}{0.05} \approx 20$
The expected number is 20 pot shards.

4. (a) Geometric probability distribution, $p = 0.80$.
$P(n) = p(1-p)^{n-1}$
$P(n) = (0.80)(0.20)^{n-1}$

(b) $P(1) = (0.80)(0.20)^{1-1} = 0.80$
$P(2) = (0.80)(0.20)^{2-1} = 0.16$
$P(3) = (0.80)(0.20)^{3-1} = 0.032$

(c) $P(n \geq 4) = 1 - P(1) - P(2) - P(3)$
$= 1 - 0.80 - 0.16 - 0.032$
$= 0.008$

(d) $P(n)=(0.04)(0.96)^{n-1}$

$P(1)=(0.04)(0.96)^{1-1}=0.04$

$P(2)=(0.04)(0.96)^{2-1}=0.0384$

$P(3)=(0.04)(0.96)^{3-1}=0.0369$

$$\begin{aligned}P(n\geq 4)&=1-P(1)-P(2)-P(3)\\&=1-0.04-0.0384-0.0369\\&=0.8847\end{aligned}$$

5. (a) Geometric probability distribution, $p=0.71$.

$P(n)=p(1-p)^{n-1}$

$P(n)=(0.71)(0.29)^{n-1}$

(b) $P(1)=(0.71)(0.29)^{1-1}=0.71$

$P(2)=(0.71)(0.29)^{2-1}=0.2059$

$$\begin{aligned}P(n\geq 3)&=1-P(1)-P(2)\\&=1-0.71-0.2059\\&=0.0841\end{aligned}$$

(c) $P(n)=(0.83)(0.17)^{n-1}$

$P(1)=(0.83)(0.17)^{1-1}=0.83$

$P(2)=(0.83)(0.17)^{2-1}=0.1411$

$$\begin{aligned}P(n\geq 3)&=1-P(1)-P(2)\\&=1-0.83-0.1411\\&=0.0289\end{aligned}$$

6. (a) Geometric probability distribution, $p=0.36$.

$P(n)=p(1-p)^{n-1}$

$P(n)=(0.036)(0.964)^{n-1}$

(b) $P(3)=(0.036)(0.964)^{3-1}\approx 0.03345$

$P(5)=(0.036)(0.964)^{5-1}\approx 0.0311$

$P(12)=(0.036)(0.964)^{12-1}\approx 0.0241$

(c)
$$\begin{aligned}P(n\geq 5)&=1-P(1)-P(2)-P(3)-P(4)\\&=1-0.036-(0.036)(0.964)-(0.036)(0.964)^2-(0.036)(0.964)^3\\&=1-0.036-0.0347-0.03345-0.03225\\&=0.8636\end{aligned}$$

(d) $\mu = \frac{1}{p} = \frac{1}{0.036} \approx 27.8$

The expected number is 28 apples.

7. (a) Geometric probability distribution, $p = 0.30$.

$$P(n) = p(1-p)^{n-1}$$

$$P(n) = (0.30)(0.70)^{n-1}$$

(b) $P(3) = (0.30)(0.70)^{3-1} = 0.147$

(c)
$$\begin{aligned} P(n>3) &= 1 - P(1) - P(2) - P(3) \\ &= 1 - 0.30 - (0.30)(0.70) - 0.147 \\ &= 1 - 0.30 - 0.21 - 0.147 \\ &= 0.343 \end{aligned}$$

(d) $\mu = \frac{1}{p} = \frac{1}{0.30} = 3.33$

The expected number is 3 trips.

8. (a) The Poisson distribution would be a good choice because finding prehistoric artifacts is a relatively rare occurrence. It is reasonable to assume that the events are independent and the variable is the number of artifacts found in a fixed amount of sediment.

$$\lambda = \frac{1.5}{10\text{ L}} \cdot \frac{5}{5} = \frac{7.5}{50\text{ L}}; \ \lambda = 7.5 \text{ per 50 liters}$$

$$P(r) = \frac{e^{-\lambda}\lambda^r}{r!}$$

$$P(r) = \frac{e^{-7.5}(7.5)^r}{r!}$$

(b) $P(2) = \frac{e^{-7.5}(7.5)^2}{2!} \approx 0.0156$

$$P(3) = \frac{e^{-7.5}(7.5)^3}{3!} \approx 0.0389$$

$$P(4) = \frac{e^{-7.5}(7.5)^4}{4!} \approx 0.0729$$

(c)
$$\begin{aligned} P(r \geq 3) &= 1 - P(0) - P(1) - P(2) \\ &= 1 - 0.0006 - 0.0041 - 0.0156 \\ &= 0.9797 \end{aligned}$$

(d) $P(r<3)=P(0)+P(1)+P(2)$
$=0.0006+0.0041+0.0156$
$=0.0203$

or

$P(r<3)=1-P(r\geq 3)$
$=1-0.9797$
$=0.0203$

9. (a) The Poisson distribution would be a good choice because frequency of grooming is a relatively rare occurrence. It is reasonable to assume that the events are independent and the variable is the number of times that one otter grooms another in a fixed time interval.

$$\lambda=\frac{1.7}{10\text{ min}}\cdot\frac{3}{3}=\frac{5.1}{30\text{ min}};\ \lambda=5.1\text{ per }30\text{ min interval}$$

$$P(r)=\frac{e^{-\lambda}\lambda^r}{r!}$$

$$P(r)=\frac{e^{-5.1}(5.1)^r}{r!}$$

(b) $P(4)=\dfrac{e^{-5.1}(5.1)^4}{4!}\approx 0.1719$

$P(5)=\dfrac{e^{-5.1}(5.1)^5}{5!}\approx 0.1753$

$P(6)=\dfrac{e^{-5.1}(5.1)^6}{6!}\approx 0.1490$

(c) $P(r\geq 4)=1-P(0)-P(1)-P(2)-P(3)$
$=1-0.0061-0.0311-0.0793-0.1348$
$=0.7487$

(d) $P(r<4)=P(0)+P(1)+P(2)+P(3)$
$=0.0061-0.0311-0.0793+0.1348$
$=0.2513$

or

$P(r<4)=1-P(r\geq 4)$
$=1-0.7487$
$=0.2513$

10. (a) The Poisson distribution would be a good choice because frequency of shoplifting is a relatively rare occurrence. It is reasonable to assume that the events are independent and the variable is the number of incidents in a fixed time interval.

$$\lambda=\frac{1}{3\text{ hr}}\cdot\frac{\frac{11}{3}}{\frac{11}{3}}=\frac{\frac{11}{3}}{11\text{ hr}};\ \lambda=\frac{11}{3}\approx 3.7\text{ per 11 hours (rounded to nearest tenth)}$$

(b) $P(r \geq 1) = 1 - P(0)$
$= 1 - 0.0247$
$= 0.9753$

(c) $P(r \geq 3) = 1 - P(0) - P(1) - P(2)$
$= 1 - 0.0247 - 0.0915 - 0.1692$
$= 0.7146$

(d) $P(0) = 0.0247$

11. (a) Essay. Answer could include:

The Poisson distribution would be a good choice because frequency of births is a relatively rare occurrence. It is reasonable to assume that the events are independent and the variable is the number of births (or deaths) for a community of a given population size.

(b) For 1000 people, $\lambda = 16$ births; $\lambda = 8$ deaths

By Table 4 in Appendix II:

$$P(10 \text{ births}) = 0.0341$$
$$P(10 \text{ deaths}) = 0.0993$$
$$P(16 \text{ births}) = 0.0992$$
$$P(16 \text{ deaths}) = 0.0045$$

(c) For 1500 people,

$$\lambda = \frac{16}{1000} \cdot \frac{1.5}{1.5} = \frac{24}{1500}; \ \lambda = 24 \text{ births per 1500 people}$$
$$\lambda = \frac{8}{1000} \cdot \frac{1.5}{1.5} = \frac{12}{1500}; \ \lambda = 12 \text{ deaths per 1500 people}$$

By Table 4 or a calculator:

$$P(10 \text{ births}) = 0.00066$$
$$P(10 \text{ deaths}) = 0.1048$$
$$P(16 \text{ births}) = 0.02186$$
$$P(16 \text{ deaths}) = 0.0543$$

(d) For 750 people,

$$\lambda = \frac{16}{1000} \cdot \frac{0.75}{0.75} = \frac{12}{750}; \ \lambda = 12 \text{ births per 750 people}$$
$$\lambda = \frac{8}{1000} \cdot \frac{0.75}{0.75} = \frac{6}{750}; \ \lambda = 6 \text{ deaths per 750 people}$$

$$P(10 \text{ births}) = 0.1048$$
$$P(10 \text{ deaths}) = 0.0413$$
$$P(16 \text{ births}) = 0.0543$$
$$P(16 \text{ deaths}) = 0.0003$$

12. (a) Essay. Answer could include:

The Poisson distribution would be a good choice because frequency of hairline cracks is a relatively rare occurrence. It is reasonable to assume that the events are independent and the variable is the number of hairline cracks for a given length of retaining wall.

(b) $\lambda = \frac{4.2}{30 \text{ ft}} \cdot \frac{\frac{5}{3}}{\frac{5}{3}} = \frac{7}{50 \text{ ft}};$

$\lambda = 7$ per 50 ft

From Table 4 in Appendix II:

$$P(3) = 0.0521$$

$$\begin{aligned} P(r \geq 3) &= 1 - P(0) - P(1) - P(2) \\ &= 1 - 0.0009 - 0.0064 - 0.0223 \\ &= 0.9704 \end{aligned}$$

(c) $\lambda = \frac{4.2}{30 \text{ ft}} \cdot \frac{\frac{2}{3}}{\frac{2}{3}} = \frac{2.8}{20 \text{ ft}};$

$\lambda = 2.8$ per 20 ft

$$P(3) = 0.2225$$

$$\begin{aligned} P(r \geq 3) &= 1 - P(0) - P(1) - P(2) \\ &= 1 - 0.0608 - 0.1703 - 0.2384 \\ &= 0.5305 \end{aligned}$$

(d) $\lambda = \frac{4.2}{30 \text{ ft}} \cdot \frac{\frac{1}{15}}{\frac{1}{15}} = \frac{0.28}{2 \text{ ft}};$

$\lambda = 0.3$ per 2 ft

$$P(3) = 0.0033$$

$$\begin{aligned} P(r \geq 3) &= 1 - P(0) - P(1) - P(2) \\ &= 1 - 0.7408 - 0.2222 - 0.0333 \\ &= 0.0037 \end{aligned}$$

(e) Discussion

13. (a) Essay. Answer could include:

The Poisson distribution would be a good choice because frequency of gale-force winds is a relatively rare occurrence. It is reasonable to assume that the events are independent and the variable is the number of gale-force winds in a given time interval.

(b) $\lambda = \frac{1}{60 \text{ hr}} \cdot \frac{1.8}{1.8} = \frac{1.8}{108 \text{ hours}}$;

$\lambda = 1.8$ per 108 hours

From Table 4 in Appendix II:

$$P(2) = 0.2678$$
$$P(3) = 0.1607$$
$$P(4) = 0.0723$$
$$P(r < 2) = P(0) + P(1) = 0.1653 + 0.2975 = 0.4628$$

(c) $\lambda = \frac{1}{60 \text{ hr}} \cdot \frac{3}{3} = \frac{3}{180 \text{ hours}}$;

$\lambda = 3$ per 180 hours

$$P(3) = 0.2240$$
$$P(4) = 0.1680$$
$$P(5) = 0.1008$$
$$P(r < 2) = P(0) + P(1) + P(2) = 0.0498 + 0.1494 + 0.2240 = 0.4232$$

14. (a) Essay. Answer could include:

The Poisson distribution would be a good choice because frequency of earthquakes is a relatively rare occurrence. It is reasonable to assume that the events are independent and the variable is the number of earthquakes in a given time interval.

(b) $\lambda = 1.00$ per 22 years

$P(r \geq 1) = 0.6321$

(c) $\lambda = 1.00$ per 22 years

$P(0) = 0.3679$

(d) $\lambda = \frac{1}{22 \text{ years}} \cdot \frac{\frac{25}{11}}{\frac{25}{11}} \approx \frac{2.27}{50 \text{ years}}$;

$\lambda = 2.27$ per 50 years

$P(r \geq 1) = 0.8967$

(e) $\lambda = 2.27$ per 50 years

$P(0) = 0.1033$

15. (a) Essay. Answer could include:

The Poisson distribution would be a good choice because frequency of commercial building sales is a relatively rare occurrence. It is reasonable to assume that the events are independent and the variable is the number of buildings sold in a given time interval.

(b) $\lambda = \dfrac{8}{275 \text{ days}} \cdot \dfrac{\frac{12}{55}}{\frac{12}{55}} \approx \dfrac{\frac{96}{55}}{60 \text{ days}}$;

$\lambda = \dfrac{96}{55} \approx 1.7$ per 60 days

From Table 4 in Appendix II:

$$P(0) = 0.1827$$
$$P(1) = 0.3106$$
$$P(r \geq 2) = 1 - P(0) - P(1)$$
$$= 1 - 0.1827 - 0.3106$$
$$= 0.5067$$

(c) $\lambda = \dfrac{8}{275 \text{ days}} \cdot \dfrac{\frac{18}{55}}{\frac{18}{55}} \approx \dfrac{2.6}{90 \text{ days}}$;

$\lambda \approx 2.6$ per 90 days

$$P(0) = 0.0743$$
$$P(2) = 0.2510$$
$$P(r \geq 3) = 1 - P(0) - P(1) - P(2)$$
$$= 1 - 0.0743 - 0.1931 - 0.2510$$
$$= 0.4816$$

16. (a) Essay. Answer could include:

The problem satisfies the conditions for a binomial experiment with

n large, $n = 316$, and p small, $p = \frac{661}{100{,}000} = 0.00661$.

$np = 316(0.00661) \approx 2.1 < 10$.

The Poisson distribution would be a good approximation to the binomial.

$n = 316$, $p = 0.00661$, $\lambda = np \approx 2.1$

(b) From Table 4 in Appendix II,

$$P(0) = 0.1225$$

(c) $P(r \leq 1) = P(0) + P(1)$

$$= 0.1225 + 0.2572$$
$$= 0.3797$$

(d) $P(r \geq 2) = 1 - P(r \leq 1)$

$$= 1 - 0.3797$$
$$= 0.6203$$

17. **(a)** Essay. Answer could include:

The problem satisfies the conditions for a binomial experiment with

$$n \text{ large, } n = 1000, \text{ and } p \text{ small, } p = \frac{1}{569} \approx 0.0018.$$
$$np \approx 1000(0.0018) = 1.8 < 10.$$

The Poisson distribution would be a good approximation to the binomial.

$$\lambda = np \approx 1.8$$

(b) From Table 4 in Appendix II,

$$P(0) = 0.1653$$

(c) $$\begin{aligned} P(r > 1) &= 1 - P(0) - P(1) \\ &= 1 - 0.1653 - 0.2975 \\ &= 0.5372 \end{aligned}$$

(d) $$\begin{aligned} P(r > 2) &= P(r > 1) - P(2) \\ &= 0.5372 - 0.2678 \\ &= 0.2694 \end{aligned}$$

(e) $$\begin{aligned} P(r > 3) &= P(r > 2) - P(3) \\ &= 0.2694 - 0.1607 \\ &= 0.1087 \end{aligned}$$

18. **(a)** Essay. Answer could include:

The Poisson distribution would be a good choice because frequency of lost bags is a relatively rare occurrence. It is reasonable to assume that the events are independent and the variable is the number of bags lost per 1000 passengers.

$\lambda = 6.02$ or 6.0 per 1000 passengers

(b) From Table 4 in Appendix II:

$$P(0) = 0.0025$$
$$\begin{aligned} P(r \geq 3) &= 1 - P(0) - P(1) - P(2) \\ &= 1 - 0.0025 - 0.0149 - 0.0446 \\ &= 0.9380 \end{aligned}$$
$$\begin{aligned} P(r \geq 6) &= P(r \geq 3) - P(3) - P(4) - P(5) \\ &= 0.9380 - 0.0892 - 0.1339 - 0.1606 \\ &= 0.5543 \end{aligned}$$

(c) $\lambda = 13.0$ per 1000 passengers

$$P(0) = 0.000 \text{ (to 3 digits)}$$
$$\begin{aligned} P(r \geq 6) &= 1 - P(r \leq 5) \\ &= 1 - 0.0107 \\ &= 0.9893 \end{aligned}$$
$$\begin{aligned} P(r \geq 12) &= 1 - P(r \leq 11) \\ &= 1 - 0.3532 \\ &= 0.6468 \end{aligned}$$

19. (a) Essay. Answer could include:

The problem satisfies the conditions for a binomial experiment with n large, $n = 175$, and p small, $p = 0.005$. $np = (175)(0.005) = 0.875 < 10$. The Poisson distribution would be a good approximation to the binomial. $n = 175, p = 0.005, \lambda = np = 0.9$.

(b) From Table 4 in Appendix II,

$$P(0) = 0.4066$$

(c) $P(r \geq 1) = 1 - P(0)$

$$= 1 - 0.4066$$
$$= 0.5934$$

(d) $P(r \geq 2) = P(r \geq 1) - P(1)$

$$= 0.5934 - 0.3659$$
$$= 0.2275$$

20. (a) Essay. Answer could include:

The problem satisfies the conditions for a binomial experiment with n large, $n = 137$, and p small, $p = 0.02$. $np = (137)(0.02) = 2.74 < 10$. The Poisson distribution would be a good approximation to the binomial. $n = 175, p = 0.02, \lambda = np = 2.74 \approx 2.7$.

(b) From Table 4 in Appendix II,

$$P(0) = 0.0672$$

(c) $P(r \geq 2) = 1 - P(0) - P(1)$

$$= 1 - 0.0672 - 0.1815$$
$$= 0.7513$$

(d) $P(r \geq 4) = P(r \geq 2) - P(2) - P(3)$

$$= 0.7513 - 0.2450 - 0.2205$$
$$= 0.2858$$

21. (a) $n = 100, p = 0.02, r = 2$

$$P(r) = C_{n,r} p^r (1-p)^{n-r}$$
$$P(2) = C_{100,2} (0.02)^2 (0.98)^{100-2}$$
$$= 4950(0.0004)(0.1381)$$
$$= 0.2734$$

(b) $\lambda = np = 100(0.02) = 2$

From Table 4 in Appendix II,

$$P(2) = 0.2707$$

(c) The approximation is correct to two decimal places.

(d) $n = 100; p = 0.02; r = 3$

By the formula for the binomial distribution,

$$\begin{aligned} P(3) &= C_{100,3}(0.02)^3(0.98)^{100-3} \\ &= 161{,}700(0.000008)(0.1409) \\ &= 0.1823 \end{aligned}$$

By the Poisson approximation, $\lambda = 3$, $P(3) = 0.1804$. The approximation is correct to two decimal places.

Chapter 5 Review

1. (a)
$$\begin{aligned} \mu &= \Sigma xP(x) \\ &= 18.5(0.127) + 30.5(0.371) + 42.5(0.285) + 54.5(0.215) + 66.5(0.002) \\ &= 37.628 \\ &\approx 37.63 \end{aligned}$$

The expected lease term is about 38 months.

$$\begin{aligned} \sigma &= \sqrt{\Sigma(x-\mu)^2 P(x)} \\ &= \sqrt{(-19.13)^2(0.127) + (-7.13)^2(0.371) + (4.87)^2(0.285) + (16.87)^2(0.215) + (28.87)^2(0.002)} \\ &\approx \sqrt{134.95} \\ &\approx 11.6 \text{ (using } \mu = 37.63 \text{ in the calculations)} \end{aligned}$$

(b) Leases in Months

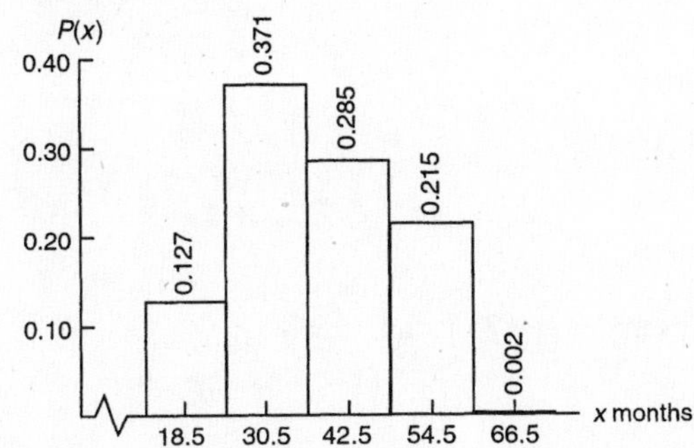

2. (a)

Number killed by Wolves	Relative Frequency	$P(x)$
112	112/296	0.378
53	53/296	0.179
73	73/296	0.247
56	56/296	0.189
2	2/296	0.007

(b) $\mu = \sum xP(x)$

$= 0.5(0.378) + 3(0.179) + 8(0.247) + 13(0.189) + 18(0.007)$

≈ 5.28 yr

$\sigma = \sqrt{\sum (x-\mu)^2 P(x)}$

$= \sqrt{(-4.78)^2 (0.378) + (-2.28)^2 (0.179) + (2.72)^2 (0.247) + (7.72)^2 (0.189) + (12.72)^2 (0.007)}$

$= \sqrt{23.8}$

≈ 4.88 yr

3. This is a binomial experiment with 10 trials. A trial consists of a claim.

Success = submitted by a male under 25 years of age.
Failure = not submitted by a male under 25 years of age.

(a) The probabilities can be taken directly from Table 3 in Appendix II, $n = 10, p = 0.55$.

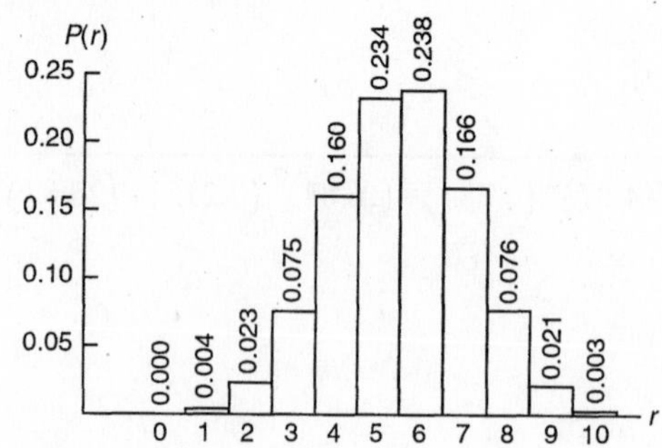

(b) $P(r \geq 6) = P(6) + P(7) + P(8) + P(9) + P(10)$

$= 0.238 + 0.166 + 0.076 + 0.021 + 0.003$

$= 0.504$

(c) $\mu = np = 10(0.55) = 5.5$

The expected number of claims made by males under age 25 is 5.5.

$\sigma = \sqrt{npq} = \sqrt{10(0.55)(0.45)} \approx 1.57$

4. (a) $n = 20, p = 0.05$

$P(r \leq 2) = P(0) + P(1) + P(2)$

$= 0.358 + 0.377 + 0.189$

$= 0.924$

(b) $n = 20, p = 0.15$

Probability accepted:

$$P(r \le 2) = P(0) + P(1) + P(2)$$
$$= 0.039 + 0.137 + 0.229$$
$$= 0.405$$

Probability not accepted:

$$1 - 0.405 = 0.595$$

5. $n = 16, p = 0.50$

(a) $P(r \ge 12) = P(12) + P(13) + P(14) + P(15) + P(16)$
$$= 0.028 + 0.009 + 0.002 + 0.000 + 0.000$$
$$= 0.039$$

(b) $P(r \le 7) = P(0) + P(1) + P(2) + P(3) + P(4) + P(5) + P(6) + P(7)$
$$= 0.000 + 0.000 + 0.002 + 0.009 + 0.028 + 0.067 + 0.122 + 0.175$$
$$= 0.403$$

(c) $\mu = np = 16(0.50) = 8$

The expected number of inmates serving time for drug dealing is 8.

6. $n = 200, p = 0.80$

$$\mu = np = 200(0.80) = 160$$

The expected number that will arrive on time is 160 flights.

$$\sigma = \sqrt{npq} = \sqrt{200(0.80)(0.20)} \approx 5.66$$

The standard deviation is 5.66 flights.

7. $n = 10, p = 0.75$

(a) The probabilities can be obtained directed from Table 3 in Appendix II.

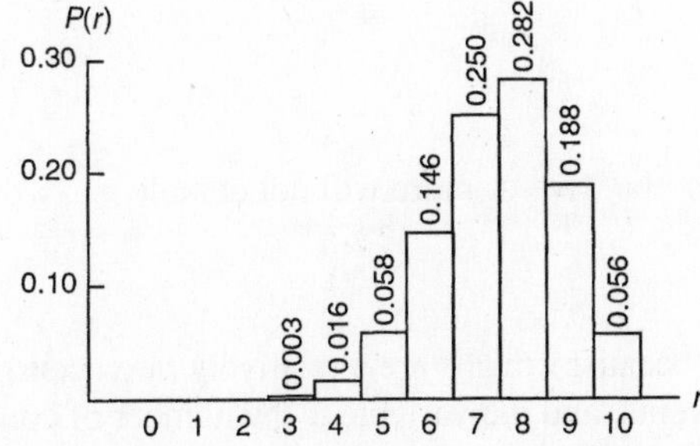

(b) No more than one bad is the same as at least nine good.

$$P(r \geq 9) = P(9) + P(10)$$
$$= 0.188 + 0.056$$
$$= 0.244$$

$$P(r \geq 1) = P(1) + P(2) + P(3) + P(4) + P(5) + P(6) + P(7) + P(8) + P(9) + P(10)$$
$$= 0.000 + 0.000 + 0.003 + 0.016 + 0.058 + 0.146 + 0.250 + 0.282 + 0.188 + 0.056$$
$$= 0.999$$

(c) $\mu = np = 10(0.75) = 7.5$

The expected number of good grapefruit in a sack is 7.5.

(d) $\sigma = \sqrt{npq} = \sqrt{10(0.75)(0.25)} \approx 1.37$

8. Let success = show up, then $p = 0.95$, $n = 82$.

$$\mu = np = 82(0.95) = 77.9$$

If 82 party reservations have been made, 77.9 or about 78 can be expected to show up.

$$\sigma = \sqrt{npq} = \sqrt{82(0.95)(0.05)} \approx 1.97$$

9. $p = 0.85$, $n = 12$

$$P(r \leq 2) = P(0) + P(1) + P(2)$$
$$= 0.000 + 0.000 + 0.000$$
$$= 0.000 \quad \text{(to 3 digits)}$$

The data seem to indicate that the percent favoring the increase in fees is less than 85%.

10. Let success = do not default, then $p = 0.50$.

Find n such that

$$P(r \geq 5) = 0.941.$$

Try $n = 15$.

$$P(r \geq 5) = 1 - [P(0) + P(1) + P(2) + P(3) + P(4)]$$
$$= 1 - (0.000 + 0.000 + 0.003 + 0.014 + 0.042)$$
$$= 1 - 0.059$$
$$= 0.941$$

You should buy 15 bonds if you want to be 94.1% sure that five or more will not default.

11. (a) Essay. Answer could include:

The Poisson distribution would be a good choice because coughs are a relatively rare occurrence. It is reasonable to assume that they are independent events, and the variable is the number of coughs in a fixed time interval.

(b) $\lambda = 11$ per 1 minute

From Table 4 in Appendix II,

$$P(r \le 3) = P(0) + P(1) + P(2) + P(3)$$
$$= 0.0000 + 0.0002 + 0.0010 + 0.0037$$
$$= 0.0049$$

(c) $\lambda = \frac{11}{60 \text{ sec}} \cdot \frac{0.5}{0.5} = \frac{5.5}{30 \text{ sec}}$; $\lambda = 5.5$ per 30 sec.

$$P(r \ge 3) = 1 - P(0) - P(1) - P(2)$$
$$= 1 - 0.0041 - 0.0225 - 0.0618$$
$$= 0.9116$$

12. (a) Essay. Answer could include:

The Poisson distribution would be a good choice because number of accidents is a relatively rare occurrence. It is reasonable to assume that they are independent events, and the variable is the number of accidents for a given number of operations.

(b) $\lambda = 2.4$ per 100,000 flight operations

From Table 4 in Appendix II,

$$P(0) = 0.0907$$

(c) $\lambda = \frac{2.4}{100{,}000} \cdot \frac{2}{2} = \frac{4.8}{200{,}000}$;

$\lambda = 4.8$ per 200,000 flight operations.

$$P(r \ge 4) = 1 - P(0) - P(1) - P(2) - P(3)$$
$$= 1 - 0.0082 - 0.0395 - 0.0948 - 0.1517$$
$$= 0.7058$$

13. The loan-default problem satisfies the conditions for a binomial experiment. Moreover, p is small, n is large, and $np < 10$. Use of the Poisson approximation to the binomial distribution is appropriate.

$$n = 300,\ p = \frac{1}{350} = 0.0029,\ \lambda = np = 300(0.0029) \approx 0.86 \approx 0.9$$

From Table 4 in Appendix II,

$$P(r \ge 2) = 1 - P(0) - P(1)$$
$$= 1 - 0.4066 - 0.3659$$
$$= 0.2275$$

14. This problem satisfies the conditions for a binomial experiment. Moreover, p is small, n is large, and $np < 10$. Use of the Poisson approximation to the binomial distribution is appropriate.

$$n = 500{,}000,\ p = \frac{1}{5{,}000{,}000},\ \lambda = np = \frac{500{,}000}{5{,}000{,}000} = 0.1$$

From Table 4 in Appendix II,

$$P(0) = 0.9048$$
$$P(1) = 0.0905$$

15. (a) Use the geometric distribution with $p = 0.5$.

$$P(n=2)=(0.5)(0.5)=(0.5)^2=0.25$$

As long as you toss the coin at least twice, it does not matter how many more times you toss it. To get the first head on the second toss, you must get a tail on the first and a head on the second.

(b)

$$P(4)=(0.5)(0.5)^3=(0.5)^4=0.0625$$

$$\begin{aligned}P(n>4)&=1-P(1)-P(2)-P(3)-P(4)\\&=1-0.5-0.5^2-0.5^3-0.5^4\\&=0.0625\end{aligned}$$

16. (a) Use the geometric distribution with $p = 0.83$.

$$P(1)=(0.83)(0.17)^{1-1}=0.83$$

(b)

$$P(2)=(0.83)(0.17)^{2-1}=0.1411$$

$$P(3)=(0.83)(0.17)^{3-1}=0.0240$$

$$P(2\text{ or }3)=0.1411+0.0240\approx 0.165$$

Chapter 6 Normal Distributions

Section 6.1

1. **(a)** not normal; left skewed instead of symmetric

   (b) not normal; curve touches and goes below x-axis instead of always being above the x-axis and being asymptotic to the x-axis in the tails

   (c) not normal; not bell-shaped, not unimodal

   (d) not normal; not a smooth curve

2. $\mu = 16$, $\sigma = 2$, $\mu + \sigma = 16 + 2 = 18$
(The mean is located directly below the peak; one standard deviation from the mean is the x-value under the point of inflection [the transition point between the curve cupping upward and cupping downward].)

3. The mean is the x-value directly below the peak; in Figure 6-16, $\mu = 10$; in Figure 6-17, $\mu = 4$. Assuming the two figures are drawn on the same scale, Figure 6-16, being shorter and more spread out, has the larger standard deviation.

4. **(a)**

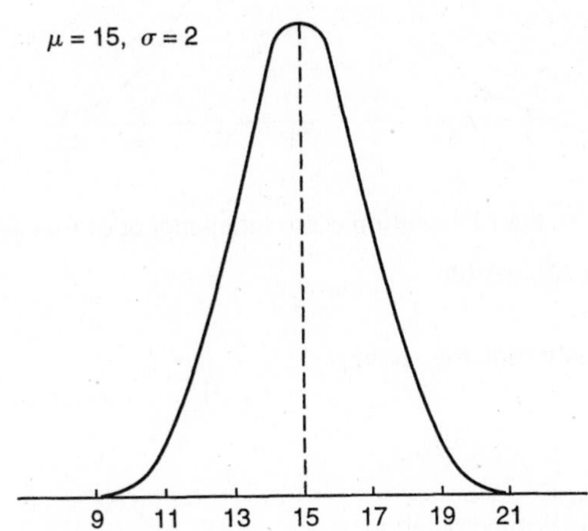

   (b)

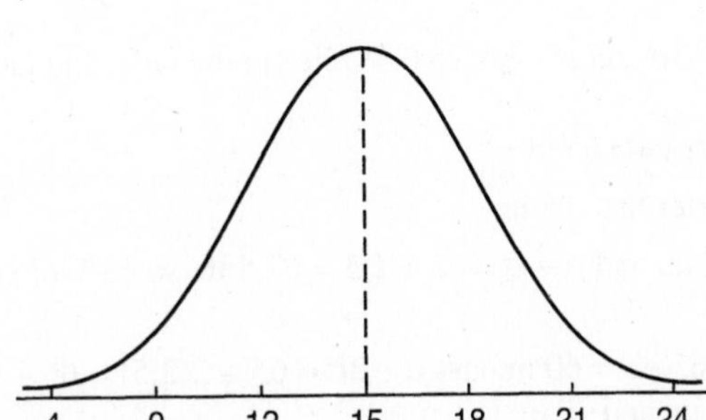

(c)

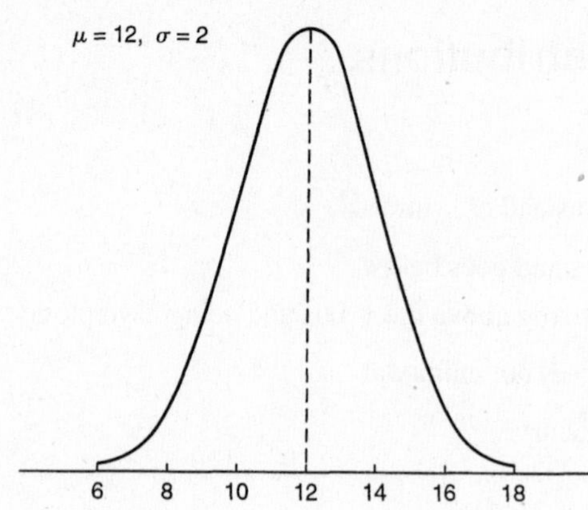

(d)

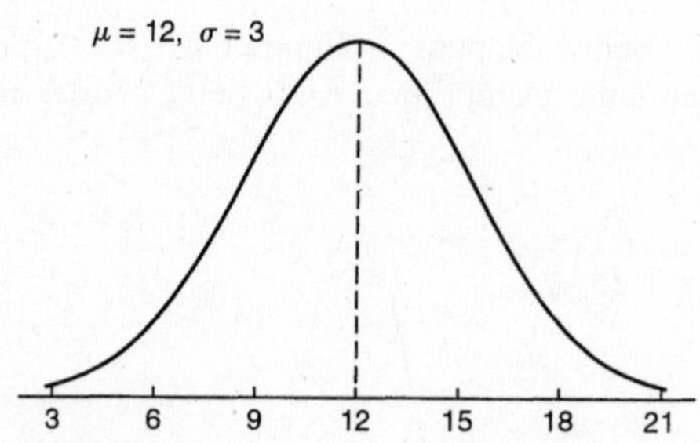

(e) No; the mean μ and the standard deviation σ are independent of one another. If $\mu_1 > \mu_2$, then $\sigma_1 > \sigma_2$, $\sigma_1 = \sigma_2$, and $\sigma_1 < \sigma_2$ are all possible.

5. (a) 50%; the normal curve is symmetric about μ

(b) 68%

(c) 99.7%

6. (a) 50%; the normal curve is symmetric about μ

(b) 95%

(c) $\frac{1}{2}(100\% - 99.7\%) = \frac{1}{2}(0.3\%) = 0.15\%$,

99.7% lies between $\mu - 3\sigma$ and $\mu + 3\sigma$, so 0.3% lies in the tails, and half of that is in the upper tail.

7. (a) $\mu = 65$, so 50% are taller than 65 in.

(b) $\mu = 65$, so 50% are shorter than 65 in.

(c) $\mu - \sigma = 65 - 2.5 = 62.5$ in. and $\mu + \sigma = 65 + 2.5 = 67.5$ in. so 68% of college women are between 62.5 in. and 67.5 in. tall.

(d) $\mu - 2\sigma = 65 - 2(2.5) = 65 - 5 = 60$ in. and $\mu - 2\sigma = 65 + 2(2.5) = 65 + 5 = 70$ in. so 95% of college women are between 60 in. and 70 in. tall.

8. (a) $\mu - 2\sigma = 21 - 2(1) = 19$ days and $\mu + 2\sigma = 21 + 2(1) = 23$ days so 95% of 1000 eggs, or 950 eggs will hatch between 19 and 23 days of incubation.

(b) $\mu - \sigma = 21 - 1 = 20$ days and $\mu + \sigma = 21 + 1 = 22$ days so 68% of 1000 eggs, or 680 eggs, will hatch between 20 and 22 days of incubation.

(c) $\mu = 21$, so 50%, or 500, of the eggs will hatch in at most 21 days.

(d) $\mu - 3\sigma = 21 - 3(1) = 21 - 3 = 18$ days and $\mu + 3\sigma = 21 + 3(1) = 21 + 3 = 24$ days so 99.7%, or 997, eggs will hatch between 18 and 24 days of incubation.

9. (a) $\mu - \sigma = 1243 - 36 = 1207$ and $\mu + \sigma = 1243 + 36 = 1279$ so about 68% of the tree rings will date between 1207 and 1279 AD.

(b) $\mu - 2\sigma = 1243 - 2(36) = 1171$ and $\mu + 2\sigma = 1243 + 2(36) = 1315$ so about 95% of the tree rings will date between 1171 and 1315 AD.

(c) $\mu - 3\sigma = 1243 - 3(36) = 1135$ and $\mu + 3\sigma = 1243 + 3(36) = 1351$ so 99.7% (almost all) of the tree rings will date between 1135 and 1351 AD.

10. (a) $\mu + \sigma = 7.6 + 0.4 = 8.0$

Since 68% of the cups filled will fall into the $\mu \pm \sigma$ range, 100% – 68% = 32% will fall outside that range and $\frac{32\%}{2} = 16\% = 0.16$ will be over $\mu + \sigma = 8$ oz. Approximately 16% of the time, the cups will overflow.

(b) 100% – 16% = 84% = 0.84 so, by the complementary event rule, 84% of the time the cups will not overflow.

(c) Since 16% of 850 = 136, we can expect approximately 136 of the cups filled by this machine will overflow.

11. (a) $\mu - \sigma = 3.15 - 1.45 = 1.70$ and $\mu + \sigma = 3.15 + 1.45 = 4.60$ so 68% of the experimental group will have millamperes pain thresholds between 1.70 and 4.60 mA.

(b) $\mu - 2\sigma = 3.15 - 2(1.45) = 0.25$ and $\mu + 2\sigma = 3.15 + 2(1.45) = 6.05$ so 95% of the experimental group will have pain thresholds between 0.25 and 6.05 mA.

12. (a)

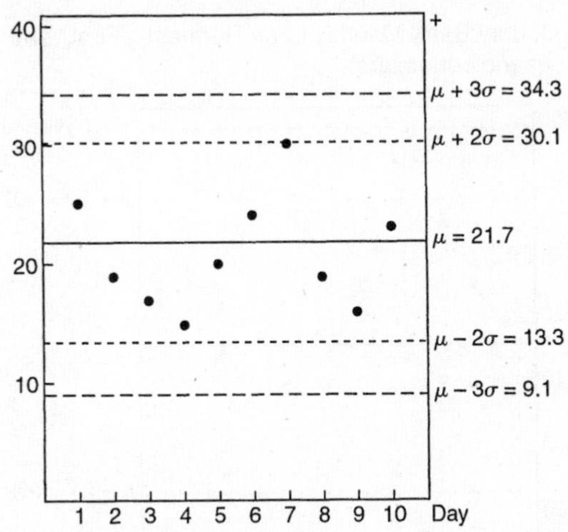

The data indicate the process is in control; none of the out-of-control warning signals are present.

(b)

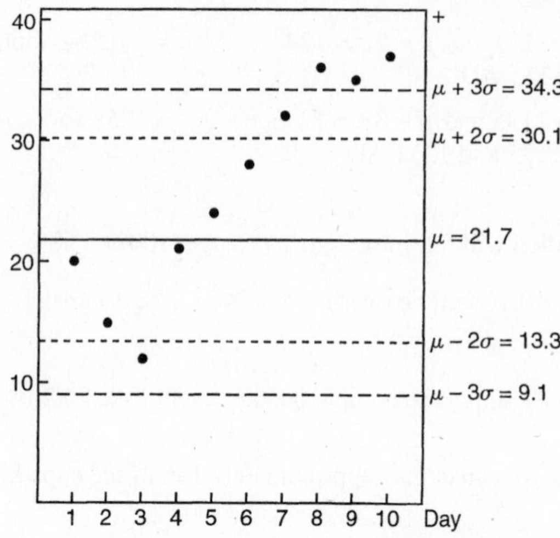

Three points fall beyond $\mu + 3\sigma = 34.3$. Four consecutive points lie beyond $\mu + 2\sigma = 30.1$. Out-of-control warning signals I and III are present; the data indicate the process is out-of-control. Under the conditions or time period (say, July 4) represented by the second 10-day period, YPMS probably needs (temporary) extra help to provide timely emergency health care for park visitors.

13. (a)

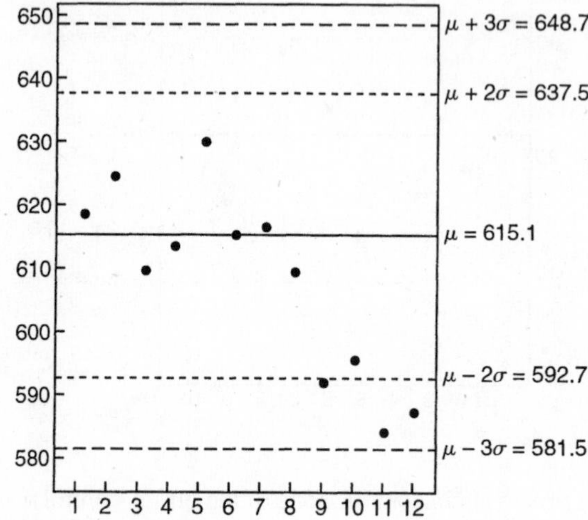

The economy would appear to be cooling off as evidenced by an overall downward trend. Out-of-control warning signal III is present: 2 of the last 3 consecutive points are below $\mu - 2\sigma = 592.7$.

(b)

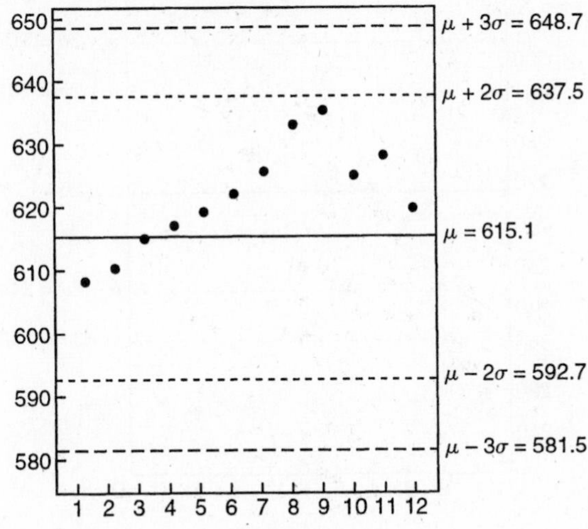

Here, it looks like the economy was heating up during months 1-9 and perhaps cooling off during months 10-12. Out-of-control warning signal II is present: there is a run of 9 consecutive points above $\mu = 615.1$.

14. (a)

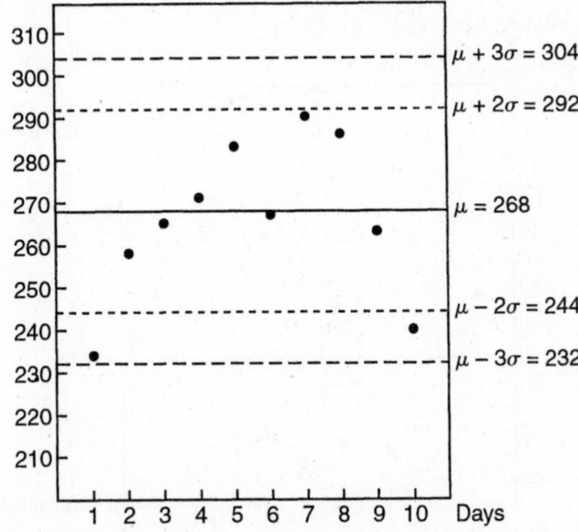

The room rentals are about what would be expected. None of the 3 out-of-control warning signals are present.

(b)

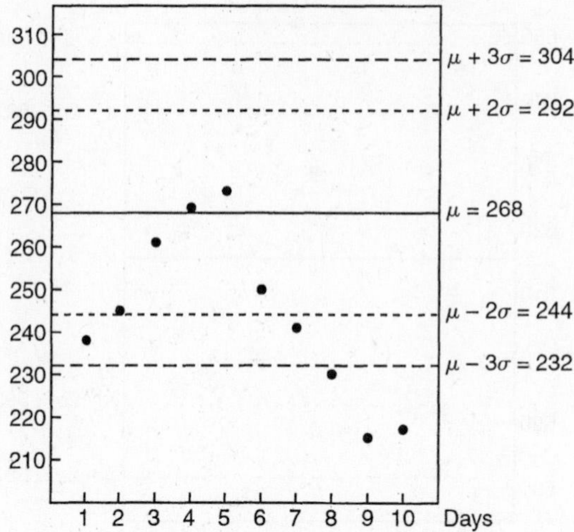

The room rentals are lower than what would be expected. Comparing (a) and (b), we see the same basic cyclical pattern (probably up on the weekends and down on the weekdays), but the pattern in (b) has been shifted down about $2\sigma = 24$ rooms rented. Out-of-control warning signals I and III are present: there are 3 points below $\mu - 3\sigma = 232$ rooms rented, and all 4 of the last 4 consecutive points are below $\mu - 2\sigma = 244$ rooms rented.

15.

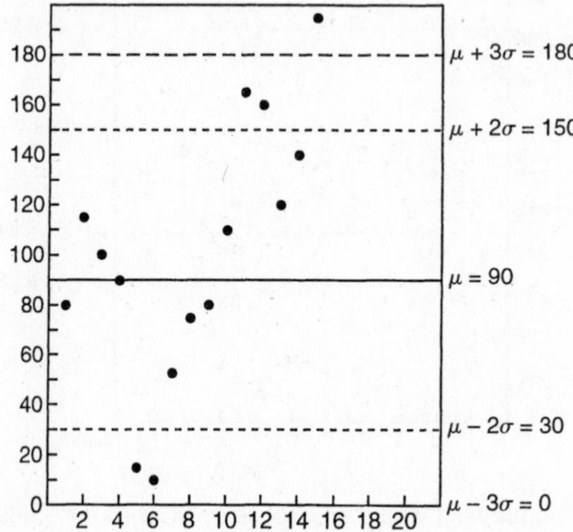

Out-of-control warning signals I and III are present. Day 15's VSI exceeds $\mu + 3\sigma$. Two of 3 consecutive points (days 10, 11, 12 or days 11, 12, 13) are about $\mu + 2\sigma = 150$, and 2 of 3 consecutive points (days 4, 5, 6 or days 5, 6, 7) are below $\mu - 2\sigma = 30$. Days 10-15 all show above average air pollution levels; days 11, 12, and 15 triggered out-of-control signals, indicating pollution abatement procedures should be in place.

Section 6.2

1. **(a)** z-scores > 0 indicate the student scored above the mean: Robert, Jane, and Linda

(b) z-scores = 0 indicates the student scored at the mean: Joel

(c) z-scores < 0 indicate the student scored below the mean: John and Susan

(d) $z = \frac{x-\mu}{\sigma}$ so $x = \mu + z\sigma$

In this case, if the student's score is x, $x = 150 + z(20)$.

Robert: $x = 150 + 1.10(20) = 172$

Joel: $x = 150 + 0(20) = 150$

Jan: $x = 150 + 1.70(20) = 184$

John: $x = 150 - 0.80(20) = 134$

Susan: $x = 150 - 2.00(20) = 110$

Linda: $x = 150 + 1.60(20) = 182$

2. Use $z = \frac{x-\mu}{\sigma}$. In this case, $z = \frac{x-0.51}{0.25}$ with x expressed as a decimal or $z = \frac{x-51\%}{25\%}$ with x expressed in percent.

(a) $z = \frac{0.45-0.51}{0.25} = -0.24$

(b) $z = \frac{0.72-0.51}{0.25} = 0.84$

(c) $z = \frac{0.75-0.51}{0.25} = 0.96$

(d) $z = \frac{65\%-51\%}{25\%} = 0.56$

(e) $z = \frac{33\%-51\%}{25\%} = -0.72$

(f) $z = \frac{55\%-51\%}{25\%} = 0.16$

3. Use $z = \frac{x-\mu}{\sigma}$. In this case, $z = \frac{x-73}{5}$.

(a) $53^\circ\text{F} < x < 93^\circ\text{F}$

$\frac{53-73}{5} < \frac{x-73}{5} < \frac{93-73}{5}$ Subtract $\mu = 73^\circ$F from each piece; divide result by $\sigma = 5^\circ$F.

$-\frac{20}{5} < z < \frac{20}{5}$

$-4.00 < z < 4.00$

(b) $x < 65^\circ\text{F}$

$x - 73 < 65 - 73$ Subtract $\mu = 73^\circ\text{F}$.

$\frac{x-73}{5} < \frac{65-73}{5}$ Divide both sides by $\sigma = 5^\circ\text{F}$.

$z < -1.6$

(c) $78^\circ\text{F} < x$

$\frac{78-73}{5} < \frac{x-73}{5}$ Subtract $\mu = 73^\circ\text{F}$ from each side; divide by $\sigma = 5^\circ\text{F}$.

$\frac{5}{5} < z$

$1.00 < z$ (or $z > 1.00$)

Since $z = \frac{x-73}{5}$, $x = 73 + 5z$.

(d) $1.75 < z$

$5(1.75) < 5z$ Multiply both sides by $\sigma = 5^\circ\text{F}$.

$73 + 5(1.75) < 73 + 5z$ Add $\mu = 73^\circ\text{F}$ to both sides.

$81.75^\circ\text{F} < x$ (or $x > 81.75$)

(e) $z < -1.90$

$5z < 5(-1.90)$ Multiply both sides by $\sigma = 5^\circ\text{F}$.

$73 + 5z < 73 + 5(-1.90)$ Add $\mu = 73^\circ\text{F}$ to both sides.

$x < 63.5^\circ\text{F}$

(f) $-1.80 < z < 1.65$

$5(-1.80) < 5z < 5(1.65)$ Multiply each part by $\sigma = 5^\circ\text{F}$.

$73 + 5(-1.80) < 73 + 5z < 73 + 5(1.65)$ Add $\mu = 73^\circ\text{F}$ to each part of the inequality.

$64^\circ\text{F} < x < 81.25^\circ\text{F}$

4. $z = \frac{x-\mu}{\sigma}$; here, $z = \frac{x-27.2}{4.3}$

(a) $x < 30$ kg

$x - 27.2 < 30 - 27.2$ Subtract $\mu = 27.2$ kg from each side.

$\frac{x-27.2}{4.3} < \frac{30-27.2}{4.3}$ Divide both sides by $\sigma = 4.3$ kg.

$z < 0.65$ (rounded to 2 decimal places)

(b) $19 \text{ kg} < x$

$19 - 27.2 < x - 27.2$ Subtract $\mu = 27.2$ kg from each side.

$\frac{19-27.2}{4.3} < \frac{x-27.2}{4.3}$ Divide both sides by $\sigma = 4.3$ kg.

$-1.91 < z$ (rounded)

(c) $32 \text{ kg} < x < 35 \text{ kg}$

$32 - 27.2 < x - 27.2 < 35 - 27.2$ Subtract $\mu = 27.2$ kg from each part.

$\frac{32-27.2}{4.3} < \frac{x-27.2}{4.3} < \frac{35-27.2}{4.3}$ Divide each part by $\sigma = 4.3$ kg.

$1.12 < z < 1.81$ (rounded)

Since $z = \frac{x-27.2}{4.3}$, $x = 27.2 + 4.3z$ kg.

(d) $-2.17 < z$

$(4.3)(-2.17) < 4.3z$ Multiply both sides by $\sigma = 4.3$ kg.

$27.2 + 4.3(-2.17) < 27.2 + 4.3z$ Add $\mu = 27.2$ kg to each side.

$17.9 \text{ kg} < x$, or $x > 17.9$ kg (rounded)

(e) $z < 1.28$

$4.3z < 4.3(1.28)$ Multiply both sides by $\sigma = 4.3$ kg.

$27.2 + 4.3z < 27.2 + 4.3(1.28)$ Add $\mu = 27.2$ kg to both sides.

$x < 32.7$ kg (rounded)

(f) $-1.99 < z < 1.44$

$4.3(-1.99) < 4.3z < 4.3(1.44)$ Multiply each part by $\sigma = 4.3$ kg.

$27.2 + 4.3(-1.99) < 27.2 + 4.3z < 27.2 + 4.3(1.44)$ Add $\mu = 27.2$ kg to each part.

$18.6 \text{ kg} < x < 33.4$ kg (rounded)

(g) 14 kg is an unusually low weight for a fawn

$$z = \frac{x - 27.2}{4.3} = \frac{14 - 27.2}{4.3} = -3.07 \text{ (rounded)}$$

(note $\mu = 27.2$ kg)

(h) An unusually large fawn would have a large positive z, such as 3.

5. $z = \dfrac{x - \mu}{\sigma}$, here $z = \dfrac{x - 4400}{620}$

(a) $3300 < x$

$3300 - 4400 < x - 4400$ Subtract $\mu = 4400$ deer.

$\dfrac{3300 - 4400}{620} < \dfrac{x - 4400}{620}$ Divide by $\sigma = 620$ deer.

$-1.77 < z$

(b) $x < 5400$

$x - 4400 < 5400 - 4400$ Subtract $\mu = 4400$ deer.

$\dfrac{x - 4400}{620} < \dfrac{5400 - 4400}{620}$ Divide by $\sigma = 620$ deer.

$z < 1.61$

(c) $3500 < x < 5300$

$3500 - 4400 < x - 4400 < 5300 - 4400$ Subtract $\mu = 4400$.

$\dfrac{3500 - 4400}{620} < \dfrac{x - 4400}{620} < \dfrac{5300 - 4400}{620}$ Divide by $\sigma = 620$.

$-1.45 < z < 1.45$

Since $z = \dfrac{x - 4400}{620}$, $x = 4400 + 620z$ deer.

(d) $-1.12 < z < 2.43$

$620(-1.12) < 620z < 620(2.43)$ Multiply by $\sigma = 620$.

$4400 + 620(-1.12) < 4400 + 620z < 4400 + 620(2.43)$ Add $\mu = 4400$ to each part.

$3706 \text{ deer} < x < 5907$ deer (rounded)

(e)

$$\begin{aligned} z &< 1.96 \\ 620z &< 620(1.96) && \text{Multiply by } \sigma. \\ 4400+620z &< 4400+620(1.96) && \text{Add } \mu. \\ x &< 5615 \text{ deer} \end{aligned}$$

(f)

$$\begin{aligned} 2.58 &< z \\ 620(2.58) &< 620z && \text{Multiply by } \sigma. \\ 4400+620(2.58) &< 4400+620z && \text{Add } \mu. \\ 6000 \text{ deer} &< x \end{aligned}$$

(g) If $x = 2800$ deer, $z = \dfrac{2800-4400}{620} = -2.58.$

This is a small z-value, so 2800 deer is quite low for the fall deer population.

If $x = 6300$ deer, $z = \dfrac{6300-4400}{620} = 3.06.$

This is a very large z-value, so 6300 deer would be an unusually large fall population size.

6. $z = \dfrac{x-\mu}{\sigma}$ so in this case, $z = \dfrac{x-7500}{1750}$.

(a)

$$\begin{aligned} 9000 &< x \\ \frac{9000-7500}{1750} &< \frac{x-7500}{1750} && \text{Subtract } \mu\text{; divide by } \sigma. \\ 0.86 &< z \end{aligned}$$

(b)

$$\begin{aligned} x &< 6000 \\ \frac{x-7500}{1750} &< \frac{6000-7500}{1750} && \text{Subtract } \mu\text{; divide by } \sigma. \\ z &< -0.86 \end{aligned}$$

(c)

$$\begin{aligned} 3500 < x &< 4500 \\ \frac{3500-7500}{1750} < \frac{x-7500}{1750} &< \frac{4500-7500}{1750} && \text{Subtract } \mu\text{; divide by } \sigma. \\ -2.29 < z &< -1.71 \end{aligned}$$

Since $z = \dfrac{x-7500}{1750}$, $x = 7500+1750z$.

(d)

$$\begin{aligned} z &< 1.15 \\ 7500+1750z &< 7500+1750(1.15) && \text{Multiply by } \sigma\text{; add } \mu. \\ x &< 9513 \end{aligned}$$

(e)

$$\begin{aligned} 2.19 &< z \\ 7500+1750(2.19) &< 7500+1750(z) && \text{Multiply by } \sigma\text{; add } \mu. \\ 11{,}333 &< x \end{aligned}$$

(f)

$$\begin{aligned} 0.25 < z &< 1.25 \\ 7500+1750(0.25) < 7500+1750z &< 7500+1750(1.25) && \text{Multiply by } \sigma\text{; add } \mu. \\ 7938 < x &< 9688 \end{aligned}$$

(g) Since $\mu = 7500$, $x = 2500$ is quite low.

$$z = \frac{x-\mu}{\sigma} = \frac{2500-7500}{1750} = -2.86 \text{ (a very small } z\text{)}$$

7. $z = \dfrac{x-\mu}{\sigma}$ so in this case, $z = \dfrac{x-4.8}{0.3}$.

(a)
$$\begin{aligned} 4.5 &< x \\ \frac{4.5-4.8}{0.3} &< \frac{x-4.8}{0.3} \quad \text{Subtract } \mu\text{; divide by } \sigma. \\ -1.00 &< z \end{aligned}$$

(b)
$$\begin{aligned} x &< 4.2 \\ \frac{x-4.8}{0.3} &< \frac{4.2-4.8}{0.3} \quad \text{Subtract } \mu\text{; divide by } \sigma. \\ z &< -2.00 \end{aligned}$$

(c)
$$\begin{gathered} 4.0 < x < 5.5 \\ \frac{4.0-4.8}{0.3} < \frac{x-4.8}{0.3} < \frac{5.5-4.8}{0.3} \quad \text{Subtract } \mu\text{; divide by } \sigma. \\ -2.67 < z < 2.33 \end{gathered}$$

Since $z = \dfrac{x-4.8}{0.3}$, $x = 4.8 + 0.3z$.

(d)
$$\begin{aligned} z &< -1.44 \\ 0.3z &< 0.3(-1.44) \quad \text{Multiply by } \sigma. \\ 4.8+0.3z &< 4.8+0.3(-1.44) \quad \text{Add } \mu. \\ x &< 4.4 \end{aligned}$$

(e)
$$\begin{aligned} 1.28 &< z \\ 0.3(1.28) &< 0.3z \quad \text{Multiply by } \sigma. \\ 4.8+0.3(1.28) &< 4.8+0.3z \quad \text{Add } \mu. \\ 5.2 &< x \end{aligned}$$

(f)
$$\begin{gathered} -2.25 < z < -1.00 \\ 0.3(-2.25) < 0.3z < 0.3(-1.00) \quad \text{Multiply by } \sigma. \\ 4.8+0.3(-2.25) < 4.8+0.3z < 4.8+0.3(-1.00) \quad \text{Add } \mu. \\ 4.1 < x < 4.5 \end{gathered}$$

(g) If the RBC was 5.9 or higher, that would be an unusually high red blood cell count.

$$\begin{aligned} x &\ge 5.9 \\ \frac{x-4.8}{0.3} &\ge \frac{5.9-4.8}{0.3} \\ z &\ge 3.67 \text{ (a very large } z\text{-value)} \end{aligned}$$

8. (a) $z = \dfrac{x-\mu}{\sigma}$

Site 1: $z_1 = \dfrac{x_1 - \mu_1}{\sigma_1}$

$z_1 = \dfrac{x_1 - 1272}{35}$

so for $x_1 = 1250$

$z_1 = \dfrac{1250-1272}{35} = -0.63$

Site 2: $z_2 = \dfrac{x_2 - \mu_2}{\sigma_2}$

$z_2 = \dfrac{x_2 - 1122}{40}$

so for $x_2 = 1234$

$z_2 = \dfrac{1234-1122}{40} = 2.80$

(b) x_2, the object dated 1234 AD, is more unusual at its site, since $z_2 = 2.8$ vs. $z_1 = -0.63$.

For problems 9–48, refer to the following sketch patterns for guidance in calculations

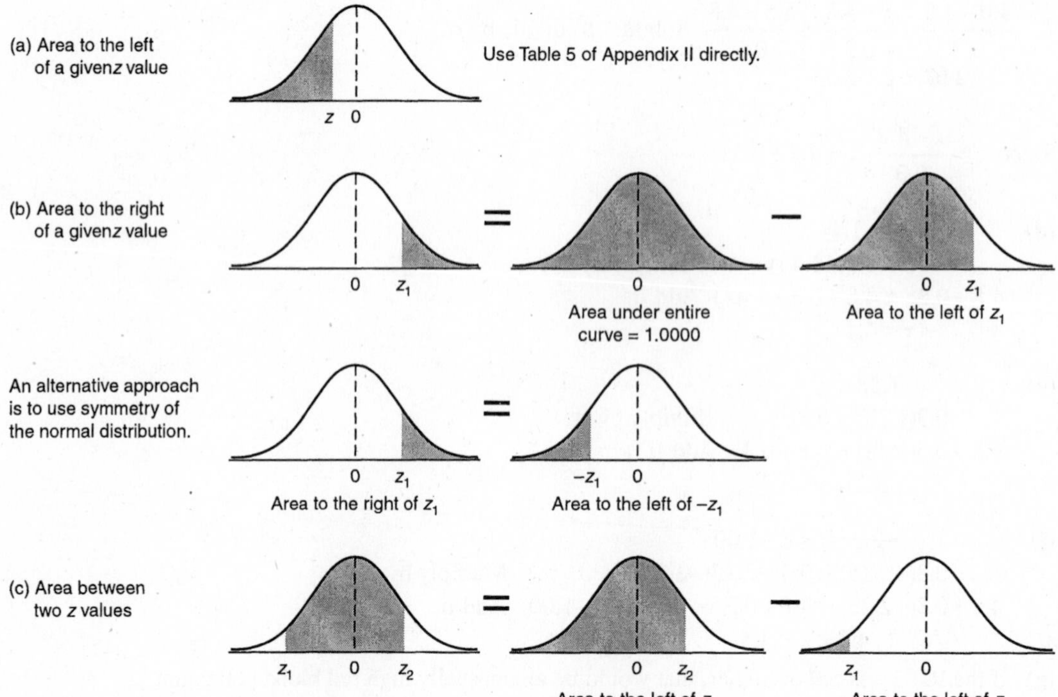

Using the left-tail style standard normal distribution table (see figures above)

(a) For areas to the *left* of a specified z value, use the table entry directly.

(b) For areas to the *right* of a specified z value, look up the table entry for z and subtract the table value from 1. (This is the complementary event rule as applied to area as probability.)

OR: Use the fact that the normal curve is symmetric about the mean, 0. The area in the right tail above a z-value is the same as the area in the left tail below the value of $-z$. So, to find the area to the right of z, look up the table value for $-z$.

(c) For areas *between* two z-values, z_1 and z_2, where $z_1 < z_2$, subtract the tabled value for z_1, from the tabled value for z_2.

These sketches and rules for finding the area for probability from the standard normal table apply for *any* z: $-\infty < z < +\infty$.

Student sketches should resemble those indicated with negative z-values to left of 0 and positive z-values to the right of zero.

9. Refer to figure (b).
The area to the right of $z = 0$ is 1 – area to left of $z = 0$, or $1 - 0.5000 = 0.5000$.

10. Refer to figure (a).
The area to the left of $z = 0$ is 0.5000 (direct read).

11. Refer to figure (a).
The area to the left of $z = -1.32$ is 0.0934.

12. Refer to figure (a).
The area to the left of $z = -0.47$ is 0.3192.

13. Refer to figure (a).
The area to left of $z = 0.45$ is 0.6736.

14. Refer to figure (a).
The area to left of $z = 0.72$ is 0.7642.

15. Refer to figure (b).
The area to right of $z = 1.52$ is $1 - 0.9357 = 0.0643$.

16. Refer to figure (b).
The area to right of $z = 0.15$ is $1 - 0.5596 = 0.4404$.

17. Refer to figure (b).
The area to right of $z = -1.22$ is $1 - 0.1112 = 0.8888$.

18. Refer to figure (b).
The area to right of $z = -2.17$ is $1 - 0.0150 = 0.9850$.

19. Refer to figure (c).
The area between $z = 0$ and $z = 3.18$ is $0.9993 - 0.5000 = 0.4993$.

20. Refer to figure (c).
The area between $z = 0$ and $z = 2.92$ is $0.9982 - 0.5000 = 0.4982$.

21. Refer to figure (c).
The area between $z = 0$ and $z = -2.01$ is $0.5000 - 0.0222 = 0.4778$.

22. Refer to figure (c).
The area between $z = 0$ and $z = -1.93$ is $0.5000 - 0.0268 = 0.4732$.

23. Refer to figure (c).
The area between $z = -2.18$ and $z = 1.34$ is $0.9099 - 0.0146 = 0.8953$.

24. Refer to figure (c).
The area between $z = -1.40$ and $z = 2.03$ is $0.9788 - 0.0808 = 0.8980$.

25. Refer to figure (c).
The area between $z = 0.32$ and $z = 1.92$ is $0.9726 - 0.6255 = 0.3471$.

26. Refer to figure (c).
The area between $z = 1.42$ and $z = 2.17$ is $0.9850 - 0.9222 = 0.0628$.

27. Refer to figure (c).
The area between $z = -2.42$ and $z = -1.77$ is $0.0384 - 0.0078 = 0.0306$.

28. Refer to figure (c).
The area between $z = -1.98$ and $z = -0.03$ is $0.4880 - 0.0239 = 0.4641$.

29. Refer to figure (a).
$P(z \le 0) = -0.5000$

30. Refer to figure (b).
$P(z \ge 0) = 1 - P(z < 0) = 1 - 0.5000 = 0.5000$

31. Refer to figure (a).
$P(z \le -0.13) = 0.4483$ (direct read)

32. Refer to figure (a).
$P(z \le -2.15) = 0.0158$

33. Refer to figure (a).
$P(z \le 1.20) = 0.8849$

34. Refer to figure (a).
$P(z \le 3.20) = 0.9993$

35. Refer to figure (b).
$P(z \ge 1.35) = 1 - P(z < 1.35) = 1 - 0.9115 = 0.0885$

36. Refer to figure (b).
$P(z \ge 2.17) = 1 - P(z < 2.17) = 1 - 0.9850 = 0.0150$

37. Refer to figure (b).
$P(x \ge -1.20) = 1 - P(z < -1.20) = 1 - 0.1151 = 0.8849$

38. Refer to figure (b).
$P(z \ge -1.50) = 1 - P(z < -1.50) = 1 - 0.0668 = 0.9332$

39. Refer to figure (c).
$P(-1.20 \le z \le 2.64) = P(z \le 2.64) - P(z < -1.20) = 0.9959 - 0.1151 = 0.8808$

40. Refer to figure (c).
$P(-2.20 \le z \le 1.04) = P(z \le 1.04) - P(z < -2.20) = 0.8508 - 0.0139 = 0.8369$

41. Refer to figure (c).
$P(-2.18 \le z \le -0.42) = P(z \le -0.42) - P(z < -2.18) = 0.3372 - 0.0146 = 0.3226$

42. Refer to figure (c).
$P(-1.78 \le z \le -1.23) = P(z \le -1.23) - P(z < -1.78) = 0.1093 - 0.0375 = 0.0718$

43. Refer to figure (c).
$P(0 \le z \le 1.62) = P(z \le 1.62) - P(z < 0) = 0.9474 - 0.5000 = 0.4474$

44. Refer to figure (c).
$P(0 \le z \le 0.54) = P(z \le 0.54) - P(z < 0) = 0.7054 - 0.5000 = 0.2054$

45. Refer to figure (c).
$P(-0.82 \le z \le 0) = P(z \le 0) - P(z < -0.82) = 0.5000 - 0.2061 = 0.2939$

46. Refer to figure (c).
$P(-2.37 \le z \le 0) = P(z \le 0) - P(z < -2.37) = 0.5000 - 0.0089 = 0.4911$

47. Refer to figure (c).
$P(-0.45 \le z \le 2.73) = P(z \le 2.73) - P(z < -0.45) = 0.9968 - 0.3264 = 0.6704$

48. Refer to figure (c).
$P(-0.73 \le z \le 3.12) = P(z \le 3.12) - P(z < -0.73) = 0.9991 - 0.2327 = 0.7664$

Section 6.3

1. We are given $\mu = 4$ and $\sigma = 2$. Since $z = \dfrac{x-\mu}{\sigma}$, we have $z = \dfrac{x-4}{2}$.

$P(3 \le x \le 6)$
$= P(3-4 \le x-4 \le 6-4)$ Subtract $\mu = 4$ from each part of the inequality.
$= P\left(\dfrac{3-4}{2} \le \dfrac{x-4}{2} \le \dfrac{6-4}{2}\right)$ Divide each part by $\sigma = 2$.
$= P\left(-\dfrac{1}{2} \le z \le \dfrac{2}{2}\right)$
$= P(-0.5 \le z \le 1)$
$= P(z \le 1) - P(z < -0.5)$ Refer to sketch (c) in the solutions for Section 6.2.
$= 0.8413 - 0.3085$
$= 0.5328$

2. We are given $\mu = 15$ and $\sigma = 4$. Since $z = \dfrac{x-\mu}{\sigma}$, we have $z = \dfrac{x-15}{4}$.

$P(10 \le x \le 26)$
$= P(10-15 \le x-15 \le 26-15)$ Subtract $\mu = 15$.
$= P\left(\dfrac{10-15}{4} \le \dfrac{x-15}{4} \le \dfrac{26-15}{4}\right)$ Divide each part of the inequality by $\sigma = 4$.
$= P(-1.25 \le z \le 2.75)$
$= P(z \le 2.75) - P(z < -1.25)$ Refer to sketch (c) in solutions for Section 6.2.
$= 0.9970 - 0.1056$
$= 0.8914$

3. We are given $\mu = 40$ and $\sigma = 15$. Since $z = \dfrac{x-\mu}{\sigma}$, we have $z = \dfrac{x-40}{15}$.

$P(50 \le x \le 70)$
$= P(50-40 \le x-40 \le 70-40)$ Subtract $\mu = 40$.
$= P\left(\dfrac{50-40}{15} \le \dfrac{x-40}{15} \le \dfrac{70-40}{15}\right)$ Divide by $\sigma = 15$.
$= P(0.67 \le z \le 2)$
$= P(z \le 2) - P(z < 0.67)$
$= 0.9772 - 0.7486 = 0.2286$

4. We are given $\mu = 5$ and $\sigma = 1.2$. Since $z = \dfrac{x-\mu}{\sigma}$, we have $z = \dfrac{x-5}{1.2}$.

$P(7 \le x \le 9)$
$= P(7-5 \le x-5 \le 9-5)$ Subtract $\mu = 5$.
$= P\left(\dfrac{7-5}{1.2} \le \dfrac{x-5}{1.2} \le \dfrac{9-5}{1.2}\right)$ Divide by $\sigma = 1.2$.
$= P(1.67 \le z \le 3.33)$
$= P(z \le 3.33) - P(z < 1.67)$
$= 0.9996 - 0.9525 = 0.0471$

5. We are given $\mu = 15$ and $\sigma = 3.2$. Since $z = \dfrac{x-\mu}{\sigma}$, we have $z = \dfrac{x-15}{3.2}$.

$P(8 \le x \le 12)$
$= P(8-15 \le x-15 \le 12-15)$ Subtract $\mu = 15$.
$= P\left(\dfrac{8-15}{3.2} \le \dfrac{x-15}{3.2} \le \dfrac{12-15}{3.2}\right)$ Divide by $\sigma = 3.2$.
$= P(-2.19 \le z \le -0.94)$
$= P(z \le -0.94) - P(z < -2.19)$
$= 0.1736 - 0.0143 = 0.1593$

6. We are given $\mu = 50$ and $\sigma = 15$. Since $z = \dfrac{x-\mu}{\sigma}$, we have $z = \dfrac{x-50}{15}$.

$$\begin{aligned} &P(40 \le x \le 47) \\ &= P(40-50 \le x-50 \le 47-50) && \text{Subtract } \mu = 50. \\ &= P\left(\frac{40-50}{15} \le \frac{x-50}{15} \le \frac{47-50}{15}\right) && \text{Divide by } \sigma = 15. \\ &= P(-0.67 \le z \le -0.20) \\ &= P(z \le -0.20) - P(z < -0.67) \\ &= 0.4207 - 0.2514 = 0.1693 \end{aligned}$$

7. We are given $\mu = 20$ and $\sigma = 3.4$. Since $z = \dfrac{x-\mu}{\sigma}$, we have $z = \dfrac{x-20}{3.4}$.

$$\begin{aligned} &P(x \ge 30) \\ &= P(x-20 \ge 30-20) && \text{Subtract } \mu = 20. \\ &= P\left(\frac{x-20}{3.4} \ge \frac{30-20}{3.4}\right) && \text{Divide by } \sigma = 3.4. \\ &= P(z \ge 2.94) \\ &= 1 - P(z < 2.94) && \text{Refer to sketch (b) in Section 6.2.} \\ &= 1 - 0.9984 = 0.0016 \end{aligned}$$

8. We are given $\mu = 100$ and $\sigma = 15$. Since $z = \dfrac{x-\mu}{\sigma}$, we have $z = \dfrac{x-100}{15}$.

$$\begin{aligned} &P(x \ge 120) \\ &= P(x-100 \ge 120-100) && \text{Subtract } \mu. \\ &= P\left(\frac{x-100}{15} \ge \frac{120-100}{15}\right) && \text{Divide by } \sigma. \\ &= P(z \ge 1.33) && \text{Refer to sketch (b) in Section 6.2.} \\ &= 1 - P(z < 1.33) \\ &= 1 - 0.9082 = 0.0918 \end{aligned}$$

9. We are given $\mu = 100$ and $\sigma = 15$. Since $z = \dfrac{x-\mu}{\sigma}$, we have $z = \dfrac{x-100}{15}$.

$$\begin{aligned} &P(x \ge 90) \\ &= P\left(\frac{x-100}{15} \ge \frac{90-100}{15}\right) && \text{Subtract } \mu\text{; divide by } \sigma. \\ &= P(z \ge -0.67) \\ &= 1 - P(z < -0.67) = 1 - 0.2514 = 0.7486 \end{aligned}$$

10. We are given $\mu = 3$ and $\sigma = 0.25$. Since $z = \dfrac{x-\mu}{\sigma}$, we have $z = \dfrac{x-3}{0.25}$.

$$\begin{aligned} &P(x \ge 2) \\ &= P\left(\frac{x-3}{0.25} \ge \frac{2-3}{0.25}\right) && \text{Subtract } \mu\text{; divide by } \sigma. \\ &= P(z \ge -4) \\ &= 1 - P(z < -4) \approx 1 - 0 = 1 \end{aligned}$$

For problems 11–20, refer to the following sketch patterns for guidance in calculation.

(a) **Left-tail case:**
The given area A is to the left of z.

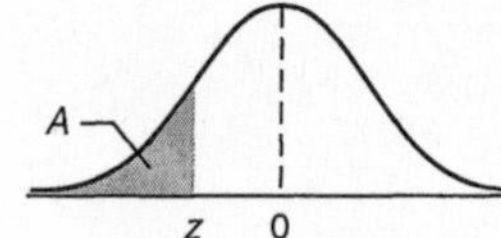

or

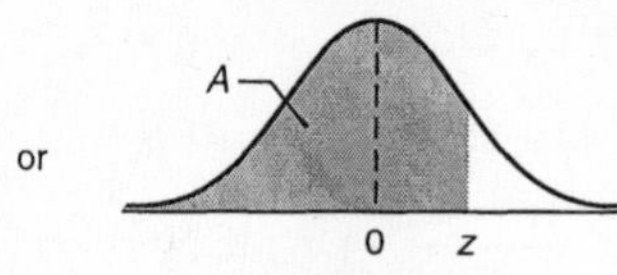

For the left-tail case, look up the number A in the body of the table and use the corresponding z value.

(b) **Right-tail case:**
The given area A is to the right of z.

1 – A A 0 z

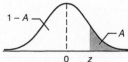

or

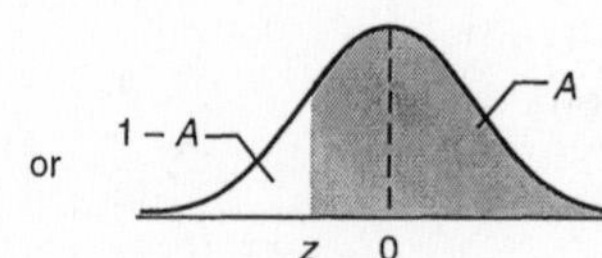

For the right-tail case, look up the number 1 – A in the body of the table and use the corresponding z value.

(c) **Center case:**
The given area A is symmetric and centered above $z = 0$. Half of A lies to the left and half lies to the right of $z = 0$.

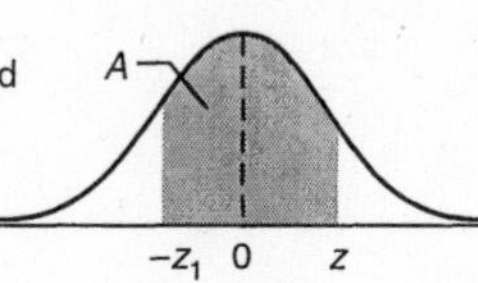

For the center case, look up the number $\frac{1-A}{2}$ in the body of the table and use the corresponding $\pm z$ value.

Student sketches should resemble the figures above, with negative z-values to the left of zero and positive z-values to the right of zero, and A written as a decimal.

11. Refer to figure (a).
Find z so that the area A to the left of z is 6% = 0.06. Since $A = 0.06$ is less than 0.5000, look for a negative z value. A to left of –1.55 is 0.0606 and A to left of –1.56 is 0.0594. Since 0.06 is in the middle of 0.0606 and 0.0594, for our z-value we will use the average of –1.55 and –1.56:

$$\frac{-1.55+(-1.56)}{2} = -1.555.$$

12. Refer to figure (a).
Find z so that the area A to the left of z is 5.2% = 0.052. Since $A = 0.052 < 0.5000$, look for a negative z value. A to the left of –1.63 is 0.0516, which is closer to 0.052 than is A to the left of –1.62 (0.0526), so $z = -1.63$.

13. Refer to figure (a).
Find z so that the area A to the left of z is 55% = 0.55. Since $A = 0.55 > 0.5000$, look for a positive z-value. The area to the left of 0.13 is 0.5517, so $z = 0.13$.

14. Refer to figure (a).
Find z so that the area A to the left of z is 97.5% = 0.975. Since $A = 0.975 > 0.5000$, look for a positive z. A to left of $z = 1.96$ is 0.9750.

15. Refer to figure (b).
Find z so that the area A to the right of z is 8% = 0.08. Since A to the right of z is 0.08, $1 - A = 1 - 0.08 = 0.92$ is to the left of z-value. The area to the left of 1.41 is 0.9207.

16. Refer to figure (b).
Find z so that the area A to the right of z is 5% = 0.05. Since A to the right of z is 0.05, $1 - A = 1 - 0.05 = 0.95$ is to the left of z. Since $1 - A = 0.95 > 0.5000$, look for a positive z-value. The area to the left of 1.64 is 0.9495, and the area to the left of 1.65 is 0.9505. Since 0.95 is halfway between 0.9495 and 0.9505, we average the two z values.

$$\frac{1.64+1.65}{2} = 1.645$$

17. Refer to figure (b).
Find z so that the area A to the right of z is 82% = 0.82. Since A to the right of z, $1 - A = 1 - 0.82 = 0.18$ is to the left of z. Since $1 - A = 0.18 < 0.5000$, look for a negative z value. The area to the left of $z = -0.92$ is 0.1788.

18. Refer to figure (b).
Find z so that the area A to the right of z is 95% = 0.95. Since A to the right of z is 0.95, $1 - A = 1 - 0.95 = 0.05$ is to the left of z. Because $1 - A = 0.05 < 0.5000$, look for a negative z value. The area to the left of −1.64 is 0.0505. The area to the left of −1.65 is 0.0495. Since 0.05 is halfway between these two area values we average the two z-values.

$$\frac{-1.64+(-1.65)}{2} = -1.645$$

19. Refer to figure (c).
Find z such that the area A between $-z$ and z is 98% = 0.98. Since A is between $-z$ and z, $1 - A = 1 - 0.98 = 0.02$ lies in the tails, and since we need $\pm z$, half of $1 - A$ lies in each tail. The area to the left of $-z$ is $\frac{1-A}{2} = \frac{0.02}{2} = 0.01$. The area to the left of −2.33 is 0.0099. Thus $-z = -2.33$ and $z = 2.33$.

20. Refer to figure (c).
Find z such that the area A between $-z$ and z is 95% = 0.95. If A between $-z$ and $z = 0.95$, then $1 - A = 1 - 0.95 = 0.05$ is the area in the tails, and that is split evenly between the two tails. Thus, the area to the left of $-z$ is $\frac{1-A}{2} = \frac{0.05}{2} = 0.025$. The area to the left of −1.96 is 0.0250, so $-z$ is −1.96 and $z = 1.96$.

21. x is approximately normal with $\mu = 85$ and $\sigma = 25$. Since $z = \frac{x-\mu}{\sigma}$, we have $z = \frac{x-85}{25}$.

(a) $P(x > 60)$

$$= P\left(\frac{x-85}{25} > \frac{60-85}{25}\right) = P(z > -1)$$
$$= 1 - P(z \le -1) = 1 - 0.1587 = 0.8413$$

(b) $P(x < 110) = P\left(\frac{x-85}{25} < \frac{110-85}{25}\right) = P(z < 1) = 0.8413.$

(c) $P(60 < x < 110)$

$$= P(-1 < z < 1) \quad \text{using (a) and (b)}$$
$$= P(z < 1) - P(z \le -1) = 0.8413 - 0.1587 = 0.6826$$

(i.e., approximately 68% of the blood glucose measurements lie within $\mu \pm \sigma$)

(d) $P(x > 140)$

$= P\left(\frac{x-85}{25} > \frac{140-85}{25}\right) = P(z > 2.2)$

$= 1 - P(z \le 2.2) = 1 - 0.9861 = 0.0139$

22. x is approximately normally distributed with $\mu = 38$ and $\sigma = 12$. Since $z = \frac{x-\mu}{\sigma}$, we have $z = \frac{x-38}{12}$.

(a) $P(x < 60) = P\left(\frac{x-38}{12} < \frac{60-38}{12}\right) = P(z < 1.83) = 0.9664$

(b) $P(x > 16) = P\left(\frac{x-38}{12} > \frac{16-38}{12}\right) = P(z > -1.83) = 1 - P(z \le -1.83) = 1 - 0.0336 = 0.9664$

(c) $P(16 < x < 60)$

$= P(-1.83 < z < 1.83)$ using (a) and (b)

$= P(z < 1.83) - P(z \le -1.83) = 0.9664 - 0.0336$

$= 0.9328$

(d) $P(x > 60)$

$= 1 - P(x \le 60)$ complementary event rule

$= 1 - 0.9664$ from (a)

$= 0.0336$

23. SAT scores, x, are normal with $\mu_x = 500$ and $\sigma_x = 100$. Since $z = \frac{x-\mu_x}{\sigma_x}$, we have $x = \frac{x-500}{100}$.

(a) $P(x > 675) = P\left(\frac{x-500}{100} > \frac{675-500}{100}\right) = P(z > 1.75) = 1 - P(z \le 1.75) = 1 - 0.9599 = 0.0401$

(b) $P(x < 450) = P\left(\frac{x-500}{100} < \frac{450-500}{100}\right) = P(z < -0.5) = 0.3085$

(c) $P(450 \le x \le 675)$

$= P(-0.5 \le z \le 1.75)$ using (a), (b)

$= P(z \le 1.75) - P(z < -0.5) = 0.9599 - 0.3085$

$= 0.6514$ using work in (a), and (b)

ACT scores, y, are normal with $\mu_y = 18$ and $\sigma_y = 6$. Since $z = \frac{y-\mu_y}{\sigma_y}$, we have $z = \frac{y-18}{6}$.

(d) $P(y > 28) = P\left(\frac{y-18}{6} > \frac{28-18}{6}\right) = P(z > 1.67) = 1 - P(z \le 1.67) = 1 - 0.9525 = 0.0475$

(e) $P(y > 12) = P\left(\frac{y-18}{6} > \frac{12-18}{6}\right) = P(z > -1) = 1 - P(z \le -1) = 1 - 0.1587 = 0.8413$

(f) $P(12 \le y \le 28)$

$= P(-1 \le z \le 1.67)$ using (a), (b)

$= P(z \le 1.67) - P(z < -1) = 0.9525 - 0.1587 = 0.7938$

24. SAT scores, x, are normal with $\mu_x = 500$ and $\sigma_x = 100$; ACT scores, y, are normal with $\mu_y = 18$ and $\sigma_x = 6$. Since $z_0 = \frac{x_0 - \mu_x}{\sigma_x}$, a little algebra shows $x_0 = \mu_x + z_0\sigma_x$ and, similarly, $y_0 = \mu_y + z_0\sigma_y$.

(a) Find the SAT score, x_0, such that $P(x \geq x_0) = 10\% = 0.10$.

$$P(x \geq x_0) = P\left(\frac{x-500}{100} \geq \frac{x_0 - 500}{100}\right) = P(z \geq z_0) = 0.10$$

(that is, find the value z_0 such that 10% of the standard normal curve lies to the right of z_0). Since 10% is to the right of z_0, $1 - 0.10 = 0.90 = 90\%$ is to the left of z_0. Because $0.90 > 0.5000$, z_0 will be a positive number.

$$P(z \leq 1.28) = 0.8997, \text{ so } z_0 = 1.28$$

$x_0 = \mu_x + z_0\sigma_x$ so here, $x_0 = 500 + 1.28(100) = 628$ students scoring 628 points or more on the SAT math exam are in the top 10%.

Similarly, find y_0 such that $P(y \geq y_0) = 0.10$. Since 10% of the standard normal curve is to the right of z_0, $100\% - 10\% = 90\% = 0.90$ is to the left of z_0. $P(z \leq 1.28) = 0.8997$, so $z_0 = 1.28$. Then $y_0 = \mu_y + z_0\sigma_y = 18 + 1.28(6) = 25.68 \approx 26$. Students scoring 26 or more points on the ACT math test are in the top 10%.

(b) Find the SAT score, x_0, and the ACT score, y_0, such that $P(x \geq x_0) = P(y \geq y_0) = 20\% = 0.20$.
First, find z_0 such that $P(z \geq z_0) = 0.20$, or $P(z < z_0) = 1 - 0.20 = 0.80$. $P(z < 0.84) = 0.7995$, so $z_0 = 0.84$. Then $x_0 = \mu_x + z_0\sigma_x = 500 + 0.84(100) = 584$ and $y_0 = \mu_y + z_0\sigma_y = 18 + 0.84(6) = 23.04 \approx 23$. Students scoring at least 584 on the SAT math test, or at least 23 on the ACT math test, are in the top 20%.

(c) Find x_0, y_0, and z_0 such that $P(x \geq x_0) = P(y \geq y_0) = P(z \geq z_0) = 60\% = 0.60$.
First, z_0: $P(z < z_0) = 1 - 0.60 = 0.40$. $P(z < -0.25) = 0.4013$, so $z_0 = -0.25$. Then $x_0 = \mu_x + z_0\sigma_x = 500 + (-0.25)(100) = 475$ and $y_0 = \mu_y + z_0\sigma_y = 18 + (-0.25)(6) = 16.5$. So students scoring at least 475 on the SAT test or at least 16.5 on the ACT test are in the top 60%.

25. Pot shard thickness, x, is approximately normally distributed with $\mu = 5.1$ and $\sigma = 0.9$ millimeters.

(a) $P(x < 3.0) = P\left(\frac{x-5.1}{0.9} < \frac{3.0-5.1}{0.9}\right) = P(z < -2.33) = 0.0099$

(b) $P(x > 7.0) = P\left(\frac{x-5.1}{0.9} > \frac{7.0-5.1}{0.9}\right) = P(z > 2.11) = 1 - P(z \leq 2.11) = 1 - 0.9826 = 0.0174$

(c) $P(3.0 \leq x \leq 7.0)$
$= P(-2.33 \leq z \leq 2.11)$ using (a), (b)
$= P(z \leq 2.11) - P(z < -2.33) = 0.9826 - 0.0099$
$= 0.9727$

26. Response time, x, is normally distributed with $\mu = 8.4$ and $\sigma = 1.7$ minutes.

(a) $P(5 \leq x \leq 10)$
$= P\left(\frac{5-8.4}{1.7} \leq \frac{x-8.4}{1.7} \leq \frac{10-8.4}{1.7}\right) = P(-2 \leq z \leq 0.94)$
$= P(z \leq 0.94) - P(z < -2) = 0.8264 - 0.0228 = 0.8036$

(b) $P(x<5)=P(z<-2)=0.0228$ using (a)

(c) $P(x>10)=P(z>0.94)=1-P(z\le 0.94)=1-0.8264=0.1736$ using (a)

27. Fuel consumption, x, is approximately normal with $\mu=3213$ and $\sigma=180$ gallons per hour.

(a) $P(3000\le x\le 3500)$

$$=P\left(\frac{3000-3213}{180}\le\frac{x-3213}{180}\le\frac{3500-3213}{180}\right)$$
$$=P(-1.18\le z\le 1.59)=P(z\le 1.59)-P(z<-1.18)$$
$$=0.9441-0.1190=0.8251$$

(b) $P(x<3000)=P(z<-1.18)=0.1190$ using (a)

(c) $P(x>3500)=P(z>1.59)=1-P(z\le 1.59)=1-0.9441=0.0559$ using (a)

28. Temperature, x, is normally distributed with $\mu=22$ and $\sigma=10°$.

(a) $P(x\ge 42)=P\left(\frac{x-22}{10}\ge\frac{42-22}{10}\right)=P(z\ge 2)=1-P(z<2)=1-0.9772=0.0228$

(b) $P(x\le 15)=P\left(\frac{x-22}{10}\le\frac{15-22}{10}\right)=P(z\le -0.70)=0.2420$

(c) $P(29\le x\le 40)$

$$=P\left(\frac{29-22}{10}\le\frac{x-22}{10}\le\frac{40-22}{10}\right)$$
$$=P(0.7\le z\le 1.8)=P(z\le 1.8)-P(z<0.7)$$
$$=0.9641-0.7580=0.2061$$

29. Lifetime, x, is normally distributed with $\mu=45$ and $\sigma=8$ months.

(a) $P(x\le 36)=P\left(\frac{x-45}{8}\le\frac{36-45}{8}\right)=P(z\le -1.125)\approx P(z\le -1.13)=0.1292$

The company will have to replace approximately 13% of its batteries.

(b) Find x_0 such that $P(x\le x_0)=10\%=0.10$. First, find z_0 such that $P(z\le z_0)=0.10$.
$P(z\le -1.28)=0.1003$, so $z_0=-1.28$. Then $x_0=\mu+z_0\sigma=45+(-1.28)(8)=34.76\approx 35$.
The company should guarantee the batteries for 35 months.

30. Lifetime, x, is normally distributed with $\mu=28$ and $\sigma=5$ months.

(a) 2 years = 24 months

$$P(x\le 24)=P\left(z\le\frac{24-28}{5}\right)=P(z\le -0.8)=0.2119$$

The company should expect to replace about 21.2% of its watches.

(b) Find x_0 such that $P(x\le x_0)=12\%=0.12$. First, find z_0 such that $P(z\le z_0)=0.12$.
$P(z\le -1.17)=0.1210$ and $P(z\le -1.18)=0.1190$. Since 0.12 is halfway between 0.1210 and 0.1190, we will average the z-values: $z_0=\frac{-1.17+(-1.18)}{2}=-1.175$.

So $x_0=\mu+z_0\sigma=28+(-1.175)(5)=22.125$.

The company should guarantee its watches for 22 months.

31. Age at replacement, x, is approximately normal with $\mu = 8$ and range = 6 years.

(a) The empirical rule says that about 95% of the data are between $\mu - 2\sigma$ and $\mu + 2\sigma$, or about 95% of the data are in a $(\mu + 2\sigma) - (\mu - 2\sigma) = 4\sigma$ range (centered around μ). Thus, the range $\approx 4\sigma$, or $\sigma \approx$ range/4. Here, we can approximate σ by 6/4 = 1.5 years.

(b) $P(x > 5) = P\left(z > \dfrac{5-8}{1.5}\right) = P(z > -2)$ using the estimate of σ from (a)

$= 1 - P(z \le -2) = 1 - 0.0228 = 0.9772$

(c) $P(x < 10) = P\left(z < \dfrac{10-8}{1.5}\right) = P(z < 1.33) = 0.9082$

(d) Find x_0 so that $P(x \le x_0) = 10\% = 0.10$. First, find z_0 such that $P(z \le z_0) = 0.10$.

$P(z \le -1.28) = 0.1003$, so $z_0 = -1.28$. Then $x_0 = \mu + z_0\sigma = 8 + (-1.28)(1.5) = 6.08$.

The company should guarantee their TVs for about 6.1 years.

32. Age at replacement, x, is approximately normal with $\mu = 14$ and a (95%) range from 9 to 19 years.

(a) From Problem 31(a), range $\approx 4\sigma$, or $\sigma = \dfrac{\text{range}}{4}$. Here range = 19 – 9 = 10 years, so

$\sigma \approx 10/4 = 2.5$ years.

(b) $P(x < 11) = P\left(z < \dfrac{11-14}{2.5}\right) = P(z < -1.2) = 0.1151$

(c) $P(x > 18) = P\left(z > \dfrac{18-14}{2.5}\right) = P(z > 1.6) = 1 - P(z \le 1.6) = 1 - 0.9452 = 0.0548$

(d) Find x_0 so that $P(x < x_0) = 5\% = 0.05$. First, find z_0 so that $P(z < z_0) = 0.05$.

$P(z < -1.64) = 0.0505$ and $P(z < -1.65) = 0.0495$.

Since 0.05 is halfway between 0.0495 and 0.0505, we will average the z-values to get

$z_0 = \dfrac{-1.64 + (-1.65)}{2} = -1.645$. Then $x_0 = \mu + z_0\sigma = 14 + (-1.645)(2.5) = 9.8875$.

The company should guarantee its refrigerator for about 9.9 years.

33. Resting heart rate, x, is approximately normal with $\mu = 46$ and (95%) range from 22 to 70 bpm.

(a) From Problem 31(a), range $\approx 4\sigma$, or $\sigma \approx$ range/4. Here range = 70 – 22 = 48, so $\sigma \approx 48/4 = 12$ bpm.

(b) $P(x < 25) = P\left(z < \dfrac{25-46}{12}\right) = P(z < -1.75) = 0.0401$

(c) $P(x > 60) = P\left(z > \dfrac{60-46}{12}\right) = P(z > 1.17) = 1 - P(z \le 1.17) = 1 - 0.8790 = 0.1210$

(d) $P(25 \le x \le 60) = P(-1.75 \le z \le 1.17)$ using (b), (c)

$= P(z \le 1.17) - P(z < -1.75)$

$= 0.8790 - 0.0401$

$= 0.8389$

(e) Find x_0 such that $P(x > x_0) = 10\% = 0.10$. First, find z_0 such that $P(z > z_0) = 0.10$.

$P(z \le z_0) = 1 - 0.10 = 0.90$

$P(z \le 1.28) = 0.8997 \approx 0.90$, so let $z_0 = 1.28$.

When $x_0 = \mu + z_0\sigma = 46 + 1.28(12) = 61.36$, so horses with resting rates of 61 bpm or more may need treatment.

34. Kitten weight x is approximately normally distributed with $\mu = 24.5$ and (95%) range from 14 to 35 oz.

(a) From Problem 31(a), $\sigma \approx$ range $\div$ 4. Here range = 35 – 14 = 21 oz, so $\sigma = \frac{21}{4} \approx 5.25$ oz.

(b) $P(x < 14) = P\left(z < \frac{14 - 24.5}{5.25}\right) = P(z < -2) = 0.0228$

(c) $P(x > 33) = P\left(z > \frac{33 - 24.5}{5.25}\right) = P(z > 1.62) = 1 - P(z \le 1.62) = 1 - 0.9474 = 0.0526$

(d) $P(14 \le x \le 33) = P(-2 \le z \le 1.62) = P(z \le 1.62) - P(z < -2) = 0.9474 - 0.0228 = 0.9246$

(e) Find x_0 such that $P(x \le x_0) = 10\% = 0.10$. First, find z_0 such that $P(z \le z_0) = 0.10$.
$P(z \le -1.28) = 0.1003 \approx 0.10$, so let $z_0 = -1.28$.

Since $z_0 = \frac{x_0 - \mu}{\sigma}$, $-1.28 = \frac{x_0 - 24.5}{5.25}$, so
$x_0 = 24.5 + (-1.28)(5.25) = 17.78$

The cutoff point is about 17.8 oz.

35. Life expectancy x is normal with $\mu = 90$ and $\sigma = 3.7$ months.

(a) The insurance company wants 99% of the microchips to last longer than x_0. Saying this another way: the insurance company wants to pay the \$50 million at most 1% of the time. So, find x_0 such that $P(x \le x_0) = 1\% = 0.01$. First, find z_0 such that $P(z \le z_0) = 0.01$. $P(z \le -2.33) = 0.0099 \approx 0.01$, so let $z_0 = -2.33$. Since $z_0 = \frac{x_0 - \mu}{\sigma}$, $x_0 = \mu + z_0\sigma = 90 + (-2.33)(3.7) = 81.379 \approx 81$ months.

(b) $P(x \le 84) = P\left(z \le \frac{84 - 90}{3.7}\right) = P(z \le -1.62) = 0.0526 \approx 5\%$.

(c) The "expected loss" is 5.26% [from (b)] of the \$50 million, or 0.0526(50,000,000) = \$2,630,000.

(d) Profit is the difference between the amount of money taken in (here, \$3 million), and the amount paid out (here, \$2.63 million, from (c)). So the company expects to profit 3,000,000 – 2,630,000 = \$370,000.

36. (Questions 1–6 in the text will be labeled (a)-(f) below.) Daily attendance, x, is normally distributed with $\mu = 8000$ and $\sigma = 500$ people.

(a) $P(x < 7200) = P\left(z < \frac{7200 - 8000}{500}\right) = P(z < -1.6) = 0.0548$

(b) $P(x > 8900) = P\left(z > \frac{8900 - 8000}{500}\right) = P(z > 1.8) = 1 - P(z \le 1.8) = 1 - 0.9641 = 0.0359$

(c) $P(7200 \le x \le 8900) = P(-1.6 \le z \le 1.8) = P(z \le 1.8) - P(z < -1.6) = 0.9641 - 0.0548 = 0.9093$

Arrival times are normal with $\mu = 3$ hours, 48 minutes and $\sigma = 52$ minutes after the doors open. Convert μ to minutes: $(3 \times 60) + 48 = 228$ minutes.

(d) Find x_0 such that $P(x \le x_0) = 90\% = 0.90$. First, find z_0 such that $P(z \le z_0) = 0.90$.
$P(z \le 1.28) = 0.8997 \approx 0.90$, so let $z_0 = 1.28$. Since $z_0 = \frac{x_0 - \mu}{\sigma}$, $x_0 = \mu + z_0\sigma = 228 + (1.28)(52)$ = 294.56 minutes, or 294.56/60 = 4.9093 ≈ 4.9 hours after the doors open.

(e) Find x_0 such that $P(x \le x_0) = 15\% = 0.15$. First, find z_0 such that $P(z \le z_0) = 0.15$. $P(z \le -1.04) = 0.1492 \approx 0.15$, so let $z_0 = -1.04$. Then $x_0 = \mu + z_0\sigma = 228 + (-1.04)(52)$ $= 173.92$ minutes, or $173/60 = 2.899 \approx 2.9$ hours after the doors open.

(f) Answers vary. Most people have Saturday off, so many may come early in the day. Most people work Friday, so most people would probably come after 5 P.M. There is no reason to think weekday and weekend arrival times would have the same distribution.

37. Waiting time, x, is approximately normal with $\mu = 18$ and $\sigma = 4$ minutes.

(a) Let A be the event that $x > 20$, and B be the event that $x > 15$. We want to find $P(\text{A, given B})$. Recall

$$P(\text{A, given B}) = \frac{P(\text{A and B})}{P(\text{B})}.$$

$$P(\text{A and B}) = P(x > 20 \text{ and } x > 15) = P(x > 20)$$

Use a number line to find where both events occur simultaneously.

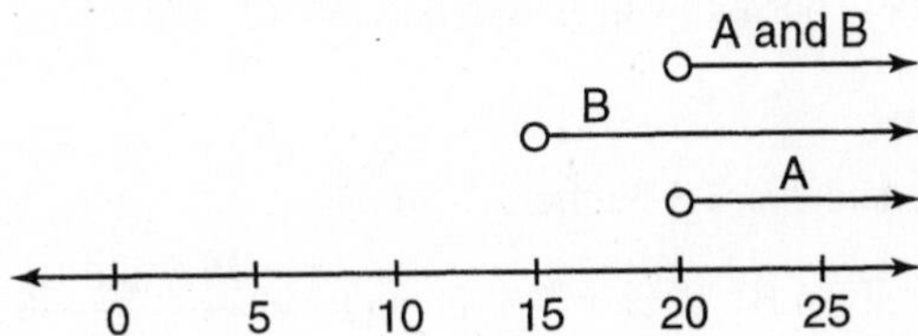

The number 20 is not included in "both A and B" because A says x is strictly greater than 20. The intervals $(15, \infty)$ and $(20, \infty)$ intersect at $(20, \infty)$.

$$P(x > 20) = P\left(z > \frac{20-18}{4}\right) = P(z > 0.5) = 1 - P(z \le 0.5) = 1 - 0.6915 = 0.3085$$

$$P(x > 15) = P\left(z > \frac{15-18}{4}\right) = P(z > -0.75) = 1 - P(z \le -0.75) = 1 - 0.2266 = 0.7734$$

$$\begin{aligned} P(x > 20, \text{ given } x > 15) &= \frac{P(x > 20) \text{ and } x > 15}{P(x > 15)} \\ &= \frac{P(x > 20)}{P(x > 15)} \\ &= \frac{0.3085}{0.7734} \\ &= 0.3989 \end{aligned}$$

(b) $P(x > 25, \text{ given } x > 18) = \dfrac{P(x > 25 \text{ and } x > 18)}{P(x > 18)}$

$$= \frac{P(x > 25)}{P(x > 18)}$$

$$= \frac{P\left(z > \frac{25-18}{4}\right)}{P\left(z > \frac{18-18}{4}\right)}$$

$$= \frac{P(z > 1.75)}{P(z > 0)}$$

$$= \frac{1 - P(z \le 1.75)}{1 - P(z \le 0)}$$

$$= \frac{(1 - 0.9599)}{(1 - 0.5000)}$$

$$= \frac{0.0401}{0.5}$$

$$= 0.0802$$

38. Cycle time, x, is approximately normal with $\mu = 45$ and $\sigma = 12$ minutes.

(a) $P(x > 60, \text{ given } x > 50)$

Let event A be $x > 60$, and event B be the $x > 50$.

The problem asks P(A, given B). Recall P(A, given B) = $\dfrac{P(\text{A and B})}{P(\text{B})}$.

Note that x is both greater than 60 and greater than 50 when x is greater than 60:

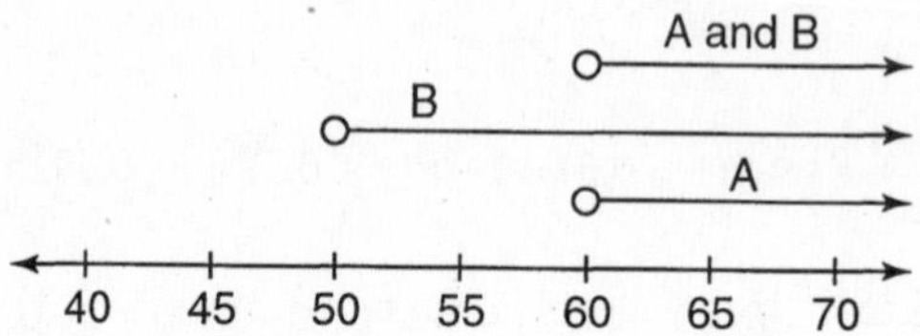

In this case, P(A and B) is the same as P(A).

The problem has been reduced to P(A, given B) = P(A)/P(B).

$P(x > 60, \text{ given } x > 50) = \dfrac{P(x > 60)}{P(x > 50)}$

$$= \frac{P\left(z > \frac{60-45}{12}\right)}{P\left(z > \frac{50-45}{12}\right)}$$

$$= \frac{P(z > 1.25)}{P(z > 0.42)}$$

$$= \frac{1 - P(z \le 1.25)}{1 - P(z \le 0.42)}$$

$$= \frac{1 - 0.8944}{1 - 0.6628}$$

$$= \frac{0.1056}{0.3372}$$

$$= 0.3132$$

(b) $P(x > 55, \text{ given } x > 40) = \dfrac{P(x > 55 \text{ and } x > 40)}{P(x > 40)}$

$$= \frac{P(x>55)}{P(x>40)}$$

$$= \frac{P\left(z > \frac{55-45}{12}\right)}{P\left(z > \frac{40-45}{12}\right)}$$

$$= \frac{P(z>0.83)}{P(z>-0.42)}$$

$$= \frac{1-P(z \le 0.83)}{1-P(z \le -0.42)}$$

$$= \frac{1-0.7967}{1-0.3372}$$

$$= \frac{0.2033}{0.6628}$$

$$= 0.3067$$

39. Maintenance cost, x, is approximately normal with $\mu = 615$ and $\sigma = 42$ dollars.

(a) $P(x > 646) = P\left(z > \dfrac{646-615}{42}\right) = P(z > 0.74) = 1 - P(z \le 0.74) = 1 - 0.7704 = 0.2296$

(b) Find x_0 such that $P(x > x_0) = 0.10$.
But, if the actual cost exceeds the budgeted amount 10% of the time, the actual cost must be within the budgeted amount 90% of the time. The problem can be rephrased as how much should be budgeted so that the probability the actual cost is less than or equal to the budgeted amount is 0.90, or find x_0 such that $P(x \le x_0) = 0.90$. First, find z_0 such that $P(z \le z_0) = 0.90$. $P(z \le 1.28) = 0.8997$, so let $z_0 = 1.28$. Since $z_0 = \frac{x_0 - \mu}{\sigma}$, $x_0 = \mu + z_0\sigma = 615 + 1.28(42) = \$668.76 \approx \$669$.

Section 6.4

Answers may vary slightly due to rounding.

1. Previously, $p = 88\% = 0.88$; now, $p = 9\% = 0.09$; $n = 200$; $r = 50$
Let a success be defined as a child with a high blood-lead level.

(a) $P(r \ge 50) = P(50 \le r) = P(49.5 \le x)$
$np = 200(0.88) = 176$; $nq = n(1-p) = 200(0.12) = 24$
Since both np and nq are greater than 5, we will use the normal approximation to the binomial with $\mu = np = 176$ and $\sigma = \sqrt{npq} = \sqrt{200(0.88)(0.12)} = \sqrt{21.12} = 4.60$.
So, $P(r \ge 50) = P(49.5 \le x) = P\left(\dfrac{49.5-176}{4.6} \le z\right) = P(-27.5 \le z)$.
Almost every z value will be greater than or equal to –27.5, so this probability is approximately 1. It is almost certain that 50 or more children a decade ago had high blood-lead levels.

(b) $P(r \geq 50) = P(50 \leq r) = P(49.5 \leq x)$

In this case, $np = 200(0.09) = 18$ and $nq = 200(0.91) = 182$, so both are greater than 5. Use the normal approximation with $\mu = np = 18$ and $\sigma = \sqrt{npq} = \sqrt{200(0.09)(0.91)} = \sqrt{16.38} = 4.05$.

So $P(49.5 \leq x) = P\left(\frac{49.5-18}{4.05} \leq z\right) = P(7.78 \leq z)$.

Almost no z values will be larger than 7.78, so this probability is approximately 0. Today, it is almost impossible that a sample of 200 children would include at least 50 with high blood-lead levels.

2. We are given $p = 0.40$ and $n = 128$. Let a success be defined as an insurance claim inflated (padded) to cover the deductible.

(a) $\frac{1}{2}(128) = 64$

$P(r \geq 64) = P(64 \leq r) = P(63.5 \leq x)$ 64 is a left endpoint $np = 128(0.4) = 51.2$ and

$nq = 128(0.6) = 76.8$ are both greater than 5, so we will use the normal approximation to the binomial

with $\mu = np = 51.2$ and $\sigma = \sqrt{npq} = \sqrt{128(0.4)(0.6)} = \sqrt{30.72} = 5.54$.

$P(63.5 \leq x) = P\left(\frac{63.5-51.2}{5.54} \leq z\right) = P(2.22 \leq z) = P(z \geq 2.22) = 1 - P(z < 2.22) = 1 - 0.9868 = 0.0132$

(b) $P(r < 45) = P(r \leq 44) = P(x \leq 44.5)$ 44 is a right endpoint.

$= P\left(z \leq \frac{44.5-51.2}{5.54}\right) = P(z \leq -1.21) = 0.1131$

(c) $P(40 \leq r \leq 64) = P(39.5 \leq x \leq 64.5)$

$$\begin{aligned} &= P\left(\frac{39.5-51.2}{5.54} \leq z \leq \frac{64.5-51.2}{5.54}\right) \\ &= P(-2.11 \leq z \leq 2.40) \\ &= P(z \leq 2.40) - P(z < -2.11) \\ &= 0.9918 - 0.0174 \\ &= 0.9744 \end{aligned}$$

(d) More than 80 *not* padded = 81 or more *not* padded, i.e., 128 – 81 = 47 or fewer *are padded.*
Method 1:

$P(r \leq 47) = P(x \leq 47.5) = P\left(z \leq \frac{47.5-51.2}{5.54}\right) = P(z \leq -0.67) = 0.2514$

Method 2:
Success is now *redefined* to mean an insurance claim that has not been padded, and p is not $1 - 0.40 = 0.60$.

$P(r \geq 81) = P(81 \leq r) = P(80.5 \leq x)$. 81 is a left endpoint. The normal approximation is still valid, since what was np in (a) is now nq and vice versa. The standard deviation is still the same, but now $\mu = np = 128(0.60) = 76.8$. So,

$P(80.5 \leq x) = P\left(\frac{80.5-76.8}{5.54} \leq z\right) = P(0.67 \leq z) = P(z \geq 0.67) = 1 - P(z < 0.67) = 1 - 0.7486 = 0.2514$.

3. We are given $n = 125$ and $p = 17\% = 0.17$. Let a success be defined as the police receiving enough information to locate and arrest a fugitive within 1 week.

(a) $P(r \geq 15) = P(15 \leq r) = P(14.5 \leq x)$. 15 is a left endpoint. $np = 125(0.17) = 21.25$ and $nq = 125(1-0.17) = 125(0.83) = 103.75$, which are both greater than 5, so we can use the normal approximation with $\mu = np = 21.25$ and $\sigma = \sqrt{npq} = \sqrt{125(0.17)(0.83)} = \sqrt{17.6375} = 4.20$. So

$$P(14.5 \leq x) = P\left(\frac{14.5-21.25}{4.2} \leq z\right) = P(-1.61 \leq z) = P(z \geq -1.61) = 1 - P(z < -1.61) = 1 - 0.0537 = 0.9463.$$

(b) $P(r \geq 28) = P(28 \leq r)$ 28 is a left endpoint.

$$\begin{aligned}
&= P(27.5 \leq x) \\
&= P\left(\frac{27.5-21.25}{4.2} \leq z\right) \\
&= P(1.49 \leq z) \\
&= P(z \geq 1.49) \\
&= 1 - P(z < 1.49) \\
&= 1 - 0.9319 \\
&= 0.0681
\end{aligned}$$

(c) Remember, r "between" a and b is $a \leq r \leq b$.

$P(15 \leq r \leq 28) = P(14.5 \leq x \leq 28.5)$ 15 is a left endpoint and 28 is a right endpoint.

$$\begin{aligned}
&= P\left(\frac{14.5-21.25}{4.2} \leq z \leq \frac{28.5-21.25}{4.2}\right) \\
&= P(-1.61 \leq z \leq 1.73) \\
&= P(z \leq 1.73) - P(z < -1.61) \\
&= 0.9582 - 0.0537 \\
&= 0.9045.
\end{aligned}$$

(d) $n = 125, p = 0.17, q = 1 - p = 1 - 0.17 = 0.83$.

np and nq are both greater than 5, so the normal approximation is appropriate.

4. $n = 316, p = 11\% = 0.11$; a success occurs when the book sold is a romance novel.

(a) $P(r < 40) = P(r \leq 39) = P(x \leq 39.5)$ 39 is a right endpoint $np = 316(0.11) = 34.76$, $nq = n(1-p) = 316(1-0.11) = 316(0.89) = 281.24$, both of which are greater than 5, so we can apply the normal approximation with $\mu = np = 34.76$ and $\sigma = \sqrt{npq} = \sqrt{316(0.11)(0.89)} = \sqrt{30.9364} = 5.56$.

$$P(x \leq 39.5) = P\left(z \leq \frac{39.5-34.76}{5.56}\right) = P(z \leq 0.85) = 0.8023$$

(b) $P(r \geq 25) = P(25 \leq r)$ 25 is a left endpoint.

$$\begin{aligned}
&= P(24.5 \leq x) \\
&= P\left(\frac{24.5-34.76}{5.56} \leq z\right) \\
&= P(-1.85 \leq z) \\
&= P(z \geq -1.85) \\
&= 1 - P(z < -1.85) \\
&= 1 - 0.0322 \\
&= 0.9678
\end{aligned}$$

(c) $P(25 \le r \le 40) = P(24.5 \le x \le 40.5)$

$$= P\left(\frac{24.5-34.76}{5.56} \le z \le \frac{40.5-34.76}{5.56}\right)$$
$$= P(-1.85 \le z \le 1.03)$$
$$= P(z \le 1.03) - P(z < -1.85)$$
$$= 0.8485 - 0.0322$$
$$= 0.8163$$

(d) $n = 316,\ p = 0.11,\ q = 1 - p = 0.89$

np and *nq* are both greater than 5, so the normal approximation to the binomial is appropriate. (See (a) above.)

5. We are given $n = 753$ and $p = 3.5\% = 0.035$; $q = 1 - p = 1 - 0.035 = 0.965$.
Let a success be a person living past age 90.

(a) $P(r \ge 15) = P(15 \le r) = P(14.5 \le x)$ 15 is a left endpoint.

Here, $np = 753(0.035) = 26.355$, and $nq = 753(0.965) = 726.645$, both of which are greater than 5; the normal approximation is appropriate, using $\mu = np = 26.355$ and

$\sigma = \sqrt{npq} = \sqrt{753(0.035)(0.965)} = \sqrt{25.4326} = 5.0431$.

$$P(14.5 \le x) = P\left(\frac{14.5-26.355}{5.0431} \le z\right)$$
$$= P(-2.35 \le z)$$
$$= P(z \ge -2.35)$$
$$= 1 - P(z < -2.35)$$
$$= 1 - 0.0094$$
$$= 0.9906$$

(b) $P(r \ge 30) = P(30 \le r)$

$$= P(29.5 \le x)$$
$$= P\left(\frac{29.5-26.355}{5.0431} \le z\right)$$
$$= P(0.62 \le z)$$
$$= P(z \ge 0.62)$$
$$= 1 - P(z < 0.62)$$
$$= 1 - 0.7324$$
$$= 0.2676$$

(c) $P(25 \le r \le 35) = P(24.5 \le x \le 35.5)$

$$= P\left(\frac{24.5-26.355}{5.0431} \le z \le \frac{35.5-26.355}{5.0431}\right)$$
$$= P(-0.37 \le z \le 1.81)$$
$$= P(z \le 1.81) - P(z < -0.37)$$
$$= 0.9649 - 0.3557$$
$$= 0.6092$$

(d) $P(r > 40) = P(r \geq 41)$
$= P(41 \leq r)$
$= P(40.5 \leq x)$
$= P\left(\frac{40.5 - 26.355}{5.0431} \leq z\right)$
$= P(2.80 \leq z)$
$= P(z \geq 2.80)$
$= 1 - P(z < 2.80)$
$= 1 - 0.9974$
$= 0.0026$

6. $n = 24$, $p = 44\% = 0.44$, $q = 1 - p = 1 - 0.44 = 0.56$
A success occurs when a billfish striking the line is caught.

(a) $P(r \leq 12) = P(x \leq 12.5)$
$np = 24(0.44) = 10.56$ and $nq = 24(0.56) = 13.44$, both of which are greater than 5, so the normal approximation is appropriate. Here, $\mu = np = 10.56$ and

$\sigma = \sqrt{npq} = \sqrt{24(0.44)(0.56)} = \sqrt{5.9136} = 2.4318.$

$P(x \leq 12.5) = P\left(z \leq \frac{12.5 - 10.56}{2.4318}\right) = P(z \leq 0.80) = 0.7881$

(b) $P(r \geq 5) = P(5 \leq r)$
$= P(4.5 \leq x)$
$= P\left(\frac{4.5 - 10.56}{2.4318} \leq z\right)$
$= P(-2.49 \leq z)$
$= P(z \geq -2.49)$
$= 1 - P(z < -2.49)$
$= 1 - 0.0064$
$= 0.9936$

(c) $P(5 \leq r \leq 12) = P(4.5 \leq x \leq 12.5)$
$= P(-2.49 \leq z \leq 0.80)$
$= P(z \leq 0.80) - P(z < -2.49)$
$= 0.7881 - 0.0064$
$= 0.7817$

(d) $n = 24$, $p = 0.44$, $q = 0.56$
Both np and $nq > 5$, so the normal approximation to the binomial is appropriate.

7. $n = 66$, $p = 80\% = 0.80$, $q = 1 - p = 1 - 0.80 = 0.20$
A success is when a new product fails within 2 years.

(a) $P(r \geq 47) = P(47 \leq r) = P(46.5 \leq x)$
$np = 66(0.80) = 52.8$, and $nq = 66(0.20) = 13.3$. Both exceed 5, so the normal approximation with $\mu = np = 52.8$ and $\sigma = \sqrt{npq} = \sqrt{66(0.8)(0.2)} = \sqrt{10.56} = 3.2496$ is appropriate.

$$\begin{aligned}P(46.5 \leq x) &= P\left(\frac{46.5-52.8}{3.2496} \leq z\right)\\ &= P(-1.94 \leq z)\\ &= P(z \geq -1.94)\\ &= 1-P(z<-1.94)\\ &= 1-0.0262\\ &= 0.9738\end{aligned}$$

(b) $P(r \leq 58) = P(x \leq 58.5) = P\left(z \leq \frac{58.5-52.8}{3.2496}\right) = P(z \leq 1.75) = 0.9599$

For (c) and (d), note we are interested now in products succeeding, so a success is redefined to be a new product staying on the market for 2 years. Here, $n = 66$, p is now 0.20 with q is now 0.80 (p and q above have been switched. Now $np = 13.2$ and $nq = 52.8$, $\mu = 13.2$, and σ stays equal to 3.2496.

(c)
$$\begin{aligned}P(r \geq 15) &= P(15 \leq r)\\ &= P(14.5 \leq x)\\ &= P\left(\frac{14.5-13.2}{3.2496} \leq z\right)\\ &= P(0.40 \leq z)\\ &= P(z \geq 0.40)\\ &= 1-P(z<0.40)\\ &= 1-0.6554\\ &= 0.3446\end{aligned}$$

(d) $P(r<10) = P(r \leq 9) = P(x \leq 9.5) = P\left(z \leq \frac{9.5-13.2}{3.2496}\right) = P(z \leq -1.14) = 0.1271$

8. $n = 63, p = 64\% = 0.64, q = 1-p = 1-0.64 = 0.36$
A success is when the murder victim knows the murderer.

(a) $P(r \geq 35) = P(35 \leq r) = P(34.5 \leq x)$
$np = 63(0.64) = 40.32$ and $nq = 63(0.36) = 22.68$
Since both np and nq are greater than 5, the normal approximation is appropriate. Use $\mu = np = 40.32$ and $\sigma = \sqrt{npq} = \sqrt{63(0.64)(0.36)} = \sqrt{14.5152} = 3.8099$. So

$$P(34.5 \leq x) = P\left(\frac{34.5-40.32}{3.8099} \leq z\right) = P(-1.53 \leq z) = 1-P(z<-1.53) = 1-0.0630 = 0.9370$$

(b) $P(r \leq 48) = P(x \leq 48.5) = P\left(z \leq \frac{48.5-40.32}{3.8099}\right) = P(z \leq 2.15) = 0.9842$

(c) If fewer than 30 victims, i.e., 29 or fewer did not know their murderer, then 63 – 29 = 34 or more victims did know their murderer.

$$\begin{aligned} P(r \geq 34) &= P(34 \leq r) \\ &= P(33.5 \leq x) \\ &= P\left(\frac{33.5-40.32}{3.8099} \leq z\right) \\ &= P(-1.79 \leq z) \\ &= 1-P(z<-1.79) \\ &= 1-0.0367 \\ &= 0.9633 \end{aligned}$$

(d) If more than 20, i.e., 21 or more, victims did not know their murdered, then 63 – 21 = 42 or fewer victims did know their murdered.

$$P(r \leq 42) = P(x \leq 42.5) = P\left(z \leq \frac{42.5-40.32}{3.8099}\right) = P(z \leq 0.57) = 0.7157$$

9. $n = 430$, $p = 70\% = 0.70$, $q = 1 - p = 1 - 0.70 = 0.30$
A success is finding the address or lost acquaintances.

(a) $P(r > 280) = P(r \geq 281) = P(281 \leq r) = P(280.5 \leq x)$
$np = 430(0.7) = 301$ and $nq = 430(0.3) = 129$
Since both np and nq are greater than 5, the normal approximation with $\mu = np = 301$ and $\sigma = \sqrt{npq} = \sqrt{430(0.7)(0.3)} = \sqrt{90.3} = 9.5026$ is appropriate.

$$P(280.5 \leq x) = P\left(\frac{280.5-301}{9.5026} \leq z\right) = P(-2.16 \leq z) = 1-P(z<-2.16) = 1-0.0154 = 0.9846$$

(b)
$$\begin{aligned} P(r \geq 320) &= P(320 \leq r) \\ &= P(319.5 \leq x) \\ &= P\left(\frac{319.5-301}{9.5026} \leq z\right) \\ &= P(1.95 \leq z) \\ &= 1-P(z>1.95) \\ &= 1-0.9744 \\ &= 0.0256 \end{aligned}$$

(c)
$$\begin{aligned} P(280 \leq r \leq 320) &= P(279.5 \leq x \leq 320.5) \\ &= P\left(\frac{279.5-301}{9.5026} \leq z \leq \frac{320.5-301}{9.5026}\right) \\ &= P(-2.26 \leq z \leq 2.05) \\ &= P(z \leq 2.05) - P(z<-2.26) \\ &= 0.9798-0.0119 \\ &= 0.9679 \end{aligned}$$

(d) $n = 430, p = 0.7, q = 0.3$
Both np and nq are greater than 5 so the normal approximation is appropriate, See (a).

10. $n = 8641, p = 61\% = 0.61, q = 1 - p = 0.39$
A success is when a pottery shard is Santa Fe black on white.

(a) $P(r < 5200) = P(r \leq 5199) = P(x \leq 5199.5)$
$np = 8641(0.61) = 5271.01$ and $nq = 3369.99$
Since both np and nq are greater than 5, we can use the normal approximation with
$\mu = np = 5271.01$ and $\sigma = \sqrt{npq} = \sqrt{8641(0.61)(0.39)} = \sqrt{2055.6939} = 45.3398$

$$P(x \leq 5199.5) = P\left(z \leq \frac{5199.5 - 5271.01}{45.3398}\right) = P(z \leq -1.58) = 0.0571$$

(b)
$$\begin{aligned} P(r > 5400) &= P(r \geq 5401) \\ &= P(5401 \leq r) \\ &= P(5400.5 \leq x) \\ &= P\left(\frac{5400.5 - 5271.01}{45.3398} \leq z\right) \\ &= P(2.86 \leq z) \\ &= 1 - P(z < 2.86) \\ &= 1 - 0.9979 \\ &= 0.0021 \end{aligned}$$

(c)
$$\begin{aligned} P(5200 \leq r \leq 5400) &= P(5199.5 \leq x \leq 5400.5) \\ &= P\left(-1.58 \leq z \leq \frac{5400.5 - 5271.01}{45.3398}\right) \\ &= P(-1.58 \leq z \leq 2.86) \\ &= P(z \leq 2.86) - P(z < -1.58) \\ &= 0.9979 - 0.0571 \\ &= 0.9408 \end{aligned}$$

(d) $n = 8641, p = 0.61, q = 0.39, np = 5271.01, nq = 3369.99$.

11. $n = 850, p = 57\% = 0.57, q = 0.43$
Success = pass Ohio bar exam

(a) $P(r \geq 540) = P(540 \leq r) = P(539.5 \leq x)$

$np = 484.5, nq = 365.5, \mu = np = 484.5, \sigma = \sqrt{npq} = \sqrt{208.335} = 14.4338$

Since both np and nq are greater than 5, use normal approximation with μ and σ as above.

$$P(539.5 \leq x) = P\left(\frac{539.5 - 484.5}{14.4338} \leq z\right) = P(3.81 \leq z) \approx 0$$

(b) $P(r \leq 500) = P(x \leq 500.5) = P\left(z \leq \frac{500.5 - 484.5}{14.4338}\right) = P(z \leq 1.11) = 0.8665$

(c)
$$\begin{aligned} P(485 \leq r \leq 525) &= P(484.5 \leq x \leq 525.5) \\ &= P\left(0 \leq z \leq \frac{525.5 - 484.5}{14.4338}\right) \\ &= P(0 \leq z \leq 2.84) \\ &= P(z \leq 2.84) - P(z < 0) \\ &= 0.9977 - 0.5 \\ &= 0.4977 \end{aligned}$$

12. $n = 5000$, $p = 3.2\% = 0.032$, $q = 0.968$
Success = coupon redeemed

(a) $P(100 < r) = P(101 \le r) = P(100.5 \le x)$
$np = 160$, $nq = 4840$, $\sigma = \sqrt{npq} = \sqrt{154.88} = 12.4451$
Since both np and nq are greater than 5, use normal approximation with $\mu = np$ and σ as shown.

$$P(100.5 \le x) = P\left(\frac{100.5-160}{12.4451} \le z\right) = P(-4.78 \le z) \approx 1$$

(b)
$$\begin{aligned} P(r < 200) &= P(r \le 199) \\ &= P(x \le 199.5) \\ &= P\left(z \le \frac{199.5-160}{12.4451}\right) \\ &= P(z \le 3.17) \\ &= 0.9992 \end{aligned}$$

(c)
$$\begin{aligned} P(100 \le r \le 200) &= P(99.5 \le x \le 200.5) \\ &= P\left(\frac{99.5-160}{12.4451} \le z \le \frac{200.5-160}{12.4451}\right) \\ &= P(-4.86 \le z \le 3.25) \\ &\approx P(z \le 3.25) \\ &= 0.9994 \end{aligned}$$

13. $n = 317$, $P(\text{buy, given sampled}) = 37\% = 0.37$, $P(\text{sampled}) = 60\% = 0.60 = p$ so $q = 0.40$

(a) $P(180 < r) = P(181 \le r) = P(180.5 \le x)$
$np = 190.2$, $nq = 126.8$, $\sigma = \sqrt{npq} = \sqrt{76.08} = 8.7224$
Since both np and np are greater than 5, use normal approximation with $\mu = np$ and $\sigma = \sqrt{npq}$.

$$P(180.5 \le x) = P\left(\frac{180.5-190.2}{8.7224} \le z\right) = P(-1.11 \le z) = 1 - P(z < -1.11) = 1 - 0.1335 = 0.8665$$

(b) $P(r < 200) = P(r \le 199) = P(x \le 199.5) = P\left(z \le \frac{199.5-190.2}{8.7224}\right) = P(z \le 1.07) = 0.8577$

(c) Let A be the event buy product; let B be the event tried free sample, Thus $P(\text{A, given B}) = 0.37$ and $P(\text{B}) = 0.60$. Since $P(\text{A and B}) = P(\text{B}) \cdot P(\text{A, given B}) = 0.60(0.37) = 0.222$, $P(\text{sample and buy}) = 0.222$.

(d) Let a success be sample and buy. Then $p = 0.222$ from (c), and $q = 0.778$.
$$P(60 \le r \le 80) = P(59.5 \le x \le 80.5)$$
Here, $np = 317(0.222) = 70.374$ and $nq = 246.626$, so use normal approximation with $\mu = np$ and $\sigma = \sqrt{npq} = \sqrt{317(0.222)(0.778)} = \sqrt{54.750972} = 7.3994$.

$$\begin{aligned} P(59.5 \le x \le 80.5) &= P\left(\frac{59.5-70.374}{7.3994} \le z \le \frac{80.5-70.374}{7.3994}\right) \\ &= P(-1.47 \le z \le 1.37) \\ &= P(z \le 1.37) - P(z < -1.47) \\ &= 0.9147 - 0.0708 \\ &= 0.8439 \end{aligned}$$

14. $n = 175$, $P(\text{vanilla}) = 25\% = 0.25$, $P(\text{chocolate}) = 9\% = 0.09$

(a) Success = buy vanilla ice cream, so $p = 0.25$ and $q = 0.75$.

$$P(50 \le r) = P(49.5 \le x)$$

$np = 43.75$, $nq = 131.25$, $\sqrt{npq} = \sqrt{32.8125} = 5.7282 = \sigma$

Since both np and nq area greater than 5, use normal approximation with $\mu = np$ and $\sigma = \sqrt{npq}$.

$$P(49.5 \le x) = P\left(\frac{49.5 - 43.75}{5.7282} \le z\right) = P(1.00 \le z) = 1 - P(z < 1) = 1 - 0.8413 = 0.1587$$

(b) Success = buy chocolate ice cream, so $p = 0.09$ and $q = 0.91$.

$$P(12 \le r) = P(11.5 \le x)$$

Since $np = 15.75 > 5$ and $nq = 175(0.91) = 159.25 > 5$, so use normal approximation with $\mu = np$ and $\sigma = \sqrt{npq} = \sqrt{14.3325} = 3.7858$.

$$P(11.5 \le x) = P\left(\frac{11.5 - 15.75}{3.7858} \le z\right) = P(-1.12 \le z) = 1 - P(z < -1.12) = 1 - 0.1314 = 0.8686$$

(c) Let V be the even the person buys vanilla ice cream and C be the event the person buys chocolate ice cream. V and C are not mutually exclusive, since a person buying vanilla can also buy chocolate ice cream. Given V and C are independent, i.e., $P(\text{V and C}) = P(\text{V}) \cdot P(\text{C})$.

$$\begin{aligned} P(\text{C or V}) &= P(\text{C}) + P(\text{V}) - P(\text{C and V}) \\ &= 0.09 + 0.25 - (0.09)(0.25) \quad \text{using (a) and (b)} \\ &= 0.3175 \end{aligned}$$

(d) Success = buy chocolate or vanilla, so $p = 0.3175$ from (c) and $q = 0.6825$.

$$P(50 \le r \le 60) = P(49.5 \le x \le 60.5)$$

Since $np = 175(0.3175) = 55.5625 > 5$ and $nq = 175(0.6825) = 119.4375 > 5$, use normal approximation with $\mu = np$ and $\sigma = \sqrt{npq} = \sqrt{175(0.3175)(0.6825)} = \sqrt{37.9214} = 6.1580$.

$$\begin{aligned} P(49.5 \le x \le 60.5) &= P\left(\frac{49.5 - 55.5625}{6.158} \le z \le \frac{60.5 - 55.5625}{6.158}\right) \\ &= P(-0.98 \le z \le 0.80) \\ &= P(z \le 0.80) - P(z < -0.98) \\ &= 0.7881 - 0.1635 \\ &= 0.6246 \end{aligned}$$

15. $n = 267$ reservations, $P(\text{show}) = 1 - 0.06 = 0.94 = p$ so $q = 0.06$.

(a) $p = 0.94$

(b) Success = show up for flight (with a reservation) seat available for all who show up means the number showing up must be ≤ 255 actual plane seats. Thus, $P(r \le 255)$.

(c) $P(r \le 255) = P(x \le 255.5)$

Since $np = 267(0.94) = 250.98 > 5$ and $nq = 267(0.06) = 16.02 > 5$, use normal approximation with $\mu = np$ and $\sigma = \sqrt{npq} = \sqrt{267(0.94)(0.06)} = \sqrt{15.0588} = 3.8806$.

$$P(x \le 255.5) = P\left(z \le \frac{255.5 - 250.98}{3.8806}\right) = P(z \le 1.16) = 0.8770$$

16. Answers vary.
The normal approximation to the binomial is appropriate (reasonably accurate) when np and nq are both greater than 5. (If $n \le 25$, say, tables of the exact binomial distribution can be used.) In this case, the normal distribution approximating the binomial has mean $\mu = np$ and standard deviation $\sigma = \sqrt{npq}$. Because the normal distribution is continuous whereas the binomial is discrete, the accuracy of the approximation is improved by using the continuity correction. The interval around the number of successes is first written as a closed interval (such as $[a, b]$ instead of (c, d) where $c + 1 = a$ and $d - 1 = b$); then the left endpoint is decreased by 0.5 and the right endpoint is increased by 0.5. (In the case of half closed intervals, such as $r \le 14$ or $r \ge 7$, only the one endpoint needs to be adjusted.)

Chapter 6 Review

1. (a) $P(0 \le z \le 1.75) = P(z \le 1.75) - P(z < 0) = 0.9599 - 0.5 = 0.4599$

(b) $P(-1.29 \le z \le 0) = P(z \le 0) - P(z < -1.29) = 0.5 - 0.0985 = 0.4015$

(c) $P(1.03 \le z \le 1.21) = P(z \le 1.21) - P(z < 1.03) = 0.8869 - 0.8485 = 0.0384$

(d) $P(z \ge 2.31) = 1 - P(z < 2.31) = 1 - 0.9896 = 0.0104$

(e) $P(z \le -1.96) = 0.0250$

(f) $P(z \le 1) = 0.8413$

2. (a) $P(0 \le z \le 0.75) = P(z \le 0.75) - P(z < 0) = 0.7734 - 0.5 = 0.2734$

(b) $P(-1.50 \le z \le 0) = P(z \le 0) - P(z < -1.50) = 0.5 - 0.0668 = 0.4332$

(c) $P(-2.67 \le z \le -1.74) = P(z \le -1.74) - P(z < -2.67) = 0.0409 - 0.0038 = 0.0371$

(d) $P(z \ge 1.56) = 1 - P(z < 1.56) = 1 - 0.9406 = 0.0594$

(e) $P(z \le -0.97) = 0.1660$

(f) $P(z \le 2.01) = 0.9778$

3. x is normal with $\mu = 47$ and $\sigma = 6.2$

(a) $P(x \le 60) = P\left(z \le \dfrac{60-47}{6.2}\right) = P(z \le 2.10) = 0.9821$

(b) $P(x \ge 50) = P\left(z \ge \dfrac{50-47}{6.2}\right) = P(z \ge 0.48) = 1 - P(z < 0.48) = 1 - 0.6844 = 0.3156$

(c) $P(50 \le x \le 60) = P(0.48 \le z \le 2.10) = P(z \le 2.10) - P(z < 0.48) = 0.9821 - 0.6844 = 0.2977$

4. x is normal with $\mu = 110$, $\sigma = 12$

(a) $P(x \le 120) = P\left(z \le \dfrac{120-110}{12}\right) = P(z \le 0.83) = 0.7967$

(b) $P(x \ge 80) = P\left(z \ge \dfrac{80-110}{12}\right) = P(z \ge -2.5) = 1 - P(z < -2.5) = 1 - 0.0062 = 0.9938$

(c) $P(108 \le x \le 117) = P\left(\dfrac{108-110}{12} \le z \le \dfrac{117-110}{12}\right) = P(-0.17 \le z \le 0.58)$
$= P(z \le 0.58) - P(z < -0.17) = 0.7190 - 0.4325 = 0.2865$

5. Find z_0 such that $P(z \geq z_0) = 5\% = 0.05$. Same as find z_0 such that $P(z < z_0) = 0.95$
$P(z < 1.645) = 0.95$, so $z_0 = 1.645$

6. Find z_0 such that $P(z \leq z_0) = 1\% = 0.01$.
$P(z \leq -2.33) = 0.0099$, so $z_0 = -2.33$

7. Find z_0 such that $P(-z_0 \leq z \leq +z_0) = 0.95$
Same as 5% of area outside $[-z_0, +z_0]$; split in half:
$P(z \leq -z_0) = 0.05/2 = 0.025$
$P(z \leq -1.96) = 0.0250$ so $-z_0 = -1.96$ and $+z_0 = 1.96$

8. Find z_0 so $P(-z_0 \leq z \leq +z_0) = 0.99$
Same as 1% outside $[-z_0, +z_0]$; divide in half.
$P(z \leq -z_0) = 0.01/2 = 0.005$.
$P(z \leq -2.575) = 0.0050$, so $\pm z_0 = \pm 2.575$, or ± 2.58

9. $\mu = 79$, $\sigma = 9$

(a) $z = \dfrac{x-\mu}{\sigma} = \dfrac{87-79}{9} = 0.89$

(b) $z = \dfrac{79-79}{9} = 0$

(c) $P(x > 85) = P\left(z > \dfrac{85-79}{9}\right) = P(z > 0.67) = 1 - P(z \leq 0.67) = 1 - 0.7486 = 0.2514$

10. $\mu = 270$, $\sigma = 35$

(a) $z = \dfrac{x-\mu}{\sigma}$ so $x = \mu + z\sigma$
here, $x = 270 + 1.9(35) = 336.5$

(b) $x = \mu + z\sigma$; here, $x = 270 + (-0.25)(35) = 261.25$

(c) $P(200 \leq x \leq 340) = P\left(\dfrac{200-270}{35} \leq z \leq \dfrac{340-270}{35}\right) = P(-2 \leq z \leq 2)$
$= P(z \leq 2) - P(z < -2) = 0.9772 - 0.0228 = 0.9544$

11. Binomial with $n = 400$, $p = 0.70$, and $q = 0.30$.
Success = can recycled

(a) $P(r \geq 300) = P(300 \leq r) = P(299.5 \leq x)$

$np = 280 > 5$, $nq = 120 > 5$, $\sqrt{npq} = \sqrt{84} = 9.1652$

Use normal approximation with $\mu = np$ and $\sigma = \sqrt{npq}$.

$P(299.5 \leq x) = P\left(\dfrac{299.5-280}{9.1652} \leq z\right) = P(2.13 \leq z) = 1 - P(z < 2.13) = 1 - 0.9834 = 0.0166$

(b) $P(260 \le r \le 300) = P(259.5 \le x \le 300.5)$

$$= P\left(\frac{259.5-280}{9.1652} \le z \le \frac{300.5-280}{9.1652}\right)$$
$$= P(-2.24 \le z \le 2.24)$$
$$= P(z \le 2.24) - P(z < -2.24)$$
$$= 0.9875 - 0.0125$$
$$= 0.9750$$

12. Lifetime x is normally distributed with $\mu = 5000$ and $\sigma = 450$ hours.

(a) $P(x \le 5000) = P(z \le 0) = 0.5000$

(b) Find x_0 such that $P(x \le x_0) = 0.05$. First, find z_0 so that $P(z \le z_0) = 0.05$.

$P(z \le -1.645) = 0.05$, so $z_0 = -1.645$

$x_0 = \mu + z_0\sigma = 5000 + (-1.645)(450) = 4259.75$

Guarantee the CD player for 4260 hours.

13. Delivery time x is normal with $\mu = 14$ and $\sigma = 2$ hours.

(a) $P(x \le 18) = P\left(z \le \frac{18-14}{2}\right) = P(z \le 2) = 0.9772$

(b) Find x_0 such that $P(x \le x_0) = 0.95$.

Find z_0 so that $P(z \le z_0) = 0.95$.

$P(z \le 1.645) = 0.95$, so $z_0 = 1.645$.

$x_0 = \mu + z_0\sigma = 14 + 1.645(2) = 17.29 \approx 17.3$ hours

14. (a)

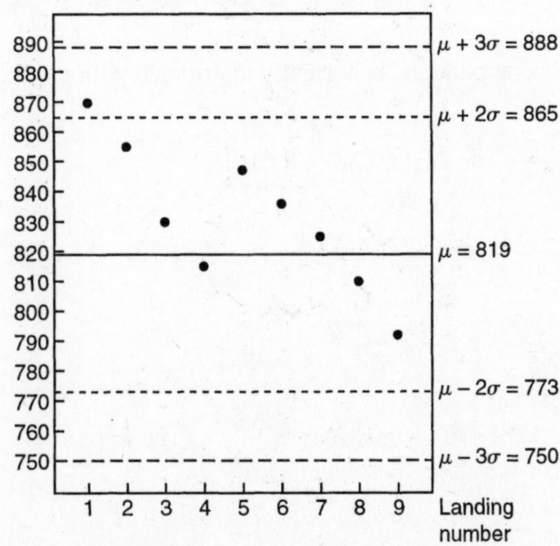

The pressure is "in control;" none of the 3 warning signals is present.

(b)

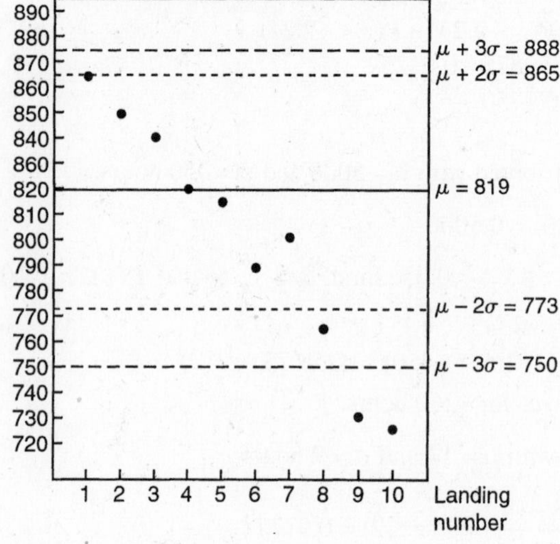

The last 2 points are below $\mu - 3\sigma$. The last 3 (consecutive) points are all below $\mu - 2\sigma$. Since warning signals I and III are present, the pressure is "out of control."

15. Scanner price errors in the store's favor are mound-shaped with $\mu = \$2.66$ and $\sigma = \$0.85$.

(a) 68% of the errors should be in the range $\mu \pm 1\sigma$, approximately, or $2.66 \pm 1(0.85)$ which is \$1.81 to \$3.51.

(b) Approximately 95% of the errors should be in the range $\mu \pm 2\sigma$, or $2.66 \pm 2(0.85)$, which is \$0.96 to \$4.36.

(c) Almost all (99.7%) of the errors should lie in the range $\mu \pm 3\sigma$, or $2.66 \pm 3(0.85)$, which is \$0.11 to \$5.21.

16. Time spent on a customer's complaint, x, is normally distributed with $\mu = 9.3$ and $\sigma = 2.5$ minutes.

(a) $P(x < 10) = P\left(z < \frac{10 - 9.3}{2.5}\right) = P(z < 0.28) = 0.6103$

(b) $P(x > 5) = P\left(z > \frac{5 - 9.3}{2.5}\right) = P(z > -1.72) = 1 - P(z \le -1.72) = 1 - 0.0427 = 0.9573$

(c)
$$\begin{aligned} P(8 \le x \le 15) &= P\left(\frac{8 - 9.3}{2.5} \le z \le \frac{15 - 9.3}{2.5}\right) \\ &= P(-0.52 \le z \le 2.28) \\ &= P(z \le 2.28) - P(z < -0.52) \\ &= 0.9887 - 0.3015 \\ &= 0.6872 \end{aligned}$$

17. Response time, x, is normally distributed with $\mu = 42$ and $\sigma = 8$ minutes.

(a) $$\begin{aligned} P(30 \le x \le 45) &= P\left(\frac{30-42}{8} \le z \le \frac{45-42}{8}\right) \\ &= P(-1.5 \le z \le 0.375) \\ &= P(z \le 0.38) - P(z < -1.5) \\ &= 0.6480 - 0.0668 \\ &= 0.5812 \end{aligned}$$

(b) $P(x < 30) = P(z < -1.5) = 0.0668$

(c) $P(x > 60) = P\left(z > \frac{60-42}{8}\right) = P(z > 2.25) = 1 - P(z \le 2.25) = 1 - 0.9878 = 0.0122$

18. Success = unlisted phone number
$n = 150$, $p = 68\% = 0.68$, $q = 1 - p = 0.32$
$np = 150(0.68) = 102$, $nq = 48$, $npq = 150(0.68)(0.32) = 32.64$

(a) $P(r \ge 100) = P(100 \le r) = P(99.5 \le x)$

Since np and nq are both greater than 5, we can use the normal approximation with $\mu = np = 102$ and $\sigma = \sqrt{npq} = \sqrt{32.64} = 5.7131$.

$P(99.5 \le x) = P\left(\frac{99.5-102}{5.7131} \le z\right) = P(-0.44 \le z) = 1 - P(z < -0.44) = 1 - 0.3300 = 0.6700$

(b) $P(r < 100) = P(r \le 99) = P(x \le 99.5) = P\left(z \le \frac{99.5-102}{5.7131}\right) = P(z \le -0.44) = 0.3300$

(c) Success is redefined to be a listed phone number, so $n = 150$, $p = 0.32$, $q = 0.68$, $np = 48$, $nq = 102$, and $\sqrt{npq} = \sqrt{32.64} = 5.7131 = \sigma$; μ is now 48; normal approximation is still appropriate.

$$\begin{aligned} P(50 \le r \le 65) &= P(49.5 \le x \le 65.5) \\ &= P\left(\frac{49.5-48}{5.7131} \le z \le \frac{65.5-48}{5.7131}\right) \\ &= P(0.26 \le z \le 3.06) \\ &= P(z \le 3.06) - P(z < 0.26) \\ &= 0.9989 - 0.6026 \\ &= 0.3963 \end{aligned}$$

19. Success = having blood type AB
$n = 250$, $p = 3\% = 0.03$, $q = 1 - p = 0.97$, $np = 7.5$, $nq = 242.5$, $npq = 7.275$

(a) $P(5 \le r) = P(4.5 \le x)$

$np > 7.5$ and $\sigma = \sqrt{npq} = \sqrt{7.275} = 2.6972$

$P(4.5 \le x) = P\left(\frac{4.5-7.5}{2.6972} \le z\right) = P(-1.11 \le z) = 1 - P(z < -1.11) = 1 - 0.1335 = 0.8665$

(b) $$\begin{aligned} P(5 \le r \le 10) &= P(4.5 \le x \le 10.5) \\ &= P\left(-1.11 \le z \le \frac{10.5-7.5}{2.6972}\right) \\ &= P(-1.11 \le z \le 1.11) \\ &= 1 - 2P(z < -1.11) \\ &= 1 - 2(0.1335) \\ &= 0.7330 \end{aligned}$$

Chapter 7 Introduction to Sampling Distributions

Section 7.1

1. Answers vary. Students should identify the individuals (subjects) and variable involved. Answers may include: A population is a set of measurements or counts either existing or conceptual. For example, the population of all ages of all people in Colorado; the population of weights of all students in your school; the population count of all antelope in Wyoming.

2. See Section 1.2. Answer may include:

A simple random sample of n measurements from a population is a subset of the population selected in a manner such that

(a) every sample of size n from the population has an equal chance of being selected and

(b) every member of the population has an equal chance of being included in the sample.

3. A population parameter is a numerical descriptive measure of a population, such as μ, the population mean; σ, the population standard deviation; σ^2, the population variance; p, the population proportion; ρ (rho) the population correlation coefficient for those who have already studied linear regression from Chapter 10.

4. A sample statistic is a numerical descriptive measure of a sample such as $\overline{x}$, the sample mean; s, the sample standard deviation; s^2, the sample variance; $\hat{p}$, the sample proportion; r, the sample correlation coefficient for those who have already studied linear regression from Chapter 10.

5. A statistical inference is a conclusion about the value of a population parameter based on information about the corresponding sample statistic and probability. We will do both estimation and testing.

6. A sampling distribution is a probability distribution for a sample statistic.

7. They help us visualize the sampling distribution by using tables and graphs that approximately represent the sampling distribution.

8. Relative frequencies can be thought of as a measure or estimate of the likelihood of a certain statistic falling within the class bounds.

9. We studied the sampling distribution of mean trout lengths based on samples of size 5. Other such sampling distributions abound. Notice that the sample size remains the same for each sample in a sampling distribution.

Section 7.2

Note: Answers may vary slightly depending on the number of digits carried in the standard deviation.

1. (a) $\mu_{\bar{x}} = \mu = 15$

$$\sigma_{\bar{x}} = \frac{\sigma}{\sqrt{n}} = \frac{14}{\sqrt{49}} = 2.0$$

Because $n = 49 \geq 30$, by the central limit theorem, we can assume that the distribution of $\bar{x}$ is approximately normal.

$$z = \frac{\bar{x} - \mu}{\sigma_{\bar{x}}} = \frac{\bar{x} - 15}{2.0}$$

$\bar{x} = 15$ converts to $z = \frac{15 - 15}{2.0} = 0$

$\bar{x} = 17$ converts to $z = \frac{17 - 15}{2.0} = 1$

$$\begin{aligned} P(15 \leq \bar{x} \leq 17) &= P(0 \leq z \leq 1) \\ &= P(z \leq 1) - P(z \leq 0) \\ &= 0.8413 - 0.5000 \\ &= 0.3413 \end{aligned}$$

(b) $\mu_{\bar{x}} = \mu = 15$

$$\sigma_{\bar{x}} = \frac{\sigma}{\sqrt{n}} = \frac{14}{\sqrt{64}} = 1.75$$

Because $n = 64 \geq 30$, by the central limit theorem, we can assume that the distribution of $\bar{x}$ is approximately normal.

$$z = \frac{\bar{x} - \mu}{\sigma_{\bar{x}}} = \frac{\bar{x} - 15}{1.75}$$

$\bar{x} = 15$ converts to $z = \frac{15 - 15}{1.75} = 0$

$\bar{x} = 17$ converts to $z = \frac{17 - 15}{1.75} = 1.14$

$$\begin{aligned} P(15 \leq \bar{x} \leq 17) &= P(0 \leq z \leq 1.14) \\ &= P(z \leq 1.14) - P(z \leq 0) \\ &= 0.8729 - 0.5000 \\ &= 0.3729 \end{aligned}$$

(c) The standard deviation of part (b) is smaller because of the larger sample size. Therefore, the distribution about $\mu_{\bar{x}}$ is narrower in part (b).

2. (a) $\mu_{\bar{x}} = \mu = 100$

$$\sigma_{\bar{x}} = \frac{\sigma}{\sqrt{n}} = \frac{48}{\sqrt{81}} = 5.33$$

Because $n = 81 \geq 30$, by the central limit theorem, we can assume that the distribution of $\bar{x}$ is approximately normal.

$$z = \frac{\bar{x} - \mu}{\sigma_{\bar{x}}} = \frac{\bar{x} - 100}{5.33}$$

$\bar{x} = 92$ converts to $z = \dfrac{92 - 100}{5.33} = -1.50$

$\bar{x} = 100$ converts to $z = \dfrac{100 - 100}{5.33} = 0$

$$\begin{aligned} P(92 \le \bar{x} \le 100) &= P(-1.50 \le z \le 0) \\ &= P(z \le 0) - P(z \le -1.50) \\ &= 0.5000 - 0.0668 \\ &= 0.4332 \end{aligned}$$

(b) $\mu_{\bar{x}} = \mu = 100$

$$\sigma_{\bar{x}} = \frac{\sigma}{\sqrt{n}} = \frac{48}{\sqrt{121}} = 4.36$$

Because $n = 121 \ge 30$, by the central limit theorem, we can assume that the distribution of $\bar{x}$ is approximately normal.

$$z = \frac{\bar{x} - \mu}{\sigma_{\bar{x}}} = \frac{\bar{x} - 100}{4.36}$$

$\bar{x} = 92$ converts to $z = \dfrac{92 - 100}{4.36} = -1.83$

$\bar{x} = 100$ converts to $z = \dfrac{100 - 100}{4.36} = 0$

$$\begin{aligned} P(92 \le \bar{x} \le 100) &= P(-1.83 \le z \le 0) \\ &= P(z \le 0) - P(z \le -1.83) \\ &= 0.5000 - 0.0336 \\ &= 0.4664 \end{aligned}$$

(c) The probability of part (b) is greater than that of part (a). The standard deviation of part (b) is smaller because of the larger sample size. Therefore, the distribution about $\mu_{\bar{x}}$ is narrower in part (b).

3. (a) No, we cannot say anything about the distribution of sample means because the sample size is only 9 and so it is too small to apply the central limit theorem.

(b) Yes, now we can say that the $\bar{x}$ distribution will also be normal with

$$\mu_{\bar{x}} = \mu = 25 \text{ and } \sigma_{\bar{x}} = \frac{\sigma}{\sqrt{n}} = \frac{3.5}{\sqrt{9}} = 1.17.$$

$$z = \frac{\bar{x} - \mu}{\sigma_{\bar{x}}} = \frac{\bar{x} - 25}{1.17}$$

$$\begin{aligned} P(23 \le \bar{x} \le 26) &= P\left(\frac{23 - 25}{1.17} \le z \le \frac{26 - 25}{1.17}\right) \\ &= P(-1.71 \le z \le 0.86) \\ &= P(z \le 0.86) - P(z \le -1.71) \\ &= 0.8051 - 0.0436 \\ &= 0.7615 \end{aligned}$$

4. (a) No, we cannot say anything about the distribution of sample means because the sample size is only 16 and so it is too small to apply the central limit theorem.

(b) Yes, now we can say that the $\overline{x}$ distribution will also be normal with

$$\mu_{\overline{x}} = \mu = 72 \text{ and } \sigma_{\overline{x}} = \frac{\sigma}{\sqrt{n}} = \frac{8}{\sqrt{16}} = 2.$$

$$z = \frac{\overline{x} - \mu}{\sigma_{\overline{x}}} = \frac{\overline{x} - 72}{2}$$

$$\begin{aligned} P(68 \le \overline{x} \le 73) &= P\left(\frac{68-72}{2} \le z \le \frac{73-72}{2}\right) \\ &= (-2 \le z \le 0.5) \\ &= P(z \le 0.5) - P(z \le -2) \\ &= 0.6915 - 0.0228 \\ &= 0.6687 \end{aligned}$$

5. (a) $\mu = 75,\ \sigma = 0.8$

$$\begin{aligned} P(x < 74.5) &= P\left(z < \frac{74.5-75}{0.8}\right) \\ &= P(z < -0.63) \\ &= 0.2643 \end{aligned}$$

(b) $\mu_{\overline{x}} = 75,\ \sigma_{\overline{x}} = \frac{\sigma}{\sqrt{n}} = \frac{0.8}{\sqrt{20}} = 0.179$

$$\begin{aligned} P(\overline{x} < 74.5) &= P\left(z < \frac{74.5-75}{0.179}\right) \\ &= P(z < -2.79) \\ &= 0.0026 \end{aligned}$$

(c) No. If the weight of only one car were less than 74.5 tons, we cannot conclude that the loader is out of adjustment. If the mean weight for a sample of 20 cars were less than 74.5 tons, we would suspect that the loader is malfunctioning. As we see in part (b), the probability of this happening is very low if the loader is correctly adjusted.

6. (a) $\mu = 68,\ \sigma = 3$

$$\begin{aligned} P(67 \le x \le 69) &= P\left(\frac{67-68}{3} \le z \le \frac{69-68}{3}\right) \\ &= P(-0.33 \le z \le 0.33) \\ &= P(z \le 0.33) - P(z \le -0.33) \\ &= 0.6293 - 0.3707 \\ &= 0.2586 \end{aligned}$$

(b) $\mu_{\bar{x}} = 68,\ \sigma_{\bar{x}} = \frac{\sigma}{\sqrt{n}} = \frac{3}{\sqrt{9}} = 1$

$$\begin{aligned} P(67 \le \bar{x} \le 69) &= P\left(\frac{67-68}{1} \le z \le \frac{69-68}{1}\right) \\ &= P(-1 \le z \le 1) \\ &= P(z \le 1) - P(z \le -1) \\ &= 0.8413 - 0.1587 \\ &= 0.6826 \end{aligned}$$

(c) The probability in part (b) is much higher because the standard deviation is smaller for the $\bar{x}$ distribution.

7. (a) $\mu = 85,\ \sigma = 25$

$$\begin{aligned} P(x < 40) &= P\left(z < \frac{40-85}{25}\right) \\ &= P(z < -1.8) \\ &= 0.0359 \end{aligned}$$

(b) The probability distribution of $\bar{x}$ is approximately normal with $\mu_{\bar{x}} = 85; \sigma_{\bar{x}} = \frac{\sigma}{\sqrt{n}} = \frac{25}{\sqrt{2}} = 17.68$.

$$\begin{aligned} P(\bar{x} < 40) &= P\left(z < \frac{40-85}{17.68}\right) \\ &= P(z < -2.55) \\ &= 0.0054 \end{aligned}$$

(c) $\mu_{\bar{x}} = 85,\ \sigma_{\bar{x}} = \frac{\sigma}{\sqrt{n}} = \frac{25}{\sqrt{3}} = 14.43$

$$\begin{aligned} P(\bar{x} < 40) &= P\left(z < \frac{40-85}{14.43}\right) \\ &= P(z < -3.12) \\ &= 0.0009 \end{aligned}$$

(d) $\mu_{\bar{x}} = 85,\ \sigma_{\bar{x}} = \frac{\sigma}{\sqrt{n}} = \frac{25}{\sqrt{5}} = 11.2$

$$\begin{aligned} P(\bar{x} < 40) &= P\left(z < \frac{40-85}{11.2}\right) \\ &= P(z < -4.02) \\ &\approx 0 \end{aligned}$$

(e) Yes; If the average value based on five tests were less than 40, the patient is almost certain to have excess insulin.

8. $\mu = 7500,\ \sigma = 1750$

(a) $P(x < 3500) = P\left(z < \frac{3500 - 7500}{1750}\right)$
$= P(z < -2.29)$
$= 0.0110$

(b) The probability distribution of $\bar{x}$ is approximately normal with

$\mu_{\bar{x}} = 7500;\ \sigma_{\bar{x}} = \frac{\sigma}{\sqrt{n}} = \frac{1750}{\sqrt{2}} = 1237.44.$

$P(\bar{x} < 3500) = P\left(z < \frac{3500 - 7500}{1237.44}\right)$
$= P(z < -3.23)$
$= 0.0006$

(c) $\mu_{\bar{x}} = 7500,\ \sigma_{\bar{x}} = \frac{\sigma}{\sqrt{n}} = \frac{1750}{\sqrt{3}} = 1010.36$

$P(\bar{x} < 3500) = P\left(z < \frac{3500 - 7500}{1010.36}\right)$
$= P(z < -3.96)$
≈ 0

(d) The probabilities decreased as n increased. It would be an extremely rare event for a person to have two or three tests below 3500 purely by chance; the person probably has leukopenia.

9. (a) $\mu = 63.0,\ \sigma = 7.1$

$P(x < 54) = P\left(z < \frac{54 - 63.0}{7.1}\right)$
$= P(z < -1.27)$
$= 0.1020$

(b) The expected number undernourished is 2200(0.1020) = 224.4, or about 224.

(c) $\mu_{\bar{x}} = 63.0,\ \sigma_{\bar{x}} = \frac{\sigma}{\sqrt{n}} = \frac{7.1}{\sqrt{50}} = 1.004$

$P(\bar{x} < 60) = P\left(z < \frac{60 - 63.0}{1.004}\right)$
$= P(z < -2.99)$
$= 0.0014$

(d) $\mu_{\bar{x}} = 63.0,\ \sigma_{\bar{x}} = 1.004$

$P(\bar{x} < 64.2) = P\left(z < \frac{64.2 - 63.0}{1.004}\right)$
$= P(z < 1.20)$
$= 0.8849$

Since the sample average is above the mean, it is quite unlikely that the doe population is undernourished.

10. (a) From the Central Limit Theorem, we expect the $\bar{x}$ distribution to be approximately normal with the mean $\mu_{\bar{x}} = \mu = 16$ and standard deviation $\sigma_{\bar{x}} = \frac{\sigma}{\sqrt{n}} = \frac{2}{\sqrt{30}} = 0.3651$.

(b) $\mu_{\bar{x}} = 16,\ \sigma_{\bar{x}} = 0.3651$

$$\begin{aligned} P(16 \le \bar{x} \le 17) &= P\left(\frac{16-16}{0.3651} \le z \le \frac{17-16}{0.3651}\right) \\ &= P(0 \le z \le 2.74) \\ &= P(z \le 2.74) - P(z \le 0) \\ &= 0.9969 - 0.5000 \\ &= 0.4969 \end{aligned}$$

(c) $\mu_{\bar{x}} = 16,\ \sigma_{\bar{x}} = 0.3651$

$$\begin{aligned} P(\bar{x} < 15) &= P\left(z < \frac{15-16}{0.3651}\right) \\ &= P(z < -2.74) \\ &= 0.0031 \end{aligned}$$

11. (a) The random variable x is itself an average based on the number of stocks or bonds in the fund. Since x itself represents a sample mean return based on a large (random) sample of stocks or bonds, x has a distribution that is approximately normal (Central Limit Theorem).

(b) $\mu_{\bar{x}} = 1.6\%,\ \sigma_{\bar{x}} = \frac{\sigma}{\sqrt{n}} = \frac{0.9\%}{\sqrt{6}} = 0.367\%$

$$\begin{aligned} P(1\% \le \bar{x} \le 2\%) &= P\left(\frac{1\% - 1.6\%}{0.367\%} \le z \le \frac{2\% - 1.6\%}{0.367\%}\right) \\ &= P(-1.63 \le z \le 1.09) \\ &= P(z \le 1.09) - P(z \le -1.63) \\ &= 0.8621 - 0.0516 \\ &= 0.8105 \end{aligned}$$

Note: It does not matter whether you solve the problem using percents or their decimal equivalents as long as you are consistent.

(c) Note: 2 years = 24 months; x is <u>monthly</u> percentage return.

$\mu_{\bar{x}} = 1.6\%,\ \sigma_{\bar{x}} = \frac{\sigma}{\sqrt{n}} = \frac{0.9\%}{\sqrt{24}} = 0.1837\%$

$$\begin{aligned} P(1\% \le \bar{x} \le 2\%) &= P\left(\frac{1\% - 1.6\%}{0.1837\%} \le z \le \frac{2\% - 1.6\%}{0.1837\%}\right) \\ &= P(-3.27 \le z \le 2.18) \\ &= P(z \le 2.18) - P(z \le -3.27) \\ &= 0.9854 - 0.0005 \\ &= 0.9849 \end{aligned}$$

(d) Yes. The probability increases as the standard deviation decreases. The standard deviation decreases as the sample size increases.

(e) $\mu_{\bar{x}} = 1.6\%,\ \sigma_{\bar{x}} = 0.1837\%$

$$P(\bar{x} < 1\%) = P\left(z < \frac{1\% - 1.6\%}{0.1837\%}\right)$$
$$= P(z < -3.27)$$
$$= 0.0005$$

This is very unlikely if $\mu = 1.6\%$. One would suspect that μ has slipped below 1.6%.

12. (a) The random variable x is itself an average based on the number of stocks in the fund. Since x itself represents a sample mean return based on a large (random) sample of stocks, x has a distribution that is approximately normal (Central Limit Theorem).

(b) $\mu_{\bar{x}} = 1.4\%,\ \sigma_{\bar{x}} = \frac{\sigma}{\sqrt{n}} = \frac{0.8\%}{\sqrt{9}} = 0.2667\%$

$$P(1\% \le \bar{x} \le 2\%) = P\left(\frac{1\% - 1.4\%}{0.2667\%} \le z \le \frac{2\% - 1.4\%}{0.2667\%}\right)$$
$$= P(-1.50 \le z \le 2.25)$$
$$= P(z \le 2.25) - P(z \le -1.50)$$
$$= 0.9878 - 0.0668$$
$$= 0.9210$$

Note: It does not matter whether you solve the problem using percents or their decimal equivalents as long as you are consistent.

(c) $\mu_{\bar{x}} = 1.4\%,\ \sigma_{\bar{x}} = \frac{\sigma}{\sqrt{n}} = \frac{0.8\%}{\sqrt{18}} = 0.1886\%$

$$P(1\% \le \bar{x} \le 2\%) = P\left(\frac{1\% - 1.4\%}{0.1886\%} \le z \le \frac{2\% - 1.4\%}{0.1886\%}\right)$$
$$= P(-2.12 \le z \le 3.18)$$
$$= P(z \le 3.18) - P(z \le -2.12)$$
$$= 0.9993 - 0.0170$$
$$= 0.9823$$

(d) Yes. The probability increases as the standard deviation decreases. The standard deviation decreases as the sample size increases.

(e) $\mu_{\bar{x}} = 1.4\%,\ \sigma_{\bar{x}} = 0.1886\%$

$$P(\bar{x} > 2\%) = P\left(z > \frac{2\% - 1.4\%}{0.1886\%}\right)$$
$$= P(z > 3.18)$$
$$= 1 - P(z \le 3.18)$$
$$= 1 - 0.9993$$
$$= 0.0007$$

This is very unlikely if $\mu = 1.4\%$. One would suspect that the European stock market may be heating up, i.e., μ is greater than 1.4%.

13. (a) Since x itself represents a sample mean from a large $n \approx 80$ (random) sample of bonds, x is approximately normally distributed according to the Central Limit Theorem.

(b) $\mu_{\bar{x}} = 10.8\%,\ \sigma_{\bar{x}} = \frac{\sigma}{\sqrt{n}} = \frac{4.9\%}{\sqrt{5}} = 2.19\%$

$$P(\bar{x} < 6\%) = P\left(z < \frac{6\% - 10.8\%}{2.19\%}\right)$$
$$= P(z < -2.19)$$
$$= 0.0143$$

Yes. Since this probability is so small, it is very unlikely that $\bar{x}$ would be less than 6% if $\mu = 10.8\%$. The junk bond market appears to be weaker, i.e., μ is less than 10.8%.

(c) $\mu_{\bar{x}} = 10.8\%,\ \sigma_{\bar{x}} = 2.19\%$

$$P(\bar{x} > 16\%) = P\left(z > \frac{16\% - 10.8\%}{2.19\%}\right)$$
$$= P(z > 2.37)$$
$$= 1 - P(z \le 2.37)$$
$$= 1 - 0.9911$$
$$= 0.0089$$

Yes. Since this probability is so small, it is very unlikely that $\bar{x}$ would be greater than 16% if μ = 10.8%. The junk bond market may be heating up, i.e., μ is greater than 10.8%.

14. (a) $\mu_{\bar{x}} = 6.4,\ \sigma_{\bar{x}} = \frac{\sigma}{\sqrt{n}} = \frac{1.5}{\sqrt{40}} = 0.2372$

$$P(6 \le \bar{x} \le 7) = P\left(\frac{6 - 6.4}{0.2372} \le z \le \frac{7 - 6.4}{0.2372}\right)$$
$$= P(-1.69 \le z \le 2.53)$$
$$= P(z \le 2.53) - P(z \le -1.69)$$
$$= 0.9943 - 0.0455$$
$$= 0.9488$$

(b) $\mu_{\bar{x}} = 6.4,\ \sigma_{\bar{x}} = \frac{\sigma}{\sqrt{n}} = \frac{1.5}{\sqrt{80}} = 0.1677$

$$P(6 \le \bar{x} \le 7) = P\left(\frac{6 - 6.4}{0.1677} \le z \le \frac{7 - 6.4}{0.1677}\right)$$
$$= P(-2.39 \le z \le 3.58)$$
$$= P(z \le 3.58) - P(z \le -2.39)$$
$$\approx 1 - 0.0084$$
$$= 0.9916$$

(c) Yes. Since this is such a large probability, the chances of $\bar{x}$ not being in this time interval is extremely unlikely. A second security guard should drop in for a look.

15. (a) The sample size should be 30 or more.

(b) No. If the distribution of x is normal, the distribution of $\bar{x}$ is also normal, regardless of the sample size.

16. (a) By the Central Limit Theorem, the sampling distribution of $\overline{x}$ is approximately normal with mean $\mu_{\overline{x}} = \mu = \$20$ and standard error $\sigma_{\overline{x}} = \frac{\sigma}{\sqrt{n}} = \frac{\$7}{\sqrt{100}} = \$0.70$. It is not necessary to make any assumption about the x distribution because n is large.

(b) $\mu_{\overline{x}} = \$20,\ \sigma_{\overline{x}} = \$0.70$

$$\begin{aligned} P(\$18 \le \overline{x} \le \$22) &= P\left(\frac{\$18-\$20}{\$0.70} \le z \le \frac{\$22-\$20}{\$0.70}\right) \\ &= P(-2.86 \le z \le 2.86) \\ &= P(z \le 2.86) - P(z \le -2.86) \\ &= 0.9979 - 0.0021 \\ &= 0.9958 \end{aligned}$$

(c) $\mu_x = \$20,\ \sigma = \$7$

$$\begin{aligned} P(\$18 \le x \le \$22) &= P\left(\frac{\$18-\$20}{\$7} \le z \le \frac{\$22-\$20}{\$7}\right) \\ &= P(-0.29 \le z \le 0.29) \\ &= 0.6141 - 0.3859 \\ &= 0.2282 \end{aligned}$$

(d) We expect the probability in part (b) to be much higher than the probability in part (c) because the standard deviation is smaller for the $\overline{x}$ distribution than it is for the x distribution. By the Central Limit Theorem, the sampling distribution of $\overline{x}$ will be approximately normal as n increases, and its standard deviation, $\sigma/\sqrt{n}$, will decrease as n increases. The standard deviation of $\overline{x}$, a.k.a. the standard error of $\overline{x}$, measures the spread of the $\overline{x}$ values; the smaller $\sigma/\sqrt{n}$ is, the less variability there is in the $\overline{x}$ values. The less variability there is in the values of $\overline{x}$, the more reliable $\overline{x}$ is as an estimate or predictor of μ. For large n, approximately 95% of the possible values of $\overline{x}$ are within $2\sigma/\sqrt{n}$ of μ. The amount x a typical customer spends on impulse buys also estimates μ (recall $\mu_{\overline{x}} = \mu_x = \mu$), but approximately 95% of individual impulse buys x are within 2σ of μ (using either the Empirical Rule for somewhat mound-shaped data, or assuming x has a distribution that is approximately normal). For a fixed interval, such as \$18 to \$22, centered at the mean, \$20 in this case, the proportion of the possible $\overline{x}$ values within the interval will be greater than the proportion of the possible x values within the same interval.

17. (a) The total checkout time for 30 customers is the sum of the checkout times for each individual customer. Thus, $w = x_1 + x_2 + \cdots + x_{30}$ and the probability that the total checkout time for the next 30 customers is less than 90 is $P(w < 90)$.

(b) If we divide both sides of $w < 90$ by 30, we get $\frac{w}{30} < 3$. However, w is the sum of 30 waiting times, so $\frac{w}{30}$ is $\overline{x}$. Therefore, $P(w < 90) = P(\overline{x} < 3)$.

(c) The probability distribution of $\overline{x}$ is approximately normal with mean $\mu_{\overline{x}} = \mu = 2.7$ and standard deviation $\sigma_{\overline{x}} = \frac{\sigma}{\sqrt{n}} = \frac{0.6}{\sqrt{30}} = 0.1095$.

(d) $P(\overline{x}<3)=P\left(z<\frac{3-2.7}{0.1095}\right)$

$=P(z<2.74)$

$=0.9969$

The probability that the total checkout time for the next 30 customers is less than 90 minutes is 0.9969, i.e., $P(w<90)=0.9969$.

18. Let $w=x_1+x_2+\ldots+x_{36}$.

(a) $w<320$ is equivalent to $\frac{w}{36}<\frac{320}{36}$ or $\overline{x}<8.889$. $\mu_{\overline{x}}=\mu=8.5$, $\sigma_{\overline{x}}=\frac{\sigma}{\sqrt{n}}=\frac{2.5}{\sqrt{36}}=0.4167$

$$\begin{aligned}P(w<320)&=P(\overline{x}<8.889)\\&=P\left(z<\frac{8.889-8.5}{0.4167}\right)\\&=P(z<0.93)\\&=0.8238\end{aligned}$$

(b) $w>275$ is equivalent to $\frac{w}{36}>\frac{275}{36}$ or $\overline{x}>7.639$. $\mu_{\overline{x}}=8.5$, $\sigma_{\overline{x}}=0.4167$

$$\begin{aligned}P(w>275)&=P(\overline{x}>7.639)\\&=P\left(z>\frac{7.639-8.5}{0.4167}\right)\\&=P(z>-2.07)\\&=1-P(z\le-2.07)\\&=1-0.0192\\&\approx0.9808\end{aligned}$$

(c)
$$\begin{aligned}P(275<w<320)&=P(7.639<\overline{x}<8.889)\\&=P(-2.07<z<0.93)\\&=P(z<0.93)-P(z<-2.07)\\&=0.8238-0.0192\\&=0.8046\end{aligned}$$

19. Let $w=x_1+x_2+\ldots+x_{45}$.

(a) $w<9500$ is equivalent to $\frac{w}{45}<\frac{9500}{45}$ or $\overline{x}<211.111$. $\mu_{\overline{x}}=240$, $\sigma_{\overline{x}}=\frac{\sigma}{\sqrt{n}}=\frac{84}{\sqrt{45}}=12.522$

$$\begin{aligned}P(w<9500)&=P(\overline{x}<211.111)\\&=P\left(z<\frac{211.111-240}{12.522}\right)\\&=P(z<-2.31)\\&=0.0104\end{aligned}$$

(b) $w < 12{,}000$ is equivalent to $\frac{w}{45} > \frac{12{,}000}{45}$ or $\overline{x} > 266.667$. $\mu_{\overline{x}} = 240,\ \sigma_{\overline{x}} = 12.522$

$$\begin{aligned} P(w > 12{,}000) &= P(\overline{x} > 266.667) \\ &= P\left(z > \frac{266.667 - 240}{12.522}\right) \\ &= P(z > 2.13) \\ &= 1 - P(z \le 2.13) \\ &= 1 - 0.9834 \\ &= 0.0166 \end{aligned}$$

(c)
$$\begin{aligned} P(9500 < w < 12{,}000) &= P(211.111 < \overline{x} < 266.667) \\ &= P(-2.31 < z < 2.13) \\ &= P(z < 2.13) - P(z < -2.31) \\ &= 0.9834 - 0.0104 \\ &= 0.9730 \end{aligned}$$

20. (a) Let $w = x_1 + x_2 + \ldots + x_9$. $\mu_{\overline{x}} = \mu = 6.3,\ \sigma_{\overline{x}} = \frac{\sigma}{\sqrt{n}} = \frac{1.2}{\sqrt{9}} = 0.4$

$$\begin{aligned} P(w < 60) &= P\left(\frac{w}{9} < \frac{60}{9}\right) \\ &= P(\overline{x} < 6.667) \\ &= P\left(z < \frac{6.667 - 6.3}{0.4}\right) \\ &= P(z < 0.92) \\ &= 0.8212 \end{aligned}$$

$$\begin{aligned} P(w > 65) &= P\left(\frac{w}{9} > \frac{65}{9}\right) \\ &= P(\overline{x} > 7.222) \\ &= P\left(z > \frac{7.222 - 6.3}{0.4}\right) \\ &= P(z > 2.31) \\ &= 1 - P(z \le 2.31) \\ &= 1 - 0.9896 \\ &= 0.0104 \end{aligned}$$

(b) Let $w = x_1 + x_2 + \ldots + x_{50}$. $\mu_{\bar{x}} = \mu = 6.3$, $\sigma_{\bar{x}} = \frac{\sigma}{\sqrt{n}} = \frac{1.2}{\sqrt{50}} = 0.170$

$$P(w < 342) = P\left(\frac{w}{50} < \frac{342}{50}\right)$$
$$P(\bar{x} < 6.84)$$
$$= P\left(z < \frac{6.84 - 6.3}{0.170}\right)$$
$$= P(z < 3.18)$$
$$= 0.9993$$

No. By the Central Limit Theorem the sample size is large enough so the sampling distribution of $\bar{x}$ is approximately normal.

Section 7.3

1. (a) Answers vary.

(b) The random variable $\hat{p}$ can be approximated by a normal random variable when both np and nq exceed 5.

$$\mu_{\hat{p}} = p, \sigma_{\hat{p}} = \sqrt{\frac{pq}{n}}$$

(c) $np = 33(0.21) = 6.93, nq = 33(0.79) = 26.07$

Yes, $\hat{p}$ can be approximated by a normal random variable since both np and nq exceed 5.

$$\mu_{\hat{p}} = p = 0.21, \sigma_{\hat{p}} = \sqrt{\frac{0.21(0.79)}{33}} \approx 0.071$$

$$\text{continuity correction} = \frac{0.5}{n} = \frac{0.5}{33} \approx 0.015$$

$$P(0.15 \le \hat{p} \le 0.25) = P(0.15 - 0.015 \le x \le 0.25 + 0.015)$$
$$= P(0.135 \le x \le 0.265)$$
$$= P\left(\frac{0.135 - 0.21}{0.071} \le z \le \frac{0.265 - 0.21}{0.071}\right)$$
$$= P(-1.06 \le z \le 0.77)$$
$$= P(z \le 0.77) - P(z \le -1.06)$$
$$= 0.7794 - 0.1446$$
$$= 0.6348$$

(d) No; $np = 25(0.15) = 3.75$ which does not exceed 5.

(e) $np = 48(0.15) = 7.2,\ nq = 48(0.85) = 40.8$

Yes, $\hat{p}$ can be approximated by a normal random variable since both np and nq exceed 5.

$$\mu_{\hat{p}} = p = 0.15,\ \sigma_{\hat{p}} = \sqrt{\frac{0.15(0.85)}{48}} \approx 0.052$$

$$\text{continuity correction} = \frac{0.5}{n} = \frac{0.5}{45} = 0.010$$

$$\begin{aligned} P(\hat{p} \ge 0.22) &= P(x \ge 0.22 - 0.010) \\ &= P(x \ge 0.21) \\ &= P\left(z \ge \frac{0.21 - 0.15}{0.052}\right) \\ &= P(z \ge 1.15) \\ &= 1 - P(z < 1.15) \\ &= 1 - 0.8749 \\ &= 0.1251 \end{aligned}$$

2. (a) $n = 50,\ p = 0.36$

$np = 50(0.36) = 18,\ nq = 50(0.64) = 32$

Approximate $\hat{p}$ by a normal random variable since both np and nq exceed 5.

$$\mu_{\hat{p}} = p = 0.36,\ \sigma_{\hat{p}} = \sqrt{\frac{0.36(0.64)}{50}} \approx 0.068$$

$$\text{continuity correction} = \frac{0.5}{n} = \frac{0.5}{50} = 0.01$$

$$\begin{aligned} P(0.30 \le \hat{p} \le 0.45) &\approx P(0.30 - 0.01 \le x \le 0.45 + 0.01) \\ &= P(0.29 \le x \le 0.46) \\ &= P\left(\frac{0.29 - 0.36}{0.068} \le z \le \frac{0.46 - 0.36}{0.068}\right) \\ &= P(-1.03 \le z \le 1.47) \\ &= P(z \le 1.47) - P(z \le -1.03) \\ &= 0.9292 - 0.1515 \\ &= 0.7777 \end{aligned}$$

(b) $n = 38,\ p = 0.25$

$np = 38(0.25) = 9.5,\ nq = 38(0.75) = 28.5$

Approximate $\hat{p}$ by a normal random variable since both np and nq exceed 5.

$$\mu_{\hat{p}} = p = 0.25,\ \sigma_{\hat{p}} = \sqrt{\frac{0.25(0.75)}{38}} \approx 0.070$$

$$\text{continuity correction} = \frac{0.5}{n} = \frac{0.5}{38} = 0.013$$

$$\begin{aligned} P(\hat{p} > 0.35) &= P(x > 0.35 - 0.013) \\ &= P(x > 0.337) \\ &= P\left(z > \frac{0.337 - 0.25}{0.070}\right) \\ &= P(z > 1.24) \\ &= 1 - P(z \le 1.24) \\ &= 1 - 0.8925 \\ &= 0.1075 \end{aligned}$$

(c) $n = 41,\ p = 0.09$

$np = 41(0.09) = 3.69$

We cannot approximate $\hat{p}$ by a normal random variable since $np < 5$.

3. $n = 30,\ p = 0.60$

$np = 30(0.60) = 18,\ nq = 30(0.40) = 12$

Approximate $\hat{p}$ by a normal random variable since both np and nq exceed 5.

$$\mu_{\hat{p}} = p = 0.6,\ \sigma_{\hat{p}} = \sqrt{\frac{0.6(0.4)}{30}} \approx 0.089$$

$$\text{continuity correction} = \frac{0.5}{n} = \frac{0.5}{30} = 0.017$$

(a)
$$\begin{aligned} P(\hat{p} \ge 0.5) &\approx P(x \ge 0.5 - 0.017) \\ &= P(x \ge 0.483) \\ &= P\left(z \ge \frac{0.483 - 0.6}{0.089}\right) \\ &= P(z \ge -1.31) \\ &= 0.9049 \end{aligned}$$

(b)
$$\begin{aligned} P(\hat{p} \ge 0.667) &\approx P(x \ge 0.667 - 0.017) \\ &= P(x \ge 0.65) \\ &= P\left(z \ge \frac{0.65 - 0.6}{0.089}\right) \\ &= P(z \ge 0.56) \\ &= 0.2877 \end{aligned}$$

(c) $P(\hat{p} \le 0.333) \approx P(x \le 0.333 + 0.017)$

$$= P(x \le 0.35)$$

$$= P\left(z \le \frac{0.35 - 0.6}{0.089}\right)$$

$$= P(z \le -2.81)$$

$$= 0.0025$$

(d) Yes, both *np* and *nq* exceed 5.

4. (a) $n = 38,\ p = 0.73$

$np = 38(0.73) = 27.74,\ nq = 38(0.27) = 10.26$

Approximate $\hat{p}$ by a normal random variable since both *np* and *nq* exceed 5.

$$\mu_{\hat{p}} = p = 0.73,\ \sigma_{\hat{p}} = \sqrt{\frac{0.73(0.27)}{38}} \approx 0.072$$

$$\text{continuity correction} = \frac{0.5}{n} = \frac{0.5}{38} = 0.013$$

$$P(\hat{p} \ge 0.667) \approx P(x \ge 0.667 - 0.013)$$

$$= P(x \ge 0.654)$$

$$= P\left(z \ge \frac{0.654 - 0.73}{0.072}\right)$$

$$= P(z \ge -1.06)$$

$$= 0.8554$$

(b) $n = 45,\ p = 0.86$

$np = 45(0.86) = 38.7,\ nq = 45(0.14) = 6.3$

Approximate $\hat{p}$ by a normal random variable since both *np* and *nq* exceed 5.

$$\mu_{\hat{p}} = p = 0.86,\ \sigma_{\hat{p}} = \sqrt{\frac{0.86(0.14)}{45}} \approx 0.052$$

$$\text{continuity correction} = \frac{0.5}{n} = \frac{0.5}{45} = 0.011$$

$$P(\hat{p} \ge 0.667) \approx P(x \ge 0.667 - 0.011)$$

$$= P(x \ge 0.656)$$

$$= P\left(z \ge \frac{0.656 - 0.86}{0.052}\right)$$

$$= P(z \ge -3.92)$$

$$\approx 1$$

(c) Yes, both *np* and *nq* exceed 5 for men and for women.

5. $n = 55,\ p = 0.11$

$np = 55(0.11) = 6.05,\ nq = 55(0.89) = 48.95$

Approximate $\hat{p}$ by a normal random variable since both np and nq exceed 5.

$$\mu_{\hat{p}} = p = 0.11,\ \sigma_{\hat{p}} = \sqrt{\frac{0.11(0.89)}{55}} \approx 0.042$$

$$\text{continuity correction} = \frac{0.5}{n} = \frac{0.5}{55} = 0.009$$

(a) $$\begin{aligned} P(\hat{p} \le 0.15) &\approx P(x \le 0.15 + 0.009) \\ &= P(x \le 0.159) \\ &= P\left(z \le \frac{0.159 - 0.11}{0.042}\right) \\ &= P(z \le 1.17) \\ &= 0.8790 \end{aligned}$$

(b) $$\begin{aligned} P(0.10 \le \hat{p} \le 0.15) &\approx P(0.10 - 0.009 \le x \le 0.15 + 0.009) \\ &= P(0.091 \le x \le 0.159) \\ &= P\left(\frac{0.091 - 0.11}{0.042} \le z \le \frac{0.159 - 0.11}{0.042}\right) \\ &= P(-0.45 \le z \le 1.17) \\ &= P(z \le 1.17) - P(z \le -0.45) \\ &= 0.8790 - 0.3264 \\ &= 0.5526 \end{aligned}$$

(c) Yes, both np and nq exceed 5.

6. $n = 28,\ p = 0.31$

$np = 28(0.31) = 8.68,\ nq = 28(0.69) = 19.32$

Approximate $\hat{p}$ by a normal random variable since both np and nq exceed 5.

$$\mu_{\hat{p}} = p = 0.31,\ \sigma_{\hat{p}} = \sqrt{\frac{0.31(0.69)}{28}} \approx 0.087$$

$$\text{continuity correction} = \frac{0.5}{n} = \frac{0.5}{28} = 0.018$$

(a) $$\begin{aligned} P(\hat{p} \ge 0.25) &\approx P(x \ge 0.25 - 0.018) \\ &= P(x \ge 0.232) \\ &= P\left(z \ge \frac{0.232 - 0.31}{0.087}\right) \\ &= P(z \ge -0.90) \\ &= 0.8159 \end{aligned}$$

(b) $P(0.25 \le \hat{p} \le 0.50) \approx P(0.25 - 0.018 \le x \le 0.50 + 0.018)$

$= P(0.232 \le x \le 0.518)$

$= P\left(\dfrac{0.232 - 0.31}{0.087} \le z \le \dfrac{0.518 - 0.31}{0.087}\right)$

$= P(-0.90 \le z \le 2.39)$

$= P(z \le 2.39) - P(z \le -0.90)$

$= 0.9916 - 0.1841$

$= 0.8075$

(c) Yes, both np and nq exceed 5.

7. (a) $n = 100,\ p = 0.06$

$np = 100(0.06) = 6,\ nq = 100(0.94) = 94$

$\hat{p}$ can be approximated by a normal random variable since both np and nq exceed 5.

$$\mu_{\hat{p}} = p = 0.06,\ \sigma_{\hat{p}} = \sqrt{\frac{0.06(0.94)}{100}} \approx 0.024$$

$$\text{continuity correction} = \frac{0.5}{100} = 0.005$$

(b) $P(\hat{p} \ge 0.07) \approx P(x \ge 0.07 - 0.005)$

$= P(x \ge 0.065)$

$= P\left(z \ge \dfrac{0.065 - 0.06}{0.024}\right)$

$= P(z \ge 0.21)$

$= 0.4168$

(c) $P(\hat{p} \ge 0.11) \approx P(x \ge 0.11 - 0.005)$

$= P(x \ge 0.105)$

$= P\left(z \ge \dfrac{0.105 - 0.06}{0.024}\right)$

$= P(z \ge 1.88)$

$= 0.0301$

Yes, since this probability is so small, it should rarely occur. The machine might need an adjustment.

8. (a) $n = 50,\ p = 0.565$

$np = 50(0.565) = 28.25,\ nq = 50(0.435) = 21.75$

$\hat{p}$ can be approximated by a normal random variable since both np and nq exceed 5.

$$\mu_{\hat{p}} = p = 0.565,\ \sigma_{\hat{p}} = \sqrt{\frac{0.565(0.435)}{50}} \approx 0.070$$

$$\text{continuity correction} = \frac{0.5}{n} = \frac{0.5}{50} = 0.01$$

(b) $P(\hat{p} \le 0.53) \approx P(x \le 0.53 + 0.01)$

$= P(x \le 0.54)$

$= P\left(z \le \dfrac{0.54 - 0.565}{0.070}\right)$

$= P(z \le -0.36)$

$= 0.3594$

(c) $P(\hat{p} \le 0.41) \approx P(x \le 0.41 + 0.01)$

$= P(x \le 0.42)$

$= P\left(z \le \dfrac{0.42 - 0.565}{0.070}\right)$

$= P(z \le -2.07)$

$= 0.0192$

(d) Meredith has the more serious case because the probability of having such a low reading in a healthy person is less than 2%.

9. $\overline{p} = \dfrac{\text{total number of successes from all 12 quarters}}{\text{total number of families from all 12 quarters}}$

$= \dfrac{11 + 14 + \ldots + 19}{12(92)}$

$= \dfrac{206}{1104}$

$= 0.1866$

$\overline{q} = 1 - \overline{p} = 1 - 0.1866 = 0.8134$

$\mu_{\hat{p}} = p \approx \overline{p} = 0.1866$

$\sigma_{\hat{p}} = \sqrt{\dfrac{pq}{n}} \approx \sqrt{\dfrac{\overline{p}\overline{q}}{n}} = \sqrt{\dfrac{0.1866(0.8134)}{92}} \approx 0.0406$

Check: $n\overline{p} = 92(0.1866) = 17.2$, $n\overline{q} = 92(0.8134) = 74.8$

Since both $n\overline{p}$ and $n\overline{q}$ exceed 5, the normal approximation should be reasonably good.

Center line $= \overline{p} = 0.1866$

Control limits at $\overline{p} \pm 2\sqrt{\dfrac{\overline{p}\overline{q}}{n}}$

$= 0.1866 \pm 2(0.0406)$

$= 0.1866 \pm 0.0812$

or 0.1054 and 0.2678

Control limits at $\overline{p} \pm 3\sqrt{\dfrac{\overline{p}\overline{q}}{n}}$

$= 0.1866 \pm 3(0.0406)$

$= 0.1866 \pm 0.1218$

or 0.0648 and 0.3084

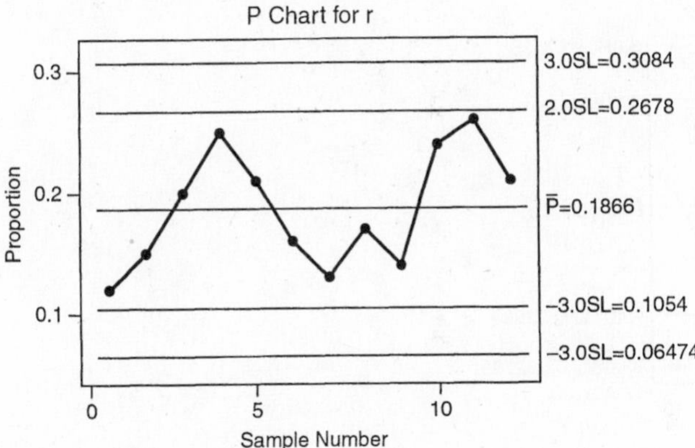

There are no out-of-control signals.

10. $\bar{p} = \dfrac{\text{total number of defective cans}}{\text{total number of cans}}$

$= \dfrac{8+11+\ldots+10}{110(15)}$

$= \dfrac{133}{1650}$

$= 0.08061$

$\bar{q} = 1 - \bar{p} = 1 - 0.08061 = 0.91939$

$\mu_{\hat{p}} = p \approx \bar{p} = 0.08061$

$\sigma_{\hat{p}} = \sqrt{\dfrac{pq}{n}} \approx \sqrt{\dfrac{\bar{p}\bar{q}}{n}} = \sqrt{\dfrac{(0.08061)(0.91939)}{110}} \approx 0.02596$

Check: $n\bar{p} = 110(0.08061) = 8.9$, $n\bar{q} = 110(0.91939) = 101.1$

Since both $n\bar{p}$ and $n\bar{q}$ exceed 5, the normal approximation should be reasonably good.

Center line $= \bar{p} = 0.08061$

Control limits at $\bar{p} \pm 2\sqrt{\dfrac{\bar{p}\bar{q}}{n}}$

$= 0.08061 \pm 2(0.02596)$

$= 0.08061 \pm 0.05192$

or 0.02869 and 0.1325

Control limits at $\bar{p} \pm 3\sqrt{\dfrac{\bar{p}\bar{q}}{n}}$

$= 0.08061 \pm 3(0.02596)$

$= 0.08061 \pm 0.07788$

or 0.00273 and 0.1585

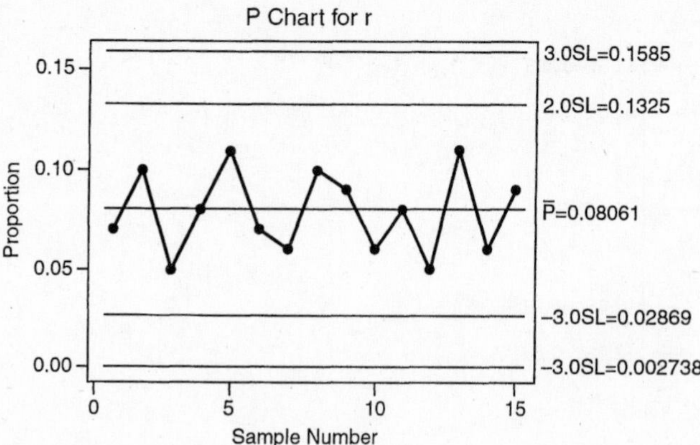

There are no out-of-control signals. It appears that the production process is in reasonable control.

11. $\overline{p} = \dfrac{\text{total number who got jobs}}{\text{total number of people}}$

$$= \frac{60+53+\ldots+58}{75(15)}$$

$$= \frac{872}{1125}$$

$$= 0.7751$$

$\overline{q} = 1 - \overline{p} = 1 - 0.7751 = 0.2249$

$\mu_{\hat{p}} = p \approx \overline{p} = 0.7751$

$$\sigma_{\hat{p}} = \sqrt{\frac{pq}{n}} \approx \sqrt{\frac{\overline{p}\overline{q}}{n}} = \sqrt{\frac{(0.7751)(0.2249)}{75}} \approx 0.0482$$

Check: $n\overline{p} = 75(0.7751) = 58.1$, $n\overline{q} = 75(0.2249) = 16.9$

Since both $n\overline{p}$ and $n\overline{q}$ exceed 5, the normal approximation should be reasonably good.

Center line $= \overline{p} = 0.7751$

Control limits at $\overline{p} \pm 2\sqrt{\dfrac{\overline{p}\overline{q}}{n}}$

$$= 0.7751 \pm 2(0.0482)$$
$$= 0.7751 \pm 0.0964$$

or 0.6787 to 0.8715

Control limits at $\overline{p} \pm 3\sqrt{\dfrac{\overline{p}\overline{q}}{n}}$

$$= 0.7751 \pm 3(0.0482)$$
$$= 0.7751 \pm 0.1446$$

or 0.6305 to 0.9197

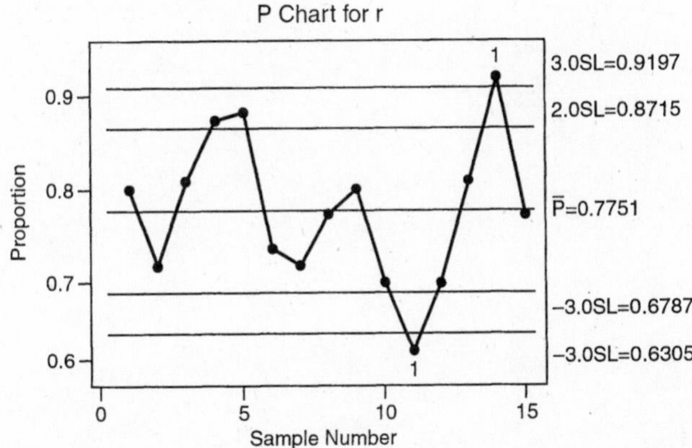

Out-of-control signal III occurs on days 4 and 5, Out-of-control signal I occurs on day 11 on the low side and day 14 on the high side. Out-of-control signals on the low side are of most concern for the homeless seeking work. The foundation should look to see what happened on that day. The foundation might take a look at the out of control periods on the high side to see if there is a possibility of cultivating more jobs.

Chapter 7 Review

1. (a) The $\overline{x}$ distribution approaches a normal distribution.

(b) The mean $\mu_{\overline{x}}$ of the $\overline{x}$ distribution equals the mean μ of the x distribution, regardless of the sample size.

(c) The standard deviation $\sigma_{\overline{x}}$ of the sampling distribution equals $\frac{\sigma}{\sqrt{n}}$, where σ is the standard deviation of the x distribution and n is the sample size.

(d) They will both be approximately normal with the same mean, but the standard deviations will be $\frac{\sigma}{\sqrt{50}}$ and $\frac{\sigma}{\sqrt{100}}$ respectively.

2. All the $\overline{x}$ distributions will be normal with mean $\mu_{\overline{x}} = \mu = 15$. The standard deviations will be:

$$n = 4:\ \sigma_{\overline{x}} = \frac{\sigma}{\sqrt{n}} = \frac{3}{\sqrt{4}} = \frac{3}{2}$$

$$n = 16:\ \sigma_{\overline{x}} = \frac{\sigma}{\sqrt{n}} = \frac{3}{\sqrt{16}} = \frac{3}{4}$$

$$n = 100:\ \sigma_{\overline{x}} = \frac{\sigma}{\sqrt{n}} = \frac{3}{\sqrt{100}} = \frac{3}{10}$$

3. (a) $\mu = 35,\ \sigma = 7$

$$\begin{aligned} P(x \geq 40) &= P\left(z \geq \frac{40-35}{7}\right) \\ &= P(z \geq 0.71) \\ &= 0.2389 \end{aligned}$$

(b) $\mu_{\bar{x}} = \mu = 35,\ \sigma_{\bar{x}} = \frac{\sigma}{\sqrt{n}} = \frac{7}{\sqrt{9}} = \frac{7}{3}$

$$P(\bar{x} \geq 40) = P\left(z \geq \frac{40-35}{\frac{7}{3}}\right)$$
$$= P(z \geq 2.14)$$
$$= 0.0162$$

4. (a) $\mu = 38,\ \sigma = 5$

$$P(x \leq 35) = P\left(z \leq \frac{35-38}{5}\right)$$
$$= P(z \leq -0.6)$$
$$= 0.2743$$

(b) $\mu_{\bar{x}} = \mu = 38,\ \sigma_{\bar{x}} = \frac{\sigma}{\sqrt{n}} = \frac{5}{\sqrt{10}} = 1.58$

$$P(\bar{x} \leq 35) = P\left(z \leq \frac{35-38}{1.58}\right)$$
$$= P(z \leq -1.90)$$
$$= 0.0287$$

(c) The probability in part (b) is much smaller because the standard deviation is smaller for the $\bar{x}$ distribution.

5. $\mu_{\bar{x}} = \mu = 100,\ \sigma_{\bar{x}} = \frac{\sigma}{\sqrt{n}} = \frac{15}{\sqrt{100}} = 1.5$

$$P(100-2 \leq \bar{x} \leq 100+2) = P(98 \leq \bar{x} \leq 102)$$
$$= P\left(\frac{98-100}{1.5} \leq z \leq \frac{102-100}{1.5}\right)$$
$$= P(-1.33 \leq z \leq 1.33)$$
$$= P(z \leq 1.33) - P(z \leq -1.33)$$
$$= 0.9082 - 0.0918$$
$$= 0.8164$$

6. $\mu_{\bar{x}} = \mu = 15,\ \sigma_{\bar{x}} = \frac{\sigma}{\sqrt{n}} = \frac{2}{\sqrt{36}} = 0.333$

$$P(15-0.5 \leq \bar{x} \leq 15+0.5) = P(14.5 \leq \bar{x} \leq 15.5)$$
$$= P\left(\frac{14.5-15}{0.333} \leq z \leq \frac{15.5-15}{0.333}\right)$$
$$= P(-1.5 \leq z \leq 1.5)$$
$$= P(z \leq 1.5) - P(z \leq -1.5)$$
$$= 0.9332 - 0.0668$$
$$= 0.8664$$

7. $\mu_{\bar{x}} = \mu = 750,\ \sigma_{\bar{x}} = \frac{\sigma}{\sqrt{n}} = \frac{20}{\sqrt{64}} = 2.5$

(a) $P(\bar{x} \geq 750) = P\left(z \geq \frac{750-750}{2.5}\right)$
$= P(z \geq 0)$
$= 0.5000$

(b) $P(745 \leq \bar{x} \leq 755) = P\left(\frac{745-750}{2.5} \leq z \leq \frac{755-750}{2.5}\right)$
$= P(-2 \leq z \leq 2)$
$= P(z \leq 2) - P(z \leq -2)$
$= 0.9772 - 0.0228$
$= 0.9544$

8. (a) Miami: $\mu = 76,\ \sigma = 1.9$

$P(x < 77) = P\left(z < \frac{77-76}{1.9}\right)$
$= P(z < 0.53)$
$= 0.7019$

Fairbanks: $\mu = 0,\ \sigma = 5.3$

$P(x < 3) = P\left(z < \frac{3-0}{5.3}\right)$
$= P(z < 0.57)$
$= 0.7157$

(b) Since x has a normal distribution, the sampling distribution of $\bar{x}$ is also normal regardless of the sample size.

Miami: $\mu_{\bar{x}} = \mu = 76,\ \sigma_{\bar{x}} = \frac{\sigma}{\sqrt{n}} = \frac{1.9}{\sqrt{7}} = 0.718$

$P(\bar{x} < 77) = P\left(z < \frac{77-76}{0.718}\right)$
$= P(z < 1.39)$
$= 0.9177$

Fairbanks: $\mu_{\bar{x}} = \mu = 0,\ \sigma_{\bar{x}} = \frac{\sigma}{\sqrt{n}} = \frac{5.3}{\sqrt{7}} = 2.003$

$P(\bar{x} < 3) = P\left(z < \frac{3-0}{2.003}\right)$
$= P(z < 1.50)$
$= 0.9332$

(c) We cannot say anything about the probability distribution of $\overline{x}$, because the sample size is not 30 or greater. Consider using all 31 days.

Miami: $\mu_{\overline{x}} = \mu = 76,\ \sigma_{\overline{x}} = \frac{\sigma}{\sqrt{n}} = \frac{1.9}{\sqrt{31}} = 0.341$

$$\begin{aligned} P(\overline{x} < 77) &= P\left(z < \frac{77-76}{0.341}\right) \\ &= P(z < 2.93) \\ &= 0.9983 \end{aligned}$$

Fairbanks: $\mu_{\overline{x}} = \mu = 0,\ \sigma_{\overline{x}} = \frac{\sigma}{\sqrt{n}} = \frac{5.3}{\sqrt{31}} = 0.952$

$$\begin{aligned} P(\overline{x} < 3) &= P\left(z < \frac{3-0}{0.952}\right) \\ &= P(z < 3.15) \\ &= 0.9992 \end{aligned}$$

9. (a) $n = 50,\ p = 0.22$

$np = 50(0.22) = 11,\ nq = 50(0.78) = 39$

Approximate $\hat{p}$ by a normal random variable since both np and nq exceed 5.

$$\mu_{\hat{p}} = p = 0.22,\ \sigma_{\hat{p}} = \sqrt{\frac{0.22(0.78)}{50}} \approx 0.0586$$

$$\text{continuity correction} = \frac{0.5}{n} = \frac{0.5}{50} = 0.01$$

$$\begin{aligned} P(0.20 \le \hat{p} \le 0.25) &\approx P(0.20 - 0.01 \le x \le 0.25 + 0.01) \\ &= P(0.19 \le x \le 0.26) \\ &= P\left(\frac{0.19-0.22}{0.0586} \le z \le \frac{0.26-0.22}{0.0586}\right) \\ &= P(-0.51 \le z \le 0.68) \\ &= P(z \le 0.68) - P(z \le -0.51) \\ &= 0.7517 - 0.3050 \\ &= 0.4467 \end{aligned}$$

(b) $n = 38,\ p = 0.27$

$np = 38(0.27) = 10.26,\ nq = 38(0.73) = 27.74$

Approximate $\hat{p}$ by a normal random variable since both np and nq exceed 5.

$$\mu_{\hat{p}} = p = 0.27,\ \sigma_{\hat{p}} = \sqrt{\frac{(0.27)(0.73)}{38}} \approx 0.0720$$

$$\text{continuity correction} = \frac{0.5}{n} = \frac{0.5}{38} = 0.013$$

$$\begin{aligned} P(\hat{p} \geq 0.35) &\approx P(x \geq 0.35 - 0.013) \\ &= P(x \geq 0.337) \\ &= P\left(z \geq \frac{0.337 - 0.27}{0.0720}\right) \\ &= P(z \geq 0.93) \\ &= 0.1762 \end{aligned}$$

(c) $n = 51,\ p = 0.05$

$np = 51(0.05) = 2.55$

No, we cannot approximate $\hat{p}$ by a normal random variable since $np < 5$.

Chapter 8 Estimation

Section 8.1

Answers may vary slightly due to rounding.

1. (a) $\overline{x}=\dfrac{\Sigma x_i}{n}=\dfrac{5128}{35}=146.5143\approx 146.5,$

$$s^2=\frac{\Sigma x_i^2-\frac{(\Sigma x_i)^2}{n}}{n-1}=\frac{756{,}820-\frac{(5128)^2}{35}}{34}=161.6101$$

$s=\sqrt{s^2}=\sqrt{161.6101}=12.7126\approx 12.7$ as stated

Since $n=35\geq 30,$ we can use s to approximate σ.

(b) $c=80\%$ so $z_c=1.28$

$\left(\overline{x}-\dfrac{z_c s}{\sqrt{n}}\right)<\mu<\left(\overline{x}+\dfrac{z_c s}{\sqrt{n}}\right),\ \left(146.5-\dfrac{1.28(12.7)}{\sqrt{35}}\right)<\mu<\left(146.5+\dfrac{1.28(12.7)}{\sqrt{35}}\right)$

$(146.5-2.7)<\mu<(146.5+2.7)$

143.8 calories $<\mu<$ 149.2 calories

(c) $c=90\%$ so $z_c=1.645$

$E\approx\dfrac{z_c s}{\sqrt{n}}=\dfrac{1.645(12.7)}{\sqrt{35}}\approx 3.5$

$(\overline{x}-E)<\mu<(\overline{x}+E)$

$(146.5-3.5)<\mu<(146.5+3.5)$

143.0 calories $<\mu<$ 150.0 calories

(d) $c=99\%$ so $t_c=2.58$

$E\approx\dfrac{z_c s}{\sqrt{n}}=\dfrac{2.58(12.7)}{\sqrt{35}}\approx 5.5;\ (\overline{x}-E)<\mu<(\overline{x}+E)$

$(146.5-5.5)<\mu<(146.5+5.5)$

141.0 calories $<\mu<$ 152.0 calories

(e)

c	z_c	Length of confidence interval
80%	1.28	149.2 – 143.8 = 5.4
90%	1.645	150.0 – 143.0 = 7.0
99%	2.58	152.0 – 141.0 = 11.0

As the confidence level, c, increases, so does z_c; therefore, all else being the same, the length of the confidence interval increases, too. We can be more confident the interval captures μ if the interval is longer.

2. (a) $n = 30, \bar{x} = 15.71$ inches, $s = 4.63$ inches, since $n = 30 \geq 30$, we can use s to approximate σ

$c = 95\%$ so $z_c = 1.96$

$$E \approx \frac{z_c s}{\sqrt{n}} = \frac{1.96(4.63)}{\sqrt{30}} = 1.66$$

$(\bar{x} - E) < \mu < (\bar{x} + E)$

$(15.71 - 1.66) < \mu < (15.71 + 1.66)$

14.05 inches $< \mu <$ 17.37 inches

(b) $n = 90$, $\bar{x} = 15.58$ inches, $s = 4.61$ inches

Since $n = 90 \geq 30$, we can use s to approximate σ.

$c = 95\%$ so $z_c = 1.96$

$$E \approx \frac{z_c s}{\sqrt{n}} = \frac{1.96(4.61)}{\sqrt{90}} = 0.95$$

$(\bar{x} - E) < \mu < (\bar{x} + E)$

$(15.58 - 0.95) < \mu < (15.58 + 0.95)$

14.63 inches $< \mu <$ 16.53 inches

(c) $n = 300$, $\bar{x} = 15.59$ inches, $s = 4.62$ inches

Since $n = 300 \geq 30$, we can use s to approximate σ.

$c = 95\%$ so $z_c = 1.96$

$$E \approx \frac{z_c s}{\sqrt{n}} = \frac{1.96(4.62)}{\sqrt{300}} = 0.52$$

$(\bar{x} - E) < \mu < (\bar{x} + E)$

$(15.59 - 0.52) < \mu < (15.59 + 0.52)$

15.07 inches $< \mu <$ 16.11 inches

(d)

Sample size, n	Length of confidence interval
30	17.37 – 14.05 = 3.32
90	16.53 – 14.63 = 1.90
300	16.11 – 15.07 = 1.04

As n increases, so does $\sqrt{n}$, which appears in the denominator of E. All else being the same, the length of the confidence interval decreases as n increases.

3. (a) $n = 42$, $\bar{x} = \frac{\Sigma x_i}{n} = \frac{1511.8}{42} = 35.9952 \approx 36.0$, as stated

$$s^2 = \frac{\Sigma x_i^2 - n\bar{x}^2}{n-1} = \frac{58{,}714.96 - 42(36.0)^2}{41} = 104.4624$$

$s^2 = \sqrt{104.4624} = 10.2207 \approx 10.2$, as stated

Since $n = 42 \geq 30$, we can use s to approximate σ.

(b) $c = 75\%$, $z_c = 1.15$

$$E \approx \frac{z_c s}{\sqrt{n}} = \frac{1.15(10.2)}{\sqrt{42}} = 1.81$$

$(\bar{x} - E) < \mu < (\bar{x} + E)$

$(36.0 - 1.81) < \mu < (36.0 + 1.81)$

$34.19 < \mu < 37.81$ thousand dollars per employee profit

(c) Since \$30 thousand per employee profit is less than the lower limit of the confidence interval (34.19), your bank profits are low, compared to other similar financial institutions.

(d) Since \$40 thousand per employee profit exceeds the upper limit of the confidence interval (37.81), your bank profit is higher than other similar financial institutions.

(e) $c = 90\%,\ z_c = 1.645$

$$E \approx \frac{z_c s}{\sqrt{n}} = \frac{1.645(10.2)}{\sqrt{42}} = 2.59$$

$(\overline{x} - E) < \mu < (\overline{x} + E)$

$(36.0 - 2.59) < \mu < (36.0 + 2.59)$

$33.41 < \mu < 38.59$ thousand dollars per employee profit

\$30 thousand is less than the lower limit of the confidence interval (33.44), so your bank's profit is less than that of other financial institutions.

\$40 thousand is more than the upper limit of the confidence interval (38.59), so your bank is doing better (profit-wise) than other financial institutions.

4. (a) $n = 35,\ \overline{x} = 5.1029 \approx 5.1,$ as stated

$s = 3.7698 \approx 3.8,$ as stated

Since $n = 35 \geq 30$, we can use s to estimate σ.

(b) $c = 80\%,\ z_c = 1.28$

$$E \approx \frac{z_c s}{\sqrt{n}} = \frac{1.28(3.8)}{\sqrt{35}} = 0.82$$

$(\overline{x} - E) < \mu < (\overline{x} + E)$

$(5.1 - 0.82) < \mu < (5.1 + 0.82)$

$4.28 < \mu < 5.92$ thousand dollars per employee profit

(c) Yes. \$3 thousand per employee profit is less than the lower limit of the confidence interval (4.28)

(d) Yes. \$6.5 thousand dollars profit per employee is larger than the upper limit of the confidence interval (5.92).

(e) $c = 95\%,\ z_c = 1.96$

$$E \approx \frac{z_c s}{\sqrt{n}} = \frac{1.96(3.8)}{\sqrt{35}} = 1.26$$

$(\overline{x} - E) < \mu < (\overline{x} + E)$

$(5.1 - 1.26) < \mu < (5.1 + 1.26)$

$3.84 < \mu < 6.36$ thousand dollars per employee profit

Yes. \$3 thousand per employee profit is less than the lower limit of the confidence interval (3.84)

Yes. \$6.5 thousand dollars profit per employee is larger than the upper limit of the confidence interval (6.36).

5. (a) $n = 40,\ \overline{x} = 51.1575 \approx 51.16,$ as stated

$s = 3.0404 \approx 3.04,$ as stated

Since $n = 40 \geq 30$, we can use s to estimate σ.

(b) $c = 90\%,\ z_c = 1.645$

$$E \approx \frac{z_c s}{\sqrt{n}} = \frac{1.645(3.04)}{\sqrt{40}} = 0.79$$

$(\overline{x} - E) < \mu < (\overline{x} + E)$

$(51.16 - 0.79) < \mu < (51.16 + 0.79)$

$50.37 < \mu < 51.95^\circ\text{F}$

(c) $c = 99\%,\ z_c = 2.58$

$E \approx \frac{z_c s}{\sqrt{n}} = \frac{2.58(3.04)}{\sqrt{40}} = 1.24$

$(\bar{x} - E) < \mu < (\bar{x} + E)$

$(51.16 - 1.24) < \mu < (51.16 + 1.24)$

$49.92^\circ\text{F} < \mu < 52.40^\circ\text{F}$

(d) Since 53°F > 52.4°F, the upper confidence interval limit, it is unlikely the average January temperature is 53°F. Plotting the data by year to see if there is an upward trend (lately or overall), and/or adding several more years of observation might provide evidence to support or refute the claim.

6. $n = 115,\ \bar{x} = \$9.74,\ s = \$2.93$

Since $n = 115 \geq 30$, we can use s to estimate σ.

(a) $c = 95\%,\ z_c = 1.96$

$E \approx \frac{z_c s}{\sqrt{n}} = \frac{1.96(2.93)}{\sqrt{115}} = 0.54$

$(\bar{x} - E) < \mu < (\bar{x} + E)$

$(9.74 - 0.54) < \mu < (9.74 + 0.54)$

$\$9.20 < \mu < \$10.28$

(b) Multiply the endpoints of the confidence interval for the average tab per customer by the number of customers. Let μ^* be the total lunch income.

$(115)(\$9.20) < \mu^* < (115)(\$10.28)$

$\$1058.00 < \mu^* < \$1182.20$

7. (a) $n = 102,\ \bar{x} = 1.2,\ s = 0.4,\ c = 99\%,\ z_c = 2.58$

Since $n = 102 \geq 30$, we can use s to estimate σ.

$E \approx \frac{z_c s}{\sqrt{n}} = \frac{2.58(0.4)}{\sqrt{102}} = 0.10$

$(\bar{x} - E) < \mu < (\bar{x} + E)$

$(1.2 - 0.10) < \mu < (1.2 + 0.10)$

$1.10 \text{ seconds} < \mu < 1.30 \text{ seconds}$

(b) $\bar{x} = 609,\ s = 248,\ c = 95\%,\ z_c = 1.96,\ n$ still 102

$E \approx \frac{z_c s}{\sqrt{n}} = \frac{1.96(248)}{\sqrt{102}} = 48.13$

$(\bar{x} - E) < \mu < (\bar{x} + E)$

$(609 - 48.13) < \mu < (609 + 48.13)$

$560.87 \text{ Hz} < \mu < 657.13 \text{ Hz}$

8. $n = 56,\ \bar{x} = 97^\circ\text{C},\ s = 17^\circ\text{C}$

Since $n = 56 \geq 30$, we can use s to estimate σ.

(a) $c = 95\%,\ z_c = 1.96$

$E \approx \frac{z_c s}{\sqrt{n}} = \frac{1.96(17)}{\sqrt{56}} = 4.5$

$(\bar{x} - E) < \mu < (\bar{x} + E)$

$(97 - 4.5) < \mu < (97 + 4.5)$

$92.5^\circ\text{C} < \mu < 101.5^\circ\text{C}$

(b) If the temperature rises, the hot air in the balloon rises, so the balloon would go up. The upper limit of the confidence interval (101.5°C) is an estimate of the (maximum) temperature at which the balloon is at equilibrium (neither going up nor down).

9. (a) $n = 38,\ \bar{x} = 2.5,\ s = 0.7,\ c = 90\%,\ z_c = 1.645$

Since $n = 38 \geq 30$, we can use s to estimate σ.

$$E \approx \frac{z_c s}{\sqrt{n}} = \frac{1.645(0.7)}{\sqrt{38}} = 0.2$$

$(\bar{x} - E) < \mu < (\bar{x} + E)$

$(2.5 - 0.2) < \mu < (2.5 + 0.2)$

2.3 minutes $< \mu <$ 2.7 minutes; length = 2.7 – 2.3 = 0.4 minute

(b) $\bar{x} = 15.2,\ s = 4.8,\ n = 38,\ c = 90\%,\ z_c = 1.645$

$$E \approx \frac{z_c s}{\sqrt{n}} = \frac{1.645(4.8)}{\sqrt{38}} = 1.3$$

$(\bar{x} - E) < \mu < (\bar{x} + E)$

$(15.2 - 1.3) < \mu < (15.2 + 1.3)$

13.9 min $< \mu <$ 16.5 min; length = 16.5 – 13.9 = 2.6 min

(c) $\bar{x} = 25.7,\ s = 8.3,\ n = 38,\ c = 90\%,\ z_c = 1.645$

$$E \approx \frac{z_c s}{\sqrt{n}} = \frac{1.645(8.3)}{\sqrt{38}} = 2.2$$

$(\bar{x} - E) < \mu < (\bar{x} + E)$

$(25.7 - 2.2) < \mu < (25.7 + 2.2)$

23.5 min $< \mu <$ 27.9 min, length = 27.9 – 23.5 = 4.4 min

(d)

length	s
0.4	0.7
2.6	4.8
4.4	8.3

As s increases, so does the length of the interval. This is because s is in the numerator of E and the length of any confidence interval is $(\bar{x} + E) - (\bar{x} - E) = 2E$.

10. $n = 50 \geq 30$, so we can use s to estimate σ.

(a) $\bar{x} = 5.55,\ s = 0.57,\ c = 85\%,\ z_c = 1.44$

$$E \approx \frac{z_c s}{\sqrt{n}} = \frac{1.44(0.57)}{\sqrt{50}} = 0.12$$

$(\bar{x} - E) < \mu < (\bar{x} + E)$

$(5.55 - 0.12) < \mu < (5.55 + 0.12)$

5.43 cm $< \mu <$ 5.67 cm

(b) $\bar{x} = 2.03,\ s = 0.27,\ c = 90\%,\ z_c = 1.645$

$$E \approx \frac{z_c s}{\sqrt{n}} = \frac{1.645(0.27)}{\sqrt{50}} = 0.06$$

$(\bar{x} - E) < \mu < (\bar{x} + E)$

$(2.03 - 0.06) < \mu < (2.03 + 0.06)$

1.97 cm $< \mu <$ 2.09 cm

11. $n = 56, \bar{x} = 3.4, s = 1.2, c = 85\%, z_c = 1.44$

Since $n = 56 \geq 30$, we can use s to estimate σ.

$E \approx \frac{z_c s}{\sqrt{n}} = \frac{1.44(1.2)}{\sqrt{56}} = 0.23$

$(\bar{x} - E) < \mu < (\bar{x} + E)$

$(3.4 - 0.23) < \mu < (3.4 + 0.23)$

3.17 years $< \mu < 3.63$ years

12. (a) $n = 75, \bar{x} = 19.5, s = 2.25, c = 95\%, z_c = 1.96$

Since $n = 75 \geq 30$, we can use s to estimate σ.

$E \approx \frac{z_c s}{\sqrt{n}} = \frac{1.96(2.25)}{\sqrt{75}} = 0.51$

$(\bar{x} - E) < \mu < (\bar{x} + E)$

$(19.5 - 0.51) < \mu < (19.5 + 0.51)$

18.99 years $< \mu < 20.01$ years

(b) $n = 89, \bar{x} = 22.8, s = 2.79, c = 99\%, z_c = 2.58$

Since $n = 89 \geq 30$, we can use s to estimate σ.

$E \approx \frac{z_c s}{\sqrt{n}} = \frac{2.58(2.79)}{\sqrt{89}} = 0.76$

$(\bar{x} - E) < \mu < (\bar{x} + E)$

$(22.8 - 0.76) < \mu < (22.8 + 0.76)$

22.04 years $< \mu < 23.56$ years

13. $n = 36, \bar{x} = 16{,}000, s = 2400, c = 90\%, z_c = 1.645$

Since $n = 36 \geq 30$, we can use s to estimate σ.

$E \approx \frac{z_c s}{\sqrt{n}} = \frac{1.645(2400)}{\sqrt{36}} = 658$

$(\bar{x} - E) < \mu < (\bar{x} + E)$

$(16{,}000 - 658) < \mu < (16{,}000 + 658)$

$15{,}342$ cars $< \mu < 16{,}658$ cars

14. (a) $n = 50, \bar{x} = 98.75, s = 15.91, c = 95\%, z_c = 1.96$

Since $n = 50 \geq 30$, we can use s to estimate σ.

$E \approx \frac{z_c s}{\sqrt{n}} = \frac{1.96(15.91)}{\sqrt{50}} = 4.41$

$(\bar{x} - E) < \mu < (\bar{x} + E)$

$(98.75 - 4.41) < \mu < (98.75 + 4.41)$

$\$94.34 < \mu < \$103.16$

(b) The WSJ's figure of $111 is not in the confidence interval; it is higher than the upper limit of $103.16. The WSJ may have surveyed only upper echelon hotels, where as your survey, based on Yellow Page listings, covered a wider variety of accommodations.

15. $n = 196,\ \overline{x} = 11.9,\ s = 4.30,\ c = 95\%,\ z_c = 1.96$

Since $n = 196 \geq 30$, we can use s to estimate σ.

$$E \approx \frac{z_c s}{\sqrt{n}} = \frac{1.96(4.30)}{\sqrt{196}} = 0.6$$

$(\overline{x} - E) < \mu < (\overline{x} + E)$

$(11.9 - 0.6) < \mu < (11.9 + 0.6)$

11.3 mg/liter $< \mu <$ 12.5 mg/liter

16. $n = 99,\ \overline{x} = 10.5,\ s = 3.2,\ c = 95\%,\ z_c = 1.96$

Since $n = 99 \geq 30$, we can use s to estimate σ.

$$E \approx \frac{z_c s}{\sqrt{n}} = \frac{1.96(3.2)}{\sqrt{99}} = 0.63$$

$(\overline{x} - E) < \mu < (\overline{x} + E)$

$(10.5 - 0.63) < \mu < (10.5 + 0.63)$

9.87 mg/liter $< \mu <$ 11.13 mg/liter

17. **(a)** $n = 40,\ \overline{x} = 287.4,\ s = 15.543 \approx 15.5,$ as stated

(b) Since $n = 40 \geq 30$, we can use s to estimate σ.

$c = 85\%,\ z_c = 1.44$

$$E \approx \frac{z_c s}{\sqrt{n}} = \frac{1.44(15.5)}{\sqrt{40}} = 3.5$$

$(\overline{x} - E) < \mu < (\overline{x} + E)$

$(287.4 - 3.5) < \mu < (287.4 + 3.5)$

283.9 pounds $< \mu <$ 290.9 pounds

(c) Yes; 200 pounds is considerably below the lower limit of the confidence interval (283.9).

(d) Yes; 291 pounds is just barely above the upper limit of the confidence interval (290.0), which rounds to 291. His weight is appropriate for such positions.

(e) $c = 95\%,\ z_c = 1.96$

$$E \approx \frac{z_c s}{\sqrt{n}} = \frac{1.96(15.5)}{\sqrt{40}} = 4.8$$

$(\overline{x} - E) < \mu < (\overline{x} + E)$

$(287.4 - 4.8) < \mu < (287.4 + 4.8)$

282.6 pounds $< \mu <$ 292.2 pounds

Yes; 200 pounds is still much smaller than the lower limit.

Yes; 291 pounds is now within the confidence interval.

18. **(a)** $n = 40,\ \overline{x} = 27.775 \approx 27.8$ as stated, $s = 3.7994 \approx 3.8$, as stated.

(b) $c = 80\%,\ z_c = 1.28$

$$E \approx \frac{z_c s}{\sqrt{n}} = \frac{1.28(3.8)}{\sqrt{40}} = 0.77$$

$(\overline{x} - E) < \mu < (\overline{x} + E)$

$(27.8 - 0.77) < \mu < (27.8 + 0.77)$

27.03 years $< \mu <$ 28.57 years

(c) Yes, he would be somewhat old for such a position because 33 is higher than the upper limit of the confidence interval (28.57).

(d) $c = 99\%,\ z_c = 2.58$

$$E \approx \frac{z_c s}{\sqrt{n}} = \frac{2.58(3.8)}{\sqrt{40}} = 1.55$$

$(\overline{x} - E) < \mu < (\overline{x} + E)$

$(27.8 - 1.55) < \mu < (27.8 + 1.55)$

26.25 years $< \mu < 29.35$ years

33 years is still quite "old," it is above the upper limit of 29.35 years.

Section 8.2

Answers may vary slightly due to rounding.

1. $n = 18$ so $d.f. = n - 1 = 18 - 1 = 17$, $c = 0.95$
$t_c = t_{0.95} = 2.110$

2. $n = 4$ so $d.f. = n - 1 = 4 - 1 = 3$, $c = 0.99$
$t_c = t_{0.99} = 5.841$

3. $n = 22$ so $d.f. = n - 1 = 22 - 1 = 21$, $c = 0.90$
$t_c = t_{0.90} = 1.721$

4. $n = 12$ so $d.f. = n - 1 = 12 - 1 = 11$, $c = 0.95$
$t_c = t_{0.95} = 2.201$

5. $n = 9$ so $d.f. = n - 1 = 9 - 1 = 8$

(a) $\overline{x} = \frac{\Sigma x}{n} = \frac{11,450}{9} \approx 1272$, as stated

$$s^2 = \frac{\Sigma x_i^2 - \frac{(\Sigma x_i)^2}{n}}{n-1} = \frac{14,577,854 - \frac{(11,450)^2}{9}}{8} = 1363.6944$$

$s = \sqrt{1363.6944} = 36.9282 \approx 37$, as stated

(b) $c = 90\%,\ t_c = t_{0.90}$ with $8\ d.f. = 1.860$

$$E = \frac{t_c s}{\sqrt{n}} = \frac{1.86(37)}{\sqrt{9}} = 22.94 \approx 23$$

$(\overline{x} - E) < \mu < (\overline{x} + E)$

$(1272 - 23) < \mu < (1272 + 23)$

1249 A.D. $< \mu <$ 1295 A.D.

6. $n = 16$ so $d.f. = n - 1 = 15$

(a) $\overline{x} = \frac{\Sigma x_i}{n} = \frac{57.2}{16} = 3.575 \approx 3.58$, as stated

$$s^2 = \frac{\Sigma x_i^2 - n\overline{x}^2}{n-1} = \frac{256.02 - 16(3.575)^2}{15} = 3.4353$$

$s = \sqrt{3.4353} = 1.853 \approx 1.85$, as stated

(b) $c = 95\%$, so $t_{0.95}$ with 15 $d.f. = 2.131$

$E = \frac{t_c s}{\sqrt{n}} = \frac{2.131(1.85)}{\sqrt{16}} \approx 0.99$

$(\bar{x} - E) < \mu < (\bar{x} + E)$

$(3.58 - 0.99) < \mu < (3.58 + 0.99)$

2.59 hours $< \mu <$ 4.57 hours

7. $n = 12$ so $d.f. = n - 1 = 11$

(a) $\bar{x} = 148.3333 \approx 148.33$, as stated

$s = 53.0151 \approx 53.02$, as stated

(b) $c = 90\%$, so $t_{0.90}$ with 11 $d.f. = 1.796$

$E = \frac{t_c s}{\sqrt{n}} = \frac{1.796(53.02)}{\sqrt{12}} \approx 27.49$

$(\bar{x} - E) < \mu < (\bar{x} + E)$

$(148.33 - 27.49) < \mu < (148.33 + 27.49)$

$\$120.84 < \mu < \$175.82$

8. $n = 20$ so $d.f. = n - 1 = 19$

(a) $\bar{x} = 83.75$, as stated

$s = 28.9662 \approx 28.97$, as stated

(b) $c = 90\%$, so $t_{0.90}$ with 19 $d.f. = 1.729$

$E = \frac{t_c s}{\sqrt{n}} = \frac{1.729(28.97)}{\sqrt{20}} \approx 11.20$

$(\bar{x} - E) < \mu < (\bar{x} + E)$

$(83.75 - 11.20) < \mu < (83.75 + 11.20)$

$\$72.55 < \mu < \$94.95$

9. $n = 6$ so $d.f. = n - 1 = 5$

(a) $\bar{x} = 91.0$, as stated

$s = 30.7181 \approx 30.7$, as stated

(b) $c = 75\%$, so $t_{0.75}$ with 5 $d.f. = 1.301$

$E = \frac{t_c s}{\sqrt{n}} = \frac{1.301(30.7)}{\sqrt{6}} \approx 16.3$

$(\bar{x} - E) < \mu < (\bar{x} + E)$

$(91.0 - 16.3) < \mu < (91.0 + 16.3)$

74.7 pounds $< \mu <$ 107.3 pounds

10. $n = 16$ so $d.f. = n - 1 = 15$

(a) $\bar{x} = 5.625 \approx 5.63$, as stated

$s = 1.7842 \approx 1.78$, as stated

(b) $c = 85\%$, so $t_{0.85}$ with 15 $d.f. = 1.517$

$E = \frac{t_c s}{\sqrt{n}} = \frac{1.517(1.78)}{\sqrt{16}} \approx 0.68$

$(\bar{x} - E) < \mu < (\bar{x} + E)$

$(5.63 - 0.68) < \mu < (5.63 + 0.68)$

4.95 pups $< \mu <$ 6.31 pups

11. $n = 6$ so $d.f. = n - 1 = 5$
$\bar{x} = 79.25,\ s = 5.33$
$c = 80\%$, so $t_{0.80}$ with 5 $d.f. = 1.476$
$$E = \frac{t_c s}{\sqrt{n}} = \frac{1.476(5.33)}{\sqrt{6}} \approx 3.21$$
$(\bar{x} - E) < \mu < (\bar{x} + E)$
$(79.25 - 3.21) < \mu < (79.25 + 3.21)$
$76.04 \text{ cm} < \mu < 82.46 \text{ cm}$

12. $n = 8$, so $d.f. = n - 1 = 7$
$\bar{x} = 244.5,\ s = 21.73,\ c = 99\%$
$t_{0.99}$ with 7 $d.f. = 3.499$
$$E = \frac{t_c s}{\sqrt{n}} = \frac{3.499(21.73)}{\sqrt{8}} = 26.8818 \approx 26.9$$
$(\bar{x} - E) < \mu < (\bar{x} + E)$
$(244.5 - 26.9) < \mu < (244.5 + 26.9)$
$217.6 \text{ calories} < \mu < 271.4 \text{ calories}$

13. $n = 8$, so $d.f. = n - 1 = 7$

(a) $\bar{x} = 12.3475 \approx 12.35$, as stated
$s = 2.2487 \approx 2.25$, as stated

(b) $c = 90\%$, so $t_{0.90}$ with 7 $d.f. = 1.895$
$$E = \frac{t_c s}{\sqrt{n}} = \frac{1.895(2.25)}{\sqrt{8}} = 1.5075 \approx 1.51$$
$(\bar{x} - E) < \mu < (\bar{x} + E)$
$(12.35 - 1.51) < \mu < (12.35 + 1.51)$
$\$10.84 < \mu < \$13.86$

14. $n = 9$, $d.f. = n - 1 = 8$
$\bar{x} = 106.8889 \approx 106.9$, as stated
$s = 29.4425 \approx 29.4$, as stated
$c = 90\%$, so $t_{0.90}$ with 8 $d.f. = 1.860$
$$E = \frac{t_c s}{\sqrt{n}} = \frac{1.860(29.4)}{\sqrt{9}} = 18.228 \approx 18.2$$
$(\bar{x} - E) < \mu < (\bar{x} + E)$
$(106.9 - 18.2) < \mu < (106.9 + 18.2)$
$\$88.7 \text{ thousand} < \mu < \$125.1 \text{ thousand}$

15. (a) $n = 19$, $d.f. = n - 1 = 18$, $c = 90\%$, $t_{0.90}$ with 18 $d.f. = 1.734$
$\bar{x} = 9.8421 \approx 9.8$, as stated
$s = 3.3001 \approx 3.3$, as stated
$$E = \frac{t_c s}{\sqrt{n}} = \frac{1.734(3.3)}{\sqrt{19}} \approx 1.3$$
$(\bar{x} - E) < \mu < (\bar{x} + E)$
$(9.8 - 1.3) < \mu < (9.8 + 1.3)$
$8.5 \text{ inches} < \mu < 11.1 \text{ inches}$

(b) $n = 7$, $d.f. = n - 1 = 6$, $c = 80\%$, $t_{0.80}$ with 6 $d.f.$ = 1.440

$\bar{x} = 17.0714 \approx 17.1$, as stated

$s = 2.4568 \approx 2.5$, as stated

$$E = \frac{t_c s}{\sqrt{n}} = \frac{1.440(2.5)}{\sqrt{7}} \approx 1.4$$

$(\bar{x} - E) < \mu < (\bar{x} + E)$

$(17.1 - 1.4) < \mu < (17.1 + 1.4)$

15.7 inches $< \mu <$ 18.5 inches

16. (a) $n = 12$, $d.f. = n - 1 = 6$, $c = 90\%$, $t_{0.90}$ with 11 $d.f.$ = 1.796

$\bar{x} = 4.70$, as stated

$s = 1.9781 \approx 1.98$, as stated

$$E = \frac{t_c s}{\sqrt{n}} = \frac{1.796(1.98)}{\sqrt{12}} \approx 1.03$$

$(\bar{x} - E) < \mu < (\bar{x} + E)$

$(4.70 - 1.03) < \mu < (4.70 + 1.03)$

$3.67\% < \mu < 5.73\%$

(b) $n = 14$, $d.f. = n - 1 = 13$, $c = 90\%$, $t_{0.90}$ with 13 $d.f.$ = 1.771

$\bar{x} = 3.1786 \approx 3.18$, as stated

$s = 1.3429 \approx 1.34$, as stated

$$E = \frac{t_c s}{\sqrt{n}} = \frac{1.771(1.34)}{\sqrt{12}} \approx 0.63$$

$(\bar{x} - E) < \mu < (\bar{x} + E)$

$(3.18 - 0.63) < \mu < (3.18 + 0.63)$

$2.55\% < \mu < 3.81\%$

17. (a) $n = 8$, $d.f. = n - 1 = 7$, $c = 85\%$, $t_{0.85}$ with 7 $d.f.$ = 1.617

$\bar{x} = 33.125 \approx 33.1$, as stated

$s = 6.3852 \approx 6.4$, as stated

$$E = \frac{t_c s}{\sqrt{n}} = \frac{1.617(6.4)}{\sqrt{8}} = 3.65885 \approx 3.7$$

$(\bar{x} - E) < \mu < (\bar{x} + E)$

$(33.1 - 3.7) < \mu < (33.1 + 3.7)$

\$29.4 thousand $< \mu <$ \$36.8 thousand

(b) $n = 9$, $d.f. = n - 1 = 8$, $c = 99\%$, $t_{0.99}$ with 8 $d.f.$ = 3.355

$\bar{x} = 20.8222 \approx 20.8$, as stated

$s = 2.5228 \approx 2.5$, as stated

$$E = \frac{t_c s}{\sqrt{n}} = \frac{3.355(2.5)}{\sqrt{9}} \approx 2.8$$

$(\bar{x} - E) < \mu < (\bar{x} + E)$

$(20.8 - 2.8) < \mu < (20.8 + 2.8)$

\$18.0 thousand $< \mu <$ \$23.6 thousand

18. (a) $n = 15$, $d.f. = n - 1 = 14$, $c = 99\%$, $t_{0.99}$ with 14 $d.f. = 2.977$

$\bar{x} = 7.2867 \approx 7.3$, as stated

$s = 0.7954 \approx 0.8$, as stated

$$E = \frac{t_c s}{\sqrt{n}} = \frac{2.977(0.8)}{\sqrt{15}} \approx 0.6$$

$(\bar{x} - E) < \mu < (\bar{x} + E)$

$(7.3 - 0.6) < \mu < (7.3 + 0.6)$

6.7 days $< \mu <$ 7.9 days

(b) $n = 10$, $d.f. = n - 1 = 9$, $c = 90\%$, $t_{0.90}$ with 9 $d.f. = 1.833$

$\bar{x} = 62.26 \approx 62.3$, as stated

$s = 8.0185 \approx 8.0$, as stated

$$E = \frac{t_c s}{\sqrt{n}} = \frac{1.833(8.0)}{\sqrt{10}} \approx 4.6$$

$(\bar{x} - E) < \mu < (\bar{x} + E)$

$(62.3 - 4.6) < \mu < (62.3 + 4.6)$

$57.7\% < \mu < 66.9\%$

19. Notice that the four figures are drawn on different scales.

(a) The box plots differ in range (distance between whisker ends), in interquartile range (distance between box ends), in medians (line through boxes), in symmetry (indicated by the placement of the median within the box, and by the placement of the median relative to the whisker endpoints), in whisker lengths, and in the presence/absence of outliers. These differences are to be expected since each box plot represents a different sample of size 20. (Although the data sets were all selected as samples of size $n = 20$ from a normal distribution with $\mu = 68$ and $\sigma = 3$, it is very interesting that Sample 2, figure (b), shows 2 outliers.)

(b)

Sample	Confidence interval width	Includes $\mu = 68$?
1	69.407 – 66.692 = 2.715	Yes
2	69.426 – 66.490 = 2.936	Yes
3	69.211 – 66.741 = 2.470	Yes
4	68.050 – 65.766 = 2.284	Yes (barely)

The intervals differ in length; all 4 cover/capture/enclose $\mu = 68$. If many additional samples of size 20 were generated from this distribution, we would expect about 95% of the confidence intervals created from these samples to cover/capture/enclose the number 68; in approximately 5% of the intervals, 68 would be outside the confidence interval, i.e., 68 would be less than the lower limit or greater than the upper limit. Drawing all these samples (at least conceptually) and checking whether or not the confidence intervals include the number 68, keeping track of the percentage that do, is an illustration of the definition of (95%) confidence intervals.

Section 8.3

Answers may vary slightly due to rounding.

1. $r = 39$, $n = 62$, $\hat{p} = \frac{r}{n} = \frac{39}{62}$, $\hat{q} = 1 - \hat{p} = \frac{23}{62}$

(a) $\hat{p} = \frac{39}{62} = 0.6290$

(b) $c = 95\%, z_c = z_{0.95} = 1.96$
$E \approx z_c\sqrt{\hat{p}\hat{q}/n} = 1.96\sqrt{(0.6290)(1-0.6290)/62} = 0.1202$
$(\hat{p}-E) < p < (\hat{p}+E), (0.6290-0.1202) < p < (0.6290+0.1202)$
$0.5088 < p < 0.7492$ or approximately 0.51 to 0.75.
We are 95% confident that the true proportion of actors who are extroverts is between 0.51 and 0.75, approximately. In repeated sampling from the same population, approximately 95% of the samples would generate confidence intervals that would cover/capture/enclose the true value of p.

(c) $np \approx n\hat{p} = r = 39$
$nq \approx n\hat{q} = n - r = 62 - 39 = 23$
It is quite likely that np and $nq > 5$, since their estimates are much larger than 5. If np and $nq > 5$ then $\hat{p}$ is approximately normal with $\mu = p$ and $\sigma = \sqrt{pq/n}$. This forms the basis for the large sample confidence interval derivation.

2. $n = 519,\ r = 285$

(a) $\hat{p} = \frac{r}{n} = \frac{285}{519} = 0.5491$

(b) $c = 99\%, z_c = 2.58, \hat{q} = 1 - \hat{p} = 0.4509$
$E \approx z_c\sqrt{\hat{p}\hat{q}/n} = 2.58\sqrt{(0.5491)(0.4509)/519} = 0.0564$
$(\hat{p}-E) < p < (\hat{p}+E), (0.5491-0.0564) < p < (0.5491+0.0564)$
$0.4927 < p < 0.6055$ or approximately 0.49 to 0.61.
In repeated sampling, approximately 99% of the intervals generated from the samples would include p, the proportion of judges who are introverts.

(c) $np \approx n\hat{p} = n\left(\frac{r}{n}\right) = r = 285 > 5$

$nq, n\hat{q} = n(1-\hat{p}) = n\left(1 - \frac{r}{n}\right) = n - r = 234 > 5$

Since the estimates of np and nq are substantially greater than 5, it is quite likely np, $nq > 5$. This allows us to use the normal approximation to the distribution of $\hat{p}$, with $\mu = p$ and $\sigma = \sqrt{pq/n}$.

3. $n = 5222,\ r = 1619$

(a) $\hat{p} = \frac{r}{n} = \frac{1619}{5222} = 0.3100$
so $\hat{q} = 1 - \hat{p} = 0.6900$

(b) $c = 99\%$, so $z_c = 2.58$
$E \approx z_c\sqrt{\hat{p}\hat{q}/n} = 2.58\sqrt{(0.3100)(0.6900)/5222} = 0.0165$
$(\hat{p}-E) < p < (\hat{p}+E), (0.3100-0.0165) < p < (0.3100+0.0165)$
$0.2935 < p < 0.3265$ or approximately 0.29 to 0.33.
In repeated sampling, approximately 99% of the confidence intervals generated from the samples would include p, the proportion of judges who are hogans.

(c) $np \approx n\hat{p} = r = 1619, nq \approx n\hat{q} = n(1-\hat{p}) = n - r = 3603$
Since the estimates of np and nq are much greater than 5, it is reasonable to assume np, $nq > 5$. Then we can use the normal distribution with $\mu = p$ and $\sigma = \sqrt{pq/n}$ to approximate the distribution of $\hat{p}$.

4. $n = 592$, $r = 360$

(a) $\hat{p} = \frac{r}{n} = \frac{360}{592} = 0.6081$
so $\hat{q} = 1 - \hat{p} = 0.3919$

(b) $c = 95\%$, $z_c = 1.96$
$E \approx z_c\sqrt{\hat{p}\hat{q}/n} = 1.96\sqrt{(0.6081)(0.3919)/592} = 0.0393$
$(\hat{p} - E) < p < (\hat{p} + E)$
$(0.6081 - 0.0393) < p < (0.6081 + 0.0393)$
$0.5688 < p < 0.6474$, or approximately 0.57 to 0.65.
In repeated sampling from this population, approximately 95% of the samples would generate confidence intervals capturing p, the population proportion of Santa Fe black on white potsherds at the excavation site.

(c) $np \approx n\hat{p} = r = 360 > 5$
$nq \approx n\hat{q} = n(1 - \hat{p}) = n - r = 592 - 360 = 232 > 5$
Since the estimates of np and nq are both greater than 5, it is reasonable to assume that np, nq are also greater than 5. We can then approximate the sampling distribution of $\hat{p}$ with a normal distribution with $\mu = p$ and $\sigma = \sqrt{pq/n}$.

5. $n = 5792$, $r = 3139$

(a) $\hat{p} = \frac{r}{n} = \frac{3139}{5792} = 0.5420$
so $\hat{q} = 1 - \hat{p} = 0.4580$

(b) $c = 99\%$, so $z_c = 2.58$
$E \approx z_c\sqrt{\hat{p}\hat{q}/n} = 2.58\sqrt{(0.5420)(0.4580)/5792} = 0.0169$
$(\hat{p} - E) < p < (\hat{p} + E)$
$(0.5420 - 0.0169) < p < (0.5420 + 0.0169)$
$0.5251 < p < 0.5589$, or approximately 0.53 to 0.56.
If we drew many samples of size 5792 physicians from those in Colorado, and generated a confidence interval from each sample, we would expect approximately 99% of the intervals to include the true proportion of Colorado physicians providing at least some charity care.

(c) $np \approx n\hat{p} = r = 3139 > 5; nq \approx n\hat{q} = n - r = 2653 > 5.$
Since the estimates of np and nq are much larger than 5, it is reasonable to assume np and nq are both greater than 5. Under the circumstances, it is appropriate to approximate the distribution of $\hat{p}$ with a normal distribution with $\mu = p$ and $\sigma = \sqrt{pq/n}$.

6. $n = 250$, $r = 40$

(a) $\hat{p} = \frac{r}{n} = \frac{40}{250} = 0.1600$
so $\hat{q} = 1 - \hat{p} = 0.8400$

(b) $c = 90\%$, so $z_c = 1.645$

$E \approx z_c\sqrt{\hat{p}\hat{q}/n} = 1.645\sqrt{(0.1600)(0.8400)/250} = 0.0381$

$(\hat{p} - E) < p < (\hat{p} + E)$

$(0.1600 - 0.0381) < p < (0.1600 + 0.0381)$

$0.1219 < p < 0.1981$, or approximately 0.12 to 0.20.

In repeated sampling, approximately 90% of the confidence intervals generated from the samples would include p, the true proportion of egg cartons with at least one broken egg.

(c) $np \approx n\hat{p} = r = 40 > 5; nq \approx n\hat{q} = n - r = 250 - 40 = 210 > 5.$

Since the estimates of np and nq are larger than 5, it is reasonable to assume np and $nq > 5$. When np and $nq > 5$, the normal distribution with $\mu = p$ and $\sigma = \sqrt{pq/n}$ provides a good approximation to the distribution of $\hat{p}$.

7. $n = 99, r = 17$

(a) $\hat{p} = \frac{r}{n} = \frac{17}{99} = 0.1717$

so $\hat{q} = 0.8283$

(b) $c = 85\%$, so $z_c = 1.44$

$E \approx z_c\sqrt{\hat{p}\hat{q}/n} = 1.44\sqrt{(0.1717)(0.8283)/99} = 0.0546$

$(\hat{p} - E) < p < (\hat{p} + E)$

$(0.1717 - 0.0546) < p < (0.1717 + 0.0546)$

$0.1171 < p < 0.2263$, or approximately 0.12 to 0.23.

In repeated sampling from this population about 85% of the intervals generated from these samples would include p, the proportion of fugitives arrested after their photographs appeared in the newspaper.

(c) $np \approx n\hat{p} = r = 17 > 5; nq \approx n\hat{q} = n - r = 82 > 5.$

Since the estimates of np and $nq > 5$, it is reasonable to assume np, $nq > 5$. If np and $nq > 5$, the normal distribution with $\mu = p$ and $\sigma = \sqrt{pq/n}$ provides a good approximation to the distribution of $\hat{p}$.

8. $n = 10{,}351, r = 7867$

(a) $\hat{p} = \frac{r}{n} = \frac{7867}{10{,}351} = 0.7600$

so $\hat{q} = 1 - \hat{p} = 0.2400$

(b) $c = 99\%$, so $z_c = 2.58$

$E \approx z_c\sqrt{\hat{p}\hat{q}/n} = 2.58\sqrt{(0.7600)(0.2400)/10{,}351} = 0.0108$

$(\hat{p} - E) < p < (\hat{p} + E)$

$(0.7600 - 0.0108) < p < (0.7600 + 0.0108)$

$0.7492 < p < 0.7708$, or approximately 0.75 to 0.77.

In repeated sampling from the population of convicts who escaped from U.S. prisons, approximately 99% of the confidence intervals created from those samples would include p, the proportion of recaptured escaped convicts.

(c) $np \approx n\hat{p} = r = 7867 > 5; nq \approx n\hat{q} = n(1 - \hat{p}) = n - r = 2484 > 5.$

Since the estimates of np and nq are each considerably greater than 5, it is reasonable to assume that np and $nq > 5$. When np and $nq > 5$, the distribution of $\hat{p}$ can be quite accurately approximated by a normal distribution with $\mu = p$ and $\sigma = \sqrt{pq/n}$.

9. $n = 855, r = 26$

(a) $\hat{p} = \frac{r}{n} = \frac{26}{855} = 0.0304$
so $\hat{q} = 1 - \hat{p} = 0.9696$

(b) $c = 99\%$, so $z_c = 2.58$
$E \approx z_c\sqrt{\hat{p}\hat{q}/n} = 2.58\sqrt{(0.0304)(0.9696)/855} = 0.0151$
$(\hat{p} - E) < p < (\hat{p} + E)$
$(0.0304 - 0.0151) < p < (0.0304 + 0.0151)$
$0.0153 < p < 0.0455$, or approximately 0.02 to 0.05.

If many additional samples of size n = 855 were drawn from this fish population, and a confidence interval was created from each such sample, approximately 99% of those confidence intervals would contain p, the catch-and-release mortality rate (barbless hooks removed).

(c) $np \approx n\hat{p} = r = 26 > 5; nq \approx n\hat{q} = n - r = 829 > 5.$

Based on the estimates of np and nq, it is safe to assume both np and $nq > 5$. When np and $nq > 5$, the distribution of $\hat{p}$ can be accurately approximated by a normal distribution with $\mu = p$ and $\sigma = \sqrt{pq/n}$.

10. $n = 200, r = 58$

(a) $\hat{p} = \frac{r}{n} = \frac{58}{200} = 0.2900$
so $\hat{q} = 1 - \hat{p} = 0.7100$

(b) $c = 95\%$, so $z_c = 1.96$
$E \approx z_c\sqrt{\hat{p}\hat{q}/n} = 1.96\sqrt{(0.2900)(0.7100)/200} = 0.0629$
$(\hat{p} - E) < p < (\hat{p} + E)$
$(0.2900 - 0.0629) < p < (0.2900 + 0.0629)$
$0.2271 < p < 0.3529$, or approximately 0.23 to 0.35.

If many additional samples of size $n = 200$ were drawn from this fish population, and if a confidence interval was created from each of these samples, approximately 95% of the intervals would include the true value of p, the catch-and-release mortality rate (barbed hooks not removed).

(c) $np \approx n\hat{p} = r = 58 > 5; nq \approx n\hat{q} = n - r = 200 - 58 = 142 > 5.$

Based on these estimates, it is reasonable to assume np, $nq > 5$, and when np and $nq > 5$, the normal distribution with $\mu = p$ and $\sigma = \sqrt{pq/n}$ closely approximates the actual distribution of $\hat{p}$, and can be used instead of the actual distribution of $\hat{p}$.

11. $n = 900, r = 54, n - r = 846$; both np and $nq > 5$.

(a) $\hat{p} = \frac{r}{n} = \frac{54}{900} = 0.0600$
so $\hat{q} = 1 - \hat{p} = 0.9400$

(b) $c = 99\%$, so $z_c = 2.58$
$E \approx z_c\sqrt{\hat{p}\hat{q}/n} = 2.58\sqrt{(0.0600)(0.9400)/900} = 0.0204$
$(\hat{p} - E) < p < (\hat{p} + E)$
$(0.0600 - 0.0204) < p < (0.0600 + 0.0204)$
$0.0396 < p < 0.0804$, or about 0.04 to 0.08.

12. $n = 1000$, $r = 590$, $n - r = 410$; both np and $nq > 5$.

(a) $\hat{p} = \frac{r}{n} = \frac{590}{1000} = 0.5900$
so $\hat{q} = 0.4100$

(b) $c = 99\%$, so $z_c = 2.58$
$E \approx z_c\sqrt{\hat{p}\hat{q}/n} = 2.58\sqrt{(0.5900)(0.4100)/1000} = 0.0401$
$(\hat{p} - E) < p < (\hat{p} + E)$
$(0.5900 - 0.0401) < p < (0.5900 + 0.0401)$
$0.5499 < p < 0.6301$, or about 0.55 to 0.63.

13. $n = 2000$, $r = 382$, $n - r = 1618$; both np and $nq > 5$.

(a) $\hat{p} = \frac{r}{n} = \frac{382}{2000} = 0.1910$, so $\hat{q} = 0.8090$

(b) $c = 80\%$, so $z_c = 1.28$
$E \approx z_c\sqrt{\hat{p}\hat{q}/n} = 1.28\sqrt{(0.1910)(0.8090)/2000} = 0.0112$
$(\hat{p} - E) < p < (\hat{p} + E)$
$(0.1910 - 0.0112) < p < (0.1910 + 0.0112)$
$0.1798 < p < 0.2022$, or about 0.18 to 0.20.

14. $n = 328$, $r = 171$, $n - r = 157$; both np and $nq > 5$.

(a) $\hat{p} = \frac{r}{n} = \frac{171}{328} = 0.5213$, so $\hat{q} = 0.4787$

(b) $c = 95\%$, so $z_c = 1.96$
$E \approx z_c\sqrt{\hat{p}\hat{q}/n} = 1.96\sqrt{(0.5213)(0.4787)/328} = 0.0541$
$(\hat{p} - E) < p < (\hat{p} + E)$
$(0.5213 - 0.0541) < p < (0.5213 + 0.0541)$
$0.4672 < p < 0.5754$, or about 0.47 to 0.58.
In repeated sampling, approximately 95% of the intervals created from these samples would include p, the proportion of M.D.s with solo practices.

(c) Margin of error $= E = 0.0541 \approx 5.4\%$
A recent study published by the American Medical Association showed that approximately 52% of M.D.s have solo practices. The study has a margin of error of 5.4 percentage points.

15. $n = 730$, $r = 628$, $n - r = 102$; both np and $nq > 5$.

(a) $\hat{p} = \frac{r}{n} = \frac{628}{730} = 0.8603$, so $\hat{q} = 0.1397$

(b) $c = 95\%$, so $z_c = 1.96$
$E \approx z_c\sqrt{\hat{p}\hat{q}/n} = 1.96\sqrt{(0.8603)(0.1397)/730} = 0.0251$
$(\hat{p} - E) < p < (\hat{p} + E)$
$(0.8603 - 0.0251) < p < (0.8603 + 0.0251)$
$0.8352 < p < 0.8854$, or about 0.84 to 0.89.
In repeated sampling, approximately 95% of the intervals created from the samples would include p, the proportion of loyal women shoppers.

(c) Margin of error $= E \approx 2.5\%$
A recent study by the Food Marketing Institute showed that about 86% of women shoppers remained loyal to their favorite supermarket last year. The study's margin of error is 2.5 percentage points.

16. $n = 1001$, $r = 273$, $n - r = 728$; both np and $nq > 5$.

(a) $\hat{p} = \frac{r}{n} = \frac{273}{1001} = 0.2727$, so $\hat{q} = 0.7273$

(b) $c = 95\%$, so $z_c = 1.96$
$E \approx z_c\sqrt{\hat{p}\hat{q}/n} = 1.96\sqrt{(0.2727)(0.7273)/1001} = 0.0276$
$(\hat{p} - E) < p < (\hat{p} + E)$
$(0.2727 - 0.0276) < p < (0.2727 + 0.0276)$
$0.2451 < p < 0.3003$, or about 0.25 to 0.30.

If many additional samples of size $n = 1001$ were drawn from this population, about 95% of the confidence intervals created from these samples would include p, the proportion of shoppers who stock up on bargains.

(c) Margin of error $= E \approx 2.8\%$
The Food Marketing Institute reported that, based on a recent study, 27.3% of shoppers stock up on an item when it is a real bargain. The study had a margin of error of 2.8 percentage points.

17. $n = 1000$, $r = 250$, $n - r = 750$; both np and $nq > 5$.

(a) $\hat{p} = \frac{r}{n} = \frac{250}{1000} = 0.2500$, so $\hat{q} = 0.7500$

(b) $c = 95\%$, so $z_c = 1.96$
$E \approx z_c\sqrt{\hat{p}\hat{q}/n} = 1.96\sqrt{(0.2500)(0.7500)/1000} = 0.0268$
$(\hat{p} - E) < p < (\hat{p} + E)$
$(0.2500 - 0.0268) < p < (0.2500 + 0.0268)$
$0.2232 < p < 0.2768$, or about 0.22 to 0.28.

(c) Margin of error $= E \approx 2.7\%$
In a survey reported in *USA Today*, 25% of large corporations interviewed admitted that, given a choice between equally qualified applicants, they would offer the job to the nonsmoker. The survey's margin of error was 2.7 percentage points.

18. $\hat{p} = 19\% = 0.19$, margin of sampling error $E = 3\% = 0.03$ confidence interval is $(\hat{p} - E) < p < (\hat{p} + E)$ so $(0.19 - 0.03) < p < (0.19 + 0.03)$, or 0.16 to 0.22.

Section 8.4

1. The goal is to estimate μ, the population mean number of new lodgepole pine saplings in a 50 square meter plot in Yellowstone National Park. Use $n = (z_c\sigma / E)^2$, where $c = 95\%$, $z_c = 1.96$, $\sigma = 44$, and $E = 10$.

$$n \approx \left[\frac{1.96(44)}{10}\right]^2 = 74.37, \text{ “round up” to 75 plots.}$$

2. The goal is to estimate the mean root depth, μ, in glacial outwash soil.
Use $n = (z_c\sigma / E)^2$ with $c = 90\%$, $z_c = 1.645, E = 0.5$, and $\sigma = 8.94$.
$n \approx [1.645(8.94)/0.5]^2 = 865.10$; “roundup” to 866 plants.

3. The goal is to estimate the proportion, p, of people in your neighborhood who go to McDonald's. Use $n = pq(z_c/E)^2$.

(a) $c = 85\%, z_c = 1.44, E = 0.05$

With no preliminary estimate of p, we will use $p = q = 0.5$, which maximizes the value of $pq = p(1-p)$, and, therefore, maximizes the value of n; no other choice of p would give a larger n. The "worst case" scenario, when pq and n are the largest values possible, occurs when $p = q = \frac{1}{2} = 0.5$.

Then, $n = pq(z_c / E)^2 \approx 0.5 \cdot 0.5(z_c / E)^2 = 0.25(z_c / E)^2 = 0.25(1.44 / 0.05)^2 = 207.36$, which is rounded up to 208 people.

(b) $\hat{p} = 1/20 = 0.05$ is a preliminary estimate of $q = 1 - p$, so $\hat{q} = 1 - \hat{p} = 0.95$ is a preliminary estimate of q.

Then $n = pq(z_c / E)^2 \approx (0.05)(0.95)(1.44 / 0.05)^2 = 39.4$, or, rounded up, 40 people.

(Note that this sample size is much, much smaller than the sample size of $n = 208$ derived in part (a) where, in the absence of a preliminary estimate of p, we used the worst case estimate of $p, \hat{p} = 1/2$.)

4. The goal is to estimate μ, the mean height of NBA players; use $n = (z_c\sigma / E)^2$. Preliminary, $n = 41$. $s = 3.32$, $c = 95\%$, $z_c = 1.96, E = 0.75$.

Then $n \approx [1.96(3.32)/0.75]^2 = 75.3$, or 76 players. However, the preliminary sample had 41 players in it, so we need to sample only $76 - 41 = 35$ additional players.

5. The goal is to find μ, the mean player weight. Preliminary, $n = 56$. Use $n = (z_c\sigma / E)^2$. $s = 26.58$, $c = 90\%$, $z_c = 1.645, E = 4$.

Then $n \approx [1.645(26.58)/4]^2 = 119.5$, or 120 players. However, since 56 players have already been drawn to estimate σ, we need only $120 - 56 = 64$ additional players.

6. The goal is to estimate p, the proportion of callers who reach a business person by phone on the first call, so use $n = pq(z_c / E)^2$.

(a) $c = 80\%, z_c = 1.28, E = 0.03$

Since there is no preliminary estimate of p, we will use $\hat{p} = \hat{q} = 1/2$, the "worst case" estimate; no other choice of $\hat{p}$ would give us a larger sample size.

When $n = pq(z_c / E)^2$ becomes $n \approx 0.5 \cdot 0.5(z_c / E)^2$ or $n \approx 0.25(z_c / E)^2 = 0.25(1.28 / 0.03)^2 = 455.1$, or 456. We need to have a sample size of 456 business phone calls.

(b) $\hat{p} = 17\% = 0.17$, so $\hat{q} = 1 - \hat{p} = 1 - 0.17 = 0.83$

$n = pq(z_c / E)^2 \approx (0.17)(0.83)(1.28 / 0.03)^2 = 256.9$, or 257 business phone calls.

7. The goal is to estimate the proportion of women students; use $n = pq(z_c / E)^2$.

(a) $c = 99\%, z_c = 2.58, E = 0.05$

Since there is no preliminary estimate of p, we'll use the "worst case" estimate, $\hat{p} = \frac{1}{2}, \hat{q} = 1 - \hat{p} = \frac{1}{2}$.

$n \approx 0.5 \cdot 0.5(z_c / E)^2 = 0.25(z_c / E)^2 = 0.25(2.58 / 0.05)^2 = 665.6$, or 666 students.

(b) Preliminary estimate of p: $\hat{p} = 54\% = 0.54, \hat{q} = 1 - \hat{p} = 0.46$.

$n \approx (0.54)(0.46)(2.58 / 0.05)^2 = 661.4 \approx 662$ students.

(There is very little difference between (a) and (b) because (a) uses $\hat{p} = \frac{1}{2} = 0.50$ and (b) uses $\hat{p} = 0.54$, and the $\hat{p}s$ are approximately the same.)

8. The goal is to estimate p, the proportion of self-service gas customers; use $n = pq(z_c / E)^2$.

(a) $c = 90\%, z_c = 1.645, E = 0.08$

Since there is no preliminary estimate of p to use, we'll use the "worst case" $\hat{p} = \hat{q} = \frac{1}{2}$.

$n = pq(z_c / E)^2 \approx 0.5 \cdot 0.5(z_c / E)^2 = 0.25(z_c / E)^2 = 0.25(1.645 / 0.08)^2 = 105.7 \approx 106$ customers.

(b) $\hat{p} = 81\% = 0.81$, so $\hat{q} = 1 - \hat{p} = 0.19$.

$n \approx \hat{p}\hat{q}(z_c / E)^2 = (0.81)(0.19)(1.645 / 0.08)^2 = 65.07 \approx 66$ customers.

9. The goal is to estimate μ, the mean reconstructed clay vessel diameter, use $n = (z_c\sigma / E)^2$.

Preliminary $n = 83$, $s = 5.5$, $c = 95\%$, $z_c = 1.96$, $E = 1.0$

$n \approx [1.96(5.5) / 1.0]^2 = 116.2 \approx 117$ clay pots.

Since 83 pots were already measured, we need 117 – 83 = 34 additional reconstructed clay pots.

10. The goal is to estimate the mean weight, μ, of bighorn sheep; use $n = (z_c\sigma / E)^2$.

Preliminary $n = 37, s = 15.8, c = 90\%, z_c = 1.645, E = 2.5$.

$n \approx [1.645(15.8) / 2.5]^2 = 108.1 \approx 109$ sheep.

Since 37 bighorn sheep have already been weighed, we need 109 – 37 = 72 additional bighorn sheep for the sample.

11. The goal is to estimate the proportion, p, of pine beetle-infested trees; use $n = pq(z_c / E)^2$.

(a) $c = 85\%, z_c = 1.44, E = 0.06$

No preliminary $\hat{p}$ available, so use "worst case" estimate of $p, \hat{p} = \frac{1}{2}; \hat{q} = 1 - \hat{p} = \frac{1}{2}$.

$n \approx 0.5 \cdot 0.5(z_c / E)^2 = 0.25(z_c / E)^2 = 0.25(1.44 / 0.06)^2 = 144$ trees.

(b) Preliminary study showed $r = 19$ infested trees in a sample of $n = 58$ trees, so $\hat{p} = r / n = 19 / 58 = 0.3276; \hat{q} = 1 - \hat{p} = 0.6724$.

$n = pq(z_c / E)^2 \approx (0.3276)(0.6724)(1.44 / 0.06)^2 = 126.88 \approx 127$ trees.

Since 58 trees have already been checked for infestation, we need to check 127 – 58 = 69 additional trees.

12. The goal is to estimate the mean daily net income, μ; use $n = (z_c\sigma / E)^2$.

Preliminary sample of $n = 40$, $s = 57.19$, $E = 10$, $c = 85\%$, $z_c = 1.44$.

$n \approx [1.44(57.19) / 10]^2 = 67.8 \approx 68$ business days. Since 40 days' records have already been examined, we need to check the net income on an additional 68 – 40 = 28 days.

13. The goal is to estimate p, the proportion of voters favoring capital punishment; use $n = pq(z_c / E)^2$.

(a) $c = 99\%, z_c = 2.58, E = 0.01$

Since there is no preliminary estimate of p, we will use the "worst case" estimate, $\hat{p} = \frac{1}{2}; \hat{q} = 1 - \hat{p} = \frac{1}{2}$.

$n \approx 0.5 \cdot 0.5(z_c / E)^2 = 0.25(z_c / E)^2 = 0.25(2.58 / 0.01)^2 = 16{,}641$ people.

(b) Preliminary estimate $\hat{p} = 67\% = 0.67; \hat{q} = 1 - \hat{p} = 0.33$.

$n \approx (0.67)(0.33)(2.58/0.01)^2 = 14,717.3 \approx 14,718$ people.

(Comment: this is an exceptionally large sample size and it would cost David quite a large sum of money to survey this many people. Good surveys are often done with sample sizes of 300 to 1000. David needs to reconsider the confidence level, *c*, and the margin of error, *E*, he wants for his project. If David opted for $c = 95\%$, $z_c = 1.96$, and $E = 0.05$, he could use a sample of about 340.)

14. The goal is to estimate μ, the average of women at their first marriage; use $n = (z_c\sigma / E)^2$.

Preliminary sample of $n = 35, s = 2.3, c = 95\%, z_c = 1.96, E = 0.25$.

$n \approx [1.96(2.3)/0.25]^2 = 325.15 \approx 326$ women.

Since 35 women have already been interviewed, the sociologist needs to interview $326 - 35 = 291$ additional women.

15. The goal is to estimate μ, the average time phone customers are on hold; use $n = (z_c\sigma / E)^2$.

Preliminary sample of size $n = 167, s = 3.8$ minutes, $c = 99\%, z_c = 2.58, E = 30$ seconds $= 0.5$ minute (all time figures must be in the same units).

$n \approx [2.58(3.8)/0.5]^2 = 384.5 \approx 385$ phone calls.

Since the airline already measured the time on hold for 167 calls, it needs to measure the time on hold for $385 - 167 = 218$ more phone calls.

16. The goal is to estimate *p*, the proportion of small businesses declaring bankruptcy; use $n = pq(z_c / E)^2$.

(a) $c = 95\%, z_c = 1.96, E = 0.10$

Since there is no preliminary estimate of *p* available, use the worst case estimate, $\hat{p} = \frac{1}{2}; \hat{q} = 1 - \hat{p} = \frac{1}{2}$.

$n \approx 0.5 \cdot 0.5(z_c / E)^2 = 0.25(z_c / E)^2 = 0.25(1.96/0.10)^2 = 96.04 \approx 97$ small businesses.

(b) Preliminary sample of $n = 38$ found $r = 6$ small businesses had declared bankruptcy, so $\hat{p} = r/n = 6/38 = 0.1579, \hat{q} = 1 - \hat{p} = 0.8421$.

$n \approx (0.1579)(0.8421)(1.96/0.10)^2 = 51.08 \approx 52$ small businesses, total.

Since 38 have already been surveyed, the National Council of Small Businesses needs to survey an additional $52 - 38 = 14$ small businesses.

17. The goal is to estimate *p*, the proportion of pickup truck owners who are women; use $n = pq(z_c / E)^2$.

(a) $c = 90\%, z_c = 1.645, E = 0.1$

Since no preliminary estimate is available, use the worst case estimate, $\hat{p} = \frac{1}{2}; \hat{q} = 1 - \hat{p} = \frac{1}{2}$.

$n \approx 0.5 \cdot 0.5(z_c / E)^2 = 0.25(z_c / E)^2 = 0.25(1.645/0.1)^2 = 67.65 \approx 68$ owners.

(b) $\hat{p} = 24\% = 0.24; \hat{q} = 1 - \hat{p} = 0.76$.

$n \approx (0.24)(0.76)(1.645/0.1)^2 = 49.36 \approx 50$ owners.

18. The goal is to estimate *p*, the proportion of voters who favor the bond issue; use $n = pq(z_c / E)^2$.

(a) $c = 90\%, z_c = 1.645, E = 5\% = 0.05$

Since no preliminary estimate of *p* is available, Linda Silbers should use the worst case estimate. $\hat{p} = \frac{1}{2}; \hat{q} = 1 - \hat{p} = \frac{1}{2}$.

$n \approx 0.5 \cdot 0.5(z_c / E)^2 = 0.25(z_c / E)^2 = 0.25(1.645/0.05)^2 = 270.6 \approx 271$ voters.

(b) $\hat{p} = 73\% = 0.73; \hat{q} = 1 - \hat{p} = 0.27.$

$n \approx (0.73)(0.27)(1.645/0.05)^2 = 213.3 \approx 214$ voters.

19. (a) Hint: it is usually easier to go from the more complicated version to the easier version in showing the equality of two things. So, start with:

$$\frac{1}{4} - \left(p - \frac{1}{2}\right)^2 = \frac{1}{4} - \left[p^2 - 2p\left(\frac{1}{2}\right) + \left(\frac{1}{2}\right)^2\right] \quad \text{Recall: } (a-b)^2 = a^2 - 2ab + b^2$$
$$= \frac{1}{4} - \left[p^2 - p + \frac{1}{4}\right]$$
$$= -p^2 + p$$
$$= p - p^2 = p(1-p)$$

as was to be shown.

(b) For any number $a, a^2 \geq 0$, so

$$\left(p - \frac{1}{2}\right)^2 \geq 0$$

$$(-1)\left(p - \frac{1}{2}\right)^2 \leq (-1)(0) = 0 \quad \text{Multiply both sides by } -1\text{, remembering to reverse the order of inequality.}$$

$$-\left(p - \frac{1}{2}\right)^2 \leq 0$$

$$0 \geq -\left(p - \frac{1}{2}\right)^2$$

$$\frac{1}{4} \geq \frac{1}{4} - \left(p - \frac{1}{2}\right)^2 \quad \text{Add } \tfrac{1}{4} \text{ to both sides.}$$

but $\frac{1}{4} - \left(p - \frac{1}{2}\right)^2 = p(1-p)$ from part (a), so $\frac{1}{4} \geq p(1-p)$

[$p(1-p)$ is never greater than $1/4$ because it is always less than or equal to $1/4$.]

20. Note: all samples size calculations, after "rounding up," give the <u>minimum</u> sample size required to meet the c, E, etc., criteria.
Recall from text page 407 that the margin of error is the maximal error E of a <u>95%</u> confidence interval for p.
The problem, therefore, implies $E = 3\% = 0.03$, $c = 95\%$, $z_c = 1.96$, and since no preliminary estimate or p is given, use $\hat{p} = \frac{1}{2}; \hat{q} = 1 - \hat{p} = \frac{1}{2}$.
Because the goal is to estimate p, the proportion of registered voters who favor using lottery proceeds for park improvements, use

$$n = pq(z_c / E)^2 \approx 0.5 \cdot 0.5 (z_c / E)^2 = 0.25(z_c / E)^2 = 0.25(1.96/0.03)^2 = 1067.1 \approx 1068 \text{ registered voters.}$$

21. The goal is to estimate the proportion, p, of votes for the Democratic presidential candidate. Use $n = pq(z_c / E)^2$.

(a) $E = 0.001, c = 99\%, z_c = 2.58$

Since there is no preliminary estimate of p, use $\hat{p} = \hat{q} = \frac{1}{2}$.

$$n \approx 0.5 \cdot 0.5(z_c / E)^2 = 0.25(z_c / E)^2 = 0.25(2.58 / 0.001)^2 = 1{,}664{,}100 \text{ votes.}$$

(b) No. If the preliminary estimate of p was $\hat{p} = 0.5$, the same as the no information, worst case estimate of p, the sample size would be exactly the same as in (a). The general formula $n = pq(z_c / E)^2$ with preliminary estimates of p (and q) = 0.5 is the same as the no-information-about-p formula, $n = \frac{1}{4}(z_c / E)^2$.

[The above solutions have repeatedly used this fact, demonstrating that using $\hat{p} = \hat{q} = 0.5$ (the worst case estimates of p and q, giving the largest possible sample size that meets the stated criteria) in the special no-information about-p formula, $n = \frac{1}{4}(z_c / E)^2$, directly.]

Section 8.5

Answers may vary slightly due to rounding. For clarity, pooled estimates will be subscripted with "*p*" or the word "pooled."

1.

	Sample 1	Sample 2
n	45	40
s	0.37	0.31
$\bar{x}$	6.18	6.45

The confidence interval is for the difference in mean heights; since both n_1 and $n_2 > 30$ use large-sample technique.

(a) $c = 95\%, z_c = 1.96$

$$E = z_c\sqrt{\frac{\sigma_1^2}{n_1} + \frac{\sigma_2^2}{n_2}} \approx z_c\sqrt{\frac{s_1^2}{n_1} + \frac{s_2^2}{n_2}} = 1.96\sqrt{\frac{0.37^2}{45} + \frac{0.31^2}{40}} = 0.1446$$

$$[(\bar{x}_1 - \bar{x}_2) - E] < (\mu_1 - \mu_2) < [(\bar{x}_1 - \bar{x}_2) + E]$$
$$[(6.18 - 6.45) - 0.14] < (\mu_1 - \mu_2) < [(6.18 - 6.45) + 0.14]$$
$$-0.41 < (\mu_1 - \mu_2) < -0.13$$

(b) Since the interval values are all negative, we are 95% confident that $\mu_1 - \mu_2 < 0$, i.e., that $\mu_1 < \mu_2$. The football players appear to be between 0.13 and 0.41 feet shorter on average than the basketball players.

(c) $c = 99\%, z_c = 2.58$

$$E = 2.58\sqrt{\frac{0.37^2}{45} + \frac{0.31^2}{40}} = 0.1904$$

$$[(\bar{x}_1 - \bar{x}_2) - E] < (\mu_1 - \mu_2) < [(\bar{x}_1 - \bar{x}_2) + E]$$
$$[(6.18 - 6.45) - 0.19] < (\mu_1 - \mu_2) < [(6.18 - 6.45) + 0.19]$$
$$-0.46 < (\mu_1 - \mu_2) < -0.08$$

No; Since all the interval values are all negative, we are 99% confidence that football players are, on average, between 0.08 and 0.46 feet shorter than basketball players.

2.

	Sample 1	Sample 2
n	38	41
$\bar{x}$	31.5	30.3
s	4.4	3.8

The confidence interval is for the difference between mean ages; since n_1 and $n_2 \geq 30$, use large-sample technique.

(a) $c = 75\%, z_c = 1.15$

$$E = z_c\sqrt{\frac{\sigma_1^2}{n_1}+\frac{\sigma_2^2}{n_2}} \approx 1.15\sqrt{\frac{4.4^2}{38}+\frac{3.8^2}{41}} = 1.0675$$

$$[(\bar{x}_1-\bar{x}_2)-E] < (\mu_1-\mu_2) < [(\bar{x}_1-\bar{x}_2)+E]$$
$$[(31.5-30.3)-1.07] < (\mu_1-\mu_2) < [(31.5-30.3)+1.07]$$
$$0.13 < (\mu_1-\mu_2) < 2.27$$

(b) Because all values in the interval are positive we are 75% confident that baseball players are, on average between 0.13 and 2.27 years older than basketball players.

(c) $c = 90\%, z_c = 1.645$

$$E = 1.645\sqrt{\frac{4.4^2}{38}+\frac{3.8^2}{41}} = 1.5270$$

$$[(\bar{x}_1-\bar{x}_2)-E] < (\mu_1-\mu_2) < [(\bar{x}_1-\bar{x}_2)+E]$$
$$[(31.5-30.3)-1.53] < (\mu_1-\mu_2) < [(31.5-30.3)+1.53]$$
$$-0.33 < (\mu_1-\mu_2) < 2.73$$

Yes. Because the interval includes 0, at the 90% confidence level, there appears to be no difference in mean ages.

3. (a) $n_1 = 15, \bar{x}_1 = 5.593 \approx 5.6, s_1 = 0.9505 \approx 1.0$
$n_2 = 12, \bar{x}_2 = 2.533 \approx 2.5, s_2 = 0.8998 \approx 0.9$

(b) Since we want a confidence interval for $\mu_1 - \mu_2$, and n_1 and n_2 are both < 30, use small sample technique; $c = 99\%$

$$s_{\text{pooled}} = \sqrt{\frac{(n_1-1)s_1^2+(n_2-1)s_2^2}{n_1+n_2-2}} = \sqrt{\frac{14(1.0)^2+11(0.9)^2}{15+12-2}} = \sqrt{0.9164} = 0.9573$$

$t_c = t_{0.99} = 2.787$ with $n_1 + n_2 - 2 = 15 + 12 - 2 = 25\ d.f.$

$$E \approx t_c s_p\sqrt{\frac{1}{n_1}+\frac{1}{n_2}} = (2.787)(0.9573)\sqrt{\frac{1}{15}+\frac{1}{12}} = 1.0333 \approx 1.03$$

$$[(\bar{x}_1-\bar{x}_2)-E] < (\mu_1-\mu_2) < [(\bar{x}_1-\bar{x}_2)+E]$$
$$[(5.6-2.5)-1.03] < (\mu_1-\mu_2) < [(5.6-2.5)+1.03]$$
$$2.07 < (\mu_1-\mu_2) < 4.13$$

(c) Since all numbers in the interval are positive, we are 99% confident that the profit as a percentage of revenue is between 2.07% and 4.13% higher for the manufacturers than for the food and drugstores.

4. (a) $n_1 = 12, \bar{x}_1 = 4.425 \approx 4.4, s_1 = 1.5829 \approx 1.6$
$n_2 = 10, \bar{x}_2 = 4.62 \approx 4.6, s_2 = 1.4235 \approx 1.4$
since $n_i < 30$, use small sample technique to estimate $\mu_1 - \mu_2$.

(b) $c = 90\%, n_1 + n_2 - 2 = 12 + 10 - 2 = 20, t_{0.90}$ with 20 $d.f. = 1.725$

$$s_{\text{pooled}} = \sqrt{\frac{(n_1-1)s_1^2 + (n_2-1)s_2^2}{n_1+n_2-2}} = \sqrt{\frac{11(1.6)^2 + 9(1.4)^2}{12+10-2}} = \sqrt{2.29} = 1.5133$$

$$E \approx t_c s_p \sqrt{\frac{1}{n_1} + \frac{1}{n_2}} = (1.725)(1.5133)\sqrt{\frac{1}{12} + \frac{1}{10}} = 1.1177 \approx 1.1$$

$[(\bar{x}_1 - \bar{x}_2) - E] < (\mu_1 - \mu_2) < [(\bar{x}_1 - \bar{x}_2) + E]$
$[(4.4 - 4.6) - 1.1] < (\mu_1 - \mu_2) < [(4.4 - 4.6) + 1.1]$
$-1.3 < (\mu_1 - \mu_2) < 0.9$

(c) No; both positive and negative values are in the interval, so we are 90% confident that there is no difference in mean profit as a percentage of revenue between insurance companies and health care organizations.

5.

	Sample 1	Sample 2
n	375	571
r	289	23
$\hat{p}$	$289/375 = 0.7707$	$23/571 = 0.0403$

$n_1\hat{p}_1 = 289, n_1\hat{q}_1 = 86, n_2\hat{p}_2 = 23, n_2\hat{q}_2 = 548$
Since all four of these estimates are > 5, use the large sample technique to estimate $p_1 - p_2$.

(a) $c = 99\%, z_c = 2.58$

$$E \approx z_c\sqrt{\frac{\hat{p}_1\hat{q}_1}{n_1} + \frac{\hat{p}_2\hat{q}_2}{n_2}} = 2.58\sqrt{\frac{(0.7707)(0.2293)}{375} + \frac{(0.0403)(0.9597)}{571}} = 2.58(0.0232) = 0.0599 \approx 0.06$$

$[(\hat{p}_1 - \hat{p}_2) - E] < (p_1 - p_2) < [(\hat{p}_1 - \hat{p}_2) + E]$
$[(0.7707 - 0.0403) - 0.0599] < (p_1 - p_2) < [(0.7707 - 0.0403) + 0.0599]$
$0.6705 < (p_1 - p_2) < 0.7903$, or approximately 0.67 to 0.79

(b) Because the confidence interval contains only positive values, $p_1 > p_2$ and we can be 99% confident that $p_1 - p_2$ is between 0.67 and 0.79, inclusive.

6.

	Sample 1	Sample 2
n	375	571
r	132	217
$\hat{p}$	$132/375 = 0.3520$	$217/571 = 0.3800$

Since $n_1\hat{p}_1 = 132, n_1\hat{q}_1 = 243, n\hat{p}_2 = 217, n\hat{q}_2 = 354$ are all greater than 5, we can use large sample methods to estimate $p_1 - p_2$.

(a) $c = 90\%, z_c = 1.645$

$$E \approx z_c\sqrt{\frac{\hat{p}_1\hat{q}_1}{n_1} + \frac{\hat{p}_2\hat{q}_2}{n_2}} = 1.645\sqrt{\frac{(0.3520)(0.6480)}{375} + \frac{(0.3800)(0.6200)}{571}} = 1.645(0.0320) = 0.0526$$

$[(\hat{p}_1 - \hat{p}_2) - E] < (p_1 - p_2) < [(\hat{p}_1 - \hat{p}_2) + E]$
$[(0.3520 - 0.3800) - 0.0526] < (p_1 - p_2) < [(0.3520 - 0.3800) + 0.0526]$
$-0.0806 < (p_1 - p_2) < 0.0246$, or about -0.08 to 0.02.

(b) The confidence interval contains both positive and negative values. With 90% confidence, we can conclude there is no difference between p_1 and p_2.

7.

	Sample 1	Sample 2
n	9340	25,111
$\bar{x}$	63.3	72.1
s	9.17	12.67

Since $n_1, n_2 > 30$, we can use large sample methods to estimate $\mu_1 - \mu_2$.

(a) $c = 99\%, z_c = 2.58$

$$E \approx z_c\sqrt{\frac{s_1^2}{n_1}+\frac{s_2^2}{n_2}} = 2.58\sqrt{\frac{9.17^2}{9340}+\frac{12.67^2}{25{,}111}} = 0.3201$$

$$[(\bar{x}_1 - \bar{x}_2) - E] < (\mu_1 - \mu_2) < [(\bar{x}_1 - \bar{x}_2) + E]$$
$$[(63.3 - 72.1) - 0.3201] < (\mu_1 - \mu_2) < [(63.3 - 72.1) + 0.3201]$$
$$-9.1201 < \mu < -8.4799, \text{ or about } -9.12 \text{ to } -8.48$$

(b) The interval includes only negative numbers, leading us to believe $\mu_1 < \mu_2$. We are 99% confident that the mean interval between eruptions during the period 1983 to 1987 is between 8.48 and 9.12 minutes longer than the mean interval between Old Faithful eruptions during the period 1948 to 1952. [Comment: it is highly unlikely the data in this problem constitute the required two independent random samples. First, the data are time series observations and are probably highly correlated. It is possible the 30 year gap between time periods would be sufficient to wipe out the effects of serial correlation so that the two samples could be considered independent. However, the times within each sample are still correlated, and random samples consist of data that are independent (and identically distributed). Second, the large sample sizes, much larger than needed, might indicate a census rather than a sample of data was used.)

8.

	Sample 1	Sample 2
n	32	32
$\bar{x}$	69.44	59.00
s	11.69	11.60

Since $n_1, n_2 > 30$, we can use large sample methods to estimate $\mu_1 - \mu_2$.

(a) $c = 99\%, z_c = 2.58$

$$E \approx z_c\sqrt{\frac{s_1^2}{n_1}+\frac{s_2^2}{n_2}} = 2.58\sqrt{\frac{11.69^2}{32}+\frac{11.60^2}{32}} = 2.58(2.9113) = 7.5111$$

$$[(\bar{x}_1 - \bar{x}_2) - E] < (\mu_1 - \mu_2) < [(\bar{x}_1 - \bar{x}_2) + E]$$
$$[(69.44 - 59.00) - 7.51] < (\mu_1 - \mu_2) < [(69.44 - 59.00) + 7.51]$$
$$2.93 < (\mu_1 - \mu_2) < 17.95$$

(b) All values in the interval are positive, indicating $\mu_1 > \mu_2$. We are 99% confident that mothers score 2.93 to 17.95 points higher than fathers on the empathy scale, i.e., mothers are more sensitive to baby temperament.

9. (a) $n_1 = 14, \bar{x}_1 = 4.8571 \approx 4.9, s = 2.7695 \approx 2.8$
$n_2 = 16, \bar{x}_2 = 4.1875 \approx 4.2, s = 2.4824 \approx 2.5.$

(b) Since both sample sizes are less than 30, we will use the small sample technique to estimate $\mu_1 - \mu_2$.
$c = 95\%, n_1 + n_2 - 2 = 14 + 16 - 2 = 28, t_{0.95}$ with 28 $d.f. = 2.048$

$$s_{\text{pooled}} = \sqrt{\frac{(n_1-1)s_1^2 + (n_2-1)s_2^2}{n_1+n_2-2}} = \sqrt{\frac{13(2.8)^2 + 15(2.5)^2}{14+16-2}} = \sqrt{6.9882} = 2.6435$$

$$E \approx t_c s_p \sqrt{\frac{1}{n_1} + \frac{1}{n_2}} = 2.048(2.6435)\sqrt{\frac{1}{14} + \frac{1}{16}} = 1.9813$$

$[(\bar{x}_1 - \bar{x}_2) - E] < (\mu_1 - \mu_2) < [(\bar{x}_1 - \bar{x}_2) + E]$
$[(4.9 - 4.2) - 1.98] < (\mu_1 - \mu_2) < [(4.9 - 4.2) + 1.98]$
$-1.28 < (\mu_1 - \mu_2) < 2.68$

(c) The interval includes both positive and negative numbers. With 95% confidence, there sums to be no difference in mean number of children by income group.

10. (a) $n_1 = 10, \bar{x}_1 = 75.80, s = 8.3240 \approx 8.32$
$n_2 = 18, \bar{x}_2 = 66.8333 \approx 66.83, s_2 = 8.8667 \approx 8.87$

(b) Since both n_1 and $n_2 < 30$, we will use small sample methods to estimate $\mu_1 - \mu_2$.
$c = 85\%, n_1 + n_2 - 2 = 10 + 18 - 2 = 26, t_{0.85}$ with 26 $d.f. = 1.483$

$$s_{\text{pooled}} = \sqrt{\frac{(n_1-1)s_1^2 + (n_2-1)s_2^2}{n_1+n_2-2}} = \sqrt{\frac{9(8.32^2) + 17(8.87^2)}{10+18-2}} = 8.6836$$

$$E \approx t_c s_p \sqrt{\frac{1}{n_1} + \frac{1}{n_2}} = 1.483(8.6836)\sqrt{\frac{1}{10} + \frac{1}{18}} = 5.0791$$

$[(\bar{x}_1 - \bar{x}_2) - E] < (\mu_1 - \mu_2) < [(\bar{x}_1 - \bar{x}_2) + E]$
$[(75.80 - 66.83) - 5.0791] < (\mu_1 - \mu_2) < [(75.80 - 66.83) + 5.0791]$
$3.89 < (\mu_1 - \mu_2) < 14.05$

(c) Because the interval contains only positive numbers, we can claim $\mu_1 > \mu_2$. We are 85% confident that grey wolves in the Chihuahua Region weight 3.89 to 14.05 pounds more, on average, than grey wolves in the Durango Region.

11. $n_1 = 210, r_1 = 65, \hat{p}_1 = 65/210 = 0.3095, \hat{q}_1 = \frac{145}{210} = 0.6905$
$n_2 = 152, r_2 = 18, \hat{p}_2 = 18/152 = 0.1184, \hat{q}_2 = \frac{134}{152} = 0.8816.$

Since $n_1\hat{p}_1 = 65, n_1\hat{q}_1 = 145, n_2\hat{p}_2 = 18,$ and $n_2\hat{q}_2 = 134$ are all > 5, we will use large sample methods to estimate $p_1 - p_2$.

(a) $c = 99\%, z_c = 2.58$

$$E \approx z_c \sqrt{\frac{\hat{p}_1\hat{q}_1}{n_1} + \frac{\hat{p}_2\hat{q}_2}{n_2}} = 2.58\sqrt{\frac{0.3095(0.6905)}{210} + \frac{(0.1184)(0.8816)}{152}} = 2.58(0.0413) = 0.1065$$

$[(\hat{p}_1 - \hat{p}_2) - E] < (p_1 - p_2) < [(\hat{p}_1 - \hat{p}_2) + E]$
$[(0.3095 - 0.1184) - 0.1065] < (p_1 - p_2) < [(0.3095 - 0.1184) + 0.1065]$
$0.0846 < (p_1 - p_2) < 0.2976$, or about 0.085 to 0.298.

(b) The interval consists only of positive values, indicating $p_1 > p_2$. We are 99% confident that the difference in the percentage of traditional Navajo hogans is between 0.085 and 0.298, i.e., there are between 8.5% and 29.8% more hogans in the Fort Defiance Region than in the Indian Wells Region. If it is true that traditional Navajo tend to live in hogans, then, percentage-wise, there are more traditional Navajo at Fort Defiance than at Indian Hills.

12. $\hat{p}_1 = 69/112 = 0.6161, \hat{q}_1 = 0.3839$
$\hat{p}_2 = 26/140 = 0.1857, q_2 = 0.8143$
$n_1\hat{p}_1 = 69, n_1\hat{q}_1 = 43, n_2\hat{p}_2 = 26, n_2\hat{q}_2 = 114$
Since all four of the above estimates exceed 5, we can use large sample methods to estimate $p_1 - p_2$.

(a) $c = 99\%, z_c = 2.58$

$$E \approx z_c\sqrt{\frac{\hat{p}_1\hat{q}_1}{n_1}+\frac{\hat{p}_2\hat{q}_2}{n_2}} = 2.58\sqrt{\frac{0.6161(0.3839)}{112}+\frac{0.1857(0.8143)}{140}} = 2.58(0.0565) = 0.1458$$

$[(\hat{p}_1 - \hat{p}_2) - E] < (p_1 - p_2) < [(\hat{p}_1 - \hat{p}_2) + E]$
$[(0.6161 - 0.1857) - 0.1458] < (p_1 - p_2) < [(0.6161 - 0.1857) + 0.1458]$
$0.2846 < (p_1 - p_2) < 0.5762$, or about 0.28 to 0.58

(b) The interval contains only positive values implying $p_1 > p_2$. We are 99% confident that the difference in percentage unidentified is between 28% and 58%. The higher the altitude, the greater the percentage of unidentified artifacts, which supports the hypothesis.

13. $n_1 = 51, \bar{x}_1 = 74.04, s_1 = 17.19$
$n_2 = 36, \bar{x}_2 = 94.53, s_2 = 19.66.$

Since $n_1, n_2 \geq 30$ we will use large sample methods to estimate $\mu_1 - \mu_2$.

(a) $c = 95\%, z_c = 1.96$

$$E \approx z_c\sqrt{\frac{s_1^2}{n_1}+\frac{s_2^2}{n_2}} = 1.96\sqrt{\frac{17.19^2}{51}+\frac{19.66^2}{36}} = 7.9689$$

$[(\bar{x}_1 - \bar{x}_2) - E] < (\mu_1 - \mu_2) < [(\bar{x}_1 - \bar{x}_2) + E]$
$[(74.04 - 94.53) - 7.9689] < (\mu_1 - \mu_2) < [(74.04 - 94.53) + 7.9689]$
$-28.4589 < (\mu_1 - \mu_2) < -12.5211$, or about -28.46 to -12.52

(b) The confidence interval covers only negative values, indicating $\mu_2 > \mu_1$. We are 95% that the mean buck weight in the Mesa Verde Region is between 12.52 and 28.46 kg more than the mean buck weight in the Cache la Poudre River. More older deer and more abundant browse may help explain the size advantage in the Mesa Verde Region.

14.

	Sample 1	Sample 2
n	316	419
r	259	94
$\hat{p} = \frac{r}{n}$	$259/316 = 0.8196$	$94/419 = 0.2243$
$\hat{q} = 1 - \hat{p}$	$57/316 = 0.1804$	$325/419 = 0.7757$

Note: Sample 2, which received no plasma compress treatment, could be considered the control group.
$n_1\hat{p}_1 = 259, n_1\hat{q}_1 = 57, n_2\hat{p}_2 = 94, n_2\hat{q}_2 = 325$
Since each of these four estimates ≥ 30, we can use large sample methods to estimate $p_1 - p_2$.

(a) $c = 95\%, z_c = 1.96$

$$E \approx z_c \sqrt{\frac{\hat{p}_1\hat{q}_1}{n_1} + \frac{\hat{p}_2\hat{q}_2}{n_2}} = 1.96\sqrt{\frac{0.8196(0.1804)}{316} + \frac{0.2243(0.7757)}{419}} = 1.96(0.0297) = 0.0582$$

$[(\hat{p}_1 - \hat{p}_2) - E] < (p_1 - p_2) < [(\hat{p}_1 - \hat{p}_2) + E]$
$[(0.8196 - 0.2243) - 0.0582] < (p_1 - p_2) < [(0.8196 - 0.2243) + 0.0582]$
$0.5371 < (p_1 - p_2) < 0.6535$, or about 0.54 to 0.65.

(b) The numbers in the confidence interval are all positive, indicating $p_1 > p_2$, i.e., the proportion of patients with no visible scars is greater among those who received the plasma compress treatment than among those without this treatment. With 95% confidence we can say that the plasma compress treatment increased the proportion of patients with no visible scars by between 54 and 65 percentage points. The treatment seems to be quite effective in reducing scars, based on this data.

15. Because the original group of 45 subjects was randomly split into 3 subgroups of 15, each subgrouping can be considered a random sample, and it is independent of the other subgroups/samples. Since the sample sizes (15) are all < 30, we will use small sample procedures (based on *t*) to find estimates of $\mu_i - \mu_j$. Because the *t* distribution requires the data to be normal but is robust against some departures from normality, the authors of this study would have to make a case for their self esteem scores' distributions being at least mound-shaped (unimodal) and symmetric.
$c = 85\%, n_i + n_j - 2 = 15 + 15 - 2 = 28, t_{0.85}$ with 28 $d.f. = 1.480$
Preliminary calculations:

$\mu_i - \mu_j$	$\bar{x}_i - \bar{x}_j$	$s_{\text{pooled } ij} = \sqrt{\frac{(n_i - 1)s_i^2 + (n_j - 1)s_j^2}{n_i + n_j - 2}}$
1 *versus* 2	19.84 – 19.32 = 0.52	$\sqrt{\frac{14(3.07)^2 + 14(3.62)^2}{15 + 15 - 2}} = 3.3563$
1 *versus* 3	19.84 – 17.88 = 1.96	$\sqrt{\frac{14(3.07)^2 + 14(3.74)^2}{15 + 15 - 2}} = 3.4214$
2 *versus* 3	19.32 – 17.88 = 1.44	$\sqrt{\frac{14(3.62)^2 + 14(3.74)^2}{15 + 15 - 2}} = 3.6805$

$$E_{ij} = t_c s_{\text{spooled } ij} \sqrt{\frac{1}{n_i} + \frac{1}{n_j}} = t_c s_{\text{pooled } ij} \sqrt{\frac{1}{15} + \frac{1}{15}}$$
$$= (1.480) s_{\text{pooled } ij} (0.3651) = s_{\text{pooled } ij} (0.5403)$$

$[(\bar{x}_i - \bar{x}_j) - E_{ij}] < (\mu_i - \mu_j) < [(\bar{x}_i - \bar{x}_j) + E_{ij}]$

(a) $i = 1, j = 2$:
$[0.52 - (3.3563)(0.5403)] < (\mu_1 - \mu_2) < [0.52 + (3.3563)(0.5403)]$
$-1.2934 < (\mu_1 - \mu_2) < 2.3334$, or about -1.29 to 2.33

(b) $i = 1, j = 3$:
$[1.96 - (3.4214)(0.5403)] < (\mu_1 - \mu_3) < [1.96 + (3.4214)(0.5403)]$
$0.1114 < (\mu_1 - \mu_3) < 3.8086$, or about 0.11 to 3.81

(c) $i = 2, j = 3$:
$[1.44 - 3.6805(0.5403)] < (\mu_2 - \mu_3) < [1.44 + 3.6805(0.5403)]$
$-0.5486 < (\mu_2 - \mu_3) < 3.4286$ or about -0.55 to 3.43

(d) With 85% confidence we can say there is no significant difference between the self-esteem scores on competence and social acceptance, and no significant difference between self-esteem scores on social acceptance and physical attractiveness. However, the interval estimate for $\mu_1 - \mu_3$ contains only positive numbers, indicating that $\mu_1 > \mu_3$. With 85% confidence we can say that the self-esteem score for competence was between 0.11 and 3.81 points higher than that for physical attractiveness. Notes. (1) There are better ways to study these 3 self-esteem scores than the method used here; however, that technique is beyond the level of the text. (2) The confidence interval formula used in (a)-(c) is designed to capture the true difference, $\mu_i - \mu_j$, 85% of the time. However, the change that <u>all</u> the intervals will <u>simultaneously</u> include the true value, for there is and js is less than 85%. (For further details, consult a more advanced textbook and look up multiple comparisons, comparison wise error rate, and family-wise or experiment wise error rate, or comparison wise, family-wise, and experiment wise confidence coefficients.) (3) Although (b) showed a <u>statistically</u> significant difference (at 85%) between μ_1, and μ_3, the paper's authors would have to argue whether a difference of 0.11 to 3.81 points has any <u>practical</u> significance, especially since 3.81 is very close to s_{pooled}. Statistical significance does not necessarily mean the results have practical significance.

16. Refer to the focus problem at the beginning of this chapter.

Group I: $n_1 = 474, r_1 = 270, \hat{p}_1 = \dfrac{270}{474} = 0.5696$

Group II: $n_2 = 805, r_2 = 270, \hat{p} = \dfrac{270}{805} = 0.3354$

(a) $\hat{p}_1 = 0.5696, \hat{q}_1 = 1 - \hat{p}_1 = 0.4304, c = 95\%, z_c = 1.96$
$n_1\hat{p}_1 = 270, n_1\hat{q}_1 = 204$; since the estimate for $n_1 p_1$ and $n_1 q_1 > 5$, we can use the large sample approach to find an estimate of p_1.

$$E_1 \approx z_c\sqrt{\frac{\hat{p}_1\hat{q}_1}{n_1}} = 1.96\sqrt{\frac{(0.5696)(0.4304)}{474}} = 0.0446$$

$(\hat{p}_1 - E_1) < p_1 < (\hat{p}_1 + E_1), (0.5696 - 0.0446) < p_1 < (0.5696 + 0.0446)$
$0.5250 < p_1 < 0.6055$, or about 0.53 to 0.61

(b) $\hat{p}_2 = 0.3354, \hat{q}_2 = 1 - \hat{p}_2 = 1 - 0.3354 = 0.6646$
$n_2\hat{p}_2 = 270, n_2\hat{q}_2 = 535$; since estimates of $n_2 p_2$ and $n_2 q_2 > 5$, we will use large sample methods to find an estimate of p_2.

$$E_2 \approx z_c\sqrt{\frac{\hat{p}_2\hat{q}_2}{n_2}} = 1.96\sqrt{\frac{(0.3354)(0.6646)}{805}} = 0.0326$$

$(\hat{p}_2 - E_2) < p_2 < (\hat{p}_2 + E_2), (0.3354 - 0.0326) < p_2 < (0.3354 + 0.0326)$
$0.3028 < p_2 < 0.3680$, or about 0.30 to 0.37

(c) Since all $n_i\hat{p}_i$ and $n_i\hat{q}_i > 5$, we will use large sample methods to estimate $p_1 - p_2$.

$$E_{12} \approx z_c\sqrt{\frac{\hat{p}_1\hat{q}_1}{n_1}+\frac{\hat{p}_2\hat{q}_2}{n_2}} = 1.96\sqrt{\frac{(0.5696)(0.4304)}{474}+\frac{0.3354(0.6646)}{805}} = 1.96(0.0282) = 0.0553$$

$$[(\hat{p}_1 - \hat{p}_2) - E_{12}] < (p_1 - p_2) < [(\hat{p}_1 - \hat{p}_2) + E_{12}]$$

$$[(0.5696 - 0.3354) - 0.0553] < (p_1 - p_2) < [0.5696 - 0.3354) + 0.0553]$$

$0.1789 < (p_1 - p_2) < 0.2895$, or about 0.18 to 0.29.

Since the interval contains only positive numbers, we can say with 95% confidence that $p_1 > p_2$, i.e., the proportion of eggs hatched in well separated and well hidden nesting boxes is greater than the proportion of eggs hatches in highly visible, closely grouped nesting boxes; in fact, with type I nesting boxes, the percentage hatched is roughly 20 to 30 percentage points higher than that of type II nesting boxes.

(d) A greater proportion of wood duck eggs hatch if the eggs are laid in well separated, well hidden, nesting boxes.

17. (a) $[(\bar{x}_1 - \bar{x}_2) - E] < \mu_1 - \mu_2 < [(\bar{x}_1 - \bar{x}_2) + E]$

where $E \approx z_c\sqrt{\frac{s_1^2}{n_1}+\frac{s_2^2}{n_2}}$

$z_{0.90} = 1.645, z_{0.95} = 1.96, z_{0.99} = 2.58$

As we change from one *c* confidence interval to another, the only number that changes is z_c. The interval width is 2*E*, and it depends on z_c; if *c* increases, z_c increases, and the interval gets wider; if *c* decreases, z_c decreases, and the interval gets narrower. The larger interval (larger z_c) always includes all the points that were in a smaller interval created from a smaller z_c. All intervals are centerd at $(\bar{x}_1 - \bar{x}_2)$.

Therefore, if a 95% confidence interval includes both positive and negative numbers, the 99% confidence interval must include both positive and negative numbers. However, in going from 95% to 90%, the width of the interval decreases evenly from both sides. If $(\bar{x}_1 - \bar{x}_2)$ is near 0, the 90% confidence interval could have both positive and negative values, just like the 95% confidence interval did, and all values in the 90% confidence interval would have also been in the 95% confidence interval. However, the farther $(\bar{x}_1 - \bar{x}_2)$ is from zero, the more likely it is that the narrower 90% confidence interval will contain only positive or only negative numbers.

(b) $[(\hat{p}_1 - \hat{p}_2) - E] < (p_1 - p_2) < [(\hat{p}_1 - \hat{p}_2) + E]$

where $E \approx z_c\sqrt{\frac{\hat{p}_1\hat{q}_1}{n_1}+\frac{\hat{p}_2\hat{q}_2}{n_2}}$

As in (a), the only number that changes (and, therefore, affects the width) is z_c, and all the intervals are centered at $(\hat{p}_1 - \hat{p}_2)$.

If a 95% confidence interval contains only positive values, a 99% confidence interval could contain all positive numbers, or both positive and negative numbers, depending on how close $(\hat{p}_1 - \hat{p}_2)$ is to zero. However, with a narrower 90% confidence interval, if the 95% confidence interval had only positive values, the 90% interval will, too, and every value in the 90% interval would also have been in the 95% confidence interval.

Note: the principle is the same whether it is a confidence interval for $\mu, \mu_1 - \mu_2, p, p_1 - p_2$, etc. One can make statements paralleling those of (b) for the 95% confidence interval having only negative values.

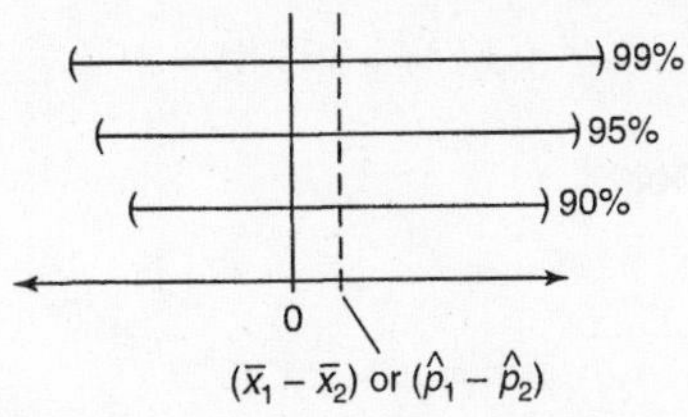

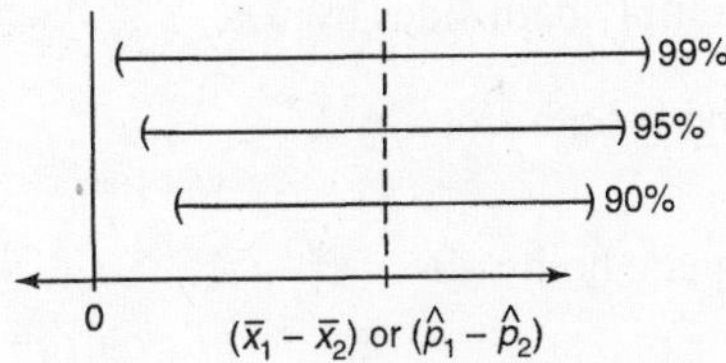

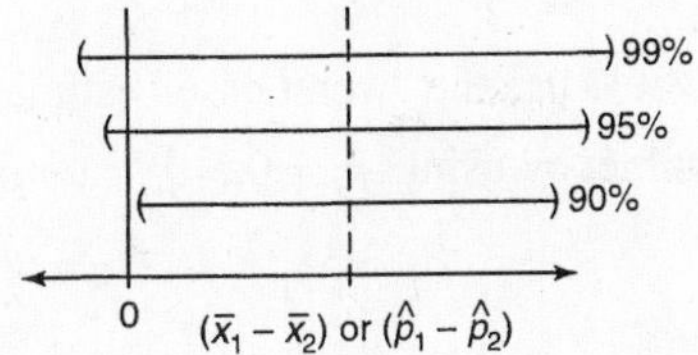

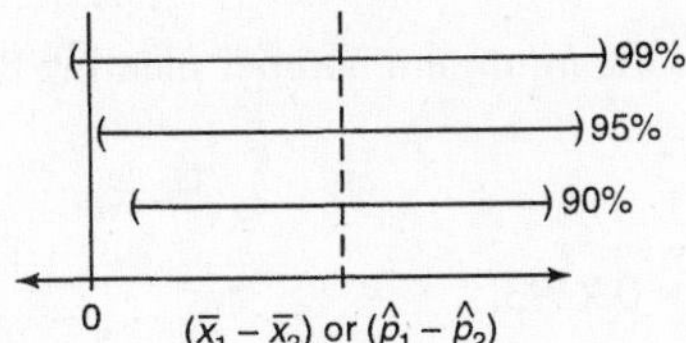

18. (a) $E = z_c\sqrt{\frac{\sigma_1^2}{n_1} + \frac{\sigma_2^2}{n_2}}$ Let $n = n_1 = n_2$; then $E = z_c\sqrt{\frac{\sigma_1^2 + \sigma_2^2}{n}} = \frac{z_c}{\sqrt{n}}\sqrt{\sigma_1^2 + \sigma_2^2}$

Solve for n:

$\sqrt{n}E = z_c\sqrt{\sigma_1^2 + \sigma_2^2}$ Multiply both sides by $\sqrt{n}$.

$\sqrt{n} = \frac{z_c}{E}\sqrt{\sigma_1^2 + \sigma_2^2}$ Divide both sides by E.

$n = \left(\frac{z_c}{E}\right)^2 (\sigma_1^2 + \sigma_2^2)$ Square both sides.

Note that this is $n_1 = n$ *and* $n_2 = n$; $2n$ units total.

(b) $c = 95\%, z_c = 1.96, E = 0.05$

$s_1 = 0.37, s_2 = 0.31$ from Problem 1 above

$$n \approx \left(\frac{z_c}{E}\right)^2 (s_1^2 + s_2^2) = \left(\frac{1.96}{0.05}\right)^2 (0.37^2 + 0.31^2) = 358.037 \approx 359$$

so n_1 and n_2 should each be 359.

(c) $c = 90\%$ so $z_c = 1.645, E = 0.5$

$s_1 = 4.4, s_2 = 3.8$ from Problem 2 above

$$n \approx \left(\frac{z_c}{E}\right)^2 (s_1^2 + s_2^2) = \left(\frac{1.645}{0.5}\right)^2 (4.4^2 + 3.8^2) = 365.85 \approx 366$$

so each n_1 and n_2 should be 366.

19. $E = z_c\sqrt{\frac{p_1q_1}{n_1} + \frac{p_2q_2}{n_2}} = \frac{z_c}{\sqrt{n}}\sqrt{p_1q_1 + p_2q_2}$ if $n = n_1 = n_2$

So $\sqrt{n}E = z_c\sqrt{p_1q_1 + p_2q_2}$ Multiply both sides by $\sqrt{n}$.

$\sqrt{n} = \frac{z_c}{E}\sqrt{p_1q_1 + p_2q_2}$ Divide both sides by E.

$n = \left(\frac{z_c}{E}\right)^2 (p_1q_1 + p_2q_2)$ Square both sides.

so $n \approx \left(\frac{z_c}{E}\right)^2 (\hat{p}_1\hat{q}_1 + \hat{p}_2\hat{q}_2)$

If we have no estimate for p_i, we would use the "worst case" estimate, i.e., the conservative approach would be to make n as large as possible, by using $\hat{p}_1 = 0.5, \hat{q}_1 = 1 - \hat{p}_1 = 0.5$
So, in this case,

$$n \approx \left(\frac{z_c}{E}\right)^2 [(0.5)(0.5) + (0.5)(0.5)] = 0.5\left(\frac{z_c}{E}\right)^2 \text{ or } \left(\frac{1}{2}\right)\left(\frac{z_c}{E}\right)^2$$

Again, all sample size estimates are the minimum number meeting the stated criteria.

(a) $c = 99\%, z_c = 2.58, E = 0.04,$

$\hat{p}_1 = \frac{289}{375} = 0.7707, \hat{q}_1 = 1 - \hat{p}_1 = 0.2293,$

$\hat{p}_2 = \frac{23}{571} = 0.0403, \hat{q}_2 = 0.9597$

(Recall the n_ip_i and n_iq_i conditions were checked in Problem 5 above.)

$$n \approx \left(\frac{z_c}{E}\right)^2 (\hat{p}_1\hat{q}_1 + \hat{p}_2\hat{q}_2) = \left(\frac{2.58}{0.04}\right)^2 [0.7707(0.2293) + 0.0403(0.9597)] = 896.107 \approx 897$$

n_1 and n_2 should each be 897 (married couples)

(b) Let $\hat{p}_i = \hat{q}_i = 0.5; c = 95\%, z_c = 1.96, E = 0.05$

$$n \approx \left(\frac{1}{2}\right)\left(\frac{z_c}{E}\right)^2 = \left(\frac{1}{2}\right)\left(\frac{1.96}{0.05}\right)^2 = 768.32 \approx 769$$

n_1 and n_2 should each be 769 (married couples)

Chapter 8 Review

1. point estimate: a single number used to estimate a population parameter
critical value: the x-axis values (arguments) of a probability density function (such as the standard normal or Student's t) which cut off an area of $c, 0 \le c \le 1$, under the curve between them. Examples: the area under the standard normal curve between $-z_c$ and $+z_c$ is c; the area under the curve of a Student's t distribution between $-t_c$ and $+t_c$ as c. The area is symmetric about the curve's mean, μ.
maximal error of estimate, E: the largest distance ("error") between the point estimate and the parameter it estimates that can be tolerated under certain circumstances; E is the half-width of a confidence interval.
confidence level, c: A measure of the reliability of an (interval) estimate: c denotes the proportion of all possible confidence interval estimates of a parameter (or difference between 2 parameters) that will cover/capture/enclose the true value being estimated. It is a statement about the probability the procedure being used has of capturing the value of interest; it cannot be considered a measure of the reliability of a specific interval, because any specific interval is either right or wrong-either it captures the parameter value, or it does not, period.
confidence interval: a procedure designed to give a range of values as an (interval) estimate of an unknown parameter value; compare point estimate. What separates confidence interval estimates from any other interval estimate (such as 4, give or take 2.8) is that the reliability of the procedure can be determined: if $c = 0.90 = 90\%$, for example, a 90% confidence interval (estimate) for μ says that it all possible samples of size n were drawn, and a 90% confidence interval for μ was created for each such sample using the prescribed method (such as $\overline{x} \pm z_c\sigma/\sqrt{n}$), then if the true value of μ became known, 90% of the confidence intervals so created would cover/capture/enclose the value of μ.
large/small samples: a large sample in our context is one that is of sufficient size to warrant using a normal approximation to the exact method, i.e., large enough that the central limit theorem can reasonably be applied and that the approximation results in sufficiently accurate estimates of the exact method results. We have said that $n \ge 30$ is large enough, in all but the most extreme cases, to say that the Student's t-distribution can be approximated by the normal and that s^2 can be used to estimate σ^2. Similarly, if np_i and nq_i are both greater than 5, the normal distribution can be used to approximate the exact binomial calculations of the probability of r successes.
Small samples are those of a size where using a normal approximation instead of the exact method would give unreliable results; the difference between the exact and appropriate answers is too large to be tolerated. For Student's t distribution, if $n < 30$, the normal approximation results are considered too crude to be useful. For the central limit theorem to be applied when estimating p or $p_1 - p_2$, or, specifically, for the normal approximation to the binomial to be applied we have said np_i and nq_i must both be >5.* Here the criteria are the products np_i and nq_i, not just the size of n. A sample of size $n = 300$ seems large enough for just about any purpose, but if $p = 0.01$, $np_i = 300(0.01) = 3 \le 5$, and $n = 300$ is not large enough for a normal approximation to be accurate enough. In general, if p (or q) is near 0 or near 1, n must be quite large before the normal approximation can be used.
*Some textbooks use other criteria or rules of thumb, such as np_i and $nq_i > 10$.

2. $n = 370 \ge 30$ is sufficiently large to use large sample procedures to estimate μ.
$\overline{x} = 750, s = 150, c = 0.90$ so $z_c = 1.645$, or $c = 0.99$ so $z_c = 2.58$

$$E \approx \frac{z_c s}{\sqrt{n}} = z_c \frac{150}{\sqrt{370}} = 7.7981 z_c$$

$(\overline{x} - E) < \mu < (\overline{x} + E)$

For $c = 0.90$: $E \approx 7.7981(1.645) = 12.8279 \approx 13$

$(750 - 13) < \mu < (750 + 13)$

$\$737 < \mu < \$763$

For $c = 0.99$: $E \approx 7.7981(2.58) = 20.1191 \approx 20$

$(750 - 20) < \mu < (750 + 20)$

$\$730 < \mu < \$770$

3. $n = 73 \geq 30$; use a large sample procedure to estimate μ.

$\bar{x} = 178.70, s = 7.81, c = 95\%, z_c = 1.96$

$E \approx \frac{z_c s}{\sqrt{n}} = \frac{1.96(7.81)}{\sqrt{73}} = 1.7916 \approx 1.79$

$(\bar{x} - E) < \mu < (\bar{x} + E)$

$(178.70 - 1.79) < \mu < (178.70 + 1.79)$

$176.91 < \mu < 180.49$

4. $c = 99\%, z_c = 2.58, E = 2, s = 7.81$ from Problem 3 above

$n = \left(\frac{z_c s}{E}\right)^2 = \left[\frac{2.58(7.81)}{2}\right]^2 = 101.5036 \approx 102$

5. (a) $\bar{x} = 74.2, s = 18.2530 \approx 18.3$, as indicated

(b) $c = 95\%, n = 15$ so use small sample procedure to estimate μ

$t_{0.95}$ with $n - 1 = 14$ *d.f.* $= 2.145$

$E \approx \frac{t_c s}{\sqrt{n}} = \frac{2.145(18.3)}{\sqrt{15}} = 10.1352 \approx 10.1$

$(\bar{x} - E) < \mu < (\bar{x} + E)$

$(74.2 - 10.1) < \mu < (74.2 + 10.1)$

64.1 centimeters $< \mu <$ 84.3 centimeters

6. (a) $n = 10, \bar{x} = 15.78 \approx 15.8, s = 3.4608 \approx 3.5$, as indicated

(b) estimate μ with small sample procedure because $n = 10 < 30$

$c = 80\%, n - 1 = 9\ d.f., t_{0.80}$ with $9\ d.f. = 1.383$

$E \approx \frac{t_c s}{\sqrt{n}} = \frac{1.383(3.5)}{\sqrt{10}} = 1.5307 \approx 1.53$

$(\bar{x} - E) < \mu < (\bar{x} + E)$

$(15.8 - 1.53) < \mu < (15.8 + 1.53)$

14.27 centimeters $< \mu <$ 17.33 centimeters

7. $n = 2958, r = 1538, \hat{p} = \frac{r}{n} = \frac{1538}{2958} = 0.5199 \approx 0.52$

$\hat{q} = 1 - \hat{p} = 0.4801, n - r = 1420, c = 90\%, z_c = 1.645$

$np \approx n\hat{p} = r = 1538 > 5, nq \approx n\hat{q} = n - r = 1420 > 5$, so use large sample method to estimate p

$E \approx z_c \sqrt{\frac{\hat{p}\hat{q}}{n}} = 1.645 \sqrt{\frac{(0.5199)(0.4801)}{2958}} = 0.0151 \approx 0.02$

$(\hat{p} - E) < p < (\hat{p} + E)$

$(0.52 - 0.02) < p < (0.52 + 0.02)$

$0.50 < p < 0.54$

8. $95\%, z_c = 1.96$, preliminary estimate $\hat{p} = 0.52$

$E = 0.01, \hat{q} = 1 - \hat{p} = 0.48$

$n = \left(\frac{z_c}{E}\right)^2 \hat{p}\hat{q} = \left(\frac{1.96}{0.01}\right)^2 (0.52)(0.48) = 9{,}588.6336$

sample size of 9589

9. $n = 167, r = 68$

(a) $\hat{p} = \frac{r}{n} = \frac{68}{167} = 0.4072, \hat{q} = 0.5928, n - r = 99$

(b) $n\hat{p} = r = 68 > 5$ and $n\hat{q} = n - r = 99 > 5$, so use large sample method to estimate p

$c = 95\%, z_c = 1.96$

$$E \approx z_c\sqrt{\frac{\hat{p}\hat{q}}{n}} = 1.96\sqrt{\frac{(0.4072)(0.5928)}{167}} = 0.0745$$

$(\hat{p} - E) < p < (\hat{p} + E)$

$(0.4072 - 0.0745) < p < (0.4072 + 0.0745)$

$0.3327 < p < 0.4817$, or about 0.333 to 0.482

10. $c = 95\%, z_c = 1.96, E = 0.06, \hat{p} = 0.4072, \hat{q} = 0.5928$ from Problem 9

$$n \approx \left(\frac{z_c}{E}\right)^2 \hat{p}\hat{q} = \left(\frac{1.96}{0.06}\right)^2 (0.4072)(0.5928) = 257.5880 \approx 258 \text{ potshards}$$

Since Problem 9 says 167 potshards have already been collected, we need 258 – 167 = 91 additional potshards to be collected.

11. $n_1 = 43, \bar{x}_1 = 3.6, s_1 = 1.8$

$n_2 = 40, \bar{x}_2 = 3.3, s_2 = 1.7$

(a) Since $n_i \geq 30$, we can use a large sample approach to estimating $\mu_1 - \mu_2$

$c = 90\%,\ z_c = 1.645$

$$E \approx z_c\sqrt{\frac{s_1^2}{n_1} + \frac{s_2^2}{n_2}} = 1.645\sqrt{\frac{1.8^2}{43} + \frac{1.7^2}{40}} = 0.6320$$

$[(\bar{x}_1 - \bar{x}_2) - E] < (\mu_1 - \mu_2) < [(\bar{x}_1 - \bar{x}_2) + E]$

$[(3.6 - 3.3) + 0.632] < (\mu_1 - \mu_2) < [(3.6 - 3.3) + 0.632]$

-0.332 percent $< (\mu_1 - \mu_2) < 0.932$ percent

(negative value means a salary decrease)

(b) Since the interval contains both positive and negative values, with confidence 90%, there appears to be no significant difference in percent salary increases between western and eastern colleges.

12. $n_1 = 32, \bar{x}_1 = 13.7, s_1 = 4.1$

$n_2 = 34, \bar{x}_2 = 10.1, s_2 = 2.7$

(a) Since $n_i \geq 30$, we can use large sample procedures to estimating $\mu_1 - \mu_2$.

$c = 95\%,\ z_c = 1.96$

$$E \approx z_c\sqrt{\frac{s_1^2}{n_1} + \frac{s_2^2}{n_2}} = 1.96\sqrt{\frac{4.1^2}{32} + \frac{2.7^2}{34}} = 1.6857 \approx 1.69$$

$[(\bar{x}_1 - \bar{x}_2) - E] < (\mu_1 - \mu_2) < [(\bar{x}_1 - \bar{x}_2) + E]$

$[(13.7 - 10.1) - 1.69] < (\mu_1 - \mu_2) < [(13.7 - 10.1) + 1.69]$

1.91 percent of stockholder equity $< (\mu_1 - \mu_2) < 5.29$ percent of stockholder equity

(b) Since all interval values are positive it appears $\mu_1 > \mu_2$, i.e., in terms of profit as a percentage of stockholder equity, retail stores do better than utilities. The difference is estimated to be between 1.9 and 5.3 percentage points, with 95% confidence.

13. $n_1 = 18, \bar{x}_1 = 98, s_1 = 6.5$
$n_2 = 24, \bar{x}_2 = 90, s_2 = 7.3$

(a) Since $n_i < 30$, use small sample procedures to estimate $\mu_1 - \mu_2$.
$c = 75\%,\ n_1 + n_2 - 2 = 40, t_{0.75}$ with 40 $d.f. = 1.167$

$$s_{\text{pooled}} = \sqrt{\frac{(n_1-1)s_1^2 + (n_2-1)s_2^2}{n_1+n_2-2}} = \sqrt{\frac{17(6.5)^2 + 23(7.3)^2}{18+24-2}} = 6.9712$$

$$E \approx t_c s_p \sqrt{\frac{1}{n_1} + \frac{1}{n_2}} = 1.167(6.9712)\sqrt{\frac{1}{18} + \frac{1}{24}} = 2.5367 \approx 2.54$$

$[(\bar{x}_1 - \bar{x}_2) - E] < (\mu_1 - \mu_2) < [(\bar{x}_1 - \bar{x}_2) + E]$
$[(98-90) - 2.54] < (\mu_1 - \mu_2) < [(98-90) + 2.54]$
5.46 pounds $< (\mu_1 - \mu_2) <$ 10.54 pounds

(b) Since the interval contains only positive values, we can say with 75% confidence, that $\mu_1 > \mu_2$, i.e., that Canadian wolves weight more than Alaska wolves, and that the difference is approximately 5.5 to 10.5 pounds.

14. $n_1 = 17, \bar{x}_1 = 4.9, s_1 = 1.0$
$n_2 = 6, \bar{x}_2 = 2.8, s_2 = 1.2$
Since $n_i < 30$, use small sample procedures to estimate $\mu_1 - \mu_2$.

(a) $c = 85\%,\ n_1 + n_2 - 2 = 17 + 6 - 2 = 21, t_{0.85}$ with 21 $d.f. = 1.494$

$$s_{\text{pooled}} = \sqrt{\frac{(n_1-1)s_1^2 + (n_2-1)s_2^2}{n_1+n_2-2}} = \sqrt{\frac{16(1.0)^2 + 5(1.2)^2}{17+6-2}} = 1.0511$$

$$E \approx t_c s_p \sqrt{\frac{1}{n_1} + \frac{1}{n_2}} = 1.494(1.0511)\sqrt{\frac{1}{17} + \frac{1}{6}} = 0.7457 \approx 0.75$$

$[(\bar{x}_1 - \bar{x}_2) - E] < (\mu_1 - \mu_2) < [(\bar{x}_1 - \bar{x}_2) + E]$
$[(4.9-2.8) - 0.75] < (\mu_1 - \mu_2) < [(4.9-2.8) + 0.75]$
$1.35 < (\mu_1 - \mu_2) < 2.85$ wolf pups per litter

(b) The interval includes only positive values, so we can say $\mu_1 > \mu_2$, i.e., with 85% confidence, the average litter size in Canada is larger than that in Finland by 1.35 to 2.85 wolf pups.

15. $n_1 = 93, r_1 = 79, \hat{p}_1 = \frac{79}{93} = 0.8495, \hat{q}_1 = 0.1505, n_1 - r_1 = 14$
$n_2 = 83, r_2 = 74, \hat{p}_2 = \frac{74}{83} = 0.8916, \hat{q}_2 = 0.1084, n_2 - r_2 = 9$
Since $n_i\hat{p}_i$ and $n_i\hat{q}_i$ are all > 5, we can use large sample procedures to estimate $p_1 - p_2$.

(a) $c = 95\%, z_c = 1.96$

$$E \approx z_c \sqrt{\frac{\hat{p}_1\hat{q}_1}{n_1} + \frac{\hat{p}_2\hat{q}_2}{n_2}} = 1.96\sqrt{\frac{(0.8495)(0.1505)}{93} + \frac{(0.8916)(0.1084)}{83}} = 0.0988$$

$[(\hat{p}_1 - \hat{p}_2) - E] < (p_1 - p_2) < [(\hat{p}_1 - \hat{p}_2) + E]$
$[(0.8495 - 0.8916) - 0.0988] < (p_1 - p_2) < [(0.8495 - 0.8916) + 0.0988]$
$-0.1409 < (p_1 - p_2) < 0.0567$

(b) Since the interval contains positive and negative values, we can say, with 95% confidence, that there is no significant differences between the proportion of accurate responses for face-to-face interviews and that for telephone interviews.

16. $n_1 = 30, r_1 = 16, \hat{p}_1 = \frac{16}{30} = 0.5333, \hat{q}_1 = 0.4667, n_1 - r_1 = 14$

$n_2 = 46, r_2 = 25, \hat{p}_2 = \frac{25}{46} = 0.5435, \hat{q}_2 = 0.4565, n_2 - r_2 = 21$

Since $n_i\hat{p}_i$ and $n_i\hat{q}_i$ are all > 5, we can use large sample procedure to estimate $p_1 - p_2$.

(a) $c = 90\%, z_c = 1.645$

$$E \approx z_c\sqrt{\frac{\hat{p}_1\hat{q}_1}{n_1} + \frac{\hat{p}_2\hat{q}_2}{n_2}} = 1.645\sqrt{\frac{0.5333(0.4667)}{30} + \frac{(0.5435)(0.4565)}{46}} = 0.1925$$

$$[(\hat{p}_1 - \hat{p}_2) - E] < (p_1 - p_2) < [(\hat{p}_1 - \hat{p}_2) + E]$$
$$[(0.5333 - 0.5435) - 0.1925] < (p_1 - p_2) < [(0.5333 - 0.5435) + 0.1925]$$
$$-0.2027 < (p_1 - p_2) < 0.1823$$

(b) Since the interval contains both positive and negative values, we can conclude, with 90% confidence, that there is no significant difference between the proportion of accurate responses in face-to-face interviews and that in telephone interviews.

17. (a) $P(A_1 < \mu_1 < B_1) = 0.80$

$P(A_2 < \mu_2 < B_2) = 0.80$

i.e., the two intervals are designed so that the confidence interval procedure produces intervals A_i to B_i that capture μ_i 80% of the time.

$P(A_1 < \mu_1 < B_1 \text{ and } A_2 < \mu_2 < B_2) = P(A_1 < \mu_1 < B_1) \cdot P(A_2 < \mu_2 < B_2, \text{ given } A_1 < \mu_1 < B_1)$

but the intervals were created using independent samples, so the intervals themselves are independent, so

$= P(A_1 < \mu_1 < B_1) \cdot P(A_2 < \mu_2 < B_2)$

by the definition of independent events: if *C* and *D* are independent, *P(C, given D) = P(C)*.

$= (0.80)(0.80)$

$= 0.64$

The probability that both intervals are simultaneously correct, i.e., that both intervals capture their μ_i, is 0.64.

$P(\text{at least one interval fails to capture its } \mu_i) = 1 - P(\text{both intervals capture their } \mu_1)$

$= 1 - 0.64$

$= 0.36$

[There are 4 possible outcomes. Using the (*x*, *y*) interval notation, they are

(1) $\mu_1 \in (A_1, B_1), \mu_2 \in (A_2, B_2)$ both capture μ_i

(2) $\mu_1 \in (A_1, B_1), \mu_2 \notin (A_2, B_2)$ only μ_1, is captured

(3) $\mu_1 \notin (A_1, B_1), \mu_2 \in (A_2, B_2)$ only μ_2 is captured

(4) $\mu_1 \notin (A_1, B_1), \mu_2 \notin (A_2, B_2)$ neither μ_i is captured

By the complimentary event rule, *P*(at least 1 fails) = *P*[case (2), (3), or (4)] = 1 – *P*[case (1)]

(b) $P(A_1 < \mu_1 < B_1) = c$
$P(A_2 < \mu_2 < B_2) = c$

(Both confidence intervals are at level c.)

$$\begin{aligned} 0.90 &= P(A_1 < \mu_1 < B_1 \text{ and } A_2 < \mu_2 < B_2) \\ &= P(A_1 < \mu_1 < B_1) \cdot P(A_2 < \mu_2 < B_2) \quad \text{since the intervals are independent} \\ &= c \cdot c \\ &= c^2 \end{aligned}$$

If $0.90 = c^2$, then $\sqrt{0.90} = c = 0.9487$, or about 0.95

(c) Answers vary.
In large, complex engineering designs, each component must be within design specifications or the project will fail.
Consider the hundreds (if not thousands) of components which must function properly to launch the space shuttle, keep it orbiting, and return it safely to earth. For example, nuts, bolts, rivets, wiring, and the like must be a certain size, give or take some tiny amount. Tiles and the glue securing them must be able to withstand a huge range of temperatures, from the ambient air temperature at launch time to the extreme heat of re-entry.
Each of the design specifications can be thought of as a confidence interval. Manufacturers and suppliers want to be very, very confident their parts are well within the specifications, or they might lose their contracts to competitors. Similarly, NASA wants to be very, very, confident all the parts, as a group, meet specifications; otherwise, costly delays or catastrophic failures may occur. (Recall that much of the challenger disaster was due to o-ring failure-because NASA decided to go ahead with the launch even though they had been warned by the o-ring manufacturer that the temperature at the launch site was below the lowest temperature at which the o-rings had been tested, and that the o-rings might not completely seat at that temperature.)
If NASA will tolerate only a 1 in 1,000 or 1 in 1,000,000 chance of failure, i.e., $c = 0.999$ or $c = 0.999999$, the individual components' confidence levels, c must be (much) higher than NASA's.

Chapter 9 Hypothesis Testing

Section 9.1

1. See text for definitions. Essay may include:

(a) A working hypothesis about the population parameter in question is called the null hypothesis. The value specified in the null hypothesis is often a historical value, a claim, or a production specification.

(b) Any hypothesis that differs from the null hypothesis is called an alternate hypothesis.

(c) If we reject the null hypothesis when it is in fact true, we have an error that is called a type I error. On the other hand, if we accept (i.e., fail to reject) the null hypothesis when it is in fact false, we have made an error that is called a type II error.

(d) The probability with which we are willing to risk a type I error is called the level of significance of a test. The probability of making a type II error is denoted by β.

2. The alternate hypothesis is used to determine which type of critical region is used. An alternate hypothesis is constructed in such a way that it is the one to be accepted when the null hypothesis must be rejected.

3. No, if we fail to reject the null hypothesis, we have not proven it to be true beyond all doubt. The evidence is not sufficient to merit rejecting H_0.

4. No, if we reject the null hypothesis, we have not proven it to be false beyond all doubt. The test was conducted with a level of significance, α, which is the probability with which we are willing to risk a type I error (rejecting H_0 when it is in fact true).

5. **(a)** The claim is $\mu = 60$ kg, so you would use $H_0: \mu = 60$ kg.

(b) We want to know if the average weight is less than 60 kg, so you would use $H_1: \mu < 60$ kg.

(c) We want to know if the average weight is greater than 60 kg, so you would use $H_1: \mu > 60$ kg.

(d) We want to know if the average weight is different from (more or less than) 60 kg, so you would use $H_1: \mu \neq 60$ kg.

(e) Since part (b) is a left-tailed test, the critical region is on the left. Since part (c) is a right-tailed test, the critical region is on the right. Since part (d) is a two-tailed test, the critical region is on both sides of the mean.

6. **(a)** The claim is $\mu = 8.3$ min, so you would use $H_0: \mu = 8.3$ min. If you believe the average is less than 8.3 min, then you would use $H_1: \mu < 8.3$ min. Since this is a left-tailed test, the critical region is on the left side of the mean.

(b) The claim is $\mu = 8.3$ min, so you would use $H_0: \mu = 8.3$ min. If you believe the average is different from 8.3 min, then you would use $H_1: \mu \neq 8.3$ min. Since this is a two-tailed test, the critical region is on both sides of the mean.

(c) The claim is $\mu = 4.5$ min, so you would use $H_0: \mu = 4.5$ min. If you believe the average is more than 4.5 min, then you would use $H_1: \mu > 4.5$ min. Since this is a right-tailed test, the critical region is on the right side of the mean.

(d) The claim is $\mu = 4.5$ min, so you would use $H_0: \mu = 4.5$ min. If you believe the average is different from 4.5 min, then you would use $H_1: \mu \neq 4.5$ min. Since this is a two-tailed test, the critical region is on both sides of the mean.

7. (a) The claim is $\mu = 16.4$ ft, so $H_0: \mu = 16.4$ ft.

(b) You want to know if the average is getting larger, so $H_1: \mu > 16.4$ ft.

(c) You want to know if the average is getting smaller, so $H_1: \mu < 16.4$ ft.

(d) You want to know if the average is different from 16.4 ft, so $H_1: \mu \neq 16.4$ ft.

(e) Since part (b) is a right-tailed test, the critical region is on the right. Since part (c) is a left-tailed test, the critical region is on the left. Since part (d) is a two-tailed test, the critical region is on both sides of the mean.

8. (a) The claim is $\mu = 8.7$ sec, so $H_0: \mu = 8.7$ sec.

(b) You want to know if the average is longer (larger), so $H_1: \mu > 8.7$ sec.

(c) You want to know if the average is reduced (smaller), so $H_1: \mu < 8.7$ sec.

(d) Since part (b) is a right-tailed test, the critical region is on the right. Since part (c) is a left-tailed test, the critical region is on the left.

9. (a) The claim is $\mu = 288$ lb, so $H_0: \mu = 288$ lb.

(b) If you want to know if the average is higher (larger), $H_1: \mu > 288$ lb. Since this is a right-tailed test, the critical region is on the right.

If you want to know if the average is lower (smaller), $H_1: \mu < 288$ lb. Since this is a left-tailed test, the critical region is on the left.

If you want to know if the average is different, $H_1: \mu \neq 288$ lb. Since this is a two-tailed test, the critical region is in both tails.

Section 9.2

1. $H_0: \mu = 16.4$ ft

$H_1: \mu < 16.4$ ft

Since < is in H_1, a left-tailed test is used.

Since the sample size $n = 36$ is large, the sampling distribution of $\bar{x}$ is approximately normal by the central limit theorem, and we can estimate σ by s.

For $\alpha = 0.01$, the critical value is $z_0 = -2.33$.

$$z = \frac{\bar{x} - \mu}{\sigma/\sqrt{n}} = \frac{15.1 - 16.4}{3.2/\sqrt{36}} = -2.44$$

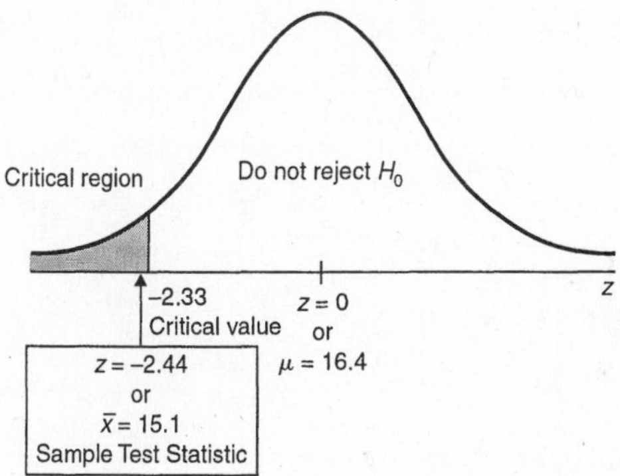

The sample test statistic falls in the critical region (−2.44 < −2.33). Therefore, we reject H_0. We conclude that the storm is lessening. The data are statistically significant.

2. H_0: $\mu = 38$ hr

H_1: $\mu < 38$ hr

Since < is in H_1, a left-tailed test is used.

Since the sample size $n = 47$ is large, the sampling distribution of $\bar{x}$ is approximately normal by the central limit theorem, and we can estimate σ by s.

For $\alpha = 0.01$, the critical value is $z_0 = -2.33$.

$$z = \frac{\bar{x} - \mu}{\sigma / \sqrt{n}} = \frac{37.5 - 38}{1.2 / \sqrt{47}} = -2.86$$

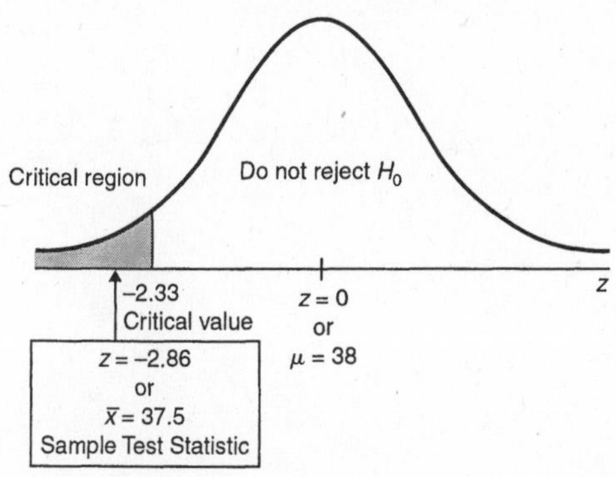

The sample test statistic falls in the critical region (−2.86 < −2.33). Therefore, we reject H_0. We conclude that the average assembly time is less. The data are statistically significant.

3. H_0: $\mu = 31.8$ calls/day

H_1: $\mu \neq 31.8$ calls/day

Since ≠ is in H_1, a two-tailed test is used.

Since the sample size $n = 63$ is large, the sampling distribution of $\bar{x}$ is approximately normal by the central limit theorem, and we can estimate σ by s.

For $\alpha = 0.01$, the critical value is $z_0 = \pm 2.58$.

$$z = \frac{\bar{x} - \mu}{\sigma / \sqrt{n}} = \frac{28.5 - 31.8}{10.7 / \sqrt{63}} = -2.45$$

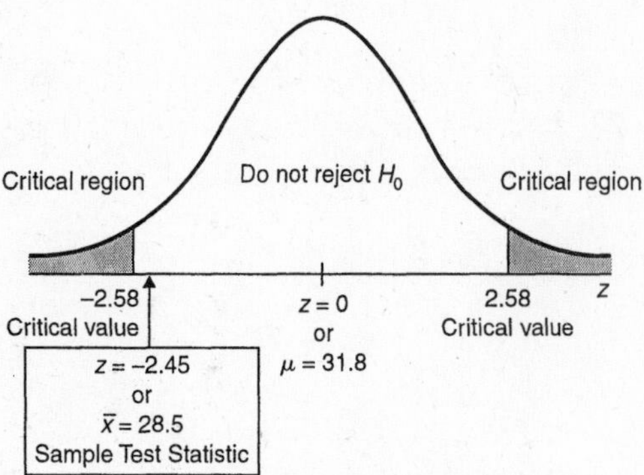

The sample test statistic does not fall in the critical region (−2.58 < −2.45 < 2.58). Therefore, we do not reject H_0. There is not enough evidence to conclude that the mean number of messages has changed. The data are not statistically significant.

4. H_0: $\mu = 3218$
   H_1: $\mu > 3218$
   Since > is in H_1, a right-tailed test is used.
   Since the sample size $n = 42$ is large, the sampling distribution of $\overline{x}$ is approximately normal by the central limit theorem, and we can estimate σ by s.
   For $\alpha = 0.01$, the critical value is $z_0 = 2.33$.

$$z = \frac{\overline{x} - \mu}{\sigma/\sqrt{n}} = \frac{3392 - 3218}{287/\sqrt{42}} = 3.93$$

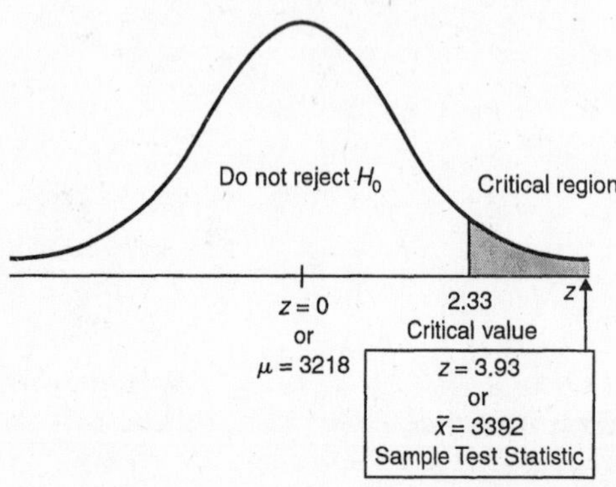

The sample test statistic falls in the critical region (3.93 > 2.33). Therefore, we reject H_0. We conclude the average number of people entering the store each day has increased. The data are statistically significant.

5. H_0: $\mu = \$4.75$
   H_1: $\mu > \$4.75$
   Since > is in H_1, a right-tailed test is used.
   Since the sample size $n = 52$ is large, the sampling distribution of $\overline{x}$ is approximately normal by the central limit theorem, and we can estimate σ by s.
   For $\alpha = 0.01$, the critical value is $z_0 = 2.33$.

$$z = \frac{\overline{x} - \mu}{\sigma/\sqrt{n}} = \frac{5.25 - 4.75}{1.15/\sqrt{52}} = 3.14$$

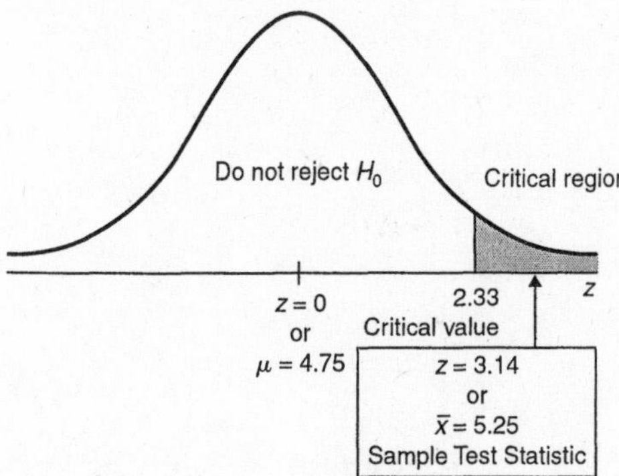

The sample test statistic falls in the critical region (3.14 > 2.33). Therefore, we reject H_0. We conclude that her average tip is more than \$4.75. The data are statistically significant.

6. H_0: $\mu = 17.2\%$

H_1: $\mu < 17.2\%$

Since < is in H_1, a left-tailed test is used.

Since the sample size $n = 50$ is large, the sampling distribution of $\bar{x}$ is approximately normal by the central limit theorem, and we can estimate σ by s.

For $\alpha = 0.05$, the critical value is $z_0 = -1.645$.

$$z = \frac{\bar{x} - \mu}{\sigma / \sqrt{n}} = \frac{15.8 - 17.2}{5.3/\sqrt{50}} = -1.87$$

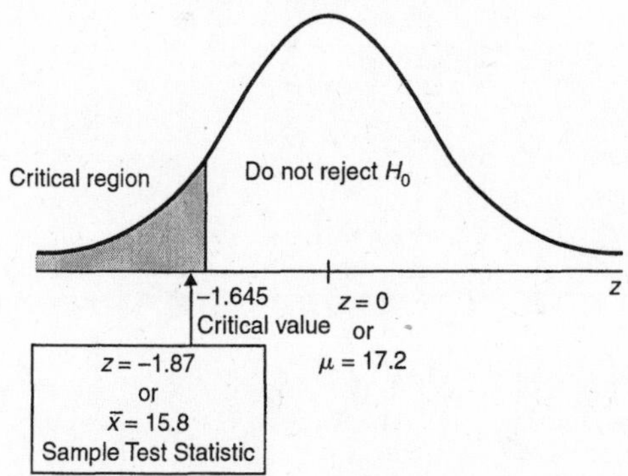

The sample test statistic falls in the critical region (−1.87 < −1.645). Therefore, we reject H_0. We conclude that this hay has lower protein content. The data are statistically significant.

7. H_0: $\mu = 10.2$ sec

H_1: $\mu < 10.2$ sec

Since < is in H_1, a left-tailed test is used.

Since the sample size $n = 41$ is large, the sampling distribution of $\bar{x}$ is approximately normal by the central limit theorem, and we can estimate σ by s.

For $\alpha = 0.05$, the critical value is $z_0 = -1.645$.

$$z = \frac{\bar{x} - \mu}{\sigma / \sqrt{n}} = \frac{9.7 - 10.2}{2.1/\sqrt{41}} = -1.52$$

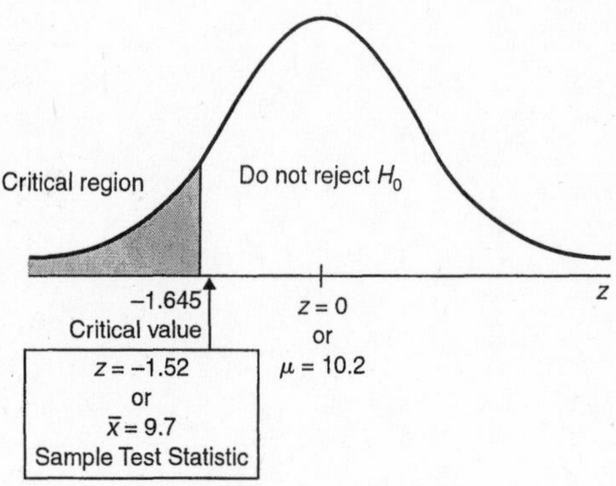

The sample test statistic does not fall in the critical region (−1.645 < −1.52). Therefore, we do not reject H_0. There is not enough evidence to conclude that the mean acceleration time is less. The data are not statistically significant.

8. H_0: $\mu = 159$ ft

H_1: $\mu < 159$ ft

Since < is in H_1, a left-tailed test is used.

Since the sample size $n = 45$ is large, the sampling distribution of $\overline{x}$ is approximately normal by the central limit theorem, and we can estimate σ by s.

For $\alpha = 0.01$, the critical value is $z_0 = -2.33$.

$$z = \frac{\overline{x} - \mu}{\sigma / \sqrt{n}} = \frac{148 - 159}{23.5/\sqrt{45}} = -3.14$$

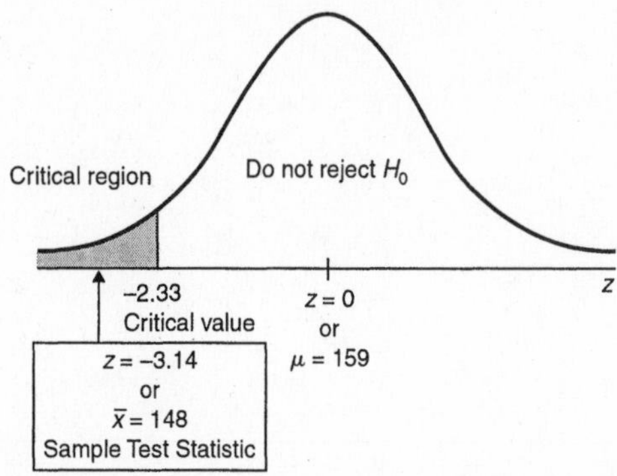

The sample test statistic falls in the critical region (−3.14 < −2.33). Therefore, we reject H_0. We conclude the mean braking distance is reduced for the new tire tread. The data are statistically significant.

9. H_0: $\mu = 19.0$ ml/dl

H_1: $\mu > 19.0$ ml/dl

Since > is in H_1, a right-tailed test is used.

Since the sample size $n = 48$ is large, the sampling distribution of $\overline{x}$ is approximately normal by the central limit theorem, and we can estimate σ by s.

For $\alpha = 0.01$, the critical value is $z_0 = 2.33$.

$$z = \frac{\overline{x} - \mu}{\sigma / \sqrt{n}} = \frac{20.7 - 19.0}{9.9/\sqrt{48}} = 1.19$$

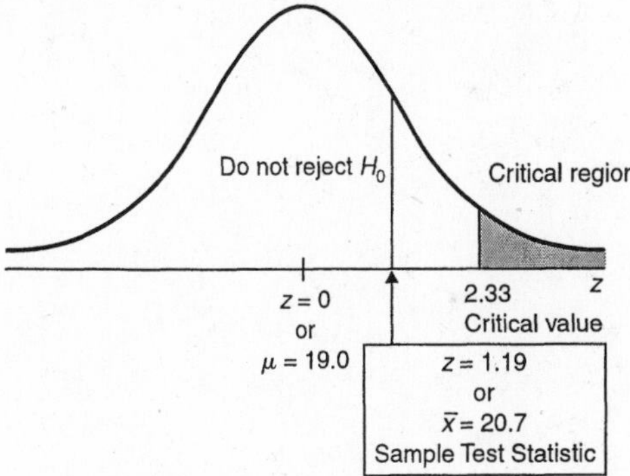

The sample test statistic does not fall in the critical region ($1.19 < 2.33$). Therefore, we do not reject H_0. There is not sufficient evidence to conclude that the average oxygen capacity has increased. The data are not statistically significant.

10. H_0: $\mu = \$1{,}789{,}556$

H_1: $\mu \neq \$1{,}789{,}556$

Since $\neq$ is in H_1, a two-tailed test is used.

Since the sample size $n = 35$ is large, the sampling distribution of $\bar{x}$ is approximately normal by the central limit theorem, and we can estimate σ by s.

For $\alpha = 0.01$, the critical values are $z_0 = \pm 2.58$.

$$z = \frac{\bar{x} - \mu}{\sigma/\sqrt{n}} = \frac{1{,}621{,}726 - 1{,}789{,}556}{591{,}218/\sqrt{35}} = -1.68$$

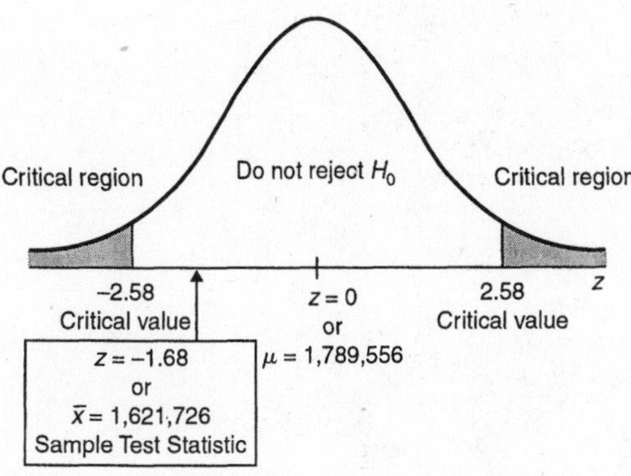

The sample test statistic does not fall in the critical region ($-2.58 < -1.68 < 2.58$). Therefore, we do not reject H_0. There is not sufficient evidence to conclude that the average salary of major league baseball players in Florida is different from the national average. The data are not statistically significant.

11. H_0: $\mu = 7.4$ pH

H_1: $\mu \neq 7.4$ pH

Since $\neq$ is in H_1, a two-tailed test is used.

Since the sample size $n = 33$ is large, the sampling distribution of $\bar{x}$ is approximately normal by the central limit theorem, and we can estimate σ by s.

For $\alpha = 0.05$, the critical values are $z_0 = \pm 1.96$.

$$z = \frac{\bar{x} - \mu}{\sigma/\sqrt{n}} = \frac{8.1 - 7.4}{1.9/\sqrt{33}} = 2.12$$

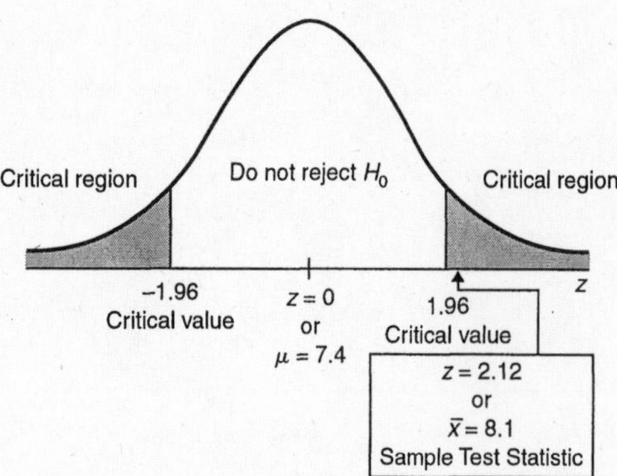

The sample test statistic falls in the critical region (2.12 > 1.96). Therefore, we reject H_0. We conclude that the drug has changed the mean pH of the blood. The data are statistically significant.

12. H_0: $\mu = 0.25$ gal

H_1: $\mu > 0.25$ gal

Since > is in H_1, a right-tailed test is used.

Since the sample size n = 100 is large, the sampling distribution of $\bar{x}$ is approximately normal by the central limit theorem, and we can estimate σ by s.

For $\alpha = 0.05$, the critical value is $z_0 = 1.645$.

$$z = \frac{\bar{x} - \mu}{\sigma/\sqrt{n}} = \frac{0.28 - 0.25}{0.10/\sqrt{100}} = 3.00$$

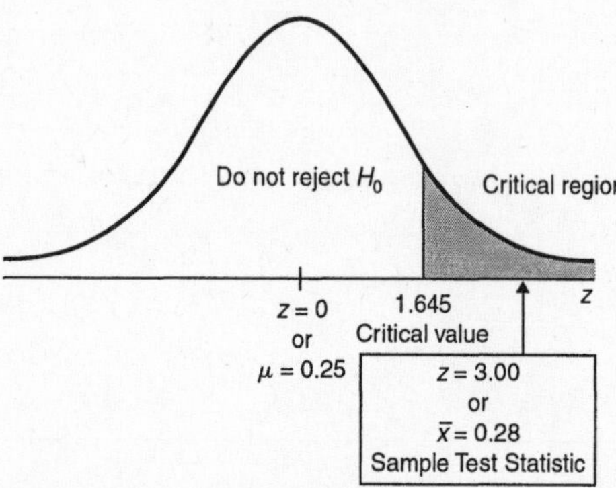

The sample test statistic falls in the critical region (3.00 > 1.645). Therefore, we reject H_0. We conclude that the supplier's claim is too low. The data are statistically significant.

13. The mean and the standard deviation round to the values given.

H_0: $\mu = \$13.9$ thousand

H_1: $\mu > \$13.9$ thousand

Since > is in H_1, a right-tailed test is used.

Since the sample size $n = 50$ is large, the sampling distribution of $\bar{x}$ is approximately normal by the central limit theorem, and we can estimate σ by s.

For $\alpha = 0.05$, the critical value is $z_0 = 1.645$.

$$z = \frac{\bar{x} - \mu}{\sigma/\sqrt{n}} = \frac{16.58 - 13.9}{8.11/\sqrt{50}} = 2.34$$

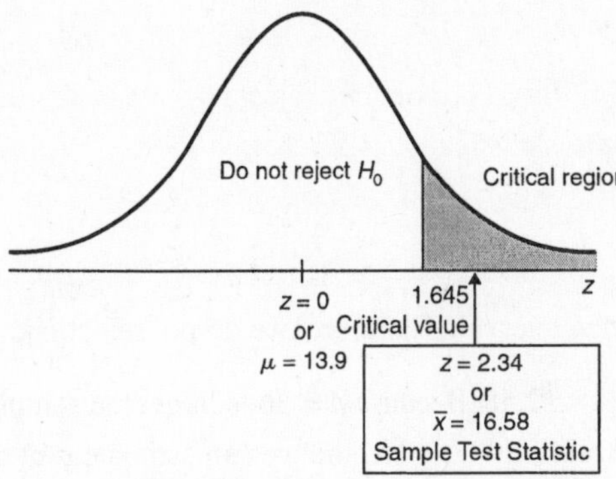

The sample test statistic falls in the critical region (2.34 > 1.645). Therefore, we reject H_0. We conclude that the mean franchise costs for pizza businesses are higher. The data are statistically significant.

14. **(a)** One-tailed test; if the null hypothesis is rejected, then one has the additional information from the test that the true population mean is larger/smaller than stated in H_0. Also, the critical value for a one-tailed test is nearer to zero than the critical values of a two-tailed test, meaning that *if* one is able to correctly surmise the direction of H_1, there is a greater chance of rejecting H_0. For example, for a right-tailed test at $\alpha = 0.05$, $z = 1.7$ would result in rejecting H_0, but in a two-tailed test at $\alpha = 0.05$ for the same $z = 1.7$, one would fail to reject H_0.

(b) Two-tailed test; for a given α-level the absolute value of the critical value for a one-tailed test is less than that of a two-tailed test, making the one-tailed test more likely to reject H_0.

(c) Yes. The rejection regions are different for one- and two-tailed tests.

15. Essay or class discussion.

16. **(a)** H_0: $\mu = 20$

H_1: $\mu \neq 20$

For $\alpha = 0.01$, $c = 1 - 0.01 = 0.99$, $s = 4$, and the critical value $z_c = 2.58$.

$$E \approx z_c \frac{s}{\sqrt{n}} = 2.58 \frac{4}{\sqrt{36}} = 1.72$$

$$\bar{x} - E < \mu < \bar{x} + E$$
$$22 - 1.72 < \mu < 22 + 1.72$$
$$20.28 < \mu < 23.72$$

The hypothesized mean $\mu = 20$ is not in the interval. Therefore, we reject H_0.

(b) For $\alpha = 0.01$, the two-tailed test's critical values are $z_0 = \pm 2.58$. Because $n = 36$ is large, the sampling distribution of $\bar{x}$ is approximately normal by the central limit theorem, and we can estimate σ by s.

$$z = \frac{\bar{x}-\mu}{\sigma/\sqrt{n}} = \frac{22-20}{4/\sqrt{36}} = 3.00$$

Since the sample test statistic falls inside the critical region (3.00 > 2.58), we reject H_0. The results are the same.

17. (a) H_0: $\mu = 21$

H_1: $\mu \neq 21$

For $\alpha = 0.01$, $c = 1 - 0.01 = 0.99$, $s = 4$, and the critical value $z_c = 2.58$.

$$E \approx z_c \frac{s}{\sqrt{n}} = 2.58 \frac{4}{\sqrt{36}} = 1.72$$

$$\bar{x} - E < \mu < \bar{x} + E$$

$$22 - 1.72 < \mu < 22 + 1.72$$

$$20.28 < \mu < 23.72$$

The hypothesized mean $\mu = 21$ falls into the confidence interval. Therefore, we do not reject H_0.

(b) For $\alpha = 0.01$, the two-tailed test's critical values are $z_0 = \pm 2.58$. Because $n = 36$ is large, the sampling distribution of $\bar{x}$ is approximately normal by the central limit theorem, and we can estimate σ by s.

$$z = \frac{\bar{x}-\mu}{\sigma/\sqrt{n}} = \frac{22-21}{4/\sqrt{36}} = 1.50$$

Since the sample test statistic falls outside the critical region (−2.58 < 1.50 < 2.58), we do not reject H_0. The results are the same.

Section 9.3

1. H_0: $\mu = 5$

H_1: $\mu > 5$

$$z = \frac{\bar{x}-\mu}{\sigma/\sqrt{n}} = \frac{6.1-5}{2.5/\sqrt{40}} = 2.78$$

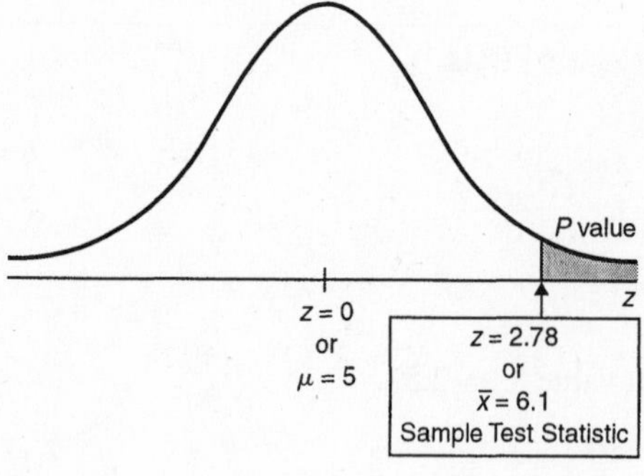

$$P \text{ value} = P(\bar{x} \geq 6.1)$$
$$= P(z \geq 2.78)$$
$$= 1 - 0.9973$$
$$= 0.0027$$

Since $0.0027 < 0.01$, the data are significant at the 1% level.

2. H_0: $\mu = 53.1$

H_1: $\mu < 53.1$

$$z = \frac{\bar{x} - \mu}{\sigma/\sqrt{n}} = \frac{52.7 - 53.1}{4.5/\sqrt{41}} = -0.57$$

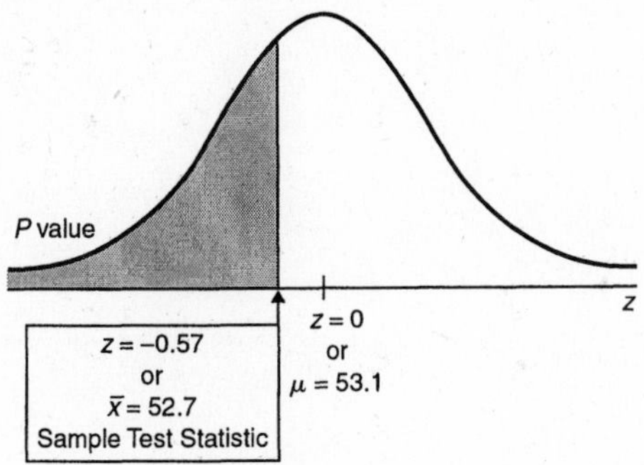

$$P \text{ value} = P(\bar{x} \leq 52.7)$$
$$= P(z \leq -0.57)$$
$$= 0.2843$$

Since $0.2843 > 0.01$, the data are not significant at the 1% level.

3. H_0: $\mu = 21.7$

H_1: $\mu \neq 21.7$

$$z = \frac{\bar{x} - \mu}{\sigma/\sqrt{n}} = \frac{20.5 - 21.7}{6.8/\sqrt{45}} = -1.18$$

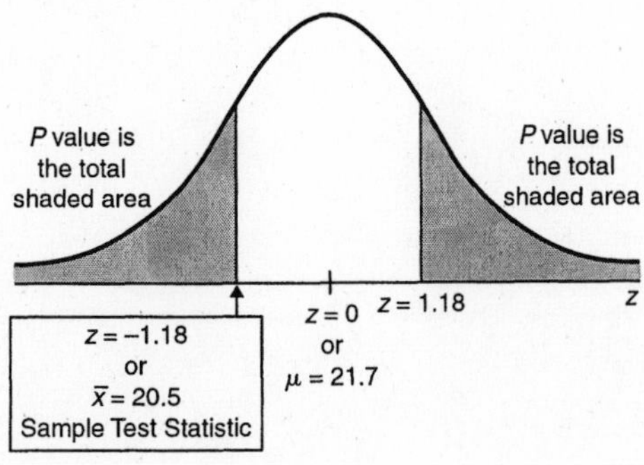

$$\begin{aligned} P \text{ value} &= 2P(\bar{x} \le 20.5) \\ &= 2P(z \le -1.18) \\ &= 2(0.1190) \\ &= 0.2380 \end{aligned}$$

Since 0.2380 > 0.05, the data are not significant at the 5% level.

4. H_0: $\mu = 18.7$

H_1: $\mu \ne 18.7$

$$z = \frac{\bar{x} - \mu}{\sigma/\sqrt{n}} = \frac{19.1 - 18.7}{5.2/\sqrt{32}} = 0.44$$

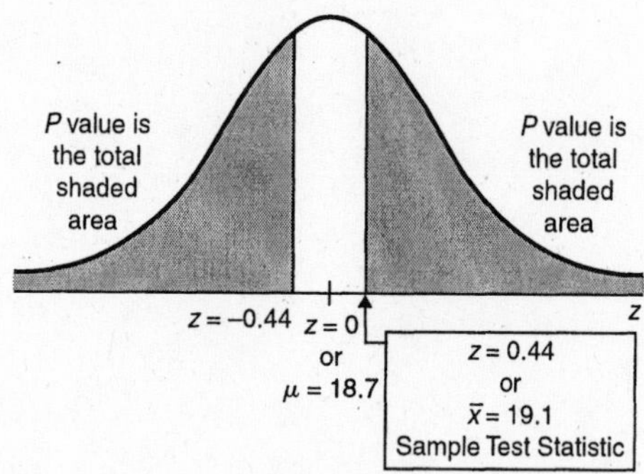

$$\begin{aligned} P \text{ value} &= 2P(\bar{x} \ge 19.1) \\ &= 2P(z \ge 0.44) \\ &= 2(1 - 0.6700) \\ &= 2(0.3300) \\ &= 0.6600 \end{aligned}$$

Since 0.6600 > 0.05, the data are not significant at the 5% level.

5. H_0: $\mu = 1.75$ yr

H_1: $\mu > 1.75$ yr

$$z = \frac{\bar{x} - \mu}{\sigma/\sqrt{n}} = \frac{2.05 - 1.75}{0.82/\sqrt{68}} = 3.02$$

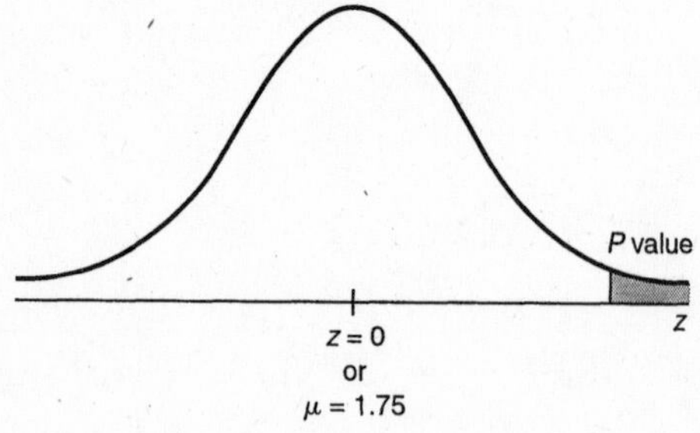

$$\begin{aligned} P \text{ value} &= P(\overline{x} \geq 2.05) \\ &= P(z \geq 3.02) \\ &= 1 - 0.9987 \\ &= 0.0013 \end{aligned}$$

Since $0.0013 < 0.01$, the data are significant at the 1% level. Coyotes in this region appear to live longer.

6. H_0: $\mu = 12 \text{ m}^2$

H_1: $\mu \neq 12\, m^2$

$$z = \frac{\overline{x} - \mu}{\sigma/\sqrt{n}} = \frac{12.3 - 12}{3.4/\sqrt{56}} = 0.66$$

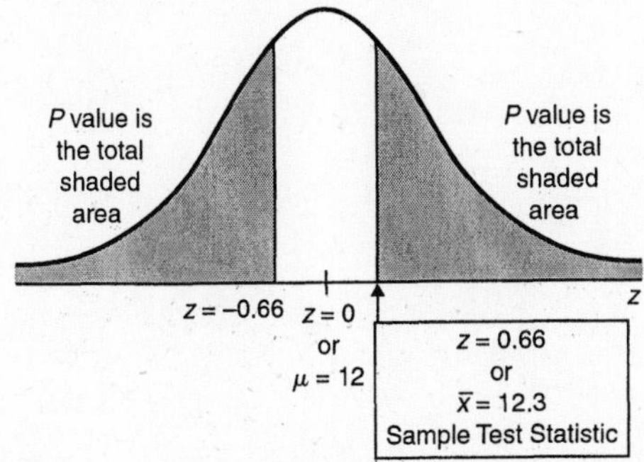

$$\begin{aligned} P \text{ value} &= 2P(\overline{x} \geq 12.3) \\ &= 2P(z \geq 0.66) \\ &= 2(1 - 0.7454) \\ &= 2(0.2546) \\ &= 0.5092 \end{aligned}$$

Since $0.5092 > 0.01$, the data are not significant at the 1% level. The evidence does not support the idea that Mesa Verdi Rivas have an average floor space size different from 12 square meters.

7. H_0: $\mu = 19$ in.

H_1: $\mu < 19$ in.

$$z = \frac{\overline{x} - \mu}{\sigma/\sqrt{n}} = \frac{18.7 - 19}{3.2/\sqrt{73}} = -0.80$$

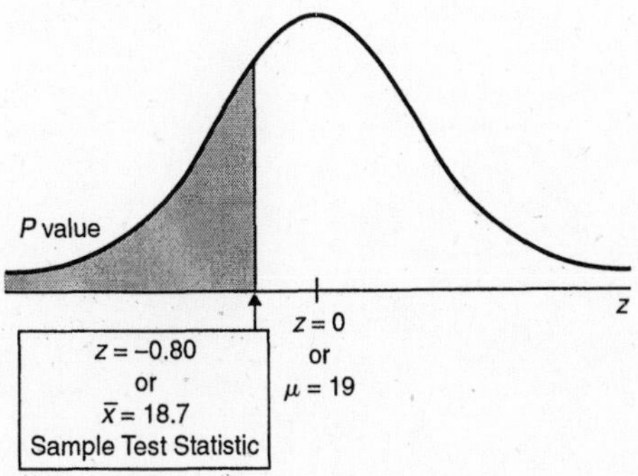

$$P \text{ value} = P(\bar{x} \le 18.7)$$
$$= P(z \le -0.80)$$
$$= 0.2119$$

Since 0.2119 > 0.05, the data are not significant at the 5% level. The data support the new hypothesis that average trout length is 19 inches.

8. H_0: $\mu = \$61{,}400$

H_1: $\mu < \$61{,}400$

$$z = \frac{\bar{x} - \mu}{\sigma/\sqrt{n}} = \frac{55{,}200 - 61{,}400}{18{,}800/\sqrt{34}} = -1.92$$

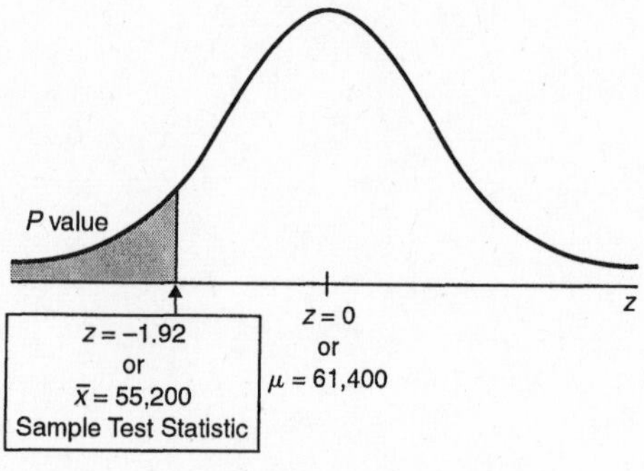

$$P \text{ value} = P(\bar{x} \le 55{,}200)$$
$$= P(z \le -1.92)$$
$$= 0.0274$$

Since 0.0274 < 0.05, the data are significant at the 5% level. The data tend to support a smaller start-up cost than $61,400.

9. H_0: $\mu = \$15.35$

H_1: $\mu < \$15.35$

$$z = \frac{\bar{x} - \mu}{\sigma/\sqrt{n}} = \frac{11.85 - 15.35}{6.21/\sqrt{34}} = -3.29$$

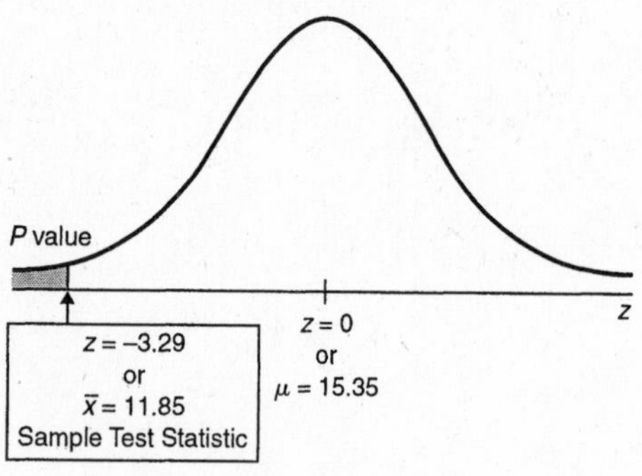

P value $= P(\overline{x} \le 11.85)$
$= P(z \le -3.29)$
$= 0.0005$

Since $0.0005 < 0.05$, the data are significant at the 5% level. The data support the claim that college students have lower daily ownership costs.

10. (a) H_0: $\mu = 19.5$ mpg
H_1: $\mu < 19.5$ mpg

The sample mean is $\overline{x} = 18.750$.
The P value is 0.047.
Reject H_0 for all $\alpha \ge 0.047$.

(b) H_0: $\mu = 19.5$ mpg
H_1: $\mu \ne 19.5$ mpg

The sample mean is $\overline{x} = 18.750$.
The P value is 0.094.
Reject H_0 for all $\alpha \ge 0.094$.

(c) The P value for a two-tailed test is twice that of the one-tailed test $[2(0.047) = 0.094]$.

Section 9.4

1. In this case we use the column headed by $\alpha' = 0.05$ and the row headed by *d.f.* $= n - 1 = 9 - 1 = 8$. This gives us $t = 1.860$. For a left-tailed test, we use symmetry of the distribution to get $t_0 = -1.860$.

2. In this case we use the column headed by $\alpha' = 0.01$ and the row headed by *d.f.* $= n - 1 = 13 - 1 = 12$. The critical value is $t_0 = 2.681$.

3. In this case we use the column headed by $\alpha'' = 0.01$ and the row headed by *d.f.* $= n - 1 = 24 - 1 = 23$. By the symmetry of the curve, the critical values are $t_0 = \pm 2.807$.

4. In this case we use the column headed by $\alpha' = 0.05$ and the row headed by *d.f.* $= n - 1 = 18 - 1 = 17$. This gives $t = 1.740$. For a left-tailed test, we use symmetry of the distribution to get $t_0 = -1.740$.

5. In this case we use the column headed by $\alpha'' = 0.05$ and the row headed by *d.f.* $= n - 1 = 12 - 1 = 11$. By the symmetry of the curve, the critical values are $t_0 = \pm 2.201$.

6. In this case we use the column headed by $\alpha' = 0.01$ and the row headed by *d.f.* $= n - 1 = 29 - 1 = 28$. The critical value is $t_0 = 2.467$.

7. (a) Answers are used in part (b).

(b) H_0: $\mu = 4.8$

H_1: $\mu < 4.8$

Since < is in H_1, a left-tailed test is used. Since the sample size is small and the data distribution is approximately normal, critical values are found using the Student's t distribution (use Table 6 in Appendix II). For a one-tailed test, look in the column headed by $\alpha' = 0.05$ and the row headed by *d.f.* $= 6 - 1 = 5$. The critical value is $t_0 = -2.015$.

$$t = \frac{\overline{x} - \mu}{s/\sqrt{n}} = \frac{4.07 - 4.8}{0.44/\sqrt{6}} = -4.06$$

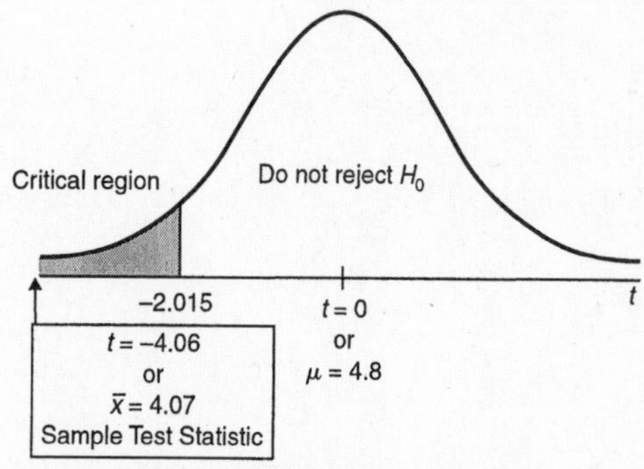

To find the P-value interval, use the α' value since our test is one-tailed and look in the row headed by *d.f.* = 5. We find that the sample t value $t = -4.06$ falls to the left of -4.032. Therefore, P value < 0.005.

The sample test statistic falls in the critical region ($-4.06 < -2.015$) and the P value is less than the level of significance $\alpha = 0.05$. Therefore, we reject H_0. We conclude at the 5% significance level that this patient's average red blood cell count is less than 4.8.

8. (a) Answers are used in part (b).

(b) H_0: $\mu = 14$

H_1: $\mu > 14$

Since > is in H_1, a right-tailed test is used. Since the sample size is small and the data distribution is approximately normal, and the data distribution is approximately normal, critical values are found using the Student's t distribution (use Table 6 in Appendix II). For a one-tailed test, look in the column headed by $\alpha' = 0.01$ and the row headed by *d.f.* $= 12 - 1 = 11$. The critical value is $t_0 = 2.718$.

$$t = \frac{\overline{x} - \mu}{s/\sqrt{n}} = \frac{18.33 - 14}{2.71/\sqrt{12}} = 5.53$$

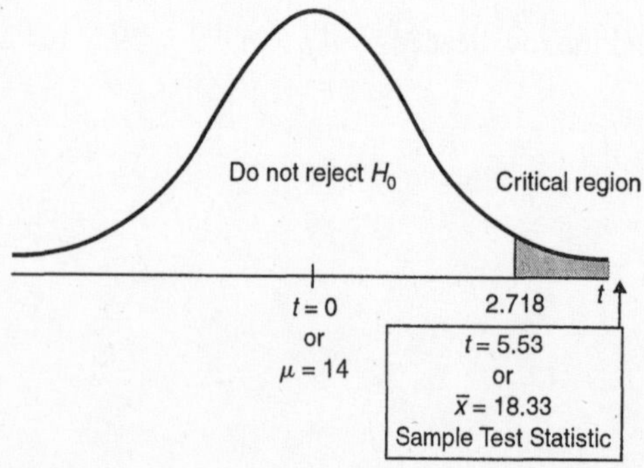

To find the P-value interval, use the α' values since our test is one-tailed and look in the row headed by $d.f. = 11$. We find that the sample t value, $t = 5.53$, falls to the right of 3.106. Therefore, P value < 0.005.

The sample test statistic falls in the critical region ($5.53 > 2.718$) and the P value is less than the level of significance $\alpha = 0.01$. Therefore, we reject H_0. We conclude that the population average HC for this patient is higher than 14.

9. (a) Answers are used in part (b).

(b) $H_0: \mu = 16.5$ days

$H_1: \mu \neq 16.5$ days

Since $\neq$ is in H_1, a two-tailed test is used. Since the sample size is small and the data distribution is approximately normal, critical values are found using the Student's t distribution (use Table 6 in Appendix II). For a two-tailed test, look in the column headed by $\alpha'' = 0.05$ and the row headed by $d.f. = 18 - 1 = 17$. The critical values are

$t_0 = \pm 2.110$.

$$t = \frac{\bar{x} - \mu}{s/\sqrt{n}} = \frac{17.83 - 16.5}{2.20/\sqrt{18}} = 2.565$$

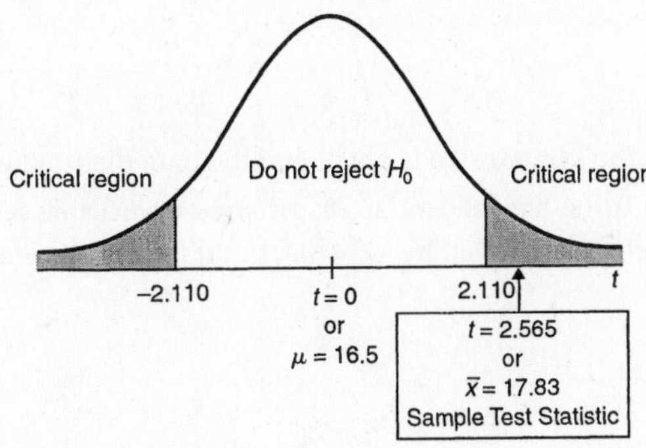

To find the P-value interval, use the α'' values since our test is two-tailed and look in the row headed by $d.f. = 17$. We find that the sample t value $t = 2.565$ falls between 2.110 and 2.567. Therefore, $0.02 < P$ value < 0.05.

The sample test statistic falls in the critical region ($2.565 > 2.110$) and the P value is less than the level of significance $\alpha = 0.05$. Therefore, we reject H_0. We conclude at the 5% significance level that the mean incubation time above 8000 feet is different from 16.5 days.

10. (a) Answers are used in part (b).

(b) $H_0: \mu = 8.8$

$H_1: \mu \neq 8.8$

Since $\neq$ is in H_1, a two-tailed test is used. Since the sample size is small and the data distribution is approximately normal, critical values are found using the Student's t distribution (use Table 6 in Appendix II). For a two-tailed test, look in the column headed by $\alpha'' = 0.05$ and the row headed by $d.f. = 14 - 1 = 13$. The critical values are

$t_0 = \pm 2.160$.

$$t = \frac{\bar{x} - \mu}{s/\sqrt{n}} = \frac{7.36 - 8.8}{4.03/\sqrt{14}} = -1.34$$

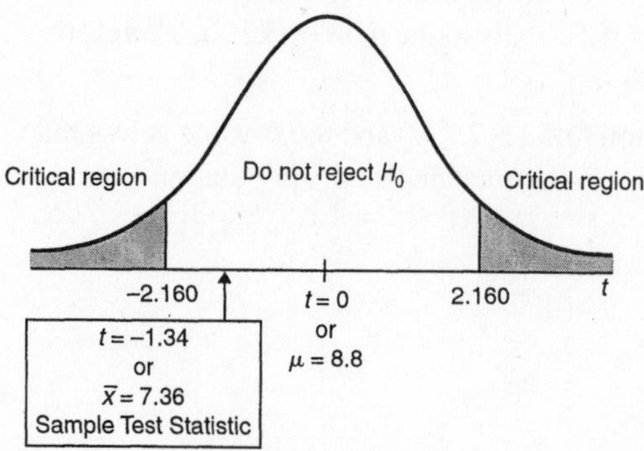

To find the *P*-value interval, use the α'' values since our test is two-tailed and look in the row headed by *d.f.* = 13. We find that the sample *t* value $t = -1.34$ falls between −1.204 and −1.350. Therefore, $0.200 < P$ value < 0.250.

The sample test statistic does not fall in the critical region $(-2.160 < -1.34 < 2.160)$ and the *P* value is greater than the level of significance $\alpha = 0.05$. Therefore, we fail to reject H_0. We cannot conclude that the average catch is different from 8.8 fish per day.

11. (a) Answers are used in part (b).

(b) H_0: $\mu = 1300$

H_1: $\mu \neq 1300$

Since $\neq$ is in H_1, a two-tailed test is used. Since the sample size is small and the data distribution is approximately normal, critical values are found using the Student's *t* distribution (use Table 6 in Appendix II). For a two-tailed test, look in the column headed by $\alpha'' = 0.01$ and the row headed by *d.f.* $= 10 - 1 = 9$. The critical values are

$t_0 = \pm 3.250$.

$$t = \frac{\bar{x} - \mu}{s/\sqrt{n}} = \frac{1268 - 1300}{37.29/\sqrt{10}} = -2.71$$

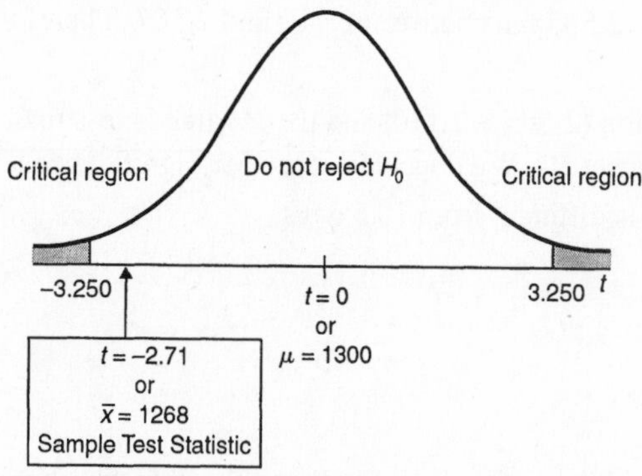

To find the *P*-value interval, use the α'' values since our test is two-tailed and look in the row headed by *d.f.* = 9. We find that the sample *t* value, $t = -2.71$, falls between −2.262 and −2.821. Therefore, $0.020 < P$ value < 0.050.

The sample test statistic does not fall in the critical region $(-3.250 < -2.71 < 3.250)$ and the *P* value is greater than the level of significance $\alpha = 0.01$. Therefore, do not reject H_0. There is not enough evidence to conclude that the population mean of tree ring dates is different from 1300.

12. (a) Answers are used in part (b).

(b) H_0: $\mu = 67$

H_1: $\mu \neq 67$

Since $\neq$ is in H_1, a two-tailed test is used. Since the sample size is small and the data distribution is approximately normal, critical values are found using the Student's *t* distribution (use Table 6 in Appendix II). For a two-tailed test, look in the column headed by $\alpha'' = 0.01$ and the row headed by *d.f.* = 16 − 1 = 15. The critical values are $t_0 = \pm 2.947$.

$$t = \frac{\bar{x} - \mu}{s/\sqrt{n}} = \frac{61.8 - 67}{10.6/\sqrt{16}} = -1.962$$

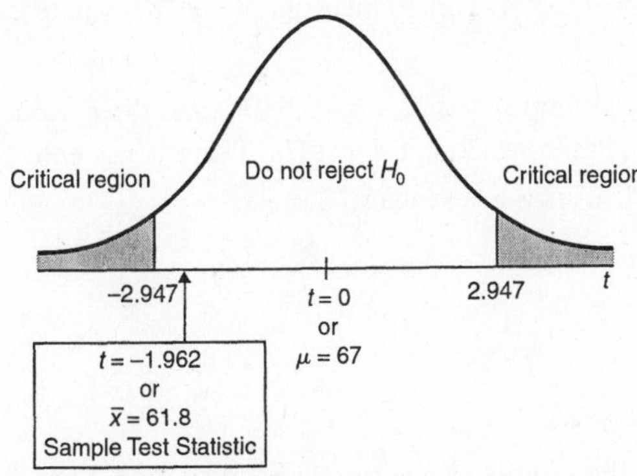

To find the *P*-value interval, use the α'' values since our test is two-tailed and look in the row headed by *d.f.* = 15. We find that the sample *t* value, $t = -1.962$, falls between −1.753 and −2.131. Therefore, $0.050 < P \text{ value} < 0.100$.

The sample test statistic does not fall in the critical region ($-2.947 < -1.962 < 2.947$) and the *P* value is greater than the level of significance $\alpha = 0.01$. Therefore, do not reject H_0. There is not enough evidence to conclude that the average thickness of slab avalanches in Vail is different from those in Canada.

13. (a) Answers are used in part (b).

(b) H_0: $\mu = 77$ yr

H_1: $\mu < 77$ yr

Since < is in H_1, a left-tailed test is used. Since the sample size is small and the data distribution is approximately normal, critical values are found using the Student's *t* distribution (use Table 6 in Appendix II). For a one-tailed test, look in the column headed by $\alpha' = 0.05$ and the row headed by *d.f.* = 20 − 1 = 19. The critical value is $t_0 = -1.729$.

$$t = \frac{\bar{x} - \mu}{s/\sqrt{n}} = \frac{74.45 - 77}{18.09/\sqrt{20}} = -0.6304$$

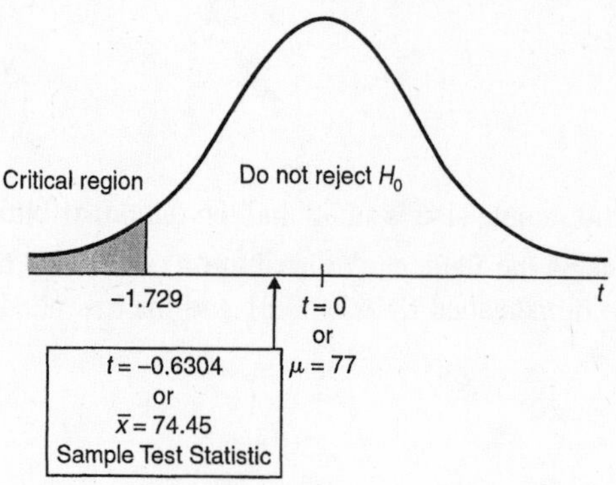

To find the *P*-value interval, use the α' values since our test is one-tailed and look in the row headed by *d.f.* = 19. We find that the sample *t* value, $t = -0.6304$, falls to the right of −1.187. Therefore, *P* value > 0.125.

The sample test statistic does not fall in the critical region ($-1.729 < -0.6304$) and the *P* value is greater than the level of significance $\alpha = 0.05$. Therefore, do not reject H_0. There is not enough evidence to conclude that the population mean life span is less than 77 years.

14. (a) Answers are used in part (b).

(b) $H_0: \mu = 40$

$H_1: \mu \neq 40$

Since ≠ is in H_1, a two-tailed test is used. Since the sample size is small and the data distribution is approximately normal, critical values are found using the Student's *t* distribution (use Table 6 in Appendix II). For a two-tailed test, look in the column headed by $\alpha'' = 0.05$ and the row headed by *d.f.* = 6 − 1 = 5. The critical values are $\pm t_0 = \pm 2.571$.

$$t = \frac{\bar{x} - \mu}{s/\sqrt{n}} = \frac{36.5 - 40}{4.2/\sqrt{6}} = -2.04$$

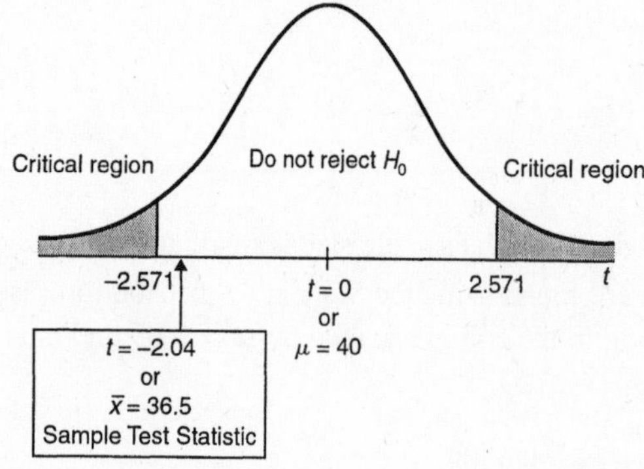

To find the *P*-value interval, use the α'' values since our test is two-tailed and look in the row headed by *d.f.* = 5. We find that the sample *t* value, $t = -2.04$, falls between −2.015 and −2.571. Therefore, 0.050 < *P* value < 0.100.

The sample test statistic does not fall in the critical region ($-2.571 < -2.04 < 2.571$) and the *P* value is greater than the level of significance $\alpha = 0.05$. Therefore, do not reject H_0. There is not enough evidence to conclude that the population average heart rate of the lion is different from 40 beats per minute.

15. **(a)** Answers are used in part (b).

(b) $H_0: \mu = 7.3$

$H_1: \mu > 7.3$

Since > is in H_1, a right-tailed test is used. Since the sample size is small and the data distribution is approximately normal, critical values are found using the Student's t distribution (use Table 6 in Appendix II). For a one-tailed test, look in the column headed by $\alpha' = 0.05$ and the row headed by $d.f.$ $= 20 - 1 = 19$. The critical value is

$t_0 = 1.729$.

$$t = \frac{\bar{x} - \mu}{s/\sqrt{n}} = \frac{8.1 - 7.3}{1.4/\sqrt{20}} = 2.556$$

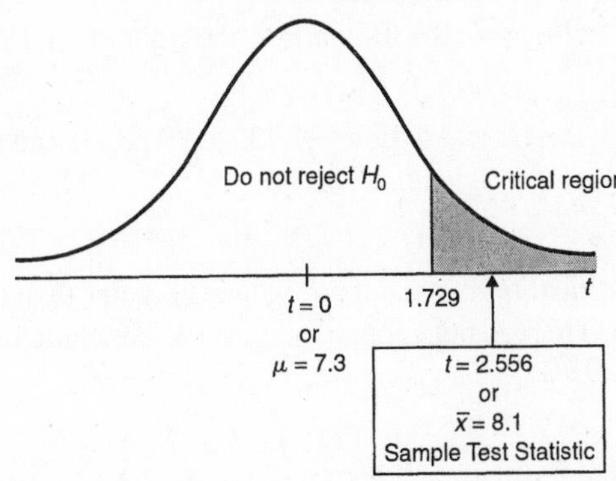

To find the P-value interval, use the α' values since our test is one-tailed and look in the row headed by $d.f. = 19$. We find that the sample t value, $t = 2.556$, falls between 2.539 and 2.861. Therefore, $0.005 < P$ value < 0.010.

The sample test statistic falls in the critical region ($2.555 > 1.729$) and the P value is less than the level of significance $\alpha = 0.05$. Therefore, reject H_0. We conclude that the evidence supports the claim that the average time women with children spend shopping in houseware stores in Cherry Creek Mall is higher than the national average.

Section 9.5

1. $H_0: p = 0.70$

$H_1: p \neq 0.70$

Since $\neq$ is in H_1, a two-tailed test is used. The $\hat{p}$ distribution is approximately normal when n is sufficiently large, which it is here, since $np = 32(0.7) = 22.4$ and $nq = 32(0.3) = 9.6$ are both > 5. For $\alpha = 0.01$, the critical values are $z_0 = \pm 2.58$.

$$\hat{p} = \frac{r}{n} = \frac{24}{32} = 0.75$$

$$z = \frac{\hat{p} - p}{\sqrt{\frac{pq}{n}}} = \frac{0.75 - 0.70}{\sqrt{\frac{0.70(0.30)}{32}}} = 0.62$$

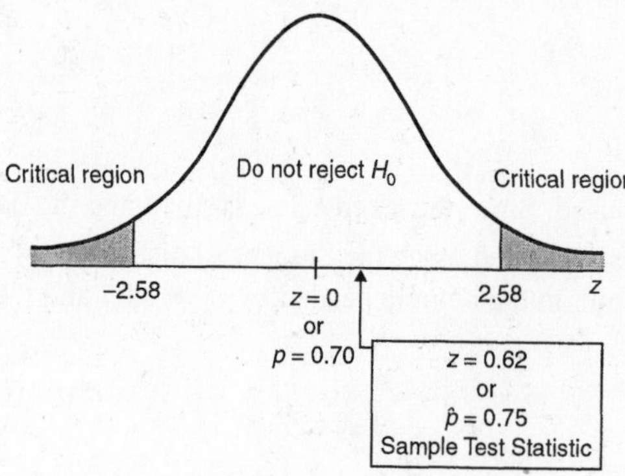

Next, find the P value associated with $z = 0.62$ and a two-tailed test.

$$\begin{aligned} P \text{ value} &= 2P(z \geq 0.62) \\ &= 2(1 - 0.7324) \\ &= 2(0.2676) \\ &= 0.5352 \end{aligned}$$

Since the sample z value falls outside the critical region and the P value is greater than the level of significance, $\alpha = 0.01$, we do not reject H_0. There is not enough evidence to conclude that the population proportion of such arrests is different from 0.70.

2. H_0: $p = 0.67$
H_1: $p < 0.67$
Since < is in H_1, a left-tailed test is used. The $\hat{p}$ distribution is approximately normal when n is sufficiently large, which it is here, since $np = 38(0.67) = 25.46$ and $nq = 38(0.33) = 12.54$ are both > 5. For $\alpha = 0.05$, the critical value is $z_0 = -1.645$.

$$\hat{p} = \frac{r}{n} = \frac{21}{38} = 0.5526$$

$$z = \frac{\hat{p} - p}{\sqrt{\frac{pq}{n}}} = \frac{0.5526 - 0.67}{\sqrt{\frac{0.67(0.33)}{38}}} = -1.54$$

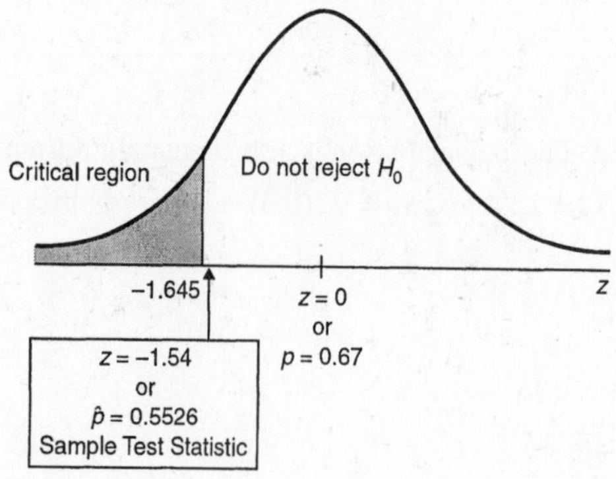

Next, find the P value associated with $z = -1.54$ and a one-tailed test.

$$\begin{aligned} P \text{ value} &= P(z \le -1.54) \\ &= 0.0618 \end{aligned}$$

Since the sample z value falls outside the critical region and the P value is greater than the level of significance, $\alpha = 0.05$, we do not reject H_0. There is not enough evidence to conclude that the population proportion of women athletes who graduate at CU Boulder is now less than 67%.

3. H_0: $p = 0.77$

H_1: $p < 0.77$

Since < is in H_1, a left-tailed test is used. The $\hat{p}$ distribution is approximately normal when n is sufficiently large, which it is here, because $np = 27(0.77) = 20.79$ and $nq = 27(0.23) = 6.21$ are both > 5. For $\alpha = 0.01$, the critical value is $z_0 = -2.3$.

$$\hat{p} = \frac{r}{n} = \frac{15}{27} = 0.5556$$

$$z = \frac{\hat{p} - p}{\sqrt{\frac{pq}{n}}} = \frac{0.5556 - 0.77}{\sqrt{\frac{0.77(0.23)}{27}}} = -2.65$$

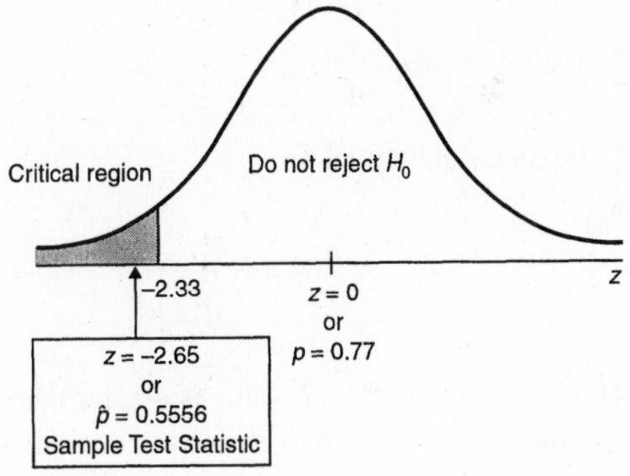

Next, find the P value associated with $z = -2.65$ and a one-tailed test.

$$\begin{aligned} P \text{ value} &= P(z \le -2.65) \\ &= 0.0040 \end{aligned}$$

Since the sample z value falls inside the critical region and the P value is less than the level of significance, $\alpha = 0.01$, we reject H_0. We conclude the population proportion of driver fatalities related to alcohol is less than 77%.

4. $H_0: p = 0.73$

$H_1: p > 0.73$

Since > is in H_1, a right-tailed test is used. The $\hat{p}$ distribution is approximately normal when n is sufficiently large, which it is here, because $np = 41(0.73) = 29.93$ and $nq = 41(0.27) = 11.07$ are both > 5. For $\alpha = 0.05$, the critical value is $z_0 = 1.645$.

$$\hat{p} = \frac{r}{n} = \frac{33}{41} = 0.8049$$

$$z = \frac{\hat{p} - p}{\sqrt{\frac{pq}{n}}} = \frac{0.8049 - 0.73}{\sqrt{\frac{0.73(0.27)}{41}}} = 108$$

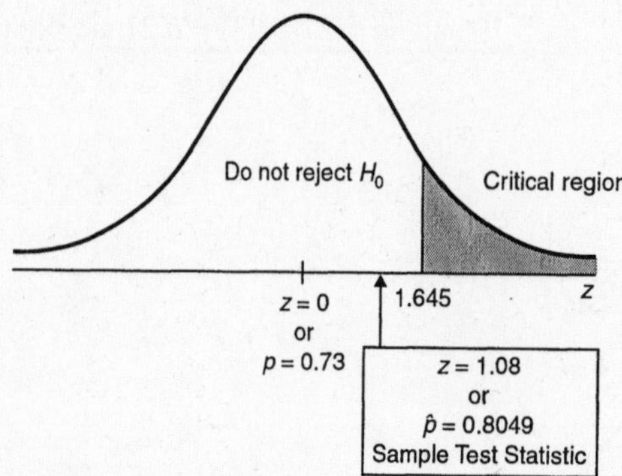

Next, find the P value associated with $z = 1.08$ and a one-tailed test.

$$\begin{aligned} P \text{ value} &= P(z \geq 1.08) \\ &= 1 - 0.8599 \\ &= 0.1401 \end{aligned}$$

Since the sample z value falls outside the critical region and the P value is greater than the level of significance, $\alpha = 0.05$, we do not reject H_0. There is not enough evidence to conclude that the population proportion of such accidents is higher than 73% in the Fargo district.

5. $H_0: p = 0.50$

$H_1: p < 0.50$

Since < is in H_1, a left-tailed test is used. The $\hat{p}$ distribution is approximately normal when n is sufficiently large, and it is here because $np = 34(0.50) = 17$ and $nq = 17$ are both > 5. For $\alpha = 0.01$, the critical value is $z_0 = -2.33$.

$$\hat{p} = \frac{r}{n} = \frac{10}{34} = 0.2941$$

$$z = \frac{\hat{p} - p}{\sqrt{\frac{pq}{n}}} = \frac{0.2941 - 0.50}{\sqrt{\frac{0.5(0.5)}{34}}} = -2.40$$

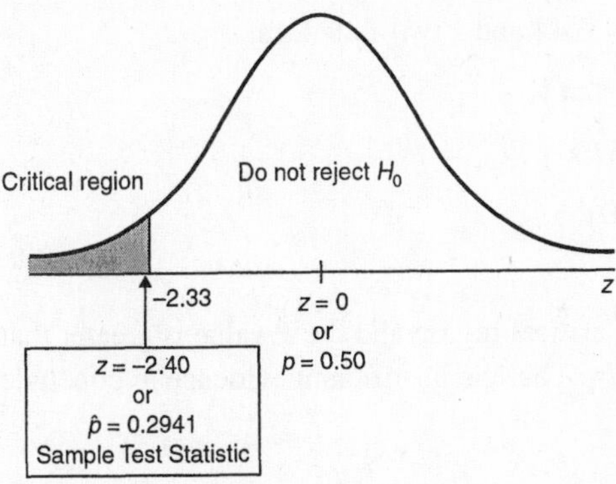

Next, find the P value associated with $z = -2.40$ and a one-tailed test.

$$\begin{aligned} P \text{ value} &= P(z \le -2.40) \\ &= 0.0082 \end{aligned}$$

Since the sample z value falls inside the critical region and the P value is less than the level of significance, $\alpha = 0.01$, we reject H_0. We conclude that the population proportion of female wolves is less than 50%.

6. $H_0: p = 0.75$
$H_1: p \ne 0.75$

Since $\ne$ is in H_1, a two-tailed test is used. The $\hat{p}$ distribution is approximately normal when n is sufficiently large, which it is here, because $np = 83(0.75) = 62.25$ and $nq = 83(0.25) = 20.75$ are both > 5. For $\alpha =$ 0.05, the critical values are $z_0 = \pm 1.96$.

$$\hat{p} = \frac{r}{n} = \frac{64}{83} = 0.7711$$

$$z = \frac{\hat{p} - p}{\sqrt{\frac{pq}{n}}} = \frac{0.7711 - 0.75}{\sqrt{\frac{0.75(0.25)}{83}}} = 0.44$$

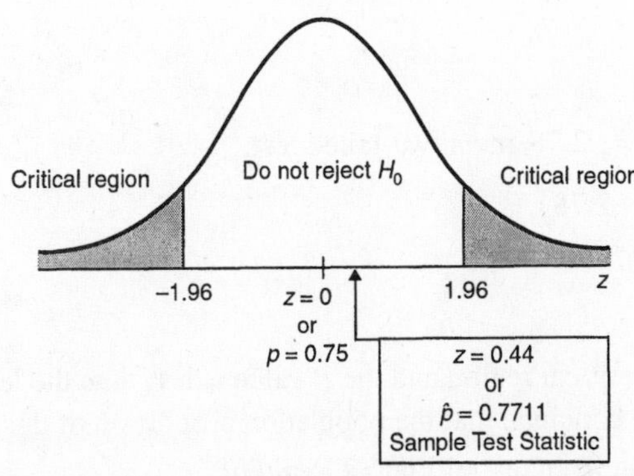

Next, find the P value associated with $z = 0.44$ and a two-tailed test.

$$\begin{aligned} P \text{ value} &= 2P(z \geq 0.44) \\ &= 2(1 - 0.6700) \\ &= 2(0.3300) \\ &= 0.6600 \end{aligned}$$

Since the sample z value falls outside the critical region and the P value is greater than the level of significance, $\alpha = 0.05$, we do not reject H_0. There is insufficient evidence to conclude that the population proportion is different from 75%.

7. H_0: $p = 0.261$
H_1: $p \neq 0.261$

Since ≠ is in H_1, a two-tailed test is used. The $\hat{p}$ distribution is approximately normal when n is sufficiently large, which it is here, because $np = 317(0.261) = 82.737$ and $nq = 317(0.739) = 234.263$ are both > 5. For $\alpha = 0.01$, the critical values are $z_0 = \pm 2.58$.

$$\hat{p} = \frac{r}{n} = \frac{61}{317} = 0.1924$$

$$z = \frac{\hat{p} - p}{\sqrt{\frac{pq}{n}}} = \frac{0.1924 - 0.261}{\sqrt{\frac{0.261(0.739)}{317}}} = -2.78$$

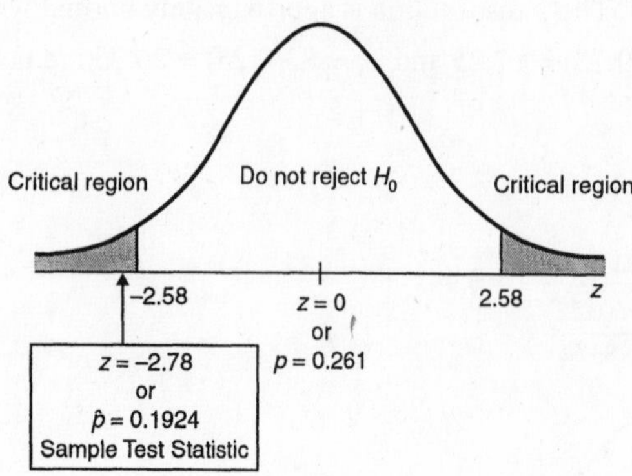

Next, find the P value associated with $z = -2.78$ and a two-tailed test.

$$\begin{aligned} P \text{ value} &= 2P(z \leq -2.78) \\ &= 2(0.0027) \\ &= 0.0054 \end{aligned}$$

Since the sample z value falls inside the critical region and the P value is less than the level of significance, $\alpha = 0.01$, we reject H_0. We conclude that the population proportion of this type of five-syllable sequence is significantly different from that of Plato's *Republic*.

8. $H_0: p = 0.214$

$H_1: p > 0.214$

Since > is in H_1, a right-tailed test is used. The $\hat{p}$ distribution is approximately normal when n is sufficiently large, which it is here, because $np = 493(0.214) = 105.502$ and $nq = 493(0.786) = 387.498$ are both > 5. For $\alpha = 0.01$, the critical value is $z_0 = 2.33$.

$$\hat{p} = \frac{r}{n} = \frac{136}{493} = 0.2759$$

$$z = \frac{\hat{p} - p}{\sqrt{\frac{pq}{n}}} = \frac{0.2759 - 0.214}{\sqrt{\frac{0.214(0.786)}{493}}} = 3.35$$

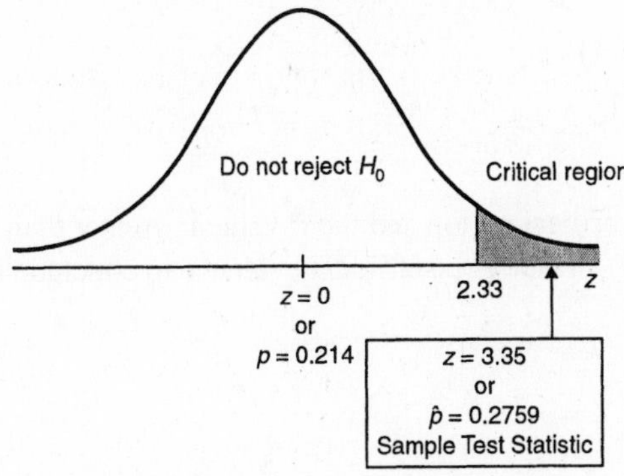

Next, find the P value associated with $z = 3.35$ and a one-tailed test.

$$\begin{aligned} P \text{ value} &= P(z \geq 3.35) \\ &= 1 - 0.9996 \\ &= 0.0004 \end{aligned}$$

Since the sample z value falls inside the critical region and the P value is less than the level of significance, $\alpha = 0.01$, we reject H_0. We conclude that the population proportion is higher than 21.4%

9. $H_0: p = 0.47$

$H_1: p > 0.47$

Since > is in H_1, a right-tailed test is used. The $\hat{p}$ distribution is approximately normal when n is sufficiently large, which it is here, because $np = 1006(0.47) = 472.82$ and $nq = 1006(0.53) = 533.18$ are both > 5. For $\alpha = 0.01$, the critical value is $z_0 = 2.33$.

$$\hat{p} = \frac{r}{n} = \frac{490}{1006} = 0.4871$$

$$z = \frac{\hat{p} - p}{\sqrt{\frac{pq}{n}}} = \frac{0.4871 - 0.47}{\sqrt{\frac{0.47(0.53)}{1006}}} = 1.09$$

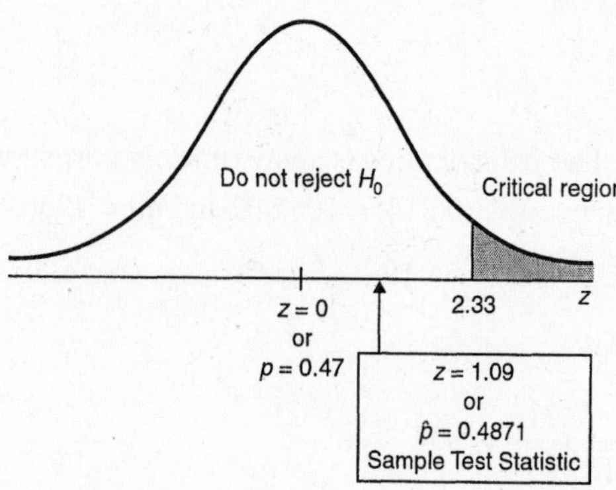

Next, find the P value associated with $z = 1.09$ and a one-tailed test.

$$\begin{aligned} P \text{ value} &= P(z \geq 1.09) \\ &= 1 - 0.8621 \\ &= 0.1379 \end{aligned}$$

Since the sample z value falls outside the critical region and the P value is greater than the level of significance, $\alpha = 0.01$, we do not reject H_0. There is insufficient evidence to conclude that the population proportion is more than 47%.

10. $H_0: p = 0.80$

$H_1: p < 0.80$

Since < is in H_1, a left-tailed test is used. The $\hat{p}$ distribution is approximately normal when n is sufficiently large, which it is here, because $np = 115(0.8) = 92$ and $nq = 115(0.2) = 23$ are both > 5. For $\alpha = 0.05$, the critical value is $z_0 = -1.645$.

$$\hat{p} = \frac{r}{n} = \frac{88}{115} = 0.7652$$

$$z = \frac{\hat{p} - p}{\sqrt{\frac{pq}{n}}} = \frac{0.7652 - 0.80}{\sqrt{\frac{0.80(0.20)}{115}}} = -0.93$$

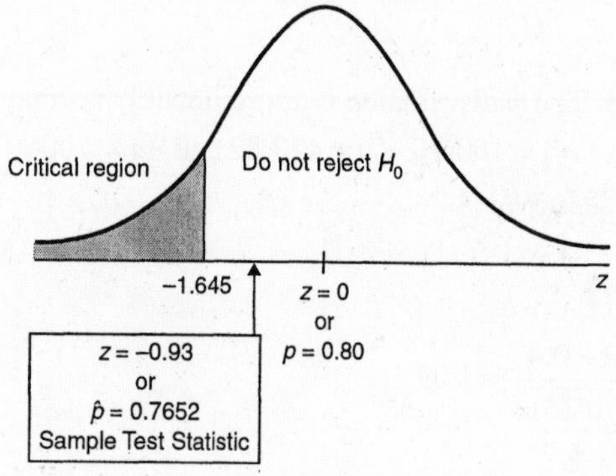

Next, find the P value associated with $z = -0.93$ and a one-tailed test.

$$P \text{ value} = P(z \le -0.93)$$
$$= 0.1762$$

Since the sample z value falls outside the critical region and the P value is greater than the level of significance, $\alpha = 0.05$, we do not reject H_0. There is insufficient evidence to conclude less than 80% of the prices in the store end in the digits 9 or 5.

11. $H_0: p = 0.092$

$H_1: p > 0.092$

Since > is in H_1, a right-tailed test is used. The $\hat{p}$ distribution is approximately normal when n is sufficiently large, which it is here, because np = 196(0.092) = 18.032 and nq = 196(0.908) = 177.968 are both > 5. For $\alpha = 0.05$, the critical value is $z_0 = 1.645$.

$$\hat{p} = \frac{r}{n} = \frac{29}{196} = 0.1480$$
$$z = \frac{\hat{p} - p}{\sqrt{\frac{pq}{n}}} = \frac{0.1480 - 0.092}{\sqrt{\frac{0.092(0.908)}{196}}} = 2.71$$

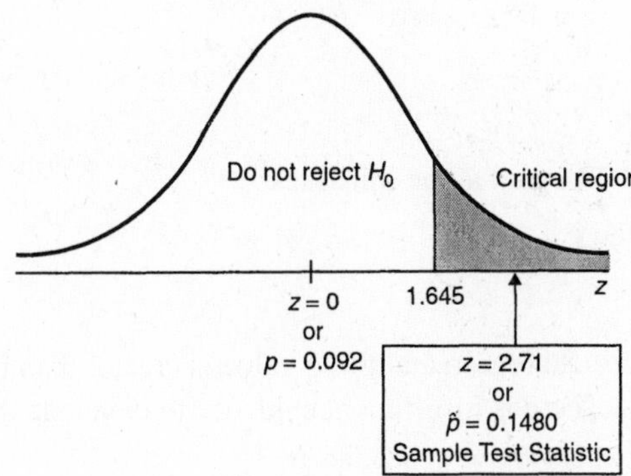

Next, find the P value associated with $z = 2.71$ and a one-tailed test.

$$P \text{ value} = P(z \ge 2.71)$$
$$= 1 - 0.9966$$
$$= 0.0034$$

Since the sample z value falls inside the critical region and the P value is less than the level of significance, $\alpha = 0.05$, we reject H_0. We conclude that the population proportion of students with hypertension during final exams week is higher than 9.2%.

12. $H_0: p = 0.12$

$H_1: p < 0.12$

Since < is in H_1, a left-tailed test is used. The $\hat{p}$ distribution is approximately normal when n is sufficiently large, which it is here, because $np = 209(0.12) = 25.08$ and $nq = 209(0.88) = 183.92$ are both > 5. For α = 0.01, the critical value is $z_0 = -2.33$.

$$\hat{p} = \frac{r}{n} = \frac{16}{209} = 0.0766$$

$$z = \frac{\hat{p} - p}{\sqrt{\frac{pq}{n}}} = \frac{0.0766 - 0.12}{\sqrt{\frac{0.12(0.88)}{209}}} = -1.93$$

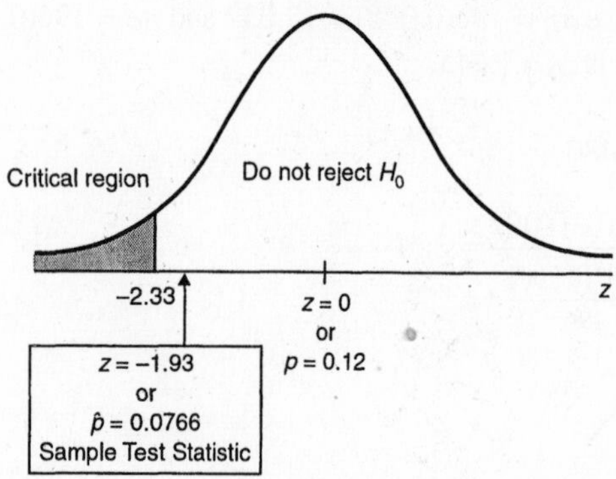

Next, find the P value associated with $z = -1.93$ and a one-tailed test.

$$P \text{ value} = P(z \le -1.93) = 0.0268$$

Since the sample z value falls outside the critical region and the P value is greater than the level of significance, $\alpha = 0.01$, we do not reject H_0. There is insufficient evidence to conclude that there has been a reduction in the population proportion of patients having headaches.

13. $H_0: p = 0.82$

$H_1: p \ne 0.82$

Since ≠ is in H_1, a two-tailed test is used. The $\hat{p}$ distribution is approximately normal when n is sufficiently large, which it is here, because $np = 73(0.82) = 59.86$ and $nq = 73(0.18) = 13.14$ are both > 5. For α = 0.01, the critical values are $z_0 = \pm 2.58$.

$$\hat{p} = \frac{r}{n} = \frac{56}{73} = 0.7671$$

$$z = \frac{\hat{p} - p}{\sqrt{\frac{pq}{n}}} = \frac{0.7671 - 0.82}{\sqrt{\frac{0.82(0.18)}{73}}} = -1.18$$

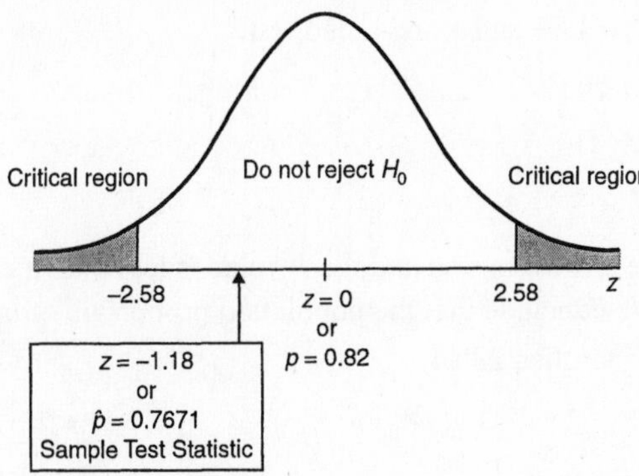

Next, find the P value associated with $z = -1.18$ and a two-tailed test.

$$\begin{aligned} P \text{ value} &= 2P(z \le -1.18) \\ &= 2(0.1190) \\ &= 0.2380 \end{aligned}$$

Since the sample z value falls outside the critical region and the P value is greater than the level of significance, $\alpha = 0.01$, we do not reject H_0. There is insufficient evidence to conclude that the population proportion is different from 82%.

14. $H_0: p = 0.28$
$H_1: p > 0.28$

Since > is in H_1, a right-tailed test is used. The $\hat{p}$ distribution is approximately normal when n is sufficiently large, which it is here, because $np = 48(0.28) = 13.44$ and $nq = 48(0.72) = 34.56$ are both > 5. For $\alpha = 0.05$, the critical value is $z_0 = 1.645$.

$$\hat{p} = \frac{r}{n} = \frac{19}{48} = 0.3958$$

$$z = \frac{\hat{p} - p}{\sqrt{\frac{pq}{n}}} = \frac{0.3958 - 0.28}{\sqrt{\frac{0.28(0.72)}{48}}} = 1.79$$

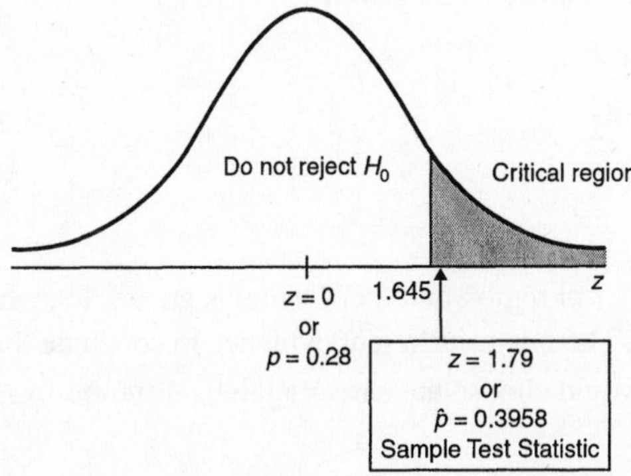

Next, find the P value associated with $z = 1.79$ and a one-tailed test.

$$\begin{aligned} P \text{ value} &= P(z \geq 1.79) \\ &= 1 - 0.9633 \\ &= 0.0367 \end{aligned}$$

Since the sample z value falls inside the critical region and the P value is less than the level of significance, $\alpha = 0.05$, we reject H_0. We conclude that the population proportion of interstate truckers who believe NAFTA benefits America is higher than 28%.

15. $H_0: p = 0.76$

$H_1: p \neq 0.76$

Since $\neq$ is in H_1, a two-tailed test is used. The $\hat{p}$ distribution is approximately normal when n is sufficiently large, which it is here, because $np = 59(0.76) = 44.84$ and $nq = 59(0.24) = 14.16$ are both > 5. For $\alpha = 0.01$, the critical values are $z_0 = \pm 2.58$.

$$\hat{p} = \frac{r}{n} = \frac{47}{59} = 0.7966$$

$$z = \frac{\hat{p} - p}{\sqrt{\frac{pq}{n}}} = \frac{0.7966 - 0.76}{\sqrt{\frac{0.76(0.24)}{59}}} = 0.66$$

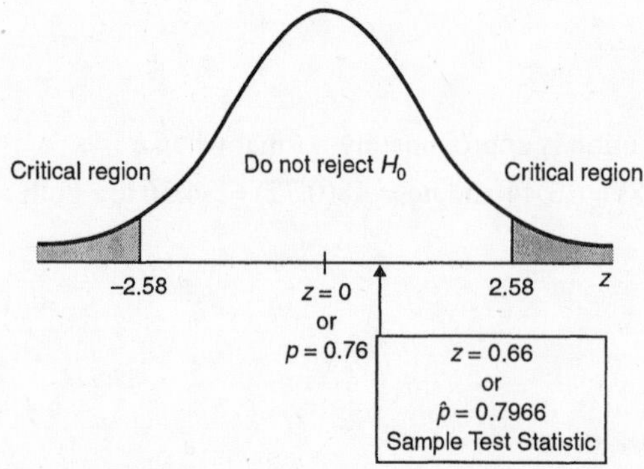

Next, find the P value associated with $z = 0.66$ and a two-tailed test.

$$\begin{aligned} P \text{ value} &= 2P(z \geq 0.66) \\ &= 2(1 - 0.7454) \\ &= 2(0.2546) \\ &= 0.5092 \end{aligned}$$

Since the sample z value falls outside the critical region and the P value is greater than the level of significance, $\alpha = 0.01$, we do not reject H_0. There is insufficient evidence to conclude that the population proportion of professors in Colorado who would choose the career again is different from 76%.

Section 9.6

Note: In the following problems, we will make the assumption that the data are (approximately) normally distributed.

1. H_0: $\mu_d = 0$

H_1: $\mu_d \neq 0$

Since ≠ is in H_1, a two-tailed test is used. Since the sample size is small, critical values are found using the Student's t distribution (use Table 6 in Appendix II). For a two-tailed test, look in the column headed by $\alpha'' = 0.05$ and the row headed by $d.f. = 8 - 1 = 7$. The critical values are $t_0 = \pm 2.365$.

$$\bar{d} = 2.25,\ s_d = 7.78$$

$$t = \frac{\bar{d} - \mu_d}{s_d/\sqrt{n}} = \frac{2.25 - 0}{7.78/\sqrt{8}} = 0.818$$

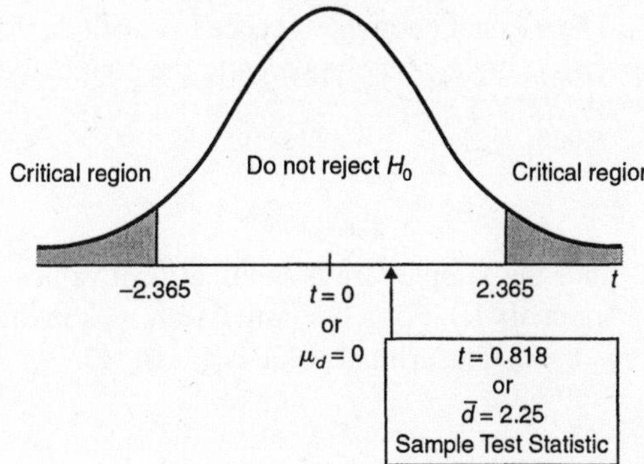

To find the P value interval, use the α'' values since the test is two-tailed and look in the row headed by $d.f. = 7$. We find that the sample t value, $t = 0.818$, falls to the left of 1.254. Therefore, P value > 0.250.

Since the sample test statistic falls outside the critical region and the P value is greater than the level of significance, $\alpha = 0.05$, we do not reject H_0. There is not enough evidence to conclude that there is a significant difference between the population mean percentage increase in corporate revenue and the population mean percentage increase in CEO salary.

2. H_0: $\mu_d = 0$

H_1: $\mu_d \neq 0$

Since ≠ is in H_1, a two-tailed test is used. Since the sample size is small, critical values are found using the Student's t distribution (use Table 6 in Appendix II). For a two-tailed test, look in the column headed by $\alpha'' = 0.01$ and the row headed by $d.f. = 7 - 1 = 6$. The critical values are $t_0 = \pm 3.707$.

$$\bar{d} = 0.37,\ s_d = 0.47$$

$$t = \frac{\bar{d} - \mu_d}{s_d/\sqrt{n}} = \frac{0.37 - 0}{0.47/\sqrt{7}} = 2.08$$

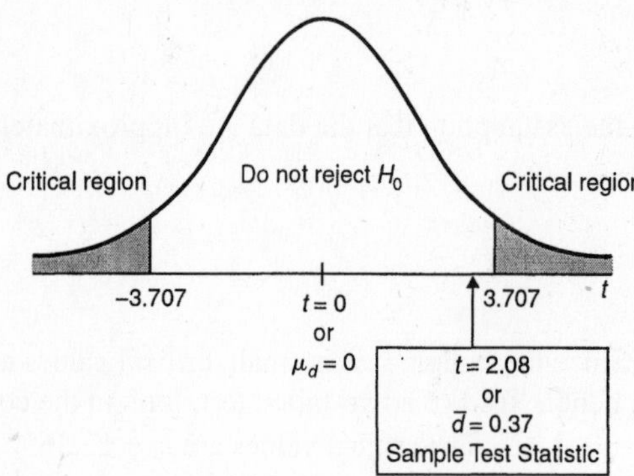

To find the P value interval, use the α'' values since the test is two-tailed and look in the row headed by *d.f.* = 6. We find that the sample t value, $t = 2.08$, falls between 1.943 and 2.447. Therefore, $0.050 < P \text{ value} < 0.100$.

Since the sample test statistic falls outside the critical region and the P value is greater than the level of significance, $\alpha = 0.01$, we do not reject H_0. There is not enough evidence to conclude that there is a difference in the population mean hours per fish using a boat compared to the population mean hours per fish fishing from the shore.

3. H_0: $\mu_d = 0$

H_1: $\mu_d > 0$

Since > is in H_1, a right-tailed test is used. Since the sample size is small, critical values are found using the Student's t distribution (use Table 6 in Appendix II). For a one-tailed test, look in the column headed by $\alpha' = 0.01$ and the row headed by *d.f.* = 5 − 1 = 4. The critical value is $t_0 = 3.747$.

$$\bar{d} = 12.6,\ s_d = 22.66$$

$$t = \frac{\bar{d} - \mu_d}{s_d/\sqrt{n}} = \frac{12.6 - 0}{22.66/\sqrt{5}} = 1.243$$

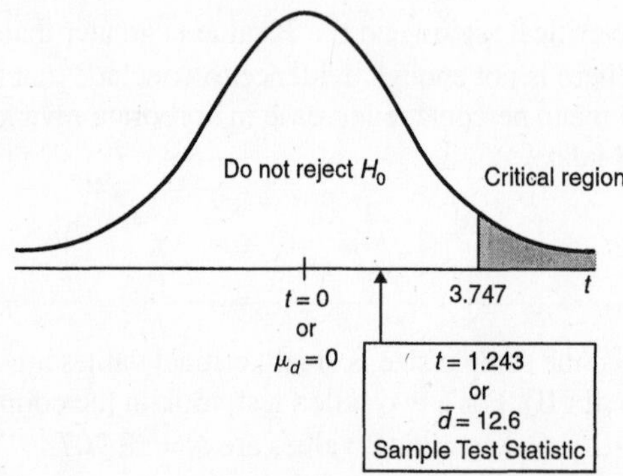

To find the P value interval, use the α' values since the test is one-tailed and look in the row headed by *d.f.* = 4. We find that the sample t value, $t = 1.243$, falls to the left of 1.344. Therefore, $P \text{ value} > 0.125$.

Since the sample test statistic falls outside the critical region and the P value is greater than the level of significance, $\alpha = 0.01$, we do not reject H_0. There is insufficient evidence to conclude that, on average, peak wind gusts are higher in January than they are in April.

4. $H_0: \mu_d = 0$

$H_1: \mu_d > 0$

Since > is in H_1, a right-tailed test is used. Since the sample size is small, critical values are found using the Student's t distribution (use Table 6 in Appendix II). For a one-tailed test, look in the column headed by $\alpha' = 0.01$ and the row headed by $d.f. = 10 - 1 = 9$. The critical value is $t_0 = 2.821$.

$$\bar{d} = 0.08,\ s_d = 1.701$$

$$t = \frac{\bar{d} - \mu_d}{s_d/\sqrt{n}} = \frac{0.08 - 0}{1.701/\sqrt{10}} = 0.1487$$

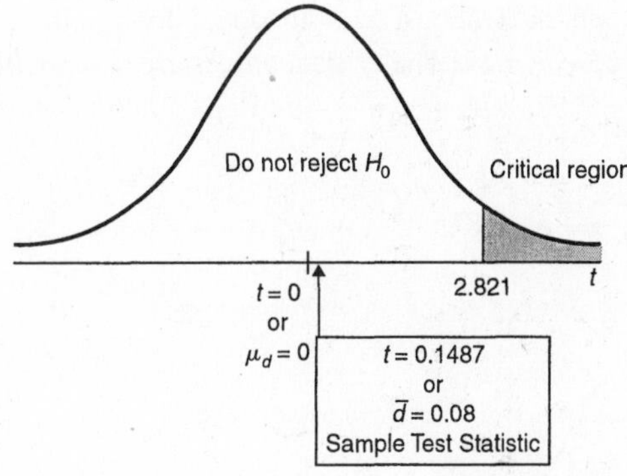

To find the P value interval, use the α' values since the test is one-tailed and look in the row headed by $d.f. = 9$. We find that the sample t value, $t = 0.1487$, falls to the left of 1.230. Therefore, P value > 0.125.

Since the sample test statistic falls outside the critical region and the P value is greater than the level of significance, $\alpha = 0.01$, we do not reject H_0. There is insufficient evidence to conclude that the January population mean has dropped.

5. $H_0: \mu_d = 0$

$H_1: \mu_d > 0$

Since > is in H_1, right-tailed test is used. Since the sample size is small, critical values are found using the Student's t distribution (use Table 6 in Appendix II). For a one-tailed test, look in the column headed by $\alpha' = 0.05$ and the row headed by $d.f. = 8 - 1 = 7$. The critical value is $t_0 = 1.895$.

$$\bar{d} = 6.125,\ s_d = 9.83$$

$$t = \frac{\bar{d} - \mu_d}{s_d/\sqrt{n}} = \frac{6.125 - 0}{9.83/\sqrt{8}} = 1.76$$

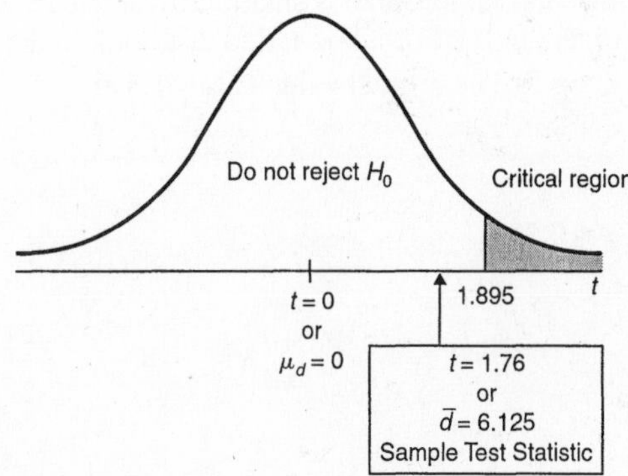

To find the P value interval, use the α' values since the test is one-tailed and look in the row headed by $d.f. = 7$. We find that the sample t value, $t = 1.76$, falls between 1.617 and 1.895. Therefore, $0.050 < P \text{ value} < 0.075$.

Since the sample test statistic falls outside the critical region and the P value is greater than the level of significance, $\alpha = 0.05$, we do not reject H_0. There is not enough evidence to conclude that average percentage of males in a wolf pack is higher in winter.

6. $H_0: \mu_d = 0$

$H_1: \mu_d \neq 0$

Since $\neq$ is in H_1, a two-tailed test is used. Since the sample size is small, critical values are found using the Student's t distribution (use Table 6 in Appendix II). For a two-tailed test, look in the column headed by $\alpha'' = 0.01$ and the row headed by $d.f. = 12 - 1 = 11$. The critical values are $t_0 = \pm 3.106$.

$$\bar{d} = -0.84,\ s_d = 3.57$$

$$t = \frac{\bar{d} - \mu_d}{s_d/\sqrt{n}} = \frac{-0.84 - 0}{3.57/\sqrt{12}} = -0.815$$

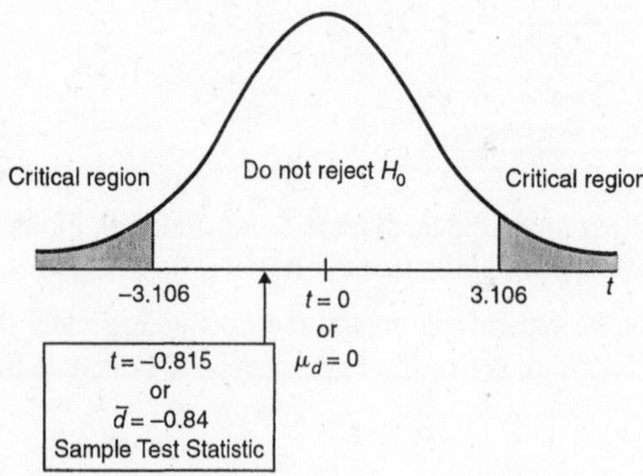

To find the P value interval, use the α'' values since the test is two-tailed and look in the row headed by $d.f. = 11$. We find that the sample t value, $t = -0.815$, falls to the right of -1.214. Therefore, $P \text{ value} > 0.250$.

Since the sample test statistic falls outside the critical region and the P value is greater than the level of significance, $\alpha = 0.01$, we do not reject H_0. There is insufficient evidence to conclude that the average temperature in Miami is different from that in Honolulu.

7. $H_0: \mu_d = 0$

$H_1: \mu_d > 0$

Since $>$ is in H_1, a right-tailed test is used. Since the sample size is small, critical values are found using the Student's t distribution (use Table 6 in Appendix II). For a one-tailed test, look in the column headed by $\alpha' = 0.05$ and the row headed by $d.f. = 8 - 1 = 7$. The critical value is $t_0 = 1.895$.

$$\bar{d} = 6,\ s_d = 21.5$$

$$t = \frac{\bar{d} - \mu_d}{s_d/\sqrt{n}} = \frac{6 - 0}{21.5/\sqrt{8}} = 0.789$$

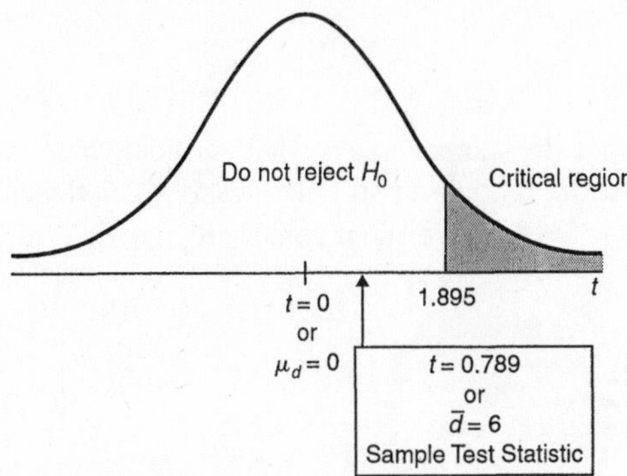

To find the P value interval, use the α' values since the test is one-tailed and look in the row headed by $d.f. = 7$. We find that the sample t value, $t = 0.789$, falls to the left of 1.254. Therefore, P value > 0.125.

Since the sample test statistic falls outside the critical region and the P value is greater than the level of significance, $\alpha = 0.05$, we do not reject H_0. We do not have enough evidence to conclude that the average number of inhabited houses is greater than the average number of inhabited hogans on the Navajo Reservation.

8. H_0: $\mu_d = 0$

H_1: $\mu_d > 0$

Since > is in H_1, a right-tailed test is used. Since the sample size is small, critical values are found using the Student's t distribution (use Table 6 in Appendix II). For a one-tailed test, look in the column headed by $\alpha' = 0.05$ and the row headed by $d.f. = 7 - 1 = 6$. The critical value is $t_0 = 1.943$.

$$\bar{d} = 0.0, \quad s_d = 8.76$$

$$t = \frac{\bar{d} - \mu_d}{s_d/\sqrt{n}} = \frac{0.0 - 0}{8.76/\sqrt{7}} = 0.000$$

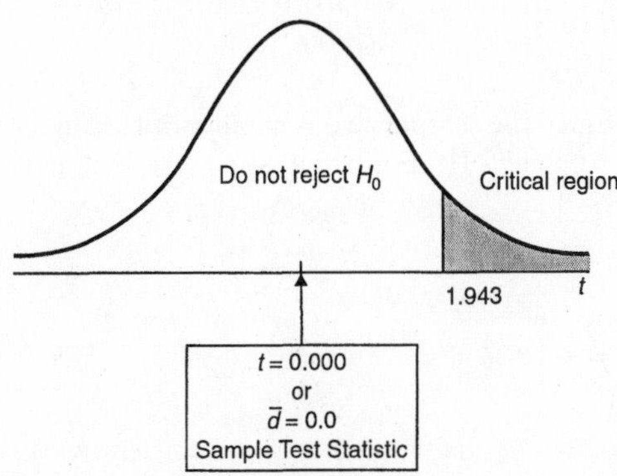

To find the P value interval, use the α' values since the test is one-tailed and look in the row headed by $d.f. = 6$. We find that the sample t value, $t = 0$, falls to the left of 1.273. Therefore, P value > 0.125.

Since the sample test statistic falls outside the critical region and the P value is greater than the level of significance, $\alpha = 0.05$, we do not reject H_0. We do not have enough evidence to conclude that there tend to be more flaked stone tools than nonflaked stone tools at this excavation site. Note: In fact, there is no reason to do a hypothesis test or "find" the P value for this data. Since d = the hypothesized mean, there is absolutely no evidence for H_1.

9. $H_0: \mu_d = 0$

$H_1: \mu_d \neq 0$

Since $\neq$ is in H_1, a two-tailed test is used. Since the sample size is small, critical values are found using the Student's *t* distribution (use Table 6 in Appendix II). For a two-tailed test, look in the column headed by $\alpha'' = 0.05$ and the row headed by $d.f. = 5 - 1 = 4$. The critical values are $t_0 = \pm 2.776$.

$$\bar{d} = 1.0, \ s_d = 5.24$$

$$t = \frac{\bar{d} - \mu_d}{s_d/\sqrt{n}} = \frac{1.0 - 0}{5.24/\sqrt{5}} = 0.427$$

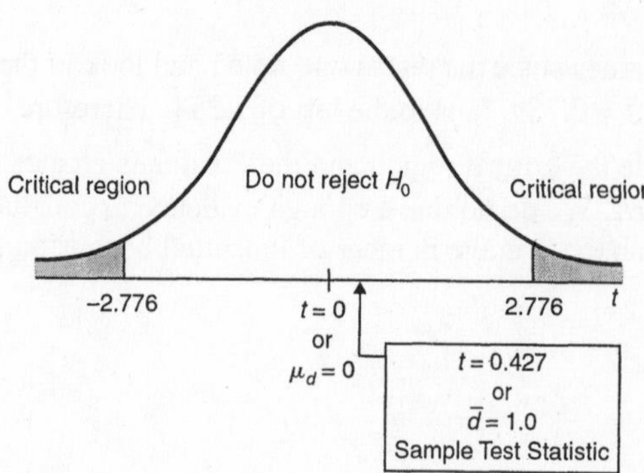

To find the *P* value interval, use the α'' values since the test is two-tailed and look in the row headed by $d.f. = 4$. We find that the sample *t* value, $t = 0.427$, falls to the left of 1.344. Therefore, *P* value > 0.250.

Since the sample test statistic falls outside the critical region and the *P* value is greater than the level of significance, $\alpha = 0.05$, we do not reject H_0. There is not enough evidence to conclude that there is a difference in the average number of service ware sherds in subarea 1 compared to subarea 2.

10. $H_0: \mu_d = 0$

$H_1: \mu_d > 0$

Since > is in H_1, a right-tailed test is used. Since the sample size is small, critical values are found using the Student's *t* distribution (use Table 6 in Appendix II). For a one-tailed test, look in the column headed by $\alpha' = 0.05$ and the row headed by $d.f. = 8 - 1 = 7$. The critical value is $t_0 = 1.895$.

$$\bar{d} = 1.25, \ s_d = 1.91$$

$$t = \frac{\bar{d} - \mu_d}{s_d/\sqrt{n}} = \frac{1.25 - 0}{1.91/\sqrt{8}} = 1.851$$

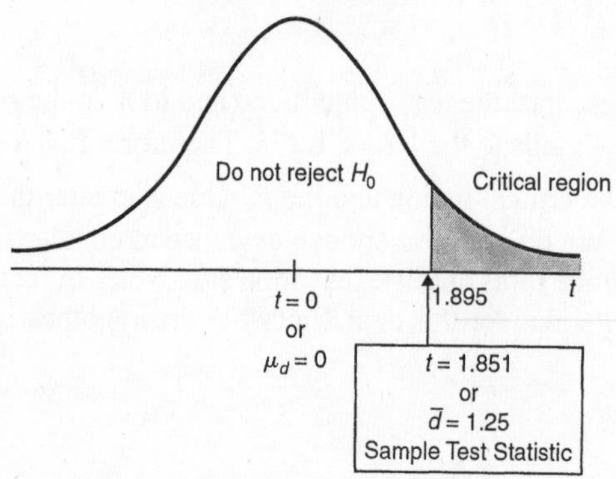

To find the P value interval, use the α' values since the test is one-tailed and look in the row headed by $d.f. = 7$. We find that the sample t value, $t = 1.851$, falls between 1.617 and 1.895. Therefore, $0.050 < P \text{ value} < 0.075$.

Since the sample test statistic falls outside the critical region and the P value is greater than the level of significance, $\alpha = 0.05$, we do not reject H_0. We do not have sufficient evidence to conclude that the mothers are more successful in picking out their own babies when a hunger cry is involved.

11. H_0: $\mu_d = 0$
H_1: $\mu_d < 0$

Since < is in H_1, a left-tailed test is used. Since the sample size is small, critical values are found using the Student's t distribution (use Table 6 in Appendix II). For a one-tailed test, look in the column headed by $\alpha' = 0.05$ and the row headed by $d.f. = 6 - 1 = 5$. The critical value is $t_0 = -2.015$.

$$\bar{d} = -10.5, \; s_d = 5.17$$

$$t = \frac{\bar{d} - \mu_d}{s_d/\sqrt{n}} = \frac{-10.5 - 0}{5.17/\sqrt{6}} = -4.97$$

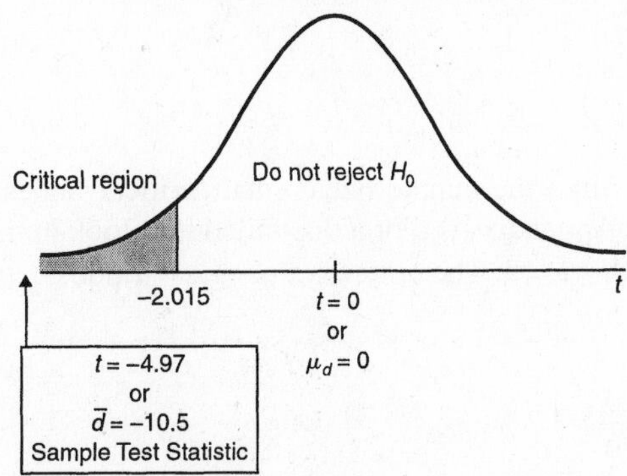

To find the P value interval, use the α' values since the test is one-tailed and look in the row headed by $d.f. = 5$. We find that the sample t value, $t = -4.97$, falls to the left of -4.032. Therefore, $P \text{ value} > 0.005$.

Since the sample test statistic falls inside the critical region and the P value is less than the level of significance, $\alpha = 0.05$, we reject H_0. We conclude that the population mean heart rate after the test is higher than that before the test.

12. H_0: $\mu_d = 0$
H_1: $\mu_d \neq 0$

Since ≠ is in H_1, a two-tailed test is used. Since the sample size is small, critical values are found using the Student's t distribution (use Table 6 in Appendix II). For a two-tailed test, look in the column headed by $\alpha'' = 0.05$ and the row headed by $d.f. = 6 - 1 = 5$. The critical values are $t_0 = \pm 2.571$.

$$\bar{d} = -3.33, \; s_d = 7.34$$

$$t = \frac{\bar{d} - \mu_d}{s_d/\sqrt{n}} = \frac{-3.33 - 0}{7.34/\sqrt{6}} = -1.111$$

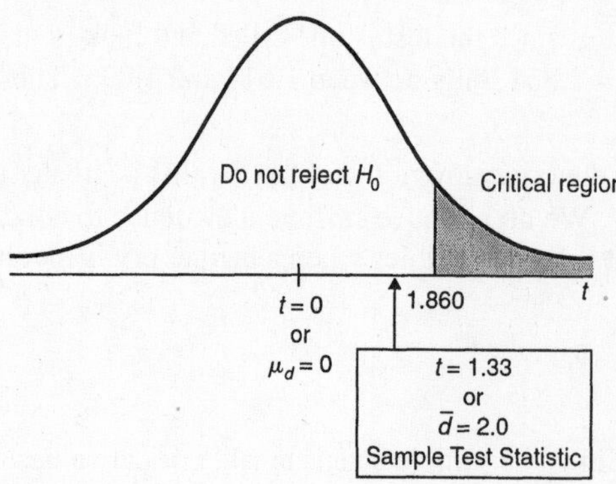

To find the P value interval, use the α'' values since the test is two-tailed and look in the row headed by $d.f. = 5$. We find that the sample t value, $t = -1.111$, falls to the right of -1.301. Therefore, P value > 0.250.

Since the sample test statistic falls outside the critical region and the P value is greater than the level of significance, $\alpha = 0.05$, we do not reject H_0. There is insufficient evidence to conclude that the population mean systolic blood pressure is different before and 6 minutes after the treadmill test.

13. H_0: $\mu_d = 0$

H_1: $\mu_d > 0$

Since > is in H_1, a right-tailed test is used. Since the sample size is small, critical values are found using the Student's t distribution (use Table 6 in Appendix II). For a one-tailed test, look in the column headed by $\alpha' = 0.05$ and the row headed by $d.f. = 9 - 1 = 8$. The critical value is $t_0 = 1.860$.

$$\bar{d} = 2.0,\ s_d = 4.5$$

$$t = \frac{\bar{d} - \mu_d}{s_d/\sqrt{n}} = \frac{2.0 - 0}{4.5/\sqrt{9}} = 1.33$$

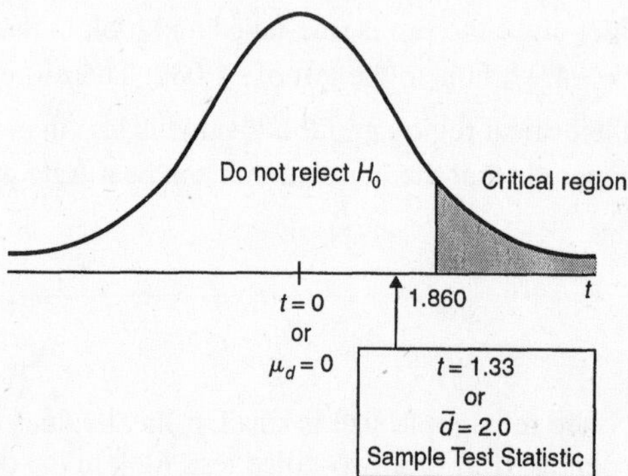

To find the P value interval, use the α' values since the test is one-tailed and look in the row headed by $d.f. = 8$. We find that the sample t value, $t = 1.33$, falls between 1.240 and 1.397. Therefore, $0.100 < P$ value < 0.125.

Since the sample test statistic falls outside the critical region and the P value is greater than the level of significance, $\alpha = 0.05$, we do not reject H_0. There is insufficient evidence to conclude that the population mean score on the last round is significantly higher than the population mean score on the first round.

14. $H_0: \mu_d = 0$

$H_1: \mu_d > 0$

Since > is in H_1, a right-tailed test is used. Since the sample size is small, critical values are found using the Student's t distribution (use Table 6 in Appendix II). For a one-tailed test, look in the column headed by $\alpha' = 0.05$ and the row headed by $d.f. = 6 - 1 = 5$. The critical value is $t_0 = 2.015$.

$$\bar{d} = 0.4,\ s_d = 0.447$$

$$t = \frac{\bar{d} - \mu_d}{s_d/\sqrt{n}} = \frac{0.4 - 0}{0.447/\sqrt{6}} = 2.192$$

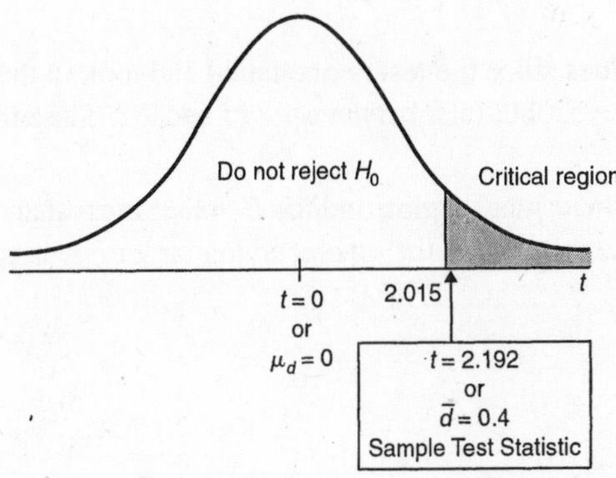

To find the P value interval, use the α' values since the test is one-tailed and look in the row headed by $d.f. = 5$. We find that the sample t value, $t = 2.192$, falls between 2.015 and 2.571. Therefore, $0.025 < P$ value < 0.050.

Since the sample test statistic falls inside the critical region and the P value is less than the level of significance, $\alpha = 0.05$, we reject H_0. We conclude that the rats receiving larger rewards tend to run the maze in less time.

15. $H_0: \mu_d = 0$

$H_1: \mu_d > 0$

Since > is in H_1, a right-tailed test is used. Since the sample size is small, critical values are found using the Student's t distribution (use Table 6 in Appendix II). For a one-tailed test, look in the column headed by $\alpha' = 0.05$ and the row headed by $d.f. = 8 - 1 = 7$. The critical value is $t_0 = 1.895$.

$$\bar{d} = 0.775,\ s_d = 1.0539$$

$$t = \frac{\bar{d} - \mu_d}{s_d/\sqrt{n}} = \frac{0.775 - 0}{1.0539/\sqrt{8}} = 2.080$$

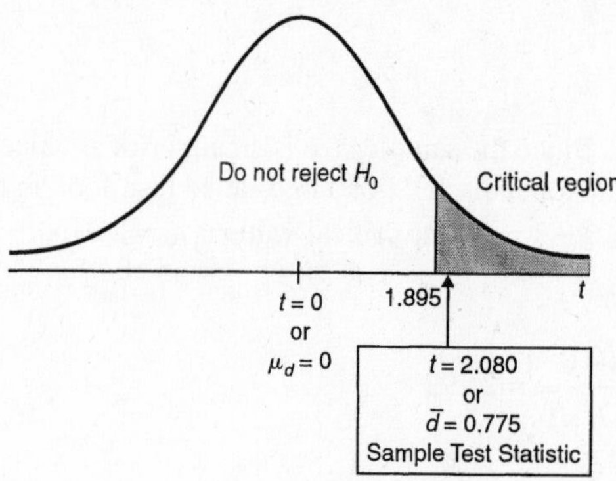

To find the P value interval, use the α' values since the test is one-tailed and look in the row headed by $d.f. = 7$. We find that the sample t value, $t = 2.080$, falls between 1.895 and 2.365. Therefore, $0.025 < P$ value < 0.050.

Since the sample test statistic falls inside the critical region and the P value is less than the level of significance, $\alpha = 0.05$, we reject H_0. We conclude that the rats receiving larger rewards tend to perform the ladder climb in less time.

16. $H_0: \mu_d = 0$

$H_1: \mu_d \neq 0$

Since $\neq$ is in H_1, a two-tailed test is used. Since the sample size is small, critical values are found using the Student's t distribution (use Table 6 in Appendix II). For a two-tailed test, look in the column headed by $\alpha'' = 0.05$ and the row headed by $d.f. = 9 - 1 = 8$. The critical values are $t_0 = \pm 2.306$.

$$\bar{d} = 0.1111, \quad s_d = 5.2784$$

$$t = \frac{\bar{d} - \mu_d}{s_d/\sqrt{n}} = \frac{0.1111 - 0}{5.2784/\sqrt{9}} = 0.0631$$

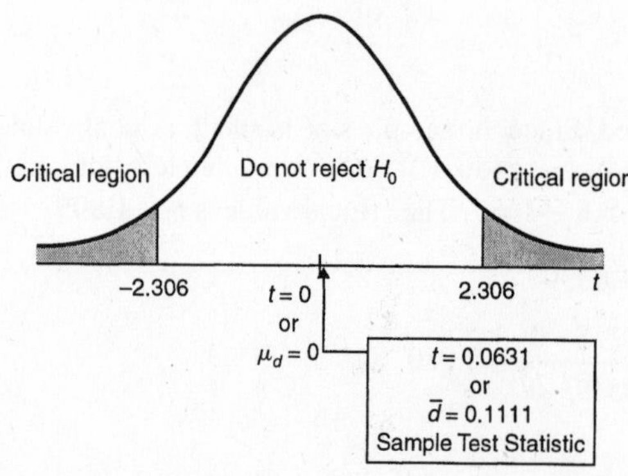

To find the P value interval, use the α'' values since the test is two-tailed and look in the row headed by $d.f. = 8$. We find that the sample t value, $t = 0.0631$, falls to the left of 1.240. Therefore, P value > 0.250.

Since the sample test statistic falls outside the critical region and the P value is greater than the level of significance, $\alpha = 0.05$, we do not reject H_0. There is insufficient evidence to conclude that there is a difference in the population mean of male versus female assistant professors.

Section 9.7

1. H_0: $\mu_1 = \mu_2$

H_1: $\mu_1 > \mu_2$

Since > is in H_1, a right-tailed test is used. Since the samples are both large, we use the normal distribution and approximate σ_1^2 and σ_2^2 by s_1^2 and s_2^2, respectively. For $\alpha = 0.01$, the critical value is $z_0 = 2.33$.

$$\bar{x}_1 - \bar{x}_2 = 2.6 - 1.9 = 0.7$$

$$z = \frac{(\bar{x}_1 - \bar{x}_2) - (\mu_1 - \mu_2)}{\sqrt{\frac{\sigma_1^2}{n_1} + \frac{\sigma_2^2}{n_2}}} = \frac{0.7 - 0}{\sqrt{\frac{0.5^2}{33} + \frac{0.8^2}{32}}} = 4.22$$

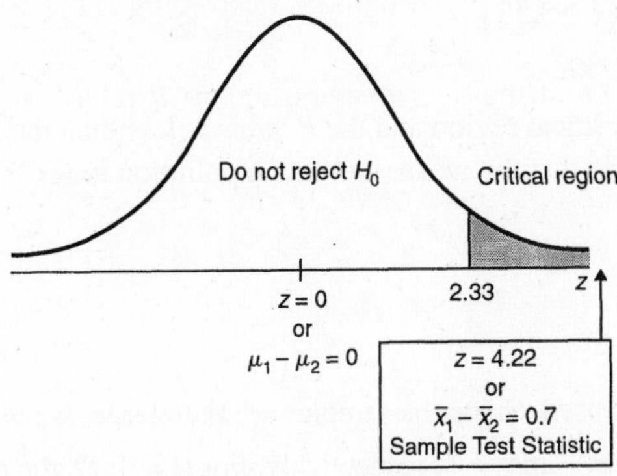

Next, find the P value associated with $z = 4.22$ and a one-tailed test.

$$P \text{ value} = P(z > 4.22) \approx 0$$

Since the sample z falls inside the critical region and the P value is less than the level of significance $\alpha = 0.01$, we reject H_0. We conclude that, on average, 10-year-old children have more REM sleep than do 35-year-old adults.

2. H_0: $\mu_1 = \mu_2$

H_1: $\mu_1 > \mu_2$

Since > is in H_1, a right-tailed test is used. Since the samples are both large, we use the normal distribution and approximate σ_1^2 and σ_2^2 by s_1^2 and s_2^2, respectively. For $\alpha = 0.01$, the critical value is $z_0 = 2.33$.

$$\bar{x}_1 - \bar{x}_2 = 43 - 30 = 13$$

$$z = \frac{(\bar{x}_1 - \bar{x}_2) - (\mu_1 - \mu_2)}{\sqrt{\frac{\sigma_1^2}{n_1} + \frac{\sigma_2^2}{n_2}}} = \frac{13 - 0}{\sqrt{\frac{22^2}{45} + \frac{12^2}{47}}} = 3.50$$

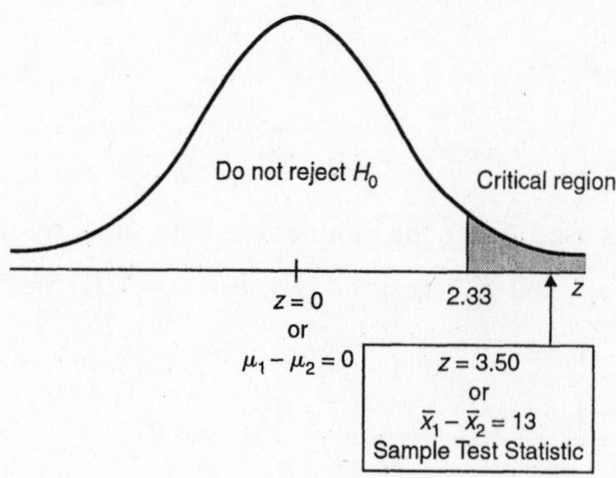

Next, find the P value associated with $z = 3.50$ and a one-tailed test.

$$P \text{ value} = P(z \geq 3.50)$$
$$< 0.0002$$

Since the sample z falls inside the critical region and the P value is less than the level of significance $\alpha = 0.01$, we reject H_0. We conclude that the mean population pollution index for Englewood is less than that for Denver in the winter.

3. $H_0: \mu_1 = \mu_2$
   $H_1: \mu_1 \neq \mu_2$

   Since $\neq$ is in H_1, a two-tailed test is used. Since the samples are both large, we use the normal distribution and approximate σ_1^2 and σ_2^2 by s_1^2 and s_2^2, respectively. For $\alpha = 0.01$, the critical values are $z_0 = \pm 2.58$.

$$\bar{x}_1 - \bar{x}_2 = 4.7 - 4.2 = 0.5$$

$$z = \frac{(\bar{x}_1 - \bar{x}_2) - (\mu_1 - \mu_2)}{\sqrt{\frac{\sigma_1^2}{n_1} + \frac{\sigma_2^2}{n_2}}} = \frac{0.5 - 0}{\sqrt{\frac{1.1^2}{201} + \frac{1.4^2}{135}}} = 3.49$$

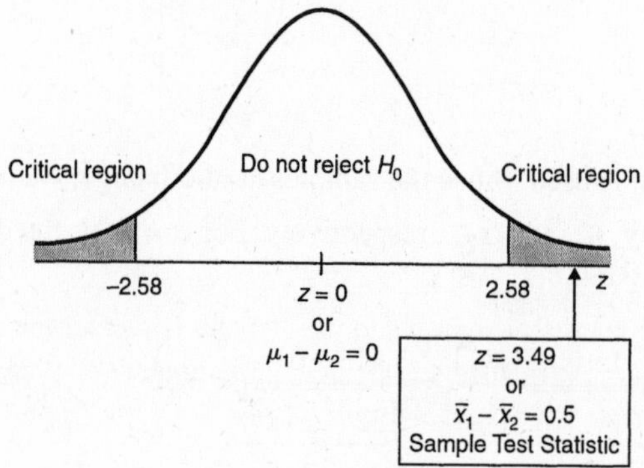

Next, find the P value associated with $z = 3.49$ and a two-tailed test.

$$\begin{aligned} P \text{ value} &= 2P(z \geq 3.49) \\ &= 2(1-0.9998) \\ &= 2(0.0002) \\ &= 0.0004 \end{aligned}$$

Since the sample z falls inside the critical region and the P value is less than the level of significance $\alpha = 0.01$, we reject H_0. We conclude that a difference exists regarding preference for camping or preference for fishing as an outdoor activity.

4. $H_0: \mu_1 = \mu_2$

$H_1: \mu_1 > \mu_2$

Since > is in H_1, a right-tailed test is used. Since the samples are both large, we use the normal distribution and approximate σ_1^2 and σ_2^2 by s_1^2 and s_2^2, respectively. For $\alpha = 0.01$, the critical value is $z_0 = 2.33$.

$$\bar{x}_1 - \bar{x}_2 = 4.3 - 4.0 = 0.3$$

$$z = \frac{(\bar{x}_1 - \bar{x}_2) - (\mu_1 - \mu_2)}{\sqrt{\frac{\sigma_1^2}{n_1} + \frac{\sigma_2^2}{n_2}}} = \frac{0.3 - 0}{\sqrt{\frac{1.3^2}{122} + \frac{1.3^2}{104}}} = 1.73$$

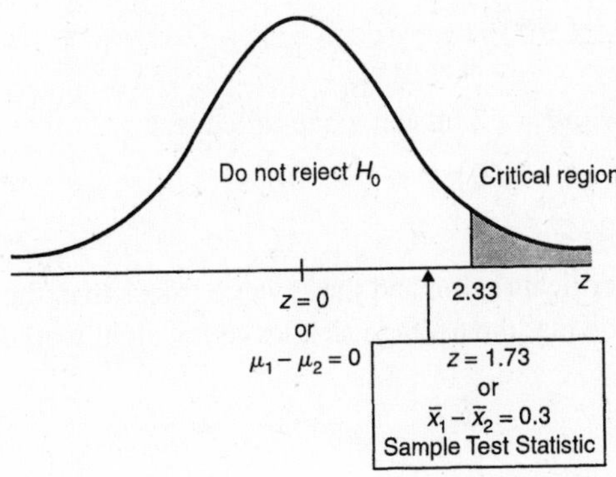

Next, find the P value associated with $z = 1.73$ and a one-tailed test.

$$\begin{aligned} P \text{ value} &= P(z \geq 1.73) \\ &= 1 - 0.9582 \\ &= 0.0418 \end{aligned}$$

Since the sample z falls outside the critical region and the P value is greater than the level of significance $\alpha = 0.01$, we do not reject H_0. There is insufficient evidence to conclude that the population mean preference for lake fishing is greater than the population mean preference for stream fishing.

5. $H_0\colon \mu_1 = \mu_2$

$H_1\colon \mu_1 < \mu_2$

Since < is in H_1, a left-tailed test is used. Since the samples are both large, we use the normal distribution and approximate σ_1^2 and σ_2^2 by s_1^2 and s_2^2, respectively. For $\alpha = 0.05$, the critical value is $z_0 = -1.645$.

$$\bar{x}_1 - \bar{x}_2 = 10.6 - 12.9 = -2.3$$

$$z = \frac{(\bar{x}_1 - \bar{x}_2) - (\mu_1 - \mu_2)}{\sqrt{\frac{\sigma_1^2}{n_1} + \frac{\sigma_2^2}{n_2}}} = \frac{-2.3 - 0}{\sqrt{\frac{3.3^2}{38} + \frac{4.5^2}{41}}} = -2.60$$

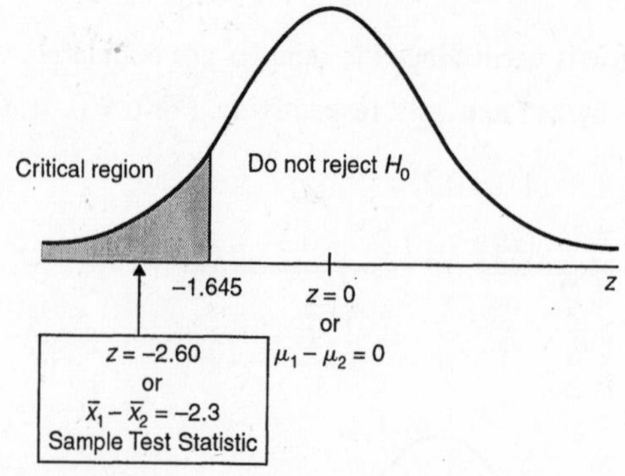

Next, find the P value associated with $z = -2.60$ and a one-tailed test.

$$P \text{ value} = P(z \le -2.60)$$
$$= 0.0047$$

Since the sample z falls inside the critical region and the P value is less than the level of significance $\alpha = 0.05$, we reject H_0. We conclude that the average sick leave for night workers is more than that for day workers.

6. $H_0\colon \mu_1 = \mu_2$

$H_1\colon \mu_1 \ne \mu_2$

Since ≠ is in H_1, a two-tailed test is used. Since the samples are both large, we use the normal distribution and approximate σ_1^2 and σ_2^2 by s_1^2 and s_2^2, respectively. For $\alpha = 0.01$, the critical values are $\pm z_0 = \pm 2.58$.

$$\bar{x}_1 - \bar{x}_2 = 4.7 - 5.1 = -0.4$$

$$z = \frac{(\bar{x}_1 - \bar{x}_2) - (\mu_1 - \mu_2)}{\sqrt{\frac{\sigma_1^2}{n_1} + \frac{\sigma_2^2}{n_2}}} = \frac{-0.4 - 0}{\sqrt{\frac{2.1^2}{53} + \frac{2.5^2}{46}}} = -0.85$$

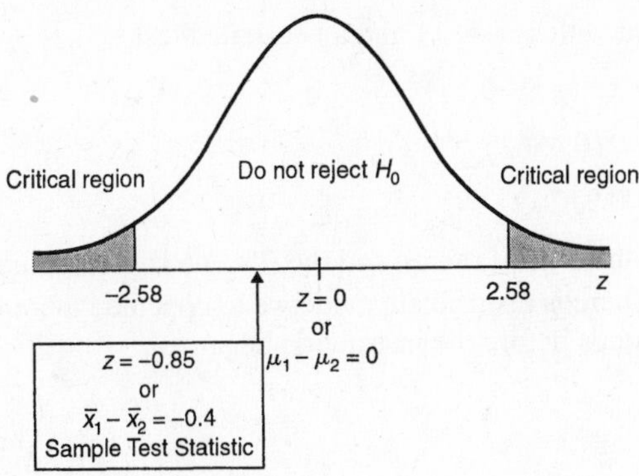

Next, find the P value associated with $z = -0.85$ and a two-tailed test.

$$\begin{aligned} P \text{ value} &= 2P(z \le -0.85) \\ &= 2(0.1977) \\ &= 0.3954 \end{aligned}$$

Since the sample z falls outside the critical region and the P value is greater than the level of significance $\alpha = 0.01$, we do not reject H_0. There is insufficient evidence to conclude that a difference exists between student opinion and community opinion about this bill.

7. H_0: $\mu_1 = \mu_2$

H_1: $\mu_1 \ne \mu_2$

Since $\ne$ is in H_1, a two-tailed test is used. Since the samples are both large, we use the normal distribution and approximate $\sigma_1{}^2$ and $\sigma_2{}^2$ by $s_1{}^2$ and $s_2{}^2$, respectively. For $\alpha = 0.05$, the critical values are $z_0 = 1.96$.

$$\bar{x}_1 - \bar{x}_2 = 344.5 - 345.9 = -1.4$$

$$z = \frac{(\bar{x}_1 - \bar{x}_2) - (\mu_1 - \mu_2)}{\sqrt{\frac{\sigma_1^2}{n_1} + \frac{\sigma_2^2}{n_2}}} = \frac{-1.4 - 0}{\sqrt{\frac{49.1^2}{30} + \frac{50.9^2}{30}}} = -0.11$$

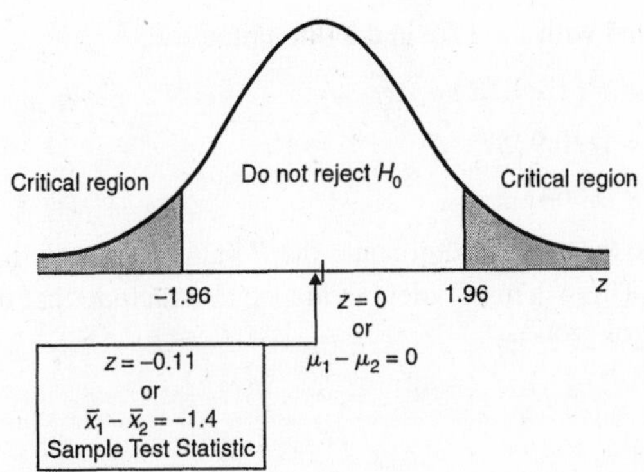

Next, find the P value associated with $z = -0.11$ and a two-tailed test.

$$\begin{aligned} P \text{ value} &= 2P(z \le -0.11) \\ &= 2(0.4562) \\ &= 0.9124 \end{aligned}$$

Since the sample z falls outside the critical region and the P value is greater than the level of significance $\alpha = 0.05$, we do not reject H_0. There is insufficient evidence to conclude there is a difference in the vocabulary scores of the two groups before the instruction began.

8. H_0: $\mu_1 = \mu_2$

H_1: $\mu_1 > \mu_2$

Let Group 1 be the experimental group and group 2 be the control group as in problem 7 above. Since > is in H_1, a right-tailed test is used. Since the samples are both large, we use the normal distribution and approximate $\sigma_1{}^2$ and $\sigma_2{}^2$ by $s_1{}^2$ and $s_2{}^2$, respectively. For $\alpha = 0.01$, the critical value is $z_0 = 2.33$.

$$\bar{x}_1 - \bar{x}_2 = 368.4 - 349.2 = 19.2$$

$$z = \frac{(\bar{x}_1 - \bar{x}_2) - (\mu_1 - \mu_2)}{\sqrt{\frac{\sigma_1^2}{n_1} + \frac{\sigma_2^2}{n_2}}} = \frac{19.2 - 0}{\sqrt{\frac{39.5^2}{30} + \frac{56.6^2}{30}}} = 1.52$$

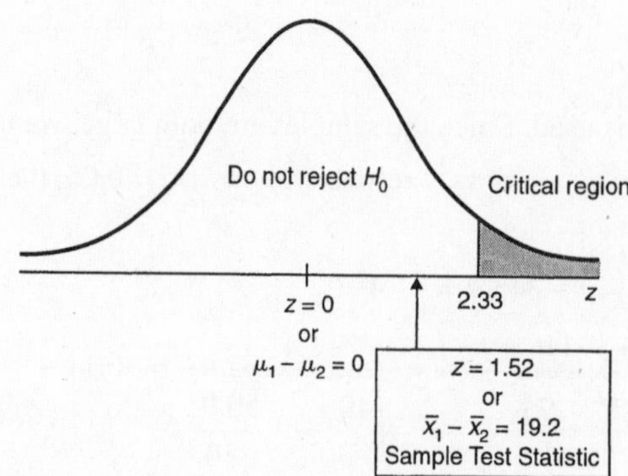

Next, find the P value associated with $z = 1.52$ and a one-tailed test.

$$\begin{aligned} P \text{ value} &= P(z \ge 1.52) \\ &= 1 - 0.9357 \\ &= 0.0643 \end{aligned}$$

Since the sample z falls outside the critical region and the P value is greater than the level of significance $\alpha = 0.01$, we do not reject H_0. There is insufficient evidence to conclude that the experimental group performed better than the control group.

9. (a) The means and standard deviations round to the results given.

(b) H_0: $\mu_1 = \mu_2$

H_1: $\mu_1 \neq \mu_2$

Since $\neq$ is in H_1, a two-tailed test is used. Since the samples are both small, we use the Student's t distribution. For $\alpha'' = 0.05$ and $d.f. = 16 + 15 - 2 = 29$, the critical values are $t_0 = \pm 2.045$.

$$s = \sqrt{\frac{(n_1-1)s_1^2 + (n_2-1)s_2^2}{n_1+n_2-2}} = \sqrt{\frac{15(2.82)^2 + 14(2.43)^2}{16+15-2}} = 2.6389$$

$$\bar{x}_1 - \bar{x}_2 = 4.75 - 3.93 = 0.82$$

$$t = \frac{(\bar{x}_1 - \bar{x}_2) - (\mu_1 - \mu_2)}{s\sqrt{\frac{1}{n_1} + \frac{1}{n_2}}} = \frac{0.82 - 0}{2.6389\sqrt{\frac{1}{16} + \frac{1}{15}}} = 0.865$$

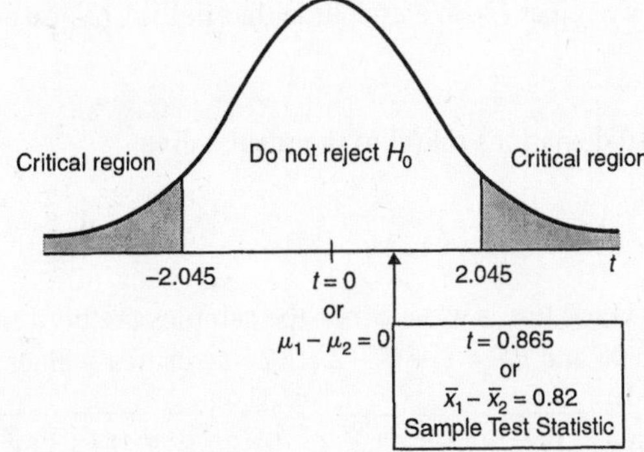

Next, find the P value interval using the α'' values and the row headed by $d.f. = 29$. We find the sample t value, $t = 0.85$, falls to the left of 1.174. Therefore, P value > 0.250.

Since the sample test statistic falls outside the critical region and the P value is greater than the level of significance $\alpha = 0.05$, we do not reject H_0. There is insufficient evidence to conclude a difference exists in the mean number of cases of fox rabies between the two regions.

10. (a) The means and standard deviations round to the results given.

(b) H_0: $\mu_1 = \mu_2$

H_1: $\mu_1 > \mu_2$

Since $>$ is in H_1, a right-tailed test is used. Since the samples are both small, we use the Student's t distribution. For $\alpha' = 0.05$ and $d.f. = 14 + 15 - 2 = 27$, the critical value is $t_0 = 1.703$.

$$s = \sqrt{\frac{(n_1-1)s_1^2 + (n_2-1)s_2^2}{n_1+n_2-2}} = \sqrt{\frac{13(2.39)^2 + 14(2.44)^2}{14+15-2}} = 2.416$$

$$\bar{x}_1 - \bar{x}_2 = 12.53 - 10.65 = 1.88$$

$$t = \frac{(\bar{x}_1 - \bar{x}_2) - (\mu_1 - \mu_2)}{s\sqrt{\frac{1}{n_1} + \frac{1}{n_2}}} = \frac{1.88 - 0}{2.416\sqrt{\frac{1}{14} + \frac{1}{15}}} = 2.09$$

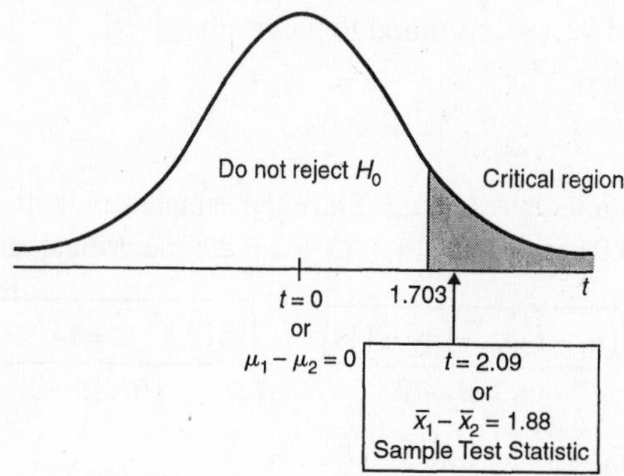

Next, find the P value interval using the α' values and the row headed by $d.f. = 27$. We find the sample t value, $t = 2.09$, falls between 2.052 and 2.473. Therefore, $0.010 < P \text{ value} < 0.025$.

Since the sample test statistic falls inside the critical region and the P value is less than the level of significance $\alpha = 0.05$, we reject H_0. We conclude that field A has on average higher soil water content than field B.

11. (a) The means and standard deviations round to the results given.

(b) H_0: $\mu_1 = \mu_2$

H_1: $\mu_1 \neq \mu_2$

Since $\neq$ is in H_1, a two-tailed test is used. Since the samples are both small, we use the Student's t distribution. For $\alpha'' = 0.05$ and $d.f. = 7 + 7 - 2 = 12$, the critical values are $t_0 = \pm 2.179$.

$$s = \sqrt{\frac{(n_1 - 1)s_1^2 + (n_2 - 1)s_2^2}{n_1 + n_2 - 2}} = \sqrt{\frac{6(3.18)^2 + 6(4.11)^2}{7 + 7 - 2}} = 3.6745$$

$$\bar{x}_1 - \bar{x}_2 = 4.86 - 4.71 = 0.15$$

$$t = \frac{(\bar{x}_1 - \bar{x}_2) - (\mu_1 - \mu_2)}{s\sqrt{\frac{1}{n_1} + \frac{1}{n_2}}} = \frac{0.15 - 0}{3.6745\sqrt{\frac{1}{7} + \frac{1}{7}}} = 0.0764$$

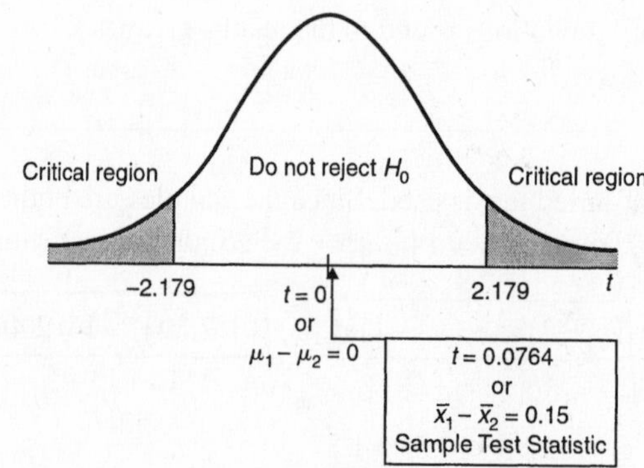

Next, find the P value interval using the α'' values and the row headed by $d.f. = 12$. We find the sample t value, $t = 0.0764$, falls to the left of 1.209. Therefore, $P \text{ value} > 0.250$.

Since the sample test statistic falls outside the critical region and the P value is greater than the level of significance $\alpha = 0.05$, we do not reject H_0. There is insufficient evidence to conclude that the population mean time lost for hot tempers is different from that lost due to disputes.

12. (a) The means and standard deviations round to the results given.

(b) $H_0: \mu_1 = \mu_2$

$H_1: \mu_1 < \mu_2$

Since < is in H_1, a left-tailed test is used. Since the samples are both small, we use the Student's t distribution. For $\alpha' = 0.05$ and $d.f. = 7 + 7 - 2 = 12$, the critical value is $t_0 = -1.782$.

$$s = \sqrt{\frac{(n_1-1)s_1^2+(n_2-1)s_2^2}{n_1+n_2-2}} = \sqrt{\frac{6(2.38)^2+6(2.69)^2}{7+7-2}} = 2.5397$$

$$\bar{x}_1 - \bar{x}_2 = 4.00 - 4.29 = -0.29$$

$$t = \frac{(\bar{x}_1-\bar{x}_2)-(\mu_1-\mu_2)}{s\sqrt{\frac{1}{n_1}+\frac{1}{n_2}}} = \frac{-0.29-0}{2.5397\sqrt{\frac{1}{7}+\frac{1}{7}}} = -0.214$$

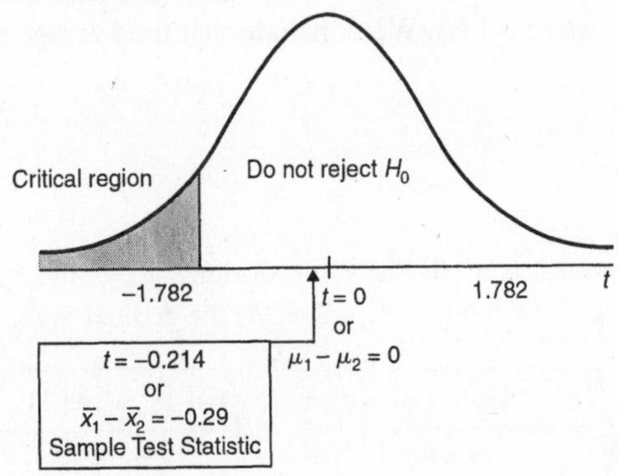

Next, find the P value interval using the α' values and the row headed by $d.f. = 12$. We find the sample t value, $t = -0.214$, falls to the right of -1.209. Therefore, P value > 0.125.

Since the sample test statistic falls outside the critical region and the P value is greater than the level of significance $\alpha = 0.05$, we fail to reject H_0. There is insufficient evidence to conclude that the population mean time lost due to stressors is greater than the population mean time lost due to intimidators.

13. (a)-(b) The means and standard deviations round to the results given.

(c) $H_0: \mu_1 = \mu_2$

$H_1: \mu_1 < \mu_2$

Since < is in H_1, a left-tailed test is used. Since the samples are both small, we use the Student's t distribution. For $\alpha' = 0.05$ and $d.f. = 10 + 12 - 2 = 20$, the critical value is $t_0 = -1.725$.

$$s = \sqrt{\frac{(n_1-1)s_1^2+(n_2-1)s_2^2}{n_1+n_2-2}} = \sqrt{\frac{9(2.7)^2+11(2.5)^2}{10+12-2}} = 2.592$$

$$\bar{x}_1 - \bar{x}_2 = 7.2 - 10.8 = -3.6$$

$$t = \frac{(\bar{x}_1-\bar{x}_2)-(\mu_1-\mu_2)}{s\sqrt{\frac{1}{n_1}+\frac{1}{n_2}}} = \frac{-3.6-0}{2.592\sqrt{\frac{1}{10}+\frac{1}{12}}} = -3.244$$

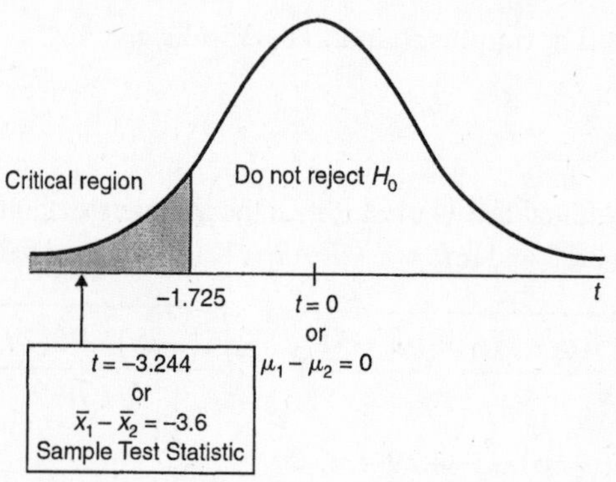

Next, find the P value interval using the α' values and the row headed by $d.f. = 20$. We find the sample t value, $t = -3.244$, falls to the left of -2.845. Therefore, P value < 0.005.

Since the sample test statistic falls inside the critical region and the P value is less than the level of significance $\alpha = 0.05$, we reject H_0. We conclude that the average change in water temperature has increased.

14. $H_0: \mu_1 = \mu_2$

$H_1: \mu_1 < \mu_2$

Since < is in H_1, a left-tailed test is used. Since the samples are both small, we use the Student's t distribution. For $\alpha' = 0.01$ and $d.f. = 11 + 15 - 2 = 24$, the critical value is $t_0 = -2.492$.

$$s = \sqrt{\frac{(n_1-1)s_1^2 + (n_2-1)s_2^2}{n_1+n_2-2}} = \sqrt{\frac{10(9)^2 + 14(7)^2}{11+15-2}} = 7.895$$

$$\bar{x}_1 - \bar{x}_2 = 76 - 82 = -6$$

$$t = \frac{(\bar{x}_1 - \bar{x}_2) - (\mu_1 - \mu_2)}{s\sqrt{\frac{1}{n_1} + \frac{1}{n_2}}} = \frac{-6-0}{7.895\sqrt{\frac{1}{11} + \frac{1}{15}}} = -1.914$$

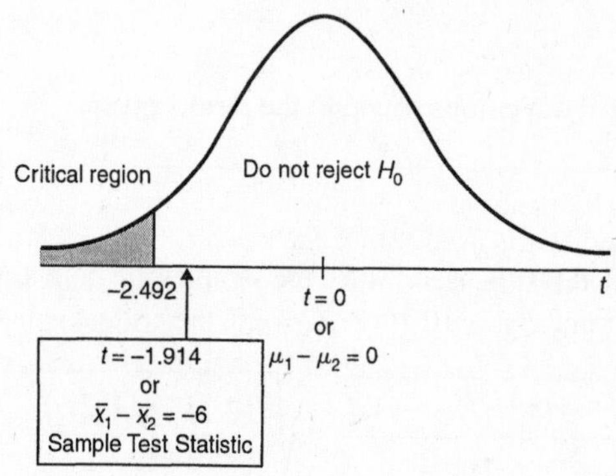

Next, find the P value interval using the α' values and the row headed by $d.f. = 24$. We find the sample t value, $t = -1.914$, falls between -1.711 and -2.064. Therefore, $0.025 < P$ value < 0.050.

Since the sample test statistic falls outside the critical region and the P value is greater than the level of significance $\alpha = 0.01$, we do not reject H_0. We have insufficient evidence to conclude that airplane pilots are less susceptible to perceptual illusions than the general population.

15. (a)-(b) The means and standard deviations round to the results given.

(c) $H_0: \mu_1 = \mu_2$

$H_1: \mu_1 \neq \mu_2$

Since $\neq$ is in H_1, a two-tailed test is used. Since the samples are both small, we use the Student's t distribution. For $\alpha'' = 0.01$ and $d.f. = 7 + 7 - 2 = 12$, the critical values are $t_0 = \pm 3.055$.

$$s = \sqrt{\frac{(n_1-1)s_1^2 + (n_2-1)s_2^2}{n_1+n_2-2}} = \sqrt{\frac{6(10.47)^2 + 6(10.78)^2}{7+7-2}} = 10.626$$

$$\bar{x}_1 - \bar{x}_2 = 72 - 77.7 = -5.7$$

$$t = \frac{(\bar{x}_1 - \bar{x}_2) - (\mu_1 - \mu_2)}{s\sqrt{\frac{1}{n_1} + \frac{1}{n_2}}} = \frac{-5.7 - 0}{10.626\sqrt{\frac{1}{7} + \frac{1}{7}}} = -1.004$$

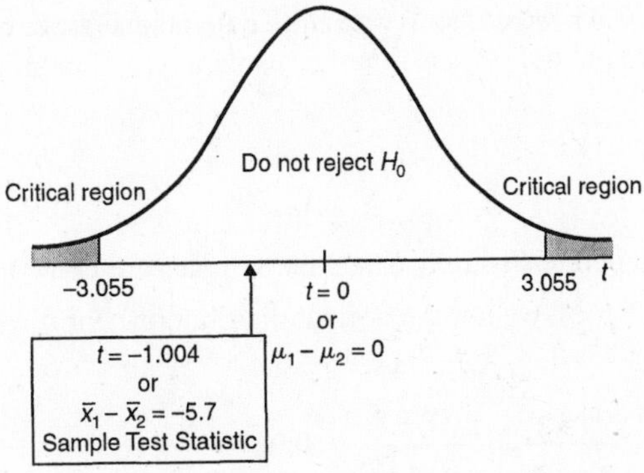

Next, find the P value interval using the α'' values and the row headed by $d.f. = 12$. We find the sample t value, $t = -1.004$, falls to the right of -1.209. Therefore, P value > 0.250.

Since the sample test statistic falls outside the critical region and the P value is greater than the level of significance $\alpha = 0.01$, we do not reject H_0. There is not sufficient evidence to conclude that the average number of emergency calls during the day differs from the average number at night.

16. (a)-(b) The means and standard deviations round to the results given.

(b) $H_0: \mu_1 = \mu_2$

$H_1: \mu_1 < \mu_2$

Since $<$ is in H_1, a left-tailed test is used. Since the samples are both small, we use the Student's t distribution. For $\alpha' = 0.05$ and $d.f. = 6 + 6 - 2 = 10$, the critical value is $t_0 = -1.812$.

$$s = \sqrt{\frac{(n_1-1)s_1^2 + (n_2-1)s_2^2}{n_1+n_2-2}} = \sqrt{\frac{5(2.8)^2 + 5(2.8)^2}{6+6-2}} = 2.8$$

$$\bar{x}_1 - \bar{x}_2 = 12.2 - 15.0 = -2.8$$

$$t = \frac{(\bar{x}_1 - \bar{x}_2) - (\mu_1 - \mu_2)}{s\sqrt{\frac{1}{n_1} + \frac{1}{n_2}}} = \frac{-2.8 - 0}{2.8\sqrt{\frac{1}{6} + \frac{1}{6}}} = -1.732$$

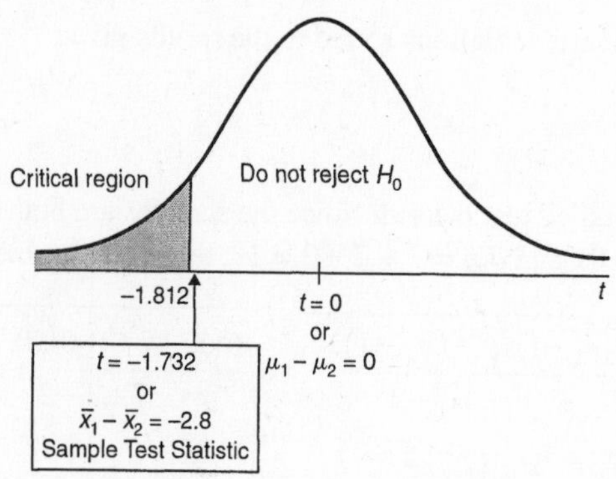

Next, find the P value interval using the α' values and the row headed by $d.f. = 10$. We find the sample t value, $t = -1.732$, falls between -1.559 and -1.812. Therefore, $0.050 < P \text{ value} < 0.075$.

Since the sample test statistic falls outside the critical region and the P value is greater than the level of significance $\alpha = 0.05$, we do not reject H_0. There is insufficient evidence to conclude that it takes longer on average to put out the gasoline fire using a type II extinguisher.

17. $H_0: p_1 = p_2$

$H_1: p_1 \neq p_2$

Since $\neq$ is in H_1, a two-tailed test is used. Since the samples are both large ($n_2\hat{p} = 8.7807 > 5$ so $n_1\hat{p}$, $n_1\hat{q}$, and $n_2\hat{q}$ are > 5 too), we use the normal distribution. For $\alpha = 0.01$, the critical values are $z_0 = \pm 2.58$.

$$\hat{p} = \frac{r_1 + r_2}{n_1 + n_2} = \frac{12+7}{153+128} = 0.0676$$

$$\hat{q} = 1 - \hat{p} = 1 - 0.0676 = 0.9324$$

$$\hat{p}_1 - \hat{p}_2 = \frac{r_1}{n_1} - \frac{r_2}{n_2} = \frac{12}{153} - \frac{7}{128} = 0.0237$$

$$z = \frac{(\hat{p}_1 - \hat{p}_2) - (p_1 - p_2)}{\sqrt{\frac{\hat{p}\hat{q}}{n_1} + \frac{\hat{p}\hat{q}}{n_2}}} = \frac{0.0237 - 0}{\sqrt{\frac{0.0676(0.9324)}{153} + \frac{0.0676(0.9324)}{128}}} = 0.79$$

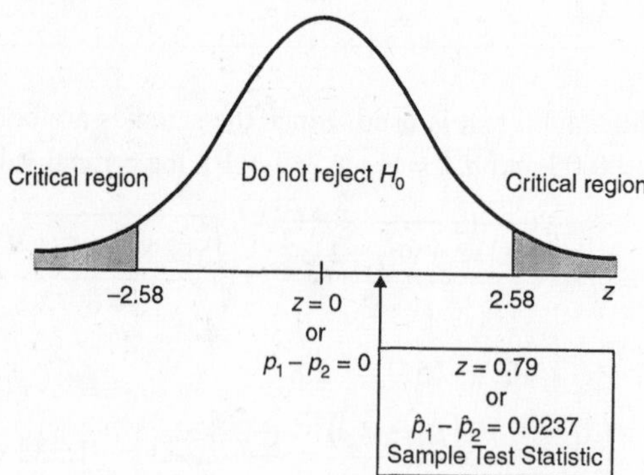

Next, find the P value associated with $z = -0.79$ and a two-tailed test.

$$\begin{aligned} P \text{ value} &= 2P(z \geq 0.79) \\ &= 2(1-0.7852) \\ &= 2(0.2148) \\ &= 0.4296 \end{aligned}$$

Since the sample z falls outside the critical region and the P value is greater than the level of significance $\alpha = 0.01$, we do not reject H_0. There is insufficient evidence to conclude that the population proportions of high school dropouts are different.

18. $H_0: p_1 = p_2$

$H_1: p_1 < p_2$

Since < is in H_1, a left-tailed test is used. Since the samples are both large ($n_2\hat{q} = 216(0.4722) = 101.9952 > 5$ so $n_1\hat{p}$, $n_1\hat{q}$, and $n_2\hat{p}$ are > 5), we use the normal distribution. For $\alpha = 0.05$, the critical value is $z_0 = -1.645$.

$$\hat{p} = \frac{r_1 + r_2}{n_1 + n_2} = \frac{141+125}{288+216} = 0.5278$$

$$\hat{q} = 1 - \hat{p} = 1 - 0.5278 = 0.4722$$

$$\hat{p}_1 - \hat{p}_2 = \frac{r_1}{n_1} - \frac{r_2}{n_2} = \frac{141}{288} - \frac{125}{216} = -0.0891$$

$$z = \frac{(\hat{p}_1 - \hat{p}_2) - (p_1 - p_2)}{\sqrt{\frac{\hat{p}\hat{q}}{n_1} + \frac{\hat{p}\hat{q}}{n_2}}} = \frac{-0.0891 - 0}{\sqrt{\frac{0.5278(0.4722)}{288} + \frac{0.5278(0.4722)}{216}}} = -1.98$$

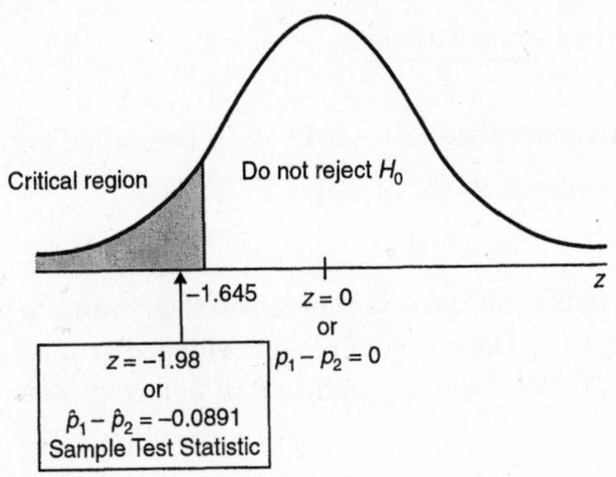

Next, find the P value associated with $z = -1.98$ and a one-tailed test.

$$\begin{aligned} P \text{ value} &= P(z \leq -1.98) \\ &= 0.0239 \end{aligned}$$

Since the sample z falls inside the critical region and the P value is less than the level of significance $\alpha = 0.01$, we reject H_0. We conclude that the population proportion of voter turnout in Colorado is higher than that in California.

19. Let p_1 = proportion who did not attend college and who believe in extraterrestrials and p_2 = proportion who did attend college and who believe in extraterrestrials.

$$H_0: p_1 = p_2$$
$$H_1: p_1 < p_2$$

Since < is in H_1, a left-tailed test is used. Since the samples are both large ($n_i \hat{p} = 100(0.42) = 42 > 5$ so $n_i \hat{q}$ is also > 5), we use the normal distribution. For $\alpha = 0.05$, the critical value is $z_0 = -2.33$.

$$\hat{p} = \frac{r_1 + r_2}{n_1 + n_2} = \frac{37 + 47}{100 + 100} = 0.42$$

$$\hat{q} = 1 - \hat{p} = 1 - 0.42 = 0.58$$

$$\hat{p}_1 - \hat{p}_2 = \frac{r_1}{n_1} - \frac{r_2}{n_2} = \frac{37}{100} - \frac{47}{100} = -0.10$$

$$z = \frac{(\hat{p}_1 - \hat{p}_2) - (p_1 - p_2)}{\sqrt{\frac{\hat{p}\hat{q}}{n_1} + \frac{\hat{p}\hat{q}}{n_2}}} = \frac{-0.10 - 0}{\sqrt{\frac{0.42(0.58)}{100} + \frac{0.42(0.58)}{100}}} = -1.43$$

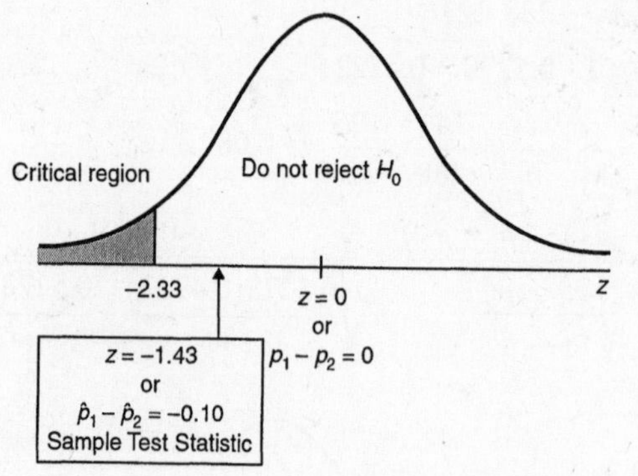

Next, find the P value associated with $z = -1.43$ and a one-tailed test.

$$P \text{ value} = P(z \le -1.43)$$
$$= 0.0764$$

Since the sample z falls outside the critical region and the P value is greater than the level of significance $\alpha = 0.01$, we do not reject H_0. There is not enough evidence to conclude that the proportion of believers who attended college is greater than the proportion of believers who did not attend college.

20. Let p_1 = proportion who would donate a loved one's organs and p_2 = proportion who would donate their own organs.

$$H_0: p_1 = p_2$$
$$H_1: p_1 > p_2$$

Since > is in H_1, a right-tailed test is used. Since the samples are both large ($n_i\hat{p} = 100(0.49) = 49 > 5$ so $n_i\hat{q}$ is also > 5), we use the normal distribution. For $\alpha = 0.01$, the critical value is $z_0 = 2.33$.

$$\hat{p} = \frac{r_1 + r_2}{n_1 + n_2} = \frac{78 + 20}{100 + 100} = 0.49$$

$$\hat{q} = 1 - \hat{p} = 1 - 0.49 = 0.51$$

$$\hat{p}_1 - \hat{p}_2 = \frac{r_1}{n_1} - \frac{r_2}{n_2} = \frac{78}{100} - \frac{20}{100} = 0.58$$

$$z = \frac{(\hat{p}_1 - \hat{p}_2) - (p_1 - p_2)}{\sqrt{\frac{\hat{p}\hat{q}}{n_1} + \frac{\hat{p}\hat{q}}{n_2}}} = \frac{0.58 - 0}{\sqrt{\frac{0.49(0.51)}{100} + \frac{0.49(0.51)}{100}}} = 8.204$$

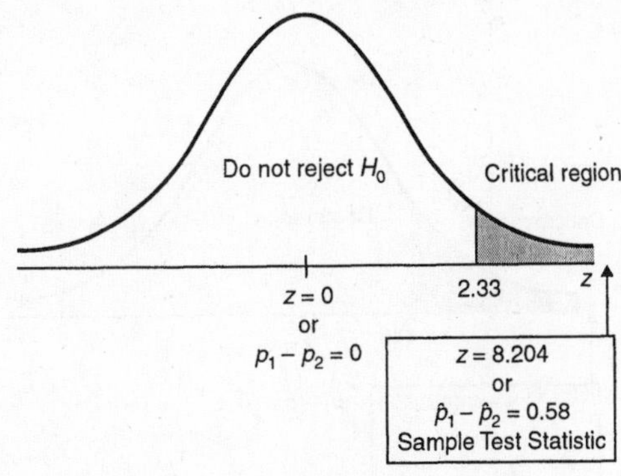

Next, find the P value associated with $z = 8.204$ and a one-tailed test.

$$P \text{ value} = P(z \geq 8.204)$$
$$\approx 0$$

Since the sample z falls inside the critical region and the P value is less than the level of significance $\alpha = 0.01$, we reject H_0. We conclude that the proportion of adult Americans who would donate a loved one's organs is higher than the proportion who would donate their own organs.

21. Let p_1 = proportion who requested nonsmoking rooms one year ago and p_2 = proportion who requested nonsmoking rooms recently.

$$H_0: p_1 = p_2$$
$$H_1: p_1 < p_2$$

Since < is in H_1, a left-tailed test is used. Since the samples are both large ($n_1\hat{q} = 378(0.5570) = 210.546 >$ 5 so $n_1\hat{p}$, $n_2\hat{p}$, and $n_2\hat{q}$ are > 5), we use the normal distribution. For $\alpha = -0.05$, the critical value is $z_0 = -1.645$.

$$\hat{p} = \frac{r_1 + r_2}{n_1 + n_2} = \frac{178 + 320}{378 + 516} = 0.5570$$

$$\hat{q} = 1 - \hat{p} = 1 - 0.5570 = 0.4430$$

$$\hat{p}_1 - \hat{p}_2 = \frac{r_1}{n_1} - \frac{r_2}{n_2} = \frac{178}{378} - \frac{320}{516} = -0.1493$$

$$z = \frac{(\hat{p}_1 - \hat{p}_2) - (p_1 - p_2)}{\sqrt{\frac{\hat{p}\hat{q}}{n_1} + \frac{\hat{p}\hat{q}}{n_2}}} = \frac{-0.1493 - 0}{\sqrt{\frac{0.5570(0.4430)}{378} + \frac{0.5570(0.4430)}{516}}} = -4.44$$

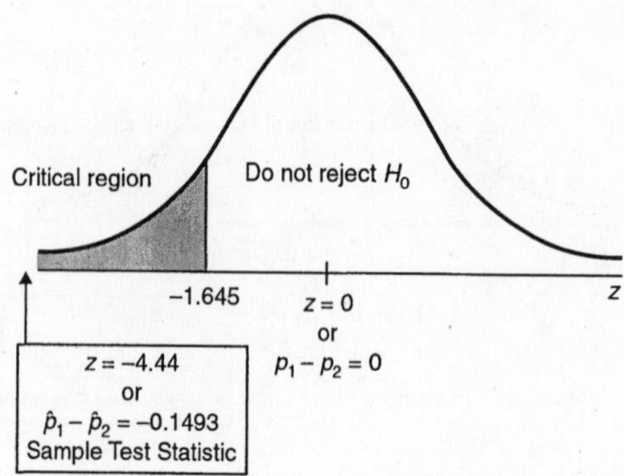

Next, find the P value associated with $z = -4.44$ and a one-tailed test.

$$P \text{ value} = P(z \le -4.44)$$
$$\approx 0$$

Since the sample z falls inside the critical region and the P value is less than the level of significance $\alpha = 0.05$, we reject H_0. We conclude that the population proportion of hotel guests requesting nonsmoking rooms has increased.

22. $H_0: p_1 = p_2$

$H_1: p_1 \neq p_2$

Since $\neq$ is in H_1, a two-tailed test is used. Since the samples are both large ($n_2\hat{p} = 326(0.0234) = 7.6284 > 5$ so $n_1\hat{p}$, $n_1\hat{q}$, and $n_2\hat{q}$ are > 5), we use the normal distribution. For $\alpha = 0.05$, the critical values are $z_0 = \pm 1.96$.

$$\hat{p} = \frac{r_1 + r_2}{n_1 + n_2} = \frac{10+8}{444+326} = 0.0234$$

$$\hat{q} = 1 - \hat{p} = 1 - 0.0234 = 0.9766$$

$$\hat{p}_1 - \hat{p}_2 = \frac{r_1}{n_1} - \frac{r_2}{n_2} = \frac{10}{444} - \frac{8}{326} = -0.0020$$

$$z = \frac{(\hat{p}_1 - \hat{p}_2) - (p_1 - p_2)}{\sqrt{\frac{\hat{p}\hat{q}}{n_1} + \frac{\hat{p}\hat{q}}{n_2}}} = \frac{-0.002 - 0}{\sqrt{\frac{0.0234(0.9766)}{444} + \frac{0.0234(0.9766)}{326}}} = -0.18$$

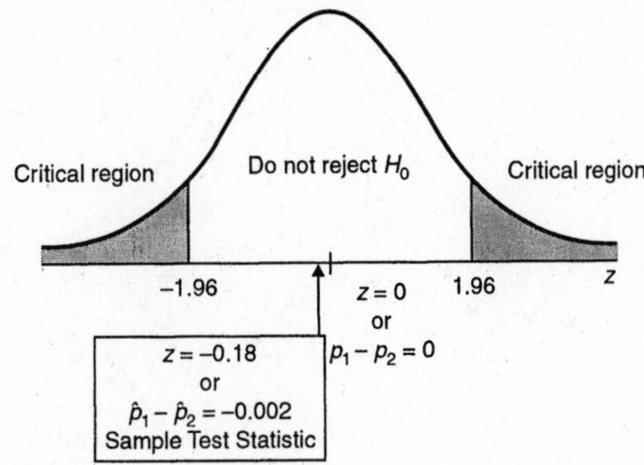

Next, find the P value associated with $z = -0.18$ and a two-tailed test.

$$\begin{aligned} P \text{ value} &= 2P(z \leq -0.18) \\ &= 2(0.4286) \\ &= 0.8572 \end{aligned}$$

Since the sample z falls outside the critical region and the P value is greater than the level of significance $\alpha = 0.05$, we do not reject H_0. We have insufficient evidence to conclude that the population proportions of this category of artifacts are different.

23. H_0: $p_1 = p_2$
H_1: $p_1 > p_2$

Since > is in H_1, a right-tailed test is used. Since the samples are both large ($n_2\hat{p} = 329(0.0405) = 13.3245 > 5$ so $n_1\hat{p}$, $n_1\hat{q}$, and $n_2\hat{q}$ are all > 5), we use the normal distribution. For $\alpha = 0.05$, the critical value is $z_0 = 1.645$.

$$\hat{p} = \frac{r_1 + r_2}{n_1 + n_2} = \frac{18+9}{338+329} = 0.0405$$

$$\hat{q} = 1 - \hat{p} = 1 - 0.0405 = 0.9595$$

$$\hat{p}_1 - \hat{p}_2 = \frac{r_1}{n_1} - \frac{r_2}{n_2} = \frac{18}{338} - \frac{9}{329} = 0.0259$$

$$z = \frac{(\hat{p}_1 - \hat{p}_2) - (p_1 - p_2)}{\sqrt{\frac{\hat{p}\hat{q}}{n_1} + \frac{\hat{p}\hat{q}}{n_2}}} = \frac{0.0259 - 0}{\sqrt{\frac{0.0405(0.9595)}{338} + \frac{0.0405(0.9595)}{329}}} = 1.70$$

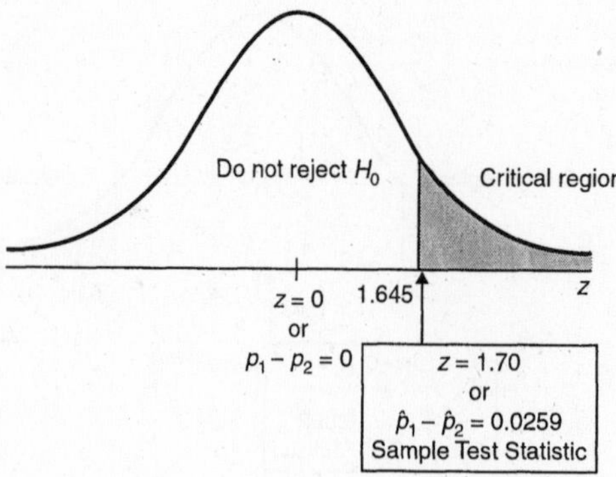

Next, find the P value associated with $z = 1.70$ and a one-tailed test.

$$\begin{aligned} P \text{ value} &= P(z \geq 1.70) \\ &= 1 - 0.9554 \\ &= 0.0446 \end{aligned}$$

Since the sample z falls inside the critical region and the P value is less than the level of significance $\alpha = 0.05$, we reject H_0. We conclude that the population proportion of such artifacts is higher in the general region around the first site.

Chapter 9 Review

1. We are testing a single mean with a large sample.

$$H_0: \mu = 11.1$$
$$H_1: \mu \neq 11.1$$

Since ≠ is in H_1, a two-tailed test is used. For $\alpha = 0.05$, the critical values are $z_0 = \pm 1.96$.

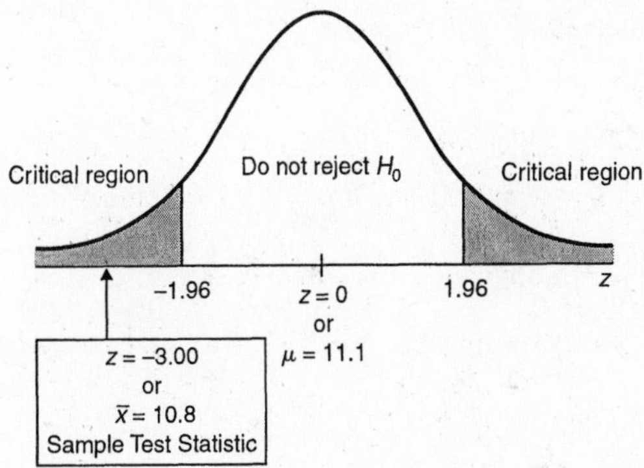

Next, find the P value associated with $z = -3.00$ and a two-tailed test.

$$\begin{aligned} P \text{ value} &= 2P(z \le -3.00) \\ &= 2(0.0013) \\ &= 0.0026 \end{aligned}$$

Since the sample z falls inside the critical region and the P value is less than $\alpha = 0.05$, we reject H_0. We conclude that the average number of miles driven per vehicle is different from the national average.

2. We are testing a single proportion with a large sample.

$$H_0: p = 0.35$$
$$H_1: p > 0.35$$

Since > is in H_1, a right-tailed test is used. For $\alpha = 0.05$, the critical value is $z_0 = 1.645$.

$$\hat{p} = \frac{r}{n} = \frac{39}{81} = 0.4815$$

$$z = \frac{\hat{p} - p}{\sqrt{\frac{pq}{n}}} = \frac{0.4815 - 0.35}{\sqrt{\frac{0.35(0.65)}{81}}} = 2.48$$

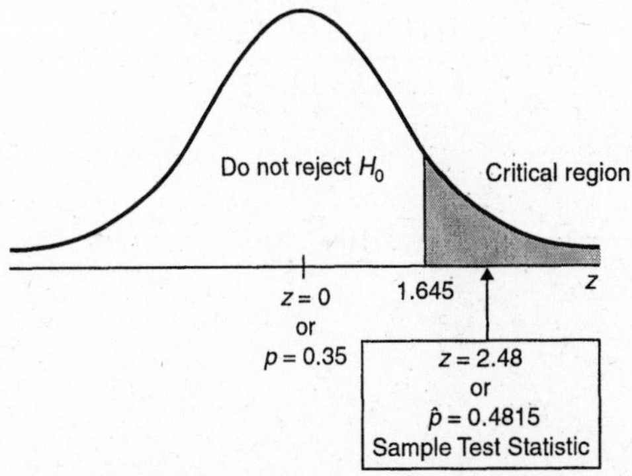

Next, find the P value associated with $z = 2.48$ and a one-tailed test.

$$\begin{aligned} P \text{ value} &= P(z \ge 2.48) \\ &= 0.0066 \end{aligned}$$

Since the sample z falls inside the critical region and the P value is less than $\alpha = 0.05$, we reject H_0. We conclude that more than 35% of the students have jobs.

3. We are testing a single mean with a small sample.

$$H_0: \mu = 0.8$$
$$H_1: \mu > 0.8$$

Since > is in H_1, a right-tailed test is used. For $\alpha' = 0.01$ and $d.f. = 9 - 1 = 8$, the critical value is $t_0 = 2.896$.

$$t = \frac{\bar{x} - \mu}{s/\sqrt{n}} = \frac{1.6 - 0.8}{0.41/\sqrt{9}} = 5.854$$

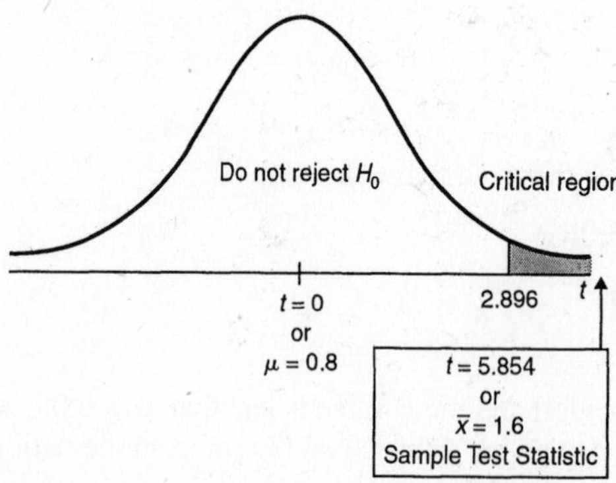

Next, find the P value interval using the α' values and the row headed by $d.f. = 8$. We find that the sample t value, $t = 5.854$, falls to the right of 3.355. Therefore, $P < 0.005$.

Since the sample t falls inside the critical region and the P value is less than $\alpha = 0.01$, we reject H_0. We conclude that the Toylot claim is too low.

4. We are testing the difference of means with small independent samples.

$$H_0: \mu_1 = \mu_2$$
$$H_1: \mu_1 > \mu_2$$

Since > is in H_1, a right-tailed test is used. For $\alpha' = 0.01$ and $d.f. = 12 + 12 - 2 = 22$, the critical value is $t_0 = 2.508$.

$$s = \sqrt{\frac{(n_1 - 1)s_1^2 + (n_2 - 1)s_2^2}{n_1 + n_2 - 2}} = \sqrt{\frac{11(2.1)^2 + 11(2.0)^2}{12 + 12 - 2}} = 2.0506$$

$$\bar{x}_1 - \bar{x}_2 = 9.4 - 6.8 = 2.6$$

$$t = \frac{\bar{x}_1 - \bar{x}_2}{s\sqrt{\frac{1}{n_1} + \frac{1}{n_2}}} = \frac{2.6}{2.0506\sqrt{\frac{1}{12} + \frac{1}{12}}} = 3.106$$

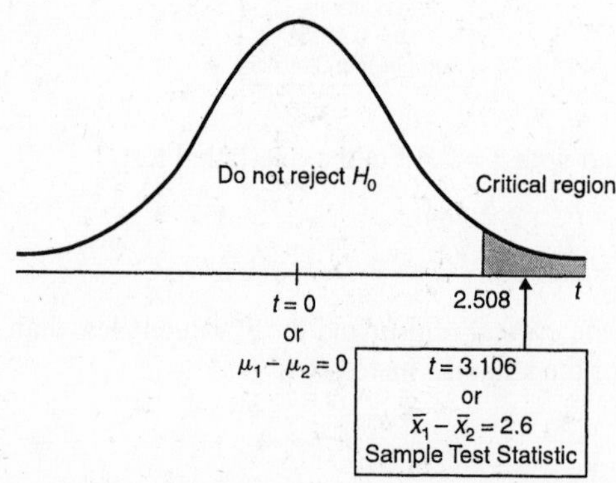

Next, find the P value interval using the α' values and the row headed by $d.f. = 22$. We find the sample t value, $t = 3.106$, falls to the right of 2.819. Therefore, P value < 0.005.

Since the sample t falls inside the critical region and the P value is less than $\alpha = 0.01$, we reject H_0. We conclude that the yellow paint has less visibility after 1 year.

5. We are testing a single proportion with a large sample.

$$H_0: p = 0.60$$
$$H_1: p < 0.60$$

Since < is in H_1, a left-tailed test is used. For $\alpha = 0.01$, the critical value is $z_0 = -2.33$.

$$\hat{p} = \frac{r}{n} = \frac{40}{90} = 0.4444$$

$$z = \frac{\hat{p} - p}{\sqrt{\frac{pq}{n}}} = \frac{0.4444 - 0.60}{\sqrt{\frac{0.60(0.40)}{90}}} = -3.01$$

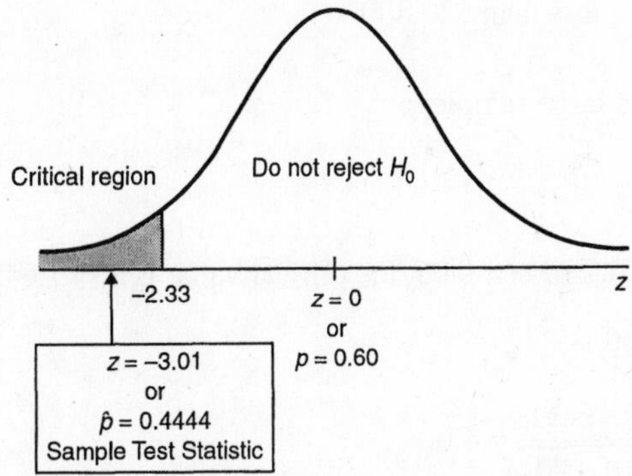

Next, find the P value associated with $z = 3.01$ and a one-tailed test.

$$P \text{ value} = P(z \le -3.01)$$
$$= 0.0013$$

Since the sample z falls inside the critical region and the P value is less than $\alpha = 0.01$, we reject H_0. We conclude that the population mortality rate has dropped.

6. We are testing a single mean with a large sample.

$$H_0: \mu = 29{,}800$$
$$H_1: \mu < 29{,}800$$

Since < is in H_1, a left-tailed test is used. For $\alpha = 0.05$, the critical value is $z_0 = -1.645$.

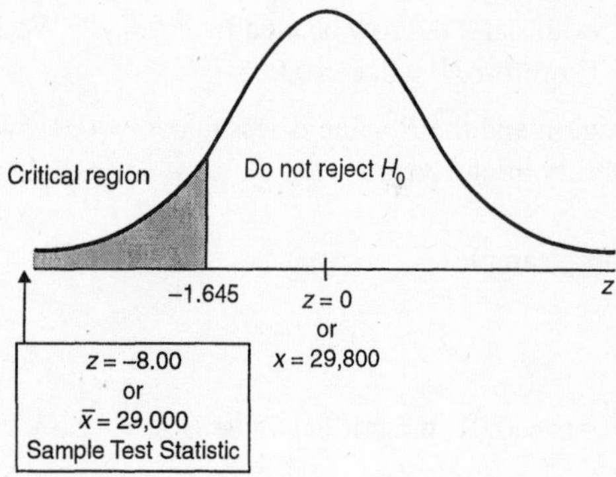

Next, find the P value associated with $z = -8.00$ and a two-tailed test.

$$P \text{ value} = P(z \le -8.00)$$
$$< 0.0001$$

Since the sample z falls inside the critical region and the P value is less than $\alpha = 0.05$, we reject H_0. We conclude that the average yearly salary is less than $29,800.

7. We are testing a single proportion with a large sample.

$$H_0: p = 0.20$$
$$H_1: p > 0.20$$

Since > is in H_1, a right-tailed test is used. For $\alpha = 0.05$, the critical value is $z_0 = 1.645$.

$$\hat{p} = \frac{r}{n} = \frac{77}{256} = 0.30$$

$$z = \frac{\hat{p} - p}{\sqrt{\frac{pq}{n}}} = \frac{0.30 - 0.20}{\sqrt{\frac{0.20(0.80)}{256}}} = 4.00$$

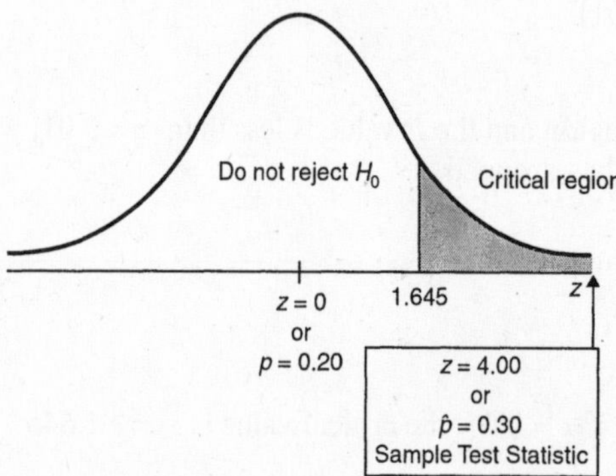

Next, find the P value associated with $z = 4.00$ and a one-tailed test.

$$P \text{ value} = P(z \ge 4.00)$$
$$\approx 0.0001$$

Since the sample z falls inside the critical region and the P value is less than $\alpha = 0.05$, we reject H_0. We conclude that the proportion of students who read the poetry magazine is more than 20%.

8. We are testing the difference of means with large independent samples.

$$H_0: \mu_1 = \mu_2$$
$$H_1: \mu_1 \neq \mu_2$$

Since $\neq$ is in H_1, a two-tailed test is used. For $\alpha = 0.05$, the critical values are $z_0 = \pm 1.96$.

$$\bar{x}_1 - \bar{x}_2 = 53 - 62 = -9$$

$$z = \frac{(\bar{x}_1 - \bar{x}_2) - (\mu_1 - \mu_2)}{\sqrt{\frac{\sigma_1^2}{n_1} + \frac{\sigma_2^2}{n_2}}} = \frac{-9 - 0}{\sqrt{\frac{19^2}{81} + \frac{15^2}{100}}} = -3.48$$

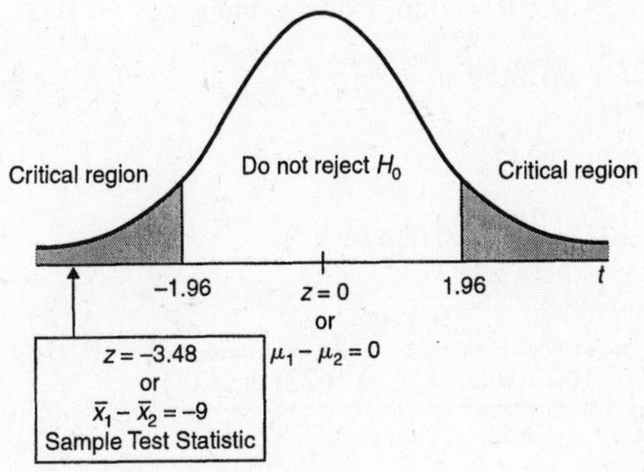

Next, find the P value associated with $z = -3.48$ and a two-tailed test.

$$P \text{ value} = 2P(z \leq -3.48)$$
$$= 2(0.0003)$$
$$= 0.0006$$

Since the sample z falls inside the critical region and the P value is less than $\alpha = 0.05$, we reject H_0. We conclude that a significant difference exists in average off-schedule times.

9. We are testing a single mean with a large sample.

$$H_0: \mu = 40$$
$$H_1: \mu > 40$$

Since $>$ is in H_1, a right-tailed test is used. For $\alpha = 0.01$, the critical value is $z_0 = 2.33$.

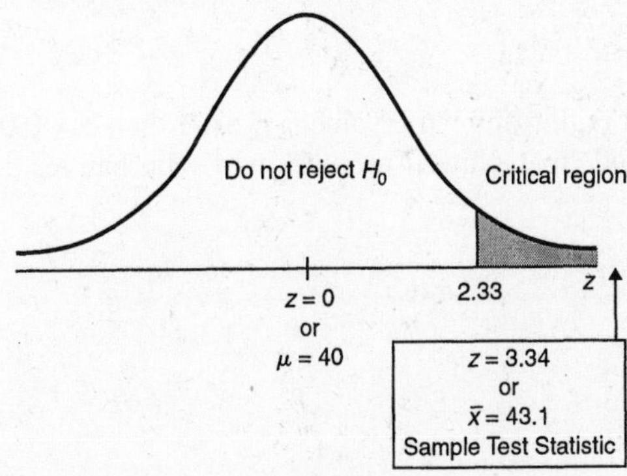

Next, find the P value associated with $z = 3.34$ and a one-tailed test.

$$P \text{ value} = P(z \geq 3.34)$$
$$= 0.0004$$

Since the sample z falls inside the critical region and the P value is less than $\alpha = 0.01$, we reject H_0. We conclude that the mean number of matches per box is more than 40.

10. We are testing a single mean with a large sample.

$$H_0\text{: } p_1 = p_2$$
$$H_1\text{: } p_1 < p_2$$

Since < is in H_1, a left-tailed test is used. For $\alpha = 0.05$, the critical value is $z_0 = -1.645$.

$$\hat{p} = \frac{r_1 + r_2}{n_1 + n_2} = \frac{12+18}{88+97} = 0.1622$$

$$\hat{q} = 1 - \hat{p} = 1 - 0.1622 = 0.8378$$

$$\hat{p}_1 - \hat{p}_2 = \frac{r_1}{n_1} - \frac{r_2}{n_2} = \frac{12}{88} - \frac{18}{97} = -0.0492$$

$$z = \frac{\hat{p}_1 - \hat{p}_2}{\sqrt{\frac{\hat{p}\hat{q}}{n_1} + \frac{\hat{p}\hat{q}}{n_2}}} = \frac{-0.0492}{\sqrt{\frac{0.1622(0.8378)}{88} + \frac{0.1622(0.8378)}{97}}} = -0.91$$

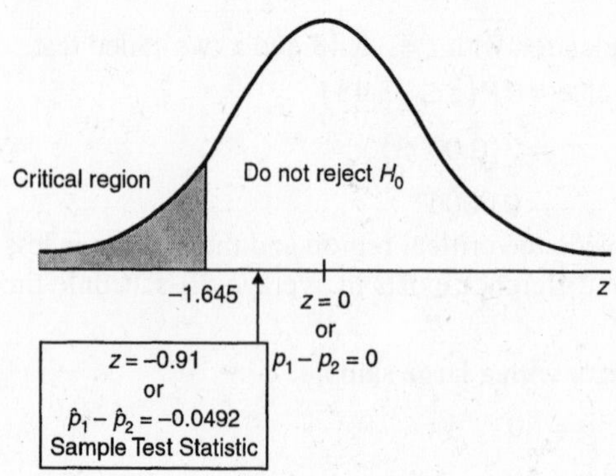

Next, find the P value associated with $z = -0.91$ and a one-tailed test.

$$P \text{ value} = P(z \leq -0.91)$$
$$= 0.1814$$

Since the sample z falls outside the critical region and the P value is greater than $\alpha = 0.05$, we do not reject H_0. There is insufficient evidence to conclude that a higher proportion of suburban residents subscribe to *Sporting News.*

11. We are testing the difference of means with small independent samples.

$$H_0: \mu_1 = \mu_2$$
$$H_1: \mu_1 \neq \mu_2$$

Since $\neq$ is in H_1, a two-tailed test is used. For $\alpha'' = 0.05$ and $d.f. = 16 + 14 - 2 = 28$, the critical values are $t_0 = \pm 2.048$.

$$s = \sqrt{\frac{(n_1-1)s_1^2+(n_2-1)s_2^2}{n_1+n_2-2}} = \sqrt{\frac{15(2.0)^2+13(1.8)^2}{16+14-2}} = 1.9097$$

$$\bar{x}_1 - \bar{x}_2 = 4.8 - 5.2 = -0.4$$

$$t = \frac{\bar{x}_1 - \bar{x}_2}{s\sqrt{\frac{1}{n_1}+\frac{1}{n_2}}} = \frac{-0.4}{1.9097\sqrt{\frac{1}{16}+\frac{1}{14}}} = -0.5723$$

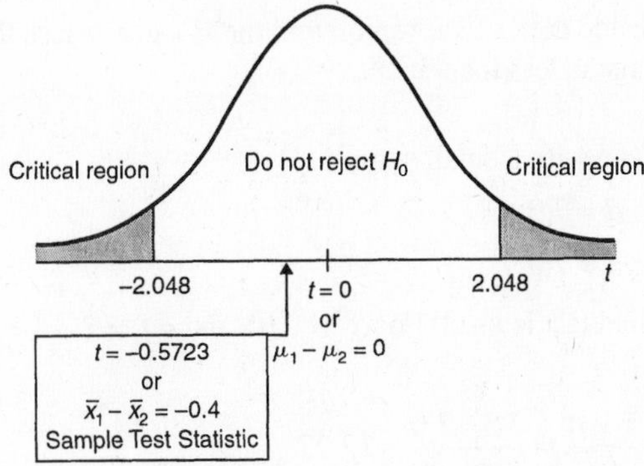

Next, find the P value interval using the α'' values and the row headed by $d.f. = 28$. We find the sample t value, $t = -0.5723$, falls to the right of -1.175. Therefore, P value > 0.250.

Since the sample test statistic falls outside the critical region and the P value is greater than $\alpha = 0.05$, we do not reject H_0. There is insufficient evidence to conclude a difference in average waiting time.

12. We are testing a single proportion with a large sample.

$$H_0: p = 0.36$$
$$H_1: p < 0.36$$

Since $<$ is in H_1, a left-tailed test is used. For $\alpha = 0.05$, the critical value is $z_0 = -1.645$.

$$\hat{p} = \frac{r}{n} = \frac{33}{120} = 0.275$$

$$z = \frac{\hat{p}-p}{\sqrt{\frac{pq}{n}}} = \frac{0.275-0.36}{\sqrt{\frac{0.36(0.64)}{120}}} = -1.94$$

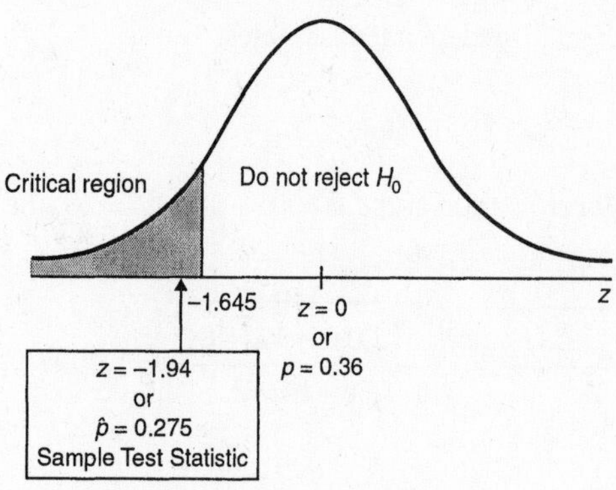

Next, find the P value associated with $z = -1.94$ and a one-tailed test.

$$P \text{ value} = P(z \le -1.94)$$
$$= 0.0262$$

Since the sample z falls inside the critical region and the P value is less than $\alpha = 0.05$, we reject H_0. We conclude that the percentage is less than 36%.

13. We are testing a single mean with a small sample.

$$H_0: \mu = 7.0$$
$$H_1: \mu \ne 7.0$$

Since $\ne$ is in H_1, a two-tailed test is used. For $\alpha'' = 0.05$ and $d.f. = 8 - 1 = 7$, the critical values are $t_0 = \pm 2.365$.

$$t = \frac{\bar{x} - \mu}{s/\sqrt{n}} = \frac{7.3 - 7.0}{0.5/\sqrt{8}} = 1.697$$

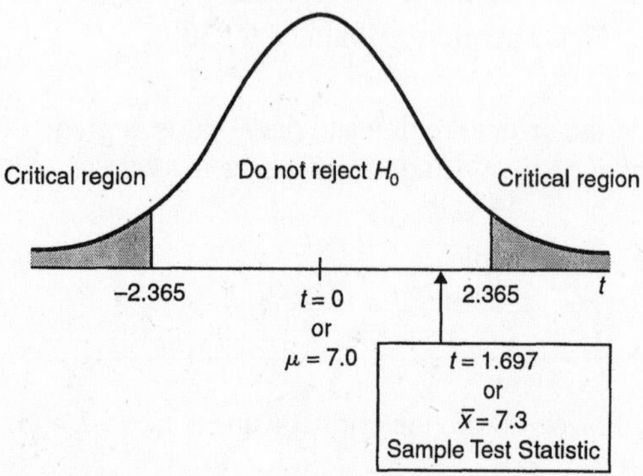

Next, find the P value interval using the α'' values and the row headed by $d.f. = 7$. We find that the sample t value, $t = 1.697$, falls between 1.617 and 1.895. Therefore, $0.10 < P < 0.15$.

Since the sample t falls outside the critical region and the P value is greater than $\alpha = 0.05$, we do not reject H_0. There is not enough evidence to conclude that the machine has slipped out of adjustment.

14. We are performing a paired difference test with small samples.

$$H_0: \mu_d = 0$$
$$H_1: \mu_d > 0$$

Since > is in H_1, a right-tailed test is used. For $\alpha' = 0.01$ and $d.f. = 6 - 1 = 5$, the critical value is $t_0 = 3.365$.

$$\bar{d} = 9.83$$
$$t = \frac{\bar{d} - \mu_d}{s_d/\sqrt{n}} = \frac{9.83 - 0}{3.97/\sqrt{6}} = 6.07$$

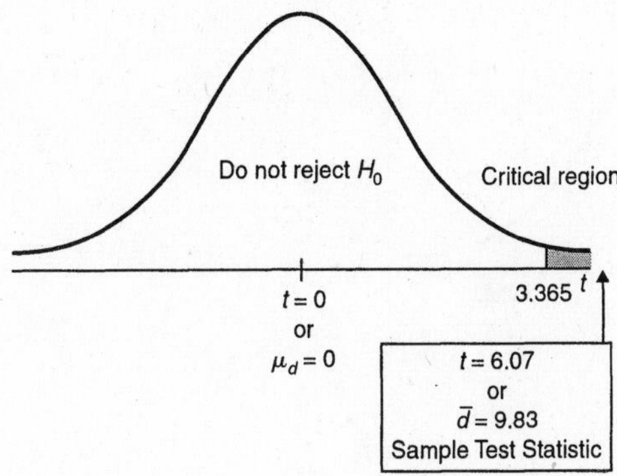

Next, find the *P* value interval using the α' values and the row headed by $d.f. = 5$. We find the sample *t* value, $t = 6.07$, falls to the right of 4.032. Therefore, *P* value < 0.005.

Since the sample *t* falls inside the critical region and the *P* value is less than $\alpha = 0.01$, we reject H_0. We conclude that the program of the experimental group did promote creative problem solving.

15. We are performing a paired difference test with small samples.

$$H_0: \mu_d = 0$$
$$H_1: \mu_d < 0$$

Since < is in H_1, a left-tailed test is used. For $\alpha' = 0.05$ and $d.f. = 5 - 1 = 4$, the critical value is $t_0 = -2.132$.

$$\bar{d} = -4.94$$
$$t = \frac{\bar{d} - \mu_d}{s_d/\sqrt{n}} = \frac{-4.94 - 0}{3.90/\sqrt{5}} = -2.832$$

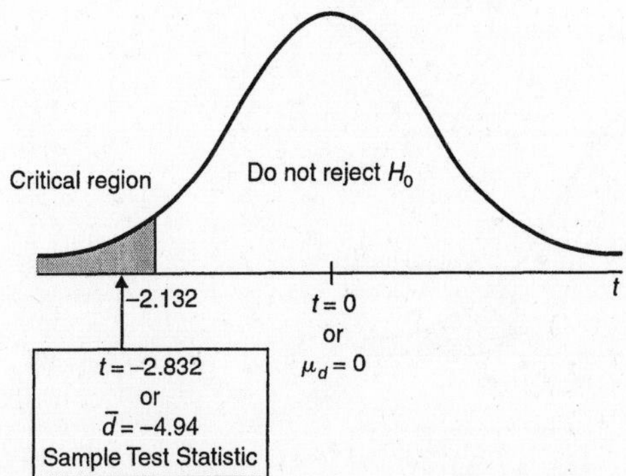

Next, find the *P* value interval using the α' values and the row headed by $d.f. = 4$. We find the sample *t* value, $t = 2.832$, falls between -2.776 and -3.747. Therefore, $0.010 < P$ value < 0.025.

Since the sample *t* falls inside the critical region and the *P* value is less than $\alpha = 0.05$, we reject H_0. We conclude that the average net sales have improved.

16. (a) The mean and standard deviation round to the results given.

(b) We are testing a single mean with a small sample.

$$H_0: \mu_d = 48$$
$$H_1: \mu_d < 48$$

Since < is in H_1, a left-tailed test is used. For $\alpha' = 0.05$ and $d.f. = 10 - 1 = 9$, the critical value is $t_0 = -1.833$.

$$t = \frac{\bar{x} - \mu}{s/\sqrt{n}} = \frac{46.2 - 48}{10.85/\sqrt{10}} = -0.525$$

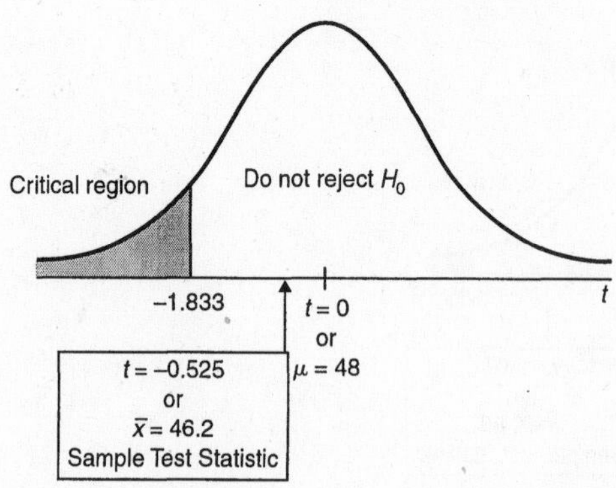

Next, find the P value interval using the α' values and the row headed by $d.f. = 9$. We find that the sample t value, $t = -0.525$, falls to the right of -1.230. Therefore, P value > 0.125.

Since the sample t falls outside the critical region and the P value is greater than $\alpha = 0.05$, we do not reject H_0. There is insufficient evidence to conclude that the average is less than 48 months.

17. We are testing the difference of means with large independent samples.

$$H_0: \mu_1 = \mu_2$$
$$H_1: \mu_1 \neq \mu_2$$

Since ≠ is in H_1, a two-tailed test is used. For $\alpha = 0.05$, the critical values are $z_0 = \pm 1.96$.

$$\bar{x}_1 - \bar{x}_2 = 3.0 - 2.7 = 0.3$$

$$z = \frac{(\bar{x}_1 - \bar{x}_2) - (\mu_1 - \mu_2)}{\sqrt{\frac{\sigma_1^2}{n_1} + \frac{\sigma_2^2}{n_2}}} = \frac{0.3 - 0}{\sqrt{\frac{0.8^2}{55} + \frac{0.9^2}{52}}} = 1.82$$

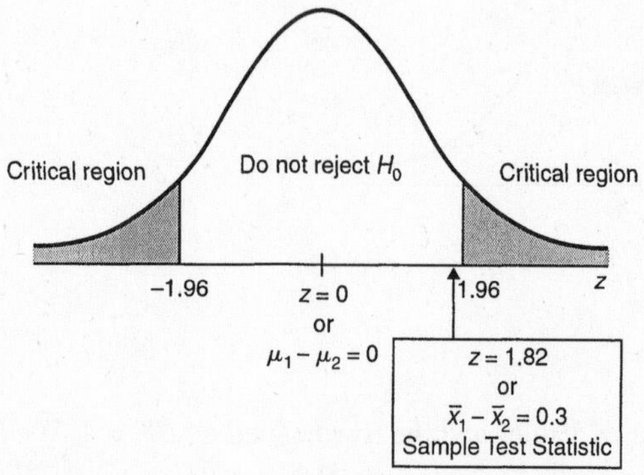

Next, find the P value associated with $z = 1.82$ and a two-tailed test.

$$\begin{aligned} P \text{ value} &= 2P(z \geq 1.82) \\ &= 2(0.0344) \\ &= 0.0688 \end{aligned}$$

Since the sample z falls outside the critical region and the P value is greater than $\alpha = 0.05$, we do not reject H_0. There is insufficient evidence to conclude that a difference exists in the population mean lengths of the two types of projectile points.

18. (a) Do not reject H_0 since P value > 0.01.

(b) Reject H_0 since P value < 0.05.

19. (a) Reject H_0 since P value < 0.01.

(b) Reject H_0 since P value < 0.05.

Chapter 10 Regression and Correlation

Section 10.1

1. The points seem close to a straight line, so there is moderate or low linear correlation.

2. No straight line is realistically a good fit, so there is no linear correlation.

3. The points seem very close to a straight line, so there is high linear correlation.

4. The points seem close to a straight line, so there is moderate or low linear correlation.

5. The points seem very close to a straight line, so there is high linear correlation.

6. No straight line is realistically a good fit, so there is no linear correlation.

7. (a)

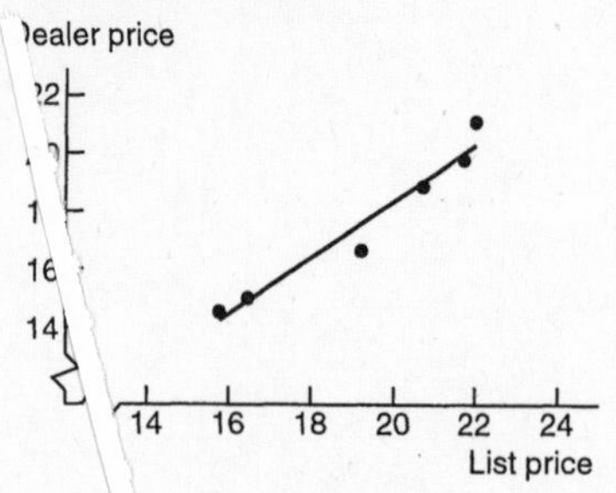

(b) Draw the line you think fits best. (Method to find equation is in Section 10.2.)

(c) Since the points are very close to a straight line, the correlation is high.

8. (a)

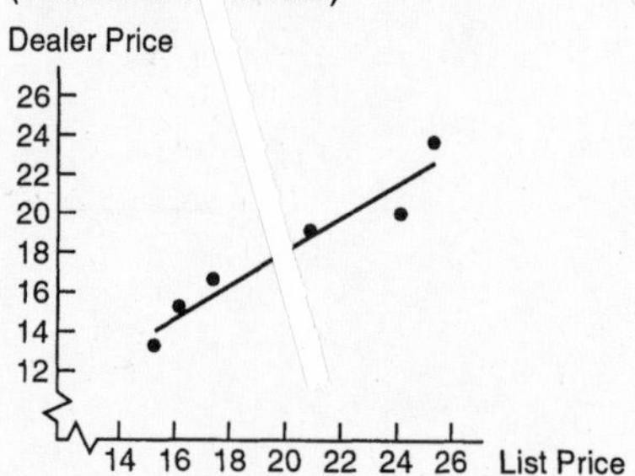

(b) Draw the line you think fits best. (Method to find equation is in Section 10.2.)

(c) Since the points are very close to a straight line, the correlation is high.

9. (a)

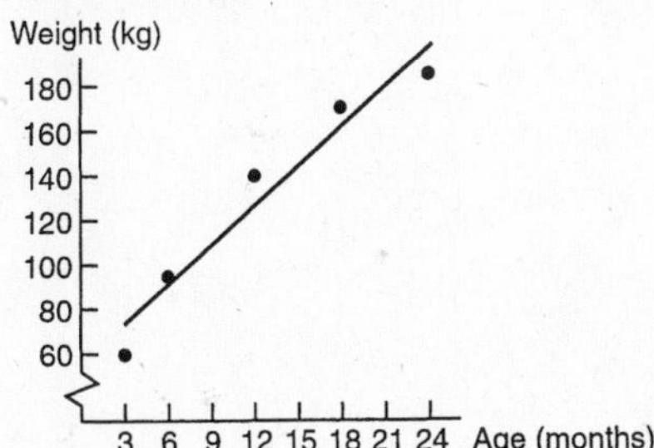

(b) Draw the line you think fits best. (Method to find equation is in Section 10.2.)

(c) Since the points are very close to a straight line, the correlation is high.

10. (a)

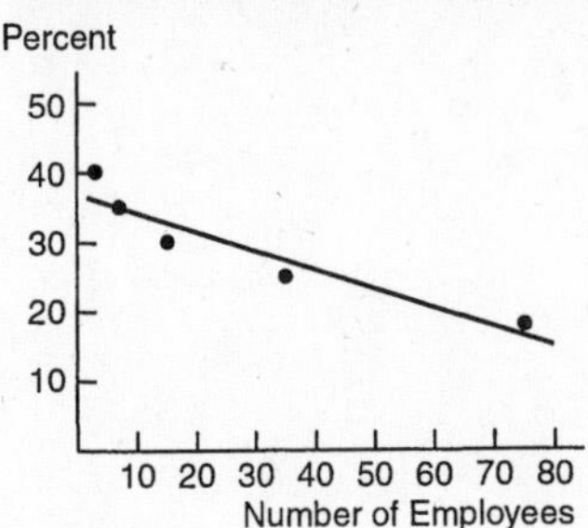

(b) Draw the line you think fits best. (Method to find equation is in Section 10.2.)

(c) Since the points are fairly close to a straight line, the correlation is moderate.

11. (a)

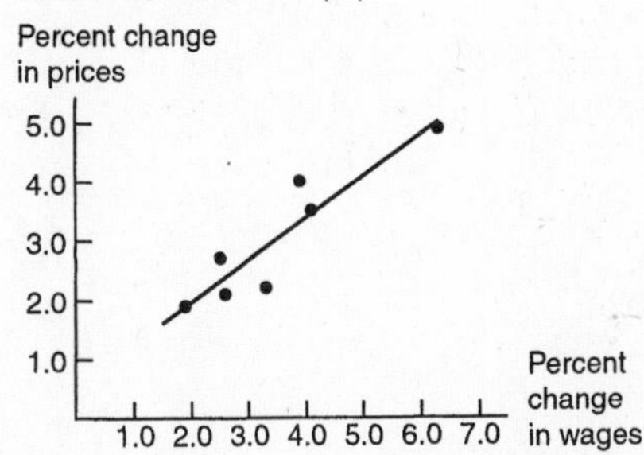

(b) Draw the line you think fits best. (Method to find equation is in Section 10.2.)

(c) Since the points are fairly close to a straight line, the correlation is moderate.

12. (a)

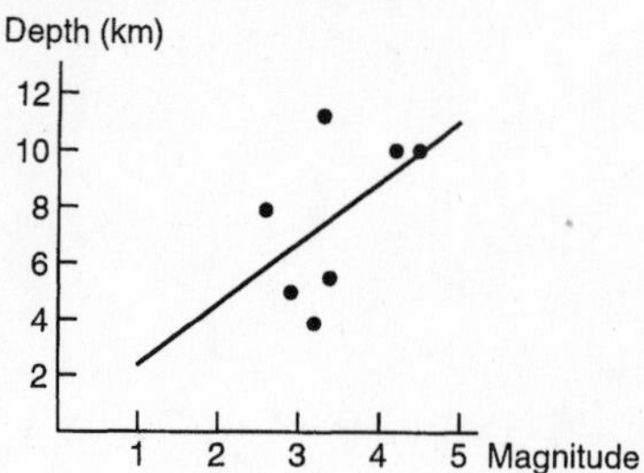

(b) Draw the line you think fits best. (Method to find equation is in Section 10.2.)

(c) Since the points are not close to a straight line, the correlation is low.

Note: One possible reason why there appears to be little, if any, linear relationship is that the Richter scale is logarithmic. An increase of 1 on the Richter scale represents a 60-fold increase in energy.

13. (a)

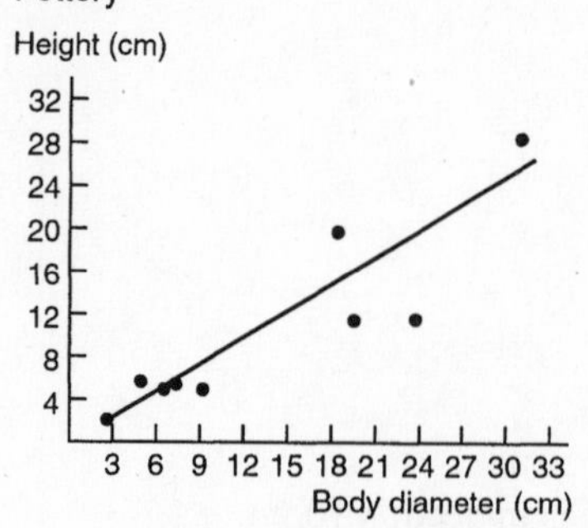

(b) Draw the line you think fits best. (Method to find equation is in Section 10.2.)

(c) Since the points are fairly close to a straight line, the correlation is moderate.

14. (a)

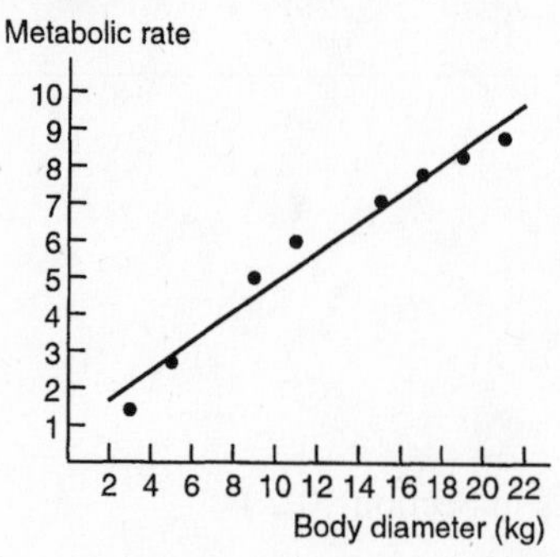

(b) Draw the line you think fits best. (Method to find equation is in Section 10.2.)

(c) Since the points are very close to a straight line, the correlation is high.

15. (a) Unit Length on y Same as That on x

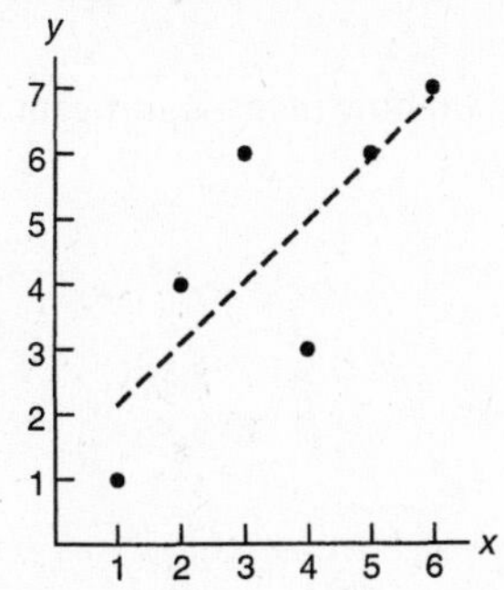

(b) Unit Length on y Twice That on x

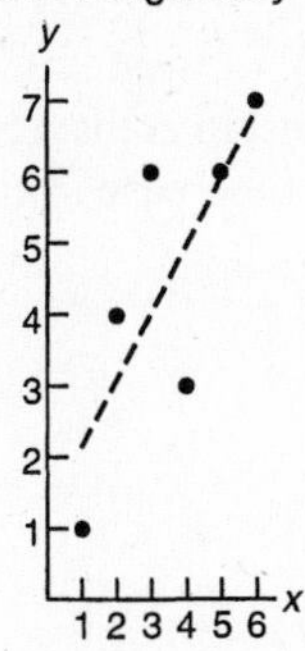

(c) Unit Length on y Half That on x

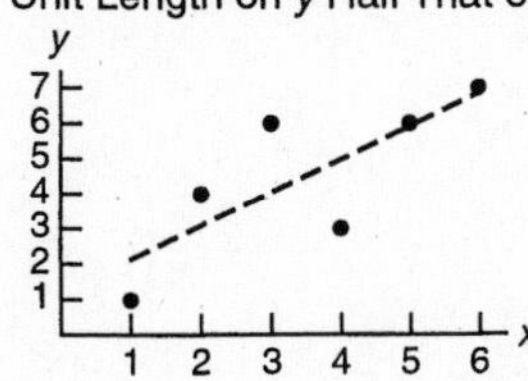

(d) Draw the lines you think best fit the data points.
Stretching the scale on the y-axis makes the line appear steeper. Shrinking the scale on the y-axis makes the line appear flatter. The slope of the line does not change. Only the appearance (visual impression) of slope changes as the scale of the y-axis changes.

Section 10.2

Note: In this section and the next two, answers may vary slightly, depending on how many significant digits are used throughout the calculations.

1. (a)

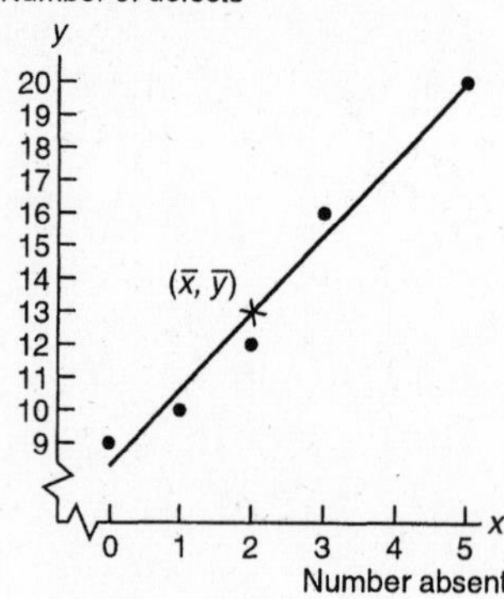

(b) $\bar{x} = \frac{\sum x}{n} = \frac{11}{5} = 2.2$

$\bar{y} = \frac{\sum y}{n} = \frac{67}{5} = 13.4$

$b = \frac{SS_{xy}}{SS_x} = \frac{34.6}{14.8} = 2.3378$

$a = \bar{y} - b\bar{x} = 13.4 - 2.3378(2.2) = 8.26$

$y = a + bx$ or $y = 8.26 + 2.338x$

(c) See figure of part (a).

(d) $S_e = \sqrt{\frac{SS_y - bSS_{xy}}{n-2}}$

$= \sqrt{\frac{83.2 - 2.3378(34.6)}{5-2}}$

$= 0.878$

(e) Use $x = 4$.

$y_p = 8.26 + 2.338(4) = 17.6$ defects

(f) $t_{0.95, 3 d.f.} = 3.182$

$$E = t_c S_e \sqrt{1 + \frac{1}{n} + \frac{(x - \bar{x})^2}{SS_x}}$$

$$= 3.182(0.878)\sqrt{1 + \frac{1}{5} + \frac{(4-2.2)^2}{14.8}}$$

$$= 3.3$$

A 95% confidence interval is

$$y_p - E \le y \le y_p + E$$
$$17.6 - 3.3 \le y \le 17.6 + 3.3$$
$$14.3 \le y \le 20.9 \text{ defects}$$

2. (a)

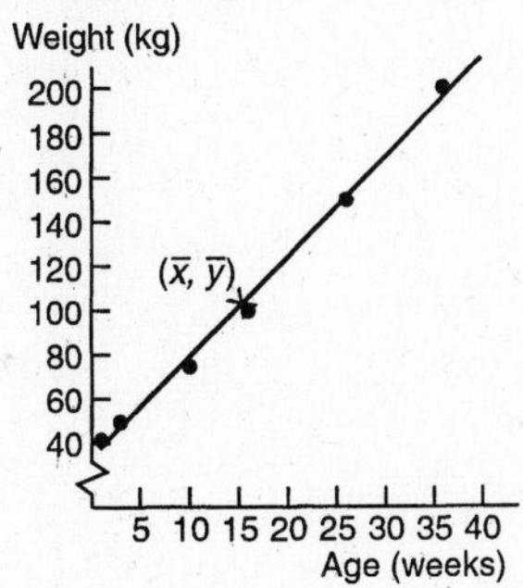

(b) $\bar{x} = \frac{\sum x}{n} = \frac{92}{6} = 15.33$

$\bar{y} = \frac{\sum y}{n} = \frac{617}{6} = 102.83$

$b = \frac{SS_{xy}}{SS_x} = \frac{4181.3}{927.3} = 4.509$

$a = \bar{y} - b\bar{x} = 102.83 - 4.509(15.33) = 33.70$

$y = a + bx$ or $y = 33.70 + 4.51x$

(c) See figure of part (a).

(d) $S_e = \sqrt{\frac{SS_y - bSS_{xy}}{n-2}}$

$= \sqrt{\frac{18940.8 - 4.509(4181.3)}{6-2}}$

$= 4.67$

(e) Use $x = 12$.

$y_p = 33.70 + 4.51(12) = 87.8$ kg

(f) $t_{0.90, 4d.f.} = 2.132$

$$E = t_c S_e \sqrt{1 + \frac{1}{n} + \frac{(x - \bar{x})^2}{SS_x}}$$

$$= 2.132(4.67)\sqrt{1 + \frac{1}{6} + \frac{(12 - 15.3)^2}{927.3}}$$

$$= 10.81$$

A 90% confidence interval for y is

$$y_p - E \le y \le y_p + E$$

$$87.8 - 10.81 \le y \le 87.8 + 10.81$$

$$76.99 \le y \le 98.61 \text{ kg}$$

3. (a)

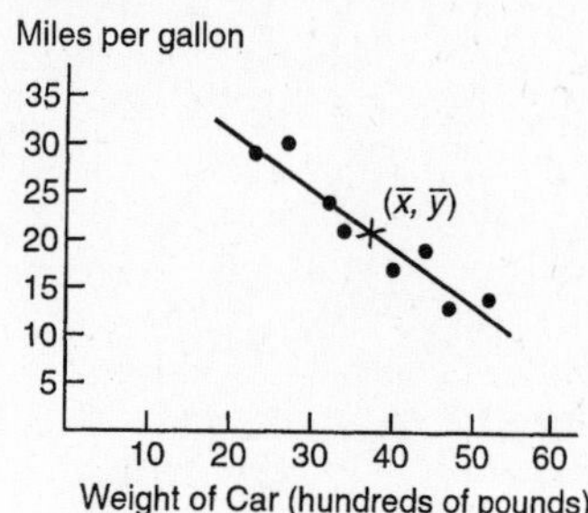

(b) $\bar{x} = \frac{\sum x}{n} = \frac{299}{8} = 37.375$

$\bar{y} = \frac{\sum y}{n} = \frac{167}{8} = 20.875$

$b = \frac{SS_{xy}}{SS_x} = \frac{-427.625}{711.875} = -0.6007$

$a = \bar{y} - b\bar{x} = 20.875 - (-0.6007)(37.375) = 43.3263$

$y = a + bx$ or $y = 43.3263 - 0.6007x$

(c) See figure of part (a).

(d) $S_e = \sqrt{\frac{SS_y - bSS_{xy}}{n-2}}$

$= \sqrt{\frac{286.875 - (-0.6007)(-427.625)}{8-2}}$

$= 2.2361$

(e) Use $x = 38$.

$y_p = 43.3263 - 0.6007(38) = 20.5$ mpg

(f) $t_{0.80, 6 d.f.} = 1.440$

$$E = t_c S_e \sqrt{1 + \frac{1}{n} + \frac{(x - \bar{x})^2}{SS_x}}$$

$$= 1.44(2.2361)\sqrt{1 + \frac{1}{8} + \frac{(38 - 37.375)^2}{711.875}}$$

$$= 3.4$$

A 80% confidence interval for y is

$$y_p - E \le y \le y_p + E$$

$$20.5 - 3.4 \le y \le 20.4 + 3.4$$

$$17.1 \le y \le 23.8 \text{ mpg}$$

4. (a) Fouls and Basketball Losses

Percent of wins

y

50
40
30
20
10

$(\bar{x}, \bar{y})$

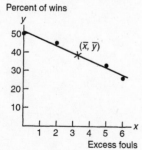

1 2 3 4 5 6 x

Excess fouls

(b) $\bar{x} = \frac{\sum x}{n} = \frac{13}{4} = 3.25$

$\bar{y} = \frac{\sum y}{n} = \frac{154}{4} = 38.5$

$b = \frac{SS_{xy}}{SS_x} = \frac{-89.5}{22.75} = -3.934$

$a = \bar{y} - b\bar{x} = 38.5 - (-3.934)(3.25) = 51.29$

$y = a + bx$ or $y = 51.29 - 3.934x$

(c) See figure of part (a).

(d) $S_e = \sqrt{\frac{SS_y - bSS_{xy}}{n-2}} = \sqrt{\frac{361-(-3.934)(-89.5)}{4-2}} = 2.11$

(e) Use $x = 4$.

$y_p = 51.29 - 3.934(4) = 35.55\%$

(f) $t_{0.80,2d.f.} = 1.886$

$$E = t_c S_e \sqrt{1 + \frac{1}{n} + \frac{(x-\bar{x})^2}{SS_x}}$$

$$= 1.886(2.11)\sqrt{1 + \frac{1}{4} + \frac{(4-3.25)^2}{22.75}} = 4.49$$

A 80% confidence interval for y is

$$y_p - E \le y \le y_p + E$$
$$35.55 - 4.49 \le y \le 35.55 + 4.49$$
$$31.06 \le y \le 40.04\%$$

5. (a) Education and Income in Small Cities

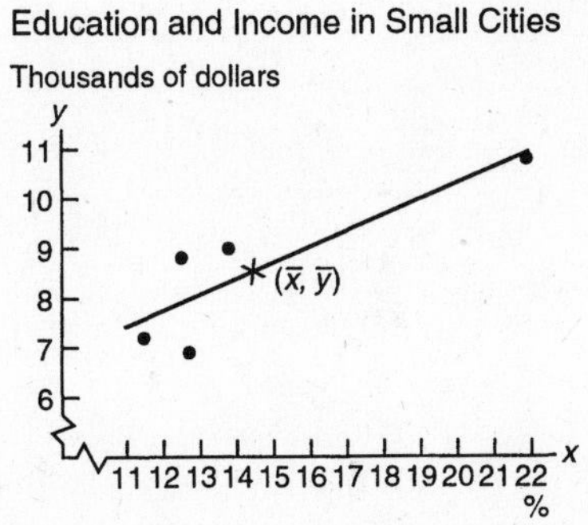

(b) $\bar{x} = \frac{\sum x}{n} = \frac{72.4}{5} = 14.48$

$\bar{y} = \frac{\sum y}{n} = \frac{42.7}{5} = 8.54$

$b = \frac{SS_{xy}}{SS_x} = \frac{22.854}{71.448} = 0.320$

$a = \bar{y} - b\bar{x} = 8.54 - 0.320(14.48) = 3.91$

$y = a + bx$ or $y = 3.91 + 0.320x$

(c) See figure of part (a).

Note that the regression line would be much steeper if (21.9, 10.8) were eliminated from the data set [which would also affect $(\bar{x}, \bar{y})$]. Not all outliers (this point is an outlier in both x (probably) and y) have this effect; however, when the parameter estimates a and b depend heavily on a particular observation, as is the case here, the point is called "influential," and conclusions drawn are shaky at best when influential observations remain in the data. For further information, refer to a more advanced textbook such as Applied Regression Analysis by Draper and Smith.

(d) $S_e = \sqrt{\dfrac{SS_y - bSS_{xy}}{n-2}}$

$= \sqrt{\dfrac{9.872 - 0.320(22.854)}{5-2}}$

$= 0.924$

(e) Use $x = 20$.

$y_p = 3.91 + 0.320(20) = 10.31$ i.e., 10.31 thousand dollars

(f) $t_{0.80, 3 d.f} = 1.638$

$$E = t_c S_e \sqrt{1 + \frac{1}{n} + \frac{(x-\bar{x})^2}{SS_x}}$$

$$= 1.638(0.924)\sqrt{1 + \frac{1}{5} + \frac{(20-14.48)^2}{71.448}}$$

$$= 1.93$$

A 80% confidence interval for y is

$$y_p - E \le y \le y_p + E$$
$$10.31 - 1.93 \le y \le 10.31 + 1.93$$
$$8.4 \le y \le 12.2$$

or 8.4 thousand dollars to 12.2 thousand dollars

6. (a) Percentage of 16 to 19-Year-Olds Not in School and per Capita Income (thousands of dollars)

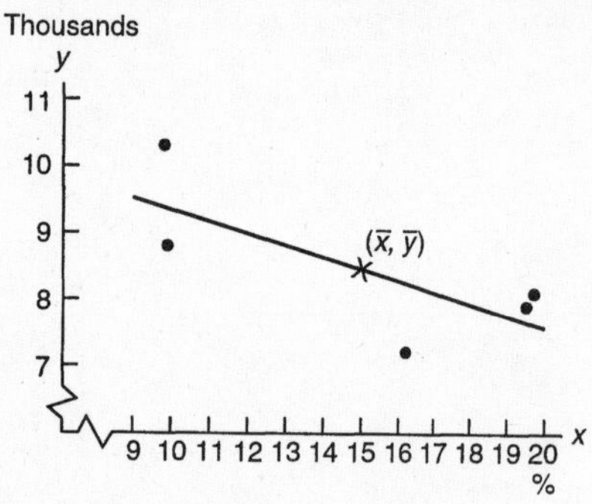

(b) $\bar{x} = \dfrac{\Sigma x}{n} = \dfrac{75.1}{5} = 15.02$

$\bar{y} = \dfrac{\Sigma y}{n} = \dfrac{42.3}{5} = 8.46$

$b = \dfrac{SS_{xy}}{SS_x} = \dfrac{-17.026}{96.828} = -0.1758$

$a = \bar{y} - b\bar{x} = 8.46 - (-0.1758)15.02 = 11.10$

$y = a + bx$ or $y = 11.10 - 0.176x$

(c) See figure of part (a).

(d) $S_e = \sqrt{\dfrac{SS_y - bSS_{xy}}{n-2}}$

$= \sqrt{\dfrac{5.532-(-0.1758)(-17.026)}{5-2}}$

$= 0.9199$

(e) Use $x = 17$.

$y_p = 11.10 - 0.176(17) = 8.11$ thousand dollars

(f) $t_{0.75,3.d.f.} = 1.423$

$E = t_c S_e \sqrt{1+\dfrac{1}{n}+\dfrac{(x-\bar{x})^2}{SS_x}}$

$= 1.423(0.9199)\sqrt{1+\dfrac{1}{5}+\dfrac{(17-15.02)^2}{96.828}}$

$= 1.46$

A 75% confidence interval for y is

$y_p - E \le y \le y_p + E$

$8.11 - 1.46 \le y \le 8.11 + 1.46$

$6.65 \le y \le 9.57$ thousand dollars

7. (a) Per Capita Income and Per Capita Retail Sales in Small Cities (thousands of dollars)

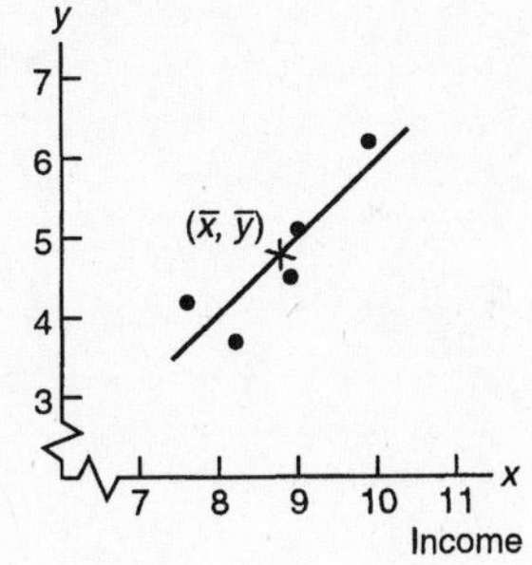

(b) $\bar{x} = \dfrac{\Sigma x}{n} = \dfrac{43.6}{5} = 8.72$

$\bar{y} = \dfrac{\Sigma y}{n} = \dfrac{23.7}{5} = 4.74$

$b = \dfrac{SS_{xy}}{SS_x} = \dfrac{2.926}{3.028} = 0.966314$

$a = \bar{y} - b\bar{x} = 4.74 - (0.966314)(8.72) = -3.69$

$y = a + bx$ or $y = -3.69 + 0.966x$

(c) See figure of part (a).

(d) $S_e = \sqrt{\dfrac{SS_y - bSS_{xy}}{n-2}}$

$= \sqrt{\dfrac{3.692 - 0.966314(2.926)}{5-2}}$

$= 0.5368$

(e) Use $x = 9.5$.

$y_p = -3.69 + 0.966(9.5) = 5.49$ thousand dollars

(f) $t_{0.80,3d.f.} = 1.638$

$$E = t_c S_e \sqrt{1 + \frac{1}{n} + \frac{(x-\bar{x})^2}{SS_x}}$$

$$= 1.638(0.5368)\sqrt{1 + \frac{1}{5} + \frac{(9.5-8.72)^2}{3.028}}$$

$$= 1.04$$

A 80% confidence interval for y is

$$y_p - E \le y \le y_p + E$$

$$5.49 - 1.04 \le y \le 5.49 + 1.04$$

$$4.45 \le y \le 6.53 \text{ thousand dollars}$$

8. (a) List and Dealer Price for GMC Sierra (thousands of dollars)

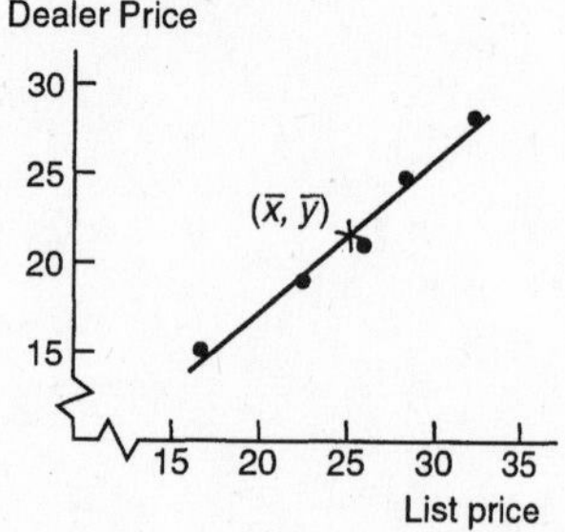

(b) $\bar{x} = \frac{\Sigma x}{n} = \frac{125.6}{5} = 25.12$

$\bar{y} = \frac{\Sigma y}{n} = \frac{108.1}{5} = 21.62$

$b = \frac{SS_{xy}}{SS_x} = \frac{117.978}{138.608} = 0.85116$

$a = \bar{y} - b\bar{x} = 21.62 - 0.85116(25.12) = 0.239$

$y = a + bx$ or $y = 0.239 + 0.851x$

(c) See figure of part (a).

(d) $S_e = \sqrt{\frac{SS_y - bSS_{xy}}{n-2}}$

$= \sqrt{\frac{103.168 - (0.85116)(117.978)}{5-2}}$

$= 0.957$

(e) Use $x = 23.5$.

$y_p = 0.239 + 0.851(23.5) = 20.24$ thousand dollars

(f) $t_{0.75,3d.f.} = 1.423$

$$E = t_c S_e \sqrt{1 + \frac{1}{n} + \frac{(x-\bar{x})^2}{SS_x}}$$

$$= 1.423(0.957)\sqrt{1 + \frac{1}{5} + \frac{(23.5-25.12)^2}{138.608}}$$

$$= 1.504$$

A 75% confidence interval for y is

$$y_p - E \le y \le y_p + E$$

$$20.24 - 1.504 \le y \le 20.24 + 1.504$$

$$18.74 \le y \le 21.74 \text{ thousand dollars}$$

9. (a) List and Dealer Price for Chevrolet Silverado (thousands of dollars)

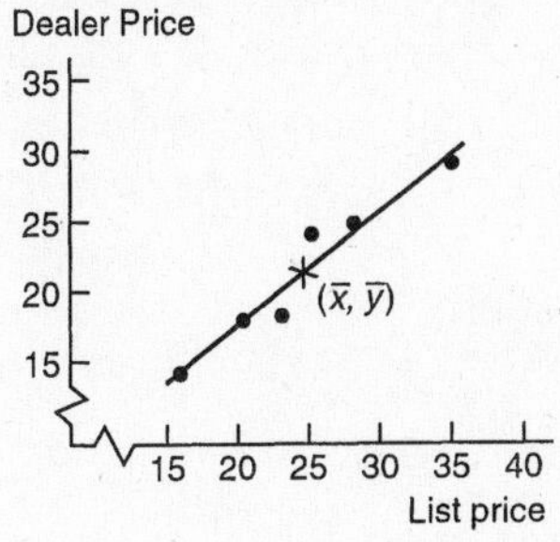

Dealer Price

35 30 25 20 15

$(\bar{x}, \bar{y})$

15 20 25 30 35 40

List price

(b) $\bar{x} = \dfrac{\sum x}{n} = \dfrac{148.4}{6} = 24.73$

$\bar{y} = \dfrac{\sum y}{n} = \dfrac{128.1}{6} = 21.35$

$b = \dfrac{SS_{xy}}{SS_x} = \dfrac{174.99}{217.053} = 0.8062$

$a = \bar{y} - b\bar{x} = 21.35 - 0.8062(24.73) = 1.41$

$y = a + bx$ or $y = 1.41 + 0.806x$

(c) See figure of part (a).

(d) $S_e = \sqrt{\dfrac{SS_y - bSS_{xy}}{n-2}}$

$= \sqrt{\dfrac{150.395 - 0.8062(174.99)}{6-2}}$

$= 1.526$

(e) Use $x = 22.9$.

$y_p = 1.41 + 0.806(22.9) = 19.87$ thousand dollars

(f) $t_{0.80, 4 d.f.} = 1.533$

$E = t_c S_e \sqrt{1 + \dfrac{1}{n} + \dfrac{(x - \bar{x})^2}{SS_x}}$

$= 1.533(1.526)\sqrt{1 + \dfrac{1}{6} + \dfrac{(22.9 - 24.73)^2}{217.053}}$

$= 2.54$

A 80% confidence interval for y is

$$y_p - E \le y \le y_p + E$$

$$19.87 - 2.54 \le y \le 19.87 + 2.54$$

$$17.33 \le y \le 22.41 \quad \text{thousand dollars}$$

10. (a) Number of Research Programs and Mean Number of Patents per Program

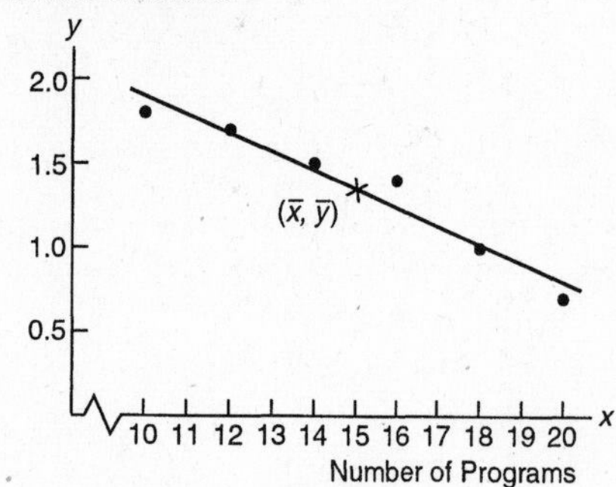

(b) $\bar{x} = \frac{\sum x}{n} = \frac{90}{6} = 15.0$

$\bar{y} = \frac{\sum y}{n} = \frac{8.1}{6} = 1.35$

$b = \frac{SS_{xy}}{SS_x} = \frac{-7.7}{70} = -0.1100$

$a = \bar{y} - b\bar{x} = 1.35 - (-0.1100)(15.0) = 3.0$

$y = a + bx$ or $y = 3.0 - 0.11x$

(c) See figure of part (a).

(d) $S_e = \sqrt{\frac{SS_y - bSS_{xy}}{n-2}}$

$= \sqrt{\frac{0.895 - (-0.11)(-7.7)}{6-2}}$

$= 0.1095$

(e) Use $x = 15$.

$y_p = 3.0 - 0.11(15) = 1.35$ patents

(f) $t_{0.85, 4d.f.} = 1.778$

$E = t_c S_e \sqrt{1 + \frac{1}{n} + \frac{(x-\bar{x})^2}{SS_x}}$

$= 1.778(0.1095)\sqrt{1 + \frac{1}{6} + \frac{(15-15)^2}{70}}$

$= 0.21$

A 85% confidence interval for y is

$$y_p - E \le y \le y_p + E$$
$$1.35 - 0.21 \le y \le 1.35 + 0.21$$
$$1.14 \le y \le 1.56 \text{ patents}$$

11. (a)

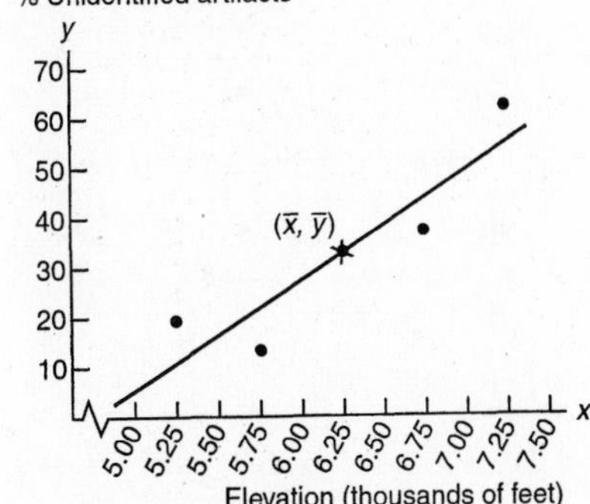

(b) $\bar{x} = \frac{\sum x}{n} = \frac{31.25}{5} = 6.25$

$\bar{y} = \frac{\sum y}{n} = \frac{164}{5} = 32.8$

$b = \frac{SS_{xy}}{SS_x} = \frac{55}{2.5} = 22.0$

$a = \bar{y} - b\bar{x} = 32.8 - 22.0(6.25) = -104.7$

$y = a + bx$ or $y = -104.7 + 22.0x$

(c) See figure of part (a).

(d) $S_e = \sqrt{\frac{SS_y - bSS_{xy}}{n-2}}$

$= \sqrt{\frac{1452.8 - (22)(55)}{5-2}}$

$= 8.996$

(e) Use $x = 6.5$.

$y_p = -104.7 + 22.0(6.5) = 38.3$ percent

(f) $t_{0.75, 3d.f.} = 1.423$

$$E = t_c S_e \sqrt{1 + \frac{1}{n} + \frac{(x-\bar{x})^2}{SS_x}}$$

$$= 1.423(8.996)\sqrt{1 + \frac{1}{5} + \frac{(6.5-6.25)^2}{2.5}}$$

$$= 14.2$$

A 75% confidence interval for y is

$$y_p - E \le y \le y_p + E$$

$$38.3 - 14.2 \le y \le 38.3 + 14.2$$

$$24.1 \le y \le 52.5 \quad \text{percent}$$

12. (a)

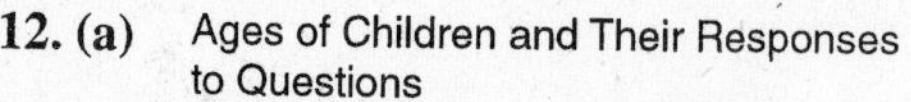

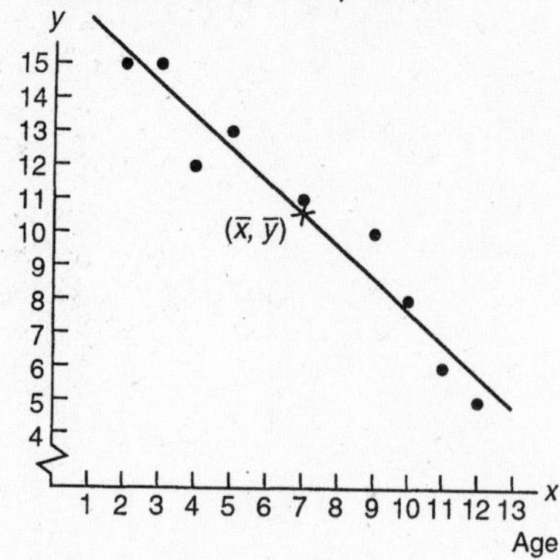

(b) $\bar{x} = \frac{\sum x}{n} = \frac{63}{9} = 7.0$

$\bar{y} = \frac{\sum y}{n} = \frac{95}{9} = 10.56$

$b = \frac{SS_{xy}}{SS_x} = \frac{-104}{108} = -0.96296$

$a = \bar{y} - b\bar{x} = 10.56 - (-0.96296)(7.0) = 17.30$

$y = a + bx$ or $y = 17.30 - 0.963x$

(c) See figure of part (a).

(d) $S_e = \sqrt{\frac{SS_y - bSS_{xy}}{n-2}}$

$= \sqrt{\frac{106.\bar{2} - (-0.96296)(-104)}{9-2}}$

$= 0.93152$

(e) Use $x = 9.5$.

$y_p = 17.30 - 0.963(9.5) = 8.15$ irrelevant responses

(f) $t_{0.99, 7 d.f.} = 3.499$

$E = t_c S_e \sqrt{1 + \frac{1}{n} + \frac{(x-\bar{x})^2}{SS_x}}$

$= 3.499(0.93152)\sqrt{1 + \frac{1}{9} + \frac{(9.5-7.0)^2}{108}}$

$= 3.52$

A 99% confidence interval for y is

$$y_p - E \le y \le y_p + E$$
$$8.15 - 3.52 \le y \le 8.15 + 3.52$$
$$4.6 \le y \le 11.7 \text{ irrelevant responses}$$

13. (a) Elevation and the Number of Frost-Free Days

Number frost-free days

y

200

150

100

50

$(\bar{x}, \bar{y})$

1 2 3 4 5 6 7 8 9 10 x

Elevation (thousands of feet)

(b) $\bar{x} = \frac{\sum x}{n} = \frac{39.6}{5} = 7.92$

$\bar{y} = \frac{\sum y}{n} = \frac{368}{5} = 73.6$

$b = \frac{SS_{xy}}{SS_x} = \frac{-352.26}{11.408} = -30.8783$

$a = \bar{y} - b\bar{x} = 73.6 - (-30.8783)(7.92) = 318.16$

$y = a + bx$ or $y = 318.16 - 30.878x$

(c) See figure of part (a).

Note: Compare this figure to that in Problem 5 above, the point (5.3, 162) is an outlier (possibly in x, definitely in y) but it is more or less along the regression line that would be drawn if it were eliminated from the data set. Thus, this is not an "influential" observation.

(d) $S_e = \sqrt{\frac{SS_y - bSS_{xy}}{n-2}}$

$= \sqrt{\frac{11,299.2 - (-30.8783)(-352.26)}{5-2}}$

$= 11.860$

(e) Use $x = 6$.

$y_p = 318.16 - 30.878(6) = 132.89$ days

(f) $t_{0.85, 3d.f.} = 1.924$

$E = t_c S_e \sqrt{1 + \frac{1}{n} + \frac{(x - \bar{x})^2}{SS_x}}$

$= 1.924(11.860)\sqrt{1 + \frac{1}{5} + \frac{(6 - 7.92)^2}{11.408}}$

$= 28.16$

A 85% confidence interval for y is

$$y_p - E \le y \le y_p + E$$
$$132.89 - 28.16 \le y \le 132.89 + 28.16$$
$$104.7 \le y \le 161.1 \text{ days}$$

14. (a)

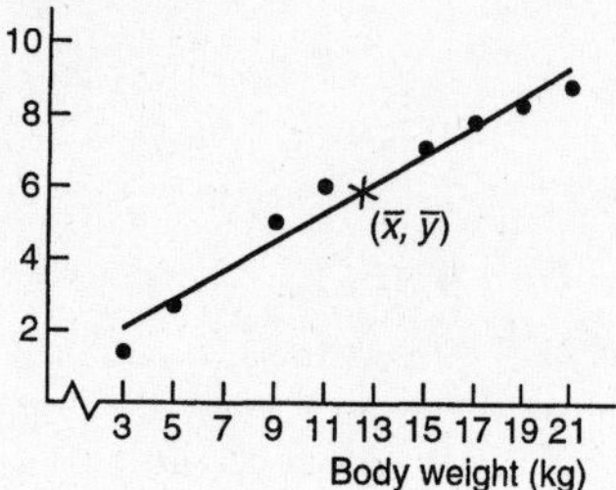

(b) $\bar{x} = \frac{\sum x}{n} = \frac{100}{8} = 12.5$

$\bar{y} = \frac{\sum y}{n} = \frac{47.1}{8} = 5.8875$

$b = \frac{SS_{xy}}{SS_x} = \frac{121.55}{302} = 0.40248$

$a = \bar{y} - b\bar{x} = 5.8875 - 0.40248(12.5) = 0.8565$

$y = a + bx$ or $y = 0.8565 + 0.4025x$

(c) See figure of part (a).

(d) $S_e = \sqrt{\frac{SS_y - bSS_{xy}}{n-2}}$

$= \sqrt{\frac{50.52875 - (0.40248)(121.55)}{8-2}}$

$= 0.5176$

(e) Use $x = 16$.

$y_p = 0.8565 + 0.4025(16) = 7.3$ (100 kcal/24 h)

(f) $t_{0.75, 6d.f.} = 1.273$

$E = t_c S_e \sqrt{1 + \frac{1}{n} + \frac{(x - \bar{x})^2}{SS_x}}$

$= 1.273(0.5176)\sqrt{1 + \frac{1}{8} + \frac{(16 - 12.5)^2}{302}}$

$= 0.7$

A 75% confidence interval for y is

$$y_p - E \le y \le y_p + E$$
$$7.3 - 0.7 \le y \le 7.3 + 0.7$$
$$6.6 \le y \le 8.0 \text{ (100 kcal/24 h)}$$

15. (a) Solubility of Carbon Dioxide in Water

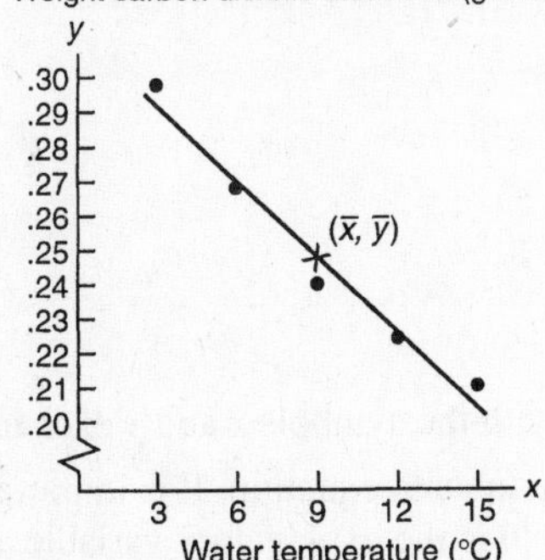

(b) $\bar{x} = \frac{\sum x}{n} = \frac{45}{5} = 9.0$

$\bar{y} = \frac{\sum y}{n} = \frac{1.24}{5} = 0.248$

$b = \frac{SS_{xy}}{SS_x} = \frac{-0.66}{90} = -0.00733$

$a = \bar{y} - b\bar{x} = 0.248 - (-0.00733)(9.0) = 0.314$

$y = a + bx$ or $y = 0.314 - 0.00733x$

(c) See figure of part (a).

(d) $S_e = \sqrt{\frac{SS_y - bSS_{xy}}{n-2}}$

$= \sqrt{\frac{0.004984 - (-0.00733)(-0.66)}{5-2}}$

$= 0.007$

(e) Use $x = 10$.

$y_p = 0.314 - 0.00733(10) = 0.241$ grams

(f) $t_{0.90,3d.f.} = 2.353$

$E = t_c S_e \sqrt{1 + \frac{1}{n} + \frac{(x-\bar{x})^2}{SS_x}}$

$= 2.353(0.007)\sqrt{1 + \frac{1}{5} + \frac{(10-9)^2}{90}}$

$= 0.018$

A 90% confidence interval for y is

$$y_p - \Sigma \le y \le y_p + E$$
$$0.241 - 0.018 \le y \le 0.241 + 0.018$$
$$0.223 \le y \le 0.259 \text{ grams}$$

16. (a) Results checks.

(b) Results checks.

(c) Yes.

(d) $y = 0.143 + 1.071x$

$$y - 0.143 = 1.071x$$

$$\frac{y - 0.143}{1.071} = x$$

$$\frac{1}{1.071}y - \frac{0.143}{1.071} = x$$

or

$$x = 0.9337y - 0.1335$$

The equation $x = 0.9337y - 0.1335$ does not match part (b), with the symbols x and y exchanged.

(e) In general, switching x and y values produces a different least-squares equation. It is important that when you perform a linear regression, you know which variable is the explanatory variable and which is the response variable.

17. (a) Yes. The pattern of residuals appears randomly scattered around the horizontal line at 0.

(b) No. There do not appear to be any outliers.

18. (a)

x	y	$y_p = 43.3263 - 0.6007x$	Residual $= y - y_p$
27	30	27.1	2.9
44	19	16.9	2.1
32	24	24.1	−0.1
47	13	15.1	−2.1
23	29	29.5	−0.5
40	17	19.3	−2.3
34	21	22.9	−1.9
52	14	12.1	1.9

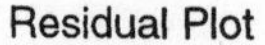

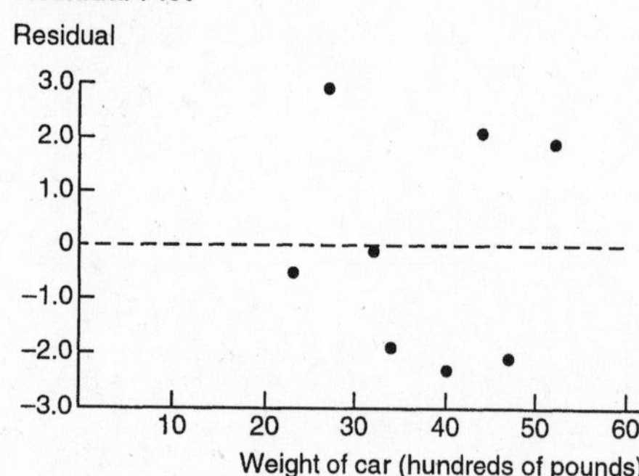

(b) The residuals seem to be scattered randomly around the horizontal line at 0. There do not appear to be any outliers.

Section 10.3

1. (a) No, high positive correlation does not mean causation.

(b) An increase in the population is a third factor that might cause traffic accidents and the number of safety stickers to increase together.

2. **(a)** No, high positive correlation does not mean causation.

(b) There is an increase in buying power due to increase in salaries.

3. **(a)** No, strong negative correlation does not mean causation.

(b) Better medical treatment is a third factor that might be decreasing infant mortalities and at the same time increasing life span.

4. **(a)** No, strong positive correlation does not mean causation.

(b) An increase in population could account for increases both in consumption of soda pop and in number of traffic accidents.

5. **(a)**

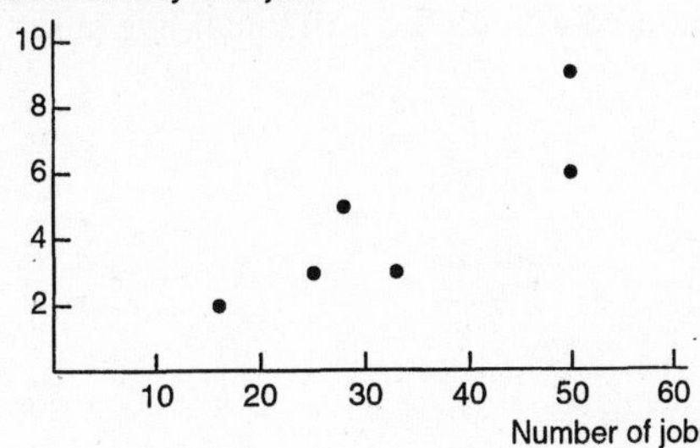

(b) r should be close to 1 because the points seem to be clustered fairly close to a straight line going up from left to right.

(c)
$$r = \frac{SS_{xy}}{\sqrt{SS_x SS_y}} = \frac{153.\overline{3}}{\sqrt{953.\overline{3}(33.\overline{3})}} = 0.860$$

$$r^2 = (0.860)^2 = 0.740$$

This means that 74.0% of the variation in y = number of entry-level jobs can be explained by the corresponding variation in x = total number of jobs using the least squares line. 100% – 74.0% = 26.0% of the variation is unexplained.

6. **(a)**

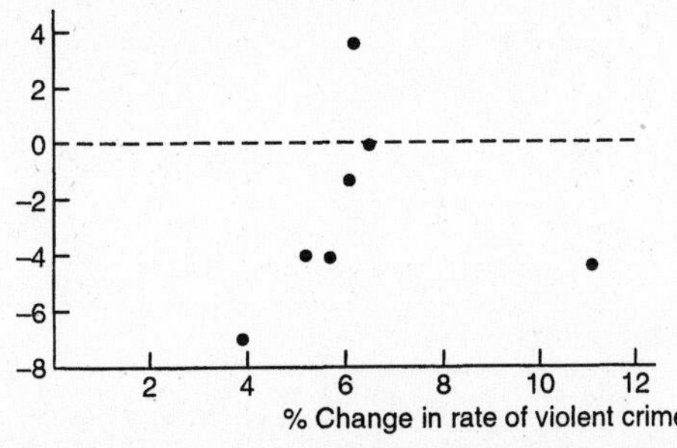

(b) r should be close to 0 because the points are not all clustered around a straight line, due to (11.1, –4.4) (which is an influential observation).

(c) $r = \frac{SS_{xy}}{\sqrt{SS_x SS_y}} = \frac{3.9314}{\sqrt{30.4086(72.8486)}} = 0.084$

$r^2 = (0.084)^2 = 0.007$

This means that 0.7% of the variation in y = percent change in the rate of imprisonment can be explained by the corresponding variation in x = percent change in the rate of violent crime using the least squares line. 100% – 0.7% = 99.3% of the variation is unexplained.

7. (a) Percentage of 16 to 19-Year-Olds Not in School and Number of Violent Crimes per 1000

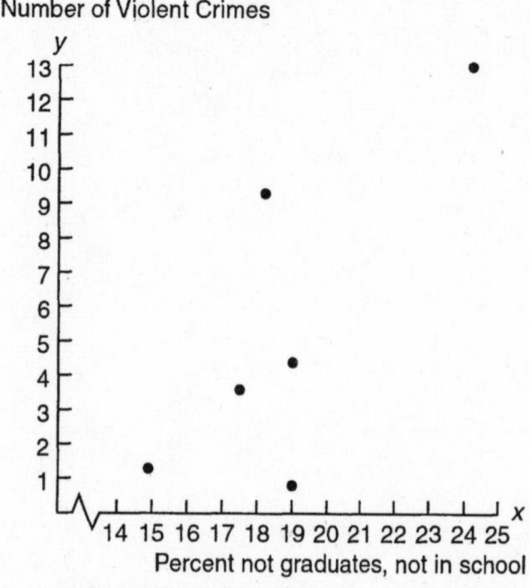

(b) r should be closer to 1 because the points are not somewhat clustered around a straight line going up from left to right.

(c) $r = \frac{SS_{xy}}{\sqrt{SS_x SS_y}} = \frac{55.91}{\sqrt{46.5(115.18)}} = 0.764$

$r^2 = (0.764)^2 = 0.584$

This means that 58.4% of the variation in y = reported violent crimes per 1000 residents can be explained by the corresponding variation in x = percentage of 16-to-19-year-olds not in school and not high school graduates using the least squares line. 100% – 58.4% = 41.6% of the variation is unexplained.

8. (a) Per Capita Income and Death Rates in Small Cities in Oregon

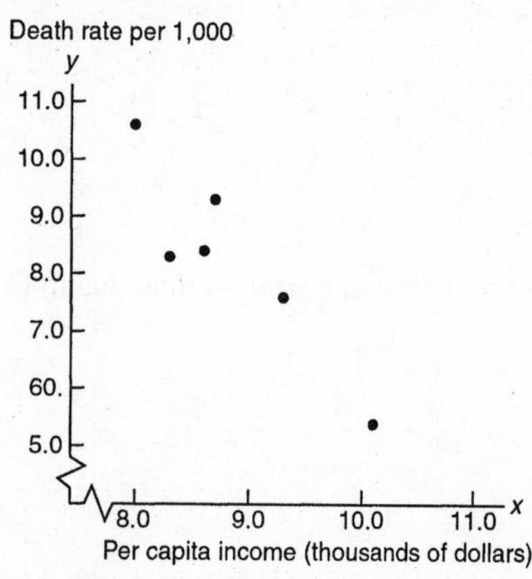

(b) r should be close to –1 because the points are clustered fairly close to a straight line going down from left to right.

(c) $r = \dfrac{SS_{xy}}{\sqrt{SS_x SS_y}} = \dfrac{-6.073}{\sqrt{2.873(15.193)}} = -0.919$

$r^2 = (-0.919)^2 = 0.845$

This means that 84.5% of the variation in y = death rate per 1000 residents can be explained by the corresponding variation in x = per capita income in thousands of dollars using the least squares line. 100% – 84.5%= 15.5% of the variation is unexplained.

9. (a) Per Capita Income and Number of Physicians per 10,000

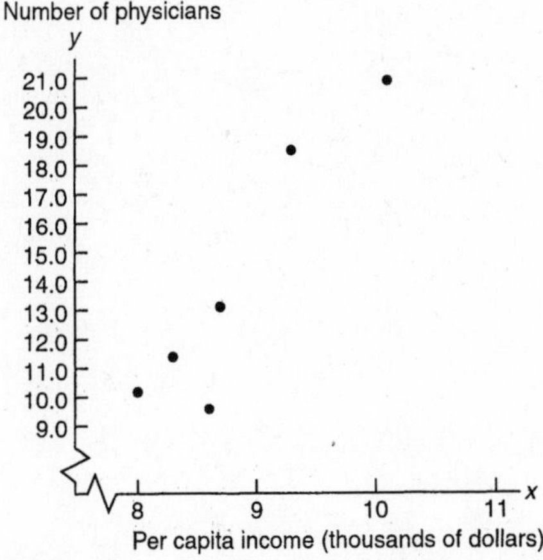

(b) r should be close to 1 because the points are clustered fairly close to a straight line going up from left to right.

(c) $r = \dfrac{SS_{xy}}{\sqrt{SS_x SS_y}} = \dfrac{16.54}{\sqrt{2.873(109.215)}} = 0.934$

$r^2 = (0.934)^2 = 0.872$

This means that 87.2% of the variation in y = number of medical doctors per 10,000 residents can be explained by the corresponding variation in x = per capita income in thousands of dollars using the least squares line. 100% – 87.2% = 12.8% of the variation is unexplained.

10. (a) Percentage of 16 to 19-Year-Olds Not in School and Death Rate per 1000 Residents

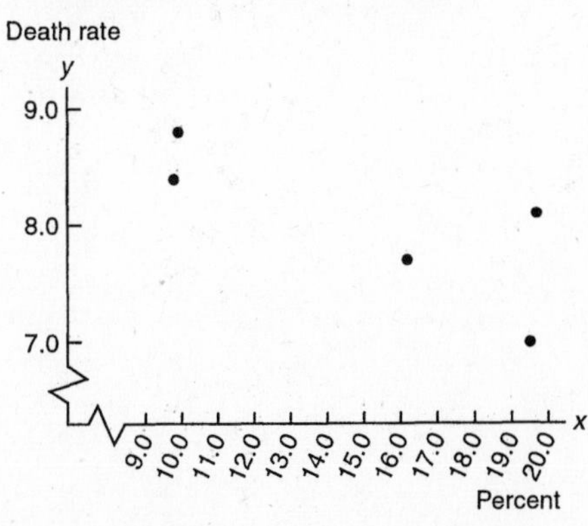

(b) r should be closer to –1 because the points are clustered some what close to a straight line going down from left to right.

(c) $r = \frac{SS_{xy}}{\sqrt{SS_x SS_y}} = \frac{-10.55}{\sqrt{96.828(1.9)}} = -0.778$

$r^2 = (-0.778)^2 = 0.605$

This means that 60.5% of the variation in y = death rate per 1000 residents can be explained by the corresponding variation in x = percentage of 16-to-19-year-olds not in school and not high school graduates using the least squares line. 100% – 60.5% = 39.5% of the variation is unexplained.

11. (a)

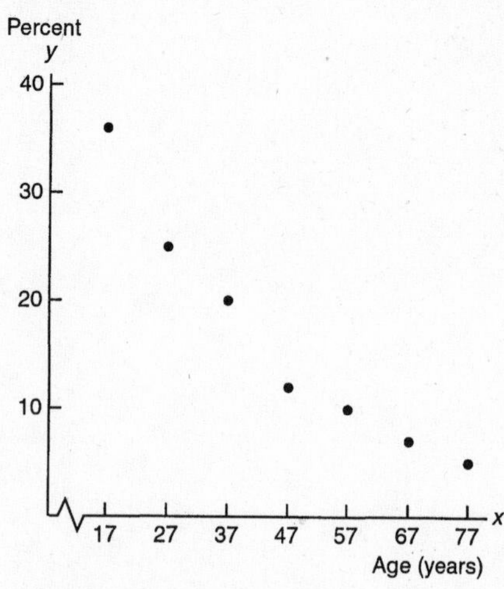

(b) r should be closer to –1 because the points are clustered very close to a straight line going down from left to right. (Note also that the data values fall nicely on a curve.)

(c) $r = \frac{SS_{xy}}{\sqrt{SS_x SS_y}} = \frac{-1390}{\sqrt{2800(749.714)}} = -0.959$

$r^2 = (-0.959)^2 = 0.920$

This means that 92% of the variation in y = percentage of all fatal accidents due to speeding can be explained by the corresponding variation in x = age in years of a licensed automobile driver using the least squares line. 100% – 92% = 8% of the variation is unexplained.

12. (a)

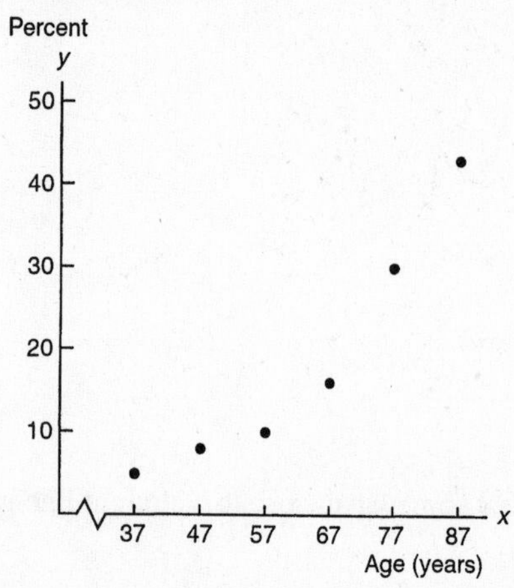

(b) r should be closer to 1 because the points are clustered very close to a straight line going up from left to right. (Note also that the data follow a curve.)

(c) $r = \frac{SS_{xy}}{\sqrt{SS_x SS_y}} = \frac{1310}{\sqrt{1750(1103.\overline{3})}} = 0.943$

$r^2 = (0.943)^2 = 0.889$

This means that 88.9% of the variation in y = percentage of fatal accidents due to failure to yield the right of way can be explained by the corresponding variation in x = age of a licensed driver in years using the least squares line. 100% – 88.9% = 11.1% of the variation is unexplained.

13. (a) Body Height and Bone Size

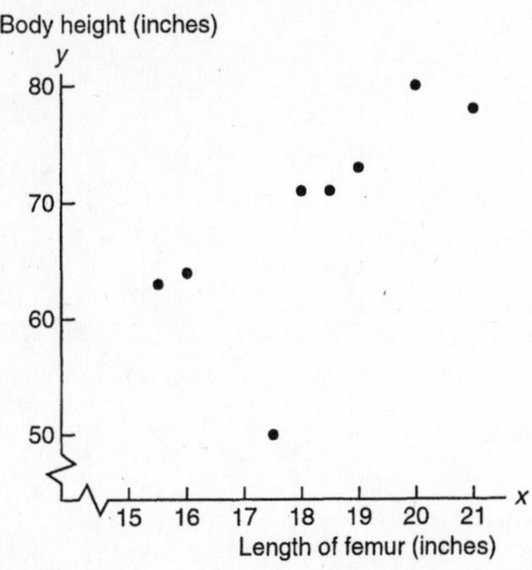

(b) r should be closer to 1 because the points are clustered close to a straight line going up from left to right.

(c) $r = \frac{SS_{xy}}{\sqrt{SS_x SS_y}} = \frac{88.875}{\sqrt{24.4688(647.5)}} = 0.7061$

$r^2 = (0.7061)^2 = 0.499$

This means that 49.9% of the variation in y = body height can be explained by the corresponding variation in x = length of femur using the least squares line. 100% – 49.9% = 50.1% of the variation is unexplained.

14. (a) Lowest Barometric Pressure and Maximum Wind Speed for Tropical Cyclones

Maximum wind speed (mph)

Lowest barometric pressure (mb)

(b) r should be closer to –1 because the points are clustered very close to a straight line going down from left to right.

(c) $r = \dfrac{SS_{xy}}{\sqrt{SS_x SS_y}} = \dfrac{-6575}{\sqrt{4557.5(9683.\overline{3})}} = -0.9897$

$r^2 = (-0.9897)^2 = 0.9795$ or 0.98

This means that 98% of the variation in y = maximum wind speed of the cyclone can be explained by the corresponding variation in x = lowest pressure as a cyclone approaches using the least squares line. 100% − 98% = 2% of the variation is unexplained.

15. (a) We get the same result.

$SS_{xy} = SS_{yx}$

(b) We get the same result.

(c) We get the same result.

(d) First set: $r = \dfrac{SS_{xy}}{\sqrt{SS_x SS_y}} = \dfrac{5}{\sqrt{4.\overline{6}(14)}} = 0.618590$

Second set: $r = \dfrac{SS_{xy}}{\sqrt{SS_x SS_y}} = \dfrac{5}{\sqrt{14(4.\overline{6})}} = 0.618590$

$r = 0.618590$ in both cases.

The least-squares equations are not necessarily the same.

16. (a) No. Interest rate probably affects both investment returns.

(b) For $w = 0.6x + 0.4y$, $a = 0.6$, $b = 0.4$

$\mu_w = a\mu_x + b\mu_y$

$\mu_w = 0.6(7.32) + 0.4(13.19)$

$\mu_w = 9.67$

$\sigma_w^2 = a^2\sigma_x^2 + b^2\sigma_y^2 + 2ab\sigma_x\sigma_y\rho$

$\sigma_w^2 = (0.6)^2(6.59)^2 + (0.4)^2(18.56)^2 + 2(0.6)(0.4)(6.59)(18.56)(0.424)$

$\sigma_w^2 = 95.64$

$\sigma_w = \sqrt{95.64} = 9.78$

(c) For $w = 0.4x + 0.6y$, $a = 0.4$, $b = 0.6$

$\mu_w = 0.4(7.32) + 0.6(13.19)$

$\mu_w = 10.84$

$\sigma_w^2 = (0.4)^2(6.59)^2 + (0.6)^2(18.56)^2 + 2(0.4)(0.6)(6.59)(18.56)(0.424)$

$\sigma_w^2 = 155.85$

$\sigma_w = \sqrt{155.85} = 12.48$

(d) $w = 0.4x + 0.6y$ produces higher returns with greater risk as measured by σ_w.

Section 10.4

1. (a) Results check.

(b) $H_0: \rho = 0$
$H_1: \rho < 0$
$$t = \frac{r\sqrt{n-2}}{\sqrt{1-r^2}} = \frac{-0.377\sqrt{8-2}}{\sqrt{1-(-0.377)^2}} = -0.997$$
$d.f. = n-2 = 8-2 = 6$

At 5% level of significance, $t_0 = -1.943$.
P value > 0.125
Since $-0.997 > -1.943$ and P value > 0.125, we fail to reject H_0. The sample evidence does not support a negative correlation.

(c) $H_0: \beta = 0$
$H_1: \beta \neq 0$
$$t = \frac{b-\beta}{\frac{S_e}{\sqrt{SS_x}}} = \frac{-0.468-0}{\frac{7.443}{\sqrt{252.40}}} = -0.999$$
$d.f. = n-2 = 8-2 = 6$

At 5% level of significance, $t_0 = \pm 2.447$.
P value > 0.250
Since $-2.447 < -0.999 < 2.447$, we fail to reject H_0. The sample evidence does not support a nonzero slope.

(d) $d.f. = 6, t_c = 1.273, b \approx -0.468$
$$E = t_c \frac{S_e}{\sqrt{SS_x}} = 1.273 \frac{7.443}{\sqrt{252.40}} = 0.596$$

A 75% confidence interval is

$$b - E < \beta < b + E$$
$$-0.468 - 0.596 < \beta < -0.468 + 0.596$$
$$-1.064 < \beta < 0.128$$

Since the confidence interval includes both positive and negative values, we conclude that the slope is zero and so faculty salaries are not tied to tuition. For a \$100 change in tuition and fees, there is essentially no change in faculty salaries.

2. (a) Results check.

(b) $H_0: \rho = 0$
$H_1: \rho \neq 0$
$$t = \frac{r\sqrt{n-2}}{\sqrt{1-r^2}} = \frac{0.187\sqrt{9-2}}{\sqrt{1-(0.187)^2}} = 0.504$$
$d.f. = n-2 = 9-2 = 7$

At 5% level of significance, $t_0 = \pm 2.365$.
P value > 0.250
Since $-2.365 < 0.504 < 2.365$ and P value > 0.250, we fail to reject H_0. The sample evidence does not support a nonzero correlation.

(c) $H_0: \beta = 0$

$H_1: \beta \neq 0$

$$t = \frac{b-\beta}{\frac{S_e}{\sqrt{SS_x}}} = \frac{0.172-0}{\frac{6.369}{\sqrt{350.70}}} = 0.506$$

$d.f. = n-2 = 9-2 = 7$

At 5% level of significance, $t_0 = \pm 2.365$.

P value > 0.250

Since $-2.365 < 0.506 < 2.365$ and P value > 0.250, we fail to reject H_0. The sample evidence does not support a nonzero slope. (The t–values in (b) and (c) differ due to roundoff error.)

(d) $d.f. = 7, t_c = 1.415, b \approx 0.172$

$$E = t_c \frac{S_e}{\sqrt{SS_x}} = 1.415 \frac{6.369}{\sqrt{350.70}} = 0.481$$

An 80% confidence interval is

$$b - E < \beta < b + E$$
$$0.172 - 0.481 < \beta < 0.172 + 0.481$$
$$-0.309 < \beta < 0.653$$

Since the confidence interval includes both positive and negative values, we conclude that the slope is zero and so faculty salaries are not tied to tuition. For a $100 change in tuition and fees, there is essentially no change in faculty salaries.

3. (a) Results check.

(b) $H_0: \rho = 0$

$H_1: \rho < 0$

$$t = \frac{r\sqrt{n-2}}{\sqrt{1-r^2}} = \frac{-0.976\sqrt{7-2}}{\sqrt{1-(-0.976)^2}} = -10.02$$

$d.f. = n-2 = 7-2 = 5$

At 1% level of significance, $t_0 = -3.365$.

P value < 0.005

Since $-10.02 < -3.365$ and P value < 0.005, we reject H_0. The sample evidence supports a negative correlation.

(c) $H_0: \beta = 0$

$H_1: \beta < 0$

$$t = \frac{b-\beta}{\frac{S_e}{\sqrt{SS_x}}} = \frac{-0.054-0}{\frac{0.166}{\sqrt{940.89}}} = -9.98$$

$d.f. = n-2 = 7-2 = 5$

At 1% level of significance, $t_0 = -3.365$.

P value < 0.005

Since $-9.98 < -3.365$ and P value < 0.005, we reject H_0. The sample evidence supports a negative slope.

(d) $d.f. = 5, t_c = 2.015, b \approx -0.054$

$$E = t_c \frac{S_e}{\sqrt{SS_x}} = 2.015 \frac{0.166}{\sqrt{940.89}} = 0.011$$

A 90% confidence interval is

$$b - E < \beta < b + E$$
$$-0.054 - 0.011 < \beta < -0.054 + 0.011$$
$$-0.065 < \beta < -0.043$$

For every meter more of depth, the optimal time decreases from about 0.04 to 0.07 hour.

4. (a) Results check.

(b) $H_0: \rho = 0$

$H_1: \rho > 0$

$$t = \frac{r\sqrt{n-2}}{\sqrt{1-r^2}} = \frac{0.984\sqrt{5-2}}{\sqrt{1-(0.984)^2}} = 9.57$$

$d.f. = n - 2 = 5 - 2 = 3$

At 1% level of significance, $t_0 = 4.541$.
P value < 0.005
Since 9.57 > 4.541 and P value < 0.005, we reject H_0. The sample evidence supports a positive correlation.

(c) $H_0: \beta = 0$

$H_1: \beta > 0$

$$t = \frac{b - \beta}{\frac{S_e}{\sqrt{SS_x}}} = \frac{6.876 - 0}{\frac{2.532}{\sqrt{12.25}}} = 9.505$$

$d.f. = n - 2 = 5 - 2 = 3$

At 1% level of significance, $t_0 = 4.541$.
P value < 0.005
Since 9.505 > 4.541 and P value < 0.005, we reject H_0. The sample evidence supports a positive slope.
Note: carrying more decimal places than shown in (b) gives $t = 9.505$, the same as in (c).

(d) $d.f. = 3, t_c = 3.182, b \approx 6.876$

$$E = t_c \frac{S_e}{\sqrt{SS_x}} = 3.182 \frac{2.532}{\sqrt{12.25}} = 2.302$$

A 95% confidence interval is

$$b - E < \beta < b + E$$
$$6.876 - 2.302 < \beta < 6.876 + 2.302$$
$$4.57 < \beta < 9.18$$

For every one unit increase in oxygen pressure breathing only available air, the oxygen pressure breathing pure oxygen increases from about 4.57 units to 9.18 units.

5. **(a)** Results check.

(b) $H_0: \rho = 0$
$H_1: \rho > 0$

$$t = \frac{r\sqrt{n-2}}{\sqrt{1-r^2}} = \frac{0.956\sqrt{6-2}}{\sqrt{1-(0.956)^2}} = 6.517$$

$d.f. = n-2 = 6-2 = 4$

At 1% level of significance, $t_0 = 3.747$.
P value < 0.005
Since $6.517 > 3.747$ and P value < 0.005, we reject H_0. The sample evidence supports a positive correlation.

(c) $H_0: \beta = 0$
$H_1: \beta > 0$

$$t = \frac{b-\beta}{\frac{S_e}{\sqrt{SS_x}}} = \frac{0.758-0}{\frac{0.1527}{\sqrt{1.733}}} = 6.535$$

$d.f. = n-2 = 6-2 = 4$

At 1% level of significance, $t_0 = 3.747$.
P value < 0.005
Since $6.535 > 3.747$ and P value < 0.005, we reject H_0. The sample evidence supports a positive slope.

(d) $d.f. = 4, t_c = 2.132, b \approx 0.758$

$$E = t_c \frac{S_e}{\sqrt{SS_x}} = 2.132 \frac{0.1527}{\sqrt{1.733}} = 0.247$$

A 90% confidence interval is

$$b - E < \beta < b + E$$
$$0.758 - 0.247 < \beta < 0.758 + 0.247$$
$$0.511 < \beta < 1.005$$

For every \$1,000 increase in list price, there is an increase in dealer price of between \$511 and \$1005.

6. **(a)** Results check.

(b) $H_0: \rho = 0$
$H_1: \rho > 0$

$$t = \frac{r\sqrt{n-2}}{\sqrt{1-r^2}} = \frac{0.977\sqrt{5-2}}{\sqrt{1-(0.977)^2}} = 7.936$$

$d.f. = n-2 = 5-2 = 3$

At 1% level of significance, $t_0 = 4.541$.
P value < 0.005
Since $7.936 > 4.541$ and P value < 0.005, we reject H_0. The sample evidence supports a positive correlation.

(c) $H_0: \beta = 0$
$H_1: \beta > 0$

$$t = \frac{b-\beta}{\frac{S_e}{\sqrt{SS_x}}} = \frac{0.879-0}{\frac{0.1522}{\sqrt{188.26}}} = 7.924$$

$d.f. = n-2 = 5-2 = 3$

At 1% level of significance, $t_0 = 4.541$.
P value < 0.005
Since 7.924 > 4.541 and P value < 0.005, we reject H_0. The sample evidence supports a positive slope.

(d) $d.f. = 3, t_c = 2.353, b \approx 0.879$

$$E = t_c \frac{S_e}{\sqrt{SS_x}} = 2.353 \frac{1.522}{\sqrt{188.26}} = 0.261$$

A 90% confidence interval is

$$b - E < \beta < b + E$$
$$0.879 - 0.261 < \beta < 0.879 + 0.261$$
$$0.618 < \beta < 1.140$$

For every increase of $1,000 in list price, the dealer price is from $618 to $1,140 higher.

7. (a) $H_0: \rho = 0$
$H_1: \rho \neq 0$

$$t = \frac{r\sqrt{n-2}}{\sqrt{1-r^2}} = \frac{0.90\sqrt{6-2}}{\sqrt{1-(0.90)^2}} = 4.129$$

$d.f. = n-2 = 6-2 = 4$

At 1% level of significance, $t_0 = \pm 4.604$.
Since $-4.604 < 4.129 < 4.604$ and $0.01 < P$ value, we do not reject H_0. The correlation coefficient ρ is not significantly different from zero at the 0.01 level of significance.

(b) $H_0: \rho = 0$
$H_1: \rho \neq 0$

$$t = \frac{r\sqrt{n-2}}{\sqrt{1-r^2}} = \frac{0.90\sqrt{10-2}}{\sqrt{1-(0.90)^2}} = 5.840$$

$d.f. = n-2 = 10-2 = 8$

At 1% level of significance, $t_0 = \pm 3.355$.

Since 5.840 > 3.355 and P value < 0.01, we reject H_0. The correlation coefficient ρ is significantly different from zero at the 0.01 level of significance.

(c) From part (a) to part (b), n increased from 6 to 10, the test statistic t increased from 4.12 to 5.840, and the critical values t_0 decreased (in absolute value) from 4.604 to 3.355. For the same $r = 0.90$ and the same level of significance $\alpha = 0.01$, we rejected H_0 for the larger n but not for the smaller n.

In general, as n increases, the degrees of freedom ($n - 2$) increase and the critical value(s) become(s) closer to zero. Also, as n increases, the test statistic $\left(t = \frac{r\sqrt{n-2}}{\sqrt{1-r^2}}\right)$ moves farther from zero. The combination of the critical value(s) approaching zero while the test statistic moves farther out into the tail of the t–distribution means we are more likely to reject H_0 for larger n (using the same r and α).

8. (a) Yes. The t values are equal (differences are due to rounding error).

(b) Essay.

A possible proof, working on the left side first, follows:

Prove: $t = \dfrac{r\sqrt{n-2}}{\sqrt{1-r^2}} = \dfrac{b\sqrt{SS_x}}{S_e}$

Proof: Begin with these versions of r, b, S_e, and r^2:

page 582 (9): $r = \dfrac{SS_{xy}}{\sqrt{SS_x\, SS_y}}$

page 561: $b = \dfrac{SS_{xy}}{SS_x}$

page 568 (7): $S_e = \sqrt{\dfrac{\Sigma(y-y_p)^2}{n-2}}$
or $\sqrt{\Sigma(y-y_p)^2} = \sqrt{n-2}\; S_e$

page 589: $r^2 = \dfrac{\Sigma(y_p-\bar{y})^2}{\Sigma(y-\bar{y})^2} = \dfrac{\Sigma(y_p-\bar{y})^2}{SS_y}$ (1)

Then from page 589: $SS_y = \Sigma(y-\bar{y})^2 = \Sigma(y_p-\bar{y})^2 + \Sigma(y-y_p)^2$
or $\Sigma(y_p-\bar{y})^2 = SS_y - \Sigma(y-y_p)^2$ (2)

So $r^2 = \dfrac{\Sigma(y_p-\bar{y})^2}{SS_y} = \dfrac{SS_y - \Sigma(y-y_p)^2}{SS_y}$ using (2)

$= 1 - \dfrac{\Sigma(y-y_p)^2}{SS_y}$

or $1-r^2 = \dfrac{\Sigma(y-y_p)^2}{SS_y}$

$\sqrt{1-r^2} = \dfrac{\sqrt{\Sigma(y-y_p)^2}}{\sqrt{SS_y}}$

$\dfrac{1}{\sqrt{1-r^2}} = \dfrac{\sqrt{SS_y}}{\sqrt{\Sigma(y-y_p)^2}} = \dfrac{\sqrt{SS_y}}{\sqrt{n-2}\; S_e}$ using (1)

Then $t = \dfrac{r\sqrt{n-2}}{\sqrt{1-r^2}} = r\left(\dfrac{1}{\sqrt{1-r^2}}\right)\sqrt{n-2} = \left(\dfrac{SS_{xy}}{\sqrt{SS_x\, SS_y}}\right)\left(\dfrac{\sqrt{SS_y}}{\sqrt{n-2}\; S_e}\right)\sqrt{n-2}$

$= \dfrac{SS_{xy}}{\sqrt{SS_x}\; S_e} = \dfrac{SS_{xy}}{\sqrt{SS_x}\; S_e}\left(\dfrac{\sqrt{SS_x}}{\sqrt{SS_x}}\right) = \left(\dfrac{SS_{xy}}{SS_x}\right)\dfrac{\sqrt{SS_x}}{S_e} = \dfrac{b\sqrt{SS_x}}{S_e}$

as was to be shown.

Section 10.5

1. $x_1 = 1.6 + 3.5x_2 - 7.9x_3 + 2.0x_4$

(a) The response variable is x_1.

(b) The constant term is 1.6.
The coefficient 3.5 goes with corresponding explanatory variable x_2.
The coefficient –7.9 goes with corresponding explanatory variable x_3.
The coefficient 2.0 goes with corresponding explanatory variable x_4.

(c) $x_2 = 2, x_3 = 1, x_4 = 5$
$x_1 = 1.6 + 3.5(2) - 7.9(1) + 2.0(5) = 10.7$
The predicted value is 10.7.

(d) In multiple regression, the coefficients of the explanatory variables can be thought of as "slopes" (the change in the response variables per unit change in the explanatory variable) if we look at one explanatory variable's coefficient at a time, while holding the other explanatory variables as arbitrary and fixed constants.
x_3 and x_4 held constant, x_2 increased by one unit:
The change in x_1 would be an increase of 3.5 units.
x_3 and x_4 held constant, x_2 increased by two units:
The change in x_1 would be an increase of 2(3.5) = 7 units.
x_3 and x_4 held constant, x_2 decreased by four units:
The change in x_1 would be an decrease of 4(3.5) = 14 units.

(e) $d.f. = n - k - 1 = 12 - 3 - 1 = 8$
A 90% confidence interval for the coefficient of x_2 is $b_2 - tS_2 < \beta_2 < b_2 + tS_2$
$3.5 - 1.86(0.419) < \beta_2 < 3.5 + 1.86(0.419)$
$2.72 < \beta_2 < 4.28$

(f) $H_0\text{: } \beta_2 = 0$
$H_1\text{: } \beta_2 \neq 0$
$$t = \frac{b_2 - \beta_2}{S_2} = \frac{3.5 - 0}{0.419} = 8.35$$
$d.f. = 8, t_0 = \pm 2.306$ for 5% level of significance.
Since 8.35 > 2.306, we reject H_0.
We conclude that $\beta_2 \neq 0$ and x_2 should be included as an explanatory variable in the least-squares equation.

2. $x_3 = -16.5 + 4.0x_1 + 9.2x_4 - 1.1x_7$

(a) The response variable is x_3.
The explanatory variables are x_1, x_4, and x_7.

(b) The constant term is -16.5.
The coefficient 4.0 goes with the corresponding explanatory variable x_1.
The coefficient 9.2 goes with the corresponding explanatory variable x_4.
The coefficient -1.1 goes with the corresponding explanatory variable x_7.

(c) $x_1 = 10, x_4 = -1, x_7 = 2$
$x_3 = -16.5 + 4.0(10) + 9.2(-1) - 1.1(2) = 12.1$
The predicted value is 12.1.

(d) In multiple regression, the coefficients of the explanatory variables can be thought of as "slopes" (the change in the response variables per unit change in the explanatory variable) if we look at one explanatory variable's coefficient at a time, while holding the other explanatory variables as arbitrary and fixed constants.

x_1 and x_7 held constant, x_4 increased by one unit:

The change in x_3 would be an increase of 9.2 units.

x_1 and x_7 held constant, x_4 increased by three units:

The change in x_3 would be an increase of 3(9.2) = 27.6 units.

x_1 and x_7 held constant, x_4 decreased by two units:

The change in x_3 would be a decrease of 2(9.2) = 18.4 units.

(e) $d.f. = n - k - 1 = 15 - 3 - 1 = 11$

A 90% confidence interval for the coefficient of x_4 is $b_4 - tS_4 < \beta_4 < b_4 + tS_4$

$9.2 - 1.796(0.921) < \beta_4 < 9.2 + 1.796(0.921)$

$7.55 < \beta_4 < 10.85$

(f) $H_0: \beta_4 = 0$
$H_1: \beta_4 \neq 0$

$$t = \frac{b_4 - \beta_4}{S_4} = \frac{9.2 - 0}{0.921} = 9.989$$

$d.f. = 11, t_0 = \pm 3.106$ for 1% level of significance.

Since 9.989 > 3.106, we reject H_0.

We conclude that $\beta_4 \neq 0$ and x_4 should be included as an explanatory variable in the least-squares equation.

3. (a)

	$\bar{x}$	s	$CV = \frac{s}{\bar{x}} \cdot 100$
x_1	150.09	13.63	9.08%
x_2	62.45	9.11	14.59%
x_3	195.0	17.31	8.88%

Relative to its mean, x_2 has the greatest spread of data values and x_3 has the smallest spread of data values.

(b) $r^2_{x_1x_2} \approx (0.979)^2 \approx 0.958$
$r^2_{x_1x_3} \approx (0.971)^2 \approx 0.943$
$r^2_{x_2x_3} \approx (0.946)^2 \approx 0.895$

The variable x_2 has the greatest influence on x_1 (0.958 > 0.943).

Yes. Both variables x_2 and x_3 show a strong influence on x_1 because 0.958 and 0.943 are close to 1.

95.8% of the variation of x_1 can be explained by the corresponding variation in x_2.

94.3% of the variation of x_1 can be explained by the corresponding variation in x_3.

(c) $R^2 = 0.977$

97.7% of the variation in x_1 can be explained by the corresponding variation in x_2 and x_3 taken together.

(d) $x_1 = 30.99 + 0.861x_2 + 0.355x_3$

In multiple regression, the coefficients of the explanatory variables can be thought of as "slopes" (the change in the response variables per unit change in the explanatory variable) if we look at one explanatory variable's coefficient at a time, while holding the other explanatory variables as arbitrary and fixed constants.

If age (x_2) were held fixed and x_3 increased by 10 pounds, the systolic blood pressure is expected to increase by 0.335(10) = 3.35.

If weight (x_3) were held fixed and x_2 increased by 10 years, the systolic blood pressure is expected to increase by 0.861(10) = 8.61.

(e) $H_0\colon \beta_i = 0$

$H_1\colon \beta_i \neq 0$

$d.f = n-k-1 = 11-2-1 = 8$

$t_0 = \pm 2.306$ for 5% level of significance.

For β_2, the sample test statistic is $t = 3.47$.

For β_3, the sample test statistic is $t = 2.56$.

Since 3.47 > 2.306 and 2.56 > 2.306, reject H_0 for each coefficient and conclude that the coefficients of x_2 and x_3 are not zero. Explanatory variables x_i whose coefficients (β_i) are nonzero contribute information in the least squares equation, i.e., without these x_i, the resulting least squares regression equation is not as good a fit to the data as is the regression equation which includes these x_i.

(f) $d.f. = 8, t = 1.86$

A 90% confidence interval for β_i is

$$b_i - tS_i < \beta_i < b_i + tS_i$$
$$0.861 - 1.86(0.2482) < \beta_2 < 0.861 + 1.86(0.2482)$$
$$0.40 < \beta_2 < 1.32$$
$$0.335 - 1.86(0.1307) < \beta_3 < 0.335 + 1.86(0.1307)$$
$$0.09 < \beta_3 < 0.58$$

(g) $x_1 = 30.99 + 0.861(68) + 0.335(192) \approx 153.9$

Michael's predicted systolic blood pressure is 153.9 and a 90% confidence interval for this new observation's value, given these x_i, i.e., the prediction interval, is 148.3 to 159.4.

4. (a)

	$\bar{x}$	s	$CV = \frac{s}{\bar{x}} \cdot 100$
x_1	79.04	12.28	15.53%
x_2	79.48	12.50	15.73%
x_3	81.48	11.77	14.44%
x_4	162.04	24.04	14.83%

Relative to its mean, each exam had about the same spread of scores. Yes; it seems that all of the exams were about the same level of difficulty.

(b) $r^2_{x_1x_2} \approx (0.901)^2 \approx 0.812$
$r^2_{x_1x_3} \approx (0.893)^2 \approx 0.797$
$r^2_{x_1x_4} \approx (0.946)^2 \approx 0.895$
$r^2_{x_2x_3} \approx (0.846)^2 \approx 0.716$
$r^2_{x_2x_4} \approx (0.929)^2 \approx 0.863$
$r^2_{x_3x_4} \approx (0.972)^2 \approx 0.945$

Exam 3 had the most influence on the final exam 4 (0.945 > 0.895 > 0.863). Even though exam 3 had more influence, the other two exams still had a lot of influence on the final because 0.895 and 0.863 are close to 1.

(c) $R^2 = 0.990$

99.0% of the variation in x_4 can be explained by the corresponding variation in x_1, x_2, and x_3 taken together.

(d) $x_4 = -4.34 + 0.356x_1 + 0.543x_2 + 1.17x_3$

In multiple regression, the coefficients of the explanatory variables can be thought of as "slopes" (the change in the response variables per unit change in the explanatory variable) if we look at one explanatory variable's coefficient at a time, while holding the other explanatory variables as arbitrary and fixed constants.

If age x_1 and x_2 are held fixed and x_3 is increased by 10 points, the final exam score is expected to increase by $10(1.17) = 11.7 \approx 12$ points.

(e) H_0: $\beta_i = 0$
H_1: $\beta_i \neq 0$
$d.f = n - k - 1 = 25 - 3 - 1 = 21$
$t_0 = \pm 2.080$ for 5% level of significance.
For β_1, the sample test statistic is $t = 2.93$.
For β_2, the sample test statistic is $t = 5.38$.
For β_3, the sample test statistic is $t = 11.33$.

Since 2.93 > 2.08, 5.38 > 2.08, and 11.33 > 2.08, reject H_0 for each coefficient and conclude that the coefficients of x_1, x_2 and x_3 are not zero. Explanatory variables x_i whose coefficients (β_i) are nonzero contribute information in the least squares equation, i.e., without these x_i, the resulting least squares regression equation is not as good a fit to the data as is the regression equation which includes these x_i.

(f) $d.f. = 21, t = 1.721$

A 90% confidence interval for β_i is

$$b_i - tS_i < \beta_i < b_i + tS_i$$

$$0.356 - 1.721(0.1214) < \beta_1 < 0.356 + 1.721(0.1214)$$
$$0.147 < \beta_1 < 0.565$$

$$0.543 - 1.721(0.1008) < \beta_2 < 0.543 + 1.721(0.1008)$$
$$0.370 < \beta_2 < 0.716$$

$$1.167 - 1.721(0.1030) < \beta_3 < 1.167 + 1.721(0.1030)$$
$$0.990 < \beta_3 < 1.344$$

(g) $x_4 = -4.34 + 0.356(68) + 0.543(72) + 1.17(75) \approx 147$
Susan's predicted score on the final exam is 147 and a 90% confidence interval for this new observation's value, given these x_i, i.e., the prediction interval, is 142 to 151, all rounded to whole numbers.

5. (a)

	$\bar{x}$	s	$CV = \frac{s}{\bar{x}} \cdot 100$
x_1	85.24	33.79	39.64%
x_2	8.74	3.89	44.51%
x_3	4.90	2.48	50.61%
x_4	9.92	5.17	52.12%

Relative to its mean, x_4 has the largest spread of data values. The larger the CV, the more we expect the variable to change relative to its average value, because a variable with a large CV has a large standard deviation, s, relative to $\bar{x}$, and s measures "spread," or variability, in the data. x_1 has a small CV because we divide by a large mean.

(b) $r^2_{x_1x_2} \approx (0.917)^2 \approx 0.841$
$r^2_{x_1x_3} \approx (0.930)^2 \approx 0.865$
$r^2_{x_1x_4} \approx (0.475)^2 \approx 0.226$
$r^2_{x_2x_3} \approx (0.790)^2 \approx 0.624$
$r^2_{x_2x_4} \approx (0.429)^2 \approx 0.184$
$r^2_{x_3x_4} \approx (0.299)^2 \approx 0.089$

The variable x_4 has the least influence on box office receipts x_1 $(0.226 < 0.841 < 0.865)$.

x_2 = production costs, $r^2_{x_1x_2} \approx 0.841$.
84.1% of the variation of box office receipts can be attributed to the corresponding variation in production costs.

(c) $R^2 = 0.967$
96.7% of the variation in x_1 can be explained by the corresponding variation in x_2, x_3, and x_4 taken together.

(d) $x_1 = 7.68 + 3.66x_2 + 7.62x_3 + 0.83x_4$
In multiple regression, the coefficients of the explanatory variables can be thought of as "slopes" (the change in the response variables per unit change in the explanatory variable) if we look at one explanatory variable's coefficient at a time, while holding the other explanatory variables as arbitrary and fixed constants.
If x_2 and x_4 were held fixed and x_3 were increased by 1 ($1 million), the corresponding change in x_1 (box office receipts) would be an increase of 7.62 or 7.62 million dollars.

(e) $H_0\colon \beta_i = 0$
$H_1\colon \beta_i \neq 0$
$d.f = n - k - 1 = 10 - 3 - 1 = 6$
$t_0 = \pm 2.447$ for 5% level of significance.
For β_2, the sample test statistic is $t = 3.28$.
For β_3, the sample test statistic is $t = 4.60$.
For β_4, the sample test statistic is $t = 1.54$
Since $3.28 > 2.447$ and $4.60 > 2.447$, reject H_0 for coefficients β_2 and β_3 and conclude that the coefficients of x_2 and x_3 are not zero.
Since $-2.447 < 1.54 < 2.447$, do not reject H_0 for the coefficient β_4 and conclude that the coefficient of x_4 could be zero. If $\beta_4 = 0$, then x_4 contributes nothing to the (population) regression line. We can eliminate the variable x_4 and fit the (estimated) regression line without it, and probably see little, if any, difference between the predicted values of x_1 based on x_2 and x_3 only and the predicted values of x_1 based on x_2, x_3, and x_4.

(f) $d.f. = 6,\ t = 1.943$
A 90% confidence interval for β_i is

$$b_i - tS_i < \beta_i < b_i + tS_i$$

$$3.662 - 1.943(1.118) < \beta_2 < 3.662 + 1.943(1.118)$$
$$1.49 < \beta_2 < 5.83$$

$$7.621 - 1.943(1.657) < \beta_3 < 7.621 + 1.943(1.657)$$
$$4.40 < \beta_3 < 10.84$$

$$0.8285 - 1.943(0.5394) < \beta_4 < 0.8285 + 1.943(0.5394)$$
$$-0.22 < \beta_4 < 1.88$$

(g) $x_1 = 7.68 + 3.66(11.4) + 7.62(4.7) + 0.83(8.1) = 91.94$
The prediction is 91.94 million dollars and a 85% confidence interval for this new observation's value, given these x_i, i.e., the prediction interval, is \$77.6 million to \$106.3 million.

(h) $x_3 = -0.650 + 0.102x_1 - 0.260x_2 - 0.0899x_4$
$x_3 = -0.650 + 0.102(100) - 0.260(12) - 0.0899(9.2)$
$x_3 = 5.63$
The prediction is 5.63 million dollars and a 80% confidence interval for this new observation's value, given these x_i, i.e., the prediction interval, is \$4.21 million to \$7.04 million.

6. (a)

	$\overline{x}$	s	$CV = \frac{s}{\overline{x}} \cdot 100$
x_1	286.574	192.062	67.02%
x_2	3.326	2.011	60.46%
x_3	387.481	191.168	49.34%
x_4	8.100	3.775	46.60%
x_5	9.693	5.140	53.03%
x_6	7.741	4.896	63.25%

Relative to its mean, x_1 has the largest spread of data values and x_4 has a smallest spread of data values.

(b) $r_{23} = 0.844$
$r_{24} = 0.749$
$r_{25} = 0.838$
$r_{26} = -0.766$
$r_{34} = 0.906$
$r_{35} = 0.864$
$r_{36} = -0.807$
$r_{45} = 0.795$
$r_{46} = -0.841$
$r_{56} = -0.870$
$r^2_{x_1x_2} \approx (0.894)^2 \approx 0.799$
$r^2_{x_1x_3} \approx (0.946)^2 \approx 0.895$
$r^2_{x_1x_4} \approx (0.914)^2 \approx 0.835$
$r^2_{x_1x_5} \approx (0.954)^2 \approx 0.910$
$r^2_{x_1x_6} \approx (-0.912)^2 \approx 0.832$

The variable x_5 has the greatest influence on annual net sales (0.910 is the largest). The variable x_2 has the least influence on annual net sales (0.799 is the smallest).

(c) $R^2 = 0.993$
99.3% of the variation in x_1 can be explained by the corresponding variation in x_2, x_3, x_4, x_5, and x_6 taken together.

(d) $x_1 = -18.9 + 16.2x_2 + 0.175x_3 + 11.5x_4 + 13.6x_5 - 5.31x_6$

In multiple regression, the coefficients of the explanatory variables can be thought of as "slopes" (the change in the response variables per unit change in the explanatory variable) if we look at one explanatory variable's coefficient at a time, while holding the other explanatory variables as arbitrary and fixed constants.
If all explanatory variables but x_6 remained fixed and x_6 increased by 2, then the annual net sales are expected to decrease by 2(5.31) = 10.62 or $10,620.
If all explanatory variables but x_4 remained fixed and x_4 increased by 1($1000), then the annual net sales are expected to increase by 11.5 or $11,500.

(e) H_0: $\beta_i = 0$
H_1: $\beta_i \neq 0$
$d.f = 27 - 5 - 1 = 21$
$t_0 = \pm 2.080$ for 5% level of significance.
For β_2, the sample test statistic is $t = 4.57$.
For β_3, the sample test statistic is $t = 3.03$.
For β_4, the sample test statistic is $t = 4.55$
For β_5, the sample test statistic is $t = 7.67$.
For β_6, the sample test statistic is $t = -3.11$.
Since all of these t values are larger than 2.080 or less than -2.080, we reject H_0 for each coefficient and conclude that the coefficients of x_2, x_3, x_4, x_5, and x_6 are not zero.

(f) The predicted annual net sales are 194.41 (or $194.41 thousand) and the 80% confidence interval for this new observation's value, given these x_i, i.e., the prediction interval, is $160.76 thousand to $228.06 thousand.

(g) $x_4 = 4.14 + 0.0431x_1 - 0.800x_2 + 0.00059x_3 - 0.661x_5 + 0.057x_6$

The predicted amount spent on local advertising is \$5.571 thousand and the 80% confidence interval for this new observation's value, given these x_i, i.e., the prediction interval, is \$4.048 thousand to \$7.094 thousand. Advertising costs for this store should be between \$4,048 and \$7,094.

Chapter 10 Review Problems

1. (a)

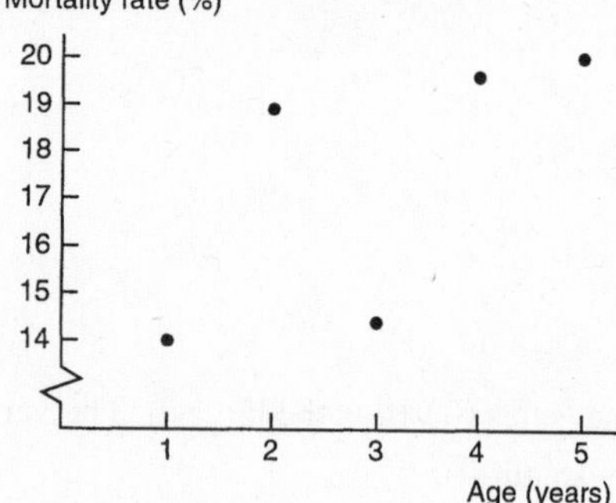

(b) $\bar{x} = \frac{\Sigma x}{n} = \frac{15}{5} = 3$

$\bar{y} = \frac{\Sigma y}{n} = \frac{86.9}{5} = 17.38$

$b = \frac{SS_{xy}}{SS_x} = \frac{12.7}{10} = 1.27$

$a = \bar{y} - b\bar{x} = 17.38 - 1.27(3) = 13.57$

$y = a + bx$ or $y = 13.57 + 1.27x$

(c) $r = \frac{SS_{xy}}{\sqrt{SS_x SS_y}} = \frac{12.7}{\sqrt{10(34.408)}} = 0.685$

$r^2 = (0.685)^2 = 0.469$

The correlation coefficient r measures the strength of the linear relationship between a bighorn sheep's age and the mortality rate. The coefficient of determination, r^2, means that 46.9% of the variation in y = mortality rate in this age groups can be explained by the corresponding variation in x = age of a bighorn sheep using the least squares line.

(d) $H_0: \rho = 0$

$H_1: \rho > 0$

$t = \frac{r\sqrt{n-2}}{\sqrt{1-r^2}} = \frac{0.685\sqrt{5-2}}{\sqrt{1-(0.685)^2}} = 1.629$

At 1% level of significance, $t_0 = 4.541$.

Since $1.629 < 4.541$, we do not reject H_0.

There does not seem to be a positive correlation between age and mortality rate of bighorn sheep.

(e) $H_0: \beta = 0$

$H_1: \beta > 0$

$$t = \frac{b-\beta}{\frac{S_e}{\sqrt{SS_x}}} = \frac{1.27-0}{\frac{2.468}{\sqrt{10}}} = 1.627$$

$d.f. = n-2 = 5-2 = 3$

At 1% level of significance, $t_0 = 4.541$.

Since $1.627 < 4.541$, we do not reject H_0.

The sample evidence does not support a positive slope.

2. (a)

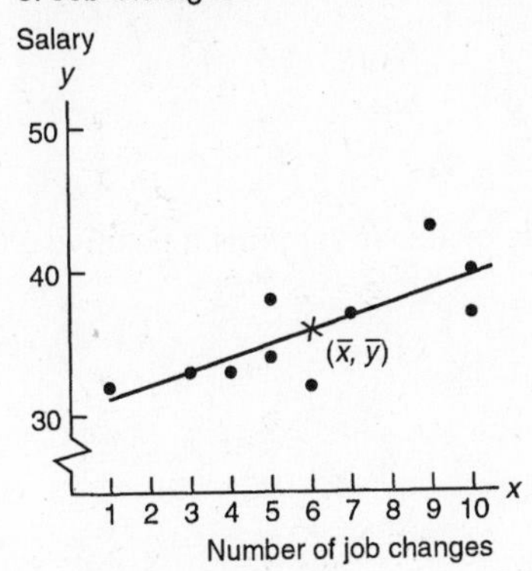

(b) $\overline{x} = \frac{\sum x}{n} = \frac{60}{10} = 6.0$

$\overline{y} = \frac{\sum y}{n} = \frac{359}{10} = 35.9$

$b = \frac{SS_{xy}}{SS_x} = \frac{77}{82} = 0.939024$

$a = \overline{y} - b\overline{x} = 35.9 - 0.939024(6.0) = 30.266$

$y = a + bx$ or $y = 30.266 + 0.939x$

(c) See the figure in part (a).

(d) Let $x = 2$.

$y_p = 30.266 + 0.939(2) = 32.14$

The predicted salary is \$32,140.

(e) $$S_e = \sqrt{\frac{SS_y - bSS_{xy}}{n-2}} = \sqrt{\frac{124.9 - 0.939024(77)}{10-2}} = 2.564058$$

(f) $$E = t_c S_e \sqrt{1 + \frac{1}{n} + \frac{(x-\overline{x})^2}{SS_x}}$$

$$= 1.860(2.564058)\sqrt{1 + \frac{1}{10} + \frac{(2-6.0)^2}{82}}$$

$= 5.43$

A 90% confidence interval for y is

$$y_p - E \le y \le y_p + E$$
$$32.14 - 5.43 \le y \le 32.14 + 5.43$$
$$26.71 \le y \le 37.57$$

(g) The correlation coefficient will be positive because the points are clustered around a straight line going up from left to right.

(h) $r = \dfrac{SS_{xy}}{\sqrt{SS_x SS_y}} = \dfrac{77}{\sqrt{82(124.9)}} = 0.761$

$r^2 = (0.761)^2 = 0.579$

This means that 57.9% of the variation in y = salary can be explained by the corresponding variation in x = number of job changes using the least squares line.

(i) $H_0: \rho = 0$

$H_1: \rho > 0$

$t = \dfrac{r\sqrt{n-2}}{\sqrt{1-r^2}} = \dfrac{0.761\sqrt{10-2}}{\sqrt{1-(0.761)^2}} = 3.318$

$d.f. = n-2 = 10-2 = 8$

At 5% level of significance, $t_0 = 1.860$.

Since 3.318 > 1.860, reject H_0 and conclude that the sample evidence supports a positive correlation.

(j) $H_0: \beta = 0$

$H_1: \beta > 0$

$t = \dfrac{b-\beta}{\frac{S_e}{\sqrt{SS_x}}} = \dfrac{0.939024-0}{\frac{2.564058}{\sqrt{82}}} = 3.316$

$d.f. = n-2 = 10-2 = 8$

At 5% level of significance, $t_0 = 1.860$.

Since 3.16 > 1.860, reject H_0 and conclude that the sample evidence supports a positive slope.

3. (a) Weight of One-Year-Old versus Weight of Adult

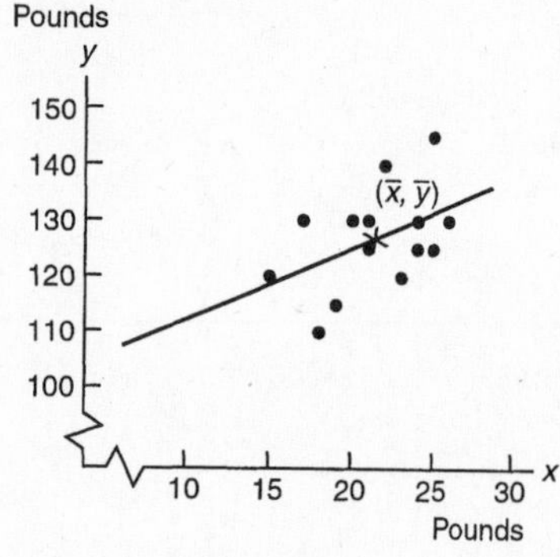

(b) $\bar{x} = \dfrac{\Sigma x}{n} = \dfrac{300}{14} = 21.43$

$\bar{y} = \dfrac{\Sigma y}{n} = \dfrac{1775}{14} = 126.79$

$b = \dfrac{SS_{xy}}{SS_x} = \dfrac{184.2857}{143.4286} = 1.285$

$a = \bar{y} - b\bar{x} = 126.79 - (1.285)(21.43) = 99.25$

$y = a + bx$ or $y = 99.25 + 1.285x$

(c) See the figure in part (a).

(d) Let $x = 20$.

$y_p = 99.25 + 1.285(20) = 124.95$

The predicted weight is 124.95 pounds.

(e) $S_e = \sqrt{\dfrac{SS_y - bSS_{xy}}{n-2}} = \sqrt{\dfrac{1080.36 - 1.285(184.2857)}{14-2}} = 8.38$

(f) $E = t_c S_e \sqrt{1 + \dfrac{1}{n} + \dfrac{(x-\overline{x})^2}{SS_x}}$

$= 2.179(8.38)\sqrt{1 + \dfrac{1}{14} + \dfrac{(20-21.43)^2}{143.4286}}$

$= 19.03$

A 95% confidence interval for y is

$$y_p - E \le y \le y_p + E$$
$$124.95 - 19.03 \le y \le 124.95 + 19.03$$
$$105.92 \le y \le 143.98$$

(g) The correlation coefficient will be positive because the points are clustered around a straight line going up from left to right.

(h) $r = \dfrac{SS_{xy}}{\sqrt{SS_x SS_y}} = \dfrac{184.2857}{\sqrt{143.4286(1080.36)}} = 0.468$

$r^2 = (0.468)^2 = 0.219$

The correlation coefficient r measures the strength of the linear relationship between a woman's weight at age 1 and at age 30. The coefficient of determination r^2 means that 21.9% of the variation in y = weight of a mature adult (30 years old) can be explained by the corresponding variation in x = weight of a 1-year-old baby using the least squares line.

(i) $H_0: \rho = 0$

$H_1: \rho > 0$

$t = \dfrac{r\sqrt{n-2}}{\sqrt{1-r^2}} = \dfrac{0.468\sqrt{14-2}}{\sqrt{1-(0.468)^2}} = 1.834$

$d.f. = n - 2 = 14 - 2 = 12$

At 1% level of significance, $t_0 = 2.681$.

Since $1.834 < 2.681$, do not reject H_0. There does not seem to be any significant positive correlation at the 1% level.

(j) $H_0: \beta = 0$

$H_1: \beta > 0$

$t = \dfrac{b - \beta}{\frac{S_e}{\sqrt{SS_x}}} = \dfrac{1.285 - 0}{\frac{8.38}{\sqrt{143.4286}}} = 1.84$

$d.f. = n - 2 = 14 - 2 = 12$

At 1% level of significance, $t_0 = 2.681$.

Since $1.84 < 2.681$, we do not reject H_0. The sample evidence does not support a positive slope.

4. (a) Number of Insurance Sales and Number of Visits

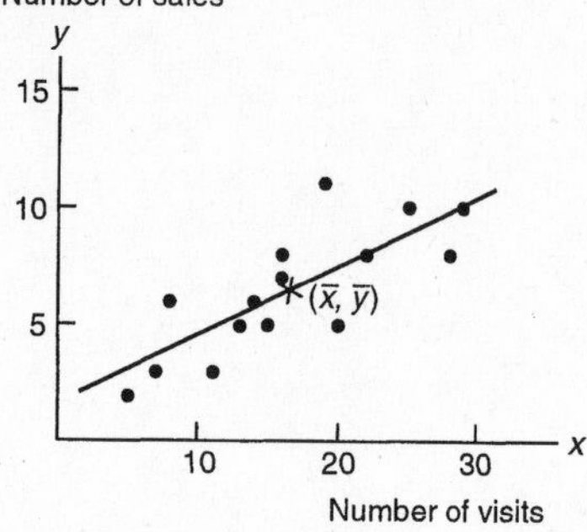

(b) $\overline{x} = \frac{\sum x}{n} = \frac{248}{15} = 16.5\overline{3} \approx 16.53$

$\overline{y} = \frac{\sum y}{n} = \frac{97}{15} = 6.4\overline{6} \approx 6.47$

$b = \frac{SS_{xy}}{SS_x} = \frac{221.2\overline{6}}{755.7\overline{3}} = 0.292784$

$a = \overline{y} - b\overline{x} = 6.4\overline{6} - 0.292784(16.5\overline{3}) = 1.626$

$y = a + bx$ or $y = 1.626 + 0.293x$

(c) See the figure in part (a).

(d) Let $x = 18$.

$y_p = 1.626 + 0.293(18) = 6.9$

The predicted number of sales is 6.9 or 7.

(e) $S_e = \sqrt{\frac{SS_y - bSS_{xy}}{n-2}} = \sqrt{\frac{103.7\overline{3} - 0.292784(221.2\overline{6})}{15-2}} = 1.730940$

(f) $E = t_c S_e \sqrt{1 + \frac{1}{n} + \frac{(x-\overline{x})^2}{SS_x}}$

$= 1.771(1.730940)\sqrt{1 + \frac{1}{15} + \frac{(18 - 16.5\overline{3})^2}{755.7\overline{3}}}$

$= 3.17$

A 90% confidence interval for y is

$$y_p - E \le y \le y_p + E$$
$$6.9 - 3.17 \le y \le 6.9 + 3.17$$
$$3.73 \le y \le 10.07$$

(g) $r = \frac{SS_{xy}}{\sqrt{SS_x SS_y}} = \frac{221.2\overline{6}}{\sqrt{755.7\overline{3}(103.7\overline{3})}} = 0.790$

$r^2 = (0.790)^2 = 0.624$

This means that 62.4% of the variation in y = number of people who bought insurance that week can be explained by the corresponding variation in x = number of visits made each week using the least squares line.

(h) $H_0\colon \rho = 0$
$H_1\colon \rho > 0$

$$t = \frac{r\sqrt{n-2}}{\sqrt{1-r^2}} = \frac{0.790\sqrt{15-2}}{\sqrt{1-(0.790)^2}} = 4.65$$

$d.f. = n-2 = 15-2 = 13$

At 1% level of significance, $t_0 = 2.650$.

Since $4.65 > 2.650$, we reject H_0 and conclude that the sample evidence supports a positive correlation.

(i) $H_0\colon \beta = 0$
$H_1\colon \beta > 0$

$$t = \frac{b-\beta}{\frac{S_e}{\sqrt{SS_x}}} = \frac{0.292784-0}{\frac{1.730940}{\sqrt{755.73}}} = 4.65$$

$d.f. = n-2 = 15-2 = 13$

At 1% level of significance, $t_0 = 2.650$.

Since $4.65 > 2.650$, we reject H_0 and conclude that the sample evidence supports a positive slope.

5. (a)

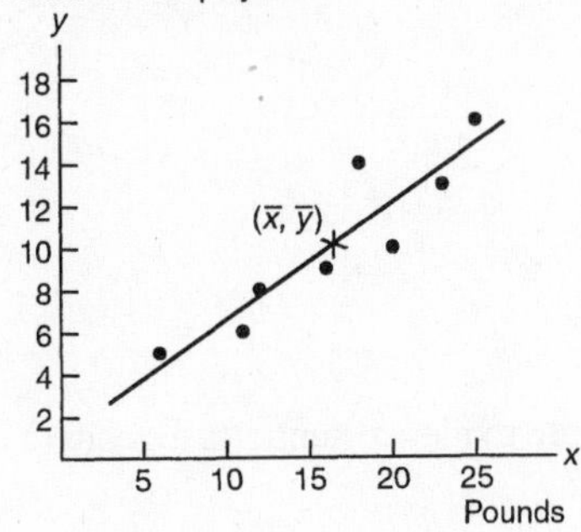

(b) $\bar{x} = \frac{\Sigma x}{n} = \frac{131}{8} = 16.375 \approx 16.38$

$\bar{y} = \frac{\Sigma y}{n} = \frac{81}{8} = 10.125 \approx 10.13$

$b = \frac{SS_{xy}}{SS_x} = \frac{160.625}{289.875} = 0.554118 \approx 0.554$

$a = \bar{y} - b\bar{x} = 10.125 - 0.554118(16.375) = 1.051$

$y = a + bx$ or $y = 1.051 + 0.544x$

(c) See the figure in part (a).

(d) Use $x = 15$.

$y_p = 1.051 + 0.544(15) = 9.36$

About 9 or 10 employees should be assigned mail duty.

(e) $$S_e = \sqrt{\frac{SS_y - bSS_{xy}}{n-2}} = \sqrt{\frac{106.875-(0.554118)(160.625)}{8-2}} = 1.73$$

(f) $E = t_c S_e \sqrt{1 + \frac{1}{n} + \frac{(x-\bar{x})^2}{SS_x}}$

$= 2.447(1.73)\sqrt{1 + \frac{1}{8} + \frac{(15-16.375)^2}{289.875}}$

$= 4.5$

A 95% confidence interval for y is

$$y_p - E \le y \le y_p + E$$
$$9.36 - 4.5 \le y \le 9.36 + 4.5$$
$$4.86 \le y \le 13.86$$

(g) $r = \frac{SS_{xy}}{\sqrt{SS_x SS_y}} = \frac{160.625}{\sqrt{289.875(106.875)}} = 0.913$

$r^2 = (0.913)^2 = 0.834$

The correlation coefficient r measures the strength of the linear association between weight of incoming mail and number of employees assigned to answer it. The coefficient of determination, r^2, means that 83.4% of the variation in y = number of employees can be explained by the corresponding variation in x = weight of incoming mail using the least squares line.

(h) $H_0: \rho = 0$

$H_1: \rho > 0$

$t = \frac{r\sqrt{n-2}}{\sqrt{1-r^2}} = \frac{0.913\sqrt{8-2}}{\sqrt{1-(0.913)^2}} = 5.48$

$d.f. = n - 2 = 8 - 2 = 6$

At 1% level of significance, $t_0 = 3.143$.

Since $5.48 > 3143$, we reject H_0 and conclude that the sample evidence supports a positive correlation coefficient.

(i) $H_0: \beta = 0$

$H_1: \beta > 0$

$t = \frac{b-\beta}{\frac{S_e}{\sqrt{SS_x}}} = \frac{0.554118-0}{\frac{1.73}{\sqrt{289.875}}} = 5.45$

$d.f. = n - 2 = 8 - 2 = 6$

At 1% level of significance, $t_0 = 3.143$.

Since $5.45 > 3.143$, we reject H_0 and conclude that the sample evidence supports a positive slope.

(j) $d.f. = 6, t_c = 1.440, b \approx 0.554$

$E = t_c \frac{S_e}{\sqrt{SS_x}} = 1.440 \frac{1.73}{\sqrt{289.875}} = 0.146$

An 80% confidence interval is

$$b - E < \beta < b + E$$
$$0.554 - 0.146 < \beta < 0.554 + 0.146$$
$$0.41 < \beta < 0.70$$

For each additional pound of mail, assign 1 employee to work from 41% to 70% of a work day on mail.

6. (a) Percent Population Change

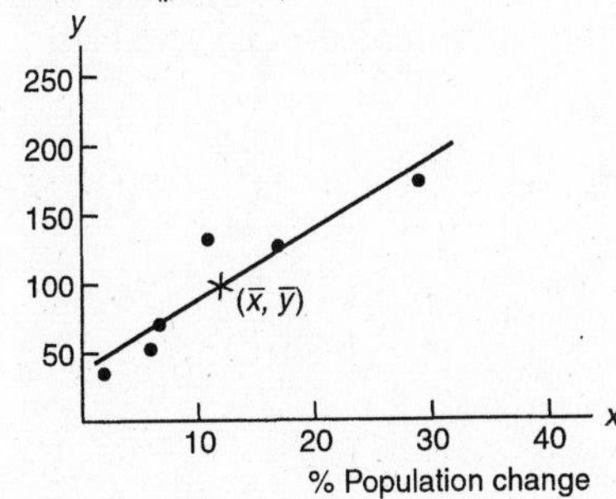

(b) $\bar{x} = \frac{\Sigma x}{n} = \frac{72}{6} = 12.0$

$\bar{y} = \frac{\Sigma y}{n} = \frac{589}{6} = 98.1\bar{6} \approx 98.17$

$b = \frac{SS_{xy}}{SS_x} = \frac{2431}{476} = 5.1071 \approx 5.11$

$a = \bar{y} - b\bar{x} = 98.1\bar{6} - 5.1071(12.0) = 36.881 \approx 36.9$

$y = a + bx$ or $y = 36.9 + 5.11x$

See the figure in part (a).

(c) Let $x = 12$

$y = 36.9 + 5.11(12) = 98.2$

The predicted crime rate is 98.2 crimes per thousand.

(d) $$S_e = \sqrt{\frac{SS_y - bSS_{xy}}{n-2}} = \sqrt{\frac{14456.8\bar{3} - 5.1071(2431)}{6-2}} = 22.59$$

$$E = t_c S_e \sqrt{1 + \frac{1}{n} + \frac{(x-\bar{x})^2}{SS_x}}$$

$$= 1.533(22.59)\sqrt{1 + \frac{1}{6} + \frac{(12-12)^2}{476}} = 37.41$$

A 80% confidence interval for y is

$$y_p - E \le y \le y_p + E$$
$$98.2 - 37.41 \le y \le 98.2 + 37.41$$
$$60.8 \le y \le 135.6$$

or about 61 to 136 crimes per thousand.

(e) $$r = \frac{SS_{xy}}{\sqrt{SS_x SS_y}} = \frac{2431}{\sqrt{476(14456.8\bar{3})}} = 0.927$$

$r^2 = (0.927)^2 = 0.859$

$H_0: \rho = 0$

$H_1: \rho \ne 0$

$$t = \frac{r\sqrt{n-2}}{\sqrt{1-r^2}} = \frac{0.927\sqrt{6-2}}{\sqrt{1-(0.927)^2}} = 4.94$$

$d.f. = n - 2 = 6 - 2 = 4$

At 1% level of significance, $t_0 = \pm 4.604$.

Since $4.94 > 4.604$, we reject H_0 and conclude that the sample evidence supports a significant correlation coefficient.

(f) High correlation does not guarantee a "cause-and-effect" situation. Before causation is estabilished, more work needs to be done taking other variables into account.
High correlation is simply an indication of a mathematical relationship between variables.

(g) $H_0: \beta = 0$
$H_1: \beta > 0$

$$t = \frac{b-\beta}{\frac{S_e}{\sqrt{SS_x}}} = \frac{5.1071-0}{\frac{22.59}{\sqrt{476}}} = 4.93$$

$d.f. = n-2 = 6-2 = 4$

At 1% level of significance, $t_0 = 3.747$.

Since 4.93 > 3.747, we reject H_0 and conclude that the sample evidence supports a positive slope.

(h) $d.f. = 4, t_c = 1.533, b \approx 5.11$

$$E = t_c \frac{S_e}{\sqrt{SS_x}} = 1.533 \frac{22.59}{\sqrt{476}} = 1.59$$

An 80% confidence interval is

$$b - E < \beta < b + E$$
$$5.11 - 1.59 < \beta < 5.11 + 1.59$$
$$3.52 < \beta < 6.70$$

For every percentage point increase in population, expect the crime rate per 1000 to increase from between 3.52 to 6.70 crimes per thousand.

Chapter 11 Chi-Square and *F* Distributions

Section 11.1

1. H_0: Myers-Briggs preference and profession are independent.

H_1: Myers-Briggs preference and profession are not independent.

$$\chi^2 = \sum\frac{(O-E)^2}{E}$$

$$= \frac{(308-241.05)^2}{241.05} + \frac{(226-292.95)^2}{292.95} + \frac{(667-723.61)^2}{723.61} + \frac{(936-879.39)^2}{879.39} + \frac{(112-122.33)^2}{122.33} + \frac{(159-148.67)^2}{148.67}$$

$$= 43.5562$$

Since there are 3 rows and 2 columns, *d.f.* = (3 – 1)(2 – 1) = 2. For $\alpha = 0.01$, the critical value is $\chi^2_{0.01} = 9.21$.

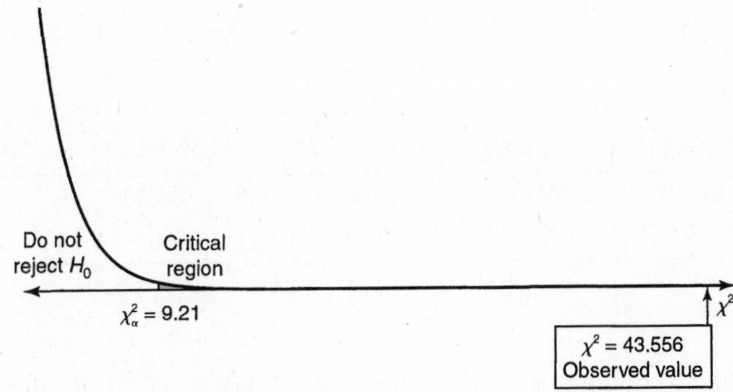

Since the sample statistic falls inside the critical region, we reject H_0. We conclude that Myers-Briggs preference and profession are not independent.

2. H_0: Myers-Briggs preference and profession are independent.

H_1: Myers-Briggs preference and profession are not independent.

$$\chi^2 = \sum\frac{(O-E)^2}{E}$$

$$= \frac{(114-238.39)^2}{238.39} + \frac{(420-295.61)^2}{295.61} + \frac{(785-715.62)^2}{715.62} + \frac{(818-887.37)^2}{887.37} + \frac{(176-120.98)^2}{120.98} + \frac{(95-150.02)^2}{150.02}$$

$$= 174.6$$

Since there are 3 rows and 2 columns, *d.f.* = (3 – 1)(2 – 1) = 2. For $\alpha = 0.01$, the critical value is $\chi^2_{0.01} = 9.21$.

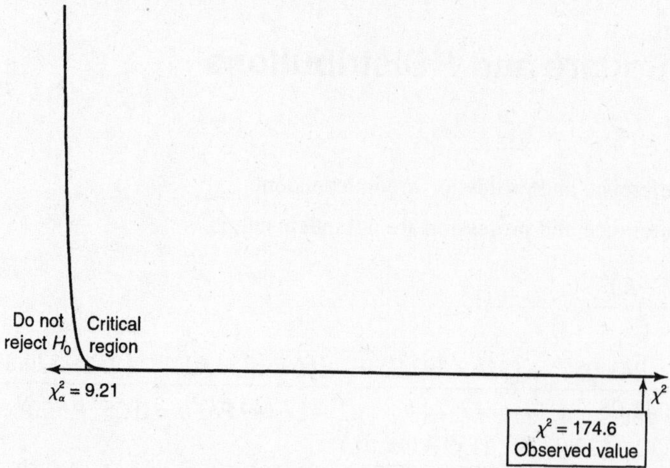

Since the sample statistic falls inside the critical region, we reject H_0. We conclude that Myers-Briggs preference and profession are not independent.

3. H_0: Site type and pottery type are independent.
   H_1: Site type and pottery type are not independent.

$$\chi^2 = \sum \frac{(O-E)^2}{E}$$

$$= \frac{(75-74.64)^2}{74.64} + \frac{(61-59.89)^2}{59.89} + \frac{(53-54.47)^2}{54.47} + \frac{(81-84.11)^2}{84.11} + \frac{(70-67.5)^2}{67.5}$$

$$+ \frac{(62-61.39)^2}{61.39} + \frac{(92-89.25)^2}{89.25} + \frac{(68-71.61)^2}{71.61} + \frac{(66-65.14)^2}{65.14}$$

$$= 0.5552$$

Since there are 3 rows and 3 columns, $d.f. = (3-1)(3-1) = 4$. For $\alpha = 0.05$, the critical value is $\chi^2_{0.05} = 9.49$.

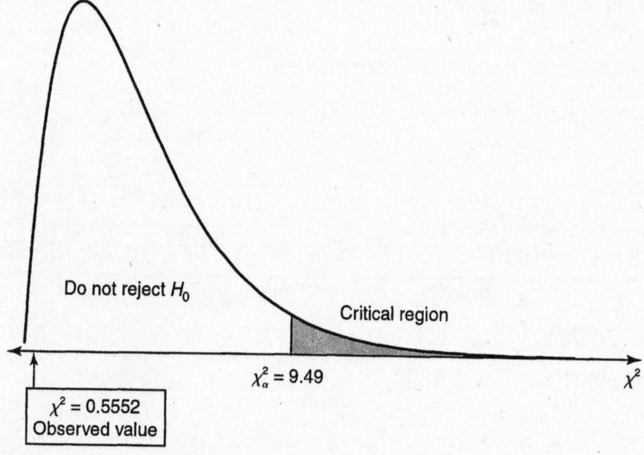

Since the sample statistic falls outside the critical region, do not reject H_0. There is insufficient evidence to conclude that site type and pottery type are not independent.

4. H_0: Ceremonial ranking and pottery type are independent.
H_1: Ceremonial ranking and pottery type are not independent.

$$\chi^2 = \sum \frac{(O-E)^2}{E}$$

$$= \frac{(242-242.61)^2}{242.61} + \frac{(26-25.39)^2}{25.39} + \frac{(658-636.41)^2}{636.41} + \frac{(45-66.59)^2}{66.59} + \frac{(371-391.98)^2}{391.98} + \frac{(62-41.02)^2}{41.02}$$

$$= 19.6079$$

Since there are 3 rows and 2 columns, *d.f.* = (3 – 1)(2 – 1) = 2. For $\alpha = 0.05$, the critical value is $\chi^2_{0.05} = 5.99$.

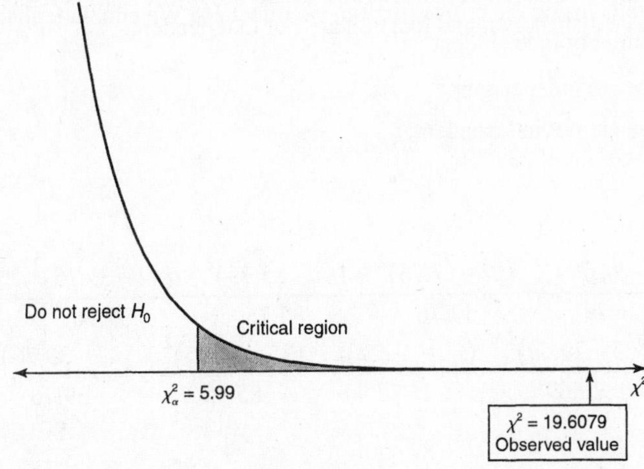

Since the sample statistic falls inside the critical region, we reject H_0. We conclude that ceremonial ranking and pottery type are not independent.

5. H_0: Age distribution and location are independent.
H_1: Age distribution and location are not independent.

$$\chi^2 = \sum \frac{(O-E)^2}{E}$$

$$= \frac{(13-14.08)^2}{14.08} + \frac{(13-12.84)^2}{12.84} + \frac{(15-14.08)^2}{14.08} + \frac{(10-11.33)^2}{11.33} + \frac{(11-10.34)^2}{10.34} + \frac{(12-11.33)^2}{11.33} + \frac{(34-31.59)^2}{31.59} + \frac{(28-28.82)^2}{28.82} + \frac{(30-31.59)^2}{31.59}$$

$$= 0.67$$

Since there are 3 rows and 3 columns, *d.f.* = (3 – 1)(3 – 1) = 4. For $\alpha = 0.05$, the critical value is $\chi^2_{0.05} = 9.49$.

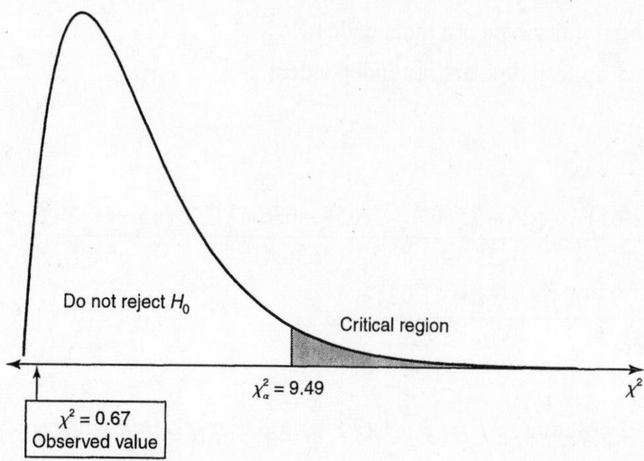

Since the sample statistic falls outside the critical region, we do not reject H_0. There is insufficient evidence to conclude that age distribution and location are not independent.

6. H_0: Type and career choice are independent.

H_1: Type and career choice are not independent.

$$\chi^2 = \sum \frac{(O-E)^2}{E}$$

$$= \frac{(64-53.46)^2}{53.46} + \frac{(15-24.79)^2}{24.79} + \frac{(17-17.76)^2}{17.76} + \frac{(82-85.75)^2}{85.75} + \frac{(42-39.76)^2}{39.76} + \frac{(30-28.49)^2}{28.49}$$
$$+ \frac{(68-64.04)^2}{64.04} + \frac{(35-29.69)^2}{29.69} + \frac{(12-21.27)^2}{21.27} + \frac{(75-85.75)^2}{85.75} + \frac{(42-39.76)^2}{39.76} + \frac{(37-28.49)^2}{28.49}$$
$$= 15.602$$

Since there are 4 rows and 3 columns, $d.f. = (4-1)(3-1) = 6$. For $\alpha = 0.01$, the critical value is $\chi^2_{0.01} = 16.81$.

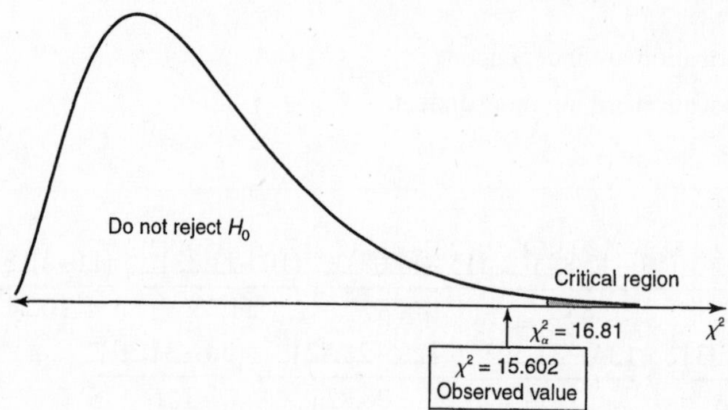

Since the sample statistic falls outside the critical region, we do not reject H_0. There is insufficient evidence to conclude that type and career choice are not independent.

7. H_0: Ages of young adults and movie preferences are independent.

H_1: Ages of young adults and movie preferences are not independent.

$$\chi^2 = \sum \frac{(O-E)^2}{E}$$

$$= \frac{(8-10.60)^2}{10.60} + \frac{(15-12.06)^2}{12.06} + \frac{(11-11.33)^2}{11.33} + \frac{(12-9.35)^2}{9.35} + \frac{(10-10.65)^2}{10.65}$$

$$+ \frac{(8-10.00)^2}{10.00} + \frac{(9-9.04)^2}{9.04} + \frac{(8-10.29)^2}{10.29} + \frac{(12-9.67)^2}{9.67}$$

$$= 3.623$$

Since there are 3 rows and 3 columns, $d.f. = (3-1)(3-1) = 4$. For $\alpha = 0.05$, the critical value is $\chi^2_{0.05} = 9.49$.

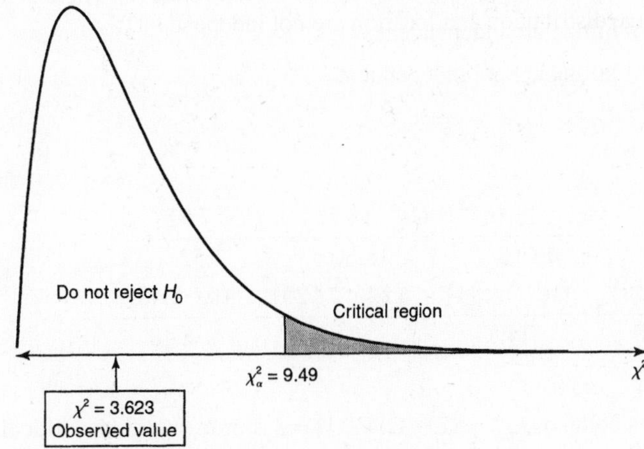

Since the sample statistic falls outside the critical region, we do not reject H_0. There is insufficient evidence to conclude that ages of young adults and movie preferences are not independent.

8. H_0: Contribution and ethnic group are independent.

H_1: Contribution and ethnic group are not independent.

$$\chi^2 = \sum \frac{(O-E)^2}{E}$$

$$= \frac{(310-441.42)^2}{441.42} + \frac{(715-569.96)^2}{569.96} + \frac{(201-244.61)^2}{244.61} + \frac{(105-86.87)^2}{86.87} + \frac{(42-30.13)^2}{30.13}$$

$$+ \frac{(619-501.86)^2}{501.86} + \frac{(511-648.01)^2}{648.01} + \frac{(312-278.10)^2}{278.10} + \frac{(97-98.77)^2}{98.77} + \frac{(22-34.26)^2}{34.26}$$

$$+ \frac{(402-439.17)^2}{439.17} + \frac{(624-567.06)^2}{567.06} + \frac{(217-243.36)^2}{243.36} + \frac{(88-86.43)^2}{86.43} + \frac{(35-29.98)^2}{29.98}$$

$$+ \frac{(544-492.54)^2}{492.54} + \frac{(571-635.97)^2}{635.97} + \frac{(309-272.93)^2}{272.93} + \frac{(79-96.93)^2}{96.93} + \frac{(29-33.62)^2}{33.62}$$

$$= 190.44$$

Since there are 4 rows and 5 columns, *d.f.* = (4 – 1)(5 – 1) = 12. For $\alpha = 0.01$, the critical value is $\chi^2_{0.01} = 26.22$.

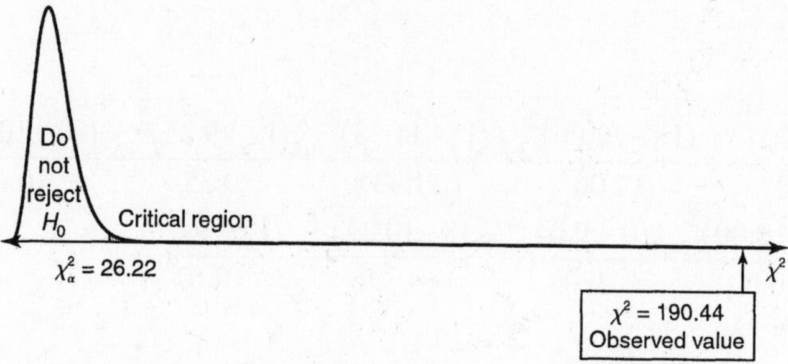

Since the sample statistic falls inside the critical region, we reject H_0. We conclude that contribution and ethnic group are not independent.

9. H_0: Ticket sales and type of billing are independent.
H_1: Ticket sales and type of billing are not independent.

$$\chi^2 = \sum \frac{(O-E)^2}{E}$$

$$= \frac{(10-7.52)^2}{7.52} + \frac{(12-13.16)^2}{13.16} + \frac{(18-18.80)^2}{18.80} + \frac{(7-7.52)^2}{7.52} + \frac{(6-8.48)^2}{8.48} + \frac{(16-14.84)^2}{14.84} + \frac{(22-21.20)^2}{21.20} + \frac{(9-8.48)^2}{8.48}$$

$$= 1.87$$

Since there are 2 rows and 4 columns, *d.f.* = (2 – 1)(4 – 1) = 3. For $\alpha = 0.05$, the critical value is $\chi^2_{0.05} = 7.81$.

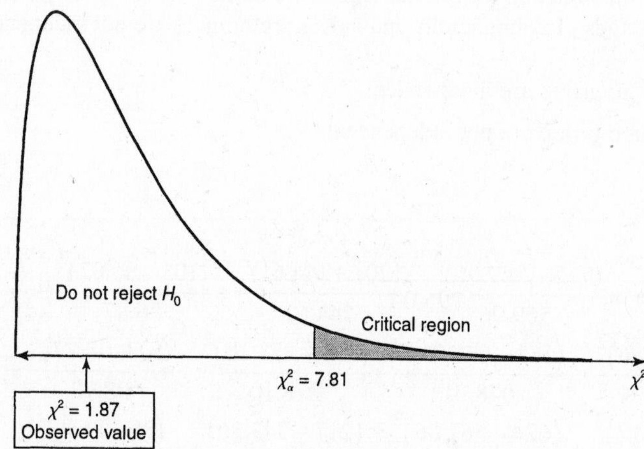

Since the sample statistic falls outside the critical region, we do not reject H_0. There is insufficient evidence to conclude that ticket sales and type of billing are not independent.

10. H_0: Party affiliation and dollars spent are independent.

H_1: Party affiliation and dollars spent are not independent.

$$\chi^2 = \sum \frac{(O-E)^2}{E}$$

$$= \frac{(8-9.78)^2}{9.78} + \frac{(15-16.63)^2}{16.63} + \frac{(22-18.59)^2}{18.59} + \frac{(12-10.22)^2}{10.22} + \frac{(19-17.37)^2}{17.37} + \frac{(16-19.41)^2}{19.41}$$

$$= 2.176$$

Since there are 2 rows and 3 columns, $d.f. = (2-1)(3-1) = 2$. For $\alpha = 0.01$, the critical value is $\chi^2_{0.01} = 9.21$.

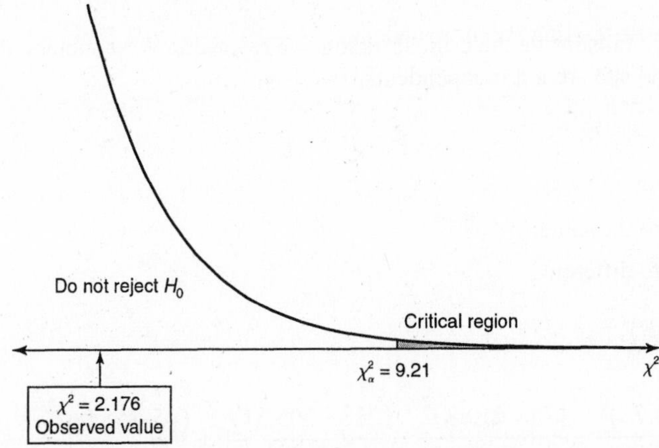

Since the sample statistic falls outside the critical region, we do not reject H_0. There is insufficient evidence to conclude that party affiliation and dollars spent are not independent.

11. H_0: Stone tool construction material and site are independent.

H_1: Stone tool construction material and site are not independent.

$$\chi^2 = \sum \frac{(O-E)^2}{E}$$

$$= \frac{(3657-4099.96)^2}{4099.96} + \frac{(1238-795.04)^2}{795.04} + \frac{(497-473.23)^2}{473.23} + \frac{(68-91.77)^2}{91.77} + \frac{(3606-3214.64)^2}{3214.64} + \frac{(232-623.36)^2}{623.36} + \frac{(357-329.17)^2}{329.17} + \frac{(36-63.83)^2}{63.83}$$

$$= 609.845$$

Since there are 4 rows and 2 columns, *d.f.* = (4 – 1)(2 – 1) = 3. For $\alpha = 0.01$, the critical value is $\chi^2_{0.01} = 11.34$.

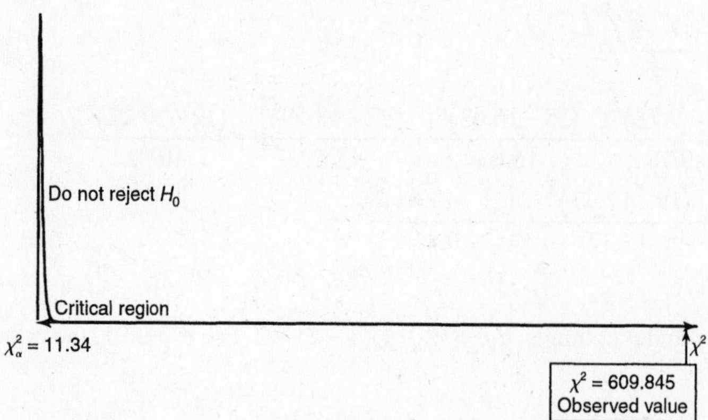

Since the sample statistic falls inside the critical region, we reject H_0. We conclude that stone tool construction material and site are not independent.

Section 11.2

1. H_0: The distributions are the same.

H_1: The distributions are different.

$$\chi^2 = \sum \frac{(O-E)^2}{E}$$

$$= \frac{(47-32.76)^2}{32.76} + \frac{(75-61.88)^2}{61.88} + \frac{(288-305.31)^2}{301.31} + \frac{(45-55.06)^2}{55.06}$$

$$= 11.79$$

d.f. = (number of *E* entries) – 1 = 4 – 1 = 3. The critical value is $\chi^2_{0.05} = 7.81$.

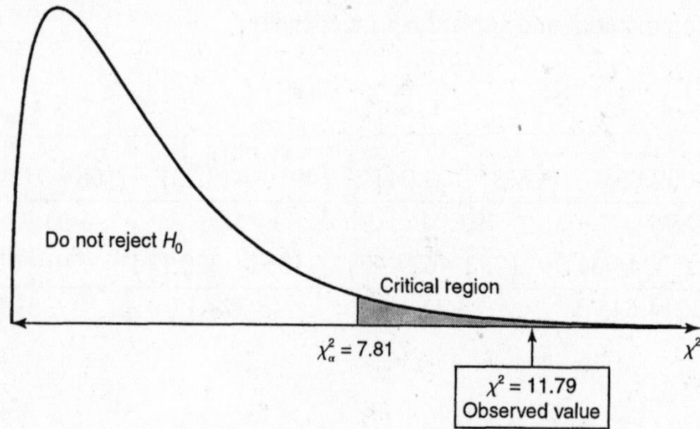

Since the sample statistic falls inside the critical region, we reject H_0. We conclude the distributions are different.

2. H_0: The distributions are the same.

H_1: The distributions are different.

$$\chi^2 = \sum \frac{(O-E)^2}{E}$$

$$= \frac{(102-106.86)^2}{106.86} + \frac{(112-119.19)^2}{119.19} + \frac{(33-36.99)^2}{36.99} + \frac{(96-102.75)^2}{102.75} + \frac{(68-45.21)^2}{45.21}$$

$$= 13.017$$

$d.f.$ = (number of E entries) − 1 = 5 − 1 = 4. The critical value is $\chi^2_{0.05} = 9.49$.

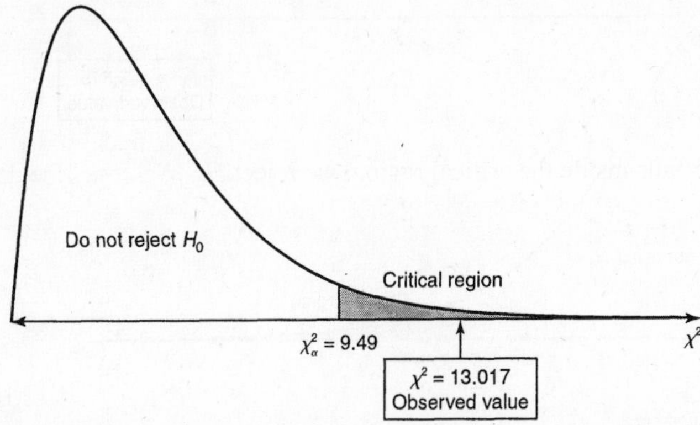

Since the sample statistic falls inside the critical region, we reject H_0. We conclude the distributions are different.

3. H_0: The distributions are the same.

H_1: The distributions are different.

$$\chi^2 = \sum \frac{(O-E)^2}{E}$$

$$= \frac{(906-910.92)^2}{910.92} + \frac{(162-157.52)^2}{157.52} + \frac{(168-169.40)^2}{169.40} + \frac{(197-194.67)^2}{194.67} + \frac{(53-53.50)^2}{53.50}$$

$$= 0.1984$$

$d.f.$ = (number of E entries) − 1 = 5 − 1 = 4. The critical value is $\chi^2_{0.01} = 13.28$.

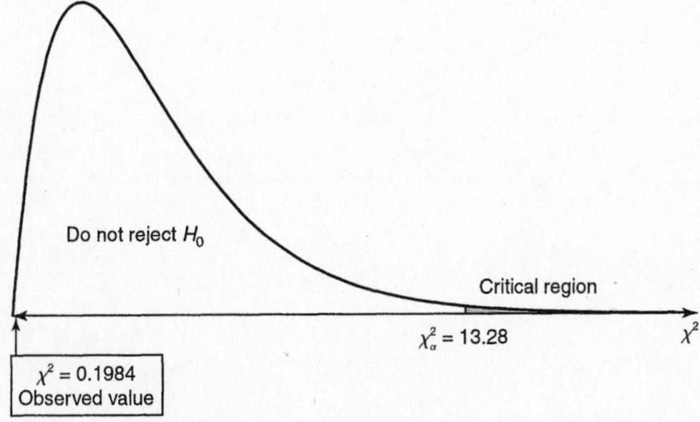

Since the sample statistic falls outside the critical region, we do not reject H_0. There is insufficient evidence to conclude that the distributions are different.

4. H_0: The distributions are the same.

H_1: The distributions are different.

$$\chi^2 = \sum \frac{(O-E)^2}{E}$$

$$= \frac{(102-102.40)^2}{102.40} + \frac{(125-123.84)^2}{123.84} + \frac{(43-38.40)^2}{38.40} + \frac{(27-29.76)^2}{29.76} + \frac{(23-25.60)^2}{25.60}$$

$$= 1.084$$

d.f. = (number of *E* entries) – 1 = 5 – 1 = 4. The critical value is $\chi^2_{0.05} = 9.49$.

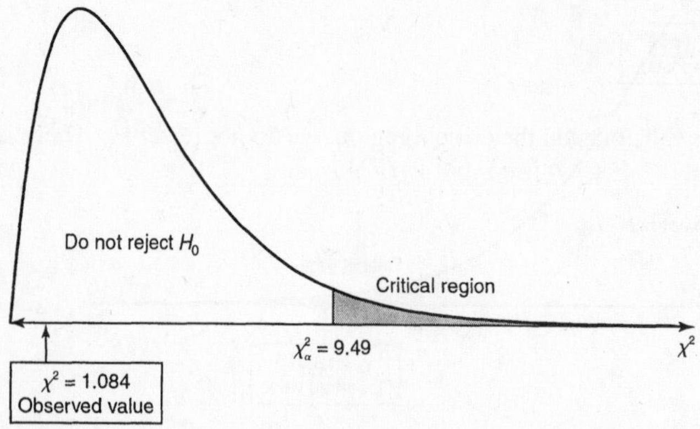

Since the sample statistic falls outside the critical region, we do not reject H_0. There is insufficient evidence to conclude that the distributions are different.

5. (a) Essay.

(b) H_0: The distributions are the same.

H_1: The distributions are different.

$$\chi^2 = \sum \frac{(O-E)^2}{E}$$

$$= \frac{(16-14.57)^2}{14.57} + \frac{(78-83.08)^2}{83.08} + \frac{(212-210.80)^2}{210.80} + \frac{(221-210.80)^2}{210.80}$$

$$+ \frac{(81-83.08)^2}{83.08} + \frac{(12-14.57)^2}{14.57}$$

$$= 1.4567$$

d.f. = (number of *E* entries) – 1 = 6 – 1 = 5. The critical value is $\chi^2_{0.01} = 15.09$.

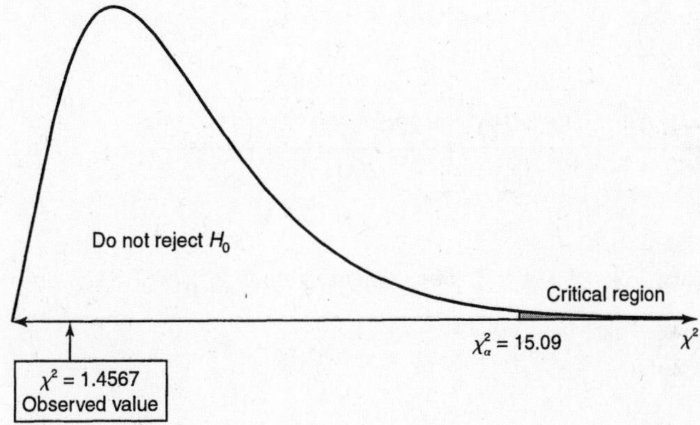

Since the sample statistic falls outside the critical region, we do not reject H_0. There is insufficient evidence to conclude that the distribution is not normal.

6. (a) Essay.

(b) H_0: The distributions are the same.

H_1: The distributions are different.

$$\chi^2 = \sum \frac{(O-E)^2}{E}$$

$$= \frac{(14-14.57)^2}{14.57} + \frac{(86-83.08)^2}{83.08} + \frac{(207-210.80)^2}{210.80} + \frac{(215-210.80)^2}{210.80}$$

$$+ \frac{(83-83.08)^2}{83.08} + \frac{(15-14.57)^2}{14.57}$$

$$= 0.26758$$

d.f. = (number of *E* entries) – 1 = 6 – 1 = 5. The critical value is $\chi^2_{0.01} = 15.09$.

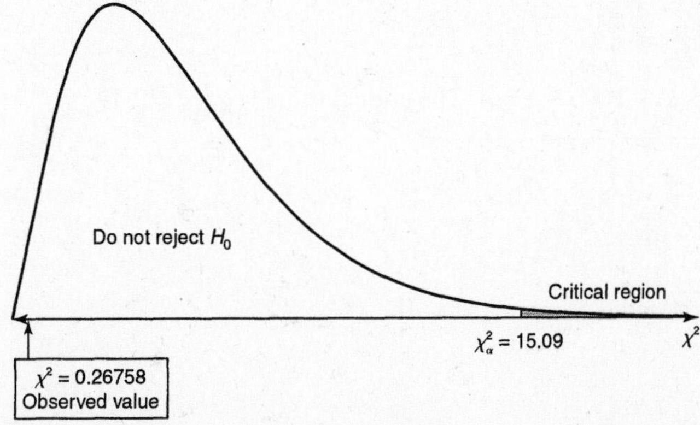

Since the sample statistic falls outside the critical region, we do not reject H_0. There is insufficient evidence to conclude that the distribution is not normal.

7. H_0: The distributions are the same.

H_1: The distributions are different.

$$\chi^2 = \sum \frac{(O-E)^2}{E}$$

$$= \frac{(120-150)^2}{150} + \frac{(85-75)^2}{75} + \frac{(220-200)^2}{200} + \frac{(75-75)^2}{75}$$

$$= 9.333$$

d.f. = (number of *E* entries) – 1 = 4 – 1 = 3. The critical value is $\chi^2_{0.05} = 7.81$.

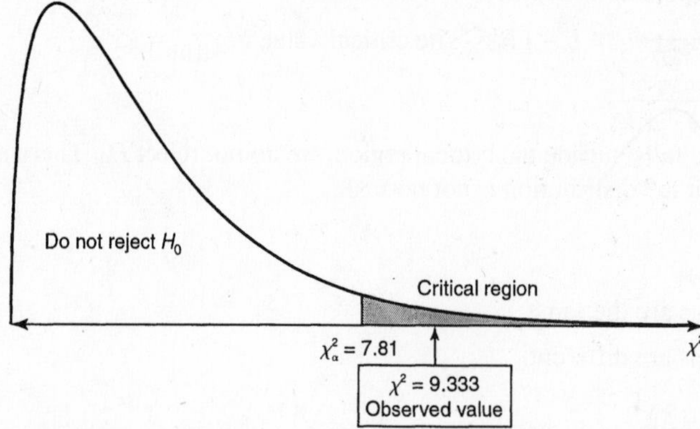

Since the sample statistic falls inside the critical region, we reject H_0. We conclude that the fish distribution has changed.

8. H_0: The distributions are the same.

H_1: The distributions are different.

$$\chi^2 = \sum \frac{(O-E)^2}{E}$$

$$= \frac{(1210-1349.44)^2}{1349.44} + \frac{(956-1054.25)^2}{1054.25} + \frac{(940-843.40)^2}{843.40} + \frac{(814-632.55)^2}{632.55} + \frac{(297-337.36)^2}{337.36}$$

$$= 91.51$$

d.f. = (number of *E* entries) – 1 = 5 – 1 = 4. The critical value is $\chi^2_{0.05} = 9.49$.

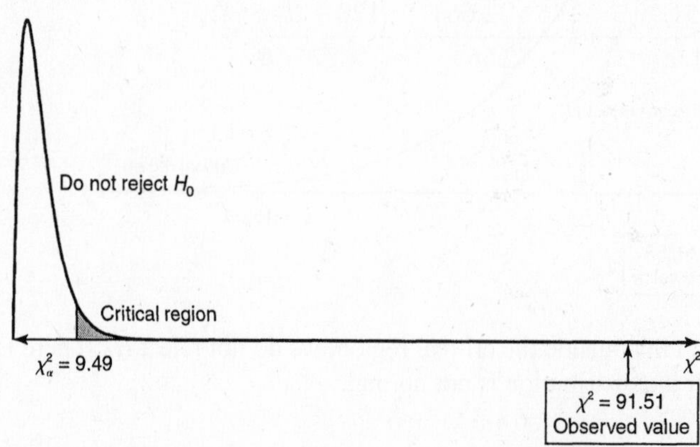

Since the sample statistic falls inside the critical region, we reject H_0. We conclude that the distributions are different.

9. H_0: The distributions are the same.

H_1: The distributions are different.

$$\chi^2 = \sum \frac{(O-E)^2}{E}$$

$$= \frac{(127-121.50)^2}{121.50} + \frac{(40-36.45)^2}{36.45} + \frac{(480-461.70)^2}{461.70} + \frac{(502-498.15)^2}{498.15} + \frac{(56-72.90)^2}{72.90} + \frac{(10-24.30)^2}{24.30}$$

$$= 13.7$$

$d.f.$ = (number of E entries) − 1 = 6 − 1 = 5. The critical value is $\chi^2_{0.01} = 15.09$.

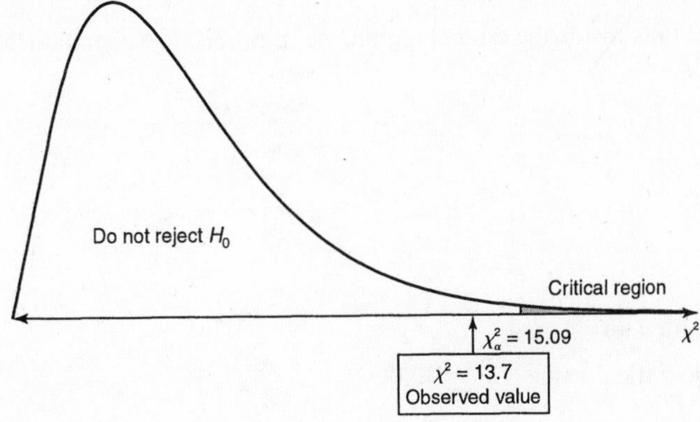

Since the sample statistic falls outside the critical region, we do not reject H_0. There is insufficient evidence to conclude that the distributions are different.

10. H_0: The distributions are the same.

H_1: The distributions are different.

$$\chi^2 = \sum \frac{(O-E)^2}{E}$$

$$= \frac{(88-62.28)^2}{62.28} + \frac{(135-150.51)^2}{150.51} + \frac{(52-57.09)^2}{57.09} + \frac{(40-51.90)^2}{51.90} + \frac{(76-72.66)^2}{72.66} + \frac{(128-124.56)^2}{124.56}$$

$$= 15.65$$

d.f. = (number of *E* entries) − 1 = 6 − 1 = 5. The critical value is $\chi^2_{0.01} = 15.09$.

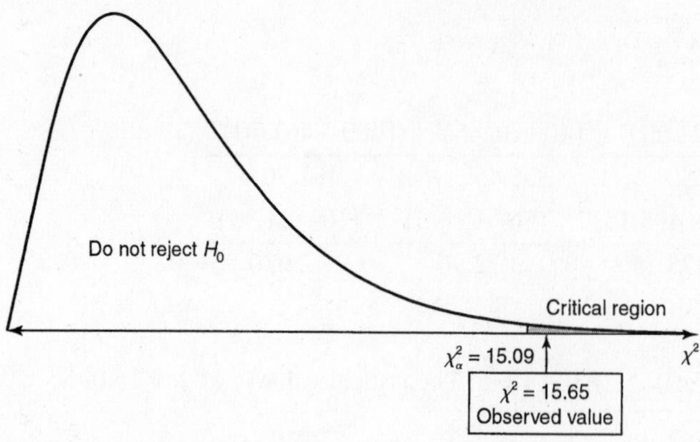

Since the sample statistic falls inside the critical region, we reject H_0. We conclude that the distributions are different.

Section 11.3

1. H_0: $\sigma^2 = 42.3$

H_1: $\sigma^2 > 42.3$

Since > is in H_1, a right-tailed test is used.

For *d.f.* = 23 − 1 = 22, the critical value is $\chi^2_{0.05} = 33.92$.

$$\chi^2 = \frac{(n-1)s^2}{\sigma^2} = \frac{(23-1)46.1}{42.3} = 23.98$$

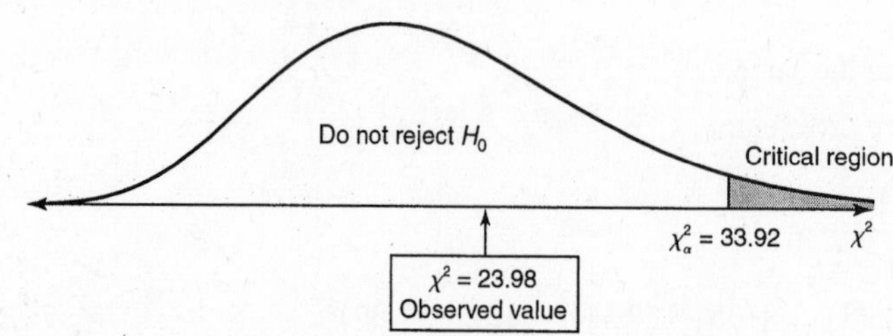

Since the sample statistic falls outside the critical region, we do not reject H_0. We have insufficient evidence to conclude that the variance in the new section is greater than 42.3.

For $d.f. = 22$ and $\alpha = \frac{1-0.95}{2} = 0.025$, $\chi^2_U = 36.78$.

For $d.f. = 22$ and $\alpha = \frac{1+0.95}{2} = 0.975$, $\chi^2_L = 10.98$.

The 95% confidence interval for σ^2 is

$$\frac{(n-1)s^2}{\chi^2_U} < \sigma^2 < \frac{(n-1)s^2}{\chi^2_L}$$

$$\frac{(23-1)46.1}{36.78} < \sigma^2 < \frac{(23-1)46.1}{10.98}$$

$$27.57 < \sigma^2 < 92.37$$

2. H_0: $\sigma^2 = 5.1$
H_1: $\sigma^2 < 5.1$
Since < is in H_1, a left-tailed test is used.
For *d.f.* = 41 − 1 = 40, the critical value is $\chi^2_{0.95} = 26.51$.

$$\chi^2 = \frac{(n-1)s^2}{\sigma^2} = \frac{(41-1)3.3}{5.1} = 25.88$$

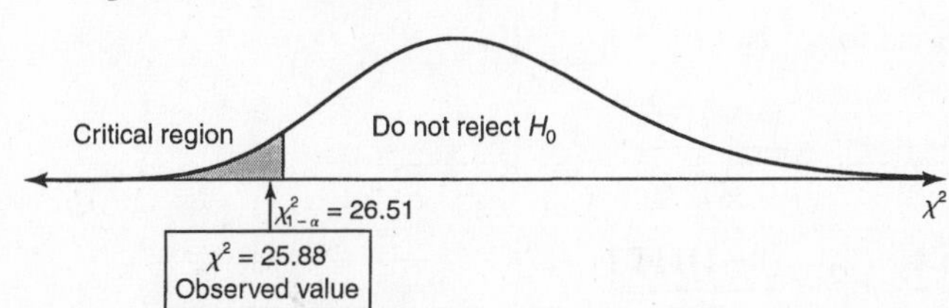

Since the sample statistic falls inside the critical region, we reject H_0. We conclude that the current variance is less than 5.1.

For $d.f. = 40$ and $\alpha = \frac{1-0.90}{2} = 0.05$, $\chi^2_U = 55.76$.

For $d.f. = 40$ and $\alpha = \frac{1+0.90}{2} = 0.95$, $\chi^2_L = 26.51$.

The 90% confidence interval for σ^2 is

$$\frac{(n-1)s^2}{\chi^2_U} < \sigma^2 < \frac{(n-1)s^2}{\chi^2_L}$$

$$\frac{(41-1)3.3}{55.76} < \sigma^2 < \frac{(41-1)3.3}{26.51}$$

$$2.37 < \sigma^2 < 4.98$$

3. H_0: $\sigma^2 = 136.2$
H_1: $\sigma^2 < 136.2$
Since < is in H_1, a left-tailed test is used.
For *d.f.* = 8 − 1 = 7, the critical value is $\chi^2_{0.99} = 1.24$.

$$\chi^2 = \frac{(n-1)s^2}{\sigma^2} = \frac{(8-1)115.1}{136.2} = 5.92$$

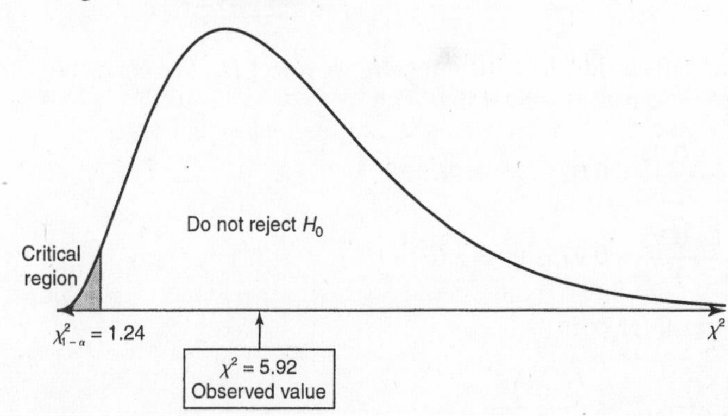

Since the sample statistic falls outside the critical region, we do not reject H_0. We have insufficient evidence to conclude that the recent variance for number of mountain-climber deaths is less than 136.1.

For $d.f. = 7$ and $\alpha = \dfrac{1-0.90}{2} = 0.05$, $\chi_U^2 = 14.07$.

For $d.f. = 7$ and $\alpha = \dfrac{1+0.90}{2} = 0.95$, $\chi_L^2 = 2.17$.

The 90% confidence interval for σ^2 is

$$\frac{(n-1)s^2}{\chi_U^2} < \sigma^2 < \frac{(n-1)s^2}{\chi_L^2}$$

$$\frac{(8-1)115.1}{14.07} < \sigma^2 < \frac{(8-1)115.1}{2.17}$$

$$57.26 < \sigma^2 < 371.29$$

4. H_0: $\sigma^2 = 47.1$

H_1: $\sigma^2 > 47.1$

Since > is in H_1, a right-tailed test is used.

For $d.f. = 15 - 1 = 14$, the critical value is $\chi_{0.05}^2 = 23.68$.

$$\chi^2 = \frac{(n-1)s^2}{\sigma^2} = \frac{(15-1)83.2}{47.1} = 24.73$$

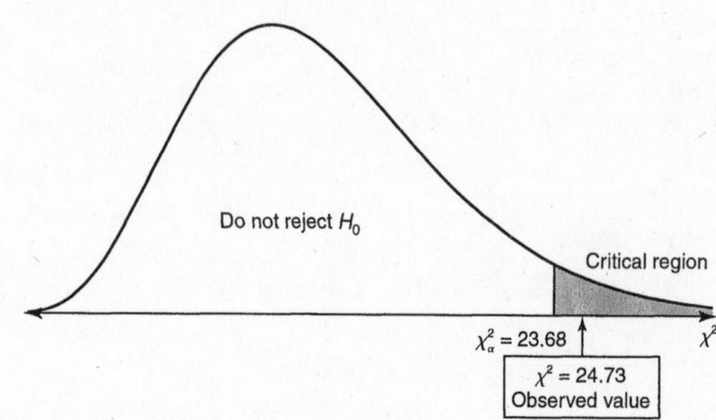

Since the sample statistic falls inside the critical region, we reject H_0. We conclude that the variance for colleges and universities in Kansas is greater than 47.1.

For $d.f. = 14$ and $\alpha = \dfrac{1-0.95}{2} = 0.025$, $\chi_U^2 = 26.12$.

For $d.f. = 14$ and $\alpha = \dfrac{1+0.95}{2} = 0.975$, $\chi_L^2 = 5.63$.

The 95% confidence interval for σ^2 is

$$\frac{(n-1)s^2}{\chi_U^2} < \sigma^2 < \frac{(n-1)s^2}{\chi_L^2}$$

$$\frac{(15-1)83.2}{26.12} < \sigma^2 < \frac{(15-1)83.2}{5.63}$$

$$44.59 < \sigma^2 < 206.89$$

5. H_0: $\sigma^2 = 9$
H_1: $\sigma^2 < 9$
Since < is in H_1, a left-tailed test is used.
For $d.f. = 24 - 1 = 23$, the critical value is $\chi^2_{0.95} = 13.09$.

$$\chi^2 = \frac{(n-1)s^2}{\sigma^2} = \frac{(24-1)(1.9)^2}{3^2} = 9.23$$

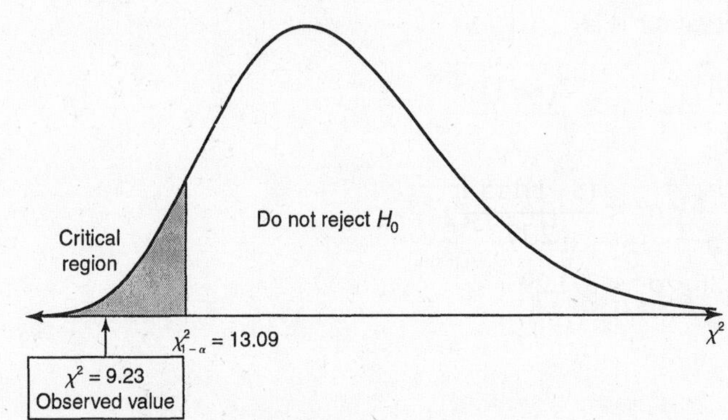

Since the sample statistic falls inside the critical region, we reject H_0. We conclude that the new typhoid shot has a smaller variance of protection times.

For $d.f. = 23$ and $\alpha = \frac{1-0.90}{2} = 0.05$, $\chi^2_U = 35.17$.

For $d.f. = 23$ and $\alpha = \frac{1+0.90}{2} = 0.95$, $\chi^2_L = 13.09$.

The 90% confidence interval for σ is

$$\sqrt{\frac{(n-1)s^2}{\chi^2_U}} < \sigma < \sqrt{\frac{(n-1)s^2}{\chi^2_L}}$$

$$\sqrt{\frac{(24-1)(1.9)^2}{35.17}} < \sigma < \sqrt{\frac{(24-1)(1.9)^2}{13.09}}$$

$$1.54 < \sigma < 2.52$$

6. H_0: $\sigma^2 = 225$
H_1: $\sigma^2 > 225$
Since > is in H_1, a right-tailed test is used.
For $d.f. = 10 - 1 = 9$, the critical value is $\chi^2_{0.01} = 21.67$.

$$\chi^2 = \frac{(n-1)s^2}{\sigma^2} = \frac{(10-1)(24)^2}{(15)^2} = 23.04$$

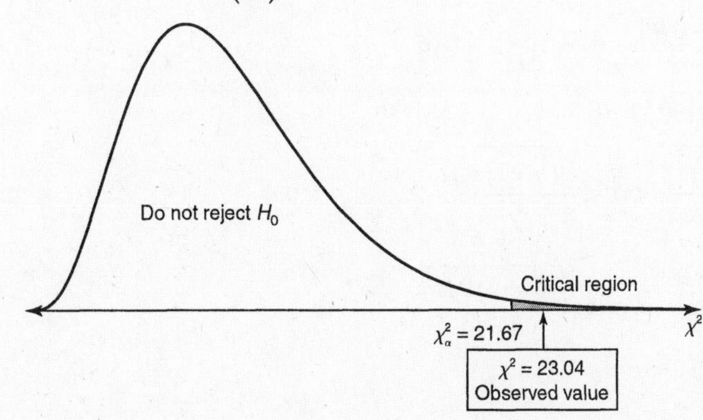

Since the sample statistic falls inside the critical region, we reject H_0. We conclude that the variance is larger than that stated in his journal.

For $d.f. = 9$ and $\alpha = \frac{1-0.95}{2} = 0.025$, $\chi_U^2 = 19.02$.

For $d.f. = 9$ and $\alpha = \frac{1+0.95}{2} = 0.975$, $\chi_L^2 = 2.70$.

The 95% confidence interval for σ is

$$\sqrt{\frac{(n-1)s^2}{\chi_U^2}} < \sigma < \sqrt{\frac{(n-1)s^2}{\chi_L^2}}$$

$$\sqrt{\frac{(10-1)(24)^2}{19.02}} < \sigma < \sqrt{\frac{(10-1)(24)^2}{2.70}}$$

$$16.5 < \sigma < 43.8$$

7. H_0: $\sigma^2 = 0.15$

H_1: $\sigma^2 > 0.15$

Since > is in H_1, a right-tailed test is used.

For $d.f. = 61 - 1 = 60$, the critical value is $\chi_{0.01}^2 = 88.38$.

$$\chi^2 = \frac{(n-1)s^2}{\sigma^2} = \frac{(61-1)0.27}{0.15} = 108$$

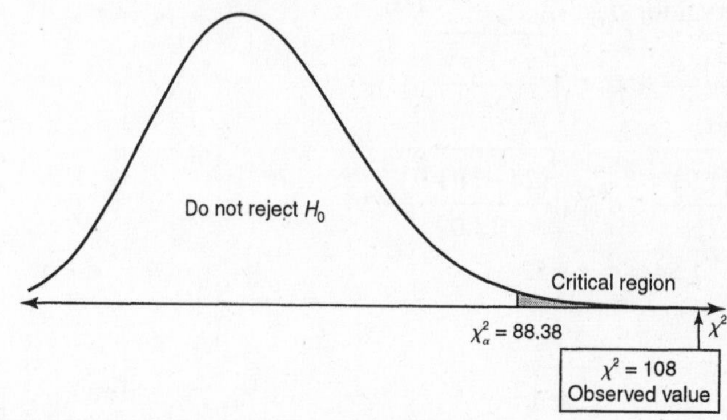

Since the sample statistic falls inside the critical region, we reject H_0. We conclude that all the engine blades must be replaced (i.e., the variance exceeds 0.15).

For $d.f. = 60$ and $\alpha = \frac{1-0.90}{2} = 0.05$, $\chi_U^2 = 79.08$.

For $d.f. = 60$ and $\alpha = \frac{1+0.90}{2} = 0.95$, $\chi_L^2 = 43.19$.

The 90% confidence interval for σ is

$$\sqrt{\frac{(n-1)s^2}{\chi_U^2}} < \sigma < \sqrt{\frac{(n-1)s^2}{\chi_L^2}}$$

$$\sqrt{\frac{(61-1)0.27}{79.08}} < \sigma < \sqrt{\frac{(61-1)0.27}{43.29}}$$

$$0.45 < \sigma < 0.61$$

8. (a) $\left.\begin{matrix} H_0\text{: } \sigma^2 = 5625 \\ H_1\text{: } \sigma^2 \neq 5625 \end{matrix}\right\}$ these hypotheses are equivalent to $\left\{\begin{matrix} H_0\text{: } \sigma = 75 \\ H_1\text{: } \sigma \neq 75 \end{matrix}\right.$

Since ≠ is in H_1, a two-tailed test is used.

For *d.f.* = 24 – 1 = 23, the critical values are $\chi^2_{0.005} = 44.18$ and $\chi^2_{0.995} = 9.26$.

$$\chi^2 = \frac{(n-1)s^2}{\sigma^2} = \frac{(24-1)(72)^2}{(75)^2} = 21.20$$

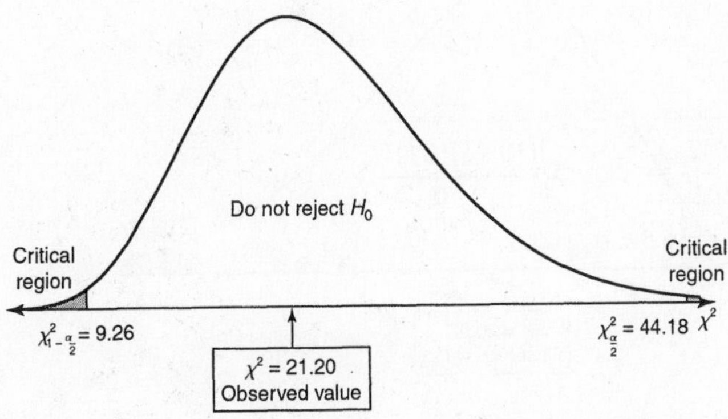

Since the sample statistic falls outside both critical regions, do not reject H_0. There is insufficient evidence to conclude that the population standard deviation for the new examination is different from 75 ($\sigma^2 = 75^2 = 5625$).

(b) For $d.f. = 23$ and $\alpha = \frac{1-0.99}{2} = 0.005$, $\chi^2_U = 44.18$.

For $d.f. = 23$ and $\alpha = \frac{1+0.99}{2} = 0.995$, $\chi^2_L = 9.26$.

The 99% confidence interval for σ^2 is

$$\frac{(n-1)s^2}{\chi^2_U} < \sigma^2 < \frac{(n-1)s^2}{\chi^2_L}$$

$$\frac{(24-1)(72)^2}{44.18} < \sigma^2 < \frac{(24-1)(72)^2}{9.26}$$

$$2698.78 < \sigma^2 < 12{,}876.03$$

(c) The 99% confidence interval for σ is

$$\sqrt{\frac{(n-1)s^2}{\chi^2_U}} < \sigma < \sqrt{\frac{(n-1)s^2}{\chi^2_L}}$$

$$\sqrt{2698.78} < \sigma < \sqrt{12{,}876.03}$$

$$51.95 < \sigma < 113.47$$

9. (a) H_0: $\sigma^2 = 15$
H_1: $\sigma^2 \neq 15$

Since $\neq$ is in H_1, a two-tailed test is used.

For *d.f.* = 22 − 1 = 21, the critical values are $\chi^2_{0.025} = 35.48$ and $\chi^2_{0.975} = 10.28$.

$$\chi^2 = \frac{(n-1)s^2}{\sigma^2} = \frac{(22-1)(14.3)}{15} = 20.02$$

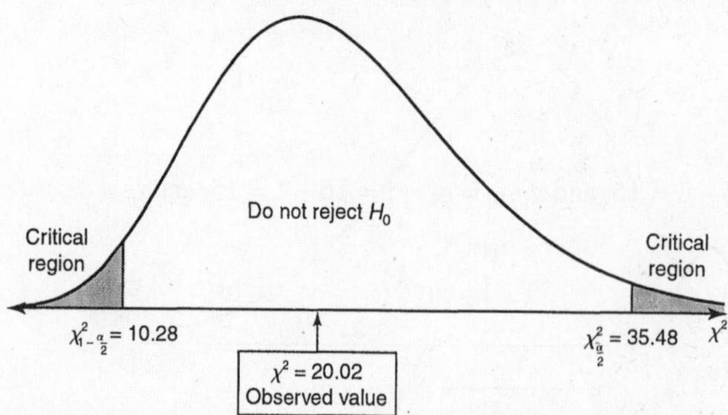

Since the sample statistic falls outside both critical regions, do not reject H_0. There is insufficient evidence to conclude that the population variance is different from 15.

(b) For $d.f. = 21$ and $\alpha = \frac{1-0.90}{2} = 0.05$, $\chi^2_U = 32.67$.

For $d.f. = 21$ and $\alpha = \frac{1+0.90}{2} = 0.95$, $\chi^2_L = 11.59$.

The 90% confidence interval for σ^2 is

$$\frac{(n-1)s^2}{\chi^2_U} < \sigma^2 < \frac{(n-1)s^2}{\chi^2_L}$$

$$\frac{(22-1)(14.3)}{32.67} < \sigma^2 < \frac{(22-1)(14.3)}{11.59}$$

$$9.19 < \sigma^2 < 25.91$$

(c) The 90% confidence interval for σ is

$$\sqrt{\frac{(n-1)s^2}{\chi^2_U}} < \sigma < \sqrt{\frac{(n-1)s^2}{\chi^2_L}}$$

$$\sqrt{9.19} < \sigma < \sqrt{25.91}$$

$$3.03 < \sigma < 5.09$$

Section 11.4

1. H_0: $\sigma_1^2 = \sigma_2^2$

H_1: $\sigma_1^2 > \sigma_2^2$

Since > is in H_1, a right-tailed test is used.
The populations follow independent normal distributions. The samples are random samples from each population.
Since $s^2 \approx 0.332$ is larger than $s^2 \approx 0.089$, we designate Population I as the first plot.

$$F = \frac{s_1^2}{s_2^2} = \frac{0.332}{0.089} = 3.73$$

Using $d.f._N = n_1 - 1 = 16 - 1 = 15$, and $d.f._D = n_2 - 1 = 16 - 1 = 15$, and $\alpha = 0.01$, the critical F value is 3.52.

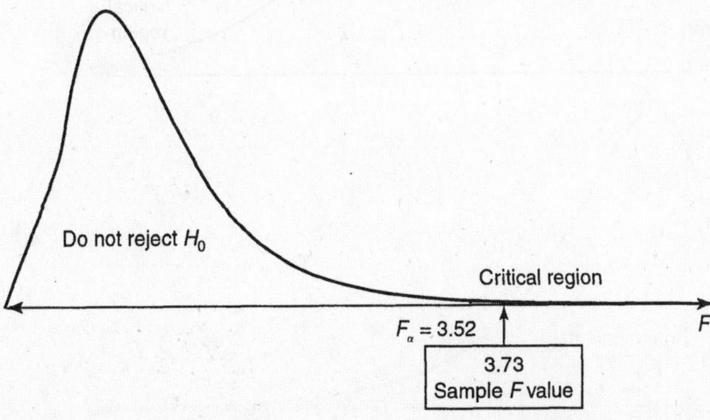

Since the sample F statistic falls inside the critical region, we reject H_0. We conclude that the variance in annual wheat production from the first plot is greater than that from the second plot.

2. H_0: $\sigma_1^2 = \sigma_2^2$

H_1: $\sigma_1^2 \neq \sigma_2^2$

Since ≠ is in H_1, a two-tailed test is used.
The populations follow independent normal distributions. The samples are random samples from each population.
Since $s^2 \approx 1.078$ is larger than $s^2 \approx 0.318$, we designate Population I as the second plot.

$$F = \frac{s_1^2}{s_2^2} = \frac{1.078}{0.318} = 3.39$$

Using $d.f._N = n_1 - 1 = 8 - 1 = 7$, and $d.f._D = n_2 - 1 = 11 - 1 = 10$, and $\alpha = 0.05$, the critical $F_{\frac{\alpha}{2}}$ value is 3.95.

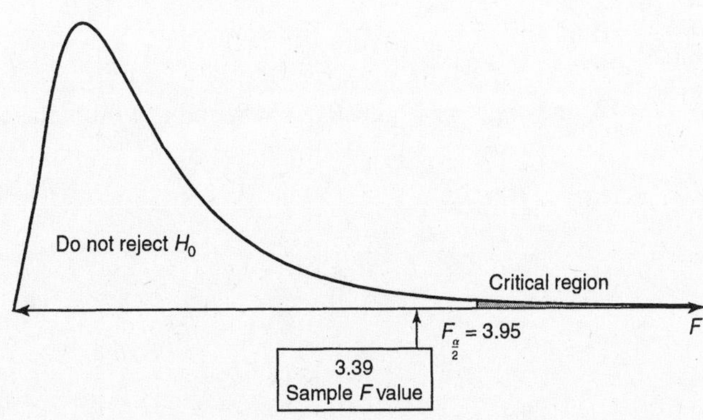

Since the sample F statistic falls outside the critical region, we do not reject H_0. There is insufficient evidence to conclude that the variance in annual wheat straw production from the first plot is different from the variance of wheat straw production from the second plot.

3. H_0: $\sigma_1^2 = \sigma_2^2$

H_1: $\sigma_1^2 \neq \sigma_2^2$

Since $\neq$ is in H_1, a two-tailed test is used.

The populations follow independent normal distributions. The samples are random samples from each population.

Since $s^2 \approx 1.786$ is larger than $s^2 \approx 1.285$, we designate Population I as France.

$$F = \frac{s_1^2}{s_2^2} = \frac{1.786}{1.285} = 1.390$$

Using $d.f._N = n_1 - 1 = 21 - 1 = 20$, and $d.f._D = n_2 - 1 = 18 - 1 = 17$, and $\alpha = 0.05$, the critical $F_{\frac{\alpha}{2}}$ value is 2.62.

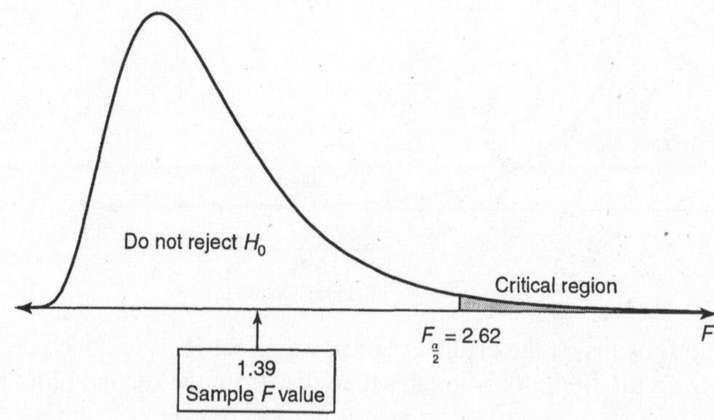

Since the sample F statistic falls outside the critical region, we do not reject H_0. There is insufficient evidence to conclude a significant difference exists in the population variances. There is no significant difference in the volatility of corporate productivity of large companies in France and in Germany.

4. H_0: $\sigma_1^2 = \sigma_2^2$

H_1: $\sigma_1^2 > \sigma_2^2$

Since $>$ is in H_1, a right-tailed test is used.

The populations follow independent normal distributions. The samples are random samples from each population.

Since $s^2 \approx 2.247$ is larger than $s^2 \approx 0.624$, we designate Population I as South Korea.

$$F = \frac{s_1^2}{s_2^2} = \frac{2.247}{0.624} = 3.60$$

Using $d.f._N = n_1 - 1 = 13 - 1 = 12$, and $d.f._D = n_2 - 1 = 9 - 1 = 8$, and $\alpha = 0.05$, the critical F value is 3.28.

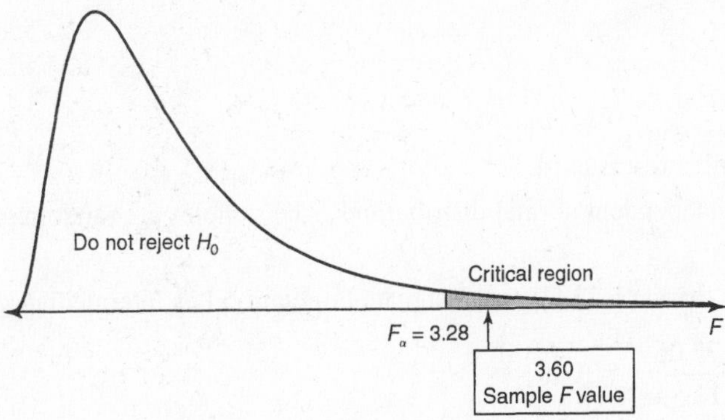

Since the sample F statistic falls inside the critical region, we reject H_0. We conclude the population variance of percentage yield on assets for South Korean companies is higher than for companies in Sweden. The volatility of corporate productivity of large companies is greater for South Korea than for Sweden.

5. H_0: $\sigma_1^2 = \sigma_2^2$

H_1: $\sigma_1^2 > \sigma_2^2$

Since > is in H_1, a right-tailed test is used.

The populations follow independent normal distributions. The samples are random samples from each population.

Since $s^2 \approx 348.43$ is larger than $s^2 \approx 137.31$, we designate Population I as aggressive growth.

$$F = \frac{s_1^2}{s_2^2} = \frac{348.43}{137.31} = 2.54$$

Using $d.f._N = n_1 - 1 = 21 - 1 = 20$, and $d.f._D = n_2 - 1 = 21 - 1 = 20$, and $\alpha = 0.05$, the critical F value is 2.12.

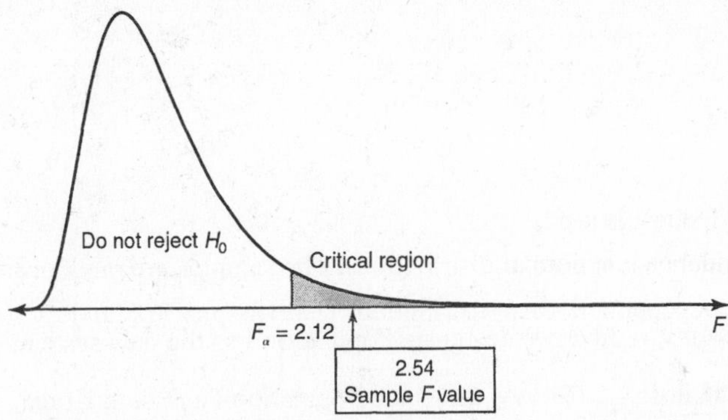

Since the sample F statistic falls inside the critical region, we reject H_0. We conclude the population variance for mutual funds holding aggressive growth small stocks is larger than that for funds holding value stocks. The smaller variance for funds holding value stocks implies they are more reliable investments.

6. H_0: $\sigma_1^2 = \sigma_2^2$

H_1: $\sigma_1^2 \neq \sigma_2^2$

Since $\neq$ is in H_1, a two-tailed test is used.

The populations follow independent normal distributions. The samples are random samples from each population.

Since $s^2 \approx 72.06$ is larger than $s^2 \approx 13.59$, we designate Population I as intermediate-term bonds.

$$F = \frac{s_1^2}{s_2^2} = \frac{72.06}{13.59} = 5.30$$

Using $d.f._N = n_1 - 1 = 16 - 1 = 15$, and $d.f._D = n_2 - 1 = 13 - 1 = 12$, and $\alpha = 0.05$, the critical $F_{\frac{\alpha}{2}}$ value is 3.18.

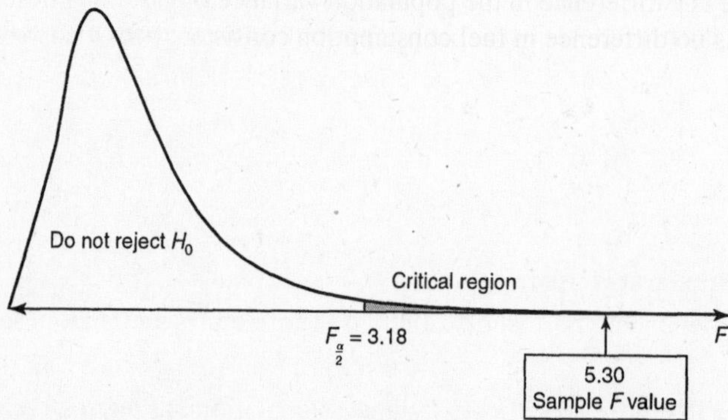

Since the sample F statistic falls inside the critical region, we reject H_0. We conclude that the population variance for annual percentage return of mutual funds holding short-term government bonds is different from the population variance for mutual funds holding intermediate-term corporate bonds. That the variances are different says only that the reliability of returns differs fund to fund. If we resort to data snooping, we would reach the conclusion, based on the sample variances, that government bond returns are more reliable.

7. H_0: $\sigma_1^2 = \sigma_2^2$

H_1: $\sigma_1^2 \neq \sigma_2^2$

Since $\neq$ is in H_1, a two-tailed test is used.

The populations follow independent normal distributions. The samples are random samples from each population.

Since $s^2 \approx 51.4$ is larger than $s^2 \approx 38.6$, we designate Population I as the new system.

$$F = \frac{s_1^2}{s_2^2} = \frac{51.4}{38.6} = 1.33$$

Using $d.f._N = n_1 - 1 = 31 - 1 = 30$, and $d.f._D = n_2 - 1 = 25 - 1 = 24$, and $\alpha = 0.05$, the critical $F_{\frac{\alpha}{2}}$ value is 2.21.

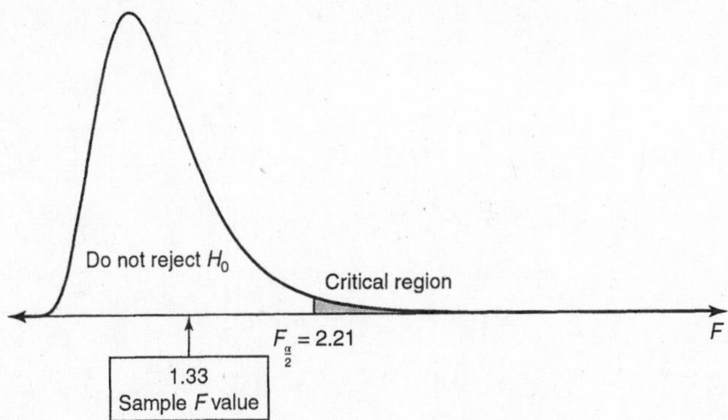

Since the sample F statistic falls outside the critical region, we do not reject H_0. There is insufficient evidence to conclude there is a difference in the population variance of gasoline consumption for the two injection systems. There is no difference in fuel consumption consistency for the two systems.

8. H_0: $\sigma_1^2 = \sigma_2^2$

H_1: $\sigma_1^2 > \sigma_2^2$

Since > is in H_1, a right-tailed test is used.

The populations follow independent normal distributions. The samples are random samples from each population.

Since $s^2 \approx 12.8$ is larger than $s^2 \approx 5.1$, we designate Population I as the old thermostat.

$$F = \frac{s_1^2}{s_2^2} = \frac{12.8}{5.1} = 2.51$$

Using $d.f._N = n_1 - 1 = 16 - 1 = 15$, and $d.f._D = n_2 - 1 = 21 - 1 = 20$, and $\alpha = 0.05$, the critical F value is 2.20.

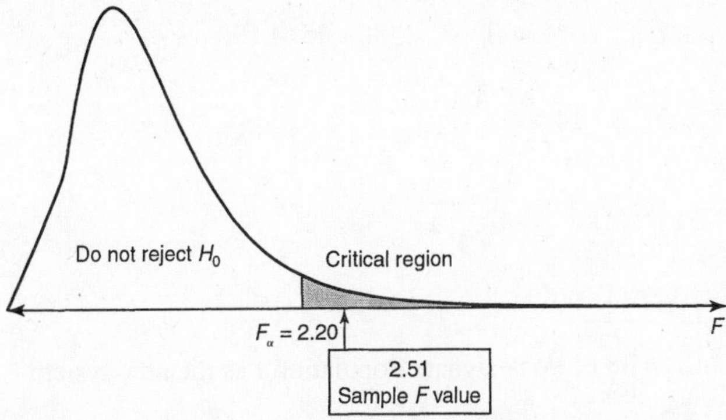

Since the sample F statistic falls inside the critical region, we reject H_0. We conclude that the population variance of the old thermostat temperature readings is larger than that for the new thermostat. The temperature readings from the old thermostat are less dependable.

Section 11.5

1. $H_0: \mu_1 = \mu_2 = \mu_3$

H_1: Not all the means are equal.

Site I	Site II	Site III
$n = 7$	$n = 4$	$n = 6$
$\sum x_1 = 286$	$\sum x_2 = 164$	$\sum x_3 = 176$
$\sum x_1^2 = 15{,}312$	$\sum x_2^2 = 8354$	$\sum x_3^2 = 7450$
$SS_1 = 3626.857$	$SS_2 = 1630$	$SS_3 = 2287.33\overline{3}$

$$\sum x_{TOT} = 286 + 164 + 176 = 626$$

$$\sum x_{TOT}^2 = 15{,}312 + 8354 + 7450 = 31{,}116$$

$$N = 7 + 4 + 6 = 17$$

$$k = 3$$

$$SS_{TOT} = \sum x_{TOT}^2 - \frac{(\sum x_{TOT})^2}{N} = 31{,}116 - \frac{(626)^2}{17} = 8064.470$$

$$SS_{BET} = \sum_{\text{all groups}} \left(\frac{(\sum x_i)^2}{n_i} \right) - \frac{(\sum x_{TOT})^2}{N}$$

$$= \frac{(286)^2}{7} + \frac{(164)^2}{4} + \frac{(176)^2}{6} - \frac{(626)^2}{17} = 520.280$$

$$SS_W = SS_1 + SS_2 + SS_3 = 3626.857 + 1630 + 2287.333 = 7544.190$$

Check that $SS_{TOT} = SS_{BET} + SS_W$: $8064.470 = 520.280 + 7544.190$

$$d.f._{BET} = k - 1 = 3 - 1 = 2$$

$$d.f._W = N - k = 17 - 3 = 14$$

$$d.f._{TOT} = N - 1 = 17 - 1 = 16$$

$$MS_{BET} = \frac{SS_{BET}}{d.f._{BET}} = \frac{520.280}{2} = 260.14$$

$$MS_W = \frac{SS_W}{d.f._W} = \frac{7544.190}{14} = 538.87$$

$$F = \frac{MS_{BET}}{MS_W} = \frac{260.14}{538.87} = 0.48$$

For $d.f._N = 2$ and $d.f._D = 14$, the critical value is $F_{0.01} = 6.51$. Since the observed F ratio is outside the critical region, we do not reject H_0. There is insufficient evidence to conclude that not all the means are equal.

Summary of ANOVA results

Source of Variation	Sum of Squares	Degrees of Freedom	MS	F Ratio	F Critical Value	Test Decision
Between groups	520.280	2	260.14	0.48	6.51	Do not reject H_0
Within groups	7544.190	14	538.87			
Total	8064.470	16				

2. $H_0: \mu_1 = \mu_2 = \mu_3 = \mu_4$

H_1: Not all the means are equal.

Site I	Site II	Site III	Site IV
$n=5$	$n=6$	$n=4$	$n=6$
$\sum x_1 = 76$	$\sum x_2 = 104$	$\sum x_3 = 112$	$\sum x_4 = 107$
$\sum x_1^2 = 1336$	$\sum x_2^2 = 2374$	$\sum x_3^2 = 3558$	$\sum x_4^2 = 2251$
$SS_1 = 180.8$	$SS_2 = 571.33\overline{3}$	$SS_3 = 422$	$SS_4 = 342.83\overline{3}$

$$\sum x_{TOT} = 76+104+112+107 = 399$$
$$\sum x_{TOT}^2 = 1336+2374+3558+2251 = 9519$$
$$N = 5+6+4+6 = 21$$
$$k = 4$$

$$SS_{TOT} = \sum x_{TOT}^2 - \frac{\left(\sum x_{TOT}\right)^2}{N} = 9519 - \frac{(399)^2}{21} = 1938$$

$$SS_{BET} = \sum_{\text{all groups}} \left(\frac{\left(\sum x_i\right)^2}{n_i}\right) - \frac{\left(\sum x_{TOT}\right)^2}{N}$$

$$= \frac{(76)^2}{5} + \frac{(104)^2}{6} + \frac{(112)^2}{4} + \frac{(107)^2}{6} - \frac{(399)^2}{21} = 421.033$$

$$SS_W = SS_1 + SS_2 + SS_3 + SS_4 = 180.8 + 571.333 + 422 + 342.833 = 1516.967$$

Check that $SS_{TOT} = SS_{BET} + SS_W : 1938 = 421.033 + 1516.967$

$$d.f._{BET} = k-1 = 4-1 = 3$$
$$d.f._W = N-k = 21-4 = 17$$
$$d.f._{TOT} = N-1 = 21-1 = 20$$

$$MS_{BET} = \frac{SS_{BET}}{d.f._{BET}} = \frac{421.033}{3} = 140.344$$

$$MS_W = \frac{SS_W}{d.f._W} = \frac{1516.967}{17} = 89.233$$

$$F = \frac{MS_{BET}}{MS_W} = \frac{140.344}{89.233} = 1.573$$

For $d.f._N = 3$ and $d.f._D = 17$, the critical value is $F_{0.05} = 3.20$. Since the observed F ratio is outside the critical region, we do not reject H_0. There is insufficient evidence to conclude that not all the means are equal.

Summary of ANOVA results

Source of Variation	Sum of Squares	Degrees of Freedom	MS	F Ratio	F Critical Value	Test Decision
Between groups	421.033	3	140.344	1.573	3.20	Do not reject H_0
Within groups	1516.967	17	89.233			
Total	1938.000	20				

3. $H_0: \mu_1 = \mu_2 = \mu_3 = \mu_4$

H_1: Not all the means are equal.

See Section 11.5 or solutions to problems 1-2 for examples of calculations from formulas.

For $d.f._N = 3$ and $d.f._D = 18$, the critical value is $F_{0.05} = 3.16$. Since the observed F ratio is outside the critical region, we do not reject H_0. There is insufficient evidence to conclude that not all the means are equal.

Summary of ANOVA results

Source of Variation	Sum of Squares	Degrees of Freedom	MS	F Ratio	F Critical Value	Test Decision
Between groups	89.637	3	29.879	0.846	3.16	Do not reject H_0
Within groups	635.827	18	35.324			
Total	725.464	21				

4. $H_0: \mu_1 = \mu_2 = \mu_3$

H_1: Not all the means are equal.

See Section 11.5 or solutions to problems 1-2 for examples of calculations from formulas.

For $d.f._N = 2$ and $d.f._D = 15$, the critical value is $F_{0.01} = 6.36$. Since the observed F ratio is outside the critical region, we do not reject H_0. There is insufficient evidence to conclude that not all the means are equal.

Summary of ANOVA results

Source of Variation	Sum of Squares	Degrees of Freedom	MS	F Ratio	F Critical Value	Test Decision
Between groups	215.680	2	107.840	0.816	6.36	Do not reject H_0
Within groups	1981.725	15	132.115			
Total	2197.405	17				

5. $H_0: \mu_1 = \mu_2 = \mu_3$

H_1: Not all the means are equal.

See Section 11.5 or solutions to problems 1-2 for examples of calculations from formulas.

For $d.f._N = 2$ and $d.f._D = 9$, the critical value is $F_{0.05} = 4.26$. Since the observed F ratio is inside the critical region, we reject H_0. We conclude that not all the means are equal.

Summary of ANOVA results

Source of Variation	Sum of Squares	Degrees of Freedom	MS	F Ratio	F Critical Value	Test Decision
Between groups	1303.167	2	651.58	5.005	4.26	Reject H_0
Within groups	1171.750	9	130.19			
Total	2474.917	11				

6. $H_0: \mu_1 = \mu_2 = \mu_3$

H_1: Not all the means are equal.

See Section 11.5 or solutions to problems 1-2 for examples of calculations from formulas.

For $d.f._N = 2$ and $d.f._D = 18$, the critical value is $F_{0.05} = 3.55$. Since the observed F ratio is outside the critical region, we do not reject H_0. There is insufficient evidence to conclude that not all the means are equal.

Summary of ANOVA results

Source of Variation	Sum of Squares	Degrees of Freedom	MS	F Ratio	F Critical Value	Test Decision
Between groups	2.442	2	1.2208	2.95	3.55	Do not reject H_0
Within groups	7.448	18	0.4138			
Total	9.890	20				

7. $H_0: \mu_1 = \mu_2 = \mu_3$

H_1: Not all the means are equal.

See Section 11.5 or solutions to problems 1-2 for examples of calculations from formulas.

For $d.f._N = 2$ and $d.f._D = 11$, the critical value is $F_{0.01} = 7.21$. Since the observed F ratio is outside the critical region, we do not reject H_0. There is insufficient evidence to conclude that not all the means are equal.

Summary of ANOVA results

Source of Variation	Sum of Squares	Degrees of Freedom	MS	F Ratio	F Critical Value	Test Decision
Between groups	2.042	2	1.021	0.336	7.21	Do not reject H_0
Within groups	33.428	11	3.039			
Total	35.470	13				

8. $H_0: \mu_1 = \mu_2 = \mu_3 = \mu_4$

H_1: Not all the means are equal.

See Section 11.5 or solutions to problems 1-2 for examples of calculations from formulas.

For $d.f._N = 3$ and $d.f._D = 13$, the critical value is $F_{0.05} = 3.41$. Since the observed F ratio is inside the critical region, we reject H_0. We conclude that not all the means are equal.

Summary of ANOVA results

Source of Variation	Sum of Squares	Degrees of Freedom	MS	F Ratio	F Critical Value	Test Decision
Between groups	18.965	3	6.322	14.910	3.41	Reject H_0
Within groups	5.517	13	0.424			
Total	24.482	16				

9. $H_0: \mu_1 = \mu_2 = \mu_3 = \mu_4$

H_1: Not all the means are equal.

See Section 11.5 or solutions to problems 1-2 for examples of calculations from formulas.

For $d.f._N = 3$ and $d.f._D = 15$, the critical value is $F_{0.05} = 3.29$. Since the observed F ratio is inside the critical region, we reject H_0. We conclude that not all the means are equal.

Summary of ANOVA results

Source of Variation	Sum of Squares	Degrees of Freedom	MS	F Ratio	F Critical Value	Test Decision
Between groups	238.225	3	79.408	4.611	3.29	Reject H_0
Within groups	258.340	15	17.223			
Total	496.565	18				

Section 11.6

1. There are two factors. One factor is *walking device* with 3 levels and the other factor is *task* with two levels. The data table has 6 cells.

2. There are two factors. One factor is *rank* with 4 levels and the other factor is *institution* with 2 levels. The data table has 8 cells.

3. Since the P value is less than 0.01, there is a significant difference in mean cadence according to the factor *walking device used.* The critical value is $F_{0.01} = 6.01$. Since the sample $F = 30.94$ is greater than $F_{0.01}$, F lies in the critical region and we reject H_0.

4. (a) There are two factors. One factor is *education level* with 4 levels and the other factor is *media type* with 5 levels.

(b) For education,
H_0: No difference in population mean index according to education level.
H_1: At least two education levels have different mean indices.

$$F_{\text{education}} = \frac{MS_{\text{education}}}{MS_{\text{error}}} = \frac{320}{108} = 2.963$$

For $d.f._N = 3$ and $d.f._D = 12$, the critical value is $F_{0.05} = 3.49$.
Since the observed F ratio is less than the critical value, F lies outside the critical region and we do not reject H_0.
The data do not indicate any differences in population mean index according to education level.

(c) For media,

H_0: No difference in population mean index by media type.
H_1: At least two types of media have different population mean indices.

$$F_{\text{media}} = \frac{MS_{\text{media}}}{MS_{\text{error}}} = \frac{1}{108} = 0.0093$$

(Minitab results are often rounded to just a few digits. For example, MS for media is 5/4 = 1.25 which has been rounded to 1.)
For $d.f._N = 4$ and $d.f._D = 12$, the critical value is $F_{0.05} = 3.26$.
Since the observed F ratio is less than the critical value, F lies outside the critical region and we do not reject H_0.
The data do not indicate any differences in population mean index according to media type.

5. **(a)** There are two factors. One factor is *income level* with 4 levels and the other factor is *media type* with 5 levels.

(b) For income,

H_0: There is no difference in population mean index based on income level.
H_1: At least two income levels have different population mean indices.

$$F_{\text{income}} = \frac{MS_{\text{income}}}{MS_{\text{error}}} = \frac{308}{160} = 1.925$$

For $d.f._N = 3$ and $d.f._D = 12$, the critical value is $F_{0.05} = 3.49$.
Since the observed F ratio is less than the critical value, F lies outside the critical region and we do not reject H_0.
The data do not indicate any differences in population mean index according to income level.

(c) For media,

H_0: No difference in population mean index by media type.
H_1: At least two media types have different population mean indices.

$$F_{\text{media}} = \frac{MS_{\text{media}}}{MS_{\text{error}}} = \frac{11}{160} = 0.069$$

For $d.f._N = 4$ and $d.f._D = 12$, the critical value is $F_{0.05} = 3.26$.
Since the observed F ratio is less than the critical value, F lies outside the critical region and we do not reject H_0.
The data do not indicate any differences in population mean index according to media type.

6. **(a)** There are two factors. One factor is *class* with 4 levels and the other factor is *gender* with 2 levels.

(b) H_0: No interaction between factors.
H_1: Some interaction between factors.

$$F_{\text{interaction}} = \frac{MS_{\text{interaction}}}{MS_{\text{error}}} = \frac{0.090}{0.221} = 0.4072$$

For $d.f._N = 3$ and $d.f._D = 24$, the critical value is $F_{0.05} = 3.01$.
Since the observed F ratio is less than the critical value, F lies outside the critical region and we do not reject H_0.
The data do not indicate any interaction between factors.

(c) H_0: No difference in population mean GPA based on class.
H_1: At least two classes have different population mean GPAs.

$$F_{\text{class}} = \frac{MS_{\text{class}}}{MS_{\text{error}}} = \frac{0.718}{0.221} = 3.2489$$

For $d.f._N = 3$ and $d.f._D = 24$, the critical value is $F_{0.05} = 3.01$.
Since the observed F ratio is greater than the critical value, F lies in the critical region and we reject H_0. We conclude at least two classes have different population mean GPAs.

(d) H_0: No difference in population mean GPA based on gender.
H_1: Some difference in population mean GPA based on gender.

$$F_{\text{gender}} = \frac{MS_{\text{gender}}}{MS_{\text{error}}} = \frac{0.300}{0.221} = 1.3575$$

For $d.f._N = 1$ and $d.f._D = 24$, the critical value is $F_{0.05} = 4.26$. Since the observed F ratio is less than the critical value, F lies outside the critical region and we do not reject H_0. The data do not indicate any difference in population mean GPA based on gender.

7.

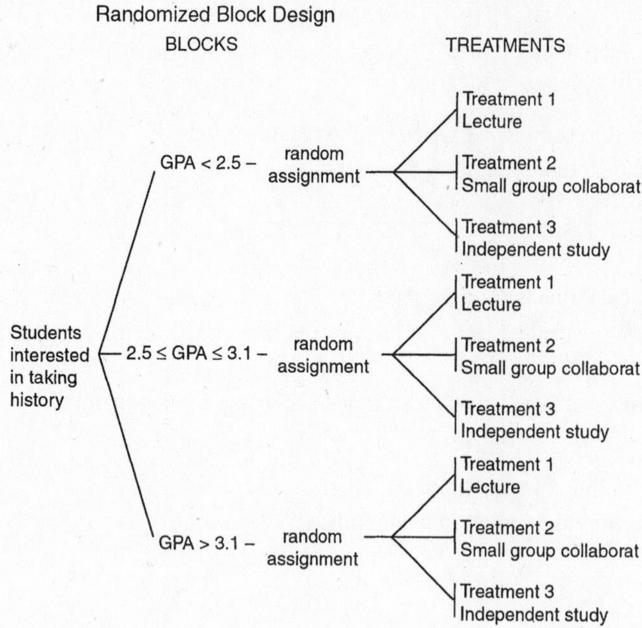

Yes; the design fits the model for randomized block design.

Chapter 11 Review

1. One-way ANOVA

H_0: $\mu_1 = \mu_2 = \mu_3 = \mu_4$

H_1: Not all the means are equal.

See Section 11.5 or solutions to problems 1-2 for examples of calculations from formulas.

For $d.f._N = 3$ and $d.f._D = 16$, the critical value is $F_{0.05} = 3.24$. Since the observed F ratio is outside the critical region, we do not reject H_0. There is insufficient evidence to conclude that not all the packaging mean sales are equal.

Summary of ANOVA results

Source of Variation	Sum of Squares	Degrees of Freedom	MS	F Ratio	F Critical Value	Test Decision
Between groups	6150	3	2050	2.63	3.24	Do not reject H_0
Within groups	12,455	16	778			
Total	18,605	19				

2. Chi-square test of independence
H_0: Time to do a test and test score are independent.
H_1: Time to do a test and test score are not independent.

$$\chi^2 = \sum \frac{(O-E)^2}{E}$$
$$= \frac{(23-18.93)^2}{18.93} + \frac{(42-42.60)^2}{42.60} + \frac{(65-71.00)^2}{71.00} + \frac{(12-9.47)^2}{9.47}$$
$$+ \frac{(17-21.07)^2}{21.07} + \frac{(48-47.40)^2}{47.40} + \frac{(85-79.00)^2}{79.00} + \frac{(8-10.53)^2}{10.53}$$
$$= 3.92$$

Since there are 2 rows and 4 columns, $d.f. = (2-1)(4-1) = 3$. For $\alpha = 0.01$, the critical value is $\chi^2_{0.01} = 11.34$.

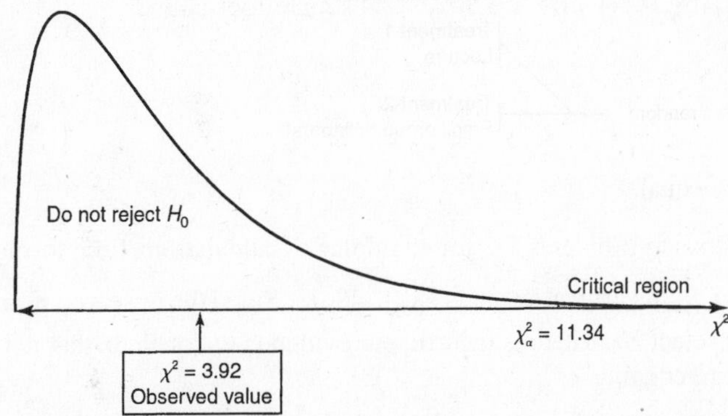

Since the sample statistic falls outside the critical region, we do not reject H_0. There is insufficient evidence to conclude that time to do a test and test score are not independent.

3. (a) Chi-square for testing σ^2

H_0: $\sigma^2 = 810{,}000$
H_1: $\sigma^2 > 810{,}000$

Since > is in H_1, a right-tailed test is used.
For $d.f. = 30 - 1 = 29$, the critical value is $\chi^2_{0.01} = 49.59$.

$$\chi^2 = \frac{(n-1)s^2}{\sigma^2} = \frac{(30-1)(1353)^2}{(900)^2} = 65.54$$

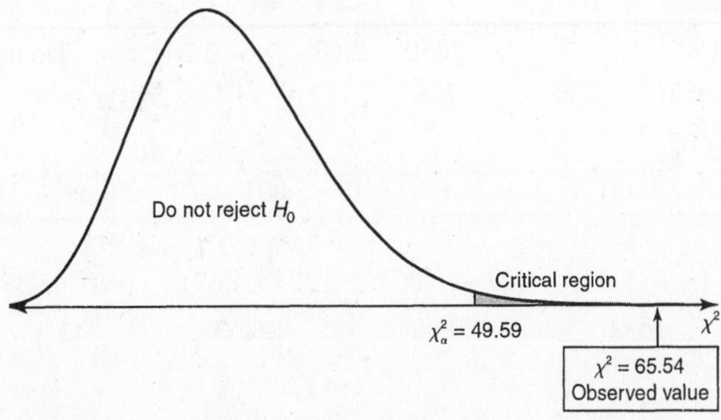

Since the sample statistic falls in the critical region, we reject H_0. We conclude that the variance of blow-out pressures is more than Soap Stone claims it is.

(b) For $d.f. = 29$ and $\alpha = \dfrac{1-0.95}{2} = 0.025$, $\chi^2_U = 45.72$.

For $d.f. = 29$ and $\alpha = \dfrac{1+0.95}{2} = 0.975$, $\chi^2_L = 16.05$.

The 95% confidence interval for σ^2 is

$$\frac{(n-1)s^2}{\chi^2_U} < \sigma^2 < \frac{(n-1)s^2}{\chi^2_L}$$

$$\frac{(30-1)(1353)^2}{45.72} < \sigma^2 < \frac{(30-1)(1353)^2}{16.05}$$

$$1{,}161{,}147.4 < \sigma^2 < 3{,}307{,}642.4 \text{ square foot-pounds}$$

4. One-way ANOVA

H_0: $\mu_1 = \mu_2 = \mu_3$

H_1: Not all the means are equal.

See Section 11.5 or solutions to problems 1-2 for examples of calculations from formulas.

For $d.f._N = 2$ and $d.f._D = 9$, the critical value is $F_{0.01} = 8.02$. Since the observed F ratio is outside the critical region, we do not reject H_0. There is insufficient evidence to conclude that not all the mean times to execute the programs are equal.

Summary of ANOVA results

Source of Variation	Sum of Squares	Degrees of Freedom	MS	F Ratio	F Critical Value	Test Decision
Between groups	1.002	2	0.501	0.443	8.02	Fail to reject H_0
Within groups	10.165	9	1.129			
Total	11.167	11				

5. Chi-square test of independence

H_0: Student grade and teacher rating are independent.

H_1: Student grade and teacher rating are not independent.

$$\chi^2 = \sum \frac{(O-E)^2}{E}$$

$$= \frac{(14-10.00)^2}{10.00} + \frac{(18-13.33)^2}{13.33} + \frac{(15-21.67)^2}{21.67} + \frac{(3-5.00)^2}{5.00} + \frac{(25-30.00)^2}{30.00} + \frac{(35-40.00)^2}{40.00}$$

$$+ \frac{(75-65.00)^2}{65.00} + \frac{(15-15.00)^2}{15.00} + \frac{(21-20.00)^2}{20.00} + \frac{(27-26.67)^2}{26.67} + \frac{(40-43.33)^2}{43.33} + \frac{(12-10.00)^2}{10.00}$$

$$= 9.8$$

Since there are 3 rows and 4 columns, $d.f. = (3-1)(4-1) = 6$. For $\alpha = 0.01$, the critical value is $\chi^2_{0.01} = 16.81$.

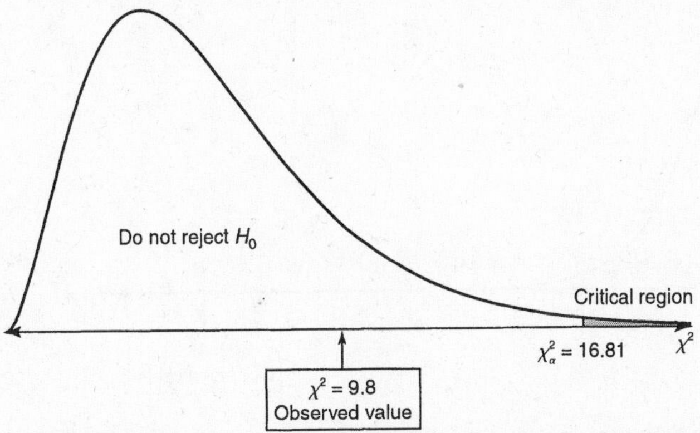

Since the sample statistic falls outside the critical region, we do not reject H_0. We have insufficient evidence to conclude that student grade and teacher rating are not independent.

6. Chi-square for testing σ^2

H_0: $\sigma^2 = 0.0625$

H_1: $\sigma^2 > 0.0625$

Since > is in H_1, a right-tailed test is used.

For $d.f.$ = 12 – 1 = 11, the critical value is $\chi^2_{0.05} = 19.68$.

$$\chi^2 = \frac{(n-1)s^2}{\sigma^2} = \frac{(12-1)(0.38)^2}{(0.25)^2} = 25.41$$

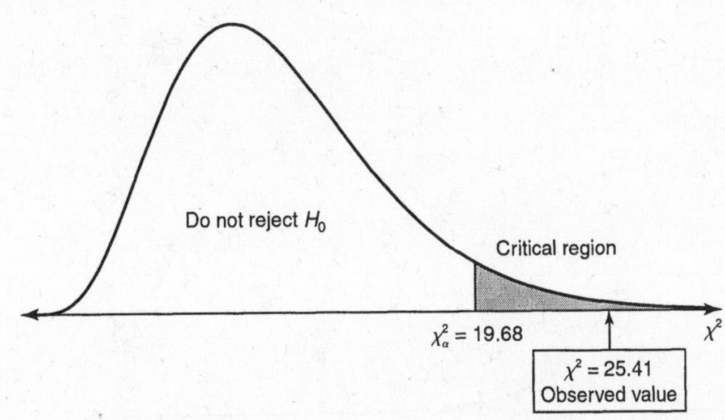

Since the sample statistic falls in the critical region, we reject H_0. We conclude that the machine needs to be adjusted (i.e., the variance has increased, $\sigma^2 > 0.25^2 > 0.0625$).

7. Chi-square goodness of fit

H_0: The distributions are the same.

H_1: The distributions are different.

$$\chi^2 = \sum \frac{(O-E)^2}{E}$$

$$= \frac{(15-42.0)^2}{42.0} + \frac{(25-31.5)^2}{31.5} + \frac{(70-63.0)^2}{63.0} + \frac{(80-52.5)^2}{52.5} + \frac{(20-21.0)^2}{21.0}$$

$$= 33.93$$

$d.f.$ = (number of E entries) – 1 = 5 – 1 = 4. The critical value is $\chi^2_{0.01} = 13.28$.

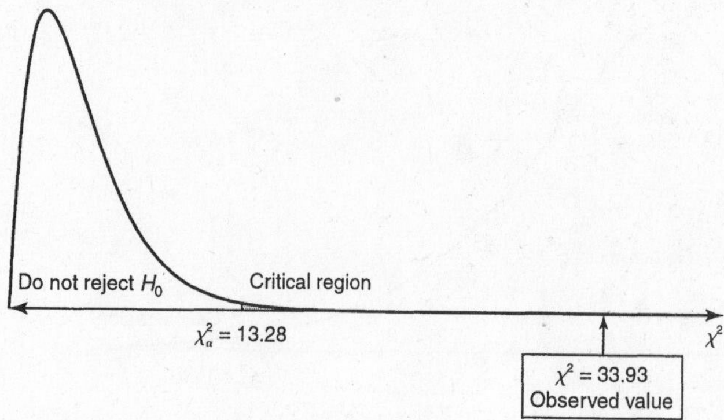

Since the sample statistic falls inside the critical region, we reject H_0. We conclude that the age distribution has changed.

8. F test for equality of two variances

H_0: $\sigma_1^2 = \sigma_2^2$

H_1: $\sigma_1^2 \neq \sigma_2^2$

Since $\neq$ is in H_1, a two-tailed test is used.

The populations follow independent normal distributions. The samples are random samples from each population.

Since $s^2 = 0.235$ is larger than $s^2 = 0.128$, we designate Population I as the old process.

$$F = \frac{s_1^2}{s_2^2} = \frac{0.235}{0.128} = 1.84$$

Using $d.f._N = n_1 - 1 = 21 - 1 = 20$, and $d.f._D = n_2 - 1 = 26 - 1 = 25$, and $\alpha = 0.05$, the critical $F_{\frac{\alpha}{2}}$ value is 2.30.

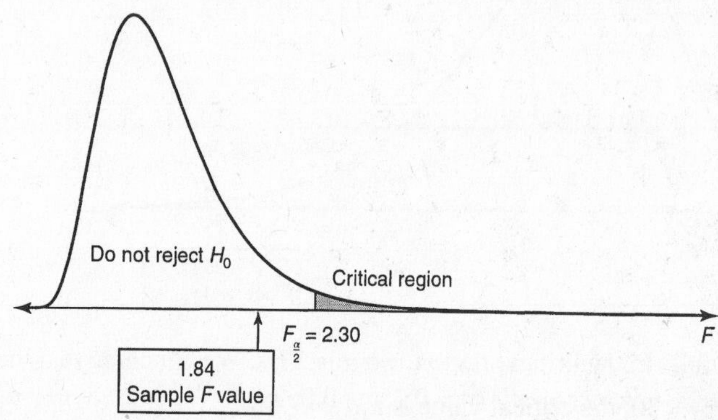

Since the sample F statistic falls outside the critical region, we do not reject H_0. There is insufficient evidence to conclude that there is a difference in the population variances for the old and the new manufacturing processes.

9. F test for the equality of two variances

H_0: $\sigma_1^2 = \sigma_2^2$

H_1: $\sigma_1^2 > \sigma_2^2$

Since $>$ is in H_1, a right-tailed test is used.

The populations follow independent normal distributions. The samples are random samples from each population.

Since $s^2 = 135.24$ is larger than $s^2 = 51.87$, we designate Population I as the new process.

$$F = \frac{s_1^2}{s_2^2} = \frac{135.24}{51.87} = 2.61$$

Using $d.f._N = n_1 - 1 = 16 - 1 = 15$, and $d.f._D = n_2 - 1 = 18 - 1 = 17$, and $\alpha = 0.05$, the critical F value is 2.31.

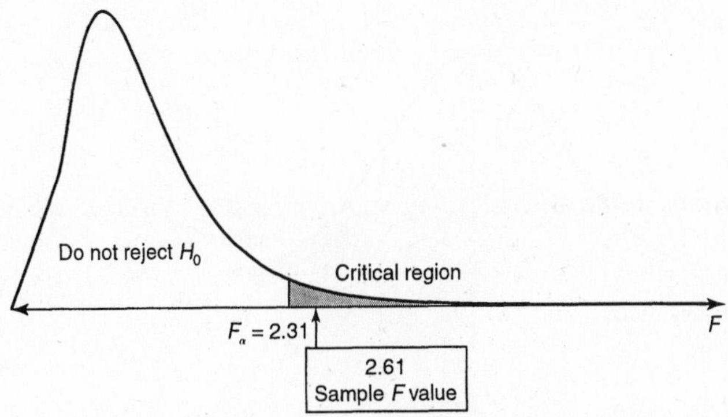

Since the sample F statistic falls inside the critical region, we reject H_0. We conclude that the population variance of life times for bulbs made by the new process is greater than that for bulbs made by the old process.

10. Two-way ANOVA

(a) There are two factors. One factor is *day* with 2 levels and the other factor is *section* with 3 levels.

(b) H_0: No interaction between day and section.
H_1: Some interaction between day and section.

$$F_{\text{interaction}} = \frac{MS_{\text{interaction}}}{MS_{\text{error}}} = \frac{19.0}{18.5} = 1.027$$

For $d.f._N = 2$ and $d.f._D = 30$, the critical value is $F_{0.01} = 5.39$.
Since the observed F ratio is less than the critical value, F lies outside the critical region and we do not reject H_0. The data do not indicate any interaction between day and section.

(c) H_0: No difference in population mean number of responses according to day.
H_1: At least two population means are different among the days.

$$F_{\text{day}} = \frac{MS_{\text{day}}}{MS_{\text{error}}} = \frac{1024.0}{18.5} = 55.35$$

For $d.f._N = 1$ and $d.f._D = 30$, the critical value is $F_{0.01} = 7.56$.
Since the observed F ratio is greater than the critical value, F lies in the critical region and we reject H_0. We conclude that the two population means differ by day.

(d) H_0: No difference in population mean number of responses according to section.
H_1: At least two population means are different among the sections.

$$F_{\text{section}} = \frac{MS_{\text{section}}}{MS_{\text{error}}} = \frac{786.8}{18.5} = 42.53$$

For $d.f._N = 2$ and $d.f._D = 30$, the critical value is $F_{0.01} = 5.39$. Since the observed F ratio is greater than the critical value, F lies in the critical region and we reject H_0. We conclude that at least two population means are different among the sections.

Chapter 12 Nonparametric Statistics

Section 12.1

For part (c) in each of the following problems, refer to sketches (a), (b) or (c) shown below.

(a)

$H_0: p = 0.5$
$H_1: p > 0.5$

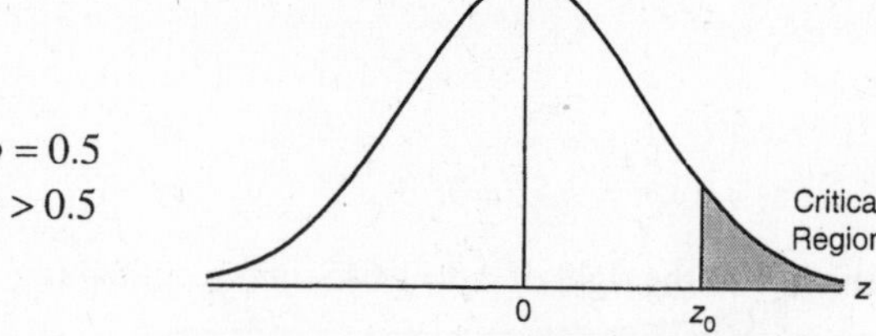

(b)

$H_0: p = 0.5$
$H_1: p < 0.5$

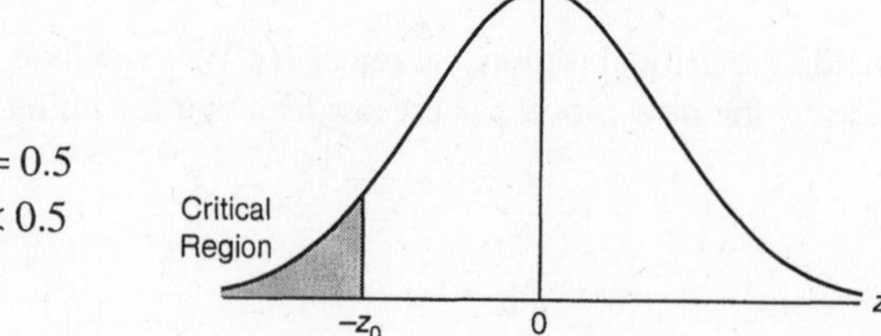

(c)

$H_0: p = 0.5$
$H_1: p \neq 0.5$

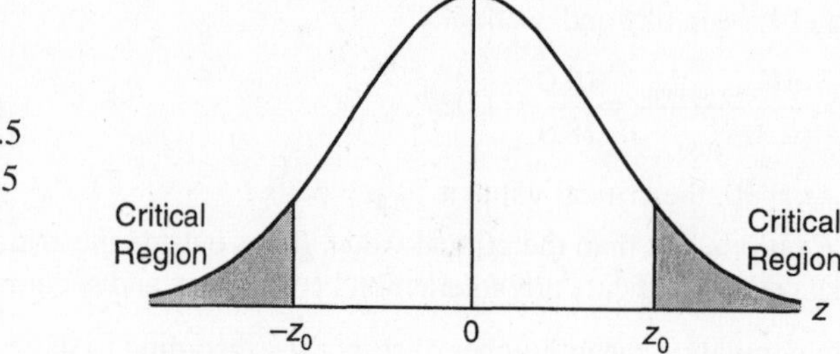

1.

Pen	New Tip	Old Tip	Sign of Difference, New – Old
1	52	50	+
2	47	55	–
3	56	51	+
4	48	45	+
5	51	57	–
6	59	54	+
7	47	46	+
8	57	53	+
9	56	52	+
10	46	40	+
11	56	49	+
12	47	51	–

(a) $H_0: p = \frac{1}{2}$; $H_1: p > \frac{1}{2}$, i.e., H_0: the distributions of writing life for the old and new pen tips are the same; H_1: the distribution of the writing life for the new pen tip is shifted to the right of that for the old pen tip; since the alternative is $p > \frac{1}{2}$, this will be a right-tailed test at level of significance $\alpha = 0.05$.

(b) Sign test with number of nonzero pairs $n = 12 \geq 12$, so use the normal approximation with $\mu = p = \frac{1}{2} = 0.5, \sigma = \sqrt{pq/n} = \sqrt{(0.5)(0.5)/12} = \sqrt{0.25/12} = 0.1443$; the critical value is $z_0 = 1.645$.

(c) Refer to Figure (a) above with $z_0 = 1.645$.

(d) $r = 9$ plus signs, $n = 12$ nonzero pairs, $x = r/n = 9/12 = 0.75$

$z = \frac{x-\mu}{\sigma} = \frac{0.75-0.5}{0.1443} = 1.73$, which is to the right of $z_0 = 1.645$, in the critical region, in the figure for part (c).

(e) Reject H_0: the data do not support the null hypothesis, but rather indicate the writing life of the new pen tip is longer than that of the old pen tip.

2.

Student	Pulse Rate Before Exam	Pulse Rate Before Ordinary Class	Sign of Difference, Exam – Ordinary Class
1	88	81	+
2	77	77	0
3	72	75	–
4	74	79	–
5	81	79	+
6	70	68	+
7	75	77	–
8	80	73	+
9	68	71	–
10	75	73	+
11	82	76	+
12	61	66	–
13	77	68	+
14	64	60	+

(a) H_0: the distribution of pulse rates is the same before an exam as it is before an ordinary class, H_1: the distribution of pulse rates before an exam is shifted to the right compared to that before an ordinary class, or H_0: $p = 0.5$, H_1:$p > 0.5$. Because the alternative is $p > 0.5$, this will be a right-tailed sign test at significance level $\alpha = 0.05$.

(b) The number of nonzero difference is $n = 13 \geq 12$, so we will use the normal approximation with $\mu = p = 0.5$, and $\sigma = \sqrt{pq/n} = \sqrt{0.5(0.5)/13} = \sqrt{0.25/13} = 0.1387$. The critical value cuts off an area of $\alpha = 0.05$ in the upper tail; $z_0 = 1.645$.

(c) Refer to Figure (a) above with $z_0 = 1.645$.

(d) $r = 8$ plus signs, $n = 13$ plus and minus signs, $x = r/n = 8/13 = 0.6154$

$z = \frac{x-\mu}{\sigma} = \frac{0.6154-0.5}{0.1387} = 0.83$, which is between 0 and $z_0 = 1.645$, in the figure for part (c); z is not in the critical region.

(e) Because z is not in the critical region, we fail to reject H_0. There is insufficient evidence to support the claim that student pulse rates increase before an exam.

3.

Student	Sign of Difference After – Before
1	–
2	+
3	+
4	+
5	–
6	0
7	–
8	+
9	–
10	+
11	+
12	+
13	–
14	+
15	–
16	+
17	0
18	+

(a) H_0: the score distributions for student awareness of current events are the same, before and after lectures, H_1: the score distributions before lectures and after lectures are different, or $H_0: p = 0.5, H_1: p \neq 0.5$. Because the alternative is $p \neq 0.5$, this will be a two-tailed sign test at level of significance $\alpha = 0.05$.

(b) Because the number of nonzero difference is $n = 16 \geq 12$, we will use the normal approximation with $\mu = p = 0.5$, and $\sigma = \sqrt{pq/n} = \sqrt{(0.5)(0.5)/16} = 0.125$. The critical value cut off a total area of $\alpha = 0.05$, half in each tail, $\pm z_0 = \pm 1.96$.

(c) Refer to Figure (c) above with $\pm z_0 = \pm 1.96$.

(d) $r = 10$ plus signs, $n = 16$ plus or minus signs, $x = r/n = 10/16 = 0.625$

$z = \dfrac{x - \mu}{\sigma} = \dfrac{0.625 - 0.5}{0.125} = 1.00$ which is between 0 and $z_0 = 1.96$; z is not in a critical region.

(e) Since z is outside the critical regions, we fail to reject H_0. There is insufficient evidence to support the claim that lectures on current events change student awareness of current events.

4.

Day	Sign of Difference, Line A – Line B
1	–
2	–
3	+
4	0
5	+
6	–
7	+
8	+
9	+
10	+
11	–
12	–
13	+
14	+
15	–

(a) H_0: the score distributions of defective lens filiters are the same for both production lines, H_1: the distribution of defective lens filters for line A is different from that for line B, or $H_0: p = 0.5, H_1: p \neq 0.5$. Because the alternative is $p \neq 0.5$, this will be a two-tailed sign test at level of significance $\alpha = 0.01$.

(b) Because the number of nonzero difference is $n = 14 \geq 12$, we will use the normal approximation with $\mu = p = 0.5$, and $\sigma = \sqrt{pq/n} = \sqrt{0.25/14} = 0.1336$. The critical values cut off a total area of $\alpha = 0.01$, half in each tail, $\pm z_0 = \pm 2.58$.

(c) Refer to Figure (c) above with $\pm z_0 = \pm 2.58$.

(d) $r = 8$ plus signs, $n = 14$ plus and minus signs, $x = r/n = 8/14 = 0.5714$

$z = \dfrac{x-\mu}{\sigma} = \dfrac{0.5714 - 0.5}{0.1336} = 0.53$, which is between 0 and $z_0 = 2.58$; z is not in a critical region.

(e) Since z is outside the critical regions, we fail to reject H_0. There is insufficient evidence to support the claim that employee experience makes a difference in the number of defective lens filters produced.

5.

Twin Pair	Sign of Difference, School A – School B
1	+
2	+
3	−
4	−
5	+
6	+
7	−
8	+
9	+
10	+
11	−
12	−

(a) H_0: the distributions of reading achievement scores are the same for both schools; H_1: the distributions are different, or $H_0: p = 0.5, H_1: p \neq 0.5$. Because the alternative is $p \neq 0.5$, this will be a two-tailed sign test at level of significance $\alpha = 0.05$.

(b) Because the number of nonzero differences is $n = 12 \geq 12$, we will use the normal approximation with $\mu = p = 0.5$, and $\sigma = \sqrt{0.25/12} = 0.1443$. The critical values cut off a total area of $\alpha = 0.05$, half in each tail, $\pm z_0 = \pm 1.96$.

(c) Refer to Figure (c) above with $\pm z_0 = \pm 1.96$.

(d) $r = 7$ plus signs, $n = 12$ plus and minus signs, $x = r/n = 7/12 = 0.5833$

$z = \dfrac{x-\mu}{\sigma} = \dfrac{0.5833 - 0.5}{0.1443} = 0.58$, which is between 0 and $z_0 = 1.96$ in the figure for part (c), z is not in a critical region.

(e) Because z is outside the critical regions, we fail to reject H_0. There is insufficient evidence to support the claim that the schools are not equally effective at teaching reading skills.

6.

Bakery	Sign of Difference, A – B
1	–
2	+
3	0
4	–
5	–
6	–
7	+
8	–
9	–
10	+
11	+
12	–
13	+
14	+
15	–
16	–
17	+
18	–
19	–
20	+

(a) H_0: the shelf life distributions are the same for preservatives A and B, H_1: the shelf life distribution for preservative B is shifted to the right of that for preservative A, or $H_0: p = 0.5, H_1: p < 0.5$. (Note that the difference is specified as A – B, so under H_1, there should be less than half plus signs.) Since the alternative is $p < 0.5$, this will be a left-tailed sign test at level of significance $\alpha = 0.05$.

(b) Because the number of nonzero differences is $n = 19 \geq 12$, we can use the normal approximation with $\mu = p = 0.5$, and $\sigma = \sqrt{pq/n} = \sqrt{0.25/19} = 0.1147$. The critical value cuts off an area of $\alpha = 0.05$, in the lower tail; $-z_0 = -1.645$.

(c) Refer to Figure (b) above with $-z_0 = -1.645$.

(d) $r = 8$ plus signs, $n = 19$ plus and minus signs, $x = r/n = 8/19 = 0.4211$.

$$z = \frac{x - \mu}{\sigma} = \frac{0.4211 - 0.5}{0.1147} = -0.69,$$

which is between $-z_0 = -1.645$ and 0; z is not in the critical region.

(e) Because z is outside the critical regions, we fail to reject H_0. There is insufficient evidence to support the claim that bread baked with preservative B will stay fresh longer.

7.

Bakery	Sign of Difference, A – B
1	0
2	–
3	–
4	0
5	+
6	–
7	–
8	+
9	–
10	–
11	–
12	–
13	+
14	–
15	–
16	–
17	–
18	–

(a) H_0: the distribution of cigarettes smoked is the same, H_1: the distribution of cigarettes smoked after hypnosis is shifted to the left of the distribution for cigarettes smoked before hypnosis, or $H_0: p = 0.5, H_1: p < 0.5$. Because the alternative is $p < 0.5$, this will be a left-tailed sign test, at significance level $\alpha = 0.01$.

(b) Because the number of nonzero differences is $n = 16 \geq 12$, we will use the normal approximation with $\mu = p = 0.5$, and $\sigma = \sqrt{pq/n} = \sqrt{0.25/16} = 0.125$. The critical value cuts off an area of $\alpha = 0.01$ in the lower tail; $-z_0 = -2.33$.

(c) Refer to Figure (b) above with $-z_0 = -2.33$.

(d) $r = 3$ plus signs, $n = 16$ plus or minus signs, $x = r/n = 3/16 = 0.1875$.

$z = \dfrac{x-\mu}{\sigma} = \dfrac{0.1875-0.5}{0.125} = -2.50$, which is to the left of $-z_0 = -2.33$ and in the critical region.

(e) Because z is in the critical region, we reject H_0. The data do not support the null hypothesis; hypnosis appear to help smokers cut back on the number of cigarettes smoked.

8.

Student	Sign of Difference, After – Before
1	–
2	–
3	–
4	–
5	0
6	+
7	–
8	–
9	–
10	+
11	–
12	–
13	–
14	–
15	–
16	+

(a) H_0: the distribution of mosquito bites is the same before as after eating garlic, H_1: the distribution of mosquito bites after eating garlic is shifted to the left of that before eating garlic, or $H_0: p = 0.5, H_1: p < 0.5$. Because the alternative is $p < 0.5$, this will be a left-tailed sign test, at level of significance $\alpha = 0.05$.

(b) Because the number of nonzero differences is $n = 15 \geq 12$, we can use the normal approximation to the distribution of p with $\mu = p = 0.5$, and $\sigma = \sqrt{pq/n} = \sqrt{0.25/15} = 0.1291$. The critical value cuts off an area of $\alpha = 0.05$ in the lower tail; $-z_0 = -1.645$.

(c) Refer to Figure (b) above with $-z_0 = -1.645$.

(d) $r = 3$ plus signs, $n = 15$ plus and minus signs, $x = r/n = 3/15 = 0.2$.

$z = \dfrac{x-\mu}{\sigma} = \dfrac{0.2-0.5}{0.1291} = -2.32$, which is below $-z_0 = -1.645$, and in the critical region.

(e) Because z is in the critical region, we reject H_0. The data do not support the null hypothesis; eating garlic appears to repel mosquitoes.

9.

Baby	Sign of Difference, After – Before
1	+
2	+
3	+
4	–
5	0
6	+
7	0
8	–
9	–
10	+
11	+
12	–
13	+
14	0
15	+
16	–
17	+

(a) H_0: the distribution of baby pulse rates is the same 24 hours before labor begins as it is 24 hours after birth, H_1: the distributions are different, or $H_0: p = 0.5, H_1: p \neq 0.5$. Because the alternative is $p \neq 0.5$, this will be a two-tailed test, at level of significance $\alpha = 0.01$.

(b) Because the number of nonzero differences is $n = 14 \geq 12$, we can use the normal approximation with mean $\mu = p = 0.5$, and standard deviation $\sigma = \sqrt{pq/n} = \sqrt{0.25/14} = 0.1336$. The critical value cuts off a total area of $\alpha = 0.01$, evenly in both tails; $\pm z_0 = \pm 2.58$.

(c) Refer to Figure (c) above with $\pm z_0 = \pm 2.58$.

(d) $r = 9$ plus signs, $n = 14$ plus and minus signs, $x = r/n = 9/14 = 0.6429$.

$z = \dfrac{x-\mu}{\sigma} = \dfrac{0.6429-0.5}{0.1336} = 1.07$, which is between 0 and $z_0 = 2.58$, and not in either critical region.

(e) Because z is outside the critical regions, we fail to reject H_0. There is insufficient evidence to support the claim that babies' pulse rates are different before and after birth.

10.

Salesperson	Sign of Difference, After – Before
1	+
2	+
3	–
4	–
5	+
6	0
7	+
8	+
9	+
10	–
11	+
12	+
13	0
14	–
15	+

(a) H_0: the distribution of the number of magazines sold is the same before TV ads aired as it was after the ads aired, H_1: the distributions are different, or $H_0: p = 0.5, H_1: p \neq 0.5$. Because the alternative is $p \neq 0.5$, this will be a two-tailed sign test, with level of significance $\alpha = 0.05$.

(b) Because the number of nonzero differences is $n = 13 \geq 12$, we can use the normal approximation with mean $\mu = p = 0.5$, and standard deviation $\sigma = \sqrt{pq/n} = \sqrt{0.25/13} = 0.1387$. The critical values cut off a total area of $\alpha = 0.05$, evenly in both tails; $\pm z_0 = \pm 1.96$.

(c) Refer to Figure (c) above with $\pm z_0 = \pm 1.96$.

(d) $r = 9$ plus signs, $n = 13$ plus and minus signs, $x = r/n = 9/13 = 0.6923$.

$z = \dfrac{x - \mu}{\sigma} = \dfrac{0.6923 - 0.5}{0.1387} = 1.39$, which is between 0 and $z_0 = 1.96$, and not in one of the critical regions.

(e) Because z is outside the critical regions, we fail to reject H_0. There is insufficient evidence to show TV ads for magazines affected magazine sales.

11.

Month	Sign of Difference, Madison – Juneau
January	–
February	–
March	–
April	+
May	+
June	+
July	+
August	+
September	+
October	+
November	+
December	–

(a) H_0: the temperature distribution is the same in Madison, Wisconsin as it is in Juneau, Alaska, H_1: the temperature distributions are different, or $H_0: p = 0.5, H_1: p \neq 0.5$. Because the alternative is $p \neq 0.5$, this will be a two-tailed sign test, with level of significance $\alpha = 0.05$.

(b) Because the number of nonzero differencess is n = 12 ≥ 12, we can use the normal approximation with $\mu = p = 0.5$, and $\sigma = \sqrt{pq/n} = \sqrt{0.25/12} = 0.1443$. The critical values cut off a total area of $\alpha = 0.05$, evenly in each tail; $\pm z_0 = \pm 1.96$.

(c) Refer to Figure (c) above with $\pm z_0 = \pm 1.96$.

(d) r = 8 plus signs, n = 12 plus and minus signs, $x = r/n = 8/12 = 0.6667$.

$z = \dfrac{x-\mu}{\sigma} = \dfrac{0.6667-0.5}{0.1443} = 1.16$, which is between 0 and $z_0 = 1.96$, and not in either critical region.

(e) Because z is outside the critical regions, we fail to reject H_0. There is insufficient evidence to support the claim that Madison and Juneau have different temperature distributions.
Note: Whereas it is true that there is no statistically significant difference in the distributions, the sign test misses one very important point: the differences are cyclical; Madison is warmer from December to March (i.e., "winter"). A "runs test" might detect this obvious pattern, whereas the sign test merely counts the number of plus signs, which would be the same if the data were ordered July to June, or April to March, etc.

Section 12.2

For problems 1-5, H_0: the distributions of the two populations are the same, H_1: the population distributions are different. Use the Wilcoxon rank sum test, two-tailed, with level of significance $\alpha = 0.05$. When n_1 and n_2 are ≥8, use the normal approximation with $\mu_R = \dfrac{n_1(n_1+n_2+1)}{2}$ and $\sigma_R = \sqrt{\dfrac{n_1 n_2(n_1+n_2+1)}{12}}$.

Let $\Sigma R_A, \Sigma R_B$ be the sum of the ranks of Groups A and B, statistic R be the sum of the ranks of the smaller sample $n_1 \le n_2$. The critical values are $\pm z_0 = \pm 1.96$. Begin by ordering and ranking the combined data:

1.

Student Score	Group	Rank
44	A	1
45	B	2
50	A	3
55	B	4
60	A	5
63	B	6
65	A	7
66	B	8
69	B	9
70	A	10
71	A	11
73	A	12
75	B	13
77	B	14
81	A	15
84	B	16
85	B	17
88	A	18
90	B	19

$n_1 = 9$ (group A), $n_2 = 10$; both are ≥ 8; use normal approximation R = sum of ranks of As $= \Sigma R_A = 82$.
(As a check: sum of ranks of Bs $= \Sigma R_B = 108$, sum of ranks of all data = 190
This should equal $(n_1 + n_2)(n_1 + n_2 + 1)/2 = 190$ ✓)

$$\mu_R = \frac{9(9+10+1)}{2} = \frac{9(20)}{2} = 90$$

$$\sigma_R = \sqrt{\frac{9(10)(9+10+1)}{12}} = \sqrt{150} = 12.2474 \approx 12.25$$

$$z \approx \frac{R - \mu_R}{\sigma_R} = \frac{82-90}{12.2474} = -0.65$$

Since z is not in either critical region, we fail to reject H_0. The data do not support the claim that the distributions of student test scores are different.

2.

Boredom Tolerance Score	Group	Rank
35	B	1
41	A	2
50	A	3
54	B	4
66	A	5
68	A	6
69	B	7
72	B	8
73	A	9
75	A	10
77	B	11
85	B	12
88	A	13
92	A	14
99	B	15
100	B	16
103	A	17
111	A	18
115	A	19
120	A	20
135	B	21
150	B	22

Group A: $n_2 = 12, \Sigma R_A = 136$
Group B: $n_1 = 10, \Sigma R_B = 117$ (Note: Group B is smaller)
[Check: $\Sigma R_A + \Sigma R_B = 136 + 117 = 253$; this should equal $(n_1 + n_2)(n_1 + n_2 + 1)/2 = 22(23)/2 = 253$ ✓]
$R = \Sigma R_B = 117$. Since n_1 and n_2 are each ≥ 8, use the normal approximation with

$$\mu_R = 10(10+12+1)/2 = 115$$

$$\sigma_R = \sqrt{10(12)(10+12+1)/12} = \sqrt{230} = 15.1658 \approx 15.17$$

$$z \approx \frac{R - \mu_R}{\sigma_R} = \frac{117-115}{15.1658} = 0.13,$$ which is not in either critical region.

Fail to reject H_0; the data do not support the claim that the distributions of boredom tolerance are different.

3.

Number of Sessions	Method	Rank
19	A	1
20	B	2
24	B	3
25	A	4
26	B	5
28	A	6
31	A	7
33	B	8
34	B	9
35	A	10
37	A	11
38	A	12
39	B	13
40	A	14
41	A	15
42	B	16
44	B	17
46	B	18
48	B	19

Method A: $n_1 = 9, \sum R_A = 80$
Method B: $n_2 = 10, \sum R_B = 110$
[Check: $\sum R_A + \sum R_B = 80 + 110 = 190$; this should equal $(n_1 + n_2)(n_1 + n_2 + 1)/2 = 19(20)/2 = 190$ ✓]
Since n_1 and n_2 are each ≥8, use the normal approximation with $\mu_R = 9(20)/2 = 90$,
$\sigma_R = \sqrt{(9)(10)(20)/12} = \sqrt{150} = 12.2474$. $z \approx \dfrac{R - \mu_R}{\sigma_R} = \dfrac{80 - 90}{12.2474} = -0.82$, which is not in either rejection region. Fail to reject H_0; there is insufficient evidence to support the claim that the distribution of the number of horse training sessions with a lead horse differs from that with no lead horse.

4.

Time	Method	Rank
15	B	$\frac{1+2}{2} = 1.5$
15	A	$\frac{1+2}{2} = 1.5$
18	A	3
19	B	4
20	A	5
22	A	6
25	A	7
28	B	8
29	B	9
30	A	$\frac{10+1}{2} = 10.5$
30	B	$\frac{10+1}{2} = 10.5$
33	A	12
40	B	13
41	A	14
44	A	15
46	B	16
55	B	17
56	A	18
58	B	19
63	B	20

(remembering to assign ties at 15 and at 30 the average of the ranks)

Method A: $n_1 = 10, \Sigma R_A = 92$

Method B: $n_2 = 10, \Sigma R_B = 118$

[Check: $\Sigma R_A + \Sigma R_B = 92 + 118 = 210$; this should equal $(n_1 + n_2)(n_1 + n_2 + 1)/2 = 20(21)/2 = 210$ ✓]

Since n_1 and $n_2 = 10 \geq 8$, use the normal approximation with $\mu_R = 10(21)/2 = 105$,

$\sigma_R = \sqrt{10(10)(21)/12} = \sqrt{175} = 13.2288$ and $R = \Sigma R_A = 92$. (Since $n_1 = n_2$, we could use $R = \Sigma R_B$ instead.)

$z \approx \frac{R - \mu_R}{\sigma_R} = \frac{92 - 105}{13.2288} = -0.98$, which is not in either critical region. Fail to reject H_0; there is insufficient evidence to support the claim that the method of teaching French verbs makes the distributions different.

(Note: using $R = \Sigma R_B$, we would get $z \approx \frac{R - \mu_R}{\sigma_R} = \frac{118 - 105}{13.2288} = +0.98$)

5.

Test Score	Group	Rank
7	A	1
8	A	2
9	B	3
10	A	4
11	B	5
12	A	6
13	A	7
14	B	8
15	A	9
16	B	10
17	A	11
18	A	12
19	B	13
22	A	14
24	B	15
27	B	16
28	B	17
29	B	18
30	B	19
31	B	20
33	B	21

Group A: $n_1 = 9, \Sigma R_A = 66$

Group B: $n_2 = 12, \Sigma R_B = 165$

[Check: $\Sigma R_A + \Sigma R_B = 66 + 165 = 231$; which should equal $(n_1 + n_2)(n_1 + n_2 + 1)/2 = 21(22)/2 = 231$ ✓]

Since $n_1, n_2 \geq 8$, use the normal approximation with $\mu_R = 9(9 + 12 + 1)/2 = 99$,

$\sigma_R = \sqrt{9(12)(22)/12} = \sqrt{198} = 14.0712$, and $R = \Sigma R_A = 66$. $z \approx \frac{R - \mu_R}{\sigma_R} = \frac{66 - 99}{14.0712} = -2.35$, which is in the (lower/left) critical region. Reject H_0; there is sufficient evidence to support the claim that the competitive and noncompetitive settings' distributions are different.

For problems 6-10: H_0: the population distributions are the same, H_1: the population distributions are different. Use a two-tailed Wilcozon rank sum test at level of significance $\alpha = 0.01$. When the sample sizes are each ≥ 8, use the normal approximation with $\mu_R = n_1(n_1 + n_2 + 1)/2$ and $\sigma_R = \sqrt{n_1(n_2)(n_1 + n_2 + 1)/12}$. Let $\Sigma R_A, \Sigma R_B$ be the sums of the ranks for data set A and data set B. Let n_1 denote the smaller sample size, and let R = sum of ranks of that group in the test statistic. The critical values are $\pm z_0 = \pm 2.58$. Begin by ranking the combined data:

6.

Test Scores	Group	Rank
42	B	1
44	B	2
52	A	3
57	B	4
60	A	$\frac{5+6}{2} = 5.5$
60	B	$\frac{5+6}{2} = 5.5$
62	B	7
65	B	8
67	A	9
68	A	10
76	A	11
79	A	12
81	A	13
82	B	14
85	A	15
86	B	16
88	A	17
90	A	18
91	B	19
93	A	20
96	B	21

Group A: $n_2 = 11, \Sigma R_A = 133.5$

Group B: $n_1 = 10, \Sigma R_B = 97.5$

[Check: $\Sigma R_A + \Sigma R_B = 133.5 + 97.5 = 231$; this should equal $(n_1 + n_2)(n_1 + n_2 + 1)/2 = 21(22)/2 = 231$ ✓]

Since both n_1 and n_2 are ≥ 8, use the normal approximation with $\mu_R = 10(22)/2 = 110$,

$\sigma_R = \sqrt{10(11)(22)/12} = 14.2009$, and $R = \Sigma R_A = 97.5$. $z \approx \frac{R - \mu_R}{\sigma_R} = \frac{97.5 - 110}{14.2009} = -0.88$, which is not in either critical region. Fail to reject H_0; there is insufficient evidence to support the claim that the distributions of test scores by diet type differ.

7.

Days Sick	Group	Rank
8	B	1
9	B	2
10	A	3
11	B	4
12	A	5
14	A	6
15	B	7
16	A	8
17	B	9
18	B	10
19	A	11
20	A	12
21	A	13
22	B	14
24	B	15
25	A	16
26	B	17
28	A	18
31	B	19

Group A: $n_1 = 9, \Sigma R_A = 92$

Group B: $n_2 = 10, \Sigma R_B = 98$

(Check: $\Sigma R_A + \Sigma R_B = 190$; this should be equal to $(n_1 + n_2)(n_1 + n_2 + 1)/2 = 19(20)/2 = 190$ ✓)

Since both n_1 and n_2 are ≥ 8, use the normal approximation with $\mu_R = 9(20)/2 = 90$,

$\sigma_R = \sqrt{9(10)(20)/12} = \sqrt{150} = 12.2474$, and $R = \Sigma R_A = 92$. $z \approx \dfrac{R - \mu_R}{\sigma_R} = \dfrac{92 - 90}{12.2474} = 0.16$, which is not in either critical region. Fail to reject H_0; there is insufficient evidence to support the claim that the distributions of duration of colds differ.

8.

Time	Group	Rank
30	B	1
31	B	2
33	A	3
36	B	4
37	B	5
38	A	6
39	B	7
40	A	8
41	A	9
42	B	10
44	B	11
45	A	12
47	A	13
50	B	14
52	A	15
55	A	16
58	A	17
61	B	18

Group A: $n_1 = 9, \Sigma R_A = 99$

Group B: $n_2 = 9, \Sigma R_B = 72$

[Check: $\Sigma R_A + \Sigma R_B = 99 + 72 = 171$; this should be equal to $(n_1 + n_2)(n_1 + n_2 + 1)/2 = 18(19)/2 = 171$ ✓]

Since both n_1 and $n_2 \geq 8$, we will use the normal approximation with $\mu_R = 9(19)/2 = 85.5$,

$\sigma_R = \sqrt{(9)(9)(19)/12} = \sqrt{128.25} = 11.3248$. Since $n_1 = n_2$, it doesn't matter which sample size is called

n_1 or whether $R = \Sigma R_A$ or $R = \Sigma R_B$, so let $R = \Sigma R_A$ and $n_A = n_1$. $z \approx \frac{R - \mu_R}{\sigma_R} = \frac{99 - 85.5}{11.3248} = 1.19$, which

is not in either critical region. Fail to reject H_0; the data do not support the claim that the distribution of skiers' times with Teflon ski bottoms is different from that of skiers' times for those who used traditional wax on their ski bottoms.

[Note: if $R = \Sigma R_B = 72, z \approx \frac{72 - 85.5}{11.3248} = -1.19$]

9.

Spelling Score	Group	Rank
61	A	1
62	B	2
63	B	3
69	A	4
70	B	5
72	B	6
75	B	7
77	A	8
79	A	9
80	B	10
81	B	11
83	A	12
85	A	13
90	B	14
92	A	15
95	A	16

Group A: $n_1 = 8, \Sigma R_A = 78$
Group B: $n_2 = 8, \Sigma R_B = 58$
[Check: $\Sigma R_A + \Sigma R_B = 78 + 58 = 136$; this should be equal to $(n_1 + n_2)(n_1 + n_2 + 1)/2 = 16(17)/2 = 136$✓]
Since $n_i = 8 \geq 8$, we will use the normal approximation with $\mu_R = 8(8 + 8 + 1)/2 = 68$, and
$\sigma_R = \sqrt{8(8)(17)/12} = \sqrt{90.6667} = 9.5219$. Since the sample sizes are the same, it doesn't matter which is n_1 or which sum of ranks is labeled R. Without loss of generality let $n_1 = n_A$ and let $R = \Sigma R_A$.
$z \approx \frac{R - \mu_R}{\sigma_R} = \frac{78 - 68}{9.5219} = 1.05$, which does not fall in either critical region. Fail to reject H_0; the data do not support the claim that the distribution of spelling scores for students taught by the phonetic method differs from that of students taught spelling by memorization.

[Note: if $R = \Sigma R_B$, then $z \approx \frac{58 - 68}{9.5219} = -1.05$.]

10.

Cement Setting Time	Group	Rank
1.4	B	1
1.6	A	2.5
1.6	B	2.5
1.8	B	4
1.9	A	5
2.2	B	6
2.4	A	7
2.5	B	8
2.7	A	9
2.8	B	10
2.9	A	11
3.4	A	12
3.6	A	13
3.8	B	14
4.0	B	15
4.1	A	16

For the ties at time = 1.6, their rank is the average of the ranks they would otherwise have received: $\frac{2+3}{2}=2.5$.

Group A: $n_1=8, \Sigma R_A=75.5$

Group B: $n_2=8, \Sigma R_B=60.5$

[Check: $\Sigma R_A+\Sigma R_B=136$; which should equal $(n_1+n_2)(n_1+n_2+1)/2=(8+8)(8+8+1)/2=136$ ✓]

Since $n_i=8\geq 8$, we can use the normal approximation with $\mu_R=8(8+8+1)/2=68$, and $\sigma_R=\sqrt{8(8)(8+8+1)/12}=\sqrt{90.6667}=9.5219$. Since the sample sizes are equal, we can chose either sample size n_1; similarly, R can equal either ΣR_A or ΣR_B. Without loss of generality let $n_1=n_A$ and $R=\Sigma R_A$.

$z\approx\frac{R-\mu_R}{\sigma_R}=\frac{75.5-68}{9.5219}=0.79$, which does not fall in either critical region. Fail to reject H_0; there is insufficient evidence to support the claim that the distribution of cement setting times for cement with no catalyst added differs from that for cement with catalyst added.

[Note: if $R=\Sigma R_B$, then $z\approx\frac{60.5-68}{9.5219}=-0.79$.]

Section 12.3

1.

Person	Class Rank, x	Sales Rank, y	$d=x-y$	d^2
1	6	4	2	4
2	8	9	−1	1
3	11	10	1	1
4	2	1	1	1
5	5	6	−1	1
6	7	7	0	0
7	3	8	−5	25
8	9	11	−2	4
9	1	3	−2	4
10	10	5	5	25
11	4	2	2	4
Sum	66	66	0	70

[Note: since there are n = 11 persons, $\sum R_x = \sum R_y = \frac{n(n+1)}{2} = \frac{11(12)}{2} = 66$ and the $\sum d$ always = 0; these can be used as checks on the calculations so far.]

$H_0: \rho_s = 0$ (there is no monotone relationship between x and y)

$H_1: \rho_s \neq 0$ (there is a monotonic relationship between x and y)

$$r_s = 1 - \frac{6\sum d^2}{n(n^2-1)} = 1 - \frac{6(70)}{11(11^2-1)} = 1 - \frac{420}{11(120)} = 0.6818 \approx 0.682$$

$\alpha = 0.05$, two-tailed test, $n = 11$, from Table 9, the critical values, call them $\pm r_0$, are ± 0.619. Since $r_s = 0.682$ is in the upper critical region, we reject H_0 and conclude that there is a monotonic relationship between x and y, the person's class rank and sales rank.

2.

Stock	Cost Rank, x	Earnings Rank, y	$d = x - y$	d^2
1	5	5	0	0
2	2	13	−11	121
3	4	1	3	9
4	7	10	−3	9
5	11	7	4	16
6	8	3	5	25
7	12	14	−2	4
8	3	6	−3	9
9	13	4	9	81
10	14	12	2	4
11	10	8	2	4
12	1	2	−1	1
13	9	11	−2	4
14	6	9	−3	9
Sum	105	105	0	296

[Check: n = 14, ΣR_x and ΣR_y should be $n(n+1)/2 = 14(15)/2 = 105$ ✓ and $\sum d$ should be 0✓]

$$r_s = 1 - \frac{6\sum d^2}{n(n^2-1)} = 1 - \frac{6(296)}{14(196-1)} = 1 - \frac{1776}{2730} = 0.349.$$

$H_0: \rho_s = 0$ (there is no monotonic relationship between x and y)

$H_1: \rho_s \neq 0$ (there is a monotonic relationship)

$\alpha = 0.01$, $n = 14$, two-tailed test; critical values, call them $\pm r_0$, are ± 0.680.

Since $r_s = 0.349$ is not in either critical region, fail to reject H_0; the data do not support the claim of a monotonic relationship between cost rank and earnings rank.

3.

Rat Colony	Population Density Rank, x	Violence Rank, y	$d = x - y$	d^2
1	3	1	2	4
2	5	3	2	4
3	6	5	1	1
4	1	2	−1	1
5	8	8	0	0
6	7	6	1	1
7	4	4	0	0
8	2	7	−5	25
Sum	36	36	0	36

$n = 8$

[Check: $\sum R_x = \sum R_y = n(n+1)/2 = 8(9)/2 = 36$ ✓ and $\sum d = 0$ ✓]

$$r_s = 1 - \frac{6\sum d^2}{n(n^2-1)} = 1 - \frac{6(36)}{8(64-1)} = 0.571.$$

H_0: $\rho_s = 0$ (there is no monotonic relationship.)

H_1: $\rho_s > 0$ (The relationship between x and y is monotone increasing; the higher population density ranks are as associated with the higher violence ranks.)

$\alpha = 0.05$, one tailed test, $n = 8$, so $r_0 = 0.620$.

Since $r_s = 0.571$ is not in the critical region, we fail to reject H_0; the data do not support the claim of a monotone-increasing relationship between the population density rankings and the violence rankings.

4. (a)

Student	Rank Order Of Finish, x	Score	Score Rank, y	$d = x - y$	d^2
1	5	73	8	−3	9
2	7	90	2	5	25
3	3	82	3.5	−0.5	0.25
4	1	95	1	0	0
5	6	65	9	−3	9
6	2	82	3.5	−1.5	2.25
7	8	78	6	2	4
8	4	75	7	−3	9
9	10	80	5	5	25
10	9	55	10	−1	1
Sum	55	-	55	0	84.5

$n = 10, n(n+1)/2 = 10(11)/2 = 55$

[Check: $\sum R_x = \sum R_y = n(n+1)/2 = 55$ ✓; $\sum d = 0$ ✓]

(Since there are two scores at 82, at rank 3 and rank 4, their ranks are $\frac{3+4}{2} = 3.5$.)

$$r_s = 1 - \frac{6\sum d^2}{n(n^2-1)} = 1 - \frac{6(84.5)}{10(99)} = 0.488.$$

(b) H_0: $\rho_s = 0$ (there is no monotonic relationship)

H_1: $\rho_s > 0$ (there is a monotone-increasing relationship)

(Here, the longer it takes a student to finish the exam, the worse his or her score.)

$\alpha = 0.05$, upper/right tailed test, $n = 10$, $r_0 = 0.564$.

Since $r_s = 0.488$ is not in the critical region, we fail to reject H_0; there is insufficient evidence to support the claim that there is a monotone-increasing relationship between order of finish and rank of exam score.

5. (a)

Soldier	Humor Test Score x	Humor Test Rank, x	Aggressiveness Test Score	Aggressiveness Rank, y	$d = x - y$	d^2
1	60	5	78	1	4	16
2	85	3	42	7	−4	16
3	78	4	68	3	1	1
4	90	2	53	5	−3	9
5	93	1	62	4	−3	9
6	45	7	50	6	1	9
7	51	6	76	2	4	1
Sum	-	28	-	28	0	68

$n = 7, n(n+1)/2 = 7(8)/2 = 28$

[Check: $\Sigma R_x = \Sigma R_y = n(n+1)/2 = 28\checkmark;\ \Sigma d = 0\checkmark$]

(b) H_0: $\rho_s = 0$ (there is no monotonic relationship)

H_1: $\rho_s < 0$ (there is a monotone-decreasing relationship between x and y)(Here, soldiers with a greater sense of humor, (smaller rank number) have lower aggression scores (large rank numbers)).

$\alpha = 0.05, n = 7$, left/lower tailed test, $r_0 = -0.715$.

$$r_s = 1 - \frac{6\Sigma d^2}{n(n^2-1)} = 1 - \frac{6(68)}{7(48)} = 1 - 1.214 = -0.214,$$

which is outside the critical region; fail to reject H_0; there is insufficient evidence to support the claim that humor rankings and aggressiveness rankings have a monotone-decreasing relationship.

6. (a)

System	Quality Rank, x	Price	Price Rank, y	$d = x - y$	d^2
1	4	690	5	−1	1
2	8	175	8	0	0
3	5	1200	1	4	16
4	2	970	2	0	0
5	7	225	7	0	0
6	6	785	4	2	4
7	1	470	6	−5	25
8	3	850	3	0	0
Sum	36	-	36	0	46

$n = 8, n(n+1)/2 = 8(9)/2 = 36$

[Check: $\Sigma R_x = \Sigma R_y = n(n+1)/2 = 36\checkmark;\ \Sigma d = 0\checkmark$]

(b) $$r_s = 1 - \frac{6\Sigma d^2}{n(n^2-1)} = 1 - \frac{6(46)}{8(64-1)} = 0.452$$

H_0: $\rho_s = 0$ (there is no monotonic relationship)

H_1: $\rho_s > 0$ (there is a monotone relationship)

$\alpha = 0.05, n = 8$, two-tailed test, $\pm r_0 = \pm 0.715$.

Since $r_s = 0.452$ is outside both critical regions, we fail to reject H_0; there is insufficient evidence to show that a monotonic relationship exists between the quality ranking and the price ranking.

7. (a)

Cadet	Aptitude Score	Aptitude Rank, x	Performance Rank, y	$d = x - y$	d^2
1	720	8	7	1	1
2	390	1	1	0	0
3	710	7	8	–1	1
4	480	3	4	–1	1
5	970	11	10	1	1
6	480	3	2	1	1
7	517	5	5	0	0
8	830	9	11	–2	4
9	690	6	6	0	0
10	850	10	9	1	1
11	480	3	3	0	0
Sum	-	66	66	0	10

The three aptitude scores of 480 will receive the average of the ranks they would otherwise receive: $\frac{2+3+4}{3}=\frac{9}{3}=3.$

$n=11, \frac{n(n+1)}{2}=\frac{11(12)}{2}=66$

[Check: $\Sigma R_x = \Sigma R_y = 66 \checkmark$; $\Sigma d = 0 \checkmark$]

(b) $r_s = 1-\frac{6\Sigma d^2}{n(n^2-1)} = 1-\frac{6(10)}{11(121-1)} = 0.955$

H_0: $\rho_s = 0$ (there is no monotonic relationship)

H_1: $\rho_s > 0$ (there is a monotone-increasing relationship between aptitude rand and performance rank)

$\alpha = 0.005$, upper/right-tailed test, $n = 11$, $r_0 = 0.764$.

Because $r_s = 0.955$ falls in the critical region, we reject H_0; the data support the claim that there is a monotone-increasing relationship between aptitude rank and performance rank.

8. (a)

Secretary	Manager A rank, x	Manager B rank, y	$d = x - y$	d^2
1	3	1	2	4
2	5	3	2	4
3	2	6	–4	16
4	1	2	–1	1
5	6	5	1	1
6	4	4	0	0
Sum	21	21	0	26

$n=6, \frac{n(n+1)}{2}=\frac{6(7)}{2}=21$

[Check: $\Sigma R_x = \Sigma R_y = 21 \checkmark$; $\Sigma d = 0 \checkmark$]

$r_s = 1-\frac{6\Sigma d^2}{n(n^2-1)} = 1-\frac{6(26)}{6(35)} = 0.257$

H_0: $\rho_s = 0$ (there is no monotonic relationship)

H_1: $\rho_s > 0$ (there is a monotone-increasing relationship)

$\alpha = 0.05 = 0.257$ upper/right-tailed test, $n = 6, r_0 = 0.829$.

Since $r_s = 0.257$ is outside the critical region, we fail to reject H_0; the data do not support the claim that there is an increasing monotone relationship between the two managers' rankings.

9. (a)

City	Insurance Sales Rank, x	Per Capita Income	Income Rank, y	$d = x - y$	d^2
1	6	17	5	1	1
2	7	18	4	3	9
3	1	19	2.5	−1.5	2.25
4	8	11	8	0	0
5	3	16	6	−3	9
6	2	20	1	1	1
7	5	15	7	−2	4
8	4	19	2.5	1.5	2.25
Sum	36	-	36	0	28.5

$n = 8, \frac{n(n+1)}{2} = \frac{8(9)}{2} = 36$

[Check: $\Sigma R_x = \Sigma R_y = 36$ ✓; $\Sigma d = 0$ ✓]

$$r_s = 1 - \frac{6\Sigma d^2}{n(n^2 - 1)} = 1 - \frac{6(28.5)}{8(64 - 1)} = 0.661$$

H_0: $\rho_s = 0$ (there is no monotonic relationship)

H_1: $\rho_s \neq 0$ (there is a monotone relationship between x and y)

$\alpha = 0.01$, two-tailed test, $n = 8$, $\pm r_0 = \pm 0.881$.

Because $r_s = 0.661$ falls outside both critical regions, we fail to reject H_0; there is insufficient evidence to support the claim of a monotone relationship between volume of insurance sales ranking and per capita income ranking.

Chapter 12 Review

No sketches of the critical region(s) will be shown in (d) below.

1. (a) Wilcoxon rank-sum test (2 independent samples)

(b) H_0: the population distributions are the same

H_1: the distributions of the populations are different.

(c) $\alpha = 0.05$, two-tailed test, $\pm z_0 = \pm 1.96$

(d)

Viscosity Index	Rank	Group
1.1	1	A
1.5	2	B
1.6	3	A
1.8	4	A
1.9	5	B
2.2	6	B
2.4	7	B
2.5	8	A
2.8	9	B
2.9	10	A
3.2	11	A
3.3	12	B
3.5	13	B
3.6	14	B
3.7	15	A
3.8	16	A
3.9	17	B
4.0	18	B
4.2	19	A
4.4	20	A
4.6	21	B

(where Group = A if the catalyst was used, and Group B if no catalyst was used)

$n_1 = n_A = 10, n_2 = n_B = 11, (n_1 + n_2)\frac{(n_1 + n_2 + 1)}{2} = \frac{21(22)}{2} = 231$

$\Sigma R_A = 107,\ \Sigma R_B = 124,\ \Sigma R_A + \Sigma R_B = 107 + 124 = 231$

$R = \Sigma R_A = 107$

Since n_1, n_2 both ≥ 8, use the normal approximation with

$$\mu_R = \frac{n_1(n_1 + n_2 + 1)}{2} = \frac{10(10 + 11 + 1)}{2} = 110$$

$$\sigma_R = \sqrt{\frac{n_1 n_2 (n_1 + n_2 + 1)}{12}} = \sqrt{\frac{10(11)(22)}{12}} = \sqrt{201.6667} = 14.2009.$$

Then

$$z = \frac{R - \mu_R}{\sigma_R} = \frac{107 - 110}{14.2009} = -0.21$$

(e) Because $z = -0.21$ falls outside both critical regions, fail to reject H_0.

(f) There is insufficient evidence to support the claim that the presence of the catalyst affects the viscosity. The distributions appear to be the same.

2. (a) Paired data (before and after memory course); sign test.

(b) H_0: the population distributions are the same

H_1: the population distribution of the last exam scores is shifted to the right of the population distribution of the first exam scores.

(c) $\alpha = 0.05$, one-tailed test, $z_0 = 1.645$

(d)

Student	Sign of Difference, Last Exam – First Exam
1	+
2	+
3	0
4	+
5	+
6	–
7	–
8	+
9	+
10	+
11	+
12	+
13	+
14	+
15	–

(d) Number of nonzero differences $n = 14 \geq 12$, so use normal approximation with $\mu = p = 0.5$ and $\sigma = \sqrt{pq/n} = \sqrt{0.25/n} = \sqrt{0.25/14} = 0.1336$. $r = 11$ plus signs, $x = r/n = 11/14 = 0.7857$.

$$z = \frac{x-\mu}{\sigma} = \frac{0.79-0.5}{0.1336} = 2.17$$

(e) Since $z = 2.17$ is in the critical region, reject H_0.

(f) There is sufficient evidence to conclude that taking the memory course improves memory exam scores, i.e., that the last exam's population distribution is shifted to the right of that for the first exam.

3. (a) Paired data, before and after; sign test.

(b) H_0: the population distributions are the same.

H_1: the population distribution of sales after mailing out advertising pamphlets is shifted to the right of the "before pamphlet" sales distribution.

(c) $\alpha = 0.01$, right-tailed test, $z_0 = 2.33$

(d)

City	Sign of Difference, After – Before
1	+
2	–
3	+
4	+
5	+
6	+
7	+
8	+
9	+
10	0
11	+
12	+
13	0
14	–
15	–

n = number of non-zero differences, 13
r = number of + signs, 10
$x = r/n = 10/13 = 0.7692 \approx 0.77$
Since $n = 13 \geq 12$, we will use the normal approximation with $\mu = p = 0.5$ and
$\sigma = \sqrt{pq/n} = \sqrt{0.25/13} = 0.1387$.

$$z = \frac{x-\mu}{\sigma} = \frac{0.77-0.5}{0.1387} = 1.95$$

(e) Since $z = 1.95$ is outside the critical region, fail to reject H_0.

(f) The data do not support the claim that advertising improved sales, i.e., there is insufficient evidence to support the claim that the "after advertising" distribution is shifted to the right of that for "before advertising."

4. (a) Two independent samples, Wilcoxon rank-sum.

(b) H_0: the population distributions are the same.
H_1: the population distributions are different.

(c) $\alpha = 0.05$, two-tailed test, $\pm z_0 = \pm 1.96$.

(d)

Number of Sessions	Group	Rank
8	A	1
9	A	2
10	A	3
11	B	4
12	A	5
13	B	6
14	A	7
15	A	8
16	A	9
17	A	10
18	B	11
19	B	12
20	A	13
21	B	14
22	B	15
23	A	16
24	B	17
25	B	18
28	B	19

where Group = A if the dog was rewarded, and Group = B otherwise.
Group A: $n_2 = 10, \Sigma R_A = 74$
Group B: $n_1 = 9, \Sigma R_B = 116$

[Check: $(n_1+n_2)(n_1+n_2+1)/2 = (9+10)(9+10+1)/2 = 190$
which should equal $\Sigma R_A + \Sigma R_B = 74 + 116 = 190$ ✓]

Since $n_i \geq 8$, we can use the normal approximation with

$$\mu_R = \frac{n_1(n_1+n_2+1)}{2} = \frac{9(9+10+1)}{2} = 90 \text{ and } \sigma_R = \sqrt{\frac{n_1 n_2(n_1+n_2+1)}{12}} = \sqrt{\frac{9(10)(9+10+1)}{12}} = \sqrt{150} = 12.2474.$$

$R = \Sigma R_B = 116$

$$z = \frac{R-\mu_R}{\sigma_R} = \frac{116-90}{12.2474} = 2.12$$

(e) Since $z = 2.12$ is in the upper critical area, reject H_0:

(f) There is sufficient evidence to show that the distribution of the number of dog training sessions with rewards is different from that for "no rewards."

5. (a) Relationship between rankings; Spearman's rank correlation test.

(b) $H_0\colon \rho_s = 0$ (there is no monotonic relationship)

$H_1\colon \rho_s > 0$ (there is a monotone-increasing relationship)

(c) $\alpha = 0.05$, right-tailed test, $n = 9$ pairs, $r_0 = 0.600$

(d)

Employee	Training Program Rank, x	Rank on the Job, y	$d = x - y$	d^2
1	8	9	−1	1
2	9	8	1	1
3	7	6	1	1
4	3	7	−4	16
5	6	5	1	1
6	4	1	3	9
7	1	3	−2	4
8	2	4	−2	4
9	5	2	3	9
Sum	45	45	0	46

[Check: $\Sigma R_x = \Sigma R_y = 45$ which should equal $n(n+1)/2 = 9(10)/2 = 45\ \checkmark$, $\Sigma d = 0\ \checkmark$]

$$r_s = 1 - \frac{6\Sigma d^2}{n(n^2-1)} = 1 - \frac{6(46)}{9(81-1)} = 0.617$$

(e) Since $r_s = 0.617$ exceeds $r_0 = 0.600$, it is in the critical region and we reject H_0.

(f) There is sufficient evidence to show that there is a monotone-increasing relationship between the training program ranking and the on-the-job performance ranking.

6. (a) (Monotonic) relationship between ranks; Spearman's rank correlation test.

(b) $H_0\colon \rho_s = 0$ (there is no monotonic relationship)

$H_1\colon \rho_s \neq 0$ (there is a monotone-increasing relationship)

(c) $\alpha = 0.10$, two-tailed test, $n = 5$ pairs, $\pm r_0 = \pm 0.900$.

Student	Chef Pierre Rank, x	Chef André Rank, y	$d = x - y$	d^2
1	4	4	0	0
2	2	1	1	1
3	3	2	1	1
4	1	3	−2	4
5	5	5	0	0
Sum	15	15	0	6

[Check: $\Sigma R_x = \Sigma R_y = 15$ which should equal $n(n+1)/2 = 5(6)/2 = 15\ \checkmark$, $\Sigma d = 0\ \checkmark$]

$$r_s = 1 - \frac{6\Sigma d^2}{n(n^2-1)} = 1 - \frac{6(6)}{5(25-1)} = 0.700$$

(e) Since $r_s = 0.7$ is outside both critical regions, fail to reject H_0.

(f) The evidence is insufficient to conclude that there is a monotone relationship between Chef Pierre's and Chef André's rankings.